Discourses on Regeneration

STEPHEN CHARNOCK

MONERGISM BOOKS

Contents

To The Reader

THE quick sale of this excellent author's former volume, viz., his Discourses upon the Existence and Attributes of God, as well as that of Divine Providence, considering how heavily the works of some others on such like subjects have gone off in our decrepit age, may be abundant evidence what acceptance they have found with the judiciously pious, who converse with books, and thereupon afford persuasive hopes that more of the genuine and useful issue of the same father, not less like to him than those born before, will yet be more favourably entertained. Wherefore, presuming we have not any way impeached our reputation by anything we wrote in the foregoing Prefaces, if thou wilt (without any repetition of the same with respect to these) but give us credit till thou hast took a distinct view by a due proportion of the several well-made parts and features here presented to thine eye by us, who were desired to perform this office of love to our deceased worthy friend, we doubt not but thou wilt easily say, As those treatises were, so these are, Judges 8:18; yea (as Joseph's brethren said, Gen. 42:11, 13), 'All sons of one man in the land of Canaan' above, each one resembling the children of him that now 'rests from his labours, and his works do follow him,' Rev. 14:13, being 'made a king and priest unto God, the Father of our Lord Jesus Christ,' Rev. 1:5, whom he served with his spirit in the gospel, Rom. 1:9, which the choice heads of evangelical truths, clearly opened and practically applied in this volume, may largely attest, and so give a supersedeas to any further recommendation of ours. The rather, when thou mayest be fully assured that a considerable part, namely, the learned and spiritual Discourses of Regeneration, were carefully copied out by one† of the former happy undertakers; and though another, who attained to the skill of perfectly reading his manuscripts, was chiefly employed in transcribing the major part of this great work from the author's own copy, yet the transcript hath been diligently compared with the original by the other‡ of the former transcribers before we read it each of us separately, and afterwards those passages conjunctly, in consultation together, wherein either of us conceived any little scruple might arise concerning the author's genuine sense, we saw re-examined, being studious to do him all the right we could, and give his own meaning in his own words unto the world, without adventuring to interpose our own conceptions. Yet after our utmost care, and the vigilant supervisal of the press by an ingenious person,§ who did much honour the author, we doubt not but had he himself survived the publication of what now appears, he would have sweetened and given grace to some lines that we presume not to alter. If, then, there should be found some things less clear, or any metaphor less pleasing, there be other things of greater weight singularly well delivered will abundantly compensate it; yea, which will greatly inform the judgment, affect the serious heart, and notably quicken to the main business of religion, and possibly, as the remains of the prophet Elisha, 2 Kings 13:21, which revived the man that was occasionally let down into his sepulchre, be a means, under God's gracious influence, to enliven some spiritually dead soul, set him upright, and enable him to run the ways of God's commandments; or, like the writing left behind Elijah, 2 Chron. 21:12, compared with 2 Kings 2:11, and 3:11, serve to warm some who are contributing to the removal of the gospel from among us. However, this later, with the former volume, will evince to those who are addicted to an over hasty censuring men of his persuasion, without any just grounds, what his great soul was mostly exercised about, namely, not matters of human policy, but the great things of the kingdom of God; not meats and drinks, i.e. mere circumstances, but the essentials and substantials of the Christian institution, righteousness, and peace, and joy in the Holy Ghost, Rom. 14:17, which we are confident he hath explained very consonant to the doctrinal articles of religion, drawn up by our first reformers, and subscribed by the minsters of the Church of England. We know not that he doth at all vary from them, or other of the reformed churches. Discipline he doth not insist on. And we suppose ingenuous readers, if they find in any little matter his sentiments different from their own, will freely give an allowance for a fair interpretation of the author's sense, at least in a posthumous work, and not wiredraw any sentences a working fancy might produce, and not review, to make them look crooked; considering what we are put in mind of in this book,* viz., every error in the head doth no more destroy the truth of faith, than every miscarriage in the life, through infirmity, nulls the being of grace; or every spot upon the face impairs the beauty and features of it.

Some who have heartily blessed God for those good things they have already received since this author's departure (and we have no small engagement upon us to be thankful to God for good books, when there be such swarms of bad ones), do with greedy eyes long to peruse his meditations upon the proposed subjects; which now appearing to their view, we are persuaded will easily gain their grateful acknowledgments that they are not disappointed, when they here find the fruitful products of the very same spirit of Mr Charnock, which was of no ordinary elevation.

And however, in the Discourse of Christ's Exaltation, there be some few materials which be of the same import with some of those in that of Reconciliation, yet handled with an acceptable variety, this might easily so fall out in the course of his celebrated preaching, not designing to lay them together in one volume, without the least disparagement; yea, now they are printed, the bottomless pit being opened, Rev. 9:2, by the papists' causing smoke to arise thence to trouble the eyes of real Chistians, the inculcating of such choice notions seems to be an angelical voice from heaven opened, Rev. 19:11, to direct God's chosen ones into that way of truth which others have not known. And if, in two or three smaller tracts, the author seem not altogether so elaborate as in his other pieces, it cannot but be granted that they were some occasional sermons composed in great straits of time; yet such as kindly savour of the same spirit with the rest, unto which it was thought fit to annex them, that there might not be any occasion to mutter that we had kept back part of what was primarily dedicated to the use of the church; or locked up in secret any pieces of so good an author, whose business, whilst he lived, was to benefit others; being happy in verifying the Arabic proverb, viz., that that learned scholar is the worst of men, who doth not profit others by his learning.

As to that discourse about The Spirit's convincing the World of Sin, the author's own notes, upon stricter search, not being found, two skilful shorthand writers,* who constantly attended his ministry, have supplied the defect, from what they both took from his own mouth, when they had compared their notes; which supply, though it should want somewhat of the accuracy of those other parts transcribed from his own manuscripts, yet those who are not over critical will find, for the completing of these discourses upon that text, not much real detriment; and upon the whole matter, not any detracting from that powerful name which the title page is adorned with. We therefore taking the freedom to advise thee, Christian reader, of those things, are not much concerned with the carping censures of supercilious critics, having, we hope, conscientiously done what was incumbent on us with all faithfulness, in emitting these writings, which might, as Peter's, be beneficial after his decease to the public, 2 Peter 1:15, which was not more the design of the deceased author in his ministry, than of his yet surviving friends, and

Thy servants, for Jesus's sake,

RICHARD ADAMS.

EDWARD VEAL.

Sept. 24. 1683.

The Necessity of Regeneration

Jesus answered and said unto him, Verily, verily, I say unto thee, Except a man be born again, he cannot see the kingdom of God. Jesus answered, Verily, verily, I say unto thee, Except a man be born of water, and of the Spirit, he cannot enter into the kingdom of God.—JOHN 3:3, 5.

These words contain the foundation of all practical religion here, and happiness hereafter. It is the principal doctrine Christ, as a prophet, came to teach, and as a king to work in the heart. It is an answer to Nicodemus his compliment, who came to him with some veneration of him. His description is in ver. 1: 'There was a man of the pharisees named Nicodemus, a ruler of the Jews.' 1. By his profession or sect, a pharisee. 2. His name, Nicodemus. 3. His quality, a ruler of the Jews; Ἄρχων, a prince, one of the great Sanhedrim, who had the supreme power in all affairs which concerned religion, even under the Roman government. His coming to Christ is described, ver. 2: 'The same came to

Jesus by night, and said unto him, Rabbi, we know that thou art a teacher come from God: for no man can do these miracles that thou doest, except God be with him.' Where we have (1.) the time of his coming, by night; (2.) the manner of coming and speaking to him with reverence, Rabbi, a title of honour. He comes to Christ; therefore is to be commended. He comes by night; hath some failure in his respect to Christ, afraid publicly to own him. Nicodemus was one of the number which believed Christ for his miracles, John 2:23. He comes hereupon to discourse with him about divine things. He acknowledges him a prophet sent by God. The reason of his acknowledgment is the consideration of his miracles, which manifested a divine power, both in the greatness and multitude of them. For he knew that God would not set the seal of his power, to one that had not his commission. Miracles are the credential letters, to signify the divine authority of any person sent upon any new dispensation by God.

Observe,

1. God doth not force any man's belief, but gives such undeniable evidences of his will and mind, that not to believe is flat contradiction to him. When he sent Moses to deliver and give a new law to the Israelites, he attended him with a miraculous power, to testify it to be his will, that what Moses delivered should be entertained. So it was with our Saviour, and in the primitive times, at the first promulgation of the gospel in several places. But when a doctrine is settled and a church established, God forbears those extraordinary works, as he did the raining down manna after the Israelites' entrance into Canaan, where they might have provision in an ordinary way of providence; and they had miracles afterward in a more scanty measure, now and then. We have now rational ways to introduce us to a belief of the Christian doctrine; and though there are no sensible miracles as before, yet there hath been in all ages, and is still, a miracle kept up in the world, greater than wrought by Christ upon the bodies of men. And that is the conversion of many obstinate sinners, and subduing them on a sudden, which in Christ's account, was the chiefest

miracle he wrought when he was upon the earth: Luke 7:22, 'Go your way, and tell John what things you have seen and heard: how that the blind see, the lame walk, the lepers are cleansed, the deaf hear, the dead are raised, to the poor the gospel is preached.' Christ had cured many in their sight; but he added in the end of the enumeration, 'To the poor the gospel is preached;' Πτωχοὶ εὐαγγελίζονται. The poor are evangelised, brought into a gospel frame, a renewed state for the kingdom of heaven, which is greater than the raising a man from a natural death to a natural life.

Nicodemus comes by night. He is fond of his own honour, loath to impair it by a free and open confession. He was a master in Israel. Had he come by day, his reputation had suffered in the vulgar opinion, who might well wonder that he, a pharisee, of a profound knowledge, should come to receive instruction from the son of a carpenter, a man despised by his fellows of the Sanhedrim. Yet he comes, though by night.

Observe,

1. It is a hard matter for us to perform a duty we are convinced of, without a flaw in it. Nicodemus is convinced by the miracles of Christ's divine authority; but he forbears an open acknowledgment of him. He creeps to him in the night, unwilling to be seen with him in the day. If Christ were not a prophet, why should he be acknowledged at all? If a prophet, why not in the day as well as in the night? Strange not to consult him in the day, whom he confesseth to have his commission from God! How weak is the faith of the best at first! How staggering between Christ and self.

2. Our own reputation will be apt to mix itself in our religious services. It is his fear of the loss of this makes him choose the darkness. This greatest piece of old Adam in us will be rising in various forms, when we are in the most spiritual exercises. What a contest is there between religion and reputation! He was willing to gratify the one, but not displease the other.

3. Ambition is the great hindrance of a thorough conversion. Nicodemus had a mind to speak to Christ, but his reputation bears too much sway in him against a thorough giving up himself to him. He was ashamed to be taken notice of in this little address he made: John 5:44, 'How can ye believe, that receive honour one of another, and seek not the honour which comes from God only?'

4. Men may have a high esteem of Christ, yet not such an esteem as amounts to a saving faith. Nicodemus acknowledges him a teacher, and that sent from God; but not the teacher, the great prophet Moses had spoken of, Deut. 18:15. He confesseth him a prophet, but not the Messiah. Look to your estimations of Christ; see whether they be supreme, superlative, the Saviour, the mediator, the Lord and King.

5. Convictions may be a long time before any appearance of conversion. If we consider Nicodemus here, only as one convinced of the divine authority of Christ, and not a thorough convert at this time; for he seems by his questions, vers. 4 and 9, to be rather a malcontent, than a convert; yet the seed then sown by our Saviour's discourse sprung up at last in fruit. He doth upon a signal occasion plead Christ's cause before a council of pharisees, probably the great Sanhedrim, yet but faintly: John 7:50, 51, 'Doth our law judge any man before it hears him, and knows what he doth?' Before, he would have no witness of his coming to Christ. Here he takes his part, as he might have done any man's upon a common principle of justice and equity, that he should not be condemned before he was heard. But there is more generous fruit afterwards, where he joins with Joseph of Arimathea in doing honour openly to our Saviour's crucified body: John 19:39, 'And there came also Nicodemus (which at the first came to Jesus by night), and brought a mixture of myrrh and aloes, about an hundred pound weight.' What grace he had seems to be in a long sleep, but is very vigorous upon its awaking.

6. True grace doth one time or other discover itself most contrary to that which was the natural crime before. In both these places, fear had

been his sin. It is now over matched by confidence. The Holy Ghost takes notice of it, 'which at the first came to Jesus by night.' He came by night before, now he comes by day. He and another never named before, Joseph of Arimathea, who being possessed with the same passion of fear, was a disciple in secret,—John 19:38, 'Being a disciple of Jesus, but secretly, for fear of the Jews,'—own him publicly at his death, when those that had been familiar with him in his life forsook him. Christ will make timorous hares to own his cause, when those that think themselves courageous lions turn their backs upon him.

Paul had the most transcendent affection to the church, who before was guilty of the smartest persecution. And Peter, after the coming of the Spirit, was as courageous as before he was cowardly in his Master's cause.

We have seen the pharisee. Let us consider our Saviour's answer: ver. 3, 'Jesus answered and said unto him, Verily, verily, I say unto thee, Except a man be born again, he cannot see the kingdom of God.'

Some think that Nicodemus asked a question which is not expressed, but may be gathered out of Christ's answer, and seems to be this, What was requisite to a man's entrance into the kingdom of heaven? Whereupon Christ tells him, that there was a necessity of being born again. Others think that Nicodemus asked no question, and that these words are a very proper reply to Nicodemus.

1. Christ answers not his compliment, but useth his authority, acknowledged by Nicodemus, of a teacher to inform him. Since you acknowledge my commission from God to be a teacher, I will teach you what I have to declare. The great design of my coming is to bring men to the kingdom of God; and the great means to this is a new birth, which can only fit you for evangelical truths here, and eternal happiness hereafter. He acknowledges Christ to be a teacher, and Christ in his reply would teach him how to become a Christian.

2. Christ frames his answer according to the pharisee's corruption. Nicodemus came by night, out of love to his credit, that might be impaired by his coming in the day-time. What would the people think? Surely this man, and the rest of his tribe, are not so knowing as they pretend to be, since he comes to Jesus to be taught, and out of fear of the pharisees, who thereby might be offended.

Christ's answer therefore very well suits him. You must become a new man, if you would have acquaintance with evangelical mysteries. Away with your old notions, and pharisaical pride. Deny your honour, credit, and whatsoever partakes of the name of self. A legal frame, and a pharisaical righteousness, will not advance you to the kingdom of God. The Jews were proud of being Abraham's children, and thought the gates of heaven could not be shut against any of that relation.

John had touched them before for this: Mat. 3:9, 'And think not to say within yourselves, We have Abraham to our father.' Christ doth tacitly here do the same, and puts him in mind of another birth, and the falseness and deceitfulness of his bottom of legal righteousness.

3. Christ frames his answer according to his weakness and ignorance. Nicodemus acknowledged him a teacher, not the Messiah. Christ would bring him to the knowledge of himself as the Messiah. Christ therefore by his answer would lift up his thoughts higher, and puts him in mind of the kingdom of God, which the Jews in their common discourse signified the kingdom of the Messiah by, and have entitled it in ages since, the kingdom of God, and the kingdom of heaven. So that Christ would bring him to the knowledge of himself as the Messiah, not only as an extraordinary prophet.

These three things evidence what relation this speech of Christ hath to that of Nicodemus.

Observe from the relation of this to Nicodemus his speech:

1. We shall gain nothing by our applaudings and praises of Christ, without a renewed nature. Nicodemus comes with much reverence,

gives Christ the title of rabbi, confesseth him to be sent of God, owns the divinity of his miracles. Christ doth not compliment him again, takes no notice of his civility, but falls roundly to his work, acquaints him with the necessity of regeneration, without which he could not see the kingdom of God, for all his fine praises of him. A glavering reverential religion is insignificant with Christ. A new birth, a likeness to Christ in nature, a conformity to him, is accounted by Christ an higher estimation of him, than all external applauses given to him.

2. No natural privilege under heaven can entitle us to the kingdom of grace or glory. It is not our carnal traduction from the best man. It is no natural birth, with the choicest privileges, gives us a right to either of them. Not the honour of having the law from God's own mouth, the glory of an outward covenant, the treasure of the oracles of God, the seal of circumcision borne in the body, that can instate this Nicodemus into this felicity. It is a birth of a higher strain, from an higher principle, a change of nature, and a removal from the old stock.

See how strangely Nicodemus replied upon this discourse of our Saviour. How strangely astonished is this great ruler in Israel at the doctrine which is absolutely necessary to an entrance into the kingdom of heaven! ver. 4, 'Nicodemus saith unto him, How can a man be born when he is old? can he enter a second time into his mother's womb, and be born?' What a childish conception hath he of this most heavenly doctrine! Can such an ancient man as I return to my first principles, dig a way into my mother's womb? It is strange that Nicodemus, being a pharisee, and so well versed in Scripture, should be so ignorant, or at least guilty of so much inadvertency, as not to think of that place, Ezek. 36, and other places, which speak of 'a new heart,' and 'an heart of flesh.' He might have considered the design of the legal purifications, which were to represent the inward holiness which ought to be in the persons so purified. Yet he hears him discourse, but doth not comprehend him. His carnal notion bears sway against spiritual truths.

Observe,

1. A man may have great knowledge in the letter of the Scripture, and yet not understand the necessary and saving doctrines in it. The doctrine of regeneration was laid down in the whole Old Testament, though not in that term. Let us take heed how we read the Scriptures; not to trouble our heads with needless and curious questions, but with the main mysteries of religion. What could all Nicodemus his knowledge profit him, if it had been ten thousand times more, without the knowledge of this doctrine, and the experience of it!

2. Nothing is more an enemy to the saving knowledge of gospel mysteries than a priding ourselves in head knowledge. Nicodemus his coming by night was not only from fear, but pride, that he might not be thought ignorant by the people. Humble men have the soundest knowledge: 'The meek will he teach his way,' Ps. 25:9.

3. How low was the interest of God in the world at that time! How had ignorance and error thrust the knowledge of God out of other parts of the world, when it languished so much in the church! How simple must the poor people be when the students in Scripture were no wiser! It is a thing to be bewailed amongst us, that wrangling knowledge hath almost thrust out spiritual. And when Christians meet, their discourses are more about unnecessary disputes than these saving mysteries of Christianity, which might produce elevations of heart to heaven.

To this exception of Nicodemus Christ makes his reply; where observe,

1. A fresh assertion of it, with an explanation: ver. 5, 'Jesus answered, Verily, verily, I say unto thee, Except a man be born of water, and of the Spirit, he cannot enter into the kingdom of God.' In the third verse, Christ lays down the necessity of the new birth; in ver. 5, the necessity of the cause, 'Except a man be born of water, and of the Spirit.' In the first speech, he lays down the doctrine; in this, he explains the principle and manner of it, to remove his false apprehensions, wherein he might mean

the transmigration of souls, which seems to be an opinion amongst the Jews.

2. A reason to back it: ver. 6, 'That which is born of the flesh is flesh; and that which is born of the Spirit is spirit.' That which is born of the flesh is flesh, and can be no more by that principle, for the effect cannot be better than the cause; but that which is born of the Spirit is spirit, i.e. hath a spiritual nature.

Flesh is taken for man corrupted: Gen. 6:3, 'For he also is flesh,' degenerate into flesh, grown a mere sensual creature by the loss of original righteousness. For upon the parting of original righteousness, the soul of man was as a body without life; a spiritual carcase, as the body is without a soul.

Flesh signifies the whole nature, as in that place, Mat. 16:17, 'Flesh and blood hath not revealed it unto thee,' &c. The incarnation of the Son of God, which is the foundation of all evangelical administrations, is above the sphere of nature to discover. Man in his natural generation is but mere nature, and cannot apprehend, cannot enjoy that which is only apprehensible and enjoyable by a spiritual nature; but man regenerated by the Spirit is spiritual, and is advanced above mere flesh, for he is made partaker of the divine nature. So that Christ's argument runs thus: No flesh can enter into the kingdom of God; but every man naturally is flesh, unless born again of the Spirit; therefore no man, unless born again of the Spirit, can enter into the kingdom of God. If you could enter into your mother's womb, and be born again, the matter would not be mended with you; you would still be but flesh, and rather worse than better; therefore that is not the birth that I mean, for the impediment would be as strong in you as before.

These two verses are an answer to Nicodemus his objection. Nicodemus understands it of a carnal birth. No, no, saith Christ, it is a spiritual birth I intend; one that is wholly divine and heavenly. That which you mean brings a man into the light of the world; that which I mean, brings a man out of the world, into the light of grace. That forms the flesh to an earthly life; this forms the soul to an heavenly. That makes you the son of man; this the son of God.*

All the difficulty lies in ver. 5, in that expression of water, &c. Some, as the papists, understand it of the elementary water of baptism, and from this place exclude all children dying without baptism from salvation. Others understand it of a metaphorical water, whereof Christ speaks, John 4:14, 'The water that I shall give him, shall be in him a well of water, springing up into everlasting life.'

Let us first see why by water cannot be meant the baptismal water.

Regeneration is the mystery and sense of that sacred ceremony. It is indeed signified, represented, and sealed in baptism; how, and in what sense, is not my present work.

1. It is strange, that when all agree that the birth here spoken of is spiritual and metaphorical, that the water here should be natural.

2. None could be saved, unless baptized, if this were meant of baptism. As if these words, John 6:53, 'Except you eat the flesh of the Son of man, and drink his blood, ye have no life in you,' were meant of the supper, none could be saved unless they did partake of it. Whereas Christ lays not the stress upon baptism, but upon faith: Mark 16:16, 'He that believeth, and is baptized, shall be saved; but he that believeth not, shall be damned.' He doth not say, He that is not baptized shall be damned, but he lays damnation wholly upon the want of faith. Many have been saved without baptism, none without faith. It is true to say, He that doth not believe shall be damned; but it is not true to say, He that is not baptized shall be damned. Christ saith the first, but not the second, though his discourse had obliged him to say so, had it been true, or had he meant this speech to Nicodemus of baptismal water. The Spirit is not tied to baptism, but he may act out of the sacraments as well as in them. Understand this of the bare want of baptism, not of the contempt or wilful neglect of it. If it were meant of baptism, it was true then, that

none could be saved without it. How did the thief upon the cross enter into paradise, which Christ promised him? So that one may enter into heaven without baptism by water, though not without the baptism of the Spirit.

3. Baptism was not then instituted as a standing sacrament in the Christian church. The institution of it we find not till after Christ's resurrection: Mat. 28:19, 'Go ye, therefore, and teach all nations, baptizing them.' And it is not likely Christ would discourse to Nicodemus of the necessity of an institution that was not yet expressly appointed by him, and which he did not appoint till after his resurrection; for he discourseth of that which was of present necessity. And if this were meant of baptism, and of that absolute necessity the papists would lay upon it from these words, then all that died before the institution of baptism by our Saviour, unbaptized, could not enter into the kingdom of heaven, though believing. Can anything be necessary before the precept for it be given? It could not be necessary before, as a means, because it is not a natural, but an instituted means. It must be therefore necessary by virtue of a command; therefore not absolutely necessary before the command, and at the time Christ spoke these words. Some say that Christ meant it, not of an absolute necessity at that time, but that it should be so after his death.* That is to give our Saviour the lie, for he spake it of the present time, some years before his death. Besides, it wrongs the goodness of our Saviour (if he had meant it of baptism), to defer the institution of it so long after, when it was at present necessary for Nicodemus his salvation. It wrongs his wisdom, too, to speak of that to be at present necessary, which was not in being, nor would be till after his death.

4. It is strange that our Saviour should speak to Nicodemus of the necessity of baptism before he had informed him of the mysteries of the gospel, whereof it is a seal. To speak of the seal before he speaks of that which is to be sealed by it, is not congruous. For the sacraments

being founded upon the doctrine on which they depend, to begin by a sacrament the instruction of a man, is to begin a building by the tiles and rafters, before you lay a foundation; and against the order expressed by our Saviour to the apostles, which puts teaching before baptizing, and was always practised in the primitive times, and is to this day in all Christian churches, to the adult and grown up. As circumcision was, amongst the Jews, not administered to any proselyte before his turning proselyte, and instruction in those laws he was to observe, and then, and not till then, his children had a right to circumcision.

5. Those that understand it of the baptismal water, and so make that of absolute necessity, do by another assertion accuse their own exposition of a falsity; for they say that the baptism of blood supplies the want of that of water, and that if either infants or adult persons be hurried away to a stake or gibbet, or killed for the Christian cause, they are certainly saved; which cannot be, if the baptism of water were to be understood in this place, and so absolutely necessary. It is water that is expressed, and blood is not water. One of these assertions must be false. A martyr dying unbaptized must be damned, and cannot enter into the kingdom of heaven, if this place be meant of the water of baptism.

6. It may also be observed that Christ, in the progress of his discourse, makes no more mention of water, but of the Spirit: 'That which is born of the Spirit is spirit;' not born of water and the Spirit, which had been very necessary, if water had been of an equal necessity with the Spirit to the new birth. And since Christ mentions it positively, that he that is born of the Spirit is spirit, will it be said, that if any be born of the Spirit, without water, he is still but flesh?

Water then here is to be taken mystically. Some by water understand the whole doctrine of the gospel; as the waters mentioned through the whole 47th of Ezekiel signify the doctrine of the gospel. To drop, in Scripture, signifies to teach, Amos 7:16; Ezek. 20:46, 'Drop thy word toward the south.' Others, by water, understand the grace of regeneration as the principle, the Spirit as the cause, as Titus 3:5, 6, 'He hath saved us by the washing of regeneration, and the renewing of the Holy Ghost.' What washing he means is expressed in the renewing of the Holy Ghost; that is, that renewing which is wholly spiritual, as proceeding from the Spirit of God, whence this grace doth flow.

By water and the Spirit are signified one and the same thing, the similitude of water shewing the cleansing and generating virtue of the Spirit; as fire and the Spirit are put together, Mat. 3:11, to signify the refining quality the Spirit hath (as fire hath to separate the dross from the good metal). Fire and the Spirit, i.e. a spirit of fire, of the force and efficacy of fire.

This water is the same which God had promised: Isa. 44:3, 'I will pour water upon him that is thirsty,' and Ezek. 36:25, 'Then will I sprinkle clean water upon you;' and ver. 27, 'I will put my Spirit within you.' He there explains water to be the Spirit: 'I will pour my Spirit upon thy seed.' And in Ezekiel he joins water and the Spirit; i.e. the water of my Spirit, or my spiritual water, my gospel grace. And Isa. 41:18, 19, God speaks of the admirable fruitfulness of this water. This shall renew you, and make you fructify in the kingdom of my Son, where none shall be received who is not born of this divine principle.

Now our Saviour having to do with a pharisee, who was acquainted with those oracles, to make him understand this truth, uses those words which the prophets had used, and ranks them in the same order; first water, then the Spirit, that the latter might clear the sense and nature of the former, to hinder Nicodemus from imagining that to be a natural water which was spiritual and mystical. Water and the Spirit signifies the water of the Spirit, or a spiritual water, as 1 Thes. 1:5, 'Our gospel came not unto you in word only, but in power, and in the Holy Ghost;' that is, in the power of the Holy Ghost.

The Spirit is compared to water in respect of its generative virtue. No fruitful plant but is produced by moisture. Water contains in it the seeds of all things. It was from water and the earth that all things in the lower world were in the first creation produced. Water is put here as exegetical of the effect of the Spirit; water being the cause of generation by its moisture, uniting the parts together.

Our Saviour in both places useth an asseveration, Verily, verily, which is spoken,

1. To shew the infallible necessity of it, the certainty of the proposition.

2. To urge a special attention. Men press those things in discourse which they would have retained.

It is to be believed because of its necessity; it is to be considered because of its excellency.

Born again. Ἄνωθεν signifies properly from above; but sometimes it is taken for again.* Nicodemus understands it so by his reply, of entering again into his mother's womb, and not of a heavenly birth.

Man was born in nature; he must be born in grace. He was born of the first Adam; he must be born of the second Adam. It is expressed in Scripture by various terms: a resurrection to life, a quickening, a new creation, the new man, the inward man, a dying to the world. It is indeed a putting off the old man, the principles and passions, the corrupt notions and affections which we derive from Adam, to devote ourselves to God, to live to Christ, to walk in newness of life.

The kingdom of God, which is sometimes taken, (1) for the kingdom of glory, (2) it is sometimes taken for the gospel state. And the same thing is signified by the kingdom of God, and the kingdom of heaven. What is called by Matthew 'the kingdom of heaven,' Mat. 4:17, is called by Mark, relating the same story, 'the kingdom of God,' Mark 1:15. And the gospel is called 'the gospel of the kingdom of God,' Mark 1:14. It is called the kingdom of God;—

1. Because it sets up the rule and government of God in the world above the devil's. The devil had been so long the God of the world, that

the interest of God seemed to be overmatched by a multitude of unclean spirits, and abominable idols; and the true God was not known to be the governor of it. The gospel discovers the true governor of the world, and sets up his rule and authority.

2. It sets up the righteousness of God,* above a legal and fleshly righteousness, much in vogue among Jews and Gentiles; but they were wholly ignorant of the righteousness of God, Rom. 10:3.

3. This kingdom is framed and set up by the Son of God; the other kingdom, under the law, was settled by God, but by the hand of Moses, a man. This is administered by him through his Spirit, his vicegerent. His royalty did not so eminently appear as in the times of the gospel.

The Father appoints the gospel state in his wisdom, the Son lays the foundation of it in his blood, the Spirit carries it on in the world by his power.

4. In respect of the service, it is high and heavenly; a serving God in spirit. The service under the legal administration was carnal; the service under the gospel administration is more spiritual, and so more suitable to the perfections of God.

5. In the end and issue of it. It is a translating us into the kingdom of Christ, Col. 1:13. The legal ceremonies could not fit men of themselves for glory; they could not make the comers thereunto perfect. But this kingdom of grace prepares us for the kingdom of glory.

Cannot see the kingdom of God. In ver. 5, he cannot enter into the kingdom of God. He cannot,

1. By reason of God's appointment.

2. In the nature of the thing itself; he hath no fitness for heaven or heavenly mysteries.

See. Seeing is taken sometimes for enjoying; not a bare sight, but fruition: John 3:36, 'He that believes not the Son shall not see life;' that is, shall not enjoy life. And Heb. 12:14, 'Without holiness, no man shall see the Lord;' they may see him in his pronouncing the sentence, but shall not see him in a way of glorious enjoyment of him.

To have a communion with Christ in a gospel state, to have an enjoyment of Christ in eternal glory, it is necessary we be stripped of the corruption of our first nature, and be clothed with another by the Spirit of God.

Observe in the verse,

1. The infallibility of the proposition: Verily, verily.

2. The necessity of regeneration: except.

3. The extension of it in regard of the subject.

(1.) Subjectum quod recipit: man, i. e. every man.

(2.) Subjectum in quo recipitur: man, i.e. the whole man, every faculty.

4. The excellency of it implied: they cannot see the kingdom of God. If he be born again, he shall enjoy the kingdom of God.

Doct. Regeneration of the soul is of absolute necessity to a gospel and glorious state.

By regeneration, I mean not a relative, but a real change of the subject, wrought in the complexion and inclinations of the soul, as in the restoring of health there is a change made in the temper and humours of the body.

As mankind was changed in Adam from what they were by a state of creation, so men must be changed in Christ from what they were in a state of corruption. As that change was not only relative but real, and the relative first introduced by the real, so must this. The relation of a child of wrath was founded upon the sin committed. Without a real change there can be no relative. Being in Christ, as freed from condemnation, is always attended with a walking in the Spirit; and walking is not before living. For the better understanding this point, I shall lay down,

I. Propositions concerning the necessity of it.

II. I shall shew that it is necessary,

1. To a gospel state.

(1.) To the performance of gospel duties.

(2.) To the enjoyment of gospel privileges.

2. To a state of glory.

I. Propositions concerning the necessity of it.

Prop. 1. There are but two states, one saving, the other damning; a state of sin and a state of righteousness; and all men are included in one of them. All men are divided into two ranks. In regard of their principle, some are in the flesh, some in the Spirit, Rom. 8:8, 9; in regard of their obedience, some walk after the flesh, some after the Spirit, Rom. 8:1; some are slaves to the flesh, others are led by the Spirit; some live only to self, some live to God. In regard of the exercise of their minds, their nobler faculty, some mind the things of the flesh, others the things of the Spirit, Rom. 8:5; some swinishly wallow in sin, others place the delights of their spirits upon better and higher objects.

The Scripture mentions no other. A state of enmity, wherein men have their inclinations contrary to God; a state of friendship and fellowship, wherein men walk before God unto all well-pleasing, and would not willingly have an inward motion swerve from his will. One is called light, the other darkness: Eph. 5:8, 'You were sometimes darkness, but now are you light;' one the children of wrath, the other the children of God. There is no medium between them, every man is in one of these states. All believers, from the bruised reed to the tallest cedar, from the smoking flax on earth to the flaming lamp in heaven, from Thomas, that would not believe without seeing, to Abraham, who would believe without staggering, all are in a state of life; and all, from the most beautiful moralist to the most venomous toad in nature's field, from the young man in the gospel, who was not far from the kingdom of heaven, to Judas, who was in the very bottom of hell, all are in a state of death. Mere nature, though never so curiously garnished, can place a man no higner; faith, though with many infirmities, puts us in a state of amity;

unbelief, though with many moralities, continues us in a state of enmity. All men are either the object of God's delight or of his abomination. The highest endowments of men remaining in corrupted nature cannot please him. The delight of God then supposeth some real change in the object which is the ground of that delight, for God is wise in his delight, and could not be pleased with anything which were not fit for his complacency. Since original nature in a man cannot displease God unless it be changed by some fault, because it was his own work, so our present nature cannot please God unless it be changed by some grace, though it be otherwise never so highly dignified. Whatsoever grows up from the old Adam is the fruit of the flesh, whatsoever grows up by the new Adam in us is the offspring of the Spirit; and upon one of these two stocks all men in the world are set. Since, therefore, one is utterly destructive, and cannot please God (Rom. 8:8, So then they that are in the flesh cannot please God), though never so well garnished (for being utterly contrary to him it cannot be approved by him), the other is absolutely necessary to salvation.

Prop. 2. It is necessary upon the account of the fall of man and the consequents of it. In Adam we died: 1 Cor. 15:22, 'As in Adam all died;' therefore in Adam we sinned: Rom. 5:19, 'By one man's disobedience many were made sinners.' Man cannot be supposed to sin in Adam unless some covenant had intervened between God and Adam,* whence there did arise in the whole human nature a debt of having righteousness transfused from the first parent to all his posterity. The want of this grace wherein his posterity are conceived is a privation, and a crime which was voluntary in the root and head. This privation of righteousness must be removed. The institution of God stands firm, that Adam and his posterity should have a pure righteousness. It is not for the honour of God to enjoin it so strictly at first, and to have no regard to it afterwards. Now this privation of righteousness, and the unrighteousness which hath taken place in the sons of Adam, cannot be removed without the infusion of grace; for without this grace he would alway want righteous-ness, and yet be alway under an obligation to have it; he would be under desires of happiness, but without it under an impossibility of attaining it.

Were there an indifferency in the soul of man, were it an abrasa tabula, the writing of moral precepts upon it by good education would sway it to walk in the paths of virtue, as an ill education doth cast it into the ways of [vice]. This is not so; for take two, let them have the same ways of education, the same precepts instilled into them, as Esau and Jacob had by their father, who were equally taught, yet how different were their lives! Esau's bad, Jacob's not without flaws. Education had not the power to root corruption out of both, no, nor out of any man in the world without a higher principle. There is some powerful principle in the soul, which leads it into by-paths contrary to those wholesome rules instilled into it. Hence ariseth a necessity of some other principle to be put into the heart to over-sway this corrupt bias. Man goes astray from the womb, as it is in Ps. 58:3, 'The wicked are estranged from the womb; they go astray as soon as they be born.' There must be something to rectify him, and expel this wandering humour.

By the fall of man there was contracted,

(1.) An unfitness to any thing that is good. Man is so immersed in wrong notions of things, that he cannot judge fully of what is good: Titus 1:16, 'To every good work reprobate.' The state of nature, or the old man, is described, Eph. 4:22, to be 'corrupt, according to deceitful lusts;' deceitful, seducing us from God, drawing us into perdition, by representing evil under the notion of good, which evidenceth our un-derstandings to be unfit to judge without a new illumination; inward and spiritual lusts, which are most deceitful, being accounted brave and generous motions; lusts or desires, which shew the corruption of the will by ill habits. Lust and sin is the mere composition of corrupted nature; the whole man is stuffed with polluting principles and filthy appetites.

What was preternatural to man in a state of innocency became natural to him after his depraved state. He is 'carnal, sold under sin,' Rom. 7:14. The spring being already out of order, cannot make the motion otherwise than depraved, as when a clock is out of order, it is natural to that present condition of it to give false intelligence of the hour of the day, and it cannot do otherwise till the wheels and weights be rectified. Our end was actively to glorify God in the service of him and obedience to him; but since man is fallen into this universal decay of his faculties, and made unfit to answer this end, there is a necessity he should be made over again, and created upon a better foundation, that some principle should be in him to oppose this universal depravation, enlighten his understanding, mollify his heart, and reduce his affections to their due order and object.

(2.) Not only an unfitness, but unwillingness to that which is good. We have not those affections to virtue as we have to vice. Are not our lives for the most part voluntarily ridiculous? Had we a full use of reason, we should judge them so. We think little of God; and when we do think of him, it is with reluctancy. This cannot be our original state, for surely, God being infinitely good, never let man come out of his hands with this actual unwillingness to acknowledge and serve him; as the apostle saith, in the case of the Galatians' errors, Gal. 5:8, 'This persuasion comes not of him which calls you,' this unwillingness comes not from him that created you. How much, therefore, do we need a restoring principle in us! We naturally fulfil the desires, or θελήματα 'of the flesh,' Eph. 2:3. There is then a necessity of some other principle in us to make us fulfil the will of God, since we were created for God, not for the flesh. We can no more be voluntarily serviceable to God while that serpentine nature and devilish habit remains in us, than we can suppose the devil can be willing to glorify God, while the nature he contracted by his fall abides powerful in him. It is as much as to say that a man can be willing against his will. Nature and will must be changed, or we for ever remain in this state.

Man is born a wild ass' colt, Job 11:12. No beast more wild and brutish than man in his natural birth, and like to remain in his wild and wilful nature without grace; a new birth can only put off the wildness of the first.

(3.) Not only unfitness and unwillingness, but inability to good. A strange force there is in a natural man, which hurries him, even against some touches of his will, to evil.

How early do men discover an affection to vice! How greedily do they embrace it, notwithstanding rebukes from superiors, good exhortations from friends, with the concurrence of the vote of conscience, giving its amen to those dissuasions! and yet carried against those arguments, deceived by sin, slain by sin, sold under it, Rom. 7:11, 14. This is the miserable state of every son of nature.

Do we not find that men sometime wrapt up in retirement, in consideration of the excellency of virtue, are so wrought upon by their solitary meditations, that they think themselves able to withstand the strongest invasion of any temptation! Yet we see oftentimes that when a pleasing temptation offers itself, though there be a conflict between reason and appetite, at length all the considerations and dictates of reason are laid aside, the former ideas laid asleep, and that committed which their own reason told them was base and sordid; so that there is something necessary, beside consideration and resolution, to the full cure of man.

No privation can be removed but by the introduction of another form; as when a man is blind, that blindness, which is a privation of sight, cannot be removed without bringing in a power of seeing again. Original sin is a privation of original righteousness, and an introduction of corrupt principles, which cannot be removed but by some powerful principle contrary to it. Since the inability upon the earth, by reason of the curse, to bring forth its fruits in such a manner as it did when man was in a state of innocency, the nature of it must be changed to reduce it to its original fruitfulness; so must man, since a general defilement from Adam hath seized upon him, be altered before he can 'bring forth fruit to God,' Rom. 7:4. We must be united to Christ, engrafted upon another stock, and partake of the power of his resurrection; without this we may bring forth fruit, but not fruit to God. There is as utter an impossibility in a man to answer the end of his creation, without righteousness, as for a man to act without life, or act strongly without health and strength. It is a contradiction to think a man can act righteously without righteousness, for without it he hath not the being of a man; that is, man in such a capacity, for those ends for which his creation intended him.

Well, then, since there is an unfitness, unwillingness, inability in a man to answer his end, there is a necessity of a new life, a new nature, a new righteousness. There is a necessity for his happiness that he should be brought back to God, live to God, be a son of God, and this cannot be without regeneration; for how can he be brought back to God without a principle of spiritual motion? How can he live to God that hath no spiritual life? How can he be fit to be a son of God who is of a brutish and diabolical nature?

Prop. 3. Hence it follows, that it is universally necessary. Necessary for all men. Our Saviour knows none without this mark. There must be a change in the soul: 2 Cor. 5:17, 'Therefore if any man be in Christ, he is a new creature.' There must be the habitation of the Spirit: Rom. 8:9, 'If any man hath not the Spirit of Christ, he is none of his.' There must be a crucifixion, not only of the corrupt affections of the flesh, but of the flesh itself: Gal. 5:24, 'They that are Christ's have crucified the flesh, with the affections and lusts.'

The old nature must be killed, with all its attendants. There is no son-ship to God without likeness, no relation of a child of God without a childlike nature. Let a man be of whatsoever quality in the world, never so high, never so low, of whatsoever age, of whatsoever moral endowments, 'except a man,' every man, &c.

And simply necessary. Our Saviour doth not say he is in danger not to see the kingdom of God, or he may come short of it; but he shall not, he cannot. There is no possible way but this for any man, no other door to creep in at but by that of a new birth; salvation cannot be attained without it, and damnation will certainly be the issue of the want of it. As there is no other name under heaven by which we can be saved but by the name of Jesus Christ, so there is no other way under heaven wherein we can be saved but by the birth of the Spirit.

It is necessary, therefore, in all places, in all professions. It is not necessary only in Europe, and not in Africa. Let a man be what he will, in any place under heaven, he must have a Jesus to save him, and an Holy Ghost to change him; it is one and the same Spirit acts in all, and produceth the same qualities in all. Let men's religion and professions be what they will (men are apt to please themselves with this and that profession and opinion, but), there is no salvation in any profession, or any kind of opinion, but by regeneration. It is not necessary our understandings should be all of one size, that our opinions should all meet in uniformity, but it is necessary we should all have one spiritual nature. It is as necessary to the being of a good man that he should be spiritual, as to the being of a man that he should be rational, though there is a great latitude and variety in the degrees of men in grace, as well as their reasons. Some are of little faith, some of great faith; some babes in Christ, some strong men. It is not necessary all should be as strong as Abraham, but it is simply necessary all should be new born, as Abraham; no age, no time excludes it.

(1.) Righteousness was necessary before the fall. The new birth is but the beginning of our restoration to that state we had before the fall. Adam could not have been happy without being innocent. The holiness of God could not create an impure creature. Without it God could take no pleasure in his work.

(2.) After the fall it was necessary, continually necessary from the first moment of the fall. This work of regeneration is included in the first promise: Gen. 3:15, 'I will put enmity between thee and the woman, between thy seed and her seed.' Naturally we have a mighty friendship to Satan, a friendship to his works, though not to his person. But if any man had interest in that promise, he must exchange that friendship for an enmity.

If Jesus Christ, who is principally meant by the seed of the woman, had an enmity to Satan, then all Christ's seed must be possessed with the same spirit. For when the seed of the woman was to break the serpent's head, it was necessary that those that would enjoy the fruit of that conquest should be enemies to the nature of the devil, and the works of the devil, otherwise they could not join with that interest which overthrows him. It is unreasonable to think the head should have an enmity, and the members an amity; and we cannot have an enmity to that which is the same with our nature, without a change of disposition. It is not a verbal enmity that is here meant. While we pretend to hate him we may do his pleasure, and Satan is never troubled to be pretendedly hated and really obeyed. As wicked men do the will of God's purpose, while they oppose the will of his precept, so they do the devil's will many times while they think they cross it; there must be a contrary nature to Satan before there can be an enmity. That foolish appetite, affected sensuality, indulgence to the flesh, the cause of our first friendship with Satan, must be changed into divine desires, affection to heavenly things, a mortification of the flesh, before a man can part with this friendship. There must be a change in the conformity of the soul to the nature of the devil before an enmity against him can be raised. We are never enemies to those that encourage us in what we affect. His nature can never be altered, by reason of the curse of God upon him; therefore ours must, if ever the league be broken.

In Isa. 65:25 it is said, 'The wolf and the lamb shall feed together, and the lion shall eat straw like an ox: and dust shall be the serpent's meat.' The nature of men may be changed by the gospel, but dust shall always be the serpent's meat. The saving some by water in the deluge was a figure of this inward baptism, which is the 'answer of a good conscience towards God,' 1 Peter 3:20, 21. As the old world was so corrupt that all must be washed away before it could be restored, so is the little world of man. The cloud and sea through which the Israelites passed signified this, as the apostle informs us: 1 Cor. 10:2, 'And were all baptized unto Moses in the cloud and the sea.' Whereupon some think there were some sprinklings of the water upon them, as they stood like two walls, to favour their passage.

(3.) Necessary in the time of the law. By the moral law this renewing was implied in the first command, of not having any other gods before him, Exod. 20:3. We cannot suppose that command only limited to a not serving an outward image. Is not the setting up self, our own reasons, our own wills, and bowing down to them, and serving them, as much a wrong to God as the bowing down to a senseless image? nay, worse than the adoring of an image, since that is senseless; but our wills corrupt, and are no more fit to be our God than an image is fit to be a representation of him. So that in the spiritual part of the command this must be included, to acknowledge nothing as the rule of perfection, but God; to set ourselves no other patterns of conformity but God, which the apostle phraseth a being new created after God, Eph. 4:24.

If all idolatry were forbidden, then that which is inward as well as that which is outward. If we were to have no other gods before him, then we were to prefer nothing inwardly before him; we were to make him our pattern, and be conformed to him; which we cannot, without another nature than that we had by corruption.

Upon this are those scriptures founded which speak of covetousness to be idolatry, Col. 3:5; that 'if any man love the world, the love of the Father is not in him,' 1 John 2:15; he doth not love God.

Now the preferring self before God is the essential part of the corrupt nature. Therefore all men, by the law of nature (which is the same with the moral law), and the Jews, to whom this law was given, were bound to have another nature than that which was derived from Adam, which essentially consisted in the making ourselves our god. Self-esteem, self-dependence, self-willedness, is denying affection and subjection to God.

By the ceremonial law more plainly. Their duty was not terminated in an external observance of the types and shadows under the law, but a heart-work God intended to signify to them in all those legal ceremonies. As sacrifices signified a necessity of expiation of sin, so their legal washings represented to them a necessity of regeneration.

Therefore God is said not to require the sacrifices of beasts: Ps. 40:6, 'Sacrifice and offering thou didst not desire' (that is, sacrifices of beasts), 'burnt-offerings and sin-offerings hast thou not required;' viz. as the ultimate object of his pleasure, but as representations of Christ, the great sacrifice. So neither did he command circumcision, and other legal purifications, for anything in themselves, or anything they could work, further than upon the body, but to signify unto them an inward work upon the heart. Hence they are said not to be commanded by God: Jer. 7:22, 23, 'For I spake not unto your fathers, nor commanded them in the day that I brought them out of the land of Egypt, concerning burnt-offerings or sacrifices; but this thing commanded I them, saying, Obey my voice.' That is, God did not principally require these as the things which did terminate his will and pleasure, but an obedience to him, and walking with him, which cannot be without an agreement of nature: 'For how can two walk together, unless they be agreed?' Amos 3:3. Hence God speaks so often to them of the circumcision of the heart, Deut. 10:16, and promises this circumcision of the heart: Deut. 30:6, 'And the Lord thy God will circumcise thy heart, and the heart of thy seed,' &c. And Paul expressly saith, Rom. 2:28, 29, that 'he was not a

Jew;' that is, a spiritual Jew, one of the spiritual seed of Abraham, who had the 'circumcision that was outward in the flesh,' but he that had 'that of the heart.'

So among us many confide in baptism, which signifieth nothing to men grown up, without an inward renewal and baptism of the heart, no more than outward circumcision did to them.

(4.) The obligation upon us is still the same.* The covenant made with Adam was made perpetually with him for all his posterity, therefore all his posterity, by that covenant, were perpetually obliged to a perfect righteousness. If God had made this covenant with Adam, that he should transfuse this original righteousness to his posterity only for such a time, then indeed, after the expiration of the term, the obligation had ceased, and none had been bound to have it as a debt required by God. The fault of wanting it had been removed without any infusion of grace, because the time being expired, and so the obligation ceasing, it had not been a fault to want it; neither could Adam's posterity have been charged with his sin, because the want of righteousness, after the expiration of the time fixed, had not been a sin. But because there was no time fixed, but that it was perpetually of force as to righteousness, which was the main intent of it, we still remain under the obligation of having a righteous nature.

Now God, seeing the impossibility of answering this obligation in our own persons, by our own strength, appoints a way whereby we may answer it in a second head, not nulling the former covenant as to the essential part of it, which was a righteous nature, but mitigating it, as the Chancery nulls not the common law, but sweetens the severity of it.

This latter covenant is called 'an everlasting covenant.' Not that the obligation of the other to righteousness is ceased, but transmitted to another head; which head cannot possibly fail, as our former did, who hath both a perfect righteousness in himself, and hath undertook for a perfect righteousness in his people, which he is able to accomplish, and to that purpose begins it here, and perfects it hereafter. To this purpose the Scripture speaks of the everlastingness of the covenant: Ps. 89:28, 'My covenant shall stand fast with him;' that is, with Christ. And if his people sin, as he expresseth it afterwards, yet 'my loving-kindness will I not utterly take from him.' In this respect Christ is called the covenant of the people: Isa. 42:6, 'I will give thee for a covenant of the people.' And the end of placing David his servant over his people, is not to give way to licentiousness and unrighteousness, and maintain men in an hostile nature against God, but that they might 'walk in his judgments, and observe his statutes,' Eze. 37:24; and that everlasting covenant of peace he would make with them is in order to sanctify them, Eze. 37:26, 28, compared together. When God would make a covenant of peace with them, an everlasting covenant, it was to set his sanctuary among them, and to let the heathen know that the Lord did sanctify Israel. And the end of the covenant is to 'put his law into the inward parts,' Jer. 31:33.

Christ undertook to keep up the honour of God, which was violated by the breach of that covenant, to 'make reconciliation for iniquity, and to bring in everlasting righteousness,' Dan. 9:24. This obligation our second head entered into for us, and in him we are complete, even as our head, and as the 'head of all principality and power,' Col. 2:10, who hath undertaken for our perfect righteousness; of our persons, by his own righteousness; of our nature, by inherent righteousness, as it follows, ver. 11, &c., 'In whom you are circumcised with the circumcision made without hands, in putting off the body of the sins of the flesh,' &c. This obligation still remains upon our head, and upon us in him, and to him we are to have recourse for a full answering of it. And this cannot be answered without a new birth here, which ends in a perfection hereafter. And Christ, by a plain precept, hath made it absolutely necessary now to all under the gospel administration.

So that no age, no time, no administration excludes it. It was as necessary to Adam, the first man, as to the last that shall be born. For being by nature spiritually dead, there must be a restoration to a spiritual life, if ever any be happy. 'God is not the God of the dead, but the God of the living.' What was alway necessary is absolutely necessary, and admits of no exception; and therefore the removal of the diabolical nature is indispensable to him and to us, since we are all the posterity of Adam, and the inheritors of his corruption. How can any, in any age, enjoy an infinite holy God, without being changed from their impurity?

Prop. 4. Hence it follows, that it is so necessary, that it is not conceivable by any man in his right wits how God can make any man happy without it. It is not for us, poor shallow creatures, to dispute what God can, and what God cannot do; what God may do by his absolute power. But yet it seems a contradiction, and it is not intelligible by as how God can make a man happy without regeneration.

What semblance of reason can be given that any one who is a slave of Satan, a child of wrath by nature, can be made the son and friend of God, without an expulsion of that nature which rendered him criminal, and restoring that in some degree which renders him innocent?

Without habitual grace, sin is not taken away; and as long as a man remains under sin, how he can be capable of any communion with God I understand not; for he cannot be at one and the same time under God's greatest wrath and his highest love. How is it possible that one can have an enjoyment of eternal life, who hath nothing in him but a relation to eternal death?

God made man's nature fit for his communion; man made himself unfit by guilt and filth. This unfitness must be removed by regeneration before this privilege man had by creation can be restored. Not that this restored righteousness is the cause of our communion with God in happiness, but a necessary requisite to it. No doubt but God might have restored this righteousness without admitting man to a converse with him, if there had been no covenant made to that purpose. That God may give grace without glory, is intelligible; but to admit a man to communion with him in glory, without grace, is not intelligible.

(1.) It is not agreeable to God's holiness to make any an inhabitant of heaven, and converse freely with him in a way of intimate love, without such a qualification of grace: Ps. 11:7, 'The righteous Lord loves righteousness; his countenance doth behold the upright.' He must, therefore, hate iniquity, and cannot love an unrighteous nature because of his love to righteousness; 'his countenance beholds the upright,' he looks upon him with a smiling eye, and therefore he cannot favourably look upon an unrighteous person, so that this necessity is not founded only in the command of God that we should be renewed, but in the very nature of the thing, because God, in regard of his holiness, cannot converse with an impure creature. God must change his nature, or the sinner's nature must be changed. There can be no friendly communion between two of different natures without the change of one of them into the likeness of the other. Wolves and sheep, darkness and light, can never agree. God cannot love a sinner as a sinner, because he hates impurity by a necessity of nature as well as a choice of will. It is as impossible for him to love it as to cease to be holy.

This change cannot be then on God's part; it must therefore be on man's part. It must therefore be by grace, whereby the sinner may be made fit for converse with God, since God cannot embrace a sinner in his dearest affections without a quality in the sinner suitable to himself. All converse is founded upon a likeness in nature and disposition; it is by grace only that the sinner is made capable of converse with God.

(2.) It is not agreeable to God's wisdom. Is it congruous to the wisdom of God to let a man be his child and the child of the devil at the same time? Is it fit to admit him to the relation of a son of God, who retains the enmity of his nature against God, to make any man happy with the dishonour of his laws, since he is not subject to the law of God, neither will be: one that cannot bear him, but abhors his honour and the apprehensions of his holiness?

Man naturally hath risings of heart against God, looks upon him under some dreadful notion, hath an utter aversion from him; alienation and enmity are inseparable: Col. 1:21, 'You who were sometimes alienated, and enemies in your minds.' It doth not consist with the wisdom of God to make any man happy against his will; God therefore first changeth the temper of the will by his powerful grace, thereby making him willing, and by degrees fitting him for happiness with him.

It is not fit corruption should inherit incorruption, or impurity be admitted to an undefiled inheritance, and therefore God brings none thither which are not first begotten by him to a lively hope, by the resurrection of Jesus Christ from the dead: 1 Peter 1:3, 4, 'Which according to his mercy hath begotten us again to a lively hope, by the resurrection of Jesus Christ from the dead, to an inheritance incorruptible, undefiled, and that fadeth not away, reserved in heaven for you.' It cannot be honourable for the wisdom of God to give a right to eternal life to one that continues a child of the devil, and bestow his love upon one that resolves to give his own heart to sin and Satan.

This which I have now discoursed is founded upon men's natural notions in their right reason. But if we look into the Scripture it is certain there is no other way but this: a man without a new birth can have no right to happiness by any covenant of God, by any truth of God, by any purchase of Christ. God never promised happiness without it; Christ never purchased it for any one without a new nature. No example is there extant of any person God hath made happy without this alteration, nor in the strictest inquiries can we conceive any other way possible; therefore if there be any one present that hath hopes to enjoy everlasting happiness without regeneration, he expects that which God never yet bestowed upon any, and which, according to our understanding, God cannot, without wrong to his holiness and wisdom, confer upon any person. I beseech you, therefore, let none of you build your hopes upon such vain foundations; you must be holy, or you shall never see God to your comfort.

Prop. 5. It is so necessary, that the coming and sufferings of our Lord and Saviour would seem insignificant without it. That this regeneration was a main end of his coming, is evident by his making this one of the main doctrines he was, as a prophet and teacher, sent from God to make known to the world, it being the first he taught Nicodemus. Jesus Christ came to glorify God, and to glorify himself in redeeming a people. And what glory can we conceive God hath, what glory can Christ have, if there be no characteristical difference between his people and the world? And what difference can there be but in a change of nature and temper, as the foundation whence all other differences do result? Sheep and goats differ in nature.

The righteousness which is given through our Mediator is the same, in the essentials and respects it bears to God, as we had at first. And his threefold office of king, priest, and prophet, is in order to it: his priestly, to reconcile and bring us to God; his prophetical, to teach us the way; and his kingly, to work in us those qualifications, and bestow that comely garb upon us that was necessary to fit us for our former converse. Our second Adam would not be like the first, if he failed in this great work of conveying his righteous nature to us, as Adam was to convey his original righteousness to his posterity. As that was to be conveyed by carnal generation, so the righteous nature of the second Adam is to be transmitted to us by spiritual regeneration. In this respect renewed men are called his seed, and counted to him for a generation, as Ps. 22:30, 'A seed shall serve him; it shall be accounted to the Lord ( )□□□□□for a generation,' to Christ; it shall be accounted as much the generation of Christ as the rest are the generation of Adam, as if they had proceeded out of his loins, as mankind did out of Adam's. As God looks upon believers as righteous through the righteousness of Christ as if it were their own, so he accounts them as if they were the generation of Jesus Christ himself.

(1.) Christ came to save from sin. Salvation from sin was more his work than barely salvation from hell: Mat. 1:21, 'He shall save his people from their sins.' From sin as the cause, from hell as the consequent. If from sin, was it only from the guilt of sin, and to leave the sinful nature unchanged? Was it only to take off punishment, and not to prepare for glory? It would have been then but the moiety of redemption, and not honourable for so great a Saviour. Can you imagine that the death of Jesus Christ, being necessary for the recovery of a sinner, was appointed for an incomplete work, to remit man's sin and continue the insolency of his nature against God? It was not his end only to save us from wrath to come, but to save us from the procuring-cause of that wrath; not forcibly and violently to save us, but in methods congruous to the honour of God's wisdom and holiness, and therefore to purify us: Tit. 2:14, 'To redeem us from all iniquity,' all parts of it, 'by purifying unto himself a peculiar people, zealous of good works,' that we might have a holy nature, whereby we might perform holy actions, and be as zealous of good works and the honour of God, as we had been of bad works and to bring dishonour to him.

It was also the end of his resurrection to 'quicken us to a newness of life,' Col. 2:12, 13, Eph. 2:5, 6. If any man without a new nature could set foot into heaven, a great intendment of the death and resurrection of Christ would be insignificant.

Christ came to take away sin, the guilt by his death, the filth by his Spirit, given us as the purchase of that death. In taking away sin he takes away also the sinful nature.

(2.) Christ came to destroy the works of the devil: 1 John 3:8, 'For this purpose the Son of God was manifested, that he might destroy the works of the devil.' These works are two, sin, and the misery consequent upon it. Upon the destruction of sin necessarily follows the dissolution of the other which was knit with it. If the sinful nature were not taken away, the devil's works would not wholly be destroyed; or if the sinful nature were taken away, and a righteous nature not planted in the stead of it, he would still have his ends against God in depriving God of the glory he ought to have from the creature. And the creature could not give God the glory he was designed by his creation to return, unless some nature were implanted in him whereby he might be enabled to do it.

Would it, then, be for the honour of this great Redeemer to come short of his end against Satan, to let all the trophies of Satan remain, in the errors of the understanding, perversity of the will, disorder of the affections, and confusion of the whole soul? Or if our Saviour had only removed these, how had the works of the devil been destroyed if we had lain open to his assaults, and been liable the next moment to be brought into the same condition, which surely would have been, were not a righteous and divine nature bestowed upon the creature.

(3.) Christ came to bring us to God: 1 Peter 3:18, 'For Christ also hath once suffered for sins, the just for the unjust, that he might bring us to God.' Was it to bring us to God with all our pollutions, which were the cause God cast us off? No; but to bring us in such a garb as that we might be fit to converse with him. Can we be so without a new nature and a spiritual likeness to God? Would that man who would bring another to a prince to introduce him into favour, bring him into his presence in a slovenly and sordid habit, such a garb which he knew was hateful to the prince? Neither will our Saviour, nor can he bring sinners in such a plight to God, because it is more contrary to the nature of God's holiness to have communion with such, than it is contrary to the nature of light to have communion with darkness, 1 John 1:5–7. Can it be thought that Christ should come to set human nature right with God, without a change of that principle which caused the first revolt from God? Besides, since the coming of Christ was to please God, and to glorify him in all his attributes, as well as to save us, how can God be pleased with the effects of

Christ's death, if he brought the creature to him without any change of nature, but with its former enmity and pollution? Will you say his mercy would be glorified? How can that be without a wrong to his purity, and a provocation to his justice? Suppose such a dispute were in God, would not holiness, wisdom, justice, joined together, over-vote mercy?

But since there can be no such dispute, how can we conceive that mercy, an infinite perfection in God, can desire anything to the prejudice of the honour of his holiness, justice, and wisdom?

Well, then, if we expect happiness without a renewed nature, we would make Christ a minister of sin as well as of righteousness, Gal. 2:17, &c. As there is a justification by him, so his intent was to plant a living principle in us, whereby we might be enabled to live to him. It is in vain, then, to think to find any benefit by the death of Christ without a new nature, any more than from God without it.

Prop. 6. The end of the Spirit's coming manifests it to be necessary. We are said therefore to be 'saved by the washing of regeneration, and renewing of the Holy Ghost,' Titus 3:5, 2 Thes. 2:13. As God by his Spirit, moving upon the face of the waters, created the world, so God by his Spirit, moving upon the face of the soul, new creates all the faculties of it. Can the coming of Christ, and the coming of the Spirit, the most signal favours of God to mankind, be intended for no other end than to convey to us the mercy of God, with the dishonour of his holiness, to change our misery without changing our nature, and putting us in a capacity both to glorify God and enjoy him? To what purpose doth the Spirit come, if not to renew? Whatsoever was the office of the Spirit, cannot be supposed to be exercised without this foundation. Can there be any seal of the Spirit without some impression made upon the soul like to the Spirit, which is the seal whereby we are sealed? Can he witness to us that we are the children of God, if there be no principle in us suitable to God as a father, no child-like frame? Is the Spirit only to bring things to remembrance for a bare speculation, without any operative effect? Is he to help us in prayer? How can that be, without giving us first a sense of what we need, and a praying heart? And how can we have a praying heart till our natures, so averse from God and his worship, be changed? He is a 'quickening Spirit,' 2 Cor. 3:6, 'the Spirit gives life.' How can that be while we lie rotting in our former death? It is a 'Spirit of holiness.' Can he dwell in a soul that hath an unholy nature? Though he find men so at his first coming, would he not quickly be weary of his house if it continued so? He comes to change our old nature, not to encourage it. What fruits of the Spirit could appear without the change of the nature of the soil?

Prop. 7. From all this it follows that this new birth is necessary in every part of the soul. There is not a faculty but is corrupted, and therefore not a faculty but must be restored. Not a wheel, not a pin in all this clock of the heart but is out of frame; not one part wherein sin and Satan have not left the marks of their feet: Titus 1:15, 'Their mind and conscience is defiled.' It is clearer to a regenerate soul that it is so, since by the light of grace he discerns a filth in every faculty. The more knowledge of God he hath, the more he discovers his ignorance; the more love to God, the more he finds and is ashamed of his enmity. And though in our imperfect regeneration here, grace and sin are in every part of the soul, as wine and water mingled together are in every part of the vessel, yet every faculty is in part renewed; and grace and sin lie not so huddled together but that the soul can distinguish them, and be able to say, this is grace, this is part of the new Adam, and this is sin, and part of the old Adam in me.

Because there was an universal depravation by the fall, regeneration must answer it in its extensiveness in every faculty. Otherwise it is not the birth of the man, but of one part only. It is but a new piece, not a new creature. This or that faculty may be said to be new, not the soul, not the man. We are all over bemired by the puddle of sin, and we must be all over washed by the water of grace. A whole sanctification is the proper fruit of reconciliation: 1 Thes. 5:23, 'The God of peace sanctify you wholly.'

Reconciliation was of the whole man, so must regeneration. Sin hath rooted itself in every part; ignorance and error in our understandings; pride, and self-love, and enmity in our wills; all must be unrooted by a new grace, and the triumphs of sin spoiled by a new birth.

Prop. 8. It is so necessary, that even the dim eye of natural reason has been apprehensive of some need of it. And, therefore, it is a wonder that there should be a need of pressing it upon men under the light of the gospel. Those doctrines that are purely intellectual and supernatural, are not so easily apprehended by men, as having no footing in reason, whereby reason is rendered unpliable to consent to them. But those doctrines that tend to the reformation of man carry a greater conviction, as having some notion of a depravation, which gives them some countenance in the minds of men, though not in their affection. Men cannot conceive any notion of God's greatness, majesty, and holiness, but they must also conceive something necessary to an enjoyment of him (wherein their felicity consists), besides those natural principles which they find in themselves. Natural reason must needs assent to this, that there must be some other complexion of the soul to fit us for a converse with so pure a majesty. The wiser sort of heathens did see themselves out of frame; the tumult and disorder in their faculties could not but be sensible to them. They found the flights of their souls too weak for their vast desires. They acknowledged the wings of it to be clipped, and that they never came so out of the hands of God. That therefore there was a necessity of some restorative above the art of man to complete the work. And I think I have read of one of them that should say, That there could not be a reformation unless God would take flesh. They had 'the work of the law written in their hearts,' Rom. 2:15. They knew such works were to be done; they found themselves unable to do them. Whence would follow that there must be some other principle to enable them than what they had by nature. To this purpose they invented their purgative virtues; and by those and other means hoped to arrive to an ὁμοίωσις τῷ θεῷ, which they much talked of as necessary to a converse with God. As they were sensible of their guilt, and therefore had sacrifices for the expiation of that, so they were sensible of their filth, and had their purifications and washings for the cleansing of that. Hence it was that they admired those men that acted in a higher sphere of moral virtue and moderation than others. Some of them have acknowledged the malady, but despaired of a remedy, judging it above the power of nature to cure. Certainly that which the wisest heathens, in the darkness of nature, without knowledge either of law or gospel, have counted necessary; and since it is seconded by so plain a declaration of our Saviour, must be indisputably necessary.* Plato in several places saith, That there was a certain divine principle in our minds at first, but that it was abolished, and God would again renew and form the soul with a kind of divinity.

How vain then are men, how inexcusably foolish, to neglect both the light of the gospel and that of reason too; that spend not one hour, one minute, in a serious consideration of it and enquiry after it; in slighting their own reason as well as the express declaration of Jesus Christ. Oh that men were sensible of this, which is of so great concernment to them.

II. I come to shew that regeneration is necessary.

1. It is necesary to a gospel state.

(1.) Nothing can exist in any state of being without a proper form. That which hath not the form of a thing is not a thing of the same species. He cannot be a man that wants a rational form of a man, a soul. And how can any man be a Christian without that which doth essentially constitute a Christian? We can no more be Christians without a Christian nature, than a man can be a man without human nature. Grace only gives being to a Christian, and constitutes him so: 1 Cor. 15:10, 'By the grace of God I am what I am: and his grace which was bestowed on me was not in vain, but I laboured more abundantly than they all.' Grace there is meant of habitual grace, because he speaks of his labour as the fruit of it. In bodily life brutes go beyond us, in the vigour of senses, greatness of strength, temperance, natural affection. In reason and moral virtues many heathens have excelled us. There is something else, then, necessary for the constitution of a Christian, and that is, Christ's living in him by a new forming of his soul by his Spirit. As the body lives by the soul, which distributes natural, vital, and animal spirits to every part of the body, for the performance of its several functions; so the soul lives by grace, which diffuseth its vigour to every part, the understanding, will, and affections.

(2.) There is no suitableness to a gospel state and government without it. In all changes of government in the world there is a change in the whole state of affairs, in those that are the instruments of government, in the principles of those that submit to the government. After the fall of man God set up a new mode of government. All judgment was committed to the Son: John 5:22, 'For the Father judges no man, but hath committed all judgment to the Son.' Ver. 27, 'And hath given him authority to execute judgment.' The whole administration of affairs is put into his hand; not excluding the Father, who still gave out his orders in the government, wherefore he saith, ver. 30, 'I can of myself do nothing; as I hear, I judge.' There must be, therefore, some agreement between the frame of this government and the subjects of it. As there is a new Adam, a new covenant, a new priesthood, a new spirit; so there must be a new heart, new compacts, new offerings, new resolutions. New administrations and old services can no more be pieced together than new cloth and old garments. The gospel state of the church is called a new heaven and a new earth. Man is by the inclinations of his corrupt nature obedient to the law of sin. There must be a cure and change of those inclinations, to make them tend to an observance of the orders of this new government, and an hearty observation of it, 2 Cor. 5:17, 'Old things are passed away; behold, all things are become new, and all things are of God' (so they were before), but now in a new manner and frame; and this is the reason rendered why every man in Christ must be a new creature.

(3.) All the subjects of this government have been brought in this way, not one excepted. Though God hath chosen some that he would bless for ever under this evangelical government, yet notwithstanding the purpose of God they are in as great unfitness for this state as the worst of men, till God exerting his power fashions them to be vessels of honour to himself. It is not God's choice of any man which puts any man into a gospel state, without the operation of the Spirit, renewing the mind and fitting him for it. All that were designed by God's eternal purpose were to be brought in by this way of the new birth, as 2 Thess. 2:13, 'God hath from the beginning chosen you to salvation, through sanctification of the Spirit and belief of the truth.' And by this they were fortified against all those workings of the mystery of iniquity, against the government of Christ and the state of the gospel, which would be damnable and destructive to many; for he had spoken of that before, upon which occasion he brings this in. 'A chosen generation, a holy nation, a peculiar people,' are joined together, 1 Peter 2:9. Peculiar they could not be, unless they had something of an intrinsic value in them above others, and a peculiar fitness for special service, and to offer spiritual sacrifices, therefore called also a royal priesthood.

(4.) The end of the particular institutions, of initiation or admission, under the two different administrations of this government, was to signify this—of circumcision under the law, and baptism under the gospel. Both signified the corruption and filthiness of nature, and the necessity of the circumcision of the heart and the purification of nature. Hence baptism is called 'the laver of regeneration,' Titus 3:5,* many understanding it of baptism. Not that these did confer this new nature in a physical way, or that it was alway conferred in the administration of them, but the necessity of having this was alway signified by them. Therefore one of the Jews,† against the opinion of his countrymen, saith absolutely, it is a madness to think that those ceremonies, under their administration, were appointed only for the purification of the body without that of the soul. And Rom. 2:29, saith the apostle, 'He is a Jew which is one inwardly, and circumcision is that of the heart in the spirit.' So that partaking of baptism, and being intrusted with the oracles of God, make a man no more a Christian than circumcision, &c., did make a man a Jew. He is only a Christian that hath a Christian nature. The necessity of this nature was evidenced and signified both by the one and by the other.

In every state there are duties to be performed and privileges to be enjoyed. So likewise in the gospel state. Without a new birth we cannot perform the one or be capable of the other.

2. It is necessary to the performance of gospel duties.

(1.) There can be no preparation to any service without it. Man's soul at first could make a spiritual music to God, till the flesh disordered the strings, and no music can be made till the Spirit puts the instrument in tune again. In Jesus Christ we are 'created to good works,' Eph. 2:10. Therefore no preparation can be before the new creation, no more than there was a preparation in the matter without form and void to become a world. What evangelical duties can be performed without an evangelical impression, without the forming of Christ and the doctrine of Christ in the heart, not only in the notion, but the operative and penetrating power of it? The heart must be first moulded, and cast into the frame of the doctrine of the gospel, before it can obey it, as Rom. 6:17, 'But ye have obeyed from the heart that form of doctrine which was delivered unto you,' or, 'unto which you were delivered.' The mould wherein a thing is cast makes it fit for the operation for which it is intended. The ship that wants any material thing in its make cannot sail well, will not obey the directions of the pilot; and he that wants grace will be carried away with the breath of every sin and temptation. All the motions and rollings naturally in ways of duty by other principles, cannot make an aptitude to divine services, no more than a thousand times flinging up a stone into the air can produce any natural fitness in it for such an elevation any more than it had at first, which was none at all. Where should we have any preparation? It cannot be from Adam; he died a spiritual death by his sin, and had no natural fitness for any spiritual service, and therefore cannot convey by nature more to his posterity than what he had by nature; what grace he had afterwards was bestowed upon his person, not upon the nature which was to be transmitted to his posterity.

(2.) Therefore we cannot act any evangelical service without a new nature. If we have no natural preparation, we can have no natural action. The law must be written in our hearts before it be formed into the life, Jer. 31:33, 34, 'I will put my law in their inward parts, and write it in their hearts.' It is then, and then only, that we have a practical and affectionate knowledge of God, 'And they shall know me from the least unto the greatest.' Restoration to a supernatural life must be before there can be supernatural actions, a just nature before a just walk, as Hosea 14:9, 'The just shall walk in them,' that is, in the ways of God. The motion of the creature is not the cause but the effect of life. The evangelical service is not the cause of righteousness but the effect. We cannot walk in one commandment of God till the law be written in our inward parts, Ezek. 36:14. Those that have not a new heart cannot walk in God's statutes. We can never answer the terms of the covenant without a new nature. For,

[1.] No act can transcend the principle of it. There is a certainty in this rule; that the elevation of an inferior nature to the acts of a superior nature cannot be without some inward participation of that superior nature. The operation of everything follows the nature of the thing. A beast cannot act like a man without partaking of the nature of a man, nor a man act like an angel without partaking of the angelical nature. How then can a man act divinely without a participation of the divine nature? Duties of a supernatural strain, as evangelic duties are, require a supernatural frame of spirit. Nothing can exceed the bounds of its nature, for then it should exceed itself in acting. Whatsoever service, therefore, doth proceed from mere nature, cannot amount to a gospel-service, because it comes not from a gospel-principle. We cannot believe without a habit of faith, nor love without a habit of love; for this only renders us able to perform such acts. Justification is necessary to our state as well as regeneration; but regeneration seems to be more necessary to our duties than the former; this principally to the performance of them, the other to the acceptance of them.

[2.] The nature doth always tincture the fruit of it. Our Saviour, by his interrogation, implies an impossibility that those that are evil should speak good things: Mat. 12:34, 'O generation of vipers, how can you, being evil, speak good things? for out of the abundance of the heart the mouth speaks.' The very hissings of a viper proceed from the malice of its nature. As the root is, so is all the fruit. From one seed many grains arise, yet all partake of the nature of that seed. Streams partake of the quality of the fountain. If the seed, root, and fountain be good, so is whatsoever springs from them. There is not one righteous man by nature, neither Jew nor Gentle, all are concluded under sin: Rom. 3:10, 'There is none righteous, no, not one;' none that 'understands and seeks God,' &c. He adds not one twice; he exempts none, not one righteous by nature, not one righteous action by nature: 'none that doth good, no, not one.' He applies it to all mankind. A poisonous nature can produce nothing but poisonous fruit. Our actions smell as rank as nature itself. Whatsoever riseth from thence, though never so spacious and well-coloured, is evil and unprofitable. If, therefore, we would produce good fruit, we must have a new root, seed, and spring. Our sour nature must be changed into a sweetness and purity. If the vine be empty, the fruit will be so too: Hosea 10:1, 'Ephraim is an empty vine, he brings forth fruit to himself,' or, 'equal to himself,' .□□□□Unless the tree be good, the fruit can never be generous: Mat. 7:17, 18, 'Neither can a corrupt tree bring forth good fruit.' We must have the Spirit before we can bring forth the fruits of the Spirit. All good services are related to this, as effects to their cause; so that what a man doth by an act of reason, and natural conscience, and good education, if his understanding and conscience remain wholly under their natural pollution, the service is not good, because the soul is corrupt; much less are those services good which are the fruit only of humour. How the soul can be habitually sinful, and yet the acts flowing from it be good, is not easily conceivable; it is against the stream of natural observation. It is true, indeed, that a man that is habituated to one kind of sin may do an action that receives no tincture from that particular habit, because it doth not proceed from it; as a drunkard gives an alms, his giving alms hath no infection inherent from that particular habit of drunkenness, but from the nature, which is wholly corrupt, it hath. 'Who can bring a clean thing out of an unclean? not one,' Job 14:4. Who can bring a clean service out of a miry heart? Not one man in the world. We cannot, therefore, perform any evangelical service if those foundations be considered.

Not spiritually, because we are flesh. God must be 'worshipped in spirit,' John 4:44; in a spiritual manner, with spiritual frames. The apostle speaks of 'walking in the spirit,' Phil. 3:3, and 'praying in the Holy Ghost,' Jude 20. None can act spiritually but those that are 'born of the Spirit;' and no action is spiritual but what proceeds from a renewed principle. The most glittering and refined flesh is but flesh in a higher sphere of flesh, therefore whatsoever springs up from that principle is fleshly, upon the former foundation, that nothing can rise higher than its nature. You may as well expect to gather grapes of thorns as spiritual duties from carnal hearts: Mat. 7:16, 'Do men gather grapes of thorns, or figs of thistles?' If a natural man 'cannot receive,' and 'cannot know the things of God, because they are spiritually discerned,' 1 Cor. 2:14, how should he perform the duties belonging to God, since they are spiritually to be performed? We are naturally more averse to motions upon our wills than to the illuminations of our minds. An appetite for knowledge, and a flight from God being both the fruits of Adam's fall, who was both curious to know, as God, and fearing to approach to God after his fall. There may be some services in natural men which may look like spiritual, but in the principle they are not so. Many acts are done by irrational creatures which look like rational acts. As the order among bees, like the acts of statesmen regulating a commonwealth; their carrying gravel in their fangs to poise them in a storm, and hinder them from being carried away by the violence of the wind; yet these are not rational acts, because they proceed not from reason, but from a natural instinct put into them by God, the supreme governor. So that as no action of an ape, though like the action of a man, can be said to be a human act, so no action of an unregenerate man, though like a spiritual action, can be called spiritual, because it proceeds not from a spiritual principle, but from a contrary one paramount in him. And all actions have their true denomination from the principle whence they flow. They may be fruits of morality, and fruits of conscience, but not spiritual fruits, which God requires.

Well, then, we must be first built up 'a spiritual house,' we must be a 'priesthood' before we can 'offer spiritual sacrifice,' 1 Peter 2:5. We must have the powerful operation of the Holy Ghost in us before we can have a tincture of the Holy Ghost upon our services. In all human acts, we should act as rational creatures; in all religious acts, as spiritual creatures. Now, as a man cannot act rationally without reason, so neither can we act spiritually without a divine spirit in us. We are indeed to serve God, and worship him as men; therefore rational acts are due to God in worship, and we are constituted in the rank of rational beings to that purpose. But since our minds are defiled, they must be purified; since our understandings are darkened, they must be enlightened. There must be a grace infused, a lamp set up, a spiritual awakening, and invigorating our reasons and wills, before we can worship God as God in a spiritual manner.

We cannot perform any evangelical service, vitally, because we are dead. Our services must be living services, if in any wise they be suitable to a living God. The apostle wishes us, Rom. 12:1, to 'present our bodies a living sacrifice.' He doth not mean only our bodies, consisting of flesh and bones, or a natural life; but he names the body as being the instrument of motion and service, or it may be synecdoche partis pro toto, a part for the whole. Present yourselves as a sacrifice consecrated to God, and living to him, and as living by him.

Upon the loss of original righteousness, another form or principle was introduced, called in Scripture flesh, and a body of death. Hence by nature we are said to be dead, Eph. 2:1, and all our works before repentance are dead works, Heb. 6:1. And these works have no true beauty in them, with whatsoever gloss they may appear to a natural eye. A dead body may have something of the features and beauty of a living, but it is but the beauty of a carcase, not of a man. A statue, by the stone-cutter's art, and the painter's skill, may be made very comely, yet it is but a statue still; where is the life? Such services are but the works of art, as flowers painted on the wall with curious colours, but where is the vegetative principle? Since man, therefore, is spiritually dead, he cannot perform a living service. As a natural death doth incapacitate for natural actions, so a spiritual death must incapacitate for spiritual actions. Otherwise, in what sense can it be called a death, if a man in a state of nature were as capable of performing spiritual actions as one in a state of grace? No vital act can be exercised without a vital principle. As Adam could not stir to perform any action, though his body was framed and perfected, till God breathed into him a living soul, so neither can we stir spiritually till God breathe into us a living grace. Spiritual motions can no more be without a spiritual life than bodily motions can be without an enlivening soul. 'The living, the living, they shall praise thee;' and Ps. 80:18, 'Quicken us, and we will call upon thy name.' There can be no living praise, nor no living prayer, without a renewed heart. If it be one effect of the blood of Christ to 'purge our consciences from dead works, to serve the living God,' as Heb. 9:14, then it is clear that till our consciences are purged from dead works we cannot serve the living God; for what suitableness can there be between a living God and dead services? Is a putrefied rank carcase a fit present for a king? or a man full of running sores and boils over his whole body fit to serve in a prince's chamber? Our best services, without a new nature, though they may appear varnished and glittering to man, yet in the sight of God they have no life, no substance, but stinking rotten dust, because coming from a dead and rotten heart.

Well, then, we must be born again; it is not a dead nature, nor a dead faith, can produce living fruit for God. We may as well read without eyes, walk without legs, act without life, as perform any service to God without a new nature; no, we cannot perform the least: a dead man can no more move his finger than his whole body.

Not graciously, because we are corrupt. By the same reason that we are to speak with grace, Col. 4:6, and to sing with grace in our hearts to the Lord, Col. 3:16, we are to do every other duty with an exercise of grace to God: and without grace, our praises are but hollowings, our prayers but howlings, as the Scripture terms them: Hosea 7:14, 'They have not cried to me with their hearts, when they howled upon their beds.' How can there be an exercise of that which is not? The skill of the musician cannot discover itself till the instrument be made tuneable. The heart must be strung with grace by the Spirit, before that Spirit can touch the strings to make harmony to God in a gospel service. Our tempers must be changed, our hearts fitted, before we can make melody to God. The principal beauty and glory of a duty lies in the internal workings of the heart; and how can that heart work graciously, that hath nothing of God and his grace in it? It is said, 'Folly is bound up in the heart of a child,' Prov. 22:15. So is corruption in the heart of a man, like poison in a bundle of stuff; it is entered into the very composition of us. A law of sin is predominant in a natural man, Rom. 7:23, which doth influence all his actions. Strong habits will interest themselves in all we go about, and all a man's services are regulated by it, for he hath no other law in his mind to check the motions of it, and to scent his duties, whereby they may carry a pleasing savour to God. The gift of prophecy, the understanding of mysteries, the depth of knowledge, the removing mountains, bestowing alms, dying for religion, are brave and noble acts; but without charity, love to God, without which, no other grace can work, all these profit nothing, 1 Cor. 13:2, 3. There is a moral goodness in feeding the poor, but no gracious goodness without charity. A little of this would make those, as a diamond doth gold wherein it is set, more valuable. If all those profit nothing without this grace of charity, they would profit much with it. How doth grace alter the very nature of services? Those acts which are sensitive in a brute, were he transformed into a man, and endued with reason, would become rational. Those actions which are but moral in a mere man, when changed into Christian, become evangelical; they would be of another nature and another value.

Well, then, look after the new birth, since it is so necessary. There cannot be gracious practices without gracious principles. Can anything fly to heaven without wings? We are to walk as Christ walked; how can we do it without a principle of kin to that which Christ had? We are bound to act from a principle of righteousness; Adam was, and his posterity are; and should we not look after that which is so necessary a perfection, requisite for our services? No doubt but the devil could find matter enough for prayer, and from the excellency of his knowledge, frame some rare strains, as some word it; but would it be a service which came from such a nature? As long as we are allied to him in our nature, our services will be of as little value. He transforms himself into an angel of light, but is still a devil; and many men do so in their religious acts, yet still remain unregenerate.

Not freely and voluntarily, because we are at enmity. A natural man's services are forced, not free. The aversion of our natures from God is as strong as their inclination to evil. We have no fervent desires to love God, and therefore no desires to do anything out of affection to him. When sensual habits are planted in the soul, there is an enmity to God in the mind: it will not be 'subject to the law of God,' Rom. 8, and whilst that habit sways, it cannot. This inclination to sin, and consequently aversion to good, is incorporated in nature, like blackness in a negro, or spots in a leopard; they are accustomed to sin, and cannot do good, Jer. 13:23. There is no agreeableness between God and man's soul, whilst there is a friendship between the heart and sin; he affects the one, and is disgusted with the other: one is his pleasure, the other his trouble; he hath no will, no heart to come to God in any service, and when he doth, he is rather dragged, than sweetly drawn. The things of God are against the bent of a natural heart; there is nothing so irksome as the most spiritual service; when men engage in them, they row against the stream of nature itself. There must, therefore, be something of a contrary efficacy to overpower this violent tide, a law of grace to renew the mind and turn the motions of the will, to another channel. Restraining grace may for a while stop the current, but not turn and change the natural course. A carnal mind conceits the things of God and his spiritual service to be foolishness, and therefore contemns them, 1 Cor. 1:23, 24. The eye of the mind must be opened to discern the wisdom of God in them, before he can affect them. The heart should be lifted up in the evangelical ways of God. Can mere flesh be thus? Force can never change nature. You may hurl lead up into the air, but it will never ascend of itself while it is lead, unless it be rarified into air or fire. Keep up iron many years in the air by the force of a loadstone, it will retain its tendency to fall to the earth if the obstacle be removed; the natural gravity is suspended, not altered. Till the nature of the will be altered, it can never move freely to any duty; there must be a power to will, before there is a will to do, as Philip. 2:13, 'It is God which works in you both to will and to do.' A supernatural renewing grace must expel corrupt habits from the will, and reduce it to its true object. When faith is planted, it brings love to work by; when the soul is renewed, there is an harmony between God and the heart, between the mind and the word, between the will and the duty; when the appetite and true taste of the soul is restored in regeneration, then spring up strong desires to apply itself to every holy service: 1 Peter 2:2, 3, 'The sincere milk of the word' is fervently desired, after it is spiritually tasted.

Well, then, there must be a change in us, or in the law. The law is spiritual, man is carnal, Rom. 7:14. The law can have no friendship for man, nor man no friendship for the law in this state, since their natures are so contrary. What the law commands is disgustful to the flesh, what the flesh desires is displeasing to the law. There must then be a change; the law must become carnal, or man become spiritual, before any agreement can be between them. Where do you think this change must light? It can never be in the law, therefore it must be in man. The wound in our wills must be cured; the tide of nature, that never carries us to God, must be turned, and altered by a stream of grace, to move us to him and his service. Man hath been a slave to his lust by the loss of grace, and is never like to be restored to his liberty in the service of God, till he be repossessed of that grace, the loss of which brought him into slavery. The gospel is a 'law of liberty,' James 1:25; a servile spirit doth not suit a free law, neither is it a fit frame for an evangelical service.

Nor delightfully. We can never perform spiritual services with delight, because we are alienated. This we are to do. Paul 'delighted in the law of God,' Rom. 7:22; and the law was the 'delights' of David, Ps. 119:92; his whole pleasure ran in this channel. Now, because of that aversion to God, there is no will and freedom in his service, much less can there be a delight. A corrupt nature can have no divine strains; a diseased man hath no delight in his own acts, his distemper makes his very motion unpleasant to him. Things that are not natural can never be delightful.

There is a mighty distance between spiritual duties and a carnal heart. Things out of their place can never be an rest. Sin is as much a natural man's element as water to a fish or air to a bird; if he be stopped in the ways of the flesh, he is restless till he return. He may indeed have some delight sometimes in a service—not as it respects God as the object, or God as the end, there is no such friendship in a natural man's heart to him—but there is an agreement between a service and some carnal end he performs it for. His delight is not terminated in the service, but in self-love, self-interest, or some external reward, anchored in it by some hopes of carnal advantage, not springing from a living love or a gracious affection to God. He hath no knowledge of God, and therefore can have no delight in God or in his service. It is impossible we can come before him without pleasure and delight, if we know how amiable he is in his person, and how gracious in his nature; but we naturally think God a hard master, and man having no delight in God, he can have none in those means which lead him to God, and as they are appointed to bring God and his soul together. He hath wrong notions of duties, looks upon them as drudgeries, not as advantages: Mal. 1:13, 'Ye said, Behold, what a weariness it is,' &c. Without a change of nature, we cannot desire communion with God, and therefore cannot delight in the means of it. We can no more do any service cheerfully than the saints without it could 'receive joyfully the spoiling of their goods,' Heb. 10:34. We can never be in a holy ecstasy without this inward principle, to make the gospel services connatural to us. This only makes high impressions upon the soul. It is the law within our hearts, which only makes us delight to do his will: Ps. 40:8, 'Thy law is within my heart,' in my bowels. He had a natural affection to it, and then a high delight in it. It made our Saviour delight to do his work; and it was the inward man of the heart, wherein the apostle's delight in the law was placed. Unless we have a divine impression of God upon us, we cannot hear his word with any joy in it; as our Saviour saith, John 8:47, 'Ye therefore hear them not,' that is, the words of God, 'because you are not of God.' Unless we have God's light and his truth sent forth into us, we can never make God our exceeding joy, or go to his altar with such a frame, Ps. 43:3, 4.

Well, then, there is a necessity of the new nature, to have a warm frame of heart in evangelical duties. What is connatural to us is only delightful. So much of weariness and bondage we have in any holy service, so much of a legal frame; so much of love and delight, so much we have of a new covenant grace. A spirit of adoption and regeneration only can make us delight to come to our father, and to cry Abba to him.

Without regeneration we cannot perform evangelical duties sincerely, because we are a lie, and in our best estate vanity. We must worship God 'in truth' as well as 'spirit,' John 4:24. God is a Spirit, and therefore must be worshipped in spirit. God is truth, and therefore must be worshipped in truth. Without a new nature we cannot worship God in truth. The old nature is in itself a lie, a mere falsity, something contrary to that nature God created. It was first introduced by a lie of the devil ('ye shall be as gods, knowing good and evil,' Gen. 3:5), and thereupon a fancy that God lied in his command. How can we serve God with this nature, which had nothing but a lie for its foundation,—a lie of the devil, a lie in our fancy? Therefore our old nature is no better than a lie. How can we serve God with that nature which is quite another thing to that of his framing? Man in his fall is a liar: Rom. 3:4, 'Let God be true, and every man a liar,' a covenant-breaker, that kept not his faith with God. God, in respect of truth, and man, in respect of lying, are set in opposition by the apostle there. No man but would slight and scorn that service from another, which he knew to be a lying service in the very frame of it. There is no truth can be in any service which is founded only upon an old nature, and performed by one that is acted by the father of lies; and so is every unregenerate man, every 'child of disobedience,' Eph. 2:2.

Now, sincerity cannot be without a new nature,

(1.) Because there are no divine motives which should sway the soul. Most services of natural men have such dirty springs, so unsuitable to that raised temper men should have in dealing with God, that they produce sacrifices not fit to be offered to an earthly governor: Mal. 1:8, 'If you offer the blind for sacrifice, is it not evil?' &c., 'offer it now unto thy governor, will he be pleased with thee?' Had they had divine motives, they had never brought such sickly services. What was not fit for themselves, they thought fit for God. Did but princes know what motives many had in their services, they would with as much scorn reject them as they do ignorantly receive them with affection. But it is otherwise with God, who knows all the springs and wards in that lock of the heart of his own framing. Do not most services take their rise from custom, or from an outward religions education barely, or at best from natural conscience, which though it be all in a man, which takes God's part, yet it is flesh, and defiled? And what pure vapours can be expected from a lake of Sodom? Titus 1:15, 'To them that are defiled and unbelieving nothing is pure; but even their mind and conscience is defiled.' The mind, which is the repository of natural light, and the conscience, which is the advocate of natural light, and applies it upon particular occasion, are defiled, and that in every unbelieving person. Can the motives which conscience takes from a dark and defiled principle, as the mind is, be divine? It is fear of death, wrath, and judgment which it mostly applies. These are the motives of defilement. Fear is the natural consequence of pollution; without sin and corruption we never had had any fear of hell. That cannot be gracious which springs naturally from the commission of sin, and can this be divine? Were there no punishment feared, there should be no duty performed. Conscience hath naturally no basis to stand upon but this. What is the principle of his fear? Self. It is not therefore obedience to God, but self-preservation, sways a man. Fear is but a servile disposition, and therefore cannot make a service good. All such extrinsic motives which arise not from a new life, are no more divine than the weights of a clock may be said to have life because they set the wheels on running. The same action may be done by several persons upon different principles and motives, for which one may be rewarded, the other not; as Mat. 10:41, 42, 'He that receives a righteous man, in the name of a righteous man, shall receive a righteous man's reward. And whosoever shall give unto one of these little ones a cup of cold water only in the name of a disciple, he shall in no wise lose his reward.' One may receive a member of Christ out of respect to Christ and the relation the person hath to him, another may receive the same person out of a common principle of humanity; the action is the same, the good redounding to the object is the same; nay, it may be greater in him that acts from a commiseration of him, as a man, than a cup of cold water from the other, because his ability is greater; but the inward respect to the object is different. One respects him as a man of the same nature with himself in misery, the other respects him as a member of Christ in misery; one respects him as a man, the other as a righteous man. The principle is different: one relieves him out of a natural compassion, common to a heathen with him, the other out of a Christian affection to his Head. The actions are therefore different, because of their motives: one is reward-able, and promised to be rewarded, the other not; one may be from grace—I do not say it always is, unless there be a constant tenor of such motives in our actions; for a natural man, under the preaching of the gospel, may do such a thing out of a present and transient respect to Christ, whom he hears so often of, and hath some presumption to be saved by, but it is not his constant frame—I say, one may be from grace, the other from nature.

Therefore from hence results a necessity of the alteration of the frame of our souls, to furnish us with divine and heavenly motives for our actions. A man may do a thing by nature from a good principle, a principle of common honesty, good in its kind (brass is good in its kind, but not so good as silver), but not evangelically good, without a renewed affection to God: John 14:15, 'If you love me, keep my commandments;' keep what I command you, out of affection to me. Where 'the imagination of the heart is evil, and only evil, and that continually,' Gen. 6:5, all the service a man in that state performs riseth from this spring, and hath some infectious imagination in it, highly abominable to God; either wrong notions of God in it, or wrong notions of the duty, or corrupt motives, something or other of the evil imagination of the heart, mixes itself with it.

(2.) Without a renewed nature, as there are no divine motives, so there can be no divine ends. We are bound to refer our natural actions, much more our religious services, to the glory of God. The end is the moral principle of every action. It is that which confers a goodness or badness upon the service: Luke 11:34, 'If the eye be evil, the whole body is full of darkness' (this is commonly understood of a man's aim). If the intention be evil, there is nothing but darkness in the whole service. The perfection of everything consists in answering the end for which it was framed. That which was the first end of our framing, ought to be the end of our acting, viz. the glory of God. But man hath taken himself off from this end, and hath been fond of making himself his chief good and ultimate end. Men naturally have corrupt ends in good duties. Pride is the cause of some men's virtue. And they are spiritually vicious in avoiding crimes, because they intrench too much upon their reputation. The pharisees made their devotion contribute to their ambition: Mat. 6:5, 'They pray to be seen of men,' and Mat. 23:5, 'But all their works they do to be seen of men.' Not one work wherein they had not respect to this. Their works might well be called the works of the devil, whose main business it was to set up pride and self. All their pretences of devotion to God, were but the adoration of some golden image. Have not many in their more splendid actions, the same end with brutes: the satisfaction of the sensitive part, covetousness, pride, emulation, sense of honour, qualities perceivable in the very brutes, as the end of some of their actions? The acting for a sensitive end is not suitable to a rational, much less can it be the end of a gracious creature. Have not men sinful ends in their religious services? in their prayers to God, in their acknowledgments of God? The devil could intreat our Saviour's leave to go into the herd of swine. Was this a prayer, though directed to Christ, when his end was to destroy and satisfy his malice in it? At best, a man without grace is like a picture in a room which eyes all, and hath no more respect to a prince than his attendants. A natural man's respect to God is but equal to a respect to all his other worldly concerns. Indeed it were well if it were so. He parcels out one part for God, one part for himself, and one part for the world; but God hath the least share, or at best, no more than the rest. And truly, as a picture cannot give a greater respect, to fix its eyes more upon a prince than a peasant, because it hath no life; so neither can a natural man pay a supreme respect to God in his service, without a spiritual life. There is a necessity then of removing those depraved ends, that man may answer the true end of his creation. The principles then upon which such ends do grow, contrary to the will of God, must be rooted out, that the soul may move purely to God in every service. We are come short of the glory of God: Rom. 3:23, 'All have sinned and come short of the glory of God;' short of aiming at it, short of his approbation of our acts. Being thus come short, our ends cannot rise higher than the frame of our soul. Grace, grace only can advance our wills to those supernatural ends for which they were first framed. We can never aim at the glory of God till we have an affection to him. We can never honour him supremely, whom we do not supremely love. An affection to God can never be had, till the nature, wherein the aversion is placed, be changed into another frame. We are to glorify God, as God. How can we do this without the knowledge of him? How can we know him but by the gospel, wherein he discovers himself? How can we have right conceptions of the gospel, till gospel impressions be made upon us? How can we act for the glory of God, to whom naturally we are enemies? There is none of us born with a spiritual love to God. There must be an alteration of the end and aim in us; our actions cannot else be good, though ordered by God himself. God employs Satan in some things, as in afflicting Job; but is his performance good? No, because his end is not the same with God's. He acts out of malice what God commands out of sovereignty, and for gracious designs. Our end without it, is not the same with the end of the action; for moral acts tend to God's glory, though the agent hath no such intention. So the action may be good in itself, but not good in the actor, because he wants a due end.

Well then, those actions only can be said to be evangelical, when the great end of God's glory, which was his end both in creation and redemption, hath a moral influence upon every service; when we have the same end in our redeemed services, as God had in his redeeming love.

Not humbly. We cannot without regeneration perform gospel duties humbly, because of natural stoutness and hardness. Evangelical duties must be performed with humility. Self-denial is the chief gospel lesson, and is to run through the veins of every service. Therefore God speaks of giving 'a heart of flesh,' in gospel times: Ezek. 11:19, 'I will take the stony heart out of their flesh, and give them a heart of flesh, that they may walk in my statutes, and keep my ordinances, and do them.' Gospel duties require a pliableness and tenderness of heart. Adam's over-valuing himself, and swelling with designs of being like God, brought an incapacity upon himself of serving his creator. And man ever since, is too much aspiring and too well opinioned of himself, to perform duties in an evangelical strain, with that meltingness, that nothingness in himself, which the gospel requires. Our swelling and admiring thoughts of our own natural righteousness, hinders Christ from saving us, and ourselves from serving him. There must then be an humble, and melting, and self-denying frame. The angels are said to cover their faces before God, Isa. 6:2, as having nothing to glory in of their own. And the chief design of the gospel is to beat down all glorying in ourselves: 1 Cor. 1:29, 31,

'That no flesh should glory in his presence; let him that glorieth, glory in the Lord.' And indeed it humbles us no more than what, upon due consideration, will appear very necessary. Nature then must be changed before this pride be rooted out. Old things must pass away, that God may be all in all in the creature. We cannot without a new nature make a true estimate of ourselves, and lie as vile and base in the presence of God. A stone, with all the hammering, cannot be made soft. Beat it into several pieces, you may sever the continuity of its parts, but not master its hardness; every little piece of it will retain the hardness of its nature. So it is with a heart of stone. The nature must be changed before it be fit for those services which require melting, humble, and admiring frames. There is a necessity of a residing grace, like fire, to keep the soul in a melting temper.

Not constantly. Without a new nature, we cannot perform gospel services constantly, because of our natural levity. Where the nature is flesh, the heart 'minds the things of the flesh,' Rom. 8:5. The mind thus habituated, will not be long employed about the things of the Spirit. There is a natural levity in man's nature. Do not many seem to begin in the Spirit and end in the flesh? seem to arise to heaven, and quickly fall down to earth? Do not our very promises vanish with the next wind of temptation, and like sparks, expire as soon as they be born, unless grace be in the heart to keep them alive. The Israelites are accused of not having a heart stedfast with God: Ps. 78:37, 'Their heart was not right with him, neither were they stedfast in his covenant.' Are our natures better than theirs? Do we not all lie under the same charge; so uncertain naturally, about divine things, as if there were nothing but wind in our composition? Nothing can be kept up in motion against its nature, but by force. A top hath no inward principle of motion, but is moved by some outward force. When that is removed, the motion languisheth. Any motion that depends only upon outward wires, expires upon the breaking of them. When external motives, which spurred men on to this or that service, cease, the service dies of course, because the spring of the motion falls. If fear of hell, terrors of death, some pressing calamity, be the spring of any duty; when these are removed, there will be no more regard to the duty they engendered. But what is natural, is constant, because the spring always remains. Interest changeth, conscience is various; and therefore the operations arising from thence, will partake of the uncertainty of them. Stony ground may bring forth blades; but for want of root, they will quickly wither: Mat. 13:5, 20. A man may mount high in religion, by the mixture of some religious passion, as meteors in the air; but by reason of the gross and earthy parts in them, will not continue their station. There is no being without, stable, but God; and no principle stable within, but grace: Heb. 13:9, 'It is a good thing that the heart be established with grace.' Whatsoever service is undertaken upon changeable motives, is as changeable as the bottom upon which it stands. If credit, slavish fear of God, worldly interest, inspire us with some seeming holy resolutions, they will all fly away upon the first removal of those props. There is therefore a necessity of a change of nature and disposition. Where there is no approbation of things that are excellent, there can be no constant operation about them. All action about an object, continues according to the affection to it, and delight in it. We shall then be filled with the fruits of righteousness, to the glory of God, when we have a sincere approbation of the excellency of them: Philip 1:10, 11, first, 'approve things that are excellent; and then follows, without offence, till the day of Christ.' A stately profession can no more hold out against the floods of temptation, than a beautiful building can stand against the winds without a good foundation under ground. It is the Spirit of the Lord within, as well as without, can only maintain the standard against temptation, Isa. 59:19.

Well then, upon the whole, there is a necessity of regeneration for the performance of gospel duties. We cannot else perform them spiritually, because we are flesh; nor vitally, because we are dead; nor graciously, because we are corrupt; nor voluntarily, because we are enmity; nor delightfully, because we are alienated; nor sincerely, because we are falsity; nor humbly, because of our stoutness; nor constantly, because of our levity. Our natures must be changed in all these respects, before we can be fit for any gospel service.

(2.) Regeneration is necessary for the enjoyment of gospel privileges.

[1.] For the favour of God, and his complacency with us. We are not fit for God's delight, without it. That person who hath his love, must have his image. If ever God could love an old nature, which he once hated, and delight in that which he once loathed, he must divest himself of his immutability. He never hated the person of any of his creatures, but for unrighteousness. And upon the removal of this cloud of separation between him and them, the beams of his love break out in their former vigour. God's love is not straitened, nor his kindness exhausted, no more than his hand is shortened, or his ear grown heavy, that he cannot hear: Isa. 59:1, 2, 'But your iniquities have separated between you and your God, and your sins have hid his face from you, that he will not hear.'

For, first, what did make the first separation, was it not sin? God told Adam before, what the issue would be, upon his eating the forbidden fruit: Gen. 2:17, 'In the day that thou eatest thereof, thou shalt surely die.' It is not a temporal death there only meant; for he should then have died that day wherein he fell, the word surely importing so much. And the punishment of a temporal death was pronounced afterwards: Gen. 3:19, 'Dust thou art, and unto dust shalt thou return.' Thou shalt surely die; thy integrity and righteousness will expire that very moment, and thou shalt die in my just displeasure. It is a spiritual death that is most properly meant. The punishment of sin is death; the chief part of this death is an 'alienation from the life of God,' Eph. 4:18; that is, not to have God, and the righteousness of God's image living in him; but to be impure, corrupt, a hater of God, and servant of sin. Now from this punishment no man can be freed, but by a contrary regeneration, the proper effect whereof is to love God, to know his name, to partake of his holiness, to imitate his virtues.* Man forfeited all God's favour upon his fall, and can challenge nothing of it.

Secondly, What then can restore man to God's favour? Can that which first deprived us of it? The cause of our destruction can never be the means of our restoration. Did the loss of Adam's integrity make him unfit for paradise, the garden of God, from whence he was expelled, as a token of God's disfavour? And can the continuance of that loss be a means to regain that love which cashiered us? It was a spiritual death; and is the carcase of a soul fit for God's complacency? There must be not only a satisfaction to his justice for the re-instating man into his favour (this is done by Jesus Christ); but a restoring of his image, this is done by the Holy Ghost. It is as impossible the soul can be beautiful without life, and without holiness, as for a body to be beautiful without a good colour and proportion of parts. Take away this, beauty must cease, and deformity succeed in the place. It is impossible, therefore, that where sin remains in its full vigour, where there is nothing of an original integrity residing, but that the soul must be monstrous, vile, and deformed in the eyes of God. To make it therefore a fit object for God's favour, it is necessary it be beautified with a holy nature, and adorned with its due proportions and vigour. The righteousness of Israel must go forth as brightness; he must be called by a new name, that is, a new nature; for what is a name without a nature? And then it should be Hephzibah, 'the Lord delights in thee.' Isa. 62:1–4, 'The righteousness thereof shall go forth as brightness, and the glory thereof as a lamp that burns.' Righteousness is the glory of a soul, as well as of a church: 'Gentiles shall see thy righteousness, and all kings thy glory: thou shalt be called by a new name;' a new nature wrought by the word of God; 'which the mouth of the Lord shall name.' Then she should be in favour with God, 'a crown of glory in the hand of the Lord, and a royal diadem in the hand of her God.' Righteousness is the glory of a soul, and God's delight and complacency is the consequent of a righteous nature.

Thirdly, The elect themselves have no interest in God's favour of delight without it. This follows upon the former; God cannot love the very top of mankind, his own choice, with a love of complacency, without regeneration, without a righteous nature. There is a favour of intention and purpose before it; there is also an executive love in the very infusing the habits of grace, which is a supernatural favour, because there is both a purpose and then an actual conferring a supernatural good. God is free, and may will to give his gifts how, and to whom he pleases. But an elect person, whilst he continues in a state of nature, is not simply beloved, though there be a purpose of love, because there is no gracious quality in him, which is the object of God's special favour. It is regeneration only which is the object of God's delight in us.

Fourthly, Hence will follow, that no privilege under heaven, without it, can bring us into God's favour; no, not if any man were related to Christ according to the flesh. The apostle Paul would not think the better of himself for a fleshly relation to Christ, for being of the same country, descended of the Jewish nation: 2 Cor. 5:16, 'Though we have known Christ after the flesh, yet henceforth know we him no more. Therefore if any man be in Christ, he is a new creature.' Though it be an honour to be of the same descent with Christ, according to the flesh, to be of the same nation and country, yet this doth not make a man any more beloved of God. Nothing avails in Christ, but a new creature; and our Saviour himself pronounceth it so. It was the highest privilege to be the mother of our Saviour, according to the flesh; yet this had been nothing, without her being born again of the Spirit: 'Who is my mother? and who are my brethren? Behold my mother and my brethren,' pointing to his disciples, Mat. 12:48, 49. 'My mother and my brethren are those which hear the word of God, and do it,' Luke 8:21. Those that hear the word, that have the gracious effect of the word wrought in them by the Spirit, are equal to my mother, and my brethren, and superior to any of my fleshly relations, if they be without it. There is a necessity of regeneration upon this account.

[2.] As there is no favour, so there is no union with God and Christ without it. Man hath some kind of natural union with all things in the world; he hath being with all creatures, rational faculties with angels, sense with animals, vegetation with plants; he wants only that with God which would beautify all the rest. And this can only be by partaking of the image of God's holiness by a new birth. There must be a capability for this union on man's part. A superior and inferior nature may be united together, but never contrary natures. There must be some proportion between the subjects to be united, which proportion consists in a commensuration of one thing to another. What proportion is there between God and our souls? There can be none without a supernatural grace infusing a pure nature. As we come out of the quarry of nature, rough and unpolished, we are not fit to be cemented with the corner-stone in the heavenly building; we must be first smoothed and altered by grace.

First, How can things be united to one another which are already united to their contraries? Separation from one body must make way for union to another. Naturally we are united to the devil as the head of the wicked world. We are by nature his members. Our understandings and wills were united with his in Adam, when Adam gave up his understanding and will to him; and ever since he 'works in the children of disobedience:' Eph. 2:2, 'Who now works in the children of disobedience,' ἐνεργοῦντος ἐν υἱοῖς. Working and working in, as a united nature to him, and principle in him. It is necessary this union should be broken before we can partake of the influence of another head. The diabolical nature and principle, therefore, which we have got by sin must be removed, and another nature, which is divine, put in the place first (in order of nature), before we can be united to Christ, and enjoy the benefits of union with him.

Secondly, How can things of a contrary nature be united together? Can fire and water be united, a good angel, and an impure devil? can heaven and hell ever meet friendly and compose one body? We are united to the first Adam by a likeness of nature; how can we be united to the second, without a likeness to him from a new principle? We were united to the first by a living soul; we must be united to the other by a quickening Spirit. We have nothing to do with the heavenly Adam, without bearing an heavenly image, 1 Cor. 15:48, 49. We are earthly as in the first Adam; we must be heavenly to be in the second, because his nature is so. If we are his members, we must have the same nature which was communicated to him by the Spirit of God, which is holiness. This nature must flow from the same principle, otherwise it is not the same nature; an old nature cannot be joined to a new Adam. There must be one spirit in both; as 1 Cor. 6:17, 'He that is joined to the Lord is one spirit;' and if it were an union barely of affections, as some would only make it, it is not conceivable how it can be without a change of disposition. But since it is an union by indwelling of the same Spirit in both (Rom. 8:9, 'If any man hath not the Spirit of Christ, he is none of his'), it is less intelligible, how it can be without an assimilation of our nature to the nature of Christ. It can never be supposed the Spirit should unite a pure head, and impure members. Such an union would make our blessed Saviour like Nebuchadnezzar's image; an head of gold, arms of silver, and feet of clay. Shall we loathe to have nasty things about us, and will the holy Jesus endure a loathesome putrefying soul to be joined to him?

Thirdly, How can anything be vitally united to another without life? It is a vital union, by virtue of which believers are called Christ (1 Cor. 11:12, 'As all the members of that one body, being many, are one body; so also is Christ'); and it is compared to the union of the members of a natural body, Rom. 12:4, 5. Members have not only life in their head, but in themselves, because the soul, which is the life of the body, is not only in the head, but in all the parts of the body, and exerciseth in every part its vital operations. The Spirit therefore, which is the band of this union, communicates life to every member wherein he resides, as well as in the head. What man would endure a dead body to be joined to him, though it were the carcase of one he never so dearly loved? If a man were united to Christ, without regeneration, Christ's body would be partly alive, partly dead, if any one member of it had not a spiritual life. A dead body and a living head, a member of Christ with a nature contrary to him, is an unconceivable paradox. Did God ever design such a monstrous union for his Son?

Upon these accounts doth result the necessity of regeneration; without it, no union with Christ.

(3.) There can be no justification without it. We are not justified by an inherent righteousness; yet we are not justified without it. We cannot be justified by it, because it is not commensurate to the law by reason of its imperfection; we cannot be justified without it, for it is not congruous to the wisdom and holiness of God, to count a person righteous, who hath nothing of righteousness in him, and whose nature is as corrupt as the worst of men. With what respect to God's honour, can it be expected that God should pardon that man's sins, whose will is not changed, who still hath the same habitualness in his will to commit sin, though he doth not at present act it. It is very congruous in a moral way, that the person offending should retract his sin, and return to his former affection. There is a distinction between justification and regeneration, though they never are asunder. Justification is relative; regeneration internally real. Union with Christ is the ground of both; Christ is the meritorious cause of both. The Father pronounceth the one, the Spirit works the other; it is the Father's sentence, and the Spirit's work. The relative and the real change are both at the same time: 1 Cor. 6:7, 'But you are sanctified, but you are justified;' both go together. We are not justified before faith, because we are justified by it, Rom. 5:1; and faith is the vital principle whereby we live: Gal. 2:20, 'The life which I now live, I live by the faith of the Son of God.' It is the root-grace, and contains the seeds of all other graces in it; it is habitually and seminally all other grace; so that unless we be new born, no justification can be expected; no justification can be evidenced. God never pardons sin, but he subdues iniquity: Micah 7:18, 19, 'Who is a God like unto thee, that pardons iniquity?' He will subdue our iniquities. The conquest cannot be made, while the nature, the root of the rebellion, remains. When he turns his compassion to us, he will turn away our hearts from iniquity. If a man were justified before he were regenerate, then he was righteous before he was alive; being 'in Christ,' as free from condemnation, is alway attended with a 'walking after the Spirit;' and walking is not before living, Rom. 8:1. Pardon would be unprofitable, unless he that were pardoned were made righteous inchoatively here, and had a right to, and hope of, a perfect righteousness hereafter. If righteousness hereafter were not imparted in this manner, it would be an argument a man were still under the law, which saith, 'He that doth them shall live in them' (which is impossible in a man that hath once sinned, though his sins are remitted). But it is clear that righteousness is imparted, since there is no man in the world whose sins are pardoned, but finds some principle in him whereby he is enabled to contest with sin more than before he was. Therefore do not deceive yourselves; there is no pardon without a righteous nature, though pardon be not given for it.

(4.) There is no adoption without regeneration. We can no more be God's sons, without spiritual regeneration, than we can be the sons and daughters of men, without natural generation. Adoption is not a mere relation without an inward form. The privilege, and the image of the sons of God, go both together. A state of adoption is never without a separation from defilement: 2 Cor. 6:17, 18, 'Come you out from among them, be you separate, and will be a father unto you, and you shall be my sons and daughters.' The new name in adoption is never given till the new creature be framed. 'As many as are led by the Spirit, they are the sons of God,' Rom. 8:14, οὗτοι, those very persons; that is the signal mark, that they are led by the Spirit; therefore first enlivened by the Spirit. A child-like relation is never without a child-like nature. The same method God observes in declaring the members his sons, as he did in declaring the head his Son, which was 'according to the Spirit of holiness, by the resurrection from the dead,' Rom. 1:4. So he declares believers to be his sons, by giving them a spirit of holiness, and by a resurrection from sin, and spiritual death. The devils may as well be adopted sons of God, as we, without a change of nature. To be the sons of the living God, was the great promise of the gospel prophesied of: Hos. 1:10, 'Ye are the sons of the living God.' How well will it suit, a living God and a dead son? God is not the God of the dead, but of the living. Our Saviour's argument from* the immortality of the soul will evidence not only a resurrection, but a necessity of spiritual life. What advantage is there in being sons of the living God, if we had no more life in us than his greatest enemies? Regeneration, as a physical act, gives us a likeness to God in our nature. Adoption, as a legal act, gives us a right to an inheritance; both the great intendments of the gospel, both accompanying one another. No sonship without a new nature.

(5). There is no acceptation of our services without it. We are not fit to perform any duty without it, and God will never accept any duty from us without it. In the 1st of Ephesians, 1. election, 2. regeneration, expressed by being holy, 3. adoption, 4. acceptation, are linked together: ver. 4–6, 'He hath chosen us that we should be holy, and without blame before him in love, having predestinated us to the adoption of children;' after follows grace 'wherein he hath made us accepted in the beloved.' Our acceptation is only upon the account of Christ; but the acceptability is upon the account of grace. Faith makes our persons and our duties acceptable, and Christ makes them both accepted. Acceptability ariseth from grace, as damnability ariseth from sin. God damns none, unless they be damnable; neither doth God accept any in Christ, unless they be acceptable.† The papists that plead for merit, acknowledge nothing of it before grace, but after grace, because then the services have a greater proportion to God, from the dignity of the person, they being acts of God's children, and wrought by his Spirit. God can love nothing but himself, and what he finds of himself in the creature. All services, without something of God's image and Spirit in them, are nothing. As the product of a million of cyphers, though you still add to them, signifies nothing; but add one figure, an unit, the Spirit, grace, it will make the product to be many millions, of high account with God. All the significancy depends upon the figure, which, if absent, the rest would be nothing. All moral perfections, without a new nature, are but cyphers in God's account: Heb. 11:6, 'Without faith it is impossible to please God.' Grace is only a good work: Philip. 1:6, 'He which hath begun a good work in you, will perform it till the day of Christ;' intimating that their morality and their natural wisdom, before their regeneration, were not good works in the sight of God. They were good in their kind; as a crab may be said to be a good crab, but not a good pippin. It is not good, unless it be fruit brought forth in Christ; neither is it ordained as good to the day of Christ, to appear glorious at the time of his triumph. God looks into our services, whether the Spirit frames them, and Christ presents them; all that we do must go through their hands before they can reach God's heart. Acceptation can never be without a renewed nature. The services of the flesh cannot please God: Rom. 8:8, 'They that are in the flesh cannot please God.' Their persons cannot, therefore their actions cannot, because they are the products of a nature at variance with him, a nature that is not, nor cannot be subject to his law; so that God must be displeased with his own spiritual law; yea, with his own holy nature, and change his judgment, and change his nature, before he can be pleased with fleshly services, for at the best, they are but refined brutishness. The image of the devil can never be grateful to God. Services flowing from nature, may seem in the outward form of them, to be as acceptable as the duties of a good man; but considering what a dunghill of filthiness the heart is, from whence they proceed, they cannot be so. Good water is sweetest, and bad water corruptest, nearest the spring or fountain; the streams may lose some of their corruption in their passage. A gracious man's duties are most pleasant to God nearest the heart; a natural man's services are most distasteful nearest the spring. When the heart is a good treasure, what comes from it is regarded as a rich gift, because it comes from a valuable treasure, Luke 6:45; hence it is that a less work, coming from a pure and holy principle in a renewed man, is more acceptable to God, than a greater work (in respect of the external glorification of him in the good of mankind), coming from an impure principle in a natural man; as a cup of cold water given to a disciple is more valuable than the gift of a prince from another principle. In the one, God sees a conformity of affection with his holiness; in the other, only a conformity with his providence. One intends God's glory, and the other only acts it, proposing some other end to himself; and we use to value gifts, rather by the affection of the friend, than the quantity of the gift. Well then, consider it; without a new nature, all our services, though they should amount to many millions in number, have no intrinsic value in them with God. For where the nature is displeasing, the actions flowing from that nature can never please him: 'He that turns away his ear from hearing the law,' that is, from a spiritual obedience to the law, 'even his prayer is an abomination,' Prov. 28:9; it is formed by a noisome soul.

(6.) There is no communion with God without a renewed soul. God is uncapable on his part, with the honour of his law and holiness, to have communion with such a creature. Man is uncapable on his part, because of the aversion rooted in his nature. What way can there be to bring God and man together without this change of nature? what communion can there be between a living God and a dead heart? God loathes sin, man loves it; God loves holiness, man loathes it. How can these contrary affections meet together in an amicable friendship? what communion with so much disagreement in affections? In all friendship there must be similitude of disposition. Justification cannot bring us into communion with God without regeneration; it may free us from punishment, discharge our sins, but not prepare us for a converse, wherein our chief happiness lies. There must be some agreement before there can be a communion. Beasts and men agree not in a life of reason, and therefore cannot converse together. God and man agree not in a life of holiness, and therefore can have no communion together. We are by sin alienated from the life of God, and therefore from his fellowship, Eph. 4:18; we must have his life restored to us before we can be instated in communion with him.

[1.] God can have no pleasure in it. God took a delight in the creation, and did rejoice in his work. Sin despoiled God of his rest. It can give God no content, no satisfaction; for to be in the flesh, is to be in that nature which was derived from Adam, which brought the displeasure of God upon all mankind. Regeneration by the Spirit restores the creature to such a state wherein God may take pleasure in him, and strips him by degrees of that sin which spoiled his delight in the work of his hands; as it grows, communion is enlarged. God made man at first after his own image, that he might have communion with him. Since the loss of that, what fitness can there be for communion, till the restoration of that which God thought fit for his delight? Suppose that some one work of a natural man may be good and pleasing to God, it will not argue a communion of God with the person: he may be pleased with the work, but not with the man; for all the goodness he hath being in the act, and the act being transient, when that is past, his goodness is as the morning dew, vanished. He cannot be the object of God's delight, because he hath no habitual goodness in him. If a man be abominable and filthy naturally, he cannot have a converse with God without a nature suitable to God, and a nature so animated, as that God may put some trust in it, and not be at uncertainty: Job 15:14–16, 'What is man, that he should be clean; he which is born of a woman, that he should be righteous? Behold, he puts no trust in his saints,' &c. No man is clean, but those that delight in sin are much more abominable, that 'drink up iniquity like water.' Now God being infinitely holy, can have no communion with that which he doth abominate; and he cannot have a fixed and a delightful communion with that which he cannot confide in. It must be therefore such a nature as is produced and preserved by his own Spirit. If the heavens are not clean in his sight, we must have a nature purer and cleaner than the heavens, before God can delightfully behold us, and pleasingly converse with us.

[2.] As God can have no pleasure in it, so man is contrary to it. Man, as he is by corruption, is at variance with God, and cannot but be at variance with him. An uncircumcised heart will not love God, or at least, will not pay him such a proportion of love, and love of such a quality, as is due to him; for if the end of the circumcision of the heart be to love the Lord with all our hearts, as Deut. 30:6, 'And the Lord thy God will circumcise thy heart, to love the Lord thy God with all thy heart,' then it will necessarily infer, that he whose heart is not circumcised, doth not love God with all his heart. Holiness and iniquity are so contrary, that no agreement can be made between them. God must deny his nature before he can deny his hatred of sin, and man must be stripped of his nature before he can leave his affection to sin. It is equally impossible for wickedness to love holiness, and for purity to love pollution. There can be no fellowship with God, whilst we walk in darkness, and he is light, 1 John 1:6, 7.

[3.] Nay, thirdly, man naturally resists all means for it. It is the Spirit only which is the bond of union, and consequently the cause of communion. The Spirit can only bring God and us together. Walking in the Spirit hinders us from fulfilling the lusts of the flesh, which make us uncapable of communion: Gal. 5:16, 'Walk in the Spirit, and you shall not fulfil the lusts of the flesh.' But every man by nature (as well as the Jews) 'resists the Holy Ghost,' Acts 7:51. And while this resistance of the great medium of it remains, this communion can never be. This resistance, therefore, must be removed, and there must be a divine stamp and impression upon our very nature, to make it pliable. You see more and more the necessity of regeneration.

(7.) As there is no communion with God without it, so no communications of Christ to our souls can be relished and improved without it. All the communications of Christ relish of that fulness of grace which was in his person, and therefore cannot be relished by any principle but that of the same nature. Whenever Jesus Christ comes to bless us with the great blessings of his purchase, he turns away our hearts from iniquity, Acts 3:26.

[1.] Ordinances cannot be improved. The word hath no place in them, John 8:37. There is no footing naturally for any divine and spiritual truth. The nature of the soil must be changed before this heavenly plant will thrive. Plants grow not upon stones, nor this heavenly plant in a stony heart. The vine and the weed draw the same moisture of the earth, which in the vine is transmuted, by the nature of the plant, into a nobler substance than that in the weed. The new nature of a good man turns the juice of the word into a nobler spirit in him; and according as the nature of a good man is enriched with grace, the more doth he concoct the word, and improve it, to the bringing forth fruit, and fruit of a diviner nature than another. The juice it affords to all is the same, but the nature of the creature turns it in the concoction. Nature must be changed then, to make any profitable improvement of the word and other institutions. A stone receives the water upon it, not into it; it falls off, or dries up as soon as ever it falls; but a new heart, a heart of flesh, sucks in the dew of the word, and grows thereby. The new birth and nature makes us suck in the milk, and grow thereby, 1 Peter 2:2.

[2.] There can be no communication of comfort. The Spirit comforts by exciting grace, and by discovering grace, not by flashes and enthusiasms. What comfort can there be when grace, the foundation, is wanting? Can the Holy Ghost ever speak a lie, and give any man comfort, and tell him he is a child of God, when he hath the nature of the devil, so contrary to him? This were to witness not with our spirits, but against the frame and habit of them, which is not the Spirit's work, Rom. 8:16. Jesus Christ will not trifle away his comforts upon such as have no conformity to him. This were to put a jewel in a swine's snout, a crown upon a beast's head. Those that are not heirs by a new nature to heaven, cannot claim any title to the first fruits and clusters of it, the comforts of the gospel. As there is a necessity of a likeness to Christ, to make us capable of communications from him in a state of glory, so it is as certainly necessary to the lower degrees of it in this world. Vessels of wrath must be changed into vessels of honour before they are capable of being filled with spiritual comforts. Our blessed Saviour keeps his choicest flowers and richest beams for his dressed garden, not for the wild desert.

(8.) We cannot be in covenant without it. This should have been first, as the foundation of all. Had not Adam had an habitual righteousness in his nature, he had not been a fit person for God to have entered into covenant with. There must therefore be a restored righteousness, that we may come into the bond of the new covenant for eternal life. The very terms of it are, a new heart, a heart of flesh, a new spirit, the law written in the heart. Without this new nature, we cannot depend on him by faith, which is the condition of the covenant. For we cannot confide in him to whom we have an enmity, and of whom we have a jealousy. We cannot have God to be our God unless we be his people, have the nature and disposition of his people, turn to him, act towards him as our God; whereas in our first defection we made the devil our God. God requires righteousness still to our being in covenant, but dispenseth with the strictness of the first covenant, and gives our Saviour a power to that end, in committing all judgment to the Son. As the covenant is spiritual, so there must be a spiritual life to answer the terms of it. Without it, we cannot walk in the way wherein we engage by covenant to walk, neither can we have any right to the promises and benefits of the covenant. Doth God promise to be our God? It is upon the condition we be his people. Doth he promise never to leave us nor forsake us? It is upon condition we continue not in our original apostasy. Doth he promise to be present with us? It is more than his holiness will endure, while we continue in our filthy nature.

2. The second general. As regeneration is necessary to a gospel state, so it is necessary to a state of glory. It seems to be typified by the strength and freshness of the Israelites when they entered into Canaan.* Not a decrepit and infirm person set foot in the promised land: none of those that came out of Egypt with an Egyptian nature, and desires for the garlick and onions thereof, with a suffering their old bondage, but dropped their carcasses in the wilderness; only the two spies, who had encouraged them against the seeming difficulties. None that retain only the old man, born in the house of bondage, but only a new regenerate creature, shall enter into the heavenly Canaan. Heaven is the inheritance of the sanctified, not of the filthy: Acts 26:18, 'That they may receive an inheritance among them which are sanctified, through faith that is in me.' So our Saviour himself phraseth it in his discourse to Paul upon his conversion by faith, the great renewing principle. Upon Adam's expulsion from paradise, a flaming sword was set to stop his re-entry into that place of happiness. As Adam, in his forlorn state, could not possess it, we also, by what we have received from Adam, cannot expect a greater privilege than our root. Had Adam retained the righteousness of his nature, he had been fit for that place, and that place for him; but poor decrepit Adam could have no leave to enter. The priest under the law could not enter into the sanctuary till he were purified, nor the people into the congregation; neither can

any man have access into the holy of holies till that be consecrated for him by the blood of Jesus, and he sprinkled by the same blood for it, Heb. 10:19, 22. It is by the blood of Jesus sprinkled upon our hearts that we enter into the holiest by a way which he hath consecrated; 'for there shall in nowise enter into it anything that defileth, neither whatsoever works abomination or a lie,' Rev. 21:17, as every unclean thing was prohibited entrance into the temple. Whosoever shall enter into the rest of God, must cease from his own works of darkness and corruption, as God did from his works of creation, Heb. 4:10. If man fell the sixth day, the day of his creation, the rest of God in his lower works was disturbed by the entrance of sin upon them, as well as it had been disturbed by the sin of the angels in heaven. God rested from his works of creation, but not in them, but in Christ, the covenant of redemption, and restoration by him. We must therefore cease from our own works, to enter into his rest. This entrance we cannot have in an unbelieving, unregenerate state, because by unbelief we approve not of that for our rest, wherein God settled his own repose; and by unregeneracy we oppose the great intendment of it, the restoration of the creature to be a fit object for God's rest and complacency. It is necessary to a state of glory.

(1.) Not that there is a natural connection between a regenerate state and glory, that in its own nature gives a right to heaven, but a gracious connection by the will of God.† Though it be morally impossible in nature that a man can have communion with God without a renewed state, yet when he hath a new nature, it is not absolutely necessary that God should love him so intensely as to give him an eternal reward, but conditionally necessary, upon the account of the covenant wherein God hath so promised. Though it be absolutely unavoidable to God to love goodness (for, because he is perfectly good, he cannot hate it), yet it is not absolutely necessary he should instate it in so unconceivable a glory. A new nature, indeed, makes a man capable of eternal glory, without which it is not possible for him to have it; but it gives him not a right to it, nor instates him in it in its own nature, but by the gracious indulgence of God. For, as I have said before, in the general foundation of this doctrine, that God may give grace without glory, is intelligible; but how he can admit a man to glory without grace is unconceivable. The very having of grace is a reward in itself. It is an ennobling of our nature, a setting us in our right station (the purity of the body is a pleasure, though a man hath no hopes upon it to be preferred to a better condition), which may appear to us upon the banishment of Adam from paradise. Had there been any natural connection, he had not been dispossessed, supposing him to have faith infused into him at the time of the promulgation of the promise; or if afterwards, he would have had a re-entry, had there been a natural connection between a new nature and a state of glory.

(2.) Nor is there any meritorious connection between a regenerate state and glory, because there is no exact proportion between a new nature and eternal glory. The papists say, that before habitual grace a man cannot merit, but after it is infused by the Spirit of God into the soul, a merit doth result from the dignity of the person brought into a state of grace. No such thing. Glory indeed is merited, but the merit results, not from the new nature, but from the new head, our Lord Jesus Christ. That righteousness whereby God is engaged to give us a crown of glory for a garland of grace, is not a commutative justice; as if grace were of equal value to glory, and heaven no more than a due compensation: 2 Tim. 4:8, 'There is laid up for me a crown of righteousness, which the Lord, the righteous Judge, shall give me at that day.' But it is the veracity and faithfulness of God which is meant by righteousness there, and otherwhere in Scripture. It is a justice due to the promise, not to the nature of the grace, and due to the covenant made with Christ, which was, that he should have a seed to serve him; upon which compact our Saviour so peremptorily demands his people's being with him in glory: John 17:24, 'Father, I will that they also whom thou hast given me be with me where I am.' As much as to say, Father, I will not remit a tittle of that article, which is part of the covenant between thee and me; I will have that performed to the full. And it is observable, though he mentions their faith, and their keeping his word, in other parts of the chapter, as arguments for God to take notice of them, and preserve them, yet his desire of the state of glory he founds upon his will, which must be grounded upon some antecedent agreement, whereby he had a right to plead for it. So that it is from the faithfulness of God to his promise, and the full merit of Christ, and thereupon his fixed resolution to have it performed, not from any meritorious dignity in the new nature itself. Grace only fits for glory, but doth not merit it.

(3.) It is necessary by a fixed determination of God. Supposing that God could in his own nature, congruously admit of an unregenerate dead creature to a fruition of him in heaven; yet since he hath decreed otherwise, and appointed other methods, God is now by his own free resolution under an immutable necessity not to admit him. As God having by a determinate counsel ordained the death of Christ as the medium to redemption, could not in our apprehensions afterwards appoint another way, because his counsel had pitched, not only upon the redemption of man, as the end, but the death of Christ as the means; and had there been a change, it must either be in the end or in the means. If in the end, and he would not have man redeemed, there had been an alteration in his love and kindness; if in the means, it must be either a worse or a better means; if a worse, and not so fit to effect redemption, it had still implied a change in his kindness; if a better means, it would argue a defect of wisdom in his first choice, that he did not foresee the best. By the like counsel and wisdom he hath settled this of regeneration as the way to glory: 'Without holiness no man shall see the Lord,' Heb. 12:14. Without a fixed and permanent holiness, which must be an holiness of nature, not only of action. Supposing any holiness in an action, without a new nature, it is yet but a transient holiness, and though it may make the action acceptable to God, yet it can never make the person that did it acceptable to him.

(4.) Regeneration is necessary in a way of aptitude and fitness for this state. A fitness in both subjects is necessary to the enjoyment of one another. Since therefore our happiness consists in an eternal fruition of God, and that naturally we are a mass and dunghill of putrefied corruption, there must be such a change as to make an agreement with that God whom to enjoy is our happiness; for all aptitude is a certain connection of the two terms whereby they may touch and receive each other. We cannot enjoy God in his ordinances without an holy nature, much less in heaven. As we are under the condemnation of the law by reason of our guilt, so we are under an unfitness for heaven by reason of our filth. We have a remote natural capacity for it, as we are creatures endued with rational faculties. But we have a moral unfitness, while we want a divine impression to make us suitable to it. Justification and adoption give us a right to the inheritance, but regeneration gives us a 'meetness to be partakers of the inheritance of the saints in light,' Col. 1:12. We are not meet for it while we are unholy, and while we are darkness, because it is an inheritance of saints, and an inheritance in light. As the body cannot be made glorious without a resurrection from a natural death, so neither can the soul, which is immortal, be made glorious without a resurrection from a spiritual death. Our corruptible bodies, 1 Cor. 15:50, cannot possess an incorruptible kingdom unless made like to the glorious body of Christ, much less our souls, which are the chief subjects of communion with him in heaven. A depraved soul is as much unfit for a purified heaven as a corruptible body is for an incorruptible glory. Our Saviour ascended not into heaven to take possession of his glory till after his resurrection from death, neither can we enter into heaven till a resurrection from sin. As Jesus Christ became like unto us, that he might be a merciful and faithful high priest for us, Heb. 2:17, 'It behoved him to be made like unto his brethren;' so it behoves us to be made like unto him, that we may be fit offerings in the hand of our high priest, to present to God, for him to take pleasure in. The father of the prodigal forgave him at the first meeting after his return, but before he admitted him into the pleasure of his house he took away his garments that smelt of draff, and put other robes upon him. God is said therefore 'to work us to this thing,' κατεργάζεσθαι, polish, that we may be fit to be clothed upon with our heavenly house, 2 Cor. 5:5. If God be happy in his nature, man cannot be happy in a nature contrary to him; for we can never expect to enjoy a felicity in such a nature, which if God himself had, he could never be happy in himself. It is holiness in God which fits him to fill heaven and earth with the beams of his glory, and it is an holy nature in us, which makes us fit to receive him. As without holiness God could not be glorious in himself: Isa. 6:3, 'Holy, holy, is the Lord of hosts: the whole earth is full of his glory;' so without holiness in our natures we could not be glorious with God. We are no more fit for heaven in a state of nature than a piece of putrefied flesh is fit to become a star. In heaven there are duties to be done, and privileges to be enjoyed. The work cannot be done, the reward cannot be received, without a new nature. The glorifying God, and enjoying him, is the glory of heaven. How can we do the one or receive the other without the change of our affections? Can God have a voluntary glory from his enemy, or can his enemy delight in the enjoyment of him?

[1.] Regeneration and the new nature is necessary to the duty of heaven. Eternity cannot free us from duty. Some duties are essential to the relation of a creature; some result only from this or that state of the creature. The alteration in the state changeth the duty proper to that state; but no place, no state, can exempt a creature from those duties which are essential to him as a creature. It is impossible to conceive any relation, without some new debt or service. From every change in relations in the world there doth arise some new duty which was not incumbent upon a man before. The relation which a regenerate man hath to God here is the same which it is in heaven, but it is manifest there in an higher degree, and a choicer fruition. Thence therefore will arise, though not any new duty that we can conceive, yet fresher obligations to those services which are proper for that place. Without a change of nature it is not possible for any man (were he admitted thither) to perform the duties of heaven. Holy work is troublesome to a natural man here; and the more heavenly it was in itself, the more disgustful to corrupt nature. What was in a little measure holy was a drudgery upon earth; and what is in a greater measure holy cannot be a satisfaction in heaven to an old frame. There are some natural motives to some duties here, and our indigency takes part with them (as in that of prayer); but those of a more elevated strain, as love, and praise, and admirations of God, our natures are more averse to. What duty can be performed without a will? It is concluded by most, that the happiness of heaven consists as much, if not more, in the frame of the will, than in that of the understanding. If the will be not new framed, what capacity is there to perform the service requisite to that happy state? We must first be made just here before we can be made perfect above: Heb. 12:23, 'Spirits of just men made perfect.' Just by an imputed righteousness, holy by an inherent righteousness, before they were transplanted to a state of perfection. Without a perfect frame none can perform the choice duties of heaven, and without righteousness here, we cannot be made perfect there.

Quest. What are the duties of heaven, that cannot be performed without a new nature?

Ans. First. Attendance on God. Some kind of service which we cannot understand in the state here below. The angels stand before God, and wait his commands; there is a pleasure of God which they do: Ps. 103:21, 'Ye ministers of his that do his pleasure.' There is a will of God done in heaven, as well as upon earth. There are acts of adoration performed by them; they cover their faces, Isa. 6; they are commanded to worship the Lord Christ, Heb. 1:6. Their holiness fits them for their attendance;

therefore called 'the holy angels.' It is against the nature of devils to perform such acts as those which the holiness of angels fits them for. Glorified souls shall be as the angels of God in heaven: Mat. 22:30, 'But are as the angels of God in heaven.' Equal to angels in their state, as they are angels in heaven; equal to angels in their work, as they are angels of God, attending on God, and ministering unto him, Dan. 7:10; though what that ministry shall be is not easily known in the extent of it. Is it usual in this world to take up a person from under an hedge, and bring him to an immediate attendance on a prince, without cleansing him, and begetting other dispositions and behaviour in him by some choice education? God picks some out for an immediate attendance on him in heaven; but he sends his Spirit to be their tutor, to breed them up, and grace their deformed souls with beautiful features, and their ulcerous and cancerous spirits, with a sound complexion, that they may be meet to stand before him. When God calls any to do him service in a particular station in the word, he gives them another heart; so he did to Saul for the kingdom, 1 Sam. 10:9. Is there not much more necessity of it for an immediate service of God in heaven? A malefactor, by pardon, is in a capacity to come into the presence of a prince, and serve him at his table; but he is not in a fitness till his noisome garments, full of his prison vermin, be taken off. Can one that is neither pardoned nor purified, one with the guilt of rebellion upon him, and a nature of rebellion in him, be fit to stand before God?

Secondly, Contemplation of God is a work in heaven. There shall be a perfect knowledge; therefore a delightful speculation. The angels behold his face, Mat. 18:10, and that alway. The saints shall see him as he is, 1 John 3:2. It is not a stupid sight, but a gazing upon the face of this sun, with a refined and ravishing delight. For this work there must be,

First, A change of judgment. The eye must be restored. It is as possible for a blind eye to behold the sun, or a blear eye to stare in the face of it, without watering, as for a blind understanding to behold God; for it is not a being in the place of heaven, but having a faculty disposed, which doth elevate us to the knowledge of him. Things that are corporal cannot know things that are spiritual. We cannot in this sensitive body view the face of an angel, and understand his nature; much less with a body of a total death, see the face of God, which is above all created beings, more than any spiritual creature is above sense. 'In heaven the saints shall know him, as they are known of him,' 1 Cor. 13:12, perfectly, as far as the capacity of a creature can extend. Has God any scales upon his eyes? Doth he not know perfectly what he knows? So shall the glorified saints. But if a natural man were admitted into heaven, what prospect could he have with a blind understanding? As men under the gospel administrations cannot see the kingdom of God, even in the midst of it, without a new birth, so neither could they see the kingdom of God in the midst of heaven itself without a new frame; if not see it, much less enjoy it.

Secondly, There must be a change of will. Men like not to retain God in their knowledge, when he is represented to them in the dark, yet pleasant glass of nature, Rom. 1:28. The apostle there speaks it of the heathens, and the wisest of them, their philosophers, who, though pleased with the contemplation of nature, yet were not pleased with the contemplation of God in nature; much less will they like him, when he discovers himself clothed with the light of holiness as a garment. That vicious eye, which is too weak to behold with any delight the image of the sun in a glass, or a pail of water, will be much more too weak to gaze upon it in its brightness in the firmament. If there be no delight to know God here, what pleasure, what fitness can there be in the same frame to contemplate him above? Let me ask you, Have you any pleasure in the study of God? What is the reason, then, that in your retirements, when you have nothing to do, your thoughts are no more upon him? What is the reason that if any motion doth offer to advise you to fix your thoughts upon him, you so soon shift it off as a troublesome companion, and some slight jolly thought is admitted with gladness into those embraces which the other courted? Can such a temper be fit for heaven, where nothing but thoughts of God run through the veins of glorified souls? If the discovery of God's glory in the gospel is accounted no better than folly by natural men, and therefore not received, 1 Cor. 2:14, the manifestation of it above would meet with no better valuation of it, unless the temper both of judgment and will were changed. They are spiritually to be discerned here, and no less spiritually to be discerned above. The weak and waterish eye must be cured by some powerful medicine before it can stare upon the light of the sun, or delight itself in its glory.

Thirdly, Love is a duty in heaven. Love is a grace that shoots the gulf with us, and attends us not only to the suburbs, but into the very heart of heaven, when other graces conduct us only to the gates, and then take their leave of us, as having no business there. 'Charity never faileth,' 1 Cor. 13:8. And, indeed, it is so essentially our duty in every place, that it is concluded that God cannot free us from the obligation of it, whilst we remain his creatures; because God being infinitely good, and therefore infinitely amiable and infinitely gracious to them, it would seem unrighteous, and inconsistent with supreme goodness, to forbid the creature an affection to that which is infinitely excellent, and a gratitude to its benefactor which can be paid only in love. Now, though we are bound to love God in the highest degree, yet every new mercy adds a fresh obligation to return our affection to him. So when we shall have the clearest beams of God's love darting upon us from heaven, we shall also have higher obligations to love him, both for his excellency, which shall be more visible, and his love, which shall be more sensible. Now, can the heart of a natural man cling about God? Can it forget its father's house, and be wholly taken up with the Creator's excellency? Can he that loved pleasures more than God in the world, 2 Tim. 3:4, love God more than pleasures in heaven, without an alteration of his soul? No. The heart must be first circumcised by God, before we can love God with all our heart, Deut. 30:6. If we will not be subject to the law of God here, how can we be subject to the love of God, which is the law of heaven? How can we cleave to God without love, or relish him without delight? No man in a natural estate could stay in heaven, because he doth not love the person whose presence only makes it heaven. How can there be a conformity to God in affection, without a conformity to his holiness? A choiceness of love, with a perverseness of will; a supremacy of delight, without a rectitude of heart; a love of God, without a loathing of sin; a fervency of love, with a violence of lust: all these are contradictions. He that hath a hatred of God, cannot perform the main duty of heaven; and therefore what should he do there?

Fourthly, Praise is a service in heaven. If a pure angel be not sufficient for so elevated a duty, how unfit then is a drossy soul? What is the angels' note, 'Holy, holy, holy, Lord God,' Isa. 6:3, can never be a natural man's; for how can he possibly praise that which he hates? What is the note of glorified saints? It is Hallelujah, Rev. 19:1, 'Salvation, and glory, and honour, and power unto the Lord our God.' And again they said, Hallelujah, ver. 3. 'Hallelujah, for the Lord God Omnipotent reigneth,' ver. 6. Nothing but hallelujah four times, ver. 1, 3, 4, 6. How can that heart frame an hallelujah, that is stuffed with jealousies of him? How can he exalt the honour of God, who was always pleased with the violations of it? How can he rejoice at the Lord's reigning, that would not have one lust subdued by his power? How can a natural man, as natural, ever be wound up to a height fit for such strains, since 'out of the abundance of the heart, the mouth speaks'? The tongue can never be framed to praise while the heart is evil. Our blessed Saviour must be glorified in us, before he can be glorified by us, 2 Thes. 1:10, 12. If a man in a mere natural state be unfit for this heavenly work, how unfit are then their tongues to sound his praise, which are always filled with reproaches of God? And how can their ears endure to hear it from others, which were never offended with the blasphemies of him? They could never rejoice in this heavenly concert were they admitted. Nay, their enmity to the work would not permit their stay. The smoke of pure incense is fitter rather to drive a swine out of the room than to invite his continuance.

[2.] The new birth is necessary, as to the duty, so to the reward of heaven. As the reward is exceeding glorious, the preparation thereto must be exceeding gracious. The rewards of heaven are something incorporated with us, inlaid in the very frame of our souls, and cannot be conceived enjoyable without a change in the nature of the subject. Man was first formed before he was brought into the garden of Eden, or pleasure: Gen. 2:8, There he 'put the man whom he had formed.' Man must be new-formed before he be brought into that place, which is the antitype of Eden, the place of eternal and spiritual pleasure. A natural man can no more relish the rewards of heaven, than a dead carcase can esteem a crown and a purple robe; or be delighted with the true pleasure of heaven, than a swine, that loves to wallow in the mire, can be delighted with a bed of roses. A disorder in nature is a prohibition to all happiness belonging to that nature; a distempered body, under the fury of a disease, can find no delight in the pleasures of the healthful; a wicked man, with a troubled and foaming sea of sin and lust in his mind, Isa. 57:20, would find no more rest in heaven than a man with his disjointed members upon a rack can in the beauty of a picture. We must be spiritually-minded before we can have either life or peace, Rom. 8:6. Righteousness in the soul is the necessary qualification for the peace and joy in the kingdom of God: Rom. 14:17, 'The kingdom of God is not meat and drink; but righteousness, and peace, and joy in the Holy Ghost.' While malice remains in the devil's nature, were he admitted into heaven he would receive a torment instead of a content. A wicked man would meet with hell in the midst of heaven as long as he carries his own rack within him, boiling and raging lusts in his heart, which can receive no contentment without objects suitable to them, let the place be what it will. Heaven, indeed, is not only a place, but a nature; and it is a contradiction to think that any can be happy with a nature contrary to the very essence of happiness.

The pleasure and reward of heaven is,

First, A perfect likeness to God and Christ. This is the great privilege of heaven, which the apostle, in the midst of his ignorance of other particulars, resolves upon as certain as that which results from regeneration, and being the sons of God, and is the full preparation for the beatific vision: 1 John 3:2, 'Now we are the sons of God; and it doth not yet appear what we shall be: but we know that, when he shall appear, we shall be like him; for we shall see him as he is.' He seems to intimate this, that we can never be like him when he doth appear, unless we be now, while we are here, the sons of God, nor ever be admitted to a sight of him. As Christ presented himself without spot to God, when he laid the foundation of our redemption, so he presents his people 'without blemish to God,' when he lays the top-stone of it in our glorification, Eph. 5:27. Now as we cannot be like to Christ in our walk here without a new birth, neither can we without it be like to Christ in glory hereafter. It is not the place makes us like to God, but there must be a likeness to God to make the place pleasant to us. When once the angels had corrupted their nature, the short stay they made in heaven did neither please them nor reform them. And when Satan appeared before God, among the angels, Job 1:6, neither God's presence nor his speaking to him did anywise better him; he came a devil, and he went away so, without any pleasure in the place or presence, but by the permission of God, to wreak his malice on holy Job. An unlikeness to God is the misery of the creature. It is therefore impossible, whilst the soul remains in that state, that it can arrive at blessedness, because it is a contradiction to think a felicity can be enjoyed in a contrariety to and separation from the fountain of it: Ps. 73:27, 'Lo, they that are far from thee shall perish.' It is by faith, beholding the glory of the Lord in the glass of the gospel here, that we must be 'transformed into his image,' before we can be 'changed into his glory,' 2 Cor. 4:18. And we cannot be like God by holy actions only, though we had performed as many of them as all the holy men in the world ever did as to the matter of them, abstracted from the principle and end; and the reason is, because God is not only holy in his actions, but holy in his nature; and, therefore, we must not only have actions materially good, but a holy nature suitable to the holiness of God, otherwise we neither are, nor never can, be like him.

Secondly, The fruition of God is a privilege of heaven, which necessarily follows this likeness. God is the eternal portion of glorified souls, upon which they live. He is the strength of their hearts, Ps. 73:25, 26. There is none but God in heaven is the chief object of their love and delight. The presence of God makes 'the fulness of joy,' Ps. 16:11. His favour and the light of his glorious countenance constitutes heaven and happiness; not the place, but the countenance. God's frown kindles hell, and his smile renders any place an heaven. Now an old nature cannot have a good look from God; for since be is infinitely holy, he must hate unholiness; infinitely true, he must hate falsity. As it is impossible a man can love truth and falsity, righteousness and unrighteousness, as such, at one and the same time, in an intense degree, therefore an impure nature cannot be happy unless God be mutable. God cannot smile on the old Adam unless he hate himself. What satisfaction can such an one possibly have in God's presence? How can he savour the society of God that never loved it? Do we naturally love any warm mention of God? Have we not a stony deadness to any heavenly motion that falls upon us? A mighty quickness to receive sinful motions in that which we love? Do not our countenances fall, and our delight take wings to itself and fly away, at any lively appearance of God? If we have such an enmity to his law, which is but a transcript of his holiness, much greater must our enmity be to the original copy. Hence in Scripture men are said to 'refuse his law,' Ps. 78:10; to 'forsake his law,' Ps. 119:53; to be 'far from his law,' Ps. 119:150. Darkness doth not more naturally vanish at the appearance of the sun, than an old nature will fly away from the glory and brightness of God. A mass of black darkness and an immense sphere of light may as soon be espoused together, as a friendly amity be struck up between God and an unrenewed man. God is light without darkness, 1 John 1:5; man is darkness itself, as if nothing else entered into the composition of his corrupt nature, Eph. 5:8. If there be therefore a disagreement, contrariety, and unwillingness on both sides, how can any pleasing correspondence be effected? If God should bring a man with his corrupt nature into local heaven, God could not please himself in it, nor such an one delight himself in God, no more than a swine can be pleased with the presence of an angel, or a mole sport itself with the beauty of flowers, or a vitiated eye rejoice at the brightness of light. We must really make God such an one as we shape him in our natural fancy, and like to us, before we can take any pleasure in converse with him. Our nature, therefore, must be changed before we can please him, or be satisfied in him. His presence else will cause fear, while our sinful state remains, an affection inconsistent with happiness.

Thirdly, The company of the saints is an adjunct of that happiness in heaven. A sitting down with Abraham, Isaac, and Jacob in the kingdom of heaven, Mat. 8:11, in a festival converse, is a part of that felicity. The coming to be with an 'innumerable company of angels, with the general assembly, and church of the first-born,' is not the least thing in the composition of this happiness, Heb. 12:22, 23. What joy is that man capable of which should be surrounded with company he hath the greatest disaffection to, where he could not meet with any one person without the holy quality he hath an antipathy against? A natural man never loved holiness, as holiness, here. The more beautiful the image of God was in any, the more burdensome was their company; the more degrees any good man wanted of perfection in righteousness, the more tolerable was a familiarity with him. If holiness in others, in a lower degree, were disaffected by you, how can you bear the perfection of it? If the mixed and dark goodness in renewed men, which was but a weak flash of the glory of heaven, were unwelcome, how will you be able to endure the lustre of it? Again, glorified saints could not have the least converse with such an one? If carnal nature were a trouble to them here, when they had many relics of corruption, much more must it be above, if they were admitted into that place of glory, because the more holy any creature is, the more it hates that which is contrary to that holiness; the more settled we are in anything, the more we loathe that which is opposite to it; all the folly in their hearts here done away, and the disagreeing principle perfected in the blessed. There must, therefore, be a change in them, to take pleasure in you; or a change in you, to take pleasure in them. They must return to the frame of old Adam, and put off the renewed image of God, before they can delight in you; or you must come up to the frame of the new Adam, and be new created after the same image, before you can delight in them. The truth is, supposing a man admitted into the heavenly place with an old nature, he could not continue there; for the saints must either leave heaven, or he must. Light and darkness cannot agree; what makes the one happy, cannot beatify the other. Saints shall not leave it, because it is their inheritance, it was prepared for them, and they for it; a natural man must, because it was never prepared for him, nor he fitted for it.

Fourthly, Spiritual delights unconceivable are in that state, which, without a new and heavenly nature, it is impossible to relish. 'In the light of God they see light,' and they 'drink of the rivers of God's pleasures,' and are 'satisfied with the fatness of his house,' Ps. 36:8, 9. Now, is it a fleshly fatness? Are the pleasures of God carnal or spiritual? What is God's pleasure shall be the pleasure of glorified souls. How can the sordid old temper be fit for spiritual delights? Flesh can never savour but the things of the flesh; another palate is necessary to relish the things of the spirit: Rom. 8:5, 'They that are after the flesh do mind the things of the flesh, but they that are after the spirit the things of the spirit;'

φρονοῦσιν signifies to savour or relish. There must be a transformation by the renewing of the mind, Rom. 12:2, which is the palate of the soul, before we can know what the will of God is, or taste what the pleasures of God are; without it we can no more relish the pleasures of God than we can know his will. All satisfaction doth not result from the intrinsic excellency of the object, or the beauty of a place, or a power in anything to affect us, but from a faculty rightly disposed to the object, and a congruity and agreement between that and the understanding, and between that and the will. Brutes cannot be delighted with intellectual pleasures, because they want a faculty, nor fools, because they want a right disposition of that faculty. Purity of heart only gives us a relish of the purity of pleasure: Tit. 1:15, 'To the pure all things are pure; but unto them that are defiled and unbelieving, is nothing pure.' An ill humour on the palate tinctures the meat, and embitters that which was sweet in itself. It must be freed from that vicious juice before it can relish the sweetness of food. Natural men, because of the impurity of their natures, savour not those spiritual delights which the word, and prayer, and other holy duties afford in themselves. What fitness, then, is there in this state for the delights of heaven, which are as much superior to those delights in duties as the sun doth surmount a star in brightness? The best unregenerate man is sunk in sense, swallowed up in sense; and what suitableness can there be between a spiritual delight and a sensual frame? True pleasures and contrary desires can never abide together. A carnal man hath no apprehensions of spiritual delights but by the measures of animal pleasures. And if there be no conception of them in the understanding, what motion to them can there be in the will, or what fitness for them in the affection? Without a new nature, a new frame, we are no more able to understand or enjoy the pleasures of heaven, than a bat is to take pleasure in a mathematician's lines or a philosopher's books. It is not conceivable how God can make any man happy against his will, because all pleasure consists in the agreeableness of the will to the object.

The whole scheme of heaven must be changed to make such men happy that have not tempers suited to its present state. The bright hangings of heaven must be taken down and others put in their place to please a vicious nature.

Use. If regeneration be absolutely necessary to a gospel state, and the enjoyment of eternal glory in heaven, then it informs us,

1. How much the nature of man is depraved; for otherwise there were no need of his being born again, and no reason could be imagined why our blessed Saviour should so pressingly urge the necessity of it, If man's nature were according to his original frame, it would please God, because it was of his own creation. But we are flesh by our natural birth, and therefore to be happy we must be spiritual by a second birth. It is not a new mending, a new repairing and patching, but a new birth. We are by sin as distant from God and grace, as death from life, as nothing from being. It is not a death in appearance, but a certain death. God foretold it to Adam: Gen. 2:17, 'But of the tree of the knowledge of good and evil, thou shalt not eat of it; for in the day thou eatest thereof, thou shalt surely die,' .□□□□ □□□I suppose there is nothing here of a corporal death meant (as I have said before), but a death of his integrity and righteous nature, upon this act of disobedience; and the reason is because a temporal death did not ensue presently. And God uses to be punctual when he fixed a time to any threatening, as here he did, in the day, at that very time thou shalt die. Had it been meant of a temporal death, he had died at that instant. When God threatened Pharaoh, to-morrow such and such a plague shall come, it was certainly so. The destruction of Nineveh in forty days had been too, had they not repented. When he promised any mercy or deliverance at such a time, it was certainly performed: the very day, at the end of the time appointed, the Israelites came out of Egypt, Exod. 12:41. And though God threatened Hezekiah with death, and bids him set his house in order, yet he fixed no time, Isa. 38:1. Besides, a temporal death was not necessary to his punishment; God might have

flung both body and soul away together into hell. Besides, a temporal death, or death of the body, was fixed after the promise of the seed, Gen. 3:12, as a punishment superadded upon his sin, as well as the rest, of his eating his bread in the sweat of his brows, and the pain of women's conception and travail, which were to put him in mind of his sin in his redeemed state; therefore I question whether a temporal death, or an obnoxiousness to it, were at all meant there, but a spiritual death, the death of his righteous nature. It is a certain death, a mighty deprivation, a loss of a noble frame, a beautiful rectitude. How may we cry, as the prophet in another case: Isa. 14:12, 'How art thou fallen from heaven, O Lucifer, son of the morning! how art thou cut down to the ground!' How is our beauty not only defaced, but changed into deformity? How dreadfully are we fallen, not only to lame ourselves, but dead ourselves, that we cannot rise again, as a man fallen may! We are so unconceivably changed from what we were, that we cannot be recovered without a new make, without a new birth. Oh that we had a true and sensible prospect of this! Give me leave to say that though the fall be the cause of all our misery, yet the true consideration and sense of it is the first step to all our happiness. And we cannot take so full a view of it in the extent of the nature of it, as in the consideration of this doctrine, viz. The necessity of regeneration.

2. If regeneration be so necessary, then how much to be lamented is the ignorance of this doctrine in the world? And strange and sad it is that it should be so little considered. The common talk is of serving God and reforming the life, but who of a thousand speaks of the necessity of a new nature? It is a sad case that, when a doctrine is so clear, men should be so stupid and deludingly damn themselves; that they should be so sottishly ignorant of this who have Bibles in their hands and houses, yet not understand this, which is the great purpose for which God even sent the Scripture among the sons of men. It is a shame not to have the knowledge of this great and necessary truth. As the apostle in another

case: 1 Cor. 15:24, 'Some have not the knowledge of God, I speak it to your shame.' How strange and uncouth doth this doctrine sound in the ears of the carnal world, which wonder at it, as Nicodemus did at our Saviour's proposal, and think all our discourses of it an heap of enthusiastic nonsense! It is as if we should speak parables, as if you should talk of astronomy to the natural fool, or read divinity in Arabic to a man who understands only his native language. How little sensible is the world of the necessity of this work! They expect Christ should change their misery into glory, without changing their hearts and fitting their spirits for it, which will never be. They think it enough for them that Christ was conceived in the womb of the virgin, without being formed again in their souls, as the poor Jews at this day expect a Messiah, not to alter the frame of their souls, but the frame of the world; not to subdue their spirits, but to conquer the nations to be their vassals. How should this stupidity of men be a matter of lamentation to us!

3. If regeneration be so absolutely necessary, how should Christian parents endeavour all they can to have their children regenerate? There is no necessity they should have great estates, and live bravely in the world; but there is a necessity, a great necessity, they should be new creatures, and live spiritually. In leaving the one to your children, you leave them but earth; in leaving the other, you convey heaven to them. There is an obligation upon you, their old polluted nature was derived from you by carnal generation; make them amends by endeavouring to derive grace to them by spiritual instruction; you made them children of wrath, why will you not endeavour to make them children of God and heirs of heaven? Education of itself will not produce this noble work, nor the bare hearing of the word, or any outward means whatsoever, by their own strength; yet the Spirit doth often bless them, and very much, and I doubt not but a great number that are regenerate had the first seeds sown in them by a religious education. And I have made this observation in many. Timothy had a religious education both by his mother and grand-

mother, though this did not renew him, for Paul, by the preaching of the gospel, was the instrument of that, he calls him 'his own son in the faith,' 1 Tim. 1:2, yet no question his religious instructions from his parents did much facilitate this work. Use all endeavour, therefore, to convince them of the necessity of a new birth, be earnest with them till you see it produced, that they may not curse you for being the instruments of their beings, but bless you for being the instruments of their spiritual life.

4. This doctrine acquaints us with the insufficiency of everything else without this to enable us to enter into the kingdom of God.

(1.) Great knowledge is not sufficient. Natural knowledge is not. All the wisdom of Solomon in a man, though it may enable him to take an exact measure of nature from the highest star to the meanest insect, doth no more fit him for heaven than the stone in the head of a toad expels his venomous nature. We have more relics of Adam's nature in knowledge than we have in righteousness. To be a philosopher, physician, or statesman, is not essential to happiness in this world, much less can it prepare a man for the happiness of another. But grace is as essential to it as natural heat and radieal moisture are to the life of a man. Jesus Christ came not to make us scholars in naturals, but to endue us with such a knowledge as is in order to eternal happiness, and with such a renewing principle as might make us capable of heaven. Knowledge and wisdom are some of the choicest flowers in nature's garden; but it will be a small advantage to descend to hell with our brains full of wit and sophistry. One saving cry from a new born infant soul is of more value than the knowledge of all philosophers. Spiritual knowledge is not, that is, the knowledge of spiritual doctrines, the knowledge of Scripture itself. Nicodemus had a good stock of this; he understood the letter of the Scripture, was well read in all the parts of the law; he was thought fit to be one of the great Sanhedrim. Something else was requisite besides this; a new birth was still wanting. What if we understood the mind of the Spirit of God in every verse in the Bible; were able to discourse profoundly of the great mysteries of the gospel; had the gift of prophecy, and knowledge of things to come; had the interpretation of the whole book of the Revelation writ in our minds; what will all this avail us? An evangelical head will be but drier fuel for eternal burning, without an evangelical impression upon the heart and the badge of a new nature. Men may prophesy in Christ's name, in his name cast devils out of bodies, and devils of errors out of men's brains, yet not be regarded by Christ; but he says to them, 'I never knew you, depart from me ye that work iniquity,' Mat. 7:22, 23. If they had had this mark and gospel impression, our Lord would have known them. Christ in heaven would have owned himself formed in the heart; he could not have been ignorant of his own nature and offspring.

Well then, a man may have all the learning of Christians and heathens stored up in his head, and not the least stamp of it in his heart; he may be wise in knowledge, and a fool in improvement. A heap and pack of knowledge is not wisdom among men, without an application of that knowledge to particular exigencies and usefulness.

(2.) Outward reformation is not sufficient. Regeneration is never without reformation of life; but this may be without that. We may be outward Christians without an inward principle, though we can never be inward Christians without an outward holiness. The new birth is properly an internal work, and shews itself externally; as the heat of the heart and vital parts will evidence itself in outward motions. 'The king's daughter is all glorious within' as well as without, Ps. 45:13. What a vanity would it be to boast of freedom from other diseases, if thou hast the plague upon thee? What a poor comfort is it to brag of thy being without gross immoralities, whilst the plague of thy nature remains un-cured? Outward reformation only (though of excellent use) is but a new appearance, not a new creature, a change of life, not of the heart; whereas this work we discourse of is a new birth in the understanding and will; it begins at the spirit and descends from thence to the body, 1 Thes. 5:23; it is a sanctification in spirit, soul, and then body. Can that which can be no evidence to us in self-examination, be of itself sufficient to waft us to heaven? If you retire to take a view of yourselves whether you belong to God, will you judge by your outward actions or inward frame? There is no characteristical difference in any external action between a true Christian and an hypocrite. That, therefore, which is not a sufficient evidence to us of a right to happiness, cannot be a sufficient preparation of ourselves for it.

This reformation may proceed either,

[1.] From force and fear. Such a reformation is from impediments, not from inclination. The cutting a bird's wings takes not away its propensity to fly, but its ability; the cutting the claws of a lion, or pulling out his teeth, changes not his lionish nature. Fear restrained Herod from putting John to death, when his will was inclined to the act, Mat. 14:5. Fear may pare the nails of sin, grace only can hinder the growth and take away its life. This doth but only stop the streams, not choke the fountain.

Or, [2.] from sense of outward interest. It may be a rational abstinence from those sordid pleasures which debase a man's esteem and prey upon his reputation; and in the mean time his inward lusts may triumph, while outward appearances are stopped. Such a splendid life may consist with those inward vermin, more contrary to the pure nature of God, and as inconsistent with a man's happiness. The river which ran in open view, may sink and run as fiercely through subterranean caverns. Men may cast out one gross devil to make way for seven more spiritual ones. The interest which restrains outward acts will not restrain inward lusts.

Well then, an outward reformation without an inward grace, can no more rectify nature, than an abstinence from luxury can cure a disease a man hath contracted through intemperance, without some other physic to pluck up the root of the distemper. Outward applications of salves and ointments will do little good in a fever, unless the spring of the disease be altered, and a new crasis wrought in the blood. All outward acts are but 'bodily exercise, which profit little,' 1 Tim. 4:3. Outward reformation doth but sweeten the conversation, but doth not purge the man. He only is a vessel unto honour who hath purged himself from these things: 2 Tim. 2:21, 'If a man therefore purge himself from those, he shall be a vessel unto honour.' Outward reformation only, it is a cleansing of our life, but not ourselves. Self-nature must be purged.

(3.) Morality is not sufficient. By morality, I mean not only an outward reformation, but some love to moral virtue, as the heathens had, raised upon the thoughts of the excellency of it. Nicodemus was a moral man; he had some affection to Christ upon the consideration of his miracles; he had never else ventured to come to him so much as by night. He had no blot upon his conversation, he had desires to be instructed. This was more than a bare abstinence from sin; yet notwithstanding, besides those moral qualifications, he must have a new birth before he can see the kingdom of God. Men may do much good, be very useful to others in their generation, yet be in the very bottom of unregeneracy. A healing witch, as well as a hurting one, is the devil's client, and in covenant with him.* There is not so great a difference between the highest degree of glory in heaven and the lowest degree of grace on earth, as there is between the lowest degree of saving grace and the highest degree of natural excellency, because the difference between these is specifical, as between a rational and irrational creature; the difference between the other is only in degree, as between an infant and a man. It is one thing to have a love to moral virtue, another thing to have a love to God in it; one thing to move for self, and another thing to move for the glory of the Creator; one thing to be animated by reason, and another thing to be inspired by the Holy Ghost. What can a moral honesty profit that man who values the world's dung above the Creator's glory? What though he be honest and useful to his neighbours, must his affection to God be measured by his honesty among men? The great business is from what principle it flows. What if he doth good to others, whilst he doth his Creator wrong by fostering any one thing in his heart above him? Can his goodness to others make a compensation for his disesteem of God? The bravest man in the whole world, who hath no other descent than from Adam, must have a new quality put into his heart before he can be happy; for if a new birth be necessary, all endowments below it are to no purpose for the attainment of that state for which it is intended. Whatsoever is of the old Adam in us, though it be a beautiful flower, must wither and die: 1 Peter 1:23, 24, 'For all flesh is as grass, and the glory of man as the flower of grass; the grass withers, and the flower thereof fadeth away.' The apostle sets in opposition the incorruptible seed whereby they were born, and the fairer flowers in nature's garden. The best thing which a man glories in is a flower, but withering; it is a glory, but the glory of the flesh; it hath no lustre in the sight of God; it is not a flower to be set in heaven. It is only the word of God, and the impressions made on us by that word, which endure for ever. As herbs cannot grow without partaking of the natural influence and beams of the sun, so nothing stands and flourishes but what partakes of the nature and spirit of Christ. Nay, it is so far from being sufficient, that it is a great hindrance of regeneration, without the overpowering grace of God, because it is the glory of a man; that is, that wherein a man glories. Men are apt to rest upon their morals without reflecting upon their naturals. They see no spots in their lives, and therefore will not believe there are any in their hearts. They are so taken up, with the pharisee, their proud thoughts of their being above others, that they never think how much they have inwardly of the publican in coming short of the glory of God. Unregenerate morality, therefore, is not sufficient. The heart must be changed before moral virtues can commence graces. When this is once done, what were moral before become divine, as having a new principle to quicken them, and a new end to direct them.

(4.) Religious professions are not sufficient. Can you, upon a serious consideration, conclude that this only is the import of all those scriptures which speak of being born of God, raised from a death in sin, quickened and led by the Spirit, created in righteousness and true holiness? Are not these things, in the very manner of speaking them, elevated above any mere profession, which may be declared to the world without any such work, which is the evident intendment of those scriptures? It is not the naming the name of Christ, but the departing from iniquity; a departing from it in our nature as well as in our actions, that is the badge whereby the Lord knows who are his: 2 Tim. 2:19, 'The Lord knows who are his: and let every one that names the name of Christ depart from iniquity.' Religious profession only is but a form, a figure, a shape of godliness: a picture made by art, without life and power, and an enlivened faculty, and a divine principle whence it should proceed; it is but a name of life at best under a state of death: Rev. 3:1, 'Thou hast a name that thou livest, and art dead.' Professions without a new nature, are no more the things God requires of us, than sacrifices under the law without a broken heart. It is not a following our Saviour in profession, but in regeneration, which gives the apostles a title to that promise of sitting upon his throne in glory: Mat. 19:28, 'Ye that have followed me in regeneration, ye shall sit upon twelve thrones, judging the twelve tribes of Israel.' Judas had followed Christ till that time, and after, in a profession, but not in the regeneration, not from a regenerated principle.

(5.) Multitudes of external religious duties and privileges are not sufficient. Men are very apt to place their security here. It was the great labour of the prophet Isaiah to bring the Jews, in his time, off from them. God doth not require attendance on ordinances as the ultimate end, but as means to the beginning and promoting a new birth: Isa. 11:16, 'To what purpose is the multitude of your sacrifices to me? Wash ye, make ye clean.' The resting in these is the manifest destruction of men's souls, when thousands of sacrifices to God cannot be acceptable without a new nature. We naturally affect an easy religion; and outward acts of worship, especially under the gospel, have no great difficulty in them. Men would rather be at great expense of sacrificing, than crucify one beloved sin;

and cringe a thousand times before the cross of Christ, than nail one corruption to it. How easy a work were it to get to heaven, if nothing else were required but to be a member of the Christian visible church? Circumcision was a privilege, but it availed nothing without a new creature, Gal. 5:6. There was another circumcision made without hands, the work of God, that was required, Col. 2:11; a new creature, without which outward circumcision signified nothing. The practice of some duties may stand with an inward hatred of them, as the abstinence from some sins may stand with an inward love to them. Outward worship is but a carcase, when the soul is not conformed to God, the object of worship, and doth not attain an union to, and communion with God, which is the end of worship. What are all acts of worship without a nature suitable to the God we approach unto in them? Judge not, therefore, of your state by any external actions; no outward act, but unregenerated persons may do, yea, they may express much zeal in them. They may have their bodies as martyrs consumed by flames, without having their corruption consumed by grace; a stinking breath may make as good music to the ear in a pipe as a sound one. There is something more necessary than a bare performance of duties.

(6.) Nay, more, convictions are not sufficient. Nicodemus was startled by our Saviour's miracles, believes him to be a prophet sent by God, acknowledgeth that God was with him, John 3:2, yet still the necessary qualification of a new birth was wanting. Your spirits may be torn in pieces by terror, the heart of stone may be rent asunder, and yet no heart of flesh appear; the ground may be ploughed, yet not sown. Sensuality and lust may be kept under by a spirit of bondage, when it is not cast out by a spirit of adoption; the sun may scorch you, and not enliven you; the knowledge of the foulness of sin, and the fierceness of wrath, is the work of the Spirit in the law; the new birth is the work of the Spirit in the gospel; the stone may be cut and hewed by the law, and yet never polished by the gospel, never brought into covenant: Hosea 6:5, 7, 'I have hewed them by my prophets, but they like men have transgressed the covenant.' It is not then great knowledge, fair-coloured fruit, oil in the lamp of life, loud professions, glittering services, or tearing convictions, which are this badge whereby Christ knows his own from all the world besides; all these will be answered, 'I know you not.' Is it not, then, a worthy work, and high time to get that new nature, whereby God will know thee to belong to him? Professions may be false, outward reformation may be but as a painted sepulchre: knowledge only elevates the understanding; but as our communion lies in the acts of the will, there must be some work upon that to fit us for our great happiness. If these things are not sufficient, then profane men cannot expect heaven by the way of hell.

Use 2. If regeneration be so absolutely necessary to salvation, how miserable is the condition of every unregenerate man! What a miserable case is it, that sinners should dream on in their delusions till everlasting burnings confute their fancies, and turn their hopes into dreadful despair. Oh, how do most men live as if this doctrine were a mere falsity, and act as if they would take heaven by the violence of their lusts, not by the industry of grace? Know you not that an unrighteous nature shall not inherit the kingdom of God? 1 Cor. 6:9, 'Know you not that the unrighteous shall not inherit the kingdom of God? be not deceived,' &c. Is it possible you should be ignorant of that which stares you in the face in every page in the Bible? If you know not this you know nothing. Be not deceived. Nothing is no natural as heart-deceit and presumptuous confidence. The apostle else would not have spoken of it with such an emphasis, but that he knew how apt men are to delude themselves with hopes of mercy in a state of sin. Self-flattery is one of the strongest branches which grows upon the pride of nature. How vain is it to fancy to yourselves a fitness for heaven, while there are only preparations for hell? Whence should such imaginations arise? Not from God; it is contrary to all his professed declarations. Is it from yourselves? What reason have you to believe your fancies in spiritual things, who are so often mistaken in temporal? Is it from the devil? What reason have you to believe your greatest enemy? If this work be wrought, he hath for ever lost you. It is he that cherishes such notions, for he hath no pleasure to undo his kingdom, and lose his subjects. Never did any man use so much diligence to get a new nature as the devil doth to hinder him.

Will you seriously consider,

1. It is highly irrational to expect security and glory in an unregenerate state. Is it for us to separate those things which God hath joined, flesh and destruction, a new birth and a kingdom? That which doth naturally tend to hell can never conduct us to heaven. Can the old nature, which frames a fit subject for eternal vengeance, ever fashion it to be a vessel of eternal glory? There is as great a tendency in the old nature to hell as there is of a stone or lead to the earth. If men may be saved in their unregeneracy,

(1.) God must be false to himself. False he must be to his truth, false to holiness, false to his Son, false to the whole tenor of the gospel. God must change the covenant of grace, blot out all his threatenings in Scripture, give the lie to all his declarations in the word, proclaim himself unwise in all his administrations, if ever such a man be happy; and is it not a damnable conceit, and a provoking wish, to desire that God should belie himself to befriend us? There must be a new gospel before any can be saved without a new nature. This cannot be. Must God change his law, or we our lusts? God hath settled and declared a decree, that none that are not born again shall enter into the kingdom of God. His decree stands irreversible, the change must necessarily therefore be on our side.

(2.) As far as I can understand, God must put himself out of heaven before that such a man can come thither. There can be no pleasure on either side with unsuitableness. If God be absent from heaven, as to his glorious presence, how can there be happiness? He loves his own righteousness better than to endure such men's presence, and they love their unrighteousness so much as not to bear his. No man cares for coming into a place which is possessed by one that he hates; they can have no pleasure to be in a heaven with God, who were delighted to be in a world without him, Eph. 2:12.

(3.) Jesus Christ must be a liar, and the gospel false, if ever there be a heaven enjoyed by an old nature. He hath asserted it, that is truth itself; and is it not a madness to imagine a possibility of coming thither in spite of him? You may upon better grounds hope to be crowned monarch of the whole world to-morrow, than to enter into heaven without being born again. Christ values his truth, though he did not his life, above our souls, and his word will stand firm against all presumptuous confidence whatsoever.

(4.) Suppose God should reverse his gospel (which cannot be), and declare another, I cannot see how the case would be mended, for what gospel can God frame, with a salvo to his own honour, without the creatures being righteous to enjoy the benefit of it? Must God conform himself to the will of our lusts? Must he cast his holiness into the depths of the sea? Must he paint himself black to agree with our hue? as the negroes picture him of their own colour. In a word, must God cease to be God that you may cease to be miserable? To desire happiness without a new nature shews a contempt of God, since it is to desire it on terms on which it is dishonourable for God to give it.

Well then, this doctrine is so certainly true, that if an angel from heaven should declare the contrary he ought not to be believed: Gal. 1:8, 'Let him be accursed;' that is, he would be more a devil than an angel, and it would be an accursed doctrine. He must found his doctrine upon another gospel, and a gospel printed in hell, but impossible to have an imprimatur from heaven. Is it possible, then, for any man, after such an assertion of our Saviour, to live under the hearing of the Christian doctrine, and fancy a heavenly glory belonging to him without a heavenly nature?

2. As it is highly irrational, so it is highly sinful to lie in an unrenewed state. To continue in it after the declaration of God's holiness, in so

eminent a manner, in the death of his Son, is a high approbation of unrighteousness, and a contempt of his infinite purity; for since he hath shewn himself a hater of sin, and the old nature of Adam in the death of the Redeemer, more than he could any other; the fostering the old nature in us is a valuing that which God hath manifested his hatred of, and a slighting all the expressions of his love. It draws a greater guilt upon our persons than Adam did by his fall upon our natures: John 15:22, 'If I had not come and spoken to them, they had not had sin.' If I had not told them those things, and preach heavenly doctrine to them, their sin had been as it were a petty larceny, in comparison of what it is now, a treason against my Father's crown and dignity; 'but now they have hated me and my Father.'

3. Hence it follows that such a man's condition must be exceeding miserable. Those that 'have a part in the first resurrection,' on them it is said 'the second death shall have no power,' Rev. 20:6; whether he means the resurrection of Christ, or the spiritual resurrection of the soul. The second death then shall have power over them that have no part in the first resurrection.

(1.) Such are peculiarly miserable. Such a man had better have been any other creature,—a toad, a serpent, a beetle, liable to be trod to death by the next comer,—than have been a man, and live and die with a serpentine nature, and without renewing grace, would be glad one day to change states with them; and it had been better to have been born in the darkest part of America than in England, and better to have lived in the blindest corner in England than in London, where he hath heard so much and so often of the necessity of the new birth, and yet cherished an old nature. It is an astonishing madness this. Better never to have been born a man than not be a real Christian, which he cannot be without this new birth, this necessary regeneration; better never to have entered by the door of baptism into the Christian society, than not have a nature answerable to the baptismal intendment. There is not the meanest beggar that creeps in the street, the most ulcerous Lazarus that lies at the door, but if renewed is infinitely happier than any one unrenewed can be with all worldly felicity.

(2.) Such are unavoidably miserable. The mercy of God can never make you happy against his truth, the righteousness of God can never do it without the necessary qualification. Is it just with God to give his worst enemies the same reward of glory with his choicest friends; to those that never endeavoured to reform their lives according to the methods of the gospel, as to those who have had the holy image of his Son drawn and wrought in their hearts? In 2 Tim. 4:8 he is said to be a 'righteous judge,' which could not be if he gave the same rewards to both the contrary qualifications. The devil may as soon be saved, as any man without a new birth. Though there be enough written against the salvation of devils, yet there is more written in the book of God against the salvation of men living and dying in an unregenerate state than against the salvation of devils. Do any expect to see the kingdom of God without it? Why, that form on which you sit, that dust under your feet, far cleaner than ourselves by nature, are fitter to be brought into that place of glory. The holiness of God can better endure them than an unrenewed man. He pronounced their kind good at the creation, but never was an unrenewed nature pronounced good by God. You can no more shun an eternal misery without it, than you can a temporal death with it; you can no more fly from hell than from yourselves. Our blessed Saviour, the redeemer of the world, will know none for admission into happiness without his badge upon them: Mat. 7:23, 'I never knew you:' you had nothing in you worthy my knowledge and affection. Where is the evangelical impression upon your soul? will be the only question then asked.

Well, then, I wish every unregenerate man would put the question to his soul, Can I dwell with everlasting burnings? Can I, with a cheerful security, meet the wrath of God in its march against me? Is eternal darkness a delightful state? Is an eternal separation from the blessed God to be desired? Is a present sensual life to be preferred before a joyful eternity? Is there any one Scripture in the whole book of God can give me comfort in this state? What, then, dost thou, O my soul, spend thy thoughts about, since there is nothing to procure thy felicity, but this new birth?

Use 3. Is of comfort. Is it so, that without regeneration there is no salvation? Then how great is the comfort of that person, who hath attained this necessary thing! What a foundation is here for the composition of new songs for spiritual exultings! What a diffusion may there be of pleasure through the whole soul! That little regenerating principle within you is more necessary than the wisdom of Solomon, the power of Nebuchadnezzar, the glory of Ahasuerus, the reaching heads of the most knowing men in the world, and shall make you happy, when others in their unrenewed wisdom and unsanctified wealth shall descend to destruction.

1. The least true grace hath comfort from hence. 'Except a man be born again, he cannot see the kingdom of God:' therefore if he be born again, he shall see it. Our Saviour doth not say, except a man hath been born so long, arrived to such a stature, but simply born again; it lies upon the essence, not upon the degree. A child that cries the first minute it is born, is in a state of life, as well as the man in the prime of his strength; a child hath the nature of a man, though attended with some strong disease and great infirmities; though every true Christian hath not the same growth, yet he hath the same birth, the same renewing Spirit. 'If a man be in Christ, he is a new creature;' the apostle doth not say, he is a strong creature, or a tall creature. St John reckons three different states of Christians, 1 John 2:13, 14, children, young men, and fathers, and all in a state of the knowledge of God.

2. Here is comfort in the ignorance of the time of the new birth. 'Except a man be born again,' not except he know the time of his being

born again; the want of the knowledge of the time hath troubled some, but it is no matter for the time, if we find the essential properties; our happiness is secured by the essence, not by the circumstance. It is the glory of those that were born in Sion, that they 'were born there,' Ps. 87:5, though the time of their birth were not exactly known by them. Many may tell the first preparations to it, the first strong conviction, the first time they found their hearts affected; this is more easy than to tell the very time when spiritual life was infused, any more than to tell the punctual time when the child was quickened in the womb; this is no more known, than that particular minute when this or that addition was made to our stature and growth, though the growth itself be discernible.

3. Such are new born to the enjoyment of God in glory. If none shall see God without it, then those shall certainly see God who have it; it is for the undefiled inheritance that God did first beget you: 1 Peter 1:3, 'He hath begotten us to a lively hope, to an inheritance undefiled, incorruptible, that fadeth not away, reserved in heaven for you.' Had not God intended you for an everlasting converse with himself, he would not have taken such pains, but have let you lie in your blood, and run down the stream of nature into the ocean of a miserable eternity with the common mass of the world. What comfort will this be, when you see the old house of your bodies full of gaps, ready to fall, that your reborn souls are ready to take possession of their eternal inheritance! Paul was one of the highest rank in Christianity, both in grace and office, yet the 'crown of righteousness' was not only laid up for him, and to be given to him, but to 'all that love the appearing' of Christ, 2 Tim. 4:8, that is, to all those that, from the principles of the new nature, aspire to that perfection, which shall be at the appearance of Christ. There is as certain a tendency, by the ordination of God, of a renewed soul to heaven, as of flame into the air. Grace and glory are in nature the same thing as a seed and a plant.

4. It is comfort upon this account, If new-born to heaven, then to all things which may further your passage thither and assist you in it. To God, as your God and king to protect you, as your Father to cherish you; to the promises as your promises, as assurances and deeds for heaven; to a sanctification of all states for a furtherance of you in your travel to and fitness for this kingdom; to a sight of God in his ordinances, and in his providences; he will not deny a beam here in his institutions to those for whom he reserves his full face hereafter; to a fellowship with God in duties of worship, as a foretaste of a perpetual communion with him; to an improvement of all graces; to the perfectest dress at last of all beautiful grace, which may completely fit you for an everlasting sight of God in heaven.

Use. 4. If without the new birth there is no entering into heaven, then it stands upon you to clear up your evidences for the new birth. If the existence of it be necessary for our felicity, the knowledge of it is necessary for our comfort. This is the great distinguishing evangelical sign; without an inward principle of life, we have not reached the intendment of the gospel: John 6:63, 'The words of Christ are spirit and life.' John 10:10, 'I am come that you might have life.' He hath no interest in the gospel that hath not this in his heart. Every man in Christ must be a new creature.

To encourage you in this work, consider,

1. It is by this you must know your justification. Justification is our blessedness: Rom. 4:8, 'Blessed is the man to whom the Lord will not impute sin.' And this is the way to know our blessedness: forgiveness of sin precedes the inheritance, and both this and that are received only by the sanctified through faith in Christ: Acts 26:18, 'That they may receive forgiveness of sin, and inheritance among them which are sanctified by faith which is in me.' The alteration of our frame is notius, more discernible to us, than that of our relative states; the new dispositions discover what relation we stand in to God. This is a certain truth, he that doth not find the draught of God's image in him, hath no reason to

conclude he hath any saving interest in the propitiatory sacrifice of the Redeemer. As the blood and water were not separated in the effusion upon the cross, neither are they in their application to the soul; water to renew us, and blood to justify us. The 'washing of regeneration' evidenceth our being justified by grace, Titus 3:5–7; the apostle infers the one from the other.

2. Therefore, by the knowledge of this only you can gain comfort. The great desire is, Oh that I were assured! Let it be your great business to clear up the new birth. It is the office of the Spirit not only to comfort but renew, and to comfort by renewing. The hope of eternal life is founded upon the renewing of the Holy Ghost, as well as on justification by grace, Titus 1:5–7; the Spirit as a comforter is to guide into all truth, John 16:13, into that truth which is sanctifying, John 17:17. The property of the Spirit is to guide us into sanctifying truth, and sanctify us by that truth; the Spirit doth witness with our spirits that we are the children of God; its witness is by something within us, not without us. There must be something in our hearts as a foundation of this testimony; what witness can there be in an old nature? Look after, therefore, those essential properties of the new nature. Christ preached duty and comfort together; his first sermon, Mat. 5, is made up of both. The clear evidence of a new life seated in the centre of the soul, will be a surer testimony of our right to, and fitness for glory, than if an angel from heaven should assure us in the name of God, that we are some of his heirs; the testimony of an angel is but that of a creature, lower then the verbal testimony of the Son of God. The evidences of the beginnings of glory, by the operations of grace and a Godlike nature, are more uncontrollable than the highest assurances all the angels in heaven can give us. Clear up this, therefore. There are many counterfeits; men may take morality, outward reformation, heaps of religious duties, to be this work, but these are all insufficient, and men without good examination may cheat themselves, and take copper for gold, and tin for silver. There is a natural or moral

integrity, and an evangelical integrity; the natural integrity God owns in Abimelech: Gen. 20:6, 'Yea, I know that thou didst this in the integrity of thy heart.' He was king of the place where Abraham thought there was no fear of God, ver. 12. And it is likely there was not. God puts none of them upon prayer for themselves, but Abraham upon praying for them.

Then ask yourselves these two or three questions.

1. How stand your hearts to God and sin? Is there a bias in the will, which doth naturally carry it to God? What light is there in your minds? what flexibleness and tenderness in the will and conscience? what sprightliness in your affections to the things of God? what readiness to meet him in his motions to you? what closing with Christ? Are there strong cries, struggling, wrestling, Jacob-like prayers? A new-born babe not to cry; a child not to call to his father, and follow him, and press to him: it is inconsistent with such a nature, since it is the first fruit of the 'spirit of adoption' received by us, to cause us to cry, Abba, Father, Rom. 8:15. How stand your hearts to sin? Are there deep humiliations for it, utter detestation of it? Are your affections dead to the flesh and the world, and alive and quick to the things of God? Rom. 8:10, 'The body is dead because of sin, and the spirit is life because of righteousness.' What humbling of inward pride, what striving against inward sins, what loathing of inward corruptions?

2. What delight have you in spiritual duties? Do your souls spring up in a service? Are your hearts in heaven before the words are out of your mouth? What is agreeable to nature is not burdensome. Spiritual services are as pleasant to a new nature, as sin is to an old, as sweet wines and delicious food is to a gluttonous disposition: Ps. 119:103, 'How sweet are thy words unto my taste! yea, sweeter than honey to my mouth!' Honey, one of the staple excellencies of Canaan, which is described to be a land flowing with milk and honey. Doth your delight in the law of God spring up from the inner man? There is a delight in doing some things of the law (the Gentiles did by nature the things contained in the law, Rom.

2:14), by a moral nature, not a new nature; if by nature, they had then a delight in them, and it was as all delight is, inward in the soul and heart, no doubt but many of them had pleasure in their morality. That is not the meaning of the apostle; but he doth distinguish his delights from theirs by the object of it, and by the subject or spring of it. It was the law of God, as it was the law of God, that he did delight in; and it was not only an inward delight, but a delight arising from an inner nature, a man distinct from that man composed of soul and body; it did arise from a spirit possessed with nobler principles and higher ends.

Well, then, is it your meat and drink to do his will? Has the glory of God been dearer to you than the dearest worldly concerns you have? Are your converses with him very delightful to you? Do the thoughts of God, and delights in him, frequently return upon you? What bears the most grateful relish in your souls? holy thoughts and duties, or sinful and foolish vanities?

3. How do you live? Have you another life 'by the faith of the Son of God?' Gal. 2:20; another faith beside the common faith, not resting in assent, but 'working by love,' Gal. 5:6. Do you live to yourselves? That is proper to a state of nature. Or do you live to God? 2 Cor. 5:13. That is proper to a state of grace: Gal. 2:19, 'I am dead to the law, that I might live unto God.' Is there a closing with Christ, not only as your Saviour, but as the principle and end of your lives? Is there a living the life of God, the life of Christ? Can Christ be formed in the heart, and there be nothing of the qualities of Christ, nothing of the spirit of Christ? Is Christ formed in the heart, a hard, low, dead, cold, dark, lifeless Christ? This frame is a quite contrary thing to Christ. If we are born of the will of God, we are born to answer the will of God. Is it the will of God that we should be loose in our hearts, and vain in our lives? That is the will of the flesh, not the will of God. According as our hearts are, so is our birth; sin or grace must have dominion in the soul; they cannot live amicably together; a man cannot be a sinner and a saint with the same

will, cannot equally love holiness and iniquity. We may as well say that a man may be in heaven and hell at the same time; not but that a renewed man may in a sudden fit do a thing against his nature, as Moses, one of a mild disposition, was transported with a strain of passion against his nature. If sin reigns in the heart, though it doth not in outward acts; if we yield ourselves servants, to obey it in the lusts thereof, though not in the outward fruit of those lusts, this new-creature principle was never settled in the heart: Rom. 6:12, 'Let not sin reign therefore in your mortal body, that you should obey it in the lusts thereof: neither yield ye your members as instruments of unrighteousness unto sin.' He makes a manifest difference between the inward lust obeyed, and the outward commission of it in the members, and places the reign of sin in one as well as the other; and, ver. 16, concludes them in a state of nature or a state of grace, according as they yield themselves servants to this or that. A regenerate practical atheist is just as true as to say a regenerate devil.

(1.) Be diligent observers, therefore, of what solid alterations you find in your spirits; what motions, starts, principles, ends you can perceive there; and if you find you have this excellent and necessary new birth, admire God's grace in you, that he should pass by so many thousands in the world and renew you; that he should leave many soaking in their sins, and swimming to destruction in their old nature, and bestow this heavenly plant upon your souls. And prize it too. Aquinas hath an excellent saying, The good of one grace is greater than the good of all nature; which words Cajetan commends as fit to be writ upon our minds, and constantly reviewed by us, to raise our admirations of God and his grace.

I speak now but little of these things, because the next discourse will lead me to speak more of them.

(2.) Seek it. If it be necessary to be had, it is necessary to be sought. We are all at this present before God in an old or new nature; and if we die in the nature we have received from old Adam, without another from the new, it is as certain that every one of us shall be excluded out of the kingdom of God, as it is certain we live and breathe in the places where we stand or sit. We are born of the earth, we must be born from heaven; we must have a spiritual as well as an animal life. Oh that every man and woman had the same thoughts of the necessity of it as they have who are past hope in hell of ever attaining it! Riches are not necessary, honours are not necessary; this is of absolute necessity. Were you like Solomon in all his glory, you could not have the privilege of entering into God's kingdom without a new nature; but a new nature without the glory of Solomon, nay, without a rag to your backs, will admit you. If those that are already renewed must be every day putting off the old and putting on the new man,*Eph. 4:22, 24, how much more need have you who have not dropped one scale, or sweat out one spirit of the old man, nor have a grain of the new man in you? As original corruption stood up in the place of original righteousness, so a gracious regenerate frame must rise up in the place of original corruption, for God will never befriend corrupt nature so much as to give a happiness to that which he hates. Men do not choose weeds but flowers to plant in their delightful gardens. God indeed doth choose weeds, but they are turned into the nature of flowers before he transplants them to glory. We must have a wedding garment to fit us for his feast, and oil in our vessels to prepare us for his nuptials.

Seek it, for,

(1.) It is an indispensable duty. God hath resolved that only 'the pure in heart shall see God,' Mat. 5:8. It is a duty incumbent on us to love God. Since we are bound to love God, we are bound to love whatsoever hath any relation to him. Therefore we must love ourselves, not with a sordid, carnal love, but as we are the image of God. Hence we are bound to do what we can to brighten and clear this image, and restore it to its primitive perfection in our souls. We are answerable to God for the presenting this image of God in the same state wherein it was when he conferred it upon Adam, and upon us in his loins. Since the

Redeemer hath undertaken to restore it, it is our duty to seek to this Redeemer for the restoration of it, for he came 'that we might have life,' John 10:16; a vital principle in us to fit us for eternal life, and to 'have it more abundantly,' in a more glorious and fixed manner than Adam had.

(2.) Seek it, for something of this nature, or equivalent to it, seems necessary to all rational and intellectual creatures. The first nature of man was sown in mutability, and there was a necessity of something equivalent to this regeneration to fix and establish his nature; as the confirmation of angels under the head Christ is in some sort a regeneration of them, for it is an alteration of their state, from mutable to immutable, not by nature, for so God only is immutable, but by grace: Eph. 1:10, 'He hath gathered together in one all things in Christ.' There is need now of it to change our nature, and afterwards to fix us in it. Most think that Adam, had he stood some time, had been confirmed in the state of innocency, and advanced to a more excellent state than that of paradise, which would have been an alteration of his state. If, then, an alteration of state was necessary for the fixing his happiness, an alteration of state is much more necessary for us for regaining the happiness we fell from.

(3.) Seek it, because in not seeking it you act against your own reason and natural experience. You have by the light of nature, improved by the light of the gospel, so much knowledge as to perceive that you are not as God first made you. You cannot but acknowledge it impossible that so filthy and disorderly a piece can come out of his hands; that there is something wanting to you. And are those relics of nature left only to shew us our indigence, and not also to spur us on to seek a remedy? Melancthon saith, I have seen many epicures who, being in some grief for their sins, have argued, How can I expect to be received by God, when I find not a new light and new virtues infused into me? When you are stilled after the rage of carnal affections or glut of pleasures, and you do in silence turn in upon yourselves, and make inquiry after your future state, if your conscience do not lie and flatter, will they not tell you to your faces that you are men of death, prepared against the day of slaughter? Besides, will not every man confess in his most raised retirements that he cannot find any real satisfaction in things below? And are there not sometimes some natural aspirings to something above these? Do not all men one time or other inquire, Ps. 4:6, 'Who will shew us any good?' Have you ever a more delightful pleasure than when you find yourselves inflamed with some desires for it? But, alas! do you not feel yourselves in a depraved state, and that these motions are but weak flutterings, and that the soul is quickly wearied in them? Is not this an evidence that there must be a more vigorous nature infused both to attain and enjoy them? Is it not then an acting against your own sentiments not to seek it? Do you not offer violence to that little reason in you to cut the wings of such motions? Let me add this too, you act in a way contrary to the nature of every thing, not to seek that state which was designed for the perfection of human nature. Is it not natural for everything to endeavour its recovery to its primitive purity, and struggle under that which is preternatural to it? A fountain will not rest till it hath wrought out the filth which hath been cast into it; so neither should man be quiet till he recover himself from the dominion of sin in his nature, and his pollution by it. Are you contented with a nasty, impure, and diseased body? are you not restless till it be cleansed and cured? and is it no trouble to you to have your souls in a dirty and foul condition? Do you not hereby act against your own nature in other things?

(4.) Not to seek it is to despise the general mercy of God, and the general kindness of the Mediator to human nature. There are in man desires for and inclinations to happiness, and some knowledge that this happiness lies in God. These desires were left in man by the mercy of God upon the interposition of the Mediator; therefore some call them not relics of nature, but restored principles, as a foundation to work upon; for upon the fall man did forfeit all, and sin despoiled himself of all de jure, but by the mediation of Christ, those were left (Col. 1:17,

'By him all things consist'), otherwise there had been no stock to work upon. These are left as foundations upon which God grafts this grace of regeneration,* as they that spin do not spin out the whole thread, but leave some end, that they may add to it another thread; so God, having a purpose to do good on man in renewing him, did not suffer the stock of nature to be wholly rooted out, but left that as a root to graft upon, to make him the better capable of happiness. Had not man had a natural desire to happiness, there were no ground to work upon him to induce him to such a thing; therefore in not seeking it you reproach God for leaving this stump in you, and seem to be so well pleased with corrupt nature as if you would not have any remainder of the former. It is a striving against the relic of original nature left in us.

(5.) Seek it, for it is as necessary as justification. You should therefore seek it with as high an esteem of it as you have of pardon; none but would desire pardon of sin. You must be as desirous of the regeneration of your nature; they are equally necessary. Those who will not have an inherent righteousness can never expect an imputed righteousness from Christ; he never came to that end. Two things happened to us by the fall: another state and another nature; the regaining of the former must be equally sought with the latter, a being in another covenant by justification (for naturally we are in the covenant with Adam), and a being beautified with another image, because naturally we are deformed by the image of Adam. As long as we are only in a state of descent from, and union with, the first Adam, we are under the strictness of his covenant and the deformity of his image; when we are united to the second Adam, and spiritually descend from him, we are in his covenant of grace, and are adorned with his image. Both, therefore, must be looked after as equally necessary: Rom. 5:21, 'That as sin hath reigned unto death, so might grace reign through righteousness unto eternal life by Jesus Christ our Lord.' Let us, then, look after this reign of grace; let not that be the last which should be first in our thoughts. Since our natural descent from Adam, we are born God's enemies: we must be spiritually new-born before our enmity can expire.

(6.) The advantages that accrue by regeneration are high. When we are renewed, we part with impurity for purity, with dross for gold, with corruption for holiness, with flesh for spirit, with nature for grace, with sin for God, and the enjoyment of him for ever. Our present nature is a nature of death and bondage; a new nature is like the new law, a law of life and liberty, James 1:25. It will put our souls in order, and set the Israelite free from the Egyptian taskmaster; it will quell the rage of sin, and diffuse a serenity in our souls. Grace and peace are not unfitly joined together by the apostle, in respect of peace in ourselves, which cannot be without habitual grace, as well as peace with God, which cannot be without his favour. It will enable us to perform spiritual services. As all natural actions flow from a natural form in the creature, so all spiritual actions flow from a spiritual nature in the soul, and without it a carnal heart can no more do any spiritual work than a rock can perform the work of a balsam-tree. It is but highly reasonable and just we should endeavour to regain that state wherein we were created, as the best for us, since the estate wherein God created us was certainly the best. It is unconceivably better to be a righteous man than to be a man.

(7.) Seek it; you will never repent your labour, because it is necessary. Necessity makes us contend with the greatest difficulties; men will do more at a pinch than they can do at other times, when no necessity is upon them. Never did any repent of it, never any will; it hath been a comfort upon a deathbed to all that had it: it never was any man's sorrow. The universal consent of all who have found it wrought should quicken our desires and endeavours for it. Ask a renewed man whether ever it troubled him that he was regenerate? whether he would be without that state rather than undergo the same pains again? Would not his answer be, No, not for all the world? When the blessed apostle Paul considered his late regeneration, he expresseth it with some regret, 1 Cor. 15:8, 'as one born out of due time.' It implies a sorrow that he was not born sooner; and Austin cries out, Sero te amavi, Domine, I have loved thee too late, Lord. So doth every renewed man repent that he was not regenerate sooner. A regenerate man come under the yoke of Christ finds such a pleasure in it, such a suitableness, such an advantage to his interest, that he would not be free from those delightful engagements, and the sweetness of that yoke, for all the delights and commodities of the world.

Exhortation 3. Seek it presently; let not a minute pass without some ejaculation to God for the new birth; and when you come home, fall upon your knees, and rise not till you find a change of resolutions and dispositions. If you did well understand the necessity of it, you would not be one hour without begging it. You have heard the necessity of it now, are you sure you shall ever hear the doctrine preached on again? Are you sure you may not be past the hope as well as the happiness of the new birth before many days be run, if the present opportunity be neglected? When God commanded Abraham to circumcise himself and his family, it is said he did it that very day wherein God commanded him, Gen. 17:23. Why should you not imitate Abraham in the ready and speedy circumcision of the heart? Though God doth wait long, it cannot be thought he should alway be courting dead souls. It must be now; there is no hope of such a change after death: 'The redemption of their soul ceaseth for ever,' Ps. 49:8; no more under the offers of a redeeming Saviour, no more under the motions of a renewing Spirit. Christ breaks the nations like a potter's vessel, Ps. 2:9. A vessel before it be burned may be macerated in water, and formed anew; but when it hath been burned in the furnace, it cannot be changed. Well, if thou wilt be new born this day, God will bless the memory of this day, for he will gain a son; Jesus Christ will by his blood put this day in red letters in his calendar, for he will gain a brother; the Spirit will rejoice, for he will gain a temple; angels will rejoice, for they will gain a fellow-servant; you will gain a fitness for an everlasting inheritance. Let me, therefore, press young men and women to this necessary and important concern; I know not when I may have so fit an opportunity or subject for it. It is not said, except an old man be born again, but except a man; therefore be not careless, as if you were not concerned in it, nor put it off to a longer day from the probability of the length of your life in a course of nature. Consider,

1. An early regeneration makes for God's honour.

(1.) In preventing much sin. How ripe are young ones, yea, even children when they are scarce green in age, as though iniquity had been their tutor in the womb! Youthful blood is the devil's tinder. Job knew it; therefore when his sons feasted he sacrificed, chap. 1:5. He was jealous of their inbred corruption, from the sense of the sins of his own youth, which we find him complaining of, Job 13:26; therefore he feared his children, having the same temptations, might fall into the same transgressions. Now, by an early regeneration, many diseases of the soul are prevented, as well as the great crack of nature cured, as the distempers of the body are prevented by altering the habit of it in the spring. Though by a late regeneration, that of an old man, the soul is fitted for heaven, yet it will be grievous to him to think that his former dishonouring of God in his natural state was not prevented. It is otherwise with the early regenerate; they cannot complain, as Paul did, Oh, how have I persecuted the church of God! how have I breathed out threatenings against Christ and his people! how have I wallowed in all kind of sin! They have indeed as much reason to complain of the stock of the old nature within them, but not of so many bitter fruits of the flesh as others. How doth the devil hang the wing when he is deprived of an active servant! As nothing makes heaven so glad, so nothing makes hell so sad, as to be frustrated of the full crop of sin it expected from such an instrument.

(2.) In doing much service for God. Young men are usually of active spirits and vigorous affections, whereas age doth freeze all youthful warmth. Such, like Peter, can 'gird themselves, and go whither they please,' John 21:18, and travel about for God; but age damps the spirits. We are not so fit for service when the vigour of our youth is spent. And would you be saved, and God have no more glory from you? Now what parts, or strength, or mettle, a young man hath, grace will bias, put into a right channel, and direct to an useful end. The early regenerate will be eminent in piety; for in a course of nature, they have a longer time to grow in. Their faith and love, by a larger exercise, will be the stronger; and the stronger the grace, the more glory will be brought to God, Rom. 4:20. Abraham, it is said, was 'strong in faith, giving glory to God.' He that rises betimes in the morning, will do more work than he that lies in bed till noon, or loiters till the sun declines.

(3.) In manifesting the power of the grace of God. An early regeneration is the great ornament of the gospel. It evidenceth the dignity and strength of habitual grace, in quenching youthful heats and powerful temptations, in making such to deny themselves, and prefer God's precepts before their own pleasures. It magnifies grace, when the devil is beat upon his own dunghill, where he had so great an interest, by reason of the corruptions such are subject to. What an elogy is it to the beauty and power of grace, to see a young flourishing plant in God's garden! It shews the power of his grace upon such to salvation, that they are strong in the power of the might of God, to wrestle against principalities and powers, as well as against flesh and blood. It manifests the power of God's grace in the work of faith, and that there is a spirit of power residing in them.

2. As an early regeneration makes for God's honour, so it makes for your own interest.

(1.) Your new birth will be the gentler. The work of conscience will be more kindly, without the horrors they have, who have lain many years soaking in the old nature. More of hell must be flashed in an old sinner's face, to awaken him from his dead sleep. Paul, who had sinned some years with an high hand, was struck to the earth. Christ, as it were, took him by the throat, and shook him: Acts 9:6, 'He trembling, and astonished, said,' &c. There will be more amazing aggravations of sin to rack the conscience, and consequently more anguish. Putrefied wounds require more lancing; and therefore are more painful in the cure than those which are but newly made. The more we are alienated from the life of God, the harder it will be to return to live that life again. The further a man is gone out of his road, the longer he must travel to come in again; and the more pains he must take in running or riding, than he that wandered but a little from it.

(2.) Your new birth will be the gratefuller to God. God loves the first fruits. He would not have the gleanings, but the first crop of everything under the law, which was laid upon the altar as God's portion. The kindness of the youth is most respected by God. He cherished Israel because they were 'the first fruits of his increase,' Jer. 2:2, 3. 'I remember the kindness of thy youth, the love of thy espousals, when thou wentest after me in the wilderness,' under many discouragements. God writes down the time of the new birth, and it runs in his mind a long time after. 'Epenetus, the first fruits of Achaia,' is saluted by Paul, just after the salutation of the whole church, with the title of well-beloved: Rom. 16:5, 'Greet the church that is in their house; salute my well-beloved Epenetus, who is the [first] fruits of Achaia unto Christ.' And surely more beloved by the Lord than by the servant. God hath most affection for such as come in at the first sound of the gospel. Daniel was a young man, yet the holiest man of his age; and God hath so great an affection to him that he joins him with Noah, that famous preacher of righteousness, and Job, that mirror of patience,—Ezek. 14:14, 'Though these three men, Noah, Daniel, and Job, were in it, they should but deliver their own souls by their righteousness,'—as those that had the greatest power with him, to keep off judgments from the place where they were.

(3.) Comfort will be the greater by an early new birth. What a long time will such an one have to enjoy the comforts of the Spirit! whereas those that are renewed later, have fewer comforts, because their grieving the Spirit hath been the longer. You will be always ready, and fit for the kingdom of God, let God call when he will. Your foretastes of heaven greater, and much acquaintance with the life of it, before you arrive at the place of full enjoyment. John, the youngest disciple, lay in Christ's bosom; he had afterwards the most spiritual illuminations, and the discoveries of the state of the church in after days revealed to him. When our sluggishness makes God wait for our return, his justice will make us wait long for his comforts. The earlier your new birth, the sweeter will be your death, as being more stored with experiences of God's grace, and goodness, and truth, wherewith to answer all the devil's affrighting charges in your departing hence. No doubt can arise, but there will be a treasure of experience whence to draw an answer. The longer acquaintance you have with God, and the longer likeness to him in your natures, the more joyful will be your passage to him, and the more confidence against the fear of death.

(4.) The earlier your new birth, the sincerer and stronger will be your grace. To row against the strong stream and tide of nature, temptations of a youthful age, the inconstancy and lightness of your humour, and the inconsiderateness of your temper, are arguments of sincerity. To seek God, when a man hath fair and frequent invitations to sin, is not so liable to suspicion, as when a man can live no longer. The latter proceeds rather from a fear of wrath than love to their Creator, or affection to his glory. Grace will be the stronger, the more full of juice. He that is new-born betimes, when he is young, will grow to a greater stature and a mighty strength in his age; for it is not with grace as it is with our bodies, the older the weaker; but as the outward man decays, the inward man grows, and is renewed day by day, 2 Cor. 4:16. A young plant in the house of God will be fat and flourishing, and fall of fruit in old age, Ps. 92:13, 14. The weakness of the body in such is the youthfulness of grace.

(5.) The earlier the new birth, the weightier will be your glory in the kingdom of God. God rewards according to our works: Rev. 2:23, 'I will give to every one of you according to your works.' Not only to the wicked, the children of the woman Jezebel, according to their works, but to them whose charity, service, faith, patience, he knew, ver. 19. The longer you are without a new life, a vital principle, the fewer will your works be, and the shorter your wages. Though God in regeneration works as a sovereign, and hath mercy on whom he will have mercy, yet, in rewarding, he acts as a righteous judge, according to the rules of justice: 2 Tim. 4:8, 'The crown which the Lord, the righteous judge, shall give me;' and so doth proportion the glory to every man's service. Young ones regenerate, that bear head against the temptations of their violent nature, shall have crowns set with more jewels. They shall not only have an entrance, but 'an abundant entrance into the everlasting kingdom of our Lord and Saviour Jesus Christ,' 2 Peter 1:11. They shall enter into the port with a full gale. The more violent storms they bear up against, the brighter will be their glory. For if he that endures temptation, but one temptation, shall have a crown, by proportion, he that endures many shall have a greater: James 1:12, 'Blessed is the man that endures temptation; for when he is tried, he shall have a crown of life.' How comfortable will it be to feel the weight of your crown and the richness of your robes, according to your years of service. If there be any sorrow in heaven, it is because they were not sooner new-born, that they might more have glorified God on earth, who bestows so much honour upon them in heaven. If any of you were sure to be regenerate after you had spent so many years after the course of the world and fulfilling the lusts of the flesh, yet how great would your loss be, both of the comforts of the Spirit in this life, and of degrees of glory in the other!

3. Deferring the seeking after this new birth till more years grow upon you is a mighty folly. It is a matter of the highest concern, the greatest necessity, in comparison of which all other things are but toys and superfluities. Is it not folly to prefer superfluous things before necessary? Is it not a madness for a man to be mending the mud-wall about his garden,

and neglect to quench the fire which hath got hold of his house? You are poisoned in your nature, you have plague-spots upon your hearts. Would it not be ridiculous for a man that hath drunk poison, and spilt some upon his clothes, to be more careful to have the stains fetched out of his garments than the poison out of his stomach? You are careful about the concerns of the body and flesh, oh be not such fools as to let the poison within get the greater head, and the plague continue in the heart.

Folly it is,

(1.) Because of the uncertainty of life. You are not lords and keepers of your own times, they are in God's hands: Ps. 31:15, 'My times are in thy hands.' What if he should fling that time out of his hand to-morrow, what would your condition be? Those that are in a dead state now, as they are here, if judgment find them so, are irrecoverable. Because thou art a child of wrath, if he take thee thus away with his stroke, as Job speaks, chap. 36:18, then a 'great ransom cannot deliver thee.' Hell followed death close at the back, Rev. 6:8. Shall sin reign in a body? That is base. But in a mortal body, a body that may drop into the grave every hour? That is folly in the highest degree. It is the apostle's exhortation: Rom. 6:12, 'Let not sin therefore reign in your mortal bodies.' Many a candle hath been put out before half burnt; how often hath a clear sun in the morning been overcast before noon! Were none of you the last week at the funeral of some strong and vigorous person? Perhaps there is no more time left you than just what will serve for to seek this new birth. God seizeth upon some suddenly, that they have not time so much as to cry out what aileth them: Job 36:13, 14, 'They cry not when he bindeth them. They die in youth, and their life is among the unclean.' It is better to be new-born many years too soon (if it can be supposed to be too soon), than to defer it one minute too late. He that defers the new birth to-day, may not have a morrow to be new born in. And to be surprised by death before you are new born, better for you had never been born at all.

(2.) It is folly, because if you neglect the present time, though you may live, yet your return to God by a new birth may be very uncertain. There is such a thing as a day of grace, shorter than the days of a man's life: Luke 19:42, 'The things of their peace' were then 'hid from their eyes,' though their destruction was deferred forty years. There is such a resolve in heaven sometimes, that 'the Spirit shall strive no longer' with this or that man: Gen. 6:3, 'My Spirit shall not always strive with man,' or 'in man,' with this or that man; 'for that he also is flesh.' It is a threatening to those in the church, in opposition to the profane world, ver. 2. The church began then to be corrupted. My Spirit shall not strive with them; though they make a profession of me, and attend upon me in worship, yet they are flesh, degenerated into mere flesh, and flesh they shall be. And sometimes it is confirmed by a solemn oath. Rev. 10:5, 6, The angel swears in a most solemn manner, 'By him that lives for ever, who created heaven and earth,' &c., 'that there should be time no longer;' that is, no time of repentance, as appears if you refer it to Rev. 9:20, 21. It is not therefore without great reason that the apostle doth double both the notes of attention, behold, and the time too, now, now, when he exhorts them not to receive the grace of God in vain; that is, sit under the gospel administration to no purpose, without having a gospel impression and signature upon their hearts: 'Behold, now is the accepted time; behold, now is the day of salvation,' 2 Cor. 6:2.

4. As it is a folly to neglect it, so if it be not presently sought, and endeavoured for, the more difficult it will be every day to attain it.

(1.) In regard of the increase of moral indisposition and unfitness. It is true indeed there is in every man a moral indisposition to a spiritual renovation, but the indisposition is greater when the habits of sin are more than ordinarily strengthened. The more the soul is frozen, the harder it will be to melt. A body dead some few hours is a subject more capable of having life breathed into it than when it is putrefied and partly mouldered to dust. A young tree may more easily be taken up and transplanted than a strong old oak, which hath spread its roots deep into the earth. The more rooted the habit of sin, the harder the alteration of the soul. Every sin in an unregenerate man is an adding a new stone to the former heap upon the grave to hinder his resurrection. It is a fetter and bond—Acts 8:23, 'bond of iniquity'—and the more new chains are put upon thee, the more unable wilt thou be to stir. The habits of sin will become more connatural to the soul, and fortify themselves with new recruits.

(2.) In regard of the industry of the devil. If you remain in a state of nature till you are old, that devil which blinds you now will have increased your blindness by that time; he will bestir himself in your age, that he may not lose that which he hath possessed so long. It is a shame for Satan, as well as for a man, deficere in ultimo actu. He that struck the first fatal blow to us, and occasioned this degenerate nature, will not want watchfulness and care to strengthen it in you. He will be diligent to keep up his own work; the longer his possession, the more difficult his departure. Judas was a devil in our Saviour's judgment all his time—John 6:70, 'One of you is a devil,'—but when he had withstood the force of our Saviour's discourses, and nourished his covetousness against his Master's frequent conviction, the devil 'entered into his heart,' John 13:27. Perhaps there had been before some strugglings of natural conscience in Judas, as there may be in some of you; but when he had, against the sight of our Saviour's miracles, the hearing of his sermons, the checks of his own conscience, continued in a natural state, Satan enters into him in a more peculiar manner, in a way of more special efficacy; and, by an uncontrollable power, breaks the bridle of conscience, which had held him in so long, and runs furiously with him to what wickedness he pleased. Satan reigned in him before; but as the regenerate, being by degrees filled with spiritual gifts, and having additions of grace, are said to be 'filled with the Spirit,' so natural men, as they increase in sin by degrees, are said to have a new entrance of Satan into them, because there is an increase of his efficacy in them, and power over them, binding them in stronger chains and fetters of iron.

(3.) In regard of spiritual judgments, which will make it impossible. Such judgments upon men that sit under the gospel, and admit not the influence of it, are more frequent than is usually imagined, though they are not so visible. Open sins God punishes many times by visible judgments, but wilful unregeneracy by spiritual. Though a man may sit under the same means of grace which God doth bless to regenerate others, they may be an accidental means to harden him: 'The miry places shall not he healed, but be given to salt,' as it is Ezek. 47:11, when others shall grow like trees on both sides the river, and bear a never-fading leaf. If once your neglects and provocations put God to his oath, and make him swear, as he once did, that you shall not enter into his rest, Heb. 3:11, his oath will be irreversible, he will blow up heaven and earth before he will break it. And that it may not be evaded that this was an oath against the Israelites, it is intimated by the apostle that even in the times of the gospel this oath is of force, ver. 12. He from thence exhorts them at that time to take heed of 'an evil heart of unbelief.' What need of this exhortation to them, if this oath did only concern the Israelites murmuring in the wilderness, and were not valid against unbelievers and unregenerate men in the time of the gospel? It is a terrible place that in Isa. 6:9, 'Make the heart of this people fat, and make their ears heavy, and shut their eyes, lest they see with their eyes, and understand with their heart, and convert, and be healed;' which dreadful place is no less than six times quoted in the New Testament, as though it belonged only to them that sit under evangelical light with a wilful unregeneracy. Certainly as the mercies of the gospel are most spiritual, so the judgments inflicted upon the neglecters of it are the most spiritual judgments. Then a man is made the centre of divine fury, and his heart sealed up from any seizure by sanctifying grace: Ezek. 24:13, 'Because I have purged thee,' that is, offered thee purging grace, 'and thou wast not purged, thou shalt not be purged from thy filthiness any more, till I have caused my fury to rest upon thee.' When God passes such a secret sentence, if all the men in the world, and all the angels in heaven, should, with their most affectionate strains of reason, attempt the persuading of you, they were not able to open an heart which God hath judicially locked up and sealed. It is observed by some, that the work of the gospel, for conversion, is usually done in those places where it comes, in the space of seven years, as to those who have sat under it so long; and they ground it upon Dan. 9:27, 'And he shall confirm the covenant with many for one week,' that is, one week of years. And that our Saviour preached three years and an half among the Jews, and the apostles three years and an half or thereabouts before the Jews were discovenanted. I will not affirm it positively, but offer it as worthy consideration to those that have sat under the gospel more than seven years without any renewing work on their souls.

Well then, let me beseech you, resolve upon this work presently. We are not to bid a poor man 'go away, and come again to-morrow,' Prov. 3:27, 28; and shall we bid the Spirit, knocking at our hearts in the gospel, go away, and come again another time? Our blessed Saviour did not defer his death for us till he was old, and shall not we live to him till we are old? As his death is an argument used by the apostle, to move us to live to him, 2 Cor. 5:14, 15, so the time of his death should be an argument to us to live to him betimes. How many hath this foolish to-morrow deceived! and many have perished to-day before the dawning of to-morrow. Defer it not therefore a night longer; reflect upon yourselves, and say, Have I lived so long, pleased with my old nature? O Lord, what had become of me without thy wonderful patience? Let your motion be as the lightning, as the prophet Ezekiel speaks of the motion of four beasts, chap. 1:14. God may make up the match between himself and you before midnight: there was less time in God's working upon the jailer.

Quest. What shall we do to get this new birth?

Ans. 1. Begin with prayer; seek it from that Saviour that first made so plain a declaration of it. 'A man cannot receive anything, unless it be given him from heaven,' John 3:27. Then from heaven beg it; let God hear of you as soon as ever you come home. God usually lets in renewing grace at the same gate at which honest prayer goes out.* Prayer is a compliance with God's grace; he never refuseth it to them that heartily desire it. Go therefore to God, give him no rest; if you do so, it may not be long before you will hear that joyful word drop from his gracious lips: 'My grace will be sufficient for you,' sufficient to renew you, sufficient to cure you. Let the fervency of your prayers be proportioned according to the necessity of the thing, and the greatness of your misery without it. Plead, therefore, with God for it; Lord, is it not better to make me thy friend than to let me continue thy enemy? Is it not more thy glory to raise a soul from sin than a Lazarus from the grave? Thy power and mercy are more illustrious in turning a dry stock into a fruitful and flourishing tree. Overcome, therefore, my base nature by thy merciful power; change me from a venomous to a dove-like nature. Oh how fain would I glorify thee, by answering the end of my creation! Glorify thyself by new-creating my heart, that I may glorify thee in a newness of life. I cannot get a new heart by my own strength; but it is a work not too hard for thy power, and suitable to thy promise. Plead the promise: Ezek. 11:19, 'I will take the stony heart out of their flesh, and I will give them an heart of flesh;' and Ezek. 36:26, 'A new heart will I give you, and a new spirit will I put within you;' but he 'will be inquired of, to do it for them,' ver. 37. Breathe and aspire after it; beg for it as earnestly as you would in extreme hunger for food for the satisfaction of your natural appetite; God will not deny it for such as breathe after it, Mat. 5:6, Hunger and thirst after righteousness, and you shall be filled; beg the operation of the Spirit. Our Saviour provided the plaster, but left the Spirit to apply it; he provided the colours, his blood, to draw his image, but none but the Spirit can lay them on. Ask therefore the Spirit of the Father in the name of Christ;

the Father sends him into the world, and sends him into the heart, but in the name of Christ. It is called a holy Spirit, because without it there can be no holy nature.

2. Be deeply sensible of the corruption of nature. The more we are sensible of our inherent depravation, the more we shall breathe after a real change. Can he ever imagine the necessity of a cure, who understands not the greatness of his disease? Be fully convinced, as Paul was, that in you, that is, 'in your flesh, dwells no good thing,' Rom. 7:18. I know; I am experimentally sensible of it. Did we but truly see the defilement of our nature, and the monstrous alteration of it from that of our creation, as we can the deformity of some monster in the world, we should loathe ourselves, we should fly, if we could, from our own nature, and send forth nothing but groans for a deliverance from the body of death, and have no rest till we were stripped of so abominable a frame. Let us, therefore, turn in upon ourselves, take a view of our condition, see if there be any suitableness between our depraved natures, and the glory of another world. There is not, unless we conceit heaven a place filled only with carnal pleasures. But reason will tell us the contrary, and a carnal soul can never, in that state, be fit for a spiritual glory.

3. View often the perfection of the law of God. This will make us sensible of the contrariety of our nature to God's holiness, and consequently make us look about for a remedy. See whether your nature answers the exactness of the law; for although you were alive without the law, yet, when the commandment and your hearts come to look upon one another, you will see sin in its life and power, and all the conceits of your own excellency will die: Rom. 7:9, 'For I was alive without the law once, but when the commandment came, sin revived, and I died.' Paul thought himself a righteous person, till he came to measure himself by the exact and spiritual image of the law. He had been instructed in the literal knowledge of the law, for he was brought up a Pharisee; his head and the law were acquainted, and then he thought himself a living

person; but when his heart and the law came to be acquainted, then he found himself dead, and his high opinion of himself fell to the ground. Consider, then, how the law requires a perfect righteousness, an inward principle. All duties it commands are not only to be done materially, but formally; for they are so commanded in such a manner, from such a principle, to such an end. Then reflect, have I such a righteousness? can I answer the law? do I come up to the measures of it in any one action? Surely I do not. Then consider further, Doth not this law stand? will God lay it in the dust? has he thrown it out of doors? Surely it is holy, just, and good, and therefore a standing rule. I must have a principle suitable to that which Jesus Christ came not to destroy, but establish. How shall I do it with this corrupt nature, wherein I do not one action that doth sincerely respect it, as the law of God, that is, accompanied with a delight in it? Certainly this temper, so contrary to the law, must be changed. I must have an inner man to delight in this law, a principle that must in some measure, though imperfectly, suit it. This orderly consideration would put you upon the seeking out for such a righteousness as may in part answer it.

4. Observe the motions of the Spirit. There is an assisting work of the Spirit, and an informing work. There is not a man but hath, or once had, the strivings of this Spirit with him. There are the knockings of Christ by his Spirit at the door; there are calls, 'Zaccheus, come down; this day is salvation come to thy house.' Did you never hear a voice from heaven, saying, 'Come to me that you may have life'? Did you never hear a groan from heaven, 'When shall it once be?' Did you never see a tear trickling down the cheek of Christ, as when he wept over Jerusalem? Did you never hear a sigh of a grieved Spirit waiting upon you? Can you see, and hear, and hear again, yet no compliance, when that is of absolute necessity you are exhorted to? Smother not these motions; answer them with suitable affections. If Christ looks upon you, as he did upon Peter, think of what you are, and weep, Mark 14:72. If the Spirit calls, answer

presently, 'Thy face, Lord, will I seek.' The neglect of the time of the Spirit's breathing is the cause of a continuance in unregeneracy. Repel not those sweet motions that strike upon your hearts.

5. Attend diligently upon all means of grace. They are the pipes through which the Spirit breathes, the lungs of the Spirit, the instruments whereby our natures are altered: 'Faith comes by hearing.' It is by the hearing of faith that the Spirit is ministered: Gal. 3:5, 'He therefore that ministers to you the Spirit, doth he it by the works of the law, or the hearing of faith?' None can expect it who will not use the means to have it, no more than men can expect to live without eating and drinking. Would we be warm? we must approach to the fire. Would we be clean? we must wash in the water. Would we be renewed? we must attend upon the breathings of the Spirit in the institutions of God. This we may do, though we cannot renew ourselves; we may read the word as well as a piece of news; we may hear the word, and attend to it, as well as to any worldly concern; we may meditate upon it, and consider it, as well as a story. This we have power to do, and it is by the word that this great work is done. By a powerful word Christ called Lazarus out of the grave, and by his word spoken by his Spirit, his great deputy he sent after him, he calls us out of our state of death. Beg of the Spirit to breathe upon you before you come to attend upon his institutions. We profit little by the word, and our old nature attends us, because we take no notice of the Spirit of God, who is appointed the principal officer in this business. It is he that is to guide us into truth, John 16:13. Though men may speak truth to us, yet the Spirit can only guide the truth into our hearts, and guide us into the heart, and bowels, and inwards of truth, to taste the marrow of it.

6. I might add, Study the gospel. Look upon Jesus Christ in that glass; this transforms us into his image; as the beholding the light of the sun in a glass, paints an image of that light in our faces; so doth the beholding Christ in the gospel: 2 Cor. 3:18, 'But ye all, with open face, beholding

as in a glass the glory of the Lord, are changed into the same image.' The gospel is the cause of our first change, and of our growth in it, 'from glory to glory,' but by the Spirit of God in the gospel, 'as by the Spirit of the Lord.' Study the promises of the gospel, and the end of the blood of Christ, which was to purge our conscience from dead works. It is by believing the promises of pardon in the blood of Christ that 'the conscience is purged from dead works,' Heb. 9:14.

A Discourse on the Nature of Regeneration

Therefore if any man be in Christ, he is a new creature: old things are passed away; behold, all things are become new.—2 COR. 5:17.

THE apostle in those words, ver. 13, 'For whether we be besides ourselves, it is to God; or whether we be sober, it is for your cause,' defends his speaking so much of his integrity; though some men would count him out of his wits for it, yet he regards not their judgment; for if he were in an ecstasy, or 'beside himself,' his purpose was to serve God and his church, and therefore he did not regard the opinion of men, whether he were accounted mad or sober, so he might perform the end of his apostleship. The sense therefore of it, as Calvin renders it, is this: Let men take it as they will, that I speak so much of my integrity, I do it not upon my own account, but have respect to God and the church in speaking of it, for I am as ready to be silent as to speak, when my silence may glorify God and advantage the church as much as my speech; 'for the love of Christ constrains me,' ver. 14, for whom I am bound to live; and so he passes on to inculcate the duty of every man that hath an interest in the death of Christ. The love of Christ constrains us actively; the love wherewith Christ hath loved us is a powerful attractive to make us live to him. It is the highest equity and justice that we should live to him who died for us. Whence observe,

The true consideration and sense of the love of Christ in his death, hath a pleasing force, and is a delightful bond and obligation upon us to devote ourselves wholly to his service and glory. There is a moral constraint upon the soul to this end: 'if one died for all, then were all dead,' then all were obnoxious to eternal death. Others* dislike this interpretation, and understand it not of the death to God brought in by the first Adam, but a death to sin and the flesh, procured by the second Adam, which death is spoken of Rom. 6:2, 'How shall we, being dead to sin,' &c., and called a suffering in the flesh, and a ceasing from sin,' 1 Peter 4:1. If one died for all, then all for whom he died are dead, jure et obligatione, dead to themselves, that they might not be under their own power, but the power of him that died for them, and rose again. Since, therefore, we are dead to sin, we should take no care to maintain the life of it. And this seems, by the following verse, to be the true meaning of it: ver. 15, 'And that he died for all, that they which live should not henceforth live unto themselves, but unto him which died for them, and rose again.' He hath redeemed us by the price of his blood, that he might have us in his own power, as his own property, so that we are no longer our own masters, and have no longer right to ourselves.* They ought to die to themselves, that they may live to Christ; it being fit they should live not to their own wills, or own honour, but to the glory and will of their Redeemer. It was to this end that Christ died, that he might have a seed to serve him, and live to him. It is ingratitude and injustice to deny him our service, since thereby we endeavour to frustrate the design of his coming, and the end of his death. Observe,

1. Self is the chief end of every natural man. 'That they which live, should not henceforth live unto themselves.' Implying that all men living, who are not under the actual benefit and efficacy of our Saviour's death, do live to themselves. The greatest distinction between a regenerate and a natural man is this, self is the end of one, and Christ the end of the other. The life of a natural man, and all the dependencies of it, is to gratify corrupt self, with the greatest detriment to his natural and moral self, the happiness and good of his soul; but the life of a new creature, with all the dependencies of it, is for the glory of God and the Redeemer. This self-dependence, and a desire of independency on God, which was the great sin of Adam, whereby he would make himself his own chief end, hath run in the veins of all his posterity, and is the bitter root upon which all the fruits of gall and wormwood grow.

2. The end of our Saviour's dying and rising again was to change the corrupt end of the creature. The end of redemption, and consequently the end of the Redeemer, must be contrary to the end of corruption and the end of the first Adam. As Adam dispossessed God of his dominion to set up self, so doth Christ pull down self to advance God to his right of being our chief end. It is called, therefore, a redemption of us to God: Rev. 5:9, 'For thou wast slain, and hast redeemed us to God by thy blood;' redeemed us from a slavery under sordid lusts, to God as our end.

3. Therefore we must be taken off from ourselves, as our end, and be fixed upon another, even upon Christ, else we answer not the end of Christ's death and resurrection: 'He bore our sins in his own body on the tree, that we being dead to sin, should live unto righteousness,' 1 Peter 2:24. And if the ends of our Saviour's death and resurrection be not accomplished upon us, the fruits of it shall not be enjoyed by us. The whole work of regeneration, and conversion, and sanctification, and the efficacy of the death of Christ in the soul, consists in these two things: a taking us off from self, and pitching us upon God and Christ as our end. The terminus a quo is self, the terminus ad quem is Christ. We are

'redeemed by the precious blood of Christ from our vain conversation received by tradition from our fathers,' 1 Peter 1:18, even from our first father Adam. This is properly to set up no other gods before him, and to abhor the grossest idolatry.

4. It is highly equitable, that if Christ died for us, and was raised for us as our happiness, we should live to his glory, and make him our end in all our actions, and the whole course of our lives. The apostle uses this consideration as an argument, and as a copy and exemplar. As Christ died not for himself, nor rose again for himself, but he died for God's glory and our redemption, to vindicate God's righteousness, and justify us in his sight, and rose again to make it appear that he had done our business in redeeming us, and went to heaven to manage our cause for us, so we are to live to keep up the honour of God's righteousness and holiness, and to justify Christ in our professions of him, and conformity to him in the design of his death and resurrection. It is a high disesteem of ourselves not to live to Christ, which is both a more rightful and a more satisfying object of our affections, who returns our living to him with a happiness to ourselves. By his dying he purchased a dominion over us; by his resurrection his dominion over us was confirmed, and thereby our obligation of love and Service increased. He died as our surety to satisfy our debts, and rose as our Saviour to justify our persons; so the apostle, Rom. 4:25, 'He was delivered for our offences, and rose again for our justification.' Therefore, as he rose to justify us, we must rise to glorify him. And indeed it is a great sign of a spiritual growth when we grow in our ends and aims for God.

5. The resurrection of Christ, as well as his death, was for us. He rose again, it must be understood, for them for whom he died; he died as a public person, bearing our sins, and rose again as a public person, and head of the believing world, acquitted from our sins: Heb. 9:24, 'He is entered into heaven, to appear in the presence of God for us.' And in a conformity to these two public acts of Christ doth our regeneration

and communion with Christ consist; in a mortification of the body of sin in conformity to his death; in newness of life, by quickening grace, in conformity to his resurrection, Col. 2:12.

The apostle proceeds on, and makes his inference in the 16th verse, 'Henceforth know we no man after the flesh; yea, though we have known Christ after the flesh, yet now henceforth know we him no more.' To know is used in Scripture for love and delight, both on God's part,—Ps. 1:6, 'The Lord knows the way of the righteous,' that is, loves and delights in the way of the righteous,—and on man's part: Hosea 4:1, 'No knowledge of God in the land,' that is, no love of God. Not to know men after the flesh then, is either not to judge of men according to the endowments, though never so glittering, which arise only from fleshy principles; to esteem no man according to his greatness, his knowledge, and worth, in the account of the world; or, not to love men for our secular interest; or, not to regard men according to those fleshly privileges of circumcision and carnal ceremonies. Not ourselves, which is included in no man; not to esteem of ourselves by our knowledge, wealth, credit, honour, or any other excellency which falls under the praise of men, but by inward grace, living to God, fruitfulness to him, which falls under the praise of God. Men esteem not their fields for the gay wild flowers in them, but for the corn and fruit; 'yea, though we have known Christ after the flesh, yet now henceforth know we him no more.' We do not glory in him because he was of kin to us, and our countryman according to the flesh; we look upon him no more only as a miraculous man, but we have more noble thoughts of him; we know him as the great Redeemer of the world; we consider him in those excellent things he hath done, those excellent graces which he hath communicated, those excellent offices he doth exercise; we know him after a spiritual manner, as the author of all grace, appointed by God for such ends, accepted by God upon such works, glorified by God for such purposes; we regard him as transacting our great affairs in heaven, where he is entered as a forerunner for us,

Heb. 6:20, and as such we serve and honour him; we desire not his company in the flesh, but in the spirit, in his heavenly appearance and glory. Observe,

1. Natural men have no delight in anything but secular concerns; love nothing, but for their own advantage; admire not any true spiritual worth; they know and love men; yea, what love they pretend to Christ is only a fleshly love, a love from education, a customary love.

2. An evidence of being taken off from ourselves and living to Christ, is our valuation either of ourselves or others, according to holiness. Though a civil respect be due to men according to their station in the world,—such a respect the writer of this epistle gave to Agrippa;—yet our inward valuations of men ought to be upon the account of the image of God in them. God, who loves righteousness, knows no man after the flesh, but as he finds the image of his own righteousness in him; and as a new creature is framed after the image of God, so his affections and valuations of men or things are according to God's affections to them, or esteem of them.

3. Our professions of Christ, serving him and loving him barely for ourselves and for fleshly ends, doth not consist with regeneration. Such a love is a love to ourselves, not to Christ, a making him only subservient to us, not ourselves subservient to Christ.

4. We should eye Christ, and arise to the knowledge of him, as he is advanced and exalted by God. Look upon him as our head, delight to come under his wing, and have our whole dependence on him, know him in his righteousness to justify us, know him not only as a Saviour risen, but in the power of his resurrection in our souls, and the fellowship of his sufferings, and to be made conformable to his death; such a knowledge the apostle aims at, Philip. 3:8–10; the other knowledge is a knowledge of him in the head, this a knowledge of him in the heart; the other is a knowledge of him after the flesh, this a knowledge of him after the spirit,

in the draught of Christ in our hearts by the Spirit, an inward conception of him in the womb of our hearts.

The text is another inference made from that position, ver. 15. If there be such an obligation upon us to live to Christ, because he hath died and rose again for us; then certainly whosoever hath an interest in the death and resurrection of Christ, as to the fruits of it, must be a new creature, a changed person; old things have passed away, all things are become new in him. Whosoever is in the kingdom of Christ, engrafted into him, under the participation of his death and resurrection, is a new creature; all other excellencies are defective, though they may be useful to the world; it is a 'new creation' only makes a man excellent and worthy of the kingdom. 'Old things are passed away,' old affections, old dispositions of Adam; those things, the ἀρχαῖα, things that are very near of as old a standing as the world. Adam would be his own rule and ruler; he would be the rule of good and evil to himself; he would be his own end. These things must pass away; we must come to a fiduciary reliance upon God, under the new head of his appointment, and make him our highest good, our chief end, our exact rule; and therefore what is called the 'new creature,' Gal. 6:15, is called 'faith working by love,' Gal. 5:6. Adam's great failures were unbelief and self-love; he would not believe God's precept and threatening; he would not depend upon God. To this is opposed faith, which is a grace that empties us of ourselves, and fixes us in our dependence on another. He would also advance himself, and be his own rule and end, to know as God; to this is opposed love, which is an acting for God and his glory. And these two are the essential parts of the new creature. Some of late would understand, by the new creature, only a conversion from idolatry to the profession of Christianity. But there must be a greater import in the words than so. The apostle makes it a qualification necessary both to Jew and Gentile, that neither the circumcision of the one did avail without it, nor the uncircumcision of the other prejudice them that possess it. Besides, men may turn from one profession to another without living to God, and directing all their actions to the glory of Christ. Some translate it, 'Let him be a new creature;' others, 'He is a new creature.' One notes his state, the other his obligation. 'Old things are passed away.' It is a reason rendered; there is a change in the whole frame of things. If you understand it of the old economy, the old legal state, then it is an argument shewing the necessity of the new creature. Old things are withered; there is a new frame in the church, in the kingdom, therefore there ought to be so in the subjects of it; for the prophets use to speak of the state of the gospel under the names of a 'new heaven and new earth,' Isa. 65:17. As old rites in the church are removed, so the old principles and the old frames of Adam should pass away. The old rubbish must be thrown out when the house is new built. And they are passed away in a regenerate man, jure, obligatione, potestate, though not wholly in actu. 'All things are become new,' but not of ourselves, but by the grace of God, ver. 18, 'and all things are of God.' It is likely the apostle expresseth himself thus, to pull down the swelling thoughts of the Corinthians which they had of themselves. They were proud of their gifts, wherein, by the apostle's own confession, they came behind no church in the world, 1 Cor. 1:7; and he discourseth to them much of the excellency of charity above knowledge, and adviseth them to 'covet the best gifts,' 2 Cor. 13. He depresseth their confidence in knowledge without grace, which doth but puff up, not edify to eternal life. He wisheth them, therefore, to look more to the new creature in them, to try themselves whether they be in Christ or no, by the change they found in their hearts. 'If any man be in Christ,' that is, be a member of Christ, engrafted into him.

In the words observe,

1. The character of a true Christian by his state, a new creature.

2. The necessity of this new creation, if any man; if he be not a new creature, he is not in Christ; he hath nothing at present to do with him, he is no true member of his body.

3. The universality, any man; not a man can be in Christ by any other way, without this new creation pass upon him.

4. The advantage of it: if he be a new creature, he is certainly in Christ, it is an infallible token that the Redeemer did die and rise again for him.

5. The nature of it.

(1.) Removal of the old form: old things are passed away.

(2.) Introduction of a new: all things are become new, as without in the church, so within in the soul.

6. The note of attention: behold, more particularly set to this passage, of all things becoming new, to remove the deceit that men are liable to. Old things in some measure may pass away, but look to that, whether new things come in the place contrary to those old, whether there be new affections, new dispositions; old things may pass away, when old sins are left, and no new frames be set up in the stead of them. The doctrine I shall insist upon is this:

Doct. Every man in Christ hath a real and mighty change wrought in him, and becomes a new creature.

I pitch upon these words to shew the nature of regeneration, the necessity of which I have already discoursed of.

It is difficult to describe exactly the nature of regeneration.

1. Because of the disputes about the nature of it; whether it be quality, or a spiritual substance; whether, if a quality, it be a habit or a power, or whether it be the Holy Ghost personally.* Many controversies the wits of men have obscured it with. The Scripture discovers it to us under the terms of the new creature, a new heart, a law put into us, the image of God, a divine nature; these, though Scripture terms, are difficult to explain.

2. It is difficult, because it is visible, not in itself, but in its effects. We know seed doth propagate itself, and produce its like, but the generative part in the seed lies covered with husks and skin, so that it is hard to tell in what atom or point the generative particle doth lie. We know we

have a soul, yet it is hard to tell what the soul is, and in what part it doth principally reside. We know there are angels, yet what mortal can give a description of that glorious nature? It is much like the wind, as our Saviour describes it: John 3:8, 'The wind bloweth where it listeth, and thou hearest the sound thereof, but canst not tell whence it comes, nor whither it goes: so is every one that is born of the Spirit.' The wind, we feel it, we see the effects of it, yet cannot tell how it ariseth, where it doth repose itself, and how it is allayed; and all the notions of philosophy about it will not satisfy a curious inquirer. So likewise it is in this business of regeneration; the effects of it are known, there are certain characters whereby to discern it; but to give a description of the nature of it is not so easy.

3. It is difficult, because of the natural ignorance which is still in the minds of the best. A man cannot understand all iniquity, for there is a 'mystery of iniquity;' neither can he fully understand this work, for there is a 'mystery of godliness,' 1 Tim. 3:16; not only in the whole scheme of it without, but in the whole frame of it in the heart. It is called the 'hidden man of the heart,' 1 Peter 3:4; hidden from the world, hidden from reason, hidden from the sight sometimes of them that have it; a man can hardly sometimes see it in his own heart, by reason of the steams of corruption; as a beautiful picture is not visible in a cloud of smoke. The blindness the god of this world hath wrapt us in, that we might not know God, or the things of God, is not wholly taken off. And even what we know of the truths of God, suffers an eclipse by our carnal conceptions of them; for all the notions we frame of them have a tincture of sense and fancy.

4. It is hard for those to conceive it who have no experience of it. If we speak of the motions of natural corruption, as wrath, passion, distrust of God, and enormous sins, men can easily understand this, because we have all sad experiments of an inward corruption; but the methods and motions of the Spirit of God in this work are not comprehended, but by

those who have felt the power of it. The motions of sin are more sensible, the motions of the Spirit more secret and inward, and men want as much the experience of the one, as they have too much of the other. Hence it is that many carnal men love to have the nature of sin ripped up and discovered; partly, perhaps, for this reason among others, that they can better understand that by the daily evidence of it in their own practices; whereas other things, out of the reach of their experience, are out of the grasp of their understanding; and therefore seem to them paradoxes and incredible things: the spiritual man is not judged or discerned by any but them that are spiritual, 1 Cor. 2:15. It is certainly true, that as a painter can better decipher a stormy and cloudy air than the serenity of a clear day, and the spectator conceive it with more pleasure: so it is more easy to represent the agitations and affections of natural corruption, than the inward frame of a soul wrought by the Spirit of God.† I shall therefore describe it consonantly to the Scripture thus: Regeneration is a mighty and powerful change, wrought in the soul by the efficacious working of the Holy Spirit, wherein a vital principle, a new habit, the law of God, and a divine nature, are put into, and framed in the heart, enabling it to act holily and pleasingly to God, and to grow up therein to eternal glory. This is included in the term of a new creature in the text. There is a change, a creation, that which was not is brought into a state of being. If a new creature, and in Christ, then surely not a dead but a living creature, having a principle of life; and if a living creature, then possessed of some power to act, and habits to make those actions easy; and if a power to act, and a habit to facilitate that act, then a law in their nature as the rule of their acting; every creature hath so. In this respect the heavens are said to have ordinances: 'knowest thou the ordinances of heaven?' Job 38:33; and they seem to act in the way of a covenant, Jer. 33:25, according to such articles as God hath pitched upon. And, lastly, as in all creatures thus endued, there is a likeness to some other things in the rank of beings; so in this new creature there is a likeness to God, whence it is called 'the image of God in holiness and righteousness,' and a 'divine nature.' So that you see the divers expressions whereby the Scripture declares this work of regeneration are included in this term of the new creature, or the new creation, as the word is, καινὴ κτίσις. It is a certain spiritual and supernatural principle, or permanent form, per modum actus primi, infused by God, whereby it is made partaker of the divine nature, and enabled to act for God.

Let us therefore see,

1. How it is differenced from other states of a Christian.

2. What it is not.

3. What it is.

1. First, How it is differenced from the other states of a Christian.

(1.) It differs from conversion. Regeneration is a spiritual change, conversion is a spiritual motion. In regeneration there is a power conferred; conversion is the exercise of this power. In regeneration there is given us a principle to turn; conversion is our actual turning; that is the principle whereby we are brought out of a state of nature into a state of grace; and conversion the actual fixing on God, as the terminus ad quem. One gives posse agere, the other actu agere.

[1.] Conversion is related to regeneration, as the effect to the cause. Life precedes motion, and is the cause of motion. In the covenant, the new heart, the new spirit, and God's putting his Spirit into them, is distinguished from their walking in his statutes, Ezek. 36:27, from the first step we take in the way of God, and is set down as the cause of our motion: 'I will cause you to walk in my statutes.' In renewing us, God gives us a power; in converting us, he excites that power. Men are naturally dead, and have a stone upon them; regeneration is a rolling away the stone from the heart, and a raising to newness of life; and then conversion is as natural to a regenerate man as motion is to a living body. A principle of activity will produce action.

[2.] In regeneration, man is wholly passive; in conversion, he is active: as a child in its first formation in the womb, contributes nothing to the first infusion of life; but after it hath life, it is active, and its motions natural. The first reviving of us is wholly the act of God, without any concurrence of the creature; but after we are revived, we do actively and voluntarily live in his sight: Hosea 6:2, 'He will revive us, he will raise us up, and then we shall live in his sight;' then we shall walk before him, then shall we 'follow on to know the Lord.' Regeneration is the motion of God in the creature; conversion is the motion of the creature to God, by virtue of that first principle; from this principle all the acts of believing, repenting, mortifying, quickening, do spring. In all these a man is active; in the other merely passive; all these are the acts of the will, by the assisting grace of God, after the infusion of the first grace. Conversion is a giving ourselves to the Lord, 2 Cor. 8:5; giving our own selves to the Lord is a voluntary act, but the power whereby we are enabled thus to give ourselves, is wholly and purely, in every part of it, from the Lord himself. A rénewed man is said to be led by the Spirit, Rom. 8:14,* not dragged, not forced; the putting a bias and aptitude in the will, is the work of the Spirit quickening it; but the moving the will to God by the strength of this bias, is voluntary, and the act of the creature. The Spirit leads, as a father doth a child by the hand; the father gave him that principle of life, and conducts him and hands him in his motion; but the child hath a principle of motion in himself, and a will to move. The day of regeneration is solely the day of God's power, wherein he makes men willing to turn to him, Ps. 110:3; so that, though in actual conversion the creature be active, it is not from the power of man, though it be from a power in man, not growing up from the impotent root in nature, but settled there by the Spirit of God.

(2.) It differs from justification. They agree in the term to which, that is God: by justification we are reconciled to God; by regeneration we are assimilated, made like to God. They alway go together. As our Saviour's resurrection, which was the justification of him from that guilt which he had taken upon himself, and a public pronouncing him to be his righteous servant, is called a new begetting him: Acts 13:33, 'God hath raised up Jesus again, as it is also written in the second Psalm: Thou art my Son, this day have I begotten thee;' because it was a manifestation of him to be the Son of God, who before, being covered with our infirmities, did not appear so to the world: so our justification from guilt, and new begetting us, and manifesting us to the angels to be the sons of God, are at one and the same time, and both are by grace; 'by grace you are justified,' Rom. 5:1, the quickening and raising us together with Christ is by grace, Eph. 2:5, 6. The blessing of Abraham, which is the application of redemption from the curse of the law, and the receiving the promise of the Spirit by faith, are both together, Gal. 3:14.

But [1.] it differs from justification in the nature of the change.

Justification is a relative change, whereby a man is brought from a state of guilt to a state of righteousness; from a state of slavery to a state of liberty; from the obligation of the covenant of works to the privilege of the covenant of grace; from being a child of wrath to be an heir of promise. Regeneration is a physical change, and real, as when a dead man is raised from death to life; it is a filling the soul with another nature, Eph. 2:1, 'And you hath he quickened, who were dead in trespasses and sins.' The translators have inserted those words, 'hath he quickened,' because those words are put in the 5th verse; but methinks the words refer better to the 23d verse of the first chapter, speaking of Christ, 'who fills all in all,' and fills you too with a spiritual life; or he passes from the power of God in raising Christ, to his power in raising us. It is a change of nature, and of that nature whereby we are children of wrath, not only by the first sin, but by a conversation according to the course of the world. And this quickening respects the change of that nature which was prone to a worldly conversation, and a fulfilling the desires of the flesh. The first is a change of a man's condition, this a change in a man's disposition.

When a man is made a magistrate there is a change in his relation; when a servant or slave is made a freeman there is an alteration of his condition; but neither the one's magistracy nor the other's liberty, fills their hearts with new principles, or plants a new frame in their nature. Relation and nature are two distinct things. In creation there is a relation of a creature to God, which results from the mere being of the creature; but there is also the nature of the creature in such a rank of being, which is added over and above to its mere being. The apostle in the verses following the text, speaks of reconciliation, or non-imputation of our trespasses, as distinct from that change wrought in us in the new creation. In justification we are freed from the guilt of sin, and so have a title to life; in regeneration we are freed from the filth of sin, and have the purity of God's image in part restored to us.*

[2.] They differ in the cause, and other ways. Justification is the immediate fruit of the blood of Christ: 'Being justified by his blood,' Rom. 5:9. Regeneration is by the immediate operation of the Spirit, therefore called 'the sanctification of the Spirit;' the matter of that is without us, the righteousness of Christ; the matter of the other within us, a gracious habit. The form of the one is imputing, the form of the other is infusing or putting into us; they differ in the end, one is from condemnation to absolution, the other from pollution to communion. In the immediate effect, one gives us a right, the other a fitness. In their qualities, the righteousness of one is perfect in our head, and imputed to us. The righteousness by regeneration is actively in us, and aspires to perfection.

(3.) It differs from adoption. Adoption follows upon justification as a dignity flowing from union to Christ, and doth suppose reconciliation. Adoption gives us the privilege of sons, regeneration the nature of sons. Adoption relates us to God as a father, regeneration engraves upon us the lineaments of a father. That makes us relatively his sons by conferring a power, John 1:12. This makes us formally his sons by conveying a principle, 1 Peter 1:23. By that we are instated in the divine affection; by this we are partakers of the divine nature. Adoption doth not constitute us the children of God by an intrinsic form, but by an extrinsic acceptation; but this gives us an intrinsic right; or adoption gives us a title, and the Spirit gives us an earnest; grace is the pledge of glory. Redemption being applied in justification, makes way for adoption. Adoption makes way for regeneration, and is the foundation of it: Gal. 4:5, 6, 'God sent forth his Son to redeem them that were under the law, that we might receive the adoption of sons. And because you are sons, God hath sent forth the Spirit of his Son into your hearts, crying, Abba, Father.' Because you are thus adopted, God will make you like his Son, by sending forth the Spirit of his Son, to intimate the likeness it shall produce in the hearts of men to Christ, that you may cry, Abba, Father, behave yourselves like sons, and have recourse to God with a childlike nature. The relation to Christ as brethren is founded upon this new creature: Heb. 2:11, 'For both he that sanctifies and they who are sanctified, are all of one;' they are all of one nature, not the divine nature which Christ had by eternal generation, but that divine nature Christ had by the Spirit's unction. And being of one nature, he is not ashamed, though glorious in heaven, to call them brethren; and being Christ's brethren by a divine nature, thence result also the relation of the sons of God.

(4.) It differs from sanctification. Habitual sanctification, indeed, is the same thing with this new creature, as habitual rectitude was the spiritual life of Adam; but actual sanctification, and the gradual progress of it, grows from this principle as from a root. Faith purifies the heart, Acts 15:9, 'purifying their hearts by faith,' and is the cause of this gradual sanctification; but faith is part of this new creature, and that which is a part cannot be the cause of the whole, for then it would be the cause of itself. We are not regenerated by faith, though we are sanctified by faith; but we are new created by the Spirit of God, infusing faith into us. Faith produceth the acts of grace, but not the habit of grace, because it is of itself a part of this habit; for all graces are but one in the habit or new creature; charity, and likewise every other grace is but the bubbling up of a pure heart and good conscience, 1 Tim. 1:5. Regeneration seems to be the life of this gradual sanctification, the health and liveliness of the soul.

2. The second thing proposed is, what it is not.

(1.) It is not a removal or taking away of the old substance or faculties of the soul. Some thought that the substance of Adam's soul was corrupted when he sinned, therefore suppose the substance of his soul to be altered when he is renewed. Sin took not away the essence, but the rectitude; the new creation therefore gives not a new faculty, but a new quality. The cure of the leprosy is not a destroying of the fabric of the body, but the disease; yet in regard of the greatness of man's corruption, the soul is so much changed by these new habits, that it is as it were a new soul, a new understanding, a new will. It is not the destroying the metal, but the old stamp upon it, to imprint a new. Human nature is preserved, but the corruption in it expelled. The substance of gold is not destroyed in the fire, though the metal and the flame mix together, and fire seems to be incorporated with every part of it; but it is made more pliable to what shape the artist will cast it into, but remains gold still. It is not the breaking the candlestick, but setting up a new light in it; not a destroying the will, but putting a new bias into it. It is a new stringing the instrument to make a new harmony. It is an humbling the loftiness, and bowing down the haughtiness of the spirit, to exalt the Lord alone in the soul, Isa. 2:11, speaking of the times of the gospel. The essential nature of man, his reason and understanding, are not taken away, but rectified. As a carver takes not away the knobs and grain in the wood, but planes and smooths it, and carves the image of a man upon it, the substance of the wood remains still; so God pares away the rugged pieces in man's understanding and will, and engraves his own image upon it; but the change is so great that the soul seems to be of another species and kind, because it is acted by that grace, which is another species from that principle which acted it before. New creation is called a resurrection. Our Saviour in his resurrection had the same body, but endued with a new quality. As in Christ's transfiguration, Mat. 17:2, neither his deity nor humanity were altered, both natures remained the same. But there was a metamorphosis (μετεμορφώθη), and a glorious brightness conferred by the deity upon the humanity which it did not partake of before. So though the essence of the soul and faculties remain the same, yet another kind of light is darted in, and other qualities implanted. It was the same Paul when he complied with the body of death, and when he complained of it, but he had not the same disposition. As Adam in a state of corruption had the same faculties for substance which he had in the state of innocency; but the power, virtue, and form in those faculties, whereby he was acceptable to God, and in a capacity to please him, was wholly abolished. We lose not our substantial form, as Moses his rod did, when it was turned into a serpent; or the water at Cana was turned into wine.* Our nature is ennobled, not destroyed; enriched, not ruined; reformed, not annihilated.

(2.) It is not a change of the essential acts of the soul, as acts. The passions and affections are the same, as to the substance and nature of the acts, but the difference lies in the object. And acts, though for substance the same, yet are specifically distinguished by the diversity of objects about which they are conversant. Whatsoever is a commendable quality in nature, and left in man by the interposition of the mediator, is not taken away; but the principle, end, and objects of those acts, arising from those restored qualities, are altered. The acts of a renewed man, and the acts of a natural man, are the same in the nature of acts, as when a man loves God and fears God, or loves man or fears man; it is the same act of love, and the same act of fear; there are the same motions of the soul, the same substantial acts simply considered; the soul stands in the same posture in the one as in the other, but the difference lies in the objects; the object of the one is supernatural, the object of the other natural.*

As when a man walks to the east or west, it is the same motion in body and joints, the same manner of going; yet they are contrary motions, because the terms to which they tend are contrary one to the other: or, as when we bless God and bless man, it is with one and the same tongue that we do both, yet these are acts specifically different, in regard of the difference of their objects. The nature of the affections still remain, though not the corruption of them, and the objects to which they are directed are different. If a man be given to thoughtfulness, grace removes not this temper, but turns his meditations to God. The solitariness of his temper is not altered, but something new offered him as the object of his meditation. If a man be hot and earnest in his temper, grace takes not away his heat, but turns it into zeal to serve the interest of God. Paul was a man of active disposition; this natural activity of his disposition and temper was not dammed up by grace, but reduced to a right channel, and pitched upon a right object; as he laboured more than any in persecuting, so afterwards he 'laboured more than any' in edifying, 1 Cor. 15:9, 10. His labour was the same, and proceeded from the same temper, but another principle in that temper, and directed to another term. As it is the same horse, and the same mettle in the beast, which carries a man to his proper stage that carried him before in a wrong way, but it is turned in respect of the term. David's poetical fancy is not abolished by this new principle in him, but employed in descanting upon the praises of God, which otherwise might have been lavished out in vanity, and foolish love-songs, and descriptions of new mistresses. So that the substance and nature of the affections and acts of a man remain; but anger is turned into zeal by virtue of a new principle, grief into repentance, fear into the fear of God, carnal love into the love of the creator, by another principle which doth bias those acts.

(3.) It is not an excitation, or awakening of some gracious principle which lay hid before in nature, under the oppression of ill habits, as corn lay hid under the chaff, but was corn still. Not a beating up something that lay sculking in nature, not an awakening as of a man from sleep; but a resurrection as of a man from death; a new creation, as of a man from nothing. It is not a stirring up old principles and new kindling of them; as a candle put out lately may be blown in again by the fire remaining in the snuff, and burn upon the old stock; or as the life which retired into the more secret parts of the body in those creatures that seem dead in winter, which is excited and called out to the extreme parts by the spring sun. Indeed, there are some sparks of moral virtues in nature, which want blowing up by a good education; the foundation of these is in nature, the exciting of them from instruction, the perfection of them from use and exercise. But there is not in man the seed of one grace, but the seeds of all sin: Rom. 7:18, 'I know that in me, that is, in my flesh, dwells no good thing.' Some good thing may be in me, but it ariseth not from my flesh; it is not from any seed sown by nature, but it is another principle put into me, which doth seminally contain in it all grace; it is a putting a new seed into the soil, and exciting it to grow, 'an incorruptible seed,' 1 Peter 1:23. Therefore the Scripture doth not represent men in a trance, or sleep, but dead; and so it is not only an awakening, but a quickening, a resurrection, Eph. 2:5; Col. 2:12; Eph. 1:19, 20. We are just in this work as our Saviour was when the devil came against him: John 14:30, 'The prince of this world cometh, and hath nothing in me.' He had nothing to work upon in Christ; but he rakes in the ashes of our nature, and finds sparks enough to blow upon; but the Spirit finds nothing in us but a stump, some confused desires for happiness; he brings all the fire from heaven, wherewith our hearts are kindled. This work, therefore, is not an awakening of good habits which lay before oppressed, but a taking off those ill habits which were so far from oppressing nature that they were connatural to it, and by incorporation with it, had quite altered it from that original rectitude and simplicity wherein God at first created it.

(4.) Nor is it an addition to nature. Christ was not an addition to Adam, but a new head by himself, called Adam, in regard of the agreement with him in the notion of an head and common person: so neither is the new creature, or Christ formed in the soul, an addition to nature. Grace grows not upon the old stock. It is not a piece of cloth sewed to an old garment, but the one is cast aside, the other wholly taken on; not one garment put upon another: but a taking off one, and a putting on another, Col. 3:9, 10, 'putting off the old man, putting on the new man.' It is a taking away what was before, 'old things are passed away,' and bestowing something that had no footing before. It is not a new varnish, nor do old things remain under a new paint, nor new plaster laid upon old; a new creature, not a mended creature. It is called light, which is not a quality added to darkness, but a quality that expels it; it is a taking away the stony heart and putting an heart of flesh in the room, Ezek. 36:26. The old nature remains, not in its strength with this addition, but is crucified, and taken away in part with its attendants: Gal. 5:24, 'They that are Christ's have crucified the flesh, with the affections and lusts.' As in the cure of a man, health is not added to the disease; or in resurrection, life added to death; but the disease is expelled, death removed, and another form and habit set in the place. Add what you will without introducing another form, it will be of no more efficacy, than flowers and perfumes strewed upon a dead carcase, can restore it to life, and remove the rottenness. Nothing is the terminus a quo, in creation; it supposeth nothing before as a subject capable; nothing in a natural man is a subject morally capable to have grace, without the expulsion of the old corrupt nature. It is called a new creature, a new man; not an improved creature, or a new-dressed man.

(5.) It is not external baptism. Many men take their baptism for regeneration. The ancients usually give it this term. One calls our Saviour's baptism his regeneration.* This confers not grace, but engageth to it: outward water cannot convey inward life. How can water, a material thing, work upon the soul in a physical manner? Neither can it be proved that ever the Spirit of God is tied by any promise, to apply himself to the soul in a gracious operation, when water is applied to the body. If it were so that all that were baptized were regenerate, then all that were baptized would be saved, or else the doctrine of perseverance falls to the ground. Baptism is a means of conveying this grace, when the Spirit is pleased to operate with it. But it doth not work as a physical cause upon the soul, as a purge doth upon the humours of the body; for it is the sacrament of regeneration, as the Lord's Supper is of nourishment. As a man cannot be said to be nourished without faith, so he cannot be said to be a new creature without faith. Put the most delicious meat into the mouth of a dead man, you do not nourish him, because he wants a principle of life to concoct and digest it. Faith only is the principle of spiritual life, and the principle which draws nourishment from the means of God's appointment. Some indeed say that regeneration is conferred in baptism upon the elect, and exerts itself afterwards in conversion. But how so active a principle as a spiritual life should lie dead, and asleep so long, even many years which intervene between baptism and conversion, is not easily conceivable.

3. Let us see what it is positively.

(1.) It is a change; and, as to the kind of it is,

[1.] A real change, real from nature to grace, as well as by grace. The term of creation is real; the form introduced in the new creature is as real as the form introduced by creation into any being. Scripture terms manifest it so. A 'divine nature,' the 'image of God,' a 'law put into the heart,' they are not nominal and notional; it is a reality the soul partakes of; it gives a real denomination, 'a new man,' 'a new heart,' 'a new spirit,' 'a new creature,'* something of a real existence; it is called a resurrection: John 5:25, 'The hour is coming, and now is, when the dead shall hear the voice of the Son of God, and they that hear shall live.' If Christ had said only that the hour shall come, it had been meant of the last resurrection;

but saying that it was already come, it must be meant of a resurrection in this life. There is as real a resurrection of the soul by the trumpet of the gospel, accompanied with the vigorous efficacy of the Holy Ghost, as there shall be of bodies by the voice of the Son of God at the sound of the trumpet of the archangel. All real operations suppose some real form whence they flow, as vision supposeth a power whereby a man sees, and also a nature wherein that power is rooted. The operations of a new creature are real, and therefore suppose a real power to act, and a real habit as the spring of them. It is such a being that enables them to produce real spiritual actions, for the 'spirit of power' is conveyed to them, 2 Tim. 1:7, whereby as when they were out of Christ they were able to do nothing, so now being in him they are able to do all things, Philip. 4:13.

[2.] It is a common change to all the children of God. 'If any man be in Christ, he is a new creature;' every man in Christ is so. It is peculiar to them, and common to all of them. The new creation gives being to all Christians. It is a new being settled in them, a new impress and signature set upon them, whereby they are distinguished from all men barely considered in their naturals. As all of the same species have the same nature, as all men have the nature of men, all lions the nature of lions, so all saints agree in one nature. The life of God is communicated to all whose names are written in the book of life. All believers, those in Africa, as well as those in Europe, those in heaven as well as those on earth, have the same essential nature and change. As they are all of one family, all acted by one spirit, the heart of one answers to the heart of another, as face to face in a glass. What is a spirit of adoption in them below is a spirit of glory in them above; what in the renewed man below is a spirit crying, Abba Father, that is in them above, a spirit rejoicing in Abba Father. The impress and change is essentially the same, though not the same in degree.

[3.] It is a change quite contrary to the former frame. What more contrary to light than darkness? Such a change it is, Eph. 5:8; instead of a black darkness there is a bright light. As contrary as flesh and spirit, John 3:6, 'that which is born of the flesh is flesh; that which is born of the Spirit is spirit.' Where both are put in the abstract, one is the composition of flesh, the other of spirit: as contrary as east to west, as the seed of the woman to the seed of the serpent, as the spirit of the world and the Spirit of God. The frame of the heart before the new creation, and the frame of the heart after, bear as great a distance from one another as heaven from earth. As God and sin are the most contrary to one another, so an affection to God and an affection to sin are the most contrary affections. It is quite another bent of heart, as if a man turn from north to south. It is a position quite contrary to what it was. The heart touched by grace stands full to God, as before to sin; it is stripped of its perverse inclinations to sin, clothed with holy affections to God. He abhors what before he loved, and loves what before he abhorred. He was alienated from the life of God, but now alienated from the life of his lusts; nothing would before serve him but God's departure from him; nothing will now please him but God's rays upon him. He was before tired with God's service, now tired with his own sin. Before, crucifying the motions of the Spirit, now crucifying the affections and lusts. That which was before his life and happiness is now his death and misery; he disaffects his foolish pastimes and sinful pleasures as much as a man doth the follies of his childhood, and is as cheerful in loathing them as before he was jolly in committing them. It is a translation from one kingdom to another: Col. 1:13, a translation 'from the power of darkness into the kingdom of his dear Son.' Μετέστησε, a word taken from the transplanting of colonies: they are in a contrary soil and climate; they have other works, other laws, other privileges, other natures. As Christ's resurrection was a state quite contrary to the former, at the time of his death he was in a state of guilt by reason of our sin; at his resurrection he is freed from it. He was before made under the law; he is then freed from the curse of it. He was before in a state of death, after his resurrection in a state of life, and lives for ever. God pulls out the heart of stone, that inflexibleness to him and his service, and plants a heart of flesh in the room, a pliableness to him and his will, Ezek. 36:26. It is as great a change as when a wolf is made a lamb; that wolfish nature is lost, and the lamb-like nature introduced. By corruption man was carnal and brutish; by the new creation he is spiritual and divine. By corruption he hath the image of the devil; by this he is restored to the image of God. By that he had the seeds of all villanies; by this the roots of all graces. That made us fly from God; this makes us return to him. That made us enemies to his authority; this subjects us to his government. That made us contemn his law; this makes us prize and obey it:* "Instead of the thorn there shall come up the fir-tree; instead of the briar shall come up the myrtle-tree,' and God will preserve it from being cut off, Isa. 55:13, speaking of the time of redemption.

[4.] It is a universal change of the whole man. It is a new creature, not only a new power or new faculty. This, as well as creation, extends to every part; understanding, will, conscience, affections, all were corrupted by sin, all are renewed by grace. Grace sets up its ensigns in all parts of the soul, surveys every corner, and triumphs over every lurking enemy; it is as large in renewing as sin was in defacing. The whole soul shall be glorified in heaven; therefore the whole soul shall be beautified by grace. The beauty of the church is described in every part, Cant. 1–4, &c.

First, This new creation bears resemblance to creation and generation. God in creation creates all parts of the creature entire. When nature forms a child in the womb, it doth not only fashion one part, leaving the other imperfect, but labours about all, to form an entire man. The Spirit is busy about every part in the formation of the new creature. Generation gives the whole shape to the child, unless it be monstrous. God doth not produce monsters in grace; there is the whole shape of the new man. You mistake much if you rest in a reformation of one part only; God will say, Such a work was none of my creation. He doth not do things by halves.

Secondly, It bears proportion to corruption. As sin expelled the whole frame of original righteousness, so regenerating grace expels the whole frame of original corruption. It was not only the head or only the heart, only the understanding or only the will, that was overcast with the blackness of sin, but every part of man did lose its original rectitude. Not a faculty could boast itself like the Pharisee, and say, It was not like this or that publican; the waves of sin had gone over the heads of every one of them. Sin, like leaven, had infected the whole mass; grace overspreads every faculty to drive out the contagion. Grace is compared to light, and light is more or less in every part of the air above the horizon, for the expulsion of darkness when the sun ariseth. The Spirit is compared to fire, and therefore pierceth every part with its warmth, as heat diffuseth itself from the fire to every part of water. The natural man is denominated from corruption, not an old understanding or an old will, but the 'old man,' Eph. 4:22. So a regenerate man is not called a new understanding, or a new will, but 'a new man,' ver. 24.

Thirdly, The proper seat of grace is the substance of the soul, and therefore it influences every faculty. It is the form whence the perfection both of understanding and will do flow; it is not therefore placed in either of them, but in the essence of the soul.* It is by this the union is made between God and the soul; but the union is not of one particular faculty, but of the whole soul. 'He that is joined to the Lord is one spirit;' it is not one particular faculty that is perfected by grace, but the substance of the soul. Besides, that is the seat of grace which is the seat of the Spirit, but this or that particular faculty is not the seat of the Holy Ghost, but the soul itself, whence the Spirit rules every particular faculty by assisting grace, like a monarch in the metropolis sending orders to all parts of his dominions. The Spirit is said to dwell in a man, Gal. 4:4, Rom. 8:9; in the whole man, as the soul doth in the body, in forming every part of it; if it dwelt only in one faculty there could be no spiritual motion of the other. The principles in the will would contradict those in the understanding; the will would act blindly if there were no spiritual light in the understanding to guide it. The light of the understanding would be useless if there were no inclination in the will to follow it, and grace in both those faculties would signify little if there remained an opposing perversity in the affections. The Spirit, therefore, is in the whole soul, like fire in the whole piece of iron, quickening, warming, mollifying, making flexible, and consuming what is contrary, like Aaron's ointment, poured upon the heart, and thence runs down to the skirts of the soul.

Fourthly, Therefore there is a gracious harmony in the whole man. As in generation two forms cannot remain in the same subject; for in the same instant wherein the new form is introduced the old is cast out; so at the first moment of infusing grace, the body of death hath its deadly wound in every faculty, understanding, will, conscience, affection. The rectitude reaches every part; and all the powers of the soul, by a strong combination, by one common principle of grace acting them, conspire together to be subject to the law of God, and advance in the ways of holiness: Ps. 119:10, it is with 'the whole heart' that God is sought. In the understanding there is light instead of darkness, whereby it yields to the wisdom of God, and searches into the will of God: the spirit of the mind is renewed, Eph. 4:23. In the will there is softness instead of hardness, humility instead of pride, whereby it yields to the will of God, and closes with the law of God. In the heart and conscience there is purity instead of filth (whereby it is purged from dead works, Heb. 9:14, settled against the approbation of sin), and a resolution to be void of offence, Acts 24:16. In the affections there is love instead of enmity, delight instead of weariness, whereby they yield to the pleasure of God, have flights into the bosom of God: 'Oh how love I thy law! it is my delight day and night.' The memory is a repository for the precepts and promises of God as the choicest treasure. It is a likeness to Christ; the whole human nature of

Christ was holy, every faculty of his soul, every member of his body, his nature holy, his heart holy. If we are not formed, Christ is not formed in us; look therefore whether your reformation you rest in be in the whole, and in every part of the soul.

Fifthly, It is principally an inward change. It is as inward as the soul itself. Not only a cleansing the outside of the cup and platter, a painting over the sepulchre, but a casting out the dead bones and putrefied flesh; of a nature different from a pharisaical and hypocritical change, Mat. 23:25–27. It is a clean heart David desires, not only clean hands, Ps. 51:10. If it were not so, there could be no outward rectified change. The spring and wheels of the clock must be mended before the hand of the dial will stand right. It may stand right two hours in the day, when the time of the day comes to it, but not from any motion or rectitude in itself. So a man may seem by one or two actions to be a changed man, but the inward spring being amiss, it is but a deceit. Sometimes there may be a change, not in the heart, but in the things which the heart was set upon, when they are not what they were. As a man whose heart was set upon uncleanness, change of beauty may change his affection; the change is not in the man, but in the object. But this change I speak of is a change in the mind, when there is none in the object; as the affection of a child to his trifles changeth with the growth of his reason, though the things his heart was set upon remain in the same condition as before.

First, It is a change of principle.

Secondly, A change of end.

First, A change of principle. The principle of a natural man in his religious actions is artificial; he is wound up to such a peg, like the spring of an engine, by some outward respects which please him; but as the motion of the engine ceaseth, when the spring is down, so a natural man's motion holds no longer than the delight those motions gave him, which first engaged him in it. But the principle in a good man is spirit, an internal principle, and the first motion of this principle is towards God, to act from God, and to act for God. He fetches his fire from heaven to kindle his service; an heat and fervency of spirit precedes his serving the Lord, Rom. 12:11. There may be a serving God from an outward heat, conveying a vigour and activity to a man, but the new creature serves God from inward and heated affections. Examine therefore by what principles do I hear, and pray, and live, and walk? For all acts are good or evil, as they savour of a good or bad root, or principle in the heart. The two principles of the new creature are faith and love. What is called the new creature, Gal. 6:15, is called 'faith working by love,' Gal. 5:6.

Faith. This is the first discovery of all spiritual life within us, and therefore the immediate principle of all spiritual motion. A splendid action without faith is but moral, whereas one of a less glittering is spiritual with it. The new creature being begotten by the seed of the word, and having thereby an evangelical frame, hath therefore that which is the prime evangelical grace, upon which all other graces grow; and consequently all the acts of the new creature spring from this principle immediately, viz., faith in the precept, as a rule; faith in the promise, as an encouragement; faith in the Mediator, as a ground of acceptation. Therefore if we have not faith in the precept, though we may do a service not point-blank against the precept, yet it is not a service according to a divine rule; if we have not faith in the promise, we do it not upon divine motives; if we act not faith in the Redeemer, we despise the way of God's ordaining the presentation of our service to him. All those that you find, Heb. 11, acting from faith, had sometimes a faith in the power of God, sometimes in the faithfulness of God; but they had not only a faith in the particular promise or precept, but it was ultimately resolved into the promise of the Messiah to come: ver. 14, 'Those all died in faith, not having received the promises, but having seen them afar off,' &c. The performance of particular promises they had received, but not the performance of this grand promise; but that their faith respected. They, as new creatures, did all in observance of God promising the Mediator;

and we are to do all in observance of God sending the Mediator, being persuaded of the agreeableness of our services to him, upon the account of the command, and of the acceptation of our services by him upon the account of the Mediator. This put a difference between Paul's prayer, after the infusion of grace into him, and before; so that our Saviour sets a particular emphasis upon it: Acts 9:11, 'Behold he prays.' Paul, no doubt, had prayed many times before his believing, but nothing of that kind was put upon the file as a prayer; before, they were prayers of a self-righteous pharisee, but these of an evangelical convert; these were prayers springing from a flexibleness to Christ, a faith in him; from a Lord, what wilt thou have me to do?

Love. There are many principles of action, hope of heaven, fear of hell, reputation, interest, force of natural conscience; some of those are inward, some outward, which are the bellows that blow up a man to some fervency in action; but the true fire, that contributes an heavenly frame to a service, is the love of God. The desire of the heart is carried out to God; his heart draws near to God, because his sole delight is in God, and his whole desire for him: Ps. 73:25, 'Whom have I in heaven but thee?' Then, ver. 28, 'But it is good for me to draw near to God.' This choice affection in the new creature spirits his services, makes his soul spring up with a wonderful liveliness. The new creation is the restoration of the soul to God from its apostasy; a casting down those rebellious principles which contended with him, and reducing his affections to the right centre; and when all the lines meet here in one centre, in God, all the returns to him flow from this affection. It is but one thing settled in the soul as the object of its earnest desire; and that should be the spring of all its inquiries and actions, the beholding the beauty of the Lord, Ps. 27:4. Things may be done out of a common affection; as when a man will raise a child fallen into the dirt, out of a common tenderness; but a father would raise him with more natural affection, which is a sphere above that common compassion. Every affection therefore is not the renewed principle, but a choice affection to God. This is a mighty ingredient in this change, and doth difference the new creature from all others. One acts out of affection to God, the other out of affection to itself. Men may be offended with sin, because it disturbs their ease, health, estate, &c. He may pray, and hear, merely out of a respect to natural conscience; but how can these be the acts of the new creature, when there is no respect to God in all this? But a new creature would quench the fire of corrupt self-love, to burn only with a spiritual and divine flame; he depresseth the one to exalt the other, and would be disengaged from the burdensome chains of self-love, that he might be moved only by the spiritual charms of the other purer affection; it is a death to him to have any steams of self-love rise up to smoke and black a service.

Secondly, A change of end as well as principle, The glory of God is the end of the new creature, self the end of the old man. Before this new creation, a man's end was to please self; now his end is to please God. A man that delights in knowledge, to pleasure his understanding, and for self-improvement, when he becomes a new creature, though his desire for knowledge is not removed, yet his end is changed, and he thirsts after knowledge, not merely to please his inquisitive disposition, but to admire and praise God, and direct himself in ways agreeable to him. As the end of the sensualist is to taste the sweetness in pleasure, so the end of a renewed man is to know more of God, to taste a sweetness in him, and in every religious duty. This is the distinguishing character of the new creature. This design for the glory of God was not to be found among any of the heathens, who were so great admirers of virtue. Most of them intended only an acquiring a reputation among their countrymen; and though some of them might esteem virtue for its native dignity, yet this was to esteem it by the moiety of it, when they referred it not to the honour of God, from whence it flowed to the world. Man was not created for himself, and to be his own end; he therefore that doth chiefly aim at his own satisfaction in anything, is not a new creature: he hath his old deformed end into which he sunk by the fall. But grace carries a man higher, and reduceth all to God, and to his well-pleasing. Col. 1:9, 10, the apostle desires they may be 'filled with the knowledge of the will' of God, that they may 'walk worthy of the Lord, unto all well-pleasing.' The very first motion of this new principle is towards God, to act for God; as the first appearance of a living seed in the ground is towards heaven; thither it casts its look, from whence its life came. What the new creature receives, is from God: 1 Thes. 2:13, 'They received it as the word of God,' and therefore what he doth is for God.

(First.) The principal intent of God in the new creation is for himself: Hosea 2:23, 'I will sow her to me,' speaking of the church in the time of the gospel; not to sin, not to the world, not for herself, but I will sow her to me. Husbandmen sow the ground for themselves, for their own use, to reap the harvest, and the corn grows up to the husbandman that sowed it. What the seed doth naturally, the new creature doth intentionally, grow up for God. Since the new creature is a divine infusion, it must needs carry the soul to please God, and aim at his glory. God would never put a principle into the creature, to drive it from himself, and conduct it to his own dishonour; this consists not with God's righteousness, this would be a deceit of the creature. It is impossible, but that which is from God in so peculiar a manner, and with gracious intentions to restore the creature to his happiness, must tend to the advancement of God. Where there are no aims at the divine glory, there is no divine nature, nothing in the soul that can claim kindred with God. Regeneration is a forming the soul for God's self, and to shew forth his praise, Isa. 43:21, hence they are said to be 'a peculiar people,' in respect of their end, as well as their state. Certainly that man, who makes not God his pattern and his end, that doth not advance the praise and glory of God, was never new formed by him. What comes from God, must naturally tend to him. Is it possible that the living image of God should disgrace the original? that a divine impression should be unconcerned in the divine author?

(Secondly.) The new creation is an evangelical impression, and therefore corresponds in its intention with the gospel. This is the instrument whereby the new creature was wrought; and this was appointed and published for the glory of God: 'Glory to God in the highest,' Luke 2:14. It is to promote holiness in the creature, which is the only way whereby we can honour God. This is the prime lesson the grace or gospel of God teaches, to live godly, Titus 2:12, to live to God. What, therefore, is produced by the efficacy of such an instrument, cannot but aim at the glory of God, which was intended in it; otherwise the gospel would work an effect contrary to itself, which no instrument doth produce when managed by a wise agent; and contrary to the end of the agent too, viz., the Spirit of God, whose end is to glorify Christ: John 16:14, 'He shall glorify me.' The frame and acts of a renewed man are like the grain or seed of the word sown in the heart. Nothing the gospel designs more than the laying self low, even as low as dust and death. The first lesson is self-denial. It is in self that the strength and heart of the body of sin and lust lies; and it is the principal end of the gospel to bring the creature to sacrifice self-love to righteousness, self-interest, self-contentment, wholly to God, and his law, and his love, that God may be all in all in the creature. Before the heart was touched with the gospel, it had not the least impulse to bring forth the virtues and excellencies of God into the world; but when it is changed, it is filled to the brim with zealous desires to have his name exalted upon a high throne among men.

(Thirdly.) A new creation is the bringing forth the soul in a likeness to God. The end, therefore, of the new creature, is the glory of God. As God is the cause, so he is the pattern of the new creature, according to which he doth frame the soul; it is 'after God created in righteousness,' &c., Eph. 4:24. There can be no likeness to God where the creature dissents from him in the chief end. Without such an agreement, there can be nothing but variance between God and the creature. All the commotions and quarrels upon earth are founded upon the difference of ends. God aims at his own glory, so doth the new creature, otherwise it were impossible he should walk with God, or follow him as a dear child. It consists also in likeness to Christ: his resurrection is the pattern and cause of our regeneration: 'Ye are risen with Christ,' Col. 3:1. What, to contrary ends? Did Christ rise only to live to himself? No; but to live to God, as the great end for which he was appointed Mediator. Did he design to glorify God on earth, and doth he live to dishonour God in heaven? No; he lives to the same end there for which he lived and died here. Our spiritual resurrection, is not only a restoring us to a spiritual life, but to the ends of this life; a living to God and Christ, and to the ends of his mediation. Surely the new creature cannot be so brutish, as not to mind the honour of that nature to which it is so near allied, the glory of that God unto whom it hath the honour to bear a resemblance. A new creature hath a mighty sprightliness, and a height of spirit in some measure, when anything in his hands concerns God, more than when it concerns himself; for his will being framed according to the will of God, is filled with an ambition for the promoting the excellency of his name.

(Fourthly.) The end of the new creation is to advance the soul. It can never be advanced by an end lower than itself, or equal to itself. Any interest lower than God would be a degrading of it, a disparagement to its state, and too sordid for the soul to drive at; for it is the excellency or sordidness of the end which doth elevate or debase a man's spirit, and his actions also: the one enlargeth, the other shrivels up the soul in its operation. All things below God are unworthy of the boundless nature of the soul of man, much more unworthy of a soul rectified by a new creation. The soul is only perfected in a tendency to this end, and disgraced and lost in the mud and dirt of lower aims. That grace that is most durable, and doth most ennoble the spirit of a man, hath this property, that it 'seeks not her own,' nor 'vaunts itself,' 1 Cor. 13:4, 5.

(Fifthly.) It is impossible the soul can have this new creation without a change of end. It is not conceivable how anything can return to that, which it doth not eye as its end. The soul, as deriving its original from God, hath an obligation in all its motions to return to him as its chief end. The new creature hath an higher obligation by grace. Doth that, therefore, deserve the name of the new creature, that is so far from answering a gracious tie, that it doth not so much as answer a natural one? That is yet below the sphere of inanimate creatures, who all run back to their fountain, and one way or other declare the glory of God. He is no new creature, therefore, who is devotedly fawning upon himself, caressing himself; he is one that is yet bemired in his old nature, and hath not yet partaken of the fruit of Christ's purchase, redeeming and renewing grace. Those that are under the efficacious influence of it, and are the temple of the Holy Spirit, 'do glorify God in their body and spirit' too, inwardly as well as outwardly, because they are God's, 1 Cor. 6:19, 20. The understanding and will are both elevated by grace. The more intelligent any creature is, the more noble is his end, or ought to be, and the more he doth intend his end. The aim of a man is higher than that of a child; the aims of men in this or that station, are still more noble than the ends of men in a lower rank. Since the new creation, therefore, endues man with the most excellent nature he is capable of, it must fix a man upon the most excellent end, which is God and his glory; it were not else a new creature, or worthy of such a title.

(Sixthly.) This change of end doth only fit the soul for its proper service. From this end doth arise a quickness and an heartiness in every service. When God and his glory is not our end, our hearts flag, and we feel our spirits tired at our entrance into any service for him. When the apostle had made the glory of God his end in testifying the gospel of the grace of God, then his life was not counted dear to him, that he might finish his course with joy, Acts 20:24. Where this end sits uppermost in the heart, all allurements to the contrary are mightily despised. What a scornful eye doth the apostle cast upon all other things! and sets no higher value upon them than he would upon dross and dung, when they were not conducing to his main end, which was the knowledge of Christ, Philip. 3:8, 10.

Well, then, this is one of the most essential properties of the new creature, and that which is the clearest discovery of this state. A new creature is as earnest in secret for the glory of God, and as industrious for God, as if the eyes of all the world were upon him; the bent of his heart alway stands this way; he glorifies God in his spirit as well as body, 1 Cor. 6:20. When men will be zealous in things that concern God before men, and negligent in their spirits and inward part of the soul, then the glory of God was not their end, but themselves. For what is a man's end, sets an edge upon his spirit in private as well as public. But a new creature is of another frame. When he finds that he hath missed of his full aim, and hath not had that single respect as he ought, he is unsatisfied and troubled that God hath been no more glorified by him. But he that is not renewed is well pleased if any concerns of self have been advanced, though God be not glorified; and his soul is at rest in that act, as it hath lived to himself, and brought in something to increase the treasure of his self-ends.

Thirdly, As it is an inward change in respect of principle and end, so, thirdly, it is a change of thoughts. Being new, he is new in the choicest faculty. As when he was after the flesh he minded the things of the flesh, so now being after the spirit he minds the things of the spirit, Rom. 8:5. As a child hath not the thoughts of a man, so neither hath a natural man the thoughts of a new creature. A principle is placed in his understanding which doth emit other beams different from that smoky light which was in it before. Though a new creature cannot hinder the first motions, yet he endeavours to suppress their proceeding any further, and excites others in his heart to make head against them; and would, as far as he could, hinder the rising of any wave, the least bubbling against right reason and the interest of God. When David had an inclination in his heart to God's statutes, the immediate effect of it is to 'hate vain thoughts:' Ps. 119:112, 113, 'I have inclined my heart to perform thy statutes;' and it follows, 'I hate vain thoughts.' The vanity of his heart was a burden to him, and he loathed all the inward excrescences, any buds from that bitter stump he still bore within him. A new creature is as careful against wickedness in the head or heart, as in the life. He would be purer in the sight of God than in the view of men. He knows none but God can see the workings of his heart or the thoughts of his head, yet he is as careful that they should not rise up as that they should not break out. The soul is so changed that it is no longer a stranger and ill-willer to the motions of the Spirit; it will welcome them upon their entrance, conduct them into the innermost room, converse familiarly with them, and delight in their company; it invites their stay, pursues them when they seem to depart, holds them fast, and will not let them go, as the church doth to Christ. He turns much in upon himself, sets his eye upon his own heart, keeps that with all diligence, to observe what issues of a spiritual life are there; as it is directed in Prov. 4:23, 'Keep thy heart with all diligence, for out of it are the issues of life.' If he perceives any weeds to spring up there, or mushrooms (as they will in a night), he cuts them up and throws them out. The understanding is more quick and sensible to discern them in the first risings, to receive good ones or check bad ones, than it was before; the new creature is sensible of any touch contrary to its interest. A corrupt mind draws to it the vilest things, and unproportionable to the true nature of the soul, as a corrupt stomach doth unwholesome food, till by a new creation it be set higher, and by a sanctified reason becomes more choice about its objects; and then, like David, the heart is filled as with marrow and fatness, when he meditates on God in the night watches, Ps. 63:5, 6. The thoughts of God are an inward spring of pleasure to him, more than the thoughts of sin can be to a deformed and depraved soul.

Fourthly, Change of comforts follows upon this. Since there is a change of nature, there is a change of his complacency. The former nature is his trouble, therefore all his delights which arise from it are its discontents and burden. Every nature hath a peculiar pleasure belonging to it: the nature of a dove will not acquiesce in that which pleases a swine, nor the new nature in that which pleases the old. The comforts of manhood are of another make than those of a child, and the comforts of a prince more elevated than those of a peasant, because he hath another spirit. That Spirit who is appointed to renew him is appointed an officer to comfort him; as therefore he gives him new principles, so he gives him new consolations. He is, as a comforter, to glorify Christ, to receive of his, and shew it unto the new creature. They are Christ's own words—'He shall glorify me: for he shall receive of mine, and shall shew it unto you'—being described before under the title of a Comforter, John 16:14. He shall receive of mine; grace from me, suitable to the grace in me, wherewith to beautify; and comforts from me, suitable to those comforts in me, wherewith to refresh you. As they are brought to live the life of God in holiness, so they are brought to live the life of God in joy and comfort. Righteousness, peace, joy are the trinity which make up the kingdom of God in the heart: Rom. 14:17, 'The kingdom of God is not meat and drink; but righteousness, and peace, and joy in the Holy Ghost.' As the grace of God is their life, so the joy of the Lord is their strength; strangers to God intermeddle not with it, and have no share in it. There is a joy put into the heart together with this new creature: 'Thou hast put gladness into my heart,' Ps. 4:7—a gladness not founded upon any worldly consideration as the joy of men, not a joy of their own putting in; but the new creature's joy is a joy of God's putting in. Other men's comforts are in the creature, the new creature's comforts in the Creator. Others cannot joy if worldly things be removed, because the foundation of their joy is without them; but these, by the loss of worldly things, have their comforts rather increased than impaired, because the foundation of their joy is within them. The comforts of a natural man are sucked from the dry breasts of creatures; the comforts of a new creature are derived from the full fountain of life, which makes their very sufferings gloriously comfortable to them, 1 Peter 4:13, 14. The prodigal by his change of mind had a change of refreshment: robes for rags, and a fatted calf for husks. It is as much his comfort to loathe himself as derived from Adam, and to love the self implanted by God, as it was before the contrary. He can never look upon the new creature in him but with delightful views, and a pleasure mingles itself with every cast of his eye upon it. For certainly from making God our end, and doing all things for his glory, flows the highest delight; since God is the only happiness of that soul that is in conjunction with him as his main end, he must needs have a share in the happiness of God as well as his nature. Felicity and consolation follow it, as the shadow doth the body; and every act of the new creature towards God is edged with comfort in the very acting.

Fifthly, As it is an inward change, so it is also an outward change. I call it outward in regard of objects, in regard of operations; though it is principally inward in regard of the prime seat of it, in regard of the form, which causeth the outward. The power of seeing is in the soul, though the vision itself be in the eye. The change our Saviour made in those he cured was in the organ, when he made the blind to see, the deaf to hear, and the lame to walk, which did necessarily infer a change of objects and a change of actions. So a man by this new creation sees the things of God, hears the voice of God, walks in the ways of God. All outward changes argue not an inward, but an inward is alway attended with an outward.

First, In regard to objects. The world and sin was before the object of his inquiries and endeavours. Now he seeks the face of God; his soul follows hard after him. The world and God are so contrary, that the love of the one is enmity to the other. From multitudes of objects which distracted him, he is come to unity, which quiets and settles him: Ps. 27:4, 'One thing have I desired of the Lord, that will I seek after; that I may dwell in the house of the Lord all the days of my life, to behold the beauty of the Lord, and to inquire in his temple.' It is no lower an object than this, that the soul is coversant about, about God himself, to embrace him; about what hath most of God in it, to value and cherish it; about the word of God, to direct him in his ways, and to do his work. The understanding is conversant about the things of God, in the apprehension of them; the will in the election, the affections in complacency in them. Spiritual objects are set up by every faculty, as the delightful things which it heartily embraceth. Before, a man had no affection to God, you might as well have persuaded a swine to love the music of a lute, as a natural man supremely to love God. All his desires were set upon the dross of the world, the customs, coarse corruptions, pleasures of the world; but a truly regenerate man can as little make the world his chief object of desire and affection, as a man used to choice viands can feed upon chaff and husks. The intendment of the gospel is to set forth God in Christ as an amiable object, as infinitely glorious. It declaims against the world, to draw men from the affectionate considerations of it. The renewed work then doth consist in fixing upon God in Christ, as the main object of desire and affection. When the heart, therefore, complies with the gospel, there must be a compliance with the chief subject of the gospel, and in such a manner as may answer the intendment of the gospel. While Paul was in his natural and pharisaical state, Christ and his truth was accounted as dung, trampled upon as dross, fit to be thrown out of the converse of mankind; but when his heart is changed, there is a change in the object of his valuation: Christ is then his treasure, his all, and other things but dross in comparison of him, Philip. 3:8.

Secondly, In regard of operations. 'Old things are passed away,' old actions as well as old affections. Operations are never constantly against nature, operari sequitur esse. The heart and the actions do not alway contradict one another. According to the abundance of the heart, the mouth speaks,' Mat. 12:24. 'According to the spring of grace in the heart will the hand of the life stand. It will vent itself more or less, according to the quantity of it. It is an inward baptism with fire, which will quickly break out and shew itself in the members: Mat. 7:20, 'By their fruits you shall know them.' New apprehensions infer new operations. An alteration of judgment cannot be without an alteration of acting. As he hath 'received Christ Jesus the Lord, so he walks in him,' Col. 2:6. The very intendment of God in the new creation was this: Eph. 2:10, 'Created in Christ to good works, which God hath before ordained, that we should walk in them.' If there be not then new works, there is no new creation, for the chief intention and aim of God cannot be frustrated. Christ formed in a man is not a sleepy and inactive being: actions will scent of him. Fruits bear the image of the root whence they spring, and upon which they flourish. A new root cannot bring forth old fruits. If the nature of a crab-tree be changed into that of a vine, it will bear no longer crabs but grapes. Where holiness is implanted in the nature, holiness will be imprinted in the life. A man that hath reason superior to sense doth use his sense rationally; a renewed man that hath grace superior to reason useth his reason graciously. The operations were rational when bare reason held the sceptre, but they are spiritual when grace ascends the throne; for it cannot be that that person who is acted by the Spirit, 'lives in the Spirit, walks in the Spirit' (Gal. 5:18, 25), should do anything without a spiritual tincture, in that wherein he is acted by it. For it is impossible but every action must be dyed of the same colour with the principle whence it flows, and by which it is directed. Actions of sensitive nature are by reason of grace ordered by a new rule, directed to a new end. He ate and drank to the flesh before, now to God, 1 Cor. 10:31. He degraded his soul to invent ways to pamper his body. Now he puts his body in its due posture to serve the soul, and both to exalt God. Yea, his religious duties are changed, not as to the matter, but the manner. He knew them before, as he did Christ, after the flesh; he now knows them and performs them after the Spirit. There is zeal instead of coldness, liveliness instead of deadness, brokenness instead of presumption, a spirit of liberty instead of the whip of conscience, confidence in God instead of confidence in duty, melting pleading of promises instead of a pharisaical pleading of works. In a word, grace instead of nature, spirit instead of flesh. Paul, of a pharisaical boaster, becomes a Christian suppliant; 'behold he prays.' This change is outward as well as inward. In a man of an exact morality it is chiefly inward; he walks in his old outward ways with a new heart. In a loose man renewed it is apparently outward; he hath left both his old ways and his old nature; but a man only outwardly reformed, without any inward change, walks in new ways with an old spirit. 'He that lacks these things,' saith the apostle, after an enumeration of several graces, 'hath forgotten that he was purged from his old sins;' for indeed he never was.

Thus have I considered this new creation in the nature of a change.

2. Let us consider it in the nature of a vital principle. This new creation is a translation from death to life: 1 John 3:14, 'We know that we have passed from death to life.' And we have not a spiritual life till we are in Christ. 'He that hath not the Son hath not life,' 1 John 5:12. When our Saviour called Lazarus out of the grave, he gave him a principle of life and motion. The same he doth when he calls men from a spiritual death in sin. Whatsoever we had from the first Adam is mortal, whatsoever we have from the second Adam is vital; the one communicates a spiritual life, as the other propagated a spiritual death. The new creature is a vital powerful principle, naturally moving the soul to the service and obedience of God, and doth animate the faculties in their several motions, as the soul doth quicken the members of the body. It is called the hidden man, the inward man, implying that it hath life and motion. As the life of the body is from the soul, as the effect from the cause, so the life of the soul is from grace. Christ is the meritorious cause of this life in his person, the efficient cause of it by his Spirit; but grace is the formal cause of this life, as God is the cause of our bodily life efficiently, and the soul the cause of it formally. It is not, then, a gilding, but a quickening; not a carving, but an enlivening. Whatsoever doth proceed from an external

cause is not life or a living motion. A piece of wood may be carved in the shape of a man, but remains wood still in such a form and figure. But a Christian hath a spiritual life breathed into him, as Adam had a natural. When Adam's body was formed of the earth, it was no more than earth, till a heavenly spark was breathed into him by God, to set him upon his feet, and enable that piece of earth to move. It is distinguished therefore from hypocrisy, which is but the shadow of Christianity. This is a living principle; that a form, this a power; that a piece of art, this a nature. A picture may have the lineaments of a man, but not the life, understanding, and affections of a man.

3. Let us consider it as a habit, and then see what light the consideration of it, as a vital principle and a habit, give us into the nature of this new creation. By habit we must not understand, as we do in common speech, a clothing, as when we say, Such a one was in such a habit; but by habit we mean an inward frame, enabling a man to act readily and easily, as when an artificer hath the habit of a trade. Since this new creation is not a destruction of the substance of the soul,* but that there is the same physical being and the same faculties in all men, and nothing is changed in its substance as far as respects the nature of man, it is necessary, therefore, that this new creation consist in gracious qualities and habits, which beautify and dispose the soul to act righteously and holily. Corruption of nature is the poison, the sickness, and deformity of our nature; grace is the beauty, health, ornament of it, and that which gives it worth and value. When a debauched man is become virtuous, we say he is another man, a new man, though he hath the same soul and body which he had before, but he hath quitted those evil habits wherewith he was possessed. It is impossible to conceive a new creature without new habits. Nothing can be changed from a state of corruption to a state of purity without them. The making darkness to become light, in the very nature of it, implies the introducing a new quality, Eph. 5:8. This is meant by the seed: 1 John 3:9, 'His seed remains in him.' As seed

makes the earth capable to bring forth good fruit, which had a nature before to bring forth, not corn, but weeds, till the grain was put into it; and it is expressed by 'a fountain of living water springing up into eternal life,' John 4:14 (πηγή).

(1.) There is such a habit. God doth provide as much for those that he loves, in order to a supernatural good, as for those creatures that he loves in order to a natural good; but God hath put into all creatures such forms and qualities, whereby they may be inclined of themselves to motions agreeable to their nature, in an easy and natural way.* Much more doth God infuse into those that he moves to the obtaining a supernatural good, some spiritual qualities, whereby they may be moved rationally, sweetly, and readily to attain that good; he puts into the soul a spirit of love, a spirit of grace, whereby, as their understandings are possessed with a knowledge of the excellency of his ways, so their wills are so seasoned by the power and sweetness of this habit, that they cannot, because they will not, act contrary thereunto. And this habit of grace hath the same spiritual force in a gracious way, as those principles in other creatures in a natural way. As the habit of sin is called flesh in regard of its nature, and death in regard of its consequent, so the habit of grace is called the new creature and spirit, Gal. 5:17, in regard of its term and consequent, life. This habitual grace is the principle of all supernatural acts, as the soul concurs as an immanent principle to all works by this or that faculty. As Christ had a body prepared him to do the work of a mediator, so the soul hath a habit prepared it to do the work of a new creature. To this purpose, there is a habit of truth or sincerity in the will, and a 'hidden wisdom' in the understanding, Ps. 51:6. As the corrupt nature is a habit of sin, so the new nature is a habit of grace; God doth not only call us to believe, love, and obey, but brings in the grace of faith, and love, and obedience, bound up together, and plants it in the soil of the heart, to grow up there unto eternal life; he gives a willingness and readiness to believe, love, and obey.

(2.) This habit is necessary. The acts of a Christian are supernatural, which cannot be done without a supernatural principle; we can no more do a gracious action without it, than the apostles could do the works of their office unless endued with power from above, which our Saviour bids them tarry at Jerusalem for, Luke 24:49. If there were not a gracious habit in the soul, no act could be gracious; or supposing it could, it could not be natural, it would be only a force. New creation is not from the Spirit compelling, but inclining; not like the throwing a stone contrary to its nature, but changing the nature, and planting other habits, whereby the actions become natural. As sin was habitual in a man by nature, so grace must be habitual in a new creature, otherwise a man is not brought into a contrary state (though the acts should be contrary) if there be not a contrary habit; for it is necessary the soul should be inclined in the same manner towards God as before it was towards sin; but the inclination to sin was habitual.

(3.) This habit is but one. For it is an entire rectitude in all the faculties, and an universal principle of working righteously. As the corrupt nature is called the 'old Adam', and a 'body of death', the gracious nature is called the 'new man,' Col. 3:9, 10. As a man is but one man, a body one body, though consisting of divers members, and several parts, all formed by one spirit, and making up but one habit, so that as all sins are parts of that body of death, so all graces are but strings of this one root. As from that primogeneal light, kindled at the first creation by God, were framed the stars and lights of heaven, which have their several appearances and motions, and are distinct from one another, though all arising from the womb of that first light, so all particular graces, though they have their stated seasons of action, and are distinct in themselves, yet all flow from, and are contained in, this habit as in a root. They are so many grapes growing upon one stalk, clusters proceeding from one root of the new nature. It is from the participation of the divine nature that all those graces arise, the exercise of which the apostle exhorts them to, 2 Peter

1:4, &c; and indeed it being a divine nature, must needs include all the perfections due to it. As the divine essence of God is one, yet contains all perfections eminently; and if there were a deficiency of any, it could not be the divine essence; so the grace infused into the heart contains in it virtually all the perfections wherein it may agree with the nature of God's holiness, otherwise it were not a divine nature, if there were any defect in the nature of the habit, I say, in the nature of the habit.* And it cannot be otherwise; for though the Spirit may give one gift to one man, another gift to another, 1 Cor. 12:8, 9, yet when he would make a new creature, there must be a nature or habit containing all graces. It could not else be a divine nature; for if the Spirit doth purpose to make a new creature, he cannot but give all grace, which belongs to the essence and constitution of that new creature, otherwise he would either wilfully or weakly cross his intention.

(4.) This habit receives various denominations, either,

[1.] From the subject. It is subjectively in the essence of the soul, but as it shews itself in the understanding, it is called the knowledge of God; as it is the will, it is a choice of God; as it is in the affections, it is a motion to God. As the body of death is in the understanding, ignorance; in the will, enmity; in the conscience, deadness; in the affections, disorder and frowardness. As diseases receive several names, as they are centred in several parts, yet are but the dyscrasy or distemper of the humours.

[2.] From the object it is diversified. As it closes with Christ dying, it is faith; as it rejoiceth in Christ living, it is love; as it lies at the feet of Christ, it is humility; as it observes the will of Christ, it is obedience; as it submits to Christ's afflicting, it is patience; as it regards Christ offended, it is grief; yet all arising from one habit, and animated by faith, so that it is the love of faith, the joy of faith, the humility of faith, the patience of faith, they all spring from one habit, seated in one soul, conversant about one object, God in Christ: such a unity there is in all these diversifications. As the holy oil wherewith the vessels of the tabernacle were anointed was but one ointment, though composed of many ingredients, Exod. 30:25, 26; as all the perfections of creatures are eminently in one God, all the evil dispositions of the creatures seminally in man by nature: so all the beauties of grace are eminently included in this habit.

Hence we may take a prospect of the nature of the new creature. It being thus a vital principle, and a habit, therefore the motion to God, and for God, must be,

1. Ready in respect of disposition. He stands ready and disposed to every good work upon God's call. As the habit of sin disposeth the soul to every evil work, so the habit of grace prepares it for every good work, and makes it meet for its master's use: 2 Tim. 2:21, 'If a man therefore purge himself from these, he shall be a vessel unto honour, sanctified, and meet for his Master's use, and prepared unto every good work.' It is just as it was with Isaiah, chap. 5:5, at the first sight of the vision he complains, 'Woe is me, a man of unclean lips,' taken up with self-reflection, no offers to act for God; but when a live coal was taken from the altar and laid upon his mouth, there is a ready answer to God's question, ver. 7, 8, 'Whom shall I send? Here am I, send me.' No demurs; it was a live coal from the altar had quickened him into a new frame for God. David doth not say he had performed the statutes of God, but he had 'inclined his heart' to perform them, Ps. 119.

That I may not grate upon any troubled spirit, consider,

(1.) This readiness is seminally in every renewed person, yet it does not always actually appear. As the old nature contains in it seminally all sins, yet every man is more prone to one than another, according to education, temper of body, or a set of temptations; so the heart of a renewed man hath an habitual disposition to the exercise of all grace, because it hath the seeds of all graces in it, yet it doth not act all alike for want of vigorous occasions. As the attributes of God, though in the highest perfection, yet in their exercise in the world, sometimes one appears more triumphant than another, sometimes more of patience, sometimes mercy, sometimes justice, sometimes wisdom, one is more eminently apparent than another; so the divine nature hath seminally in this habit all grace, and an agreeableness to every duty enjoined, a principle to send forth the fruits of all when an object is offered, and the grace excited by the Spirit of God; yet sometimes one is more visible than another, according to the call it hath to stand forth and shew itself. This habitual disposition may be when there is not a present actual fitness for some service of a higher strain, by reason of some particular commission of sin, which hath sullied the soul; as a vessel of honour in respect of its formation may be fit for use, but in respect of some foulness contracted may not be immediately fit for some noble service, till a new scouring had passed upon it. A grown Christian, who hath his senses exercised in the ways of God, doth not alway actually exercise this habit, yet he is ready upon the least motion actually to do it; as a new creature having a change of end doth habitually mind the glory of God, yet he doth not in every action actually think of it, or will it as his end; but he is ready to bring this habitual aim into exercise upon the least motion, and reaches out his arm to embrace and stand right to that point. David had an habitual repentance in him while he lay asleep in his sin, and by virtue of this habit, he doth without any resistance comply with the first touch God gave him by Nathan. His repentance flowed, and never ceased till it had done its perfect work. It was a sign of a heart of flesh; a heart of stone could not have been so flexible. Job was eminent for patience, but being a new creature, he had a disposition to all the rest, and had acted them with as high a strain, had he had the same occasions.

(2.) This readiness to every service doth not actually appear in persons newly regenerate. I think the lowest degree of this habit in one newly regenerate, is a purpose of heart to cleave unto the Lord: Acts 11:23, 'When he came, and had seen the grace of God, he was glad, and exhorted them, that with purpose of heart they would cleave unto the Lord.' Certainly when there is such a fixed and constant purpose, it is a token of the grace of God; yet to this purpose there may not alway be connexed an actual readiness to every service. For at the first beginning of the new creature there is a strong resistance; it is in a strange soil, the armies of hell are in array against it, it is like a Daniel in a lion's den, or a Lot in Sodom, only God restrains the force of these enemies. As it is in a child derived from Adam, there is a principle in the natural corruption to exert all kind of wickedness; yet it doth not presently rise to the utmost of its force, till ripened by time and other intervening causes. So though the new creature hath in it a readiness virtually to the most raised action, to be as believing and laborious as Paul, as zealous as Elijah, as patient as Job, yet it mounts not presently to this state; a time must be allowed for growth. There is an infancy in grace, as well as in manhood. And as a child, though his soul be of the same nature with that of a man, yet he cannot exercise those acts of understanding and reason, because of the predominancy of sense, and the indisposition of the organs; so neither can a young Christian: he may have a disposition equal to the best Christians, but not an equal strength; the reluctancy of the corrupt habits is more vigorous, not being much mortified; he wants also that additional strength gained by exercise. There may be a greater resistance to one grace more than to another, from the strength of some corruption particularly opposite to that grace; yet 'to will is present with him,' though he 'cannot perform that which is good,' Rom. 7:18. The posture of the soul to God was as natural to him as the posture of the heart was before to sin; as a young boy first come to school may have as strong a purpose to get learning as a man that hath taken all his degrees in the university. The first graces which appear in a renewed soul are repentance and faith; because regeneration being a rooting up from the old stock and setting up a new, as it relates to the old stock, it doth necessarily produce repentance upon the sight of his misery, and for being upon the old stock so long; and faith, as a necessary grace for closing with the Redeemer upon a sight of him, and for ingrafting him upon a new stock; and then love, admiration, and thankfulness, walk the stage, from a reflection upon the greatness of the misery escaped, and the great deliverance attained. Sprouts from a root grow up, some faster, some slower, yet all arising from the same root. So some graces appear at the very first setting this habit in the soul, other graces lie hid till new occasions draw them out. This disposition, inclination, will, readiness, purpose, is the first language of a habit.

2. A second thing wherein you have a prospect of the new creature is this; as it is ready in respect of disposition, so it is in activity of motion. Since it is a life infused by infinite activity, since it is a habit bearing the impression of God, and maintained by a union with him, it is impossible it can be sleepy and dull in a constant way. All life hath motion proper to the principle of it: rational life is attended with rational actions; sensitive life, with acts proper to sense. It is as impossible then that a spiritual life should be without acts consonant to it, as that the sun should appear in the firmament without darting forth its beams. All life is accompanied with natural heat, which is the band of it, whereby the body is enabled to a vigorous motion. The new creature is not a marble statue or a transparent piece of crystal, which hath purity, but not life. It is a living spirit, and therefore active; a pure spirit, and therefore purely active, according to the degree of it. It is the same habit in part renewed, which Adam had by creation, which was not a sluggish and unwieldy principle; it must therefore have an activity, it could not else be a proper principle to contest with the contrary principle, which is active like the sea, casting out mire and dirt. Since the old Adam conveyed such a vigorous principle of corruption, the new Adam is not wanting to endue the principle of his conveyance with a suitable activity. Grace abounds in its vigour, as well as sin hath abounded in its kind, Rom. 5:20. Upon Christ's call, Matthew left his receipt of custom; the other apostles their nets; motion presently follows an enlivening call of God. It is first a habit, then an act; first a 'spirit of grace and supplication,' then a 'looking upon him whom they have pierced,' by an act of their understanding, and a 'mourning'

by an act of the will, Zech. 12:10, 11. First a 'sanctification of the spirit,' then a 'belief of the truth,' to the obtaining of glory, 2 Thes. 2:13. When anything ceaseth to act, there is either an oppression, or a death of nature.

(1.) This principle of the new creature is naturally active. All vital motions are natural; sometimes in men there are natural actions without any actual exercise of reason, as when the spirits flow out to any part for the defence of it upon the motion of any passion, as blood starts to the face upon shame, &c, which all the reason of a man cannot hinder. It is as natural to this new habit to produce new actions, as for anything to engender according to its own likeness and species, as for a living tree to spring out in leaves and fruits. A renewed man, whose seed is within himself, brings forth fruit after its kind, as well as the herbs and the trees, Gen. 1:12. All living creatures move agreeably to their natures, with a spontaneity and freedom of nature. The bramble doth not more naturally bring forth thorns, than a habit of sin doth steam out sinful actions; nor a fountain more freely bubble up its water, than a habit of grace springs up in holy actions. For shall the workmanship of God be more unapt to the proper end of it, than the workmanship of the devil, since good works are the end of God's new creating us, that we should walk in them? Walking is a natural motion: Eph. 2:10, 'We are his workmanship, created in Christ Jesus to good works.' A well dressed vine doth not more naturally bring forth grapes, than a soul rooted in Christ doth the fruits of the spirit; neither doth the sun more naturally enlighten the world with its beams, than the new creature shoots forth its desires and affections to God; for it is impossible but this habit should tend to him, since it is planted by him. The new creature's services are his meat and drink, not his work; it is as natural to him to do it, as for a creature to desire and take its proper food; you need not hire a child to suck, by the promises of fine things, it will naturally, without imitation, take the breast. The new creature having a righteous and just nature, cannot but do righteous things; nothing can act against its nature, while nature is orderly, and not disturbed by some disease or frenzy. As God, whose image a regenerate man bears, cannot but do good, because his nature is goodness: Rom. 6:2, 'How can you that are dead to sin, live any longer therein?' He can no more naturally do it than a dead man can walk. Not but that there are some mistakes sometimes, which proceed not from nature, but from some obstructing humour. Nature doth not err in its right course unless hindered by some adversary; the errors renewed men are subject to proceed not from the regenerate principle in them, but from that remainder of corruption which by degrees is weakened by the other, and at last wholly put off.

(2.) It is voluntarily active. There is a kind of natural necessity of motion, from life and habit, yet also a voluntary choice; it is a power which constrains and inclines the will: Ps. 110:3. The apostle tells us there was a 'necessity laid upon him to preach the gospel,' 1 Cor. 9:16, yet it was not a compulsion, but a voluntary act, after his will was changed. The new creature is not constrained from without, but flows freely, is not forced; the chief work is upon the will, the proper effect of any work upon the will is voluntariness. The Spirit works to make it willing; its motion then is not by compulsion: there is a sweet necessity of the new nature, and a gracious choice of will, which meet together and kiss each other; a natural, not a coactive necessity. How freely doth the soul, winged with grace, move to and for God, as a bird in the air! With what a free and ready spirit doth the new creature go to prayer, reading, and hearing! How freely doth it breathe in the air of heaven! Not spurred by outward interest, or dragged by the threatenings of the law, nor chid to it by the clamours of conscience; but gently moved to it, and upheld by it, by a soft, and dove-like, and 'free spirit,' Ps. 51:12. How great is the difference between the flowing of a fountain and the dropping of a sponge; one is free, the other squeezed: between a statue drawn upon wheels, and a living motion; one moves, the other is moved. Our Saviour, by washing us from our sins in his own blood, 'hath made us kings and priests unto God,' Rev. 1:6. First kings, putting into the new creature a royal and magnanimous frame, as he did into Saul when he advanced him to the kingdom; and then priests, to offer sacrifices to God with this royal and generous spirit. So that it is as troublesome to a soul, having this royal spirit, to omit things proper to this frame, as it is for a legalist to do them. Therefore where there are frequent omissions of duty, or a constant dulness in it, it shews the want of this kingly frame, and consequently that we are not washed from our sins in the blood of Christ. There is both such a nature and such a choice, that as the apostle saith, 2 Cor. 13:8, 'We can do nothing against the truth, but for the truth.' So the new creature cannot but do the things which are holy, just, and good, so far as he is regenerate, were there no rule without to guide him, because he hath a habit of holiness with him, a will set to the right point. His former state made him have an aversion from holy services; this makes all spiritual duties connatural to him. So that it is as irksome for him to live without God in the world, as before it was to live with him; he can as soon strip himself of his own soul, as act, from a renewed principle, contrary to God and righteousness.

(3.) It is fervently active. The nobler the being of anything is, the greater degree of activity it is attended with; the more spiritual the quality, the more vigorous the effect. Both the spirituality of the principle, excellency of the object, and affection to the end, conspire together to increase this activity. The principle is spiritually vital; the operation therefore is vigorous: the object is God as amiable; the warmer therefore the zeal; the acts are, loving God, trusting in God, depending on God, promoting his kingdom in the heart, acts delightful in themselves, delightful in their issue, the motion in them more quick; the end is the glory of God, the happiness of the creature; the higher the end, the more elevated the soul. There is an innate principle in everything to preserve its happiness; it is as natural as life itself. Inanimate creatures are endued with this nature. The flame aspires to heaven, and waves on this and that side greedily, to catch what may supply a fuel; much more will other creatues act vehemently for that which preserves their being: the toad to its plantain, the swallow to its celandine, the babe to the breast, and the Christian to the word. There is in the new creature an impetus and force settled in the soul to do good. It is a baptism of fire following that with water. The Spirit is first as water, washing us from our filth; then as fire, quickening us with grace: Mat. 3:11, 'I baptize you with water, he shall baptize you with the Holy Ghost and with fire.' In this respect it is likened to creatures of the greatest activity, fire, wind, a spring of living water; what more active in the rank of corporeal beings than fire and wind, either above or in the bowels of the earth? Witness the many stately buildings speedily consumed by the one or overthrown by the other. The new principle in the creature fills every part, dissolves the hard, melts the lumpish leaden heart, and makes it moveable in the ways of God with a glowing heat. But above this there is a higher denomination; the new creature is called spirit: John 3:6, 'That which is born of the Spirit is spirit;' that is, a spiritual creature. The activity of a spirit doth unconceivably surmount that of a body; what vast strides can a spirit take in a moment, from heaven to earth! The habit of sin in respect of its vehemency to evil is called a spirit, 'a spirit of whoredom,' Hosea 4:12; as well as the habit of grace, in respect of its vehemency to good, 'a spirit of love,' 2 Tim. 1:7. How active is the new creature in its motion to God! It can fly in a thought from earth to heaven, enter the bosom of God, clasp about him, hold him fast, even till almightiness bids him let him alone. Where there are rivers of living water in the belly, they will flow, John 7:38; where there is a divine habit, the soul will have a paraoxysm of divine heat for the glory [of] God, Acts 17:16. Paul's spirit was stirred in him upon the sight of the Athenians' idolatry. If created to good works, then not to a dull and sluggish motion in them; this was not the intendment of the Creator, and therefore not the disposition of the creature.

(4.) It is unboundedly active. This new creature's desires are as large as his nature, he cannot be bound up in the narrow and contracted motions of his former disposition. The natural activity of the soul overflows, like a swelled river, all natural bounds, since it is possessed by a spiritual habit. A man without a habit in an art, doth but bungle at his work, is quickly tired, desponds of attaining what he would; but he that hath a habit, suppose of mathematical knowledge, finds one proposition following upon another, one deduction rising up from another, that he hath a largeness, he knows not where to end; so the new creature finds one affection coming upon the neck of another many times in transports and out-goings to God, which knows no limits. It is unboundedly active;—

[1.] In affections to God. The new creature would be as unlimited in its affections to God, as God is in his affection to him. It will not fix lower than the object it hath pitched upon in heaven; all its operations tend thither; nothing below can give them a cessation, though they may suffer an interruption; it flies up, and is pulled back; it mounts again and again, follows hard on after the Lord. His affections are larger than his ability. 'Whom have I in heaven but thee? and there is none in earth that I desire besides thee,' Ps. 73:25. He seems to scorn everything else in comparison of God, though it were an angel, like a man that makes haste to some mark, turns the impediments on this side and that side. The new creature puts by the temptations of the flesh and the world, to make its way into the bosom of God, the centre of its rest, and the boundless limit of its soul. The sun, so many thousand miles distant from us, sends its rays as far as the lowest valley of the earth; and the new creature, the dartings of his soul to the highest heavens. 'Where the Spirit of the Lord is, there is liberty,' 2 Cor. 3:16, 17, the veil is taken away, it 'beholds, as in a glass, the glory of the Lord;' like an eagle, mounts up as near as it can to the sun, peers upon it till its eyes be dazzled with its brightness; he is never glutted with the views of him; his desires for him are never bounded but by him; one breathing after another, that he may fill God, as it were, with his affections, as he is filled by him with his Spirit. In his obedience, too, he would have his 'heart enlarged,' that he may 'run,' not creep, in the ways of God's commandments, Ps. 119:32; it is his grief that he cannot keep pace with God's commandments; it is his joy that God flies upon the wings of the wind to him, and his sorrow that he cannot fly upon the wings of the wind to God. He groans under his dulness, and his pleasure consists much in a liberty in God's service.

[2.] In disaffection to sin. He hates that body of death which hinders the accomplishment of the desires of his soul, and regards it at no other rate than his fetter, disease, and torture. He is discomposed when he meets with any check in his religious course; it is a violence to his new nature, and he cannot bear it without regret. His anger and impatience rises with as much force against any obstacle to a free converse with God, as it did before against any impediment in the way of his lust. Nature is restless till it hath got the conquest of the disease and corrupt humours of the body. Neither can a new creature be at quiet, till all that is against the interest of the new nature be purged out; and to that purpose he daily knocks at heaven gates for new strength and recruits of power against sin in the spiritual conflict. It is a trouble to him that he hath not as full a sense of his own corruptions as he would, and therefore he goes frequently to God to beg new discoveries of sin, that he may fetch his enemy out of his holds and skulks, and beat it to death; for by this habit the understanding is more quick in discerning the first rising of any sinful motion, and sensible of the least touch contrary to the new interest of it.

(5.) The new nature is powerfully active. There is not only an unbounded affection, but there is a power inherent in this habit to enable the soul to act; all habits add strength to the faculty. It is therefore called 'might in the inner man,' Eph. 3:16; and a 'spirit of power,' 2 Tim. 1:7. It is put as a stock into the heart, to maintain the acts of holiness; as there is a stock of sap in the root to produce branches and fruit. A power of acting is alway united with a form, and rooted in it. In regard the new nature is implanted by a higher cause than any moral habits, even by the Spirit of God, it must be able to do more than any moral nature can; and being more excellent than moral nature, must produce more excellent operations, otherwise it were not of a more excellent kind, if it had not a more excellent power. Jesus Christ was appointed to be a quickening Spirit, to convey a powerful life, to enable us to live to God. 'The kingdom of God' in the heart, as well as that in the world, 'is not in word, but in power,' 1 Cor. 4:20. Move steel as often as you will, you can never make it of itself move towards the north; but by the impression made on it by the loadstone, there is a power derived to turn and stand that way of its own accord. By nature we are 'without strength,' Rom. 5:6, because without life, Eph. 2:1. But in the renewing there is strength conveyed together with life; an ability to walk in God's statutes, conveyed with the new heart; out of weakness the soul is made strong; and the grace within, in concurrence with the supplies of the Spirit, is sufficient for it. It is not only an outward strength, as is from a staff in a sick man's hand, but an inward might. But besides this inherent strength there is an adherent ability; for Christ, who is his life, Col. 3:4, is also his strength: Philip. 4:13, 'I can do all things through Christ which strengthens me.' So that whatsoever active power is wanting in itself can be supplied by the head. And therefore the new creature hath a kind of almighty power of activity, by the communication of another, which is called a greatness of power, and a mighty power which works towards them, or, εἰς ἡμᾶς, in them that believe, Eph. 1:19. This power doth reside in the heart, and this adherent power is ready for it, but neither of them is alway perceptible, but upon some emergency, as a sound man hath a greater power to act than he puts forth upon all occasions.

(6.) It is easily active. Since that motion to God, and for God, is connatural and voluntary, and a power and ability also in the new creature, it must follow that the motion is very easy. Habits are to strengthen the faculty, and facilitate the acting of it. Bubbling is no pain to a fountain;

rivers of water flow out of the belly easily, because naturally. The motion of this habit is as easy as the motion of the lungs, or the pulse of the artery; though constant, yet not troublesome or painful in itself, but by reason of some imparted humour settled in them. This stock of grace is called the unction: 1 John 2:20, 'But you have an unction from the Holy One;' the inward oiling the soul, as oil communicates agility to the body. This unction some understand of habitual grace conveyed from the Holy One by the Spirit. As this unction upon our Saviour was the cause of his activity for God in doing good,—Acts 10:38, 'God anointed Jesus of Nazareth with the Holy Ghost and with power; who went about doing good,'—so it being the same in the new creature, will have the like effect upon him. Supernatural motions are as easy, by the strength of a supernatural habit, as natural motions are by the strength of natural habits. A bird doth with as much ease fly upward as a beast walks upon the ground, and the seed doth with as much ease spring up, and put its ear out of the ground, as a bitter root doth its unwholesome fruits and flowers. So when the soul is filled with this new habit, the walks in the ways of God are as easy by virtue of it as a course of sin and folly was before. The yoke of itself is easy, Mat. 11:30, and the motion under a light yoke cannot be grievous. The very yoke is not a shackle and burden, but a privilege. There is indeed some reluctancy sometimes, which ariseth not from the will as renewed, but from some evil habits resident in the soul, not yet fully conquered by renewing grace. You know how the apostle Paul doth distinguish between the posture of his will, and the interruptions by that sin which dwelt in him, Rom. 7:18–20.

(7.) It is pleasantly active. Ἡδὺ μὲν τὸ κατὰ φύσιν, saith the philosopher. As all actions which flow from life are pleasant, so those which flow from a divine life in the soul. It is a joy to a just man to do judgment, Prov. 21:15. That is, the entire inclination of the soul stands right to such actions; and as much a joy to him to do judgment, when enabled thereunto by a gracious habit, as it is to a sinful man under the bonds of iniquity to commit it. His soul leaps as much at an opportunity of pleasing God, as John Baptist did in his mother's womb at the appearance of Christ, as much as his heart sprang up before at the proposal of a sinful object. Never did the sun naturally rejoice so much 'like a strong man to run its race' in the heavens, Ps. 19:5, as the new man doth spiritually rejoice to run his race to heaven. It is a mighty pleasure to have our spiritual enemies under our feet, to be estranged from them. It is the purest delight to comply with God, and be embosomed in him. He is swallowed up in these choicer pleasures, as a man that hath had his full draughts of learning is in his studies, whence his diseases cannot draw him, though in his childish time he counted them his task and burden.* The delights of an heart seasoned with habitual grace are more ravishing than all the pleasures of sense, because they arise from an habit planted in the soul by that Spirit which is a Spirit of joy as well as of grace. The fatness of God's house, the sacrifices presented by him, are his delight, and he drinks of a river of pleasure in his very acts of worship: Ps. 36:8, 'They shall be abundantly satisfied with the fatness of thy house, and thou shalt make them drink of the rivers of thy pleasures.' 'In keeping thy commandments there is great reward,' Ps. 19. He finds much sweetness in the very acts of worship. Ah, how can the motions of the habits of sin, under the quarrels of conscience, yield as much delight as the habits of grace under the breathings of the Spirit! The very marks of Christ in his body are his delight and triumph. He takes pleasure in distresses for Christ's sake: 2 Cor. 12:10, saith the apostle, 'I take pleasure in infirmities, in reproaches, in necessities, in persecutions, in distresses for Christ's sake.' The motions of his soul to Christ are his life and joy. He chides his soul that her flights to Christ are not so strong as Christ's flights to him. He would have a delight in doing the will of God's precept, as Christ had in doing the will of the mediatory command. He rejoices in his breathings after God, though he wants him, and is glad his soul can have any flights towards him though he cannot find him. The tabernacles of God are amiable, when his 'heart and his flesh cries out for the living God:' Ps. 84:1, 2, 'How amiable are thy tabernacles, O Lord! my soul longs, yea, even faints for the courts of the Lord.' And when, by reason of some distemper, he cannot move so readily, some disease fetters him, some corruption hath cast a clog upon him, yet he delights in the thoughts of what he had, as a man in the former converses with his friend, though now at a distance, and cheers up his soul with the thoughts that he will again return: Ps. 42:5, 11, 'Why art thou cast down, O my soul? hope thou in God, for I shall yet praise him.' He grieves because he at present cannot do what he would, and hopes for another frame, and rejoices in the faith that he shall repossess it: 'He will turn again,' &c., Micah 7:19. A natural man without an habit of grace may move in some ways outwardly good, but with some reluctance, and without any pleasure in the goodness of the thing enjoined, or the goodness of that God who enjoins it. He may have a sudden inclination to do a good action, but he is not pleased with that inclination itself. Ahab's humiliation was good in itself, no doubt, but Ahab was pleased with it, but not as it was a humiliation, or had a likeness to a gracious action, or a tendency to the pleasing God, but as it was a means of removing the judgment threatened, so that his pleasure was only in the issue of it; but a gracious soul is pleased with the habit itself, for he considers it as the perfection of his nature, regards it as an ancient inmate, though separated from his nature by Adam's degeneracy, as friends long absent rejoice in one another. When this rectitude is in part restored, and understood to be of kin to it by creation, but lost and now returned, there must needs be an high complacency in the soul, and a joyful compliance with it. And the stronger and more vigorous this inward rectitude is in habit, the more pleasure a man hath in the exercise of it. As God, who is infinitely righteous in all his ways and in all his works, has an infinite pleasure in the exercise of this righteousness, and an infinite loathing of what is contrary to it, because it is his infinite nature, so the stronger the habit in a man, the more contentment there is in the exercise of it, because his nature is more elevated. And what is natural is delightful; and the more natural, the more delightful. Mercy is natural to God, therefore he delights in it; and because infinitely natural, therefore he doth infinitely delight in it.

Well then, since all the motions of nature are pleasant, the new nature is not inferior in the pleasure of acting to any other nature whatsoever. It being the perfectest nature, must beget the most delightful operations. What a pleasure is it to draw near to God, to melt before him, to pour out a prayer to him, and dissolve itself into love and affection in any address to him!

(8.) It is a permanent activity. There is a spring of perpetual motion. The fountain doth constantly bubble. The sun doth constantly move, because naturally. Whatsoever is natural is constant in its posture;* fire perpetually burns, and water perpetually cools. What is the essential property of a thing doth competere semper. A man is alway rational, and ready to act reason; if there be any indisposition, it is not in the soul, but in the organ or ill habit of the body, which doth obstruct the motions of the soul, and is an unfit instrument for it to act by. This habit is not a passion, but a principle; not a motion, but a spring of uniform motion; it is wrought in the nature, and like the heart is continually beating. The principle is permanent, it is an abiding anointing, 1 John 2:27, it is settled by God, given to us in Christ, backed and assured by the earnest of the Spirit in the heart, where this habit is seated. All is expressed, 1 Cor. 1:21, 22, 'Now he which establisheth us with you in Christ, and hath anointed us, is God, who hath also (that is, beside this) sealed us, and given the earnest of the Spirit in our hearts.' It is a life and habit more fixed than that in Adam: his life depended upon the rectitude of his soul, but this depends principally upon the power of the Spirit, and the everlasting life of Christ. It is a water which quencheth all thirst, and never leaves springing till it mount up to eternal life, John 4:14; it is perpetually active and springing, till it be swallowed up in glory, as rivers in the sea. Others may move by some wires, and have some strains of a natural religion, by some sudden impulses which touch the strings and faculties of the soul; but the wires break, the touch ceaseth, and the motion with it, it hath no living spring. Nay, sometimes those motions in natural men under the gospel may be more quick, and warm, and violent for a time than the natural motion of this habit; as the motion of a stone out of a sling is quicker than that of life, but faints by degrees, because it is from a force impressed, not implanted and inherent in the nature. They are just like water heated by the fire, which hath a fit of warmth, and may heat other things; but though you should heat it a thousand times, the quality, not being natural, will vanish, and the water return to its former coldness. But the new heart being in the new creature, causeth him to walk in the statutes of God, not by fits and starts, but with an uniform and harmonical motion, Ezek. 36:27, 'Ye shall keep my judgments and do them;' you shall treasure them in your minds and act them in your lives. Not but that there are in the new creature some faintings; it is sometimes more vigorous, sometimes more weak in its motion; it hath its sicknesses; it meets with wounds, but none of them to death. Every one that is born of the Spirit is like the wind, John 3:8, it moves and blusters, and when you think it is passed away, it returns, resumes its force, and you feel as stiff a motion as you did before. A man is never weary of that which is habitual to him. There may be a weariness in duty and service, but not a weariness of it, so as to throw it off; but after he hath refreshed and recruited himself, his habit will put him upon a delightful return to it. Where the ways of God are in the heart habitually, such shall go from strength to strength, till they appear in Sion, though there may be some rests and intermissions by the way: Ps. 84:5, 6, 'In whose heart are the ways of them;' some read, 'the high way of God in their hearts,' more consonant to the Hebrew.

(9.) It is an orderly motion and activity. Natural motions are orderly. As affirmative precepts bind semper, but not ad semper, so this habit enables the soul semper, but not ad semper; I mean, not to this or that service at all times. Natural things have their stated times, places, and measures. As trees bring forth fruit in their season, so doth the new creature bring forth fruit 'in his season,' Ps. 1:3, in a season proper for that fruit. It is alway producing some fruit or other, according to the particular seasons, sometimes love, sometimes humility, sometimes patience. This habit is ready at hand, whence he draws out fruits new and old.* As God doth all things in weight, and number, and measure, so doth this habit of his own implanting. As God gives every creature meat in due season, so the new creature renders God his fruit in due season. As a wicked man is always acting sin, sometimes one, sometimes another, according to the seasons of them, so doth this habit in the new creature act grace, sometimes one, sometimes another.

From all these things put together there follows,

1. A predominancy of grace in the new creature. As a state of nature consists in the prevalency of the corrupt habit which leavens the whole man, so the state of grace in a predominancy of the gracious habit, which spreads itself over the whole soul, striving with the powerful opposite, which in part resides there still. It is a habit put in to mate and destroy that habit of sin which was there before; the soul by it is made alive from the dead: Rom. 6:13, 'Yield yourselves to God, as those that are alive from the dead.' Life triumphs over death, grace over nature, whereby the members become instruments of righteousness unto God, instead of being instruments of unrighteousness unto sin. It is put in to guide reason and will, and therefore is invested with the sovereign power. As sense was first in man, but that veiled when reason stepped into the throne, as being a more excellent principle than sense, so must reason descend and give place to grace when that comes in, as being a more excellent principle than reason. It is reason it should have the sovereignty, for it doth but regain its own right, and take possession, which by the law of creation it ought to have kept till violently ejected by man. He

that hath this habit hath a spirit of might as well as of the fear of the Lord; the same spirit which was in Christ, which is a 'spirit of might,' Isa. 11:2. 'They that are Christ's have crucified the flesh, with the affections and lusts,' Gal. 5:24: have, not shall. As soon as ever they are Christ's, which they are by this principle, a deadly wound is given to sin; such a one scorns to have anything more to do with idols, Hosea 14:8. He overcomes the world: 1 John 5:4, 'Whatsoever is born of God overcomes the world.' He can do all things: enter the lists with the strongest Goliath, repel the sharpest temptations, through Christ which strengthens him, Philip. 4:13, so that grace is predominant.

2. There follows from hence a difficulty to sin. No creature can easily act against a rooted habit; how hard is it to make a beast do that which is different from and contrary to his nature! To act contrary to nature is burdensome and intolerable. What creature would willingly change its element? Will a bird sink of its own accord into the water, or a fish delight to leap upon the land, whose only element is the water? What creature would court the destruction of its life? What man would willingly deform and gash his own body? Men never do so by nature, but when frenzy hath dispossessed them of their reason. Sin must dispossess a Christian of his grace before it can be easy for him to run into ways destructive to his nature and blessedness. That principle which is in all natures must be more eminently in the highest nature, and proportionably in every nature that is of nearest approach to it. Righteousness and holiness is the very constitution of the new creature: Eph. 4:24, 'That new man, which after God is created in righteousness and true holiness.' It is as impossible for the new creature to sin by the influence of habit, as for fire to moisten by the quality of heat, or water to burn by the quality of cold. It is as impossible for that habit to bring forth the fruits of sin, as for the sun to be the cause of darkness, or a sweet fig-tree to bring forth sour fruit. Yet as there is darkness in the air, though the sun be up, by the interposition of thick clouds, so is there darkness in the new creature from the habit of

sin in the soul, which is not only a lodger, but an unwelcome inhabitant: Rom. 7:20, 'Sin that dwells in me' still, and acts according to its nature, though much over-powered and weakened by degrees by that habit of grace. Therefore it is a hard thing for him to sin: 1 John 3:9, 'He cannot sin.' It is as hard for him to contradict the new nature as before to cross the old: 'I cannot do this wickedness,' saith Joseph; it is against the frame and disposition of my soul.

(1.) It must be difficult to sin against 'purpose of heart,' which is the lowest step of the new nature, Acts 11:23, though it be not hard to sin against a flashy resolve.

(2.) It is hard for a man to sin who hath cordially chosen God for his portion, which every new nature doth, with a fixed resolution to keep his word: Ps. 119:57, 'Thou art my portion, O Lord: I have said that I would keep thy word.' When it is carried out with a free motion to God, it cannot easily be diverted from that charming object; he cannot but value any diversion at no better a rate than that of punishment.

(3.) It is difficult for him to contradict the new habit, wherewith he is so highly pleased, and which he is assured hath nothing but happiness in the womb of it.

(4.) It must be difficult for him to act that which, by virtue of this habit, he is daily in the mortification of.

(5.) It is difficult for the habit of sin in him to do the same acts after it hath received a deadly wound, as for a wounded man to do that which he could when he was sound.

(6.) This nature cannot be in a man without an universal enmity to sin, though it may without an universal victory; this belongs to the perfection of it, but enmity to the very constitution of it: Gen. 3:15, 'I will put enmity between the seed of the woman and the seed of the serpent.' He can at the best but half sin, and scarce that; he could not commit sin very freely before, because of the reluctancy of natural conscience; he can less freely do it now, since there is a habit of grace in him, which doth more powerfully fly in the face of sin when it appears; therefore there can be but a partial will to it or delight in it. The new man in the heart can never do it; the old man remaining cannot fully do it, because of the contradiction it receives from the new habit. If he doth at any time sin, this new nature can no more be pleased with it than the nature of a man is with the poison which he hath wilfully taken, which will contest with it, and endeavour to expel it, whether a man will or no. So that if a new creature be catched at a disadvantage, and be bemired by the remaining habit of sin in the heart, his spirit is wounded, his soul bleeds, his conscience upbraids him, he is displeased with himself and with his sin, runs to God, searcheth into himself, calls heaven and earth to his assistance, sharpens his spiritual weapons, and by virtue of this habit in him is dissatisfied, and in little ease, till he hath overcome this rebellion of lust, dispossessed it, removed the guilt, and cast out the filth.

4. As we have considered this work as a change, a vital principle, a habit, so we will consider it as a law put into the heart. Every creature hath a law belonging to its nature, so hath the new creature. Man hath a law of reason, beasts a law of sense and instinct, plants a law of vegetation, inanimate creatures a law of motion. A new creature hath a law put into his heart: Jer. 31:23, 'I will put my law in their inward parts, and write it in their hearts,' cited by the apostle, Heb. 8:10. It is called the 'law of the mind,' Rom. 7:23, it beginning first in the illumination of that faculty. As sin begun first in a false judgment made of the precept of God, 'You shall be as gods, knowing good and evil.'

Now, as to this law put into the heart, you may know what is meant by it in some popositions.

(1.) This law of the mind, or law written in the heart, is not wholly the same with the law of nature. Some* indeed tell us that it is nothing but the law of right reason. But certainly they are mistaken,—it is a law of grace. The law of nature was the law of a covenant of works, this law of the mind is the law of the covenant of grace. The law of nature is in all men, this law of grace only in some; the law of nature was in Paul before his conversion, this law of the mind was in him upon his conversion. The law of nature consists not of faith in a mediator, but faith is a main part of the law of grace. The law of nature acquaints not a man with the knowledge of all sins, not with unbelief; this law of grace doth, for the conviction of this is a work of the Spirit: John 16:8, 9, 'Of sin, because they believe not in me.' The law of nature is the general work of the mediator in all men, 'who enlightens every man that comes into the world,' John. 1:9. This is the peculiar work of the Mediator, by his Spirit, in the hearts of those that believe; the law of nature doth not oppose sin as sin, this law of grace doth; the law of nature is no part of sanctification, for this is in men that are born of the flesh, are flesh still; but the law of the mind is a part of sanctification, and wars against the law of the members; there is indeed a war and a contest from the law of nature against some gross sins, but not against the law of sin in the members. As sin wars against the law of the mind, as a law of direction, so the law of the mind, or the law of grace, wars against sin, as it is a law which pretends to guide and order the ways of a man.

(2.) Yet it is the restoring of that law which was the law of nature originally. It is a renewing in the heart that law which was writ in the heart of Adam: Eph. 4:24, 'That new man, which after God is created in righteousness and true holiness;' or after God was created κτισθέντα, alluding to that righteousness wherein Adam was created, lost by him, and restored by Christ. This righteousness which Adam had was the righteousness of the law: holiness towards God, which includes the duties of the first table; righteousness, including the duties of the second table; and truth being added (as it may be referred both to holiness and righteousness), shews the sincerity of it in the manner and the end of being holy to God and righteous to man. This was the law written in the heart originally, which was defaced by the fall; and whatsoever relics there were of this law in man, were only upon the account of the mediation of

Christ; it is this law which is new engraven in the soul by regeneration. God doth not say, I will write another law in their hearts, but 'my law,' Jer. 31:33,—that which was my standing law, my law to Adam, and to your fathers. The law written in the heart is not substantially distinct from that in the nature of Adam. Man by his fall did blot this law, lost his righteousness, had an enmity in his heart to it, and to the very relics of it. He is not naturally subject to the law, nor can be, as it is the law of God, because of his enmity to God, Rom. 8:7; the law of sin had taken place instead of it. Regeneration is a taking down the law of sin, and fixing the law of God in its due place and posture.

(3.) This law is written in the heart wholly. The whole law, every command which hath the print of God upon it, is written there. As God writ his whole law in tables of stone, so he writes the whole law in the 'fleshly tables of the heart,' 2 Cor. 3:3. It is true holiness and righteousness; true, as to its essential and integral parts. God doth not write one part of the law upon the heart, and leave out another; it is not a moiety of it, the impression of one command, and the defect of another. If it were not the whole law, something belonging to the essence of a new creature would be wanting. It would not be a new creature, because it would be a monster, wanting something necessarily requisite to the constitution of it, and would not be a new creature according to the original copy. Where there is an agreeableness in one nature to another, it is to the whole nature, the nature of the soul to the nature of the law.

(4.) This law written in the heart doth not make the outward law useless, for that is still a rule. This inward law written in the heart is a conformity to the outward rule, and therefore is not a rule itself. The law in the heart is imprinted by the external word in the hand of the Spirit; and therefore to try the truth of the law within, we must have recourse to the law written. If a man hath any notions of any human law, he must consult the law written, to know whether his notions of it be right, and whether his actions be according to the letter and reason of the law or no. As the law of sin within a man is not the rule of judging of sin, but the law of God, so neither is the law of grace within the rule of judging good, but the word of God. The law within, though it be commensurate to the law in its essential parts, yet it is imperfect as yet; but a rule ought to be perfect, Ps. 19:7, and so the written law is. It is this law written in the word that we are to take heed to, for the cleansing of our ways: Ps. 119:9, 'Thy word have I hid in my heart, that I might not sin against thee.' When this writing of the law in the heart was promised, ver. 11, there was also an inward teaching promised: Jer. 31:32, 'And they shall teach no more every man his neighbour, saying, Know the Lord;' which is spoken in regard of the abundance of the knowledge which should be in the time of gospel light, above what was in the twilight of Jewish ceremonies; so that the weakest Christian under the gospel knows more of God and his attributes in Christ, than the greatest Jewish doctor did before the coming of Christ. This was not so understood by Christ, as if teaching others were utterly useless; for then why should he institute apostles, pastors, teachers, &c., and promise to be with them to the end of the world, if this promise of inward teaching made outward teaching useless? In like manner, neither doth the writing the law in the heart make the outward written law useless, but rather it doth establish and advance it, and the esteem of it. The outward law is the rule, as the model of a house is the rule by which a carpenter is to make a building, and to which he is to conform that idea he hath in his mind of it; but that idea or figure of it which he hath in his mind, is to be suited to that rule which is prescribed to him in the outward pattern; and therefore that pattern is to be consulted with. The law of God is of eternal duration; and as it is a law of holiness and love of God, doth oblige every reasonable creature, in what condition soever he be, whether of nature, grace, or glory.

Quest. Wherein doth this writing of the law in the heart consist?

Ans. (1.) In an inward knowledge of the law, and approbation of it in the understanding. The knowledge of righteousness and the being of the law in the heart, are put together as the proper character of the people of God: Isa. 51:5, 'Hearken to me, ye that, know righteousness, the people in whose heart is my law.' Lest they should think a knowledge were enough, he adds, 'In whose heart is my law;' not in the head, but in the heart. There is in a renewed understanding, a principle teaching how to make use of the law. It is like the inward skill of a pilot, who guides the ship by the compass and rudder. The outward law is the compass by which we must steer; the inward law is the practical knowledge of this; an inward skill to make application of it to particular occasions. The word of God being a seed, doth, as every seed, produce a being like itself, and like that plant whose seed it is; from the seed of corn ariseth a grain of the same nature. This seed being sown first in the understanding, is there cherished, and grows up in principles and thoughts agreeable to itself, whereby the mind becomes the epistle of Christ, 2 Cor. 3:3, and an ark to preserve the tables of the law; whence David speaks of his soul keeping God's testimonies, Ps. 119:167, and not forgetting them, ver. 16. The new creature by its new light sees an amiableness in the law, a holiness in the precepts, and a filthiness in himself thereby.

(2.) It consists in an inward conformity of the heart to the law. The soul hath a likeness to the word and doctrine of the gospel within it; it is delivered into that mould: Rom. 6:17, 'You have obeyed from the heart that form of doctrine, into which you were delivered.' He considers the gospel as a mould, and the Romans as a metal poured into it, and putting on the form of it. As melted metal poured into a mould loses its former form, and puts on a new shape, the same figure with the mould into which it is poured; the soul, which before was a servant of sin, and had the image of the law of sin, being melted by the Spirit, is cast into the figure and form of the law. As when a seal hath made its impression upon wax, the stamp in the one answers exactly to the stamp on the other, put the seal on again, and they both will meet as close as if they were one body, the wax will fill every cavity in the seal; but put this seal to any impression made by another seal, there will be an inequality, the stamp on the seal and that on the wax will not close. The law of sin and the law of God, being contrary impressions, cannot close together; but the law of grace in the heart and the law of God close, they being but one and the same stamp. So that when any command of God appears, a new creature finds something within it of kin to it; as a natural man finds something ready to close with sin upon the appearance of it. The heart answers to the law as a lock to a key, ward for ward; sometimes it may not answer but resist, as a lock doth, because of some rust or some filth got up into it; but then it needs not a new making but a new cleansing, to answer exactly to the key of the law. So that as the 'Gentiles, having not the law, are a law to themselves,' Rom. 2:14, having it writ upon their minds in those notions common to mankind, so the new creature, if he had not the written law, would be a law to himself. So natural is this conformity, that were there no law without, the renewed soul would naturally be carried out in the ways of holiness. 'The law,' saith the apostle, 'is not made for a righteous man,' 1 Tim. 1:9; it is not chiefly intended for the righteous, but for the unrighteous, who would not stir one step in any good action without it, and will hardly stir with it. There would be no need of any written law in a commonwealth, if all men had an exact justice and righteousness in their own minds, and did jointly conspire to the good of the community. But when disturbers of the peace and common welfare start up, there is need then of public laws to restrain them. But there is no need of a public enacting of a law for them that are good, because what the law enjoins they do by their own judgment and inclination. So that what a new creature dot in observance of the law, is from natural freedom, choice, and judgment, and not by the force of any threatenings annexed to it.

(3.) It consists in a strong propension to the obedience of it. As there was a strong impetus in the old nature, inclining it to sin, so there is a strong impulse in the new nature, biassing it to observe the commands of the law. In this respect it is chiefly called a law written in the heart, in regard of the efficacious virtue of this new nature, sweetly constraining and directly conducting to the performance of it. The law without us commands us, the law within constrains us. That enjoins a thing to be done, this inclines us to the doing of it.* The first law is written in the Scripture or in the conscience, whereby we judge those commands to be kept; the other consists in the propension of love, or faith working by love. As the impulse of concupiscence is called 'the law of sin,' Rom. 7:25, so the impulse of grace is called the law in the heart; not as a thing distinct from the law without, but only a counterpart of it, an indenture answering to the other. They are but two parts united between themselves, and compose one perfect law; one as the direction, the other as the practice. That lays the injunction, this embraceth it; and as naturally from the disposition of the new nature as he did embrace the law of sin from the disposition of the old. It is a powerful operative law of the Spirit of life, which 'sets us free from the law of sin and death,' Rom. 8:2; not a dead letter, but an active principle, quickening the heart to close with the law, and delivering it from that which was the great hindrance to it. As the devil doth act in men's hearts, Eph. 2:2, not personally, but by a principle in the heart, the law of sin, so doth the Spirit of life by the law of grace; for being writ by a living Spirit, it is a living law. This is the chief intent of the whole new creation, to cause us to walk in God's statutes, Ezek. 36:26, 27. Ps. 37:31, 'The law of God is in his heart, none of his steps shall slide.' The soul being thus evangelised and spiritualised, may be said to do by nature the things contained in the gospel, as the Gentiles are said to do by nature the things contained in the law, Rom. 2:14, because there was a law of nature engraven in them.

(4.) It consists in a mighty affection to the law. What is in the word a law of precept, is in the heart a law of love; what is in the one a law of command, is in the other a law of liberty. 'Love is the fulfilling of the law,' Gal. 5:14. The law of love in the heart, is the fulfilling the law of God in the Spirit. It may well be said to be written in the heart, when a man doth love it. As we say, a beloved thing is in our hearts, not physically, but morally, as Calais was said to be in Queen Mary's heart. They might have looked long enough before they could have found there the map of the town; but grief for the loss of it killed her. It is a love that is inexpressible. David delights to mention it in two verses together: Ps. 119:47, 48, 'I will delight myself in thy commandments, which I have loved: my hands will I lift up to thy commandments, which I have loved;' and often in that psalm resumes the assertion. Before the new creation, there was no affection to the law: it was not only a dead letter, but a devilish letter in the esteem of a man: he wished it razed out of the world, and another more pleasing to the flesh enacted. He would be a law to himself; but when this is written within him, he is so pleased with the inscription, that he would not for all the world be without that law, and the love of it: whereas what obedience he paid to it before, was out of fear, now out of affection; not only because of the authority of the lawgiver, but of the purity of the law itself. He would maintain it with all his might against the power of sin within, and the powers of darkness without him. He loves to view this law; regards every lineament of it, and dwells upon every feature with delightful ravishments. If his eye be off, or his foot go away, how doth he dissolve in tears, mourn and groan, till his former affection hath recovered breath, and stands upon its feet! If he finds not his heart answering the law, he longs after the precepts, as the prophet saith: Ps. 119:40, 'I have longed after thy precepts, quicken me in thy righteousness.' He longs to join hands again with the holiness of them. As his heart is inclined to obey it, so it is wounded upon any neglect of it, and never at ease, till he be reduced to his former delight in it. He hath no mind ever to part with it, because of its intrinsic goodness, as well as conveniency for him. It is his pleasure, not his confinement; his ornament, not his fetter; he hates every thing that is contrary to it. How doth Paul grieve and groan under 'the body of death,' when he considered what opposition 'the law in his members made against the law of his mind'? Rom. 7:23, 24. The law in his members 'brought him into captivity to the law of sin.' Then, 'Oh wretched man that I am!' though he knew he was in part delivered from it. How doth he long for a perfect redemption from his shackles, which hindered him from following the law of his delight! And he that never murmured at his sufferings, but could glory in persecutions and death for Christ, seems to be impatient till he could hear the last expiring groan of this enemy: all which was the effect of his 'delight in the law of God after the inward man,' ver. 22. And that this writing the law doth principally consist in this affection, those two expressions, 'putting the law into the inward parts,' and 'writing it in the heart,' intimate. The nature of man being enmity against the law of God, the writing it argues, not a change of the law, but a change of the frame of the heart to the law, that should be so fashioned, that the law should reign there, and all his affections subscribe to it. As the writing the law in the heart of Christ was nothing else but the agreeableness of the mediatory law to him, and his delight in it, Ps. 40:8, so it is with a new creature.

(5.) It consists in an actual ability to obey. Writing the law in the heart implies a putting a power and strength into the soul, enabling it to run the ways of God's commandments, as well as to incline the heart and affections to them; the promise is made to the latter times: not but that the ancient patriarchs were regenerate, but not by the law, not by any covenant of works: this ability did not reside in the law, but was transferred to them from the gospel. In this respect it is called 'a letter,' 2 Cor. 3:6, because it did only instruct the eye or ear, when read or heard: this teaches the heart; that a killing letter, this a quickening Spirit; that exacted the observance of its precepts, but writ nothing in the heart to answer it, but condemned upon neglect; this commands the observance of the law, and gives an ability evangelically to perform it. That was a ministration of condemnation, this of righteousness, 2 Cor. 3:9; that could do no other but condemn, because it gave no intrinsic power to oberve it. It is through Jesus Christ that we are enabled, by virtue of this inward writing, to serve with our minds the law of God, though in our flesh we be captivated by the law of sin. As an unregenerate man is dragged to any good, but willingly obedient to the motions of sin, so a regenerate man is sometimes under the rape of sin, but is willingly obedient to the motions of grace. So that the law is written in the heart, in respect of the assent of the understanding, consent of the will, pleasure of the affections: in the understanding, by the clearness of the light of faith; in the will, by the heat of the fire of love. In the understanding there is a judicious approbation of it; in the will, a motion to it, closing with it, and an affection to keep it; and, according to its ability, an endeavour to keep pace with it.

5. The fifth thing. As there is a vital principle, an habit, a law written in the heart, so there is a likeness to God in the new creature. Every creature hath a likeness to something or other in the rank of beings: the new creature is framed according to the most exact pattern, even God himself. In this the form of regeneration doth consist. The new creature is begotten; begotten, then, in the likeness of the begetter, which is God. As sin is the impression of Satan's image, which was drawn over all by the fall, so renewing grace is the impression of the image of God; for it is a quite contrary thing to corruption. This likeness to God was man's original happiness in creation, and is his restored happiness in redemption: Col. 2:10, 'renewed in knowledge after the image of him that created him.' His misery consisted in losing it; our felicity, therefore, doth consist in recovering it. Hence it is called a 'divine nature,' 2 Peter 1:4. Every thing receives its denomination from the better part. A man is denominated rational, though he hath both a sensitive principle common with beasts, and a vegetative, or growing principle, common with plants; so a new creature is denominated divine, because grace, a divine principle, is superior in the soul. Every perfection in the creature

is supposed to be essentially somewhere. Every impression supposeth a seal that stamped it; every stream a fountain from whence it sprang; every beam a sun from whence it is shot. Grace being the highest perfection of the creature, must be somewhere essentially. Where can that be but in God? His womb and power is the womb that bare it, and the breasts which gave it suck. It must then have a resemblance to him, as a child to the father, the copy to the original. We are said to be 'born of God,' 1 John 3:9. Now to be born of any thing is to receive a form like that, which the generating person hath. But,

(1.) It is not a likeness to God in essence: it is no participation of the essence of God. It is a nature, not the essence; a likeness in an inward disposition, not in the infinite substance, which is communicated by generation only to the Son, and by procession to the Holy Ghost. The divine essence is incommunicable to any creature. Infiniteness cannot be represented, much less communicated. Man is no more renewed according to God's image, than he was at first created according to it, Gen. 1:27; which was not a communication of the divine essence, but of a righteousness resembling the righteousness of God, according to the capacity of Adam's nature; which image of God in Adam is by the apostle restrained to that of 'righteousness and true holiness,' Eph. 4:24. The likeness in a state of glory is founded upon a sight of God as he is, 1 John 3:2; which may more properly be meant of the seeing of Christ as he is in glory; for the apostle goes on in the discourse without naming of Christ; but without question means him, ver. 5, when he saith, that 'he was manifested to take away our sins.' We shall be like him, as we shall see him; therefore not in essence. His essence is concluded by most to be invisible, even in glory. How can finite creatures behold an infinite being? He must be God that knows God's essence. We shall understand him in his bowels, as a father; in his wise acts, as a governor; in his judicial acts, as a justifier; in his merciful acts, as a reconciler. We shall see him in all his relations to us. Such a vision we shall have, whatsoever it is, which shall transform us into as high a likeness to him as a finite creature is capable of. There can be no participation of the substantial perfections of God, which are incommunicable; for then it would not be a participation but an identity, oneness, or equality. God put in one letter, and the chiefest of his name, Jehovah, ◻which is twice repeated in it, into the names of Abraham and Sarai, reckoned Nehem. 9:7, as one of his favours to Abraham, but not the whole name, that is incommunicable; and Jacob's name is changed to that of Israel, putting in ◻◻,a communicable name of God.

(2.) Yet it is a real participation. It is not a picture, but a nature: it is divine. God doth not busy himself about apparitions. It is a likeness, not only in actions, but in nature. God communicates to the creature a singular participation of the divine vision and divine love; why may he not also give some excellent participation of his nature?* There is a nature; for there is something whereby we are constituted the children of God. A bare affection to God doth not seem to do this. Love constitutes a man a friend, not a son and heir by generation. The apostle argues, 'If children, then heirs,' Rom. 8:17. He could not argue in a natural way, if friends, then heirs. And the Scripture speaks of believers being the children of God, by a spiritual generation as well as by adoption. So that grace, which doth constitute one a child of God, is another form whereby a divine nature is communicated. Generation is the production of one living thing by another, in the likeness of its nature, not only in the likeness of love; so is regeneration. Were not a real likeness attainable, why should those exhortations be, of being 'holy as God is holy, pure as he is pure'? 1 Pet. 1:15, 1 John 3:3. The new creature receives the image of God; not as a glass receives the image of a man, which is only an appearance, no real existence; and though it be like the person, yet hath no communion with its nature; but as wax receives the image of the seal, which though it receives nothing of the substance, yet receives exactly the stamp, and answers it in every part. So the Scriptures represents it:

Eph. 1:13, 'You were sealed with that holy Spirit of promise.' Something of God's perfections are in the new creature by way of quality, which are in God by way of essence. In a word, it is as real a likeness to God as the creature is capable of, laid in the first draughts of it in regeneration, and completed in the highest measures in glory.

(3.) It is the whole image of God which is drawn in the new creature. It is 'the image of God,' Col. 3:10, not a part: a foot or a finger is but the image of those parts, not of a man. The members in a child answer to those in a parent, that is but a chip from the body of his father, though not in so great a proportion. The image of a man hath not only the face, or eyes, but the other members. Though a Christian may have one or two parts of this image more beautiful than the rest, as a man may have a sparkling eye that hath not a proportionable lip, yet he hath all the members of a man. The painter's skill appears in some lineaments more than in others. So the Spirit's wisdom appears in making some eminent in one grace, some in another, acording to his good pleasure; yet the whole image of God is imprinted there; it would be else not a likeness, but a monstrous birth in defect. 'The fruit of the Spirit is in all goodness, righteousness, and truth,' Eph. 5:9; and therefore the immediate effect of the Spirit in the soul is the engraving all goodness, righteousness, and truth in the essential parts of it. As God's nature is holy, his perfections holy, his actions holy, so holiness beautifies the nature, spirits the actions, and is writ upon all the endowments of a renewed man. There is an impression of the wisdom of God in the understanding, and of the holiness of God in the will.

(4.) It is more peculiarly a likeness to Christ, wherein we partake of his nature: 'He that doth righteousness is righteous, as Christ is righteous,' 1 John 3:7. There is a real likeness to Christ in righteousness, though not an equal perfection. The new nature is a draught of Christ, something of Christ put into the soul, such a likeness to Christ, that it seems to be (as it were) another Christ, as the image of the sun seems to be another sun in a pail of water, therefore called a 'forming of Christ in us,' Gal. 4:19. Not by any communication of his substance, either of the divine or human nature, but by conveying such affections into us, which bear a likeness to the affections of Christ. Hence we are exhorted to have 'the same mind which Christ had,' Philip. 2:5, and to 'arm ourselves with the same mind,' 1 Peter 4:1, which supposeth such a mind put into the new creature which he is to excite, and put into actual exercise. And the apostle speaks of a conformity to Christ in his death and resurrection, Philip. 3:10. And God did 'predestinate' all his own 'to be conformed to the image of his Son,' Rom. 8:29, συμμόρφους, of the same form and shape. Jesus Christ conformed himself to us, by assuming the human nature; and God conforms us to Christ, by bestowing upon us a divine. Hence we are said to be the seed of Christ, Isa. 53:10; not a carnal seed as the Jews say, and therefore deny Christ to be the Messiah, because he left no posterity. Whereas seed is spiritually understood, as in the first promise, the seed of the serpent or the devil. Devils do not beget, but metaphorically, as they instil their cursed principles into men; so Christ sows his principles in us, whereby we become his seed. Hence also renewed men are called 'his fellows,' Heb. 1:9. If fellows with him in the covenant, and fellows with him in glory, fellows also with him in his disposition of loving righteousness, and hating iniquity. This disposition was the inward motive of his death, and the foundation of his advancement. Without this disposition we cannot be conformable to him in his death, and consequently not his fellows in his advancement. The new creature is a likeness to Christ, therefore called the new man; as the natural man is like to Adam, therefore called the old man. The new man and old man are titles of Christ and Adam, and transferred upon others by a figure, metonymia causæ pro effectu. These are the heads and roots of the two distinct bodies of men in the world. All are in the old Adam by nature, and so partake of the old man; all believers are in the new Adam by faith, and so partake of the nature of the new man. As we did partake of Adam's nature by our natural birth, so we partake of the nature of Christ by our spiritual: by the one we have the 'image of the earthly,' by the other the new creature hath the 'image of the heavenly,' 1 Cor. 15:48, 49; the one derives sin, the other righteousness; they both imprint their image according to the quality of their extraction. Christ is full of purity, righteousness, charity, patience, humility, truth, and in a word, all the parts of holiness; then the form and image of Christ in the new creature can be no other than a lively representation of those divine qualities, a soul glittering with goodness, humility, &c., which the apostle comprehends in two words, 'righteousness and true holiness.' Therefore, if there be not a likeness to Christ in the frame and qualities of our souls, we are not born of him. No man will say an ox, or a sheep, or a dog descends from Adam, because they have not the likeness, shape, and qualities of Adam; neither can any man without such a likeness to Christ in faith, humility, patience, love, obedience, and minding the glory of God, number himself in the spiritual seed of Christ. He retains the nature poisoned by the serpent, creeping upon the earth, feeding upon the dust, not the nature formed by the eternal Spirit.

(5.) It is a likeness to the Spirit, which is the immediate cause of it. Therefore the new creature is called spirit in the abstract, as a natural man is called flesh in the abstract: John 3:6, 'That which is born of the flesh, is flesh; and that which is born of the Spirit is spirit.' As that which is born of the flesh is like to flesh in its nature, so that which is born of the Spirit is like to the Spirit in its nature, as light in the air, being the natural effect flowing from the sun, is like to that light which is in the sun; its relishes, delights, breathings, are according to its spiritual original; its motions, purposes, dispositions, are like those of the Holy Ghost, of whom it is born. The principles and impressions in the nature must be agreeable to those the Spirit hath. The Spirit is a Spirit of holiness, grace, love and zeal to the glory of God; his office is to exalt and glorify Christ. If we are renewed, then we shall have the same draught in our hearts, the same design; the fleshly principle will be changed into spiritual. They will be habitual too, as the frame of the Holy Spirit is. A natural man may do some acts that look like spiritual by fits and starts, but there is no settled principle; whereas the spirit in a new creature is a spirit of meekness, and curbs the passions; a spirit of humility, and overthrows pride; a spirit of zeal, and fires the heart; a spirit of power, and arms the soul against sin; a holy spirit, and therefore cleanseth it; an heavenly spirit, and therefore elevates it.

Quest. Wherein doth this likeness to God chiefly consist?

Ans. 1. In a likeness of affections. God is no bodily shape; we cannot be like him in our bodies, but in our souls, as they are spirits; but if there be a dissimilitude of affection and disposition, the unlikeness to God is greater than a likeness to him in point of the natural being. There is no draught of this image in us, unless we have a conformity of affections to God; it is then chiefly evidenced by a delighting in him, by faith and love, wherein we bear a resemblance to him in his affection to himself, by delighting in his image in others, wherein we imitate his affection to his creatures. He that loves not that image of God which is visible, cannot love the invisible original, 1 John 4:12, 20, and so, having no likeness to God in his affection, can have no likeness to God in his nature. And the apostle positively affirms, that 'he that loves, is born of God,' 1 John 4:7. The new creature extends its arms to every thing which hath a resemblance of that whose image it bears. The divine nature is chiefly seen in the objects of the affections, when they are set upon the same objects, and in a like manner as God's and Christ's are. When we grieve most for sin, for this grieves the Spirit, when we desire most an inward holiness, this God most longs for: 'Oh that there were such an heart in them!' When we hate sin as God hates it, because of the inward filthiness; when we love grace as God loves it, because of its native beauty; when we can love God and Christ above all the world, and other things in order to him and his glory; when we can trust Christ with all our concerns, and

God doth trust him with his glory: then, and not till then, there is an image of God in us, which God values above all the world. When the soul is thus touched and quickened by grace, she can no more strip herself of the object and manner of her affections, than she can of the affections themselves. And when she doth reach out herself to all that is good, and hath a complacency in it, it is her happiness, because it is the great likeness to the spring of happiness. When we have the like affections with God, we have in our measure a like happiness and blessedness with God.

2. In a likeness of actions. Men by sin are 'alienated from the life of God,' Eph. 4:17; by restoring grace then they are brought to have communion with God in his life, to live as God lives. By nature men live the life of beasts and devils; by grace they come to live the life of Christ. If he lives then the life of God, he must be comfortable in his actions to the acts of God. No nature is stripped of affections and actions proper to it; it would be else a picture without breath, a body without motion, a lifeless colour. The divine image is not a painted statue, but an active being. The nearer any thing approacheth in its nature to the fountain of life, the more of liveliness and activity it must needs partake of. The communicable perfections of God are enstamped upon the soul as a pattern to imitate, and as a principle to quicken. A new creature acts like God;* as melted and inflamed gold will act after the nature of fire, by the assistance of that quality communicated by the fire to it, so doth the soul by that divine quality it partakes of. It is as impossible that this image of God can produce anything but divine acts, as that the image of the sun in a burning glass should produce a darkness and coldness in the air. There will be the manifestation of the life of Christ in the motions of our soul, as the apostle speaks in case of sufferings for him there will be in our bodies, 2 Cor. 4:10. Natural men are called the devil's children, because they resemble him in nature and works, egging on to sin, and delighting themselves in their own and others' iniquities, John 8:44; so renewed men are God's children, because they live the life of God, and abound in

the works of God, 1 Cor. 15:58. As there is the same nature and the same spirit which Christ had, there will be a following of him in his works; all creatures of the same species have the same instinct, the same nature, the same acts that the first creature of that kind had originally in its creation. Grace being a new excellency advancing the soul to a higher state, endues it with a more noble kind of operation. Nothing is lifted up to a more perfect state of being, but in order to a more perfect manner of acting; if a beast should be elevated to the nature of man, would you then expect from him the actions of a beast still? And can any have the implantation of the divine nature, who hath only the actions of a man which bear no resemblance to God?

3. This likeness to God consists principally in a likeness to him in holiness. It is only 'he that doth righteousness is born of him:' 1 John 2:29, 'If you know that he is righteous, you know that every one that doth righteousness is born of him.' It is by this the children of God are manifest from the children of the devil, 1 John 3:10 in doing righteousness. If we are unlike to God in this, we are like him in nothing; God hath not a pretence of holiness, but a real purity. He that hath not 'escaped the corruption that is in the world through lust,' is no 'partaker of the divine nature;' the apostle puts that as a necessary qualification, 2 Peter 1:4. If by afflictions good men are partakers of God's holiness, much more by regeneration: Heb. 12:10, 'He chastened us for our profit, that we might be partakers of his holiness.' If God aim in his corrections at the bringing his people to partake with him in holiness, as a father doth at the reformation of his child, that he may be a follower of his virtues, much more doth God aim at it in regeneration, when a spirit of holiness is infused into the soul. The new creation is a drawing this excellency of God in the soul; if any attribute lift up his head above another, it is this; in this we chiefly are to imitate him; this is the greatest evidence of the divine nature. By sin we 'come short of that which is the glory of God, Rom. 3:23; by the renewing of the soul we attain the glory of God; that is,

attain a state of holiness, and at last a perfection of it, a communion with him in holiness here, and a full enjoyment of it hereafter. Whatsoever our fancies, our hopes, our presumptions are, if this be not drawn in our soul, if we have not an internal holiness, we are not new creatures, and therefore not in Christ.

Use 1. It serves for information. If regeneration be such an inward change, a vital principle, a law put into the heart, the image of God and Christ in the soul; then,

1. How few in the world are truly new creatures! Is the law transcribed in many men's lives? nay, can we all read it copied in our own hearts? Cannot many see the image of the devil sooner than the image of God in their own souls? Is not the law of sin writ in text letters, and with many flourishes, when the law of God is writ in characters hardly legible, and crowded into a narrow room? How many are changed from childhood to youth, from youth to manhood, from manhood to age, and the old nature still remaining in its full strength, and the body of death more vigorous than twenty or thirty years ago! Changed years, and unchanged hearts, are a very sad spectacle.

(1.) Profane men are numerous. None will offer to rank these in the number of new creatures. Such nasty souls are no branches of Christ, nor habitations for him; we read of the devil in swine, but never of our Saviour in swinish souls. Are such regenerate? Can brambles be ever accounted vines, or thistles fig-trees? These rather look like hellish than divine creatures; diabolical, not God-like natures. A devotedness to the sins of the flesh is inconsistent with the circumcision made by Christ: Col. 2:11, Putting off the body of the sins of the flesh, by the circumcision of Christ;' that is, the body of sins which exert themselves in the flesh or natural body; whereas such have the body of sin, with an activity in every member of it.* Is the image of Christ in such men? Is not he meek as a lamb? Are not they fierce as lions? Is not he holy, and they defiled with intemperance? Did not he labour for nothing but the glory of his Father, and the salvation of souls; and they mind nothing but the dishonour of God, and the destruction of themselves and others? Did not he do good to his enemies, and they scarcely spare their friends? Alas, with this contrariety, how can they pretend the image of Christ, when they have nothing but what looks like the image of his enemy the devil? Is not the gospel counted as great a foolishness by such, as at the first times of its publishing? Are not the great mysteries of God, and the contrivances of eternity, entertained with coldness, and sometimes with scoffs, and the word, the great instrument of this change, unregarded? Are such new creatures, that contemn the very means to attain it? Surely they are so far from being near the kingdom of God, that they are in the very suburbs of hell. Is a hugging base lusts against the light of nature, a contempt of God's law and authority, the nature of Christ? Were any such spots upon our Saviour's garment? Is this to be like him who was holy, harmless, separate from sin and sinners?

(2.) Among professors, is there much evidence of a new creation? When men shall say, All that the Lord speaks to us we will do, has not God as great occasion to say as he did of old, Deut. 5:24, 'Oh that there were such a heart in them, that they would fear me, and keep my commandments!' We may find a change of language in some, a change of outward actions in others, but how few are there among many who stand up before God with the breath of life! Here and there a man or woman, wherein God may see the image of his own nature. How few are they with whom Christ can shake hands, and justly call them his fellows! Christ may be in the mouth, and the devil formed in the heart; the name of Christ may be upon them, and the nature of Christ not in them. They may be born of the will of man in a religious education, but not born of the will of God in a spiritual regeneration. Is it not a graceless Christianity in many men, a faith without holiness, a Christianity without Christ? Regeneration is never without faith, love, and righteousness. They depend upon grace, as the property upon the form.

Wherever the new creation is, these are, for they are the qualities created; wherever they are not, there is nothing of a new creature, let the pretences be never so splendid. There may be a nearness to the kingdom of God by profession, when there is no right to it for want of regeneration. Instead of humility, according to our Saviour's pattern, doth not 'pride compass men as a chain,' Ps. 73:6, counting that their ornament, which is the strength of their old nature. Instead of patience, roaring passions; instead of meekness, boiling anger; instead of love, a glowing hatred. How few then are renewed! But few shall be saved, and therefore few regenerate. How little is the report of a likeness to God believed by the incredulous world! How few are the strivings of any towards heaven! Most lie quiet without any such motions, like the dust on the ground, unless some stormy affliction raise them a little towards heaven, whence they quickly fall back to their old place.

2. It informs us that a dogmatical change, or change of opinion, is not this new creature. It is not, if any man change his opinion from Gentilism to Christianity he is a new creature, but 'if any man be in Christ,' by a vital participation from union with him. As men generally place saving faith in dogmatical assents, so they place the new creation in a change of opinion, as well from truth to error as from error to truth, though there be no spiritual knowledge of God, nor internal cordial closing with the gospel, nor practice of it. Such a change may endue the head with a knowledge which never gently slides down to the affections. It may indeed have some influence upon the life, as this or that principle comes nearest to, or is divine truth, and is settled as an opinion in the soul; yet this great change may not be wrought. That is but a change in the head, this in the heart; that of opinion, this of affection; that perfects the understanding, this both the understanding and will, and the whole soul. There is a natural desire of knowledge, but a natural aversion from grace; whence this change becomes easy, the new-creature change difficult. A hot contriving head may have a cold and sapless heart. A head

informed by the knowledge of truth may be without a heart enlivened by the Spirit of truth. A head changed in opinion only will descend into the bottomless pit, when the least grain of renewing grace shall not receive so much as a singe from those flames. A change from error to truth, without a heart framed to the truth, doth but more settle a man upon his lees, and makes him not only more regardless, but opposite to a true change to God. It stores up wrath for him, and his very judgment will be a witness for the condemnation of his practice. The knowledge of God will not justify, but condemn a practical denial of him; but for all that, they are abominable, Titus 1:16. This new-creature change is not from one doctrine to another, barely considered as doctrine, but a change to the gospel in the main intendment of it, as it is 'a doctrine according to godliness,' 1 Tim. 6:3, as it may affect, purify, and direct the soul in its motion. And by the way observe this: whenever you are solicited to a change of opinion, consider the truth of it by this rule, whether it have a tendency to encourage and promote internal godliness, since this doctrine of regeneration was the first gospel lesson taught, to which all succeeding truths refer as to their end and centre. The apostle tells us what the issue of all such doctrines are that refer not to this, 'pride, doating about questions, envy, strife, railings, and evil surmisings,' verse 4. A heap of notions may consist with a body of death in its full strength, but a spirit of grace cannot; a notionalist may speak great things, but a new creature acts them. Great speculations only are but leaves without fruit, like cedars, that by their shadows may give a refreshment, but have no fruit to fill the soul hungering after righteousness.

3. Morality is not this new-creature change; that is, moral honesty, freedom from gross vices, &c. I have before spoken something about it, shewing it insufficient, when I handled the necessity of regeneration; we cannot speak too much against it, it being a soft pillow, from whence many slide insensibly into destruction. How many, upon this account, think themselves new creatures, who are yet deeply under the image of

Satan; and though they have blown off some dust from the law of nature, yet never had a syllable of the law of grace writ in their hearts! Nay, the image of the devil may be more deeply engraven in a soul whose life is free from an outward taint. Profane men express more of the beast; a civil and moral conversation may have more of the devil and serpent within, in spiritualised wickedness.

(1.) Yet morality is to be valued. It is a comely thing among men, a beauty to human societies, satisfaction to natural conscience, security to the body, example to others: men are to be applauded for it, and encouraged in it. It is a fruit of Christ's mediation, left for the preservation of human societies, without which the world would be a mere Bedlam and shambles. The works of kindness, justice, mercy, love, pity, &c., are useful and commendable. It is a thing which our Saviour loved, yet not with such a love as eternally to reward it. He looked upon the young man with some affection, Mark 10:21, but scarce upon the Pharisees without anger and disdain.

(2.) Yet we must not set the crown belonging to grace upon the head of it, and place it in a throne equal to that of the new creation. It is too amiable for men to be beaten off from it, yet with just reason we may persuade them to arise to a higher elevation. It is a curious paint, a delightful picture, an useful artifice, but not a vital principle. A glow-worm is a lovely light, yet it is not a star. We press not men to throw off morality, but to advance it, to exchange it for Christ, that their moral virtues may commence Christian graces. It is an elevation near the kingdom of God, not a translation into the kingdom of God; it is nature improved, not nature renewed; it is a well-coloured picture without a principle of life; an outward resemblance, not an inward power, 2 Tim. 3:5; a form of godliness; as a change that is made upon cloth in the draught of a picture, but no change in it by the conveyance of life. For,

[1.] It removes not the body of death. It is a cutting away the outward luxuriances, not the inward root. It removes the stench and putrefaction, not the death; an embalmed carcase is as much dead as a putrefied one, though not so loathsome. It removes not that wherein the strength of sin lies, though it doth somewhat of the stench of sin. It may check those degenerate lusts inconsistent with the peace of natural conscience, but not heal the corrupt nature. It may be a change from scandalous to spiritual sins; from vanity in the outward life, to vanity in the mind; from debauched practices, to a vainglorious and envious spirit: Eph. 4:17, 18, 'Henceforth walk not as other Gentiles walk, in the vanity of their minds; having the understanding darkened, being alienated from the life of God.' By the Gentiles, from whom the apostle would have the Ephesians differenced, he means not the lower sort, but the whole rank, ver. 21, there was a 'truth in Jesus' which they had been 'taught;' he makes no distinction between the looser rabble, and the professors of wisdom, whom he calls fools, Rom. 1:22, the followers of the divine (as they called them) philosophers, were alienated from the life of God, and walked in the vanity of their minds. The new man he exhorts them to put on was another kind of thing than what the greatest moralists among the heathen were acquainted with. It was at best human, not divine; an old nature purified, not a new implanted; or as the apostle phraseth it, a walking in the vanity of their mind, in the darkness of their understandings, though not in a vanity of gross actions. It can never remove that body of death, which was introduced into the world while this outward morality stood. What immorality against the light of nature do you find in Adam? He did break a positive command in eating the forbidden fruit; you find nothing of drunkenness, lying, swearing; his great sin was inward pride and unbelief, nothing of those sins, the freedom from which you boast of, and rest on. Some would make Adam guilty of the breach of every command in the moral law; virtually I confess they may; expressly I do not see how they can; and also virtually the highest mere moralist is guilty of the breach of the whole; yet all his morality, after the breach of this one command, could not preserve him in paradise, nor all the morality without a new nature restore you to it. You may have Adam's morality with Adam's corruption; a freedom from gross vices, with a heap of spiritual sins in your hearts, as Adam had, but not a true righteousness without the new Adam, the quickening Spirit.

[2.] Therefore the highest morality without a new creation is but flesh; all men out of Christ agree in a fleshly nature. It is the highest thing in the rank of flesh, but it is not yet mounted to spirit. Water heated to the highest pitch is but water still; and morality in the greatest elevation of it is but refined flesh; an old nature in an higher form. A profane man reduced to a philosophical morality is putrefied flesh reduced to some sweetness, endued with a fresh colour, but wanting life as much as before; it is an old nature new mended. But a new creature is Christ formed in the soul. Moral virtue colours the skin, renewing grace enlivens the heart; that changeth the outward actions, this the inward affections; that paints the man, this quickens him; that is a change indeed in the flesh, not of the flesh into spirit; it is a new action, not a new creation. There is a difference indeed among men in this respect, as there is of cleanly lambs from a filthy swine, or a ravenous wolf; yet both are in the rank of beasts. There seems to be a difference in the wickedness and malice of devils. Our Saviour tells us of a kind that are 'not cast out but by fasting and prayer,' Mat. 17:21, intimating that there are other kinds of them, not altogether so bad or so strong, yet all agreeing in one common diabolical nature; as there is a difference in gracious men, one shining like a star, another of a lesser light, yet all agree in the nature of light, and light in the Lord. So though there be a difference among men, in point of moral virtue, yet all agree in the nature of flesh: 'That which is born of the flesh is flesh,' John 3:6. Let it be what it will, a Nicodemus as well as Judas, it is flesh, a more refined sensuality, an animal life.

[3.] It must needs be differenced from the new creature, because its birth is different. Moral virtue is gained by human industry, natural strength, frequent exercises; it is made up of habits, engendered by frequent acts. But regeneration is an habit infused, which grows not upon the stock of nature, nor is it brought forth by the strength of nature; for man being flesh, cannot prepare himself to it. That may be the fruit of education, example, philosophy; this is of the Spirit; that is a fruit of God's common grace, this of his special grace; that grows upon the stock of self-love, not from the root of faith, and a divine affection; that is like a wild flower in the field, brought forth by the strength of nature; this like a flower in the garden, transplanted from heaven, derived from Christ, set and watered by the Spirit. And therefore the other being but the work of nature, cannot bear the characters of that excellency, which the affections planted by the Spirit do. That is the product of reason, this of the Spirit; that is the awakening of natural light, this the breaking out of spiritual light and love upon it; that is the excitation of an old principle, this the infusion of a new; that a rising from sleep by the jog of conscience, this a rising from death by the breath of the Spirit, working a deep contrition, and making all new.

[4.] It differs from the new creature, in regard of the contractedness of the one, and the extensiveness of the other. That is in part a purifying of the flesh, this a purging both of flesh and spirit, 2 Cor. 7:1; that binds the hands, this clears the heart; that purgeth the body, this every part of the soul; that, at the best, is but oil in the lamp of life, this oil both in lamp and vessel; that is a change of outward postures, modes, and fashion of walking, this of nature, heart, and spirit; that seems to be a dislike of some sins, this of all. If anything in moral honesty be given to God, it is but a certain part, the greatest and best is kept back from him. That may be a casting away some iniquity, but not making a new heart, when both are commanded together: Ezek. 18:31, 'Cast away from you all your transgressions, and make you a new heart and a new spirit.' That is a casting away the loathsome works of the flesh, this a new root to bring forth the fruits of the Spirit.

[5.] It differs from the new creature in the immediate principle of it, and its tendency. That is a cleansing the outward flesh in the fear of man, out of reverence to superiors (as it is said of Jehoash, he did that which was right, while he was under the awful instructions of Jehoiada, 2 Kings 12:2). This is a 'perfecting holiness in the fear of God,' 2 Cor. 7:1. That is an outward reformation from the hearing of the word, some acts materially performed from the newness of the thing, John 5:35, this from a judicious and hearty approbation of the law and will of God; that ariseth from a natural love to reason, justice, equity, this consists of love to God; that avoids some sins, because they are loathsome, this because they are sinful; that tends not to God for himself, but for something extraneous to him; it is an acting for self, not for the praise of God. The actions of unregenerate morality, as well as loathsome profaneness, are to gratify the flesh in some part of it; they all meet in that point, as the clearest brooks, as well as the the most rapid and muddy streams, run to feed the sea.

Well, then, deceive not yourselves; conclude not yourselves new creatures by your moral honesty; it will not follow, that because you have some virtues you have therefore true grace, but it will follow that if you are new creatures, and have faith and love, you have all graces in the root; and they will appear in time, though they may lie hid a while in that seminal principle; the greater virtues contain the less, but the less do not infer the greater.

4. It will certainly follow from hence, that restraints are not this new creature. Restraining grace and renewing grace are two different things; the one is a withholding: Gen. 20:6, 'I withheld thee from sinning against me;' the other an enlivening with a free spirit against it. Restraint may be from a chastisement, attended also with something of natural conscience. Abimelech had some natural integrity in his conscience not to meddle with another man's wife, which God acknowledges: 'I know that thou didst this in the integrity of thy heart; for I also withheld thee.'

Yet without this restraint by a punishment, this natural integrity might have been baffled by the temptation. Restraints may spring from the law in the hand of the magistrate, when it doth not spring from the law of God in the heart. Men may love that which they do not act, at least they may love it in others, though not in themselves, for some extrinsic considerations, and wish they had as fair a way to commit it as others have; they may hate what they practise. Do all that hear the word, love the word, hide it in their hearts, and let it sink down into the bottom of their souls? Do all that abstain from sin, loathe what they abstain from? The restraints of many being barely outward restraints, are no more arguments of regeneration, than God's withholding the devils by the chain of his powerful providence is a sign of the new creation of them. The damned are hindered from committing many of those sins which were their pleasure upon the earth; it is not a change of their disposition, but of their condition. Neither punishments in hell, nor punishments upon the earth, alter the nature; though after lying a thousand years in hell, they should have leave to dwell upon the earth again, they would have the same inclinations without an inward change. Do we not see it daily in men's afflictions, though the sense of the smart nips a little those inclinations, yet when that sense is extinguished, those inclinations bud forth afresh? The bare pruning a tree makes it bear more fruit of the same kind as long as the root remains, rather than diminisheth it: Isa. 1:5, 'Why should you be stricken any more? you will revolt more and more: the whole head is sick, and the whole heart is faint.' While the head is sick and the heart faint, though there may be a weakness to act some sins under the stroke, yet afterwards the revoltings are more violent many times than they were before. The best that restraints work of themselves, is but a cautiousness to sin more warily. The act may be repressed, while the habit remains.

5. A serious fit of melancholy, or a sudden start of affections, is not this work of the new creature. It is an habit, a law writ in the heart; not a

transient pang, or a sudden affection; not a skipping of fancy, or a quick sparkling of passion; but a new nature, a divine frame, spreading itself over every faculty; knowing God in our understandings, complying with him by our wills, aspiring to him by a settled and perpetual flame of our affections, rising heavenward, like the fire upon the altar, conforming ourselves to him in the whole man, a denial of whole self for God. It is not a working of the imagination, or a melancholy vapour, which may quickly be removed, or a flash of joy and love; but a serious humility, a constant grief under the remainder of corruption yet unextirpated; a perpetual recourse to God, and delight in him through Jesus Christ. Are your affections raised sometimes to God? and are they not oftentimes raised higher to objects extrinsecal to God? Such affections may arise rather from the constitution of the body than alteration of the soul. They are but a taste of the heavenly gift and the good word of God, Heb. 6:4, 5; a taste, and no more, and is; but a transient work. The object about which our affections are stirred may be divine, yet the operation but merely natural. May not sometimes affections be stirred much at the hearing the sufferings of our Saviour pathetically expressed, yet only out of a natural compassion, from an agreeable impression upon the fancy? The story of Joseph in the pit, and Christ upon the cross, may be heard with the same workings of passion. And may not the same be done at a well-humoured play, or at the hearing a report of the lamentable death of a Turk or heathen, pathetically expressed? These are but the workings of natural spirits. Some affections are as moveable as quicksilver, upon the least touch; they sweat like marble in moist weather, but resemble it also in hardness. You do not find the affections to be the chief seat of the law; this would be as to write letters upon melted wax or running water, but the tenor of the covenant runs upon the mind: 'I will put my law into their minds,' Heb. 8:8, 10. And when God works upon the mind, the affections will attend the dictates of that, and the motions of the will. But a work upon the affections only, is like water in a sponge, easily sucked up, and upon the least compression squeezed out. These may be where there is no root of grace; they suddenly rise, and suddenly vanish. When unrooted notions are received only into the fancy, without any illumination of the understanding, or determination of the will, the affections to them will be as volatile as the fancy which entertained them. Those in Mat. 13:20, 21, that received the word with a sudden joy, were as suddenly offended for want of a root: 'anon with joy receives it, by and by he is offended.' The word translated anon, and by and by, ἐυθὺς, is the same, a lightning of affection, and a sudden vanishing; therefore this is not the new creature, sudden affections, or a melancholy fit. The law of God seated in the heart, mind, and will, though a constant course of affection is a very good character to judge of the new creature.

6. It informs us of the excellency of the new creature. How excellent is this new creature? It is a change, a divine nature, a likeness to God, an excellency above that of the greatest moralist under heaven. The apostle calls it a change from 'glory to glory,' 2 Cor. 3:18, implying that the first change wrought upon the soul is glorious, and a new creature excellent in its first make, more glorious in its progress, unconceivably glorious when God shall put his last hand to the completing of it. Regeneration is more excellent than creation. It is more noble to be formed a son of God by grace, than made a man by nature; nature deforms, grace beautifies. By nature we are the sons of Adam, by the new nature the members of Christ. As grace excels nature, and Christ surmounts Adam, so much more excellent is the state of a Christian, a real Christian, above that of a man. Can there be a greater excellency than to have a divine beauty, a formation of Christ, a proportion of all graces, suited to the imitable perfections of God? Man is an higher creature than others, because he hath an higher principle. A life of reason is more noble than that of sense. To live by sense, is to play the part and live the life of brutes; to live by reason, is to live the life of a man: but he that lives by the Spirit, lives the life of God, answers the end of his creation, useth his

reason, understanding, will, affection for God, by whom they were first bestowed; acts more nobly, lives more pleasantly, than the greatest angel could do without such a principle. A new creature doth exceed a rational creature, considered only as rational, more than a rational doth a brute. The apostle makes a manifest distinction between the natural or the ψυχικὸς, the rational and the spiritual man, 1 Cor. 2:14, 15. A man with the richest endowments, is no more to be compared in excellency with a regenerate man, than the top of a craggy mountain is with a well-dressed garden. That must needs be excellent, the forming of which is the end of all God's ordinances in the world, the end of the Spirit's being among the sons of men, the end of keeping up mankind, the end of his patience in forbearing his punishment upon contempt of the gospel. The end of his preserving the world, is to form Christ in the heart; and when the last new creature is formed, God hath no more to do in the world: when all that are given to him shall come to believe, Christ shall then 'come, to be admired in them,' 2 Thes. 1:10. He doth not come, therefore, till all his chosen ones are brought in to believe in him, for then he would not be admired by all those that are saints in his purpose. This, therefore, must needs be excellent. One new creature is more excellent than the whole unrenewed world with their choicest ornaments. It was never pronounced of them, that they were 'partakers of the divine nature.'

7. How much therefore should new creatures be esteemed and valued? Is anything, next to God, more worthy our esteem than that which bears his image? Is anything, next to a crucified Christ, glorified in heaven, more worthy our valuation, than Christ formed in the heart of a believer? What esteem have men had for those who have had tempers like to some heroes, some generous and useful men in the world? How much more respect should be given to them that bear the characters of God upon them, and have communion with God, and Christ, and the Spirit, in their nature! If the dead image of God in a natural man ought to be respected, much more the living image of God in a renewed man. If a

picture is to have respect, much more the life. To slight them, therefore, redounds to the slighting that infinite perfection, whose image it is. They are his living images, sent into the world to represent him. He then that disesteems them for that work, disesteems him that wrought and engraved them, by the same rule that he that despised the disciples despised Christ, and the Father that sent him, Luke 10:16: 1 Thes. 4:8, 'He therefore that despiseth you, despiseth not man but God, who hath also given us his Holy Spirit.' Yet no better must be expected here; for the contracted spirit of the world can love no other birth but its own, no other similitude but what draws near unto it: 'If you were of the world, the world would love his own; but because you are not of the world, therefore the world hates you,' John 15:19. The copy can expect no better usage than the original. The nearer any approach in likeness to Christ, the more they will be exposed to contempt and scorn in the world.

8. If the new creature be such a thing as you have heard, then the sin of a regenerate man hath a greater aggravation than the sins of any in the world. If you slip into sin, the sins of the whole unregenerate world have not so great a blackness. It is true a new creature may, and doth sin; for though a new man is created in him with all his members, and essential and integral parts, yet the body of death doth remain still with all its members, and a seed-plot still, though not in the same strength and fruitfulness as before. For the apostle Paul doth not complain of a member of death, or a piece of sin, but the whole 'body of it,' and 'the law of sin in his members,' Rom. 7. It seems it did reside there still; and so it doth in all the renewed, though but faint and feeble, an old man indeed, growing older every day, losing its teeth and strength, less able to bite, less able to assault. Yet sometimes a new creature may fall into sin, but not without great aggravation. For other men sin against natural, you against spiritual principles; others sin against an habit of common notion, you against an habit of divine grace. A natural man sins against

the light of God in his conscience, a renewed man against the life of God in his heart.* Others sin against a Christ crucified and risen from the grave; he sins against a Christ new-formed and risen in his heart. Others sin against the law of God in the word, he against the law written in his mind and word too. Such cast dirt upon the Spirit's work, cross the end of so noble a piece, bring a thief into the Spirit's temple, and grieve the Holy Spirit, who instructed him better. Whenever you sin, it must cost you more grief, because your sins are more grievous; and you must grieve the more for them, because the Spirit is grieved by them. Grief for sin is a standing grace in the new creature, and part of a likeness to the Spirit of God, whatsoever some men dream to the contrary.

Use 2. Is of comfort. There is ground of joy unspeakable and full of glory that results from this. Are you of this new creation that I have been discoursing of? Then take your portion of comfort. The jewel of comfort belongs only to the cabinet of grace. It is fit you should have the comforts of heaven in your hearts, who have a fitness for heaven in your nature. The day of the new birth was a happy day, to be brought from under the rule of sin and death in it, to the rule of the Spirit of God and life in it; from bearing fruit to death, to bringing forth fruit to God and everlasting life. If sin be a torment to the womb that bare it, no joy can reside in an unregenerate spirit; if sin be the soul's rack in its own nature, grace must be its pleasure; for it carries as much contentment and satisfaction in its bowels, as sin doth disquietness and sorrow.

1. You have, by the new creation, a relation to the blessed Trinity. Such are the sons of God, the seed of Christ, the temple of the Spirit; what a connection is there between you and the three persons! God in Christ, and Christ in you, that you may be 'made perfect in one,' John 17:23. God in Christ reconciling the world, you in Christ reconciled to God; God in Christ as a father in a son, you in Christ as members in the body; Christ in you as a head in the body, the Spirit in you as an informing and enlivening principle. It makes you related to the Father as

his friends, by the ceasing of your enmity; to the Son as his propriety, for then you are his; to the Spirit as the tutor of you and inhabitant in you; all implied, Rom. 8:8–10. By your former birth you were children of wrath; by this, children of God: by that, partakers of the serpentine nature of the destroyer; by this, partakers of the divine nature of your Creator and Redeemer: by nature you descended from the loins of Adam, and thereby were related to all the corruption of the world; by the new birth you are descended from the Son of God, and 'counted to the Lord for a generation,' Ps. 22:30, and thereby related to all the perfection of heaven; as really descended from Christ by a spiritual, as from Adam by a natural generation. What an overflowing comfort is this! To be a king's son is a higher privilege than merely to be his subject; subjects have protection, sons affection; subjects partake of the kindness of the prince, sons of his nature. As a son, he hath a right to the inheritance of the father; as a subject, not. Men are subjects by covenant, though born of others, sons by generation. By being a new creature, the regenerate man acquires a more noble relation, than by being a creature. That relation that he lost by a prodigal corruption, is restored to him in a more excellent way by his spiritual regeneration.

2. If you be new creatures, you are the delight of God. It is impossible but God should have the tenderest respect to his own likeness; he must needs take a pleasure in a resemblance to his own nature, in a habit of his Spirit's infusing. Can God despise the work of his own hand? Can he then despise the work of his heart, a likeness to himself, to his Son, to his Spirit? His delight is strengthened by a threefold cord, 'he delights not in the strength of a horse, nor takes pleasure in the legs of a man,' but 'in them that fear him, in them that hope in his mercy,' Ps. 147:10, 11. You are the first fruits of his creatures, peculiarly dedicated to him as his portion by the new birth: James 1:18, 'Of his own will begat he us, with the word of truth, that we should be a kind of first fruits of his creatures,' taken out of the mass of the world for a holy offering to himself; the

more refined part of his creation, not barely creatures, but first fruits peculiarly belonging to him, upon whom he looks with a delightful eye, and under another relation. God cannot but love himself, and therefore that which approacheth most near to himself; for nothing in the creature is a fit object for God's love, but his own living image in him. As he loves himself in himself, so he loves himself in his creature. To deny his truth, is to deny himself; to deny his love to his image, would be to deny his love to himself. He can as soon hate his Christ glorified at his hand, as hate Christ formed in the soul. If sin makes men the objects of his hatred, as being contrary to his nature, grace then makes them the objects of his love, as being agreeable to his nature. He cannot but delight in his own birth, and delight in the seals of his own Spirit. You could not but displease him by being in the flesh; 'those that are in the flesh cannot please God,' Rom. 8:8; you then please him by being in the Spirit. Shall the pleasure of the Father of spirits, in his own image, be of a lower degree than that of a natural father in his son, which bears the lineaments of his body? He hath no pleasure in anything in the world, if not in you. Sin soon deformed all after he had pronounced them good, and stopped the joy God had in his works; it is by your redemption by his Son, and regeneration by his Spirit, that the joy in his works is restored to him; if he should not delight in you, what hath he in the world to please himself with? Your services please him; a new spirit, a new beauty is added to all your addresses. A new creature prays not as before, hears not as before, he refers all to God; there is a brokenness instead of pride, every sacrifice is washed in contrition, a zeal of spirit, a heavenly warmth, a sweet and delightful savour ascends up to him. It is you only that with grace 'serve him acceptably,' Heb. 12:28, with such a godly fear and frame wherein he takes a pleasure.

Well then, the new creature is the delight of God, though the scoff of men; the pleasure of him that commands the world, though reproached by them that shall fill hell with their souls.

3. How great a foundation then is laid in this for your happiness! New creatures, divine nature, a relation to God, the delight of heaven: 'If any man be in Christ, he is a new creature; old things are passed away, behold, all things are become new.' New for them, as well as in them. Distance and dissimilitude from God is the foundation of all misery; a likeness then to him is the basis of all blessedness. Divine happiness is connatural to the divine nature, and due to it, as it were jure intrinseco; as new creatures you are heirs, as sanctified creatures you are made meet for the inheritance; you have a hereditary right, and an aptitudinary right. Can any comfort be greater, than to have right to an inheritance, and a fitness to enjoy it? 'Now are we the sons of God,' 1 John 3:2, we have this real relation; not only named so, but are so, which is a certain foundation of a happiness which doth not yet fully appear to us. But such a knowledge we have, that when the original of this new nature shall appear, our imperfect likeness shall arise to a full perfection, 'we shall be like him, for we shall see him as he is;' upon the account of this relation we know there will be an exact likeness between him and us. I suppose it is properly meant of a likeness to Christ, we shall see him as he is; for the apostle, verse 5, refers it to Christ, without altering the person he had spoke of before; so that it is not meant of a seeing the essence of God, but the sight of Christ. Where lust reigns, the natural consequence is storms and dissatisfaction; he that hath the image of the devil, hath a model of hell; the new creature having the image of God, hath a model of heaven. A drop of grace is a drop of glory; so much as there is of the new creation, so much of heaven is put into the soul. It is 'a lively hope' of heaven here, and a full enjoyment of heaven hereafter, that the soul is 'begotten unto,' 1 Peter 1:3, 4. The greater the progress in this state, the more lively are the hopes of it, and the nearer approaches of heaven to the soul; such a foundation of happiness, with the hopes and foresight of it, cannot but be attended with unconceivable pleasure.

4. How highly comfortable is it to view yourselves, and consider the draught of this image, and the progress of the new creation in your souls? How comfortable is the work of self-examination to such a soul! With what pleasure may you look upon your present estate, and be filled with ravishments at every view? When you look back upon your former condition, and think of your state of death, the noisomeness of your hearts to God, the stiffness of your souls against him, when you consider how spiritual death reigned over every part; and now see your nature changed, your souls upon a lively and quick motion to God, your relishes of the sweetness of spiritual pleasures to be greater than those of sensual; how comfortable is it to behold those diffusions of God in your souls, and to feel them full of love to him, and full of love from him! How comfortable to view the original, and copy from it, and to see how near the one doth resemble the other; to cast your eye upon the state of wrath you were in by your first birth, and upon the state of grace you are in by the latter; to consider your former drudgery under sin, and your present freedom in the service of righteousness! it would make you perform those commands so often repeated, of rejoicing in the Lord alway, and shouting for joy, since mercy doth so compass you about, Ps. 32:11, Philip. 4:4. As upon the awakenings of conscience, and the exercise of its reflective office, there must needs arise an anguish and torment in an unrenewed soul, so upon the reflections of the same faculty in a new creature, there must spring a sparkling delight. As God by the reviews of himself and contemplation of his own excellency hath an infinite joy, so the new creature by the views of itself hath a joy in its measure proportionable to that of God himself. As it is in itself the image of God, so it is a lower fruition of him. I enjoy my friend somewhat in his picture when the original is absent; and this joy is greater when a beam from heaven doth shine upon this image, and both illustrate and discover the beauty of it, which in the darkness of ignorance and mistakes cannot be seen. But take heed that in these reviews you impair not your

comfort by any proud and God-neglecting reflections, but with humble and debasing thoughts of yourselves, and thankful admirations of the grace of God, and praises of him for so excellent a draught in your hearts. It is wonderful to perceive how by such a carriage the comforts of heaven flow in upon the soul, when thus humbly and thankfully it opens itself before God in this review. And let this add to your comfort, that if the reviews of so imperfect an image in you, and the dark sight of God, whose image it is, be so delightful, how much more pleasant will it be when your souls shall be elevated to the highest perfection and the most satisfying fruition!

5. And how great a comfort it is to consider that this imperfect image, which is the foundation of happiness, will in time be perfect, and as fully resemble him whose image it is as the creature is capable of! There is a day of perfect and glorious regeneration coming, wherein you will appear in all your royalty as heirs of God. The divine nature shall glitter without any filth of sin to sully it; holiness shall hold the sceptre without any lust to shake it. There is a day wherein Christ shall make all things new in the church, and in the soul; he sits upon his throne and saith it: Rev. 21:5, 'Behold, I make all things new.' It will be so new and admirable, that when you look back upon that mean draught of it while you were in the world, you would think you never had a grain of the divine nature before in you. As the vision of God will be perfect, so will your likeness to him, 1 John 3:2; as it will be a vision without any clouds, so it will be a likeness without any dissimilitude, according to the creature's capacity. The vision of Christ here transforms us into a likeness to him in his death and resurrection, the vision hereafter transforms us into a likeness to him in glory; the close look of the soul upon God shall divest it of all carnal conceptions; the understanding shall perfectly behold the original, the will closely embrace it, the affections centre in it without distraction; the whole soul shall be changed from a less degree of glory to an unconceiveable perfection in it, changed 'from glory to glory,' 2

Cor. 3:18, when the well of living water springing up in thee to eternal life shall spring into it. This fire-baptism will not leave till it hath fully consumed your dross, and refined your souls. That Spirit that begun the work will fill the heart with the knowledge and love of God, as his promise is to fill the earth, Isa. 11:9. He will not leave despoiling you of the oldness of the flesh till there be not a mite left, and clothing you with a newness of the spirit till there be not a grain of the soul free from this new enlivening. As he began, so he will finish, in abolishing that which remains of vanity, and in filling this holy temple with the glory of the Lord. There is certainly as much power in the second Adam to perfect, as well as to begin this new creation, as there was in the first to convey his soul and defiled image to his posterity. The honour of Christ and the good of the new creature are concerned in it; the honour of Christ in point of power and affection, the good of the new creature in point of happiness; his honour would suffer if he did not perfect what he had began. As Moses pleads with God for the perfecting the Israelites' deliverance in bringing them into Canaan, that the nations might not say, God was not able to deliver them, Num. 14:16. In point of affection he loves his Father, therefore the image of his Father; he loves himself, therefore the picture of himself; he loves his Spirit which glorifies him, therefore will perfect the draught he hath made. It will, then, in time be perfect, not a lineament of God but will be illustriously drawn; there shall be no more complaints of a body of death, nor any snarlings of sin and lust.

Upon these considerations you may apply the comfort this new creation affords you,

(1.) Against troubles in the world. Old things are passed away, even the old events and issues of your afflictions, they are no longer used merely to trouble you or punish you, but to perfect this new creation, to engrave more deeply or exercise this divine image. All things are but fellow-labourers to throw out the rubbish, and blow up this divine spark:

Rom. 8:28, they 'all work together for good, to them who are called according to his purpose.' As regenerating grace gives us a relation to God, so it should expel fear: Isa. 43:1, 'Fear not: for I have redeemed thee, I have called thee by name; thou art mine.' What reason is there to fear when he hath called you by name, in a special manner, not in a general way? What reason to fear when thou hast the badge of God upon thee, who hath new created thee? The grace wherein you stand, or the state of grace, should make you not only to 'rejoice in the hope of the glory of God,' but to 'glory in tribulations also,' as well as the apostle, Rom. 5:2, 3, because it 'works patience,' &c. It dresseth up the new creature, and draws the several parts of the gracious habit into exercise. Though it seem strange, yet the 'glorying in tribulation' is as proper an effect of this new creation as 'rejoicing in hope of the glory of God.' Grace, being the foundation of your glory in heaven, cannot but be the foundation of glorying in everything else which heightens it, and pusheth it nearer to its centre. Let not affliction, crosses, reproaches, molest your new nature; be new creatures as to your respects to them as well as relation to God. Our Saviour's sonship, and the meat the world knew not of, supported him under greater injuries than we can ever be subject to. What clouds of trouble should ever sadden that heart which hath the living image of God in his soul? This alone should turn the wormwood of affliction into honey, and bitterness into sweetness.

(2.) You may apply the comfort of your new creation against temptations. Will not the power of God be employed in the defence of that which is his only image in the world, since he knows that Satan is most active against it, because it is his image? And upon the same account will not God be active for it? Surely that Spirit which begat it broods upon its own birth, and watches for the defence of it against its mighty adversaries. Satan watches to cast dirt upon the divine nature; the Spirit watches to hinder it, and if cast on, to wipe it off, and restore it to its beauty. Can it enter into the heart of an infinite affection nakedly to expose his own work, his affectionate new creature, made up of faith in him and love to him, that which maintains his honour in the world, designs all for his glory, values his honour above his own credit, yea, his life; opposeth everything that opposeth him, hates everything that is loathsome to him, would endure any misery rather than displease him; I say, shall a God of infinite tenderness expose this creature to the violences and furies of hell without any defence? What should we make of God, by entertaining such thoughts of him, but a hard master, a cruel tyrant, one that would make his own work the sport of devils, to stand by carelessly and see his image trampled upon, and leave the best subjects he hath in the world to the mercy of his mortal enemy? Let not such a thought enter into any new creature, nor let us believe that the love in the heart of the new Creator is less than the power in his hand. It was the sonship and resurrection of our Saviour secured him against the counsels of enemies: Ps. 2:2 and 7 compared, 'Thou art my Son, this day have I begotten thee.' So our communion with him in his resurrection secures us against the malicious designs of Satan. Thou art my son, this day have I regenerated thee, is the voice of God to a new creature; and by this relation his happiness is secured under the greatest assaults, if he keep up faith, which will fetch vigour from the Head. The devil by his whole legions of temptations cannot more prevail against the seed of God, than Haman could against Mordecai, because he was of the seed of the Jews, as his wife prudently advised him, Esther 6:13.

(3.) This comfort of the new creation is applicable against fears of falling away. Were grace like a moral habit, acquired by moral acts, it might sink under a force, it might be lost; but it is a divine work, a new creation in Christ, not anything gained by moral philosophy, and a road of virtuous actions. Men may seem to begin in the Spirit and end in the flesh; but doth the Spirit begin this regeneration work, to suffer it to end in the flesh? When the apostle speaks of men's works, he fears the consequence; but when he speaks of God's working in a man, he is confident of a good issue, Philip. 1:6. God never begins but he resolves to perform and finish. As it is impossible for one united to Adam in a natural way not to partake of his sinful life, so it is impossible for one united to Christ in a gracious way not to partake of his spiritual life. And as every man is really in the loins of Adam, so every believer is, in a sort, spiritually in the loins of Christ, and is as truly denominated his seed; and as no man can be cut off from the stock of Adam but by the grace of God, so no man can be taken off from the stock of Christ, when once implanted, but by the retraction of that grace, against which there is sufficient security in the covenant of grace, and several promises in Scripture, like stars in the heavens, set to give light to this truth. The new creature under the gospel shall grow in beauty as the lily, in strength like a cedar; his beauty shall be as fresh as that of the rose or lily, his root as firm as that of a cedar; and this from God, who will be as the dew unto it: Hosea 14:5, 'I will be as the dew to Israel: he shall grow up as the lily, and cast forth his roots as Lebanon.' As dew quickens the plant, so will God enliven Israel; what withering can there be under such an influence? If you have been made new creatures in Christ, you are made stable creatures, his charge is as great to preserve you as it was to renew you. Besides, the divine nature is so delightful a thing, that he that once is a possessor, hath no mind to be a loser of it. He that hath once put off the old man, and put on the new, will have little heart to make another exchange, and divest himself of his beautiful robe, to be clothed again with the old tattered rags which he hath flung upon the dunghill. The new creation is a 'fellowship with Christ in his resurrection,' Philip. 3:10, and therefore in the consequents of it. As Christ did not rise to die again, so the soul is not made new to become old again. Christ formed in the soul is like Christ incarnate in the world: the divine nature may be obscured, it may and will have its humiliations; it cannot indeed die, but though it seem to die, it will have its resurrection, and afterwards its ascension into glory.

(4.) It is comfort against weakness of grace, and strength of corruptions. The whole frame of the new creature is wrought at once: the soul is infused at once, but not as Adam was, created in his full stature, and perfect strength, and exercise of all his faculties. But as Adam's posterity were generated, first infants, then men, others may be more honourable creatures, but the weakest grace is a new creature; others may be more noble members, but every new creature is a member of the body; others may have more grace, but not a better title; the weakest is a heaven-born heir, and hath the same title by the purchase of the Redeemer, the reality of the new creation, and the spirit of adoption. I do not mean by the weakest grace a superficial desire, or a velleity not to sin, and yet a daily running into it; but a grace mating and mastering corruption, though residing with it; a grace that is daily eating into the bowels of lust, and growing up to a sharper animosity and strength against what is contrary to it; for the least degree of grace is prevalent against sin, and is not overpowered by it, though it be mightily opposed. The essence of grace is the same in every new creature, though the degrees be different: it is one thing to have the nature of fire, another thing to have the strength of it; a spark is essentially fire, and will burn, though not so much as a flame. If the frame be new, though the draughts be not so clear, nor the lineaments drawn with such lively colours, yet there is a representation; the first draught of a picture bears a likeness to the person, but it will be more lively after the second or third sitting, when the limner hath laid on his fresher colours.

[1.] If your complaints of the weakness of grace and strength of corruption be sincere, it is a comfortable sign you will hold out. Hasty pretenders and proud boasters are not durable. The seed sown in the stony ground 'presently sprung up,' Mat. 13:5; grew faster, as if it would outstrip the common harvest, but as soon withered; whereas that which was sown in the good ground sprung up leisurely to perfection, and endured the storm.

[2.] You cannot reasonably think you should presently be rid of your corruptions. Some spice of a cured disease will remain in the soul as well as the body, and a certain spiritual weakness after the raising of the new creature. The law in the mind doth not presently raze out the law of sin in the members. There is a diabolical nature as well as divine. The Platonist could say, The virtuous man who doth something, ἀπροαίρετον, is both a god and a demon.* Christ formed in the heart doth not presently dispossess the serpentine nature, but master it. A man restored to health from a sharp disease may do the actions of a sound man, yet not in that manner and soundness, for all his motions are infected with the relics of that disease which lately mastered his body. Original corruption is not as a cistern (then it may be emptied), but a spring; pump out all you can at one duty, it will rise again, you will see it, before the next service.* It is true that 'he that is born of God commits not sin,' he sins not with such a frame as he did before; but it is as true that 'If we say we have no sin, we deceive ourselves, and there is no truth' of grace 'in us,' 1 John 1:8. There will be a running issue, that you may frequently touch the hem of Christ's garment for a cure. The soul of the best is never like to be 'without spot or wrinkle' till it be glorious, Eph. 5:26.

[3.] All God's communications of grace are gradual. Doth the mustard seed spring up in an instant to the tallness of a tree? Grace is sown in an instant, but grows not up so suddenly. Christ formed in the heart is like Christ in the flesh; first in his cradle, before he be upon his legs. The new creation is not a sudden leap from corruption to perfect purity; the day dawns in the heart, but the light takes a time to expel the darkness: Prov. 4:18, 'The path of the just is as the shining light, that shineth more and more unto the perfect day.' The first appearance at the dawning is an earnest that the victory will be complete at last. God did not make a full discovery of Christ to Adam, his revelations of him grew brighter with every age; the nearer his coming, the clearer was the foresight of him. The divine nature hath its time of discovery in the creature, as it had in

Christ the original; there were forty days between his resurrection and ascension, wherein he was but in the first degree of his exaltation. Christ risen in the heart will take some time before he ascends and carries up the soul to spiritual heights with him.

[4.] Consider well how it is with thy will. It is not the having of lusts, but the fulfilling of them, wherein our danger lies: Rom. 13:14, 'We have then put on the Lord Jesus Christ, when we make no provision for the flesh, to fulfil it in the lusts thereof,' but endeavour to walk holily. The author of the Epistle to the Hebrews could pretend to little more than will: chap 13:18, 'willing to live honestly,' καλῶς, comely, beautifully. And herein Paul 'exercised' himself, Acts 24:16. He manifested this will by compliance with all seasonable occasions to that purpose. Is there grace in thy whole soul? Is there an enlightened judgment to see the foulness of sin and the loveliness of Christ? Is there a renewed will to incline to God and to close with the Redeemer? Is there a rectified affection, consisting of love, desire, delight, though yet but weak in all the faculties? Are there dissatisfactions in you upon internal reviews? Have you not strong bewailings and laments for the strength of sin and weakness of grace, and breathings after a more vigorous and active grace? Let not then your complaints of the body of death stifle your praises of God for what he hath wrought in Christ in order to your full deliverance. They did not so in Paul, Rom. 7:24, 25; let them not do so in you. Take comfort in what God hath wrought, bless him for it, and solicit him to confirm that which he hath wrought in you, Ps. 68:24. He that provides food for the ravens that cry, will not stop his ears at the voice of his own image.

(5.) It is comfort against the fear of death. If you were born only of the old Adam, you were spiritually dead, and you must eternally die; it were unavoidable, if not changed; but if born of an incorruptible seed, the dissolution of your body shall be the consummation of your glory. Death strikes the outward man, and the new creature elevates the soul.

The new nature will as naturally ascend to heaven, when it is unclothed of flesh, and hath left all the relics of corruption behind it, as the pure flame aspires into the air, and seems to long to embody itself with the sun, the first fountain of light. How joyfully will the original and copy meet: Philip. 1:23, 'to depart from hence,' is 'to be with Christ.' The truth of grace in the creature, and the infinite righteousness in the Creator, kiss each other. How affectionately will God entertain that image of himself! How delightfully will Christ view himself in the soul, and the soul view itself in the heart of Christ! The soul shall see Christ in glory, and Christ shall behold the soul in perfection, where there will be nothing but life and love, love and life for ever. Is death then to be feared, that brings the new creature to this happiness?

Use 3. Is for examination. Of all things, this deserves the strictest inquiry, in regard of its absolute necessity, and in regard of its superlative excellency.

1. It is possible to know it, and not very difficult to know it. You may know the acts of your own heart. Can you not view your own thoughts? Can you desire, or love, or hate, or grieve, but you must know that you do so? Can you not tell what is the object of your inclinations, what your affections run most greedily after? No man can be such a stranger to his own soul, if he look into it. Can you not tell whether you are the same men as before; whether you love what before you hated, and hate that which before you loved? A soul may know whether it loves God supremely or no, so as to appeal to God for the truth of it, as Peter to our Saviour: John 21:17, 'Lord, thou knowest that I love thee.' It is in this reflexive power that a man excels a brute.

2. You must inquire into the effects and operations of it. Where there is this spiritual change, there is life; where there is a spiritual life, there will be spiritual operations. You must inquire, then, what sense and motion you have, that is superior to a life of nature. This new creation is not only the taking down the old frame, but setting up a new. The old creature

frame will grow more inactive, the new creature form more sprightly. Regeneration is never without some effect; if we have not the properties, we have not the nature. If the air be dark and pitchy, that a man cannot see his way, it is a sign the sun is not up to enlighten that hemisphere. A thick darkness cannot remain with the sun's rising, The works of darkness, with their power, cannot remain with a new creature state. The old rubbish cannot wholly remain with a new building. Look well, therefore, whether old principles, aims, customs, company, affections, are passed away, and whether new affections, principles, ends, be settled in the room. Be sure to distinguish well between the form and the power, between a paint and life, and regard well your inward acts. The acts of the new creature are principally in the proper seats of it, the mind, the heart, the will, the conscience, the affections. Outward acts are no sign at all; no man can perfectly judge of another by them, nor any man judge of himself. As the strength of sin, so the strength of grace, the new creature, lies in the heart. Those waters which are bitter, are bitterest, and those which are sweet, are sweetest, at the fountain; they lose somewhat of their qualities in the streams, by the mixture of other things with them.

3. In general observe, what contrariety there is to what you were before, and the very point wherein this contrariety doth consist. It is a spiritual habit, a divine nature, the law of God in the heart. It must principally be discerned in its motion to God, in its respect to God, whose law, nature, habit it is, directly contrary to the sinful habit, the law of sin in the heart, the old serpentine nature which moved to sin. Let us see in general how it was with Paul, who speaks so much of the new creature. He was quite another man after his being in Christ than he was before. He was before an admirer of his own righteousness, a contemner of grace, a persecutor of Christ and his members. After the new creation, his pharisaical plumes fall, his own righteousness is as dross, he lays it down at the feet of Christ; grace is highly admired by him, and his whole labour is spent in glorifying Christ, and edifying his church. He abhors

that which before he delighted in: he did before his own will, and the will of his sect; now, 'Lord, what wilt thou have me to do?' He is now an admirer, where he was a despiser; his industry, passions, heart, are for Christ, as before they were against him. The doctrine of the cross is no longer folly, but wisdom: he glories as much in being persecuted for Christ, as in being a persecutor of him and his people. His ravaging wolfish nature is gone, and a lamb-like nature in the place of it; he hath as much sweetness toward the people of Christ, as he had sourness against them. Of an executioner, he becomes a martyr; and would not only lose his life, but be an Anathema, to do them good whom before he hated. Christ was his life, Christ was his joy, Christ was his all, and nothing but Christ dear to him. A quite contrary strain. And this is a new creature; and therefore examine yourselves. Is there faith instead of unbelief, the knowledge of God instead of ignorance, a constant glowing affection to him instead of enmity, or a coldness of love, the love of the Creator instead of that of the creature? This is to have the image of God instead of that of the devil.

But, in particular,

1. What fervent longings have you after a likeness to God? The first draught of this image begets strong desires for a farther perfection. The sighs and groans for a likeness to God are the first lineaments of God in the soul, and arise from some degree of affection to him, and delight in him. The breathings of the soul are 'for the living God,' as David, Ps. 42:2; Ps. 84:2, for God, as a principle of life and spirit in him. This hungering and thirsting after righteousness is a sign of righteousness already in the soul, and an earnest of a further fulness, Mat. 5. None can fervently and unweariedly long for a divine nature but such as have had some taste of it. The divine nature in the soul will be returning to that nature whence it derives its essential purity. The principle coming from God will be aspiring to that nature which it is a part of, as rivers to the sea, and swell if they be hindered. He must needs long after a full draught,

and can no more satisfy himself with imperfect lineaments, than a sick man can with an imperfect cure. It is to this end he breathes after heaven, because it is a state of perfection, not from any carnal notion of it. He knows he is not already perfect, and therefore presses forward with eager desire and endeavour, 'if by any means he may attain the resurrection from the dead,' Philip. 3:11–13, &c. He doth not only desire a freedom from sin, but to be as pure and elevated in affection to God as an angel. God is not only free from unrighteousness, but full of righteousness; and therefore those desires of a divine nature are not limited to, and centred in, a negative holiness. He would set himself no other pattern but God. It is an excellent speech of a heathen,* exhorting not only to live the life of a good man, which civil virtue and the vogue of men approved of, but to look above that to the choicest desire of a divine life; for, saith he, our endeavours should be for a likeness to God, not to good men. To endeavour to be like to man, is to make one image like another; but a new creature aims at the highest exemplar; it aspires after no lower a pattern than God himself, his will, his rule, his glory, his pleasure. Do the breathings of your spirits rise as much for it, as the steams of your lusts did before against it?

2. Put this question to yourselves, What inward authority hath God over your hearts? Is the government of God set up in your souls? Can you with joy say, The Lord reigns, and none but he shall reign over me? The new creature coming under another government, hath frames suitable to it, and delightfully owns that supreme authority, and pleases himself more in a subjection to God, than the wicked can in their slavery to sin. Do you 'yield yourselves to God, and your members as instruments of righteousness unto God'? Are the motions of your souls guided by him? You are then 'alive from the dead;' it is the apostle's assertion, Rom. 6:4. Sin doth reside; but which reigns, God or lust? An usurpation may be on sin's part, when no voluntary subjection on ours. Is it an absolute, or only a partial resignation of yourselves to him? Do you give him a moiety,

or do you give him the whole? Has he the sole sovereignty? or would you give him an associate? Are any evil ways hated, out of a respect to his word, to his authority, wisdom, goodness, or a respect to yourselves? Ps. 119:128, 'I esteem thy precepts concerning all things to be right, and I hate every false way.' Ver. 133, 'Order my steps in thy word, and let not any iniquity have dominion over me.' Are God's dictates readily obeyed? Doth a free submission to his authority govern and act thee in his ways? Do you count his yoke easy, and his burden light? Do you glory in the chain of grace, and count the service of sin as iron fetters? Is the will of God above your own wills? Do you defy the one to observe the other? Is God's will sacred with you, when it thwarts your own, or only when it suits your interest? It is not then the authority of God which prevails with you, but the authority of some extraneous thing which hath the chief moving force. If so, there is no sign of the new creature in such a frame.

3. How are your affections to God? It is a new creature we are speaking of, and that is inward chiefly. Sin may be left in the practice, and not hated: goodness may be practised, when it is not affected. Where, then, is the new creature? It is not only a change of professions. Simon Magus had changed that before his baptism, but not his heart, either before or after, Acts 8:21. The strength of sin lies in the understanding, will, and affections, and it is there that the strength of grace must appear, and set up its banners. Are your affections and lusts of your flesh crucified? They must be so, if you are Christ's new creatures, Gal. 5:24. The strong stirring of natural conscience may weaken a present resolution to an act of sin, but not an affection to it, and to the habit of sin. It may restrain from outward exercises, not from inward dispositions. Natural conscience informs of the evil, but doth not confer upon us a disaffection to that evil. What are the inclinations of your affections? Are they pitched upon God? What are they for duration? Are they constantly in motion to him? Is it your pleasure to think of him, to live to him? Are

the remainders of unlikeness to him your grief, your yet imperfect image your delight, not because it is imperfect, but because it is his image? Every sigh, or a slight affection, is not a new creature. It is a deep engravement, a constant inclination, contrary to what it was before, as white to black. Do your affections correspond with the affections of God? Do you hate everything that he hates? Or is there any one lust thou wouldst caress and hide among the stuff? Such a frame is not the new-creature frame. God loves not one sin, neither must we, if we be like him. Is the love to God and Christ more settled than love to father or mother, which is an inbred affection, born with our natures? Mat. 10:37. It must be so supreme. What desires have you to magnify his name? Do you love him so intensely, as to part with your lives to glorify and enjoy him? If you be new creatures, God and his glory will be dearer to you than friends, credit, life. He said not amiss, that no man is a true Christian who is not an habitual martyr; that is, that hath not a disposition to lay down his life for the honour of God. And that apostle who hath spoke so much of the new creature had such a raised affection, Acts 20:24, he would 'not count his life dear, so he might finish his course with joy;' which was 'to testify the gospel of the grace of God.' He could lay down his head more willingly upon a block than upon a pillow, if he might finish his course to his Master's honour, and publish his grace. Where there is no concern for the honour of God, there is little sign of a likeness to him; for this is an essential part of true Christianity. If we have a new nature, we cannot but love that nature, wherever we find it. And where we find it in a greater degree, and infinitely perfect, as in God, we cannot but love it there above all; else we offer violence to the divine nature; and in not loving it in God, we love it not in ourselves. It is impossible there can be this divine nature without spiritual affections, and that the image of God can be in us without having an intense love to him whose image it is. If anything, then, lie nearer the heart of any man than God, the image of God is not in him. Therefore look into your hearts. How doth your hatred break out against sin? How is your sorrow poured out for sin?

4. How stand your souls to inward and spiritual duties? How vile are you in your own eyes because of sin? What grief is there even for your least imperfections? Are you every day defacing your pride, and strengthening your humility? Pride is the great fort of the old man, humility the great security of the new. How are you in prayer? Are you constant, are you fervent, have you daily converses with God? I mean secret prayer and meditation: there are the most intimate converses with God. I appeal to you that neglect those duties; can you pretend to this new creation? Do you think that the image of God in the heart would not often move to its original? Can a likeness to God consist with an estrangedness from him? Can any man live the life of God that doth not care for the presence of God, either speaking to him, or thinking of him? Can that law in the heart, which is put in that we may not depart from him, consist with this which is the prime departure, never to seek him, or to seek him coldly? All the affections of the new creature bend to him, and centre in him. Can this be without a drawing near to him? The 'spirit of grace' is followed with a 'spirit of supplication:' Zech. 12:10, 'the spirit of grace and of supplication.' The Spirit is not a dumb spirit in the new creature. The first work in the heart is to cry, 'Abba, Father': Gal. 4:6, 'God hath sent forth the spirit of his Son into your hearts, crying, Abba, Father.' The first impression made by the Spirit is upon the eye of the soul to look to God, and the voice of the soul to cry to him. It is the first work of a regenerate man as regenerate. It is the argument our Saviour uses to Ananias, to have confidence that Paul was not the same man as before: Acts 9:11, 'Behold, he prays.' Our old nature being made up of aversion from God, the proper language of that is, 'Depart from us.' The new nature being made up of an inclination to God, the proper language of that is, 'It is good for me to draw near to God;' for upon this renewing grace God is the proper centre of the soul, and the same principle which

moves other things to the centre will move the soul to God. It is made the effect of a pure heart: 2 Tim. 2:22, 'Peace with them that call on the Lord out of a pure heart,' and the characteristical note of a saint: 1 Cor. 1:2, 'Saints, with all that in every place call upon the name of Jesus Christ our Lord.'

5. What valuations and relishes have you of the word and institutions of Christ? As the life is, so is the food; a spiritual appetite for spiritual food is a comfortable sign of a renewed nature. In every nature there is an aversion to what is destructive, an inclination to what is preservative. Every creature doth as much desire its proper food, as it abhors that poison that would blast it. The new nature hath a new taste, his palate is embittered to his former pleasure, and refined and prepared for his new delight: he relisheth what before he loathed, esteems that sweetest that before was unpleasantest. The law in the heart, being an impression of the word, will answer it with a choice affection. The first cleansing of the heart, and the progressive sanctification of it, is wrought by the word: Eph. 5:26, 'That he might sanctify and cleanse it with the washing of water by the word.' The image of God in the heart cannot but value the image of God in his law; since the soul is brought to a love of God, it will love his operations, and all the methods of them, and therefore his word. A rectified judgment will have a rectified affection; there will be a spiritual palate, whereby it proves and 'approves what is the good, acceptable, and perfect will of God,' Rom. 12:2. What is pleasing to God is good and pleasing to him. And the same apostle sets it as a sign of a perfect man, or a sincere new creature, to esteem that the wisdom of God which the world counts foolishness: 1 Cor. 2:6, 'We speak wisdom among them that are perfect.' The Spirit of truth in the new creature will fill it with a strong affection to those truths in the word. Truth in the heart, and truth in the word, being so near of kin, cannot be strangers or unwelcome to one another. What sympathy, then, is there between the word and your hearts? What exercise of grace in it? What improvement

of grace by it? Do you desire it to satisfy your curiosity, or to further your growth? 1 Pet. 2:2, 'As new-born babes, desire the sincere milk of the word, that you may grow thereby.' Are you like the plants, both cleansed and quickened by the showers, and discovering themselves in a fresh verdure? How do you dilate your souls for it? How do you work it upon your hearts? Do you desire it should be stamped upon you? Do you long for a more perfect intimacy with it? Do you prize it above the satisfactions of wealth and the pleasures of sense? Is it 'more excellent than gold,' Ps. 19:10, 'and sweeter than honey?' Ps. 119:103. Do you spiritually concoct it, and turn spiritual meat into a spiritual juice, as the stomach doth meat into chyle, and other parts of the body into blood? Life can only do this. Do you love to have it dwell richly in you, and bring down the highest imaginations to the foot of it? Do you cut the throat of your dearest Isaacs when the word commands you? Is it a pleasure to you to see the face of God in his ordinances? Is your pleasure raised most by the spirituality of truth? The more spiritual any truth is, the more satisfactory it is to a spiritual taste. Do your hearts burn within you at the warm breath of Christ? Are they not only warmed, but raised into a flame, and that lasting? Not like the straw, which doth blaze and vanish.

6. What holiness is there in your hearts and lives? God cannot be otherwise than holy, therefore holiness is the perpetual concomitant of the divine nature; and so the apostle makes it to consist in 'escaping the pollutions that are in the world through lust,' 2 Pet. 1:4. There is a principle which springs up in holy motions and thoughts. It is in the soul the image of God is stamped, and it is there that the new creature doth chiefly exercise and preserve it. Holiness must be the proper effect of that which is planted by the Spirit of holiness. He that pretends to a likeness to God without it, fathers an irregularity upon him, and makes him a monstrous begetter. It is not born of the will of the flesh, to follow sensual pleasures, nor of the will of man, to follow only rational delights; but of the will of God, and therefore follows that will it was born of,

John 1:13. 'Let thy kingdom come, thy will be done,' is the natural language of the new creature, and glad he is to have the Spirit point him to those ways that are most conformable to the divine will, for it is not a strained holiness, but natural, such a one as ariseth from the 'fear of God in the heart,' Jer. 32:40, and a care to please God in his walk: 2 Cor. 7:11, 'Yea, what care!' It is holy as God is holy, in some measure, and therefore like him whose infinite purity cannot endure pollution. And it can no more divest itself of its inclinations to righteousness than the soul can strip itself of its natural activity. There is a certain connection between a 'heart of flesh' and 'walking in God's statutes,' Ezek. 36:26, 27. To what purpose doth God give it? either for his own work or for the devil's? There is no need of it for the latter; the heart of stone would have done his work effectually: therefore for the service of the former, and that constantly, for the new creature is 'created to good works,' not to do them by fits and turns, but 'to walk in them,' Eph. 2:10; and he is described by the apostle to be one that 'walks after the Spirit,' Rom. 8:1, the ordinary course of his heart is spiritual. How is it with you, then? Is holiness your proper element? Is it a death to you when any thing contrary to it buds up in your hearts? Is there a purity of heart joined with a zeal for goodness, Titus 2:14? They go hand in hand, as being both the ends of our Saviour's death, and both the works of the Spirit. Is there an angry detestation of the loathsomeness of sin, and a kindly affection to the purity of grace? It will be thus if the new creation be wrought, for as in original sin there was the root of all evil, therefore all holiness may be opposed, and all sin practised; so in the habit of grace there is the root of all grace, therefore all sin will be loathed, and every part of holiness will be loved. But on the contrary, if your old lusts be rather improved than impaired; if you are more charmed by swinish pleasures, and enamoured of them; if the enmity in your hearts or the loathsomeness in your lives remain, is there anything of a new creature in you? Judge for yourselves. Do you make as rich a provision for the flesh as before? Is your heart and life set upon it with as much affection? Are you joyful when employed in its drudgery? Is this to be a new creature? Can there be such darkness, if the sun of grace were risen upon you? Such fruits evidence the standing of the old root. He that hath the black mark of the devil in his life hath no reason to think he hath the spiritual badge of Christ in his heart; and if he do, he doth deceive himself.

7. How is your disposition against those things which are contrary to a divine nature? No creature hath a greater antipathy to that which is contrary to its nature, than a regenerate man hath against that which is contrary to the divine. It is as impossible there can be a friendly neighbourood between the new man and the old, as between the ark and Dagon, between heat and cold, which are always quarrelling, yea, between Christ and Belial, 2 Cor. 5:16.

(1.) Against the motions of sin. An irreconcileable war is commenced between grace and corruption. At the first inlet flesh is in arms to hinder; the spirit in arms to maintain its standing, Gal. 5:17. The contest is in the whole man; grace being seated in the heart, sends out its commands, and despatches forces to every part to meet with its enemy,* as motion beginning at the centre diffuseth itself through the whole sphere, shaking every part to the circumference. Light will oppose darkness in every part of the air; they cannot shake hands together; the increase of one is the decrease of the other. Sensibility is a sign of life; a dead man complains not of wounds and cutting; you may take out his bowels, out limb from limb; but a living man will complain of the least prick of a pin or a pinch. Natural men cannot complain of that which they do not feel. There is a mighty friendship between a dead carcase and rottenness, nothing is noisome to it. Loads of sin may lie upon him, like mountains upon a dead body, and no complaint: 'The motions of sin work in his members' without resistance, and 'bring forth their fruit unto death,' Rom. 7:5. But the new creature counts the least sin that hath stolen in upon him his torture, like the stone in the bladder, a worm in the root, and can find no rest till he routs the beginnings of the disease. If there be no antipathy then to that which is contrary to the life and being of a Christian, it is a sure sign that there is nothing of a divine life; for as a renewed man 'esteems all the precepts of God to be right,' and 'hates every false way,' Ps. 119:128, so he must abhor every motion which would divert him from what he values, and entice him to what he hates. How are your understandings sensible of the first risings contrary to the interest of the new creature? Are they more ready to dissent from them; your wills more ready to check them than before? What counterworkings against the flesh, with its affections and lusts? Are you ready with weapons in your hand to stay the first stirrings of corruption? Are you ready to pluck those buds, and fling them away with disdain? Doth both your courage and strength increase? Can you more readily be in arms against the rising of a lust than formerly you were, and cannot without horror bear the approaches of them? Doth a little dust of sin got into your eye set you a-weeping before God?

(2.) How stand you affected to spiritual sins? Here you should lay the great stress in your examination of the new creation, for your lives may be the lives of saints, while your hearts are the hearts of devils; we may have no spots of the flesh upon our garments, and a world of them upon our souls; spiritual sins may revel where the more fleshly and sensual iniquities are excluded. There is a war in the heart of the new creature against spiritual wickedness: Eph. 6:12, 'For we wrestle not against flesh and blood, but against the rulers of the darkness of this world, against spiritual wickedness in high places;' or wickedness spiritualised in the high places, Πρὸς τὰ πνευματικὰ τῆς πονηρίας ἐν τοῖς ἐπουρανίοις, the choicest faculties of the soul. Satan doth most excite those sins in the heart, and natural conscience makes no resistance against them. It is only an enlightened conscience that understands and abhors this darkness, and loathes those steams which others cherish. Do you wrestle against these which partake most of the devil's nature? Do you dandle them in your minds, or do you groan at the appearance of them? Do you fly from them as you would do from a visible apparition of the devil? These are most contrary to the divine nature and life of God. And a renewed man can no more avoid contesting with them than the nature of a living creature can with poison. But if you can without any reluctancy play the wantons with these in your hearts; if you think pride, vain-glory, ambition, speculative wickedness, &c., no evils; if your hearts never start at the appearance of them; if you entertain them as welcome guests, though you be never so free from the filthiness of the flesh, you have yet the strength of Satan's image in you, nothing of a Christian formed. A natural man may quarrel with some sins, not with all; renewed men with all, because all are enemies to God, and to the life of grace in the heart. He is always with arms in his hand to extirpate sin, and drive the Canaanite from his forts as well as the open field.

(3.) Are you in the like manner affected against temptations and occasions of sin? The state of regeneration makes the soul more subject to the assaults of temptations than before, from the envy of Satan, who stomachs the happiness of the new creature. Do your souls start at the appearance of a temptation? Do you regard any enticement to a departure from God as your torment? Do you discountenance it at the first approach, and give it no civiller entertainment, than 'Get you behind me, Satan'? Christ in the flesh did so, and Christ formed in the heart will do no less; if he happen to come near the way of evil men, he will observe the wise man's counsel, Prov. 4:14, 15, he will 'avoid it, pass not by it, turn from it, and pass away.' His spirit will rise against anything that would intrude upon him, which looks unfriendly towards God. The nobleness of the new nature will make him disdain a sordid temptation, and inspire him with a holy generosity; and the stronger the nature, the more vigorously will it oppose that which would deform it. And if any temptation break in upon it at any time, and master it, how restless is it to be delivered from it, applies itself with all its force to heaven, complains against it, engageth God's power on its side, makes up the gap where sin hath broken in, and fortifies the place to prevent a future assault! In short, a natural man nourishes inward lusts, meets motions to sin half way, smiles upon an approaching temptation. A new creature starts at the first appearance for the most part, frowns upon Satanical suggestions, turns aways his eyes from beholding vanity. One makes provision to maintain them, the other to destroy them; one submits to the tempter, the other arms himself against him.

8. Put this question to yourselves, What delight do you find in God and his ways? This indeed is an evident sign of the new nature; by this men may judge of themselves, if they will not deceive and flatter themselves in their search. This is the greatest evidence of sincerity in all the ways of God. For the law cannot be in any man's heart, unless he delight to do the will of God: Ps. 40:8, 'Thy law is within my heart, I delight to do thy will, O my God.' He will be carried out with a spiritual joy and triumph to the acting what is spiritually good, with a mighty pleasure, as great as the body takes in eating when it is hungry, or drinking when it is thirsty. It was thus with our Saviour in the flesh, it is thus with Christ formed in the heart, it is his meat and drink to do the will of God; not so much in the new creature as it was in Christ, because in that there is a remaining principle of resistance, in Christ none. It is then he can 'delight himself in the Lord,' Isa. 58:14, and count him his 'exceeding joy,' Ps. 43:4. As it is an argument that Seneca gives of the divine original of the soul, that it is most pleased with divine speculations, it is no less an argument of the new creation, when it is delighted, not only with the speculative, but with the practical contemplation of God, when the soul that triumphed before in the pleasures of sin can burn with an ardent love to God, and solace itself in communion with him; and unless holy services be our delightful element, we have not a likeness to that God, who is not only righteous, but delights in 'righteousness, loving-kindness, and judgment,' Jer. 9:24. Every being owes so much

respect to its own welfare, as not to act sluggishly and drowsily in its main concern; for the same love which excites it to perform those things which are essential to its preservation will oblige it to act with the highest complacency; and the more conducing they are to the well-being of the creature, the more powerful is the joy which spreads itself through the whole essence of the creature; therefore holy services being as intrinsecal to a holy principle as the most inward operations of any creature can be to its nature, will be done with a vigorous frame, and an edged intenseness of spirit. Without this, in some degree, nothing requisite to the operations of a new creature can be performed; without it we have no aversion to that which is contrary to the law, nor an inclination to what is conformable to it. It is a consent of the will to the whole law, Rom. 7:16, a delight of the affections in it; a consent to it in respect of the goodness; a delight in it (ver. 22), in respect of the authority enjoining it, as it is the law of God; not principally as it is in some parts conformable to human reason, but as it is the divine will, whereby both the sovereignty, holiness, and righteousness of God is owned by the whole inward man; the understanding, will, and affections, conspiring together with a strong delight in God and his law. Hence you find David so often expressing his delight in it, Ps. 119:14, 35, 47, 70, 77, &c. And indeed so much of weariness as we have in any service, so much of an old nature and a legal frame; so much as we have of love and delight, so much we have of a new creature, and new covenant grace. A natural man cannot have any of this choice joy in any spiritual service, because it is against his nature; no more than a fish can delight to be upon the land out of its proper element; but a new creature hath little delight in anything, but as it regards God, and tends to him; other men's delights are terminated in the flesh, but the elevations of a renewed soul are highly spiritual. How then is it with you? Are the duties of religion, communion with God in them, your delightful element? Is a flight of your love to him, the acting for his glory, as pleasant as flattery to a proud nature, or gain to a covetous disposition?

Have you little satisfaction in what you do, but still breathe and strive after a higher frame, and cannot rest, till with your choice embraces of your souls you clasp about God himself? O happy man! None but a divine nature could fill thee with such pleasing transports.

Use 4. Is of exhortation.

1. To those who are new creatures, that have some comfortable evidence in their souls, that there is the image of God renewed in them.

(1.) How should you admire and glorify God? Is it possible that so noble a work can be unattended with a spirit of gratitude? How should you be filled with a sense of divine goodness, and formed to set forth his praise? Surely this of thankfulness is not one of the least good works you are created unto. Before, when you were alienated from the life of God, you were estranged from his love and his praise, you would never glorify him whom you did not affect; but since a heavenly nature is introduced, a heavenly work should become the very life of your souls; tongues and hearts should be set on fire by grace.

[1.] Has not God made you differ from the whole mass of the corrupted world? There is as great a difference between a new and an old creature as between the clearest day and the darkest night; as between Christ, who is glorified in heaven, the head of his own flock, and the devil, who is damned in hell, the head of the unbelieving world; so they are opposed by the apostle, 2 Cor. 6:14, 15. Might you not have run down the stream with others, lived only a natural life with others, and at last died an eternal death, and descended, with all your intellectual and moral endowments, to the place only due to corrupt nature? But God, the God that is blessed for ever, hath breathed into you a breath of life, caused you to stand up before him with a resemblance of his nature, set you apart for himself, wrought you for glory, and made you live another life, a life by the faith of the Son of God. And is it not reason you should differ from all the world in your praises of him, who hath made you differ so vastly in your state and condition?

[2.] Hath not God in this bestowed upon you a higher perfection than all natural perfection in the world? The lowest degree of sense is more excellent than the highest inanimate perfection; therefore a fly, in regard of life, is more excellent than a diamond, or the sun itself. The lowest degree of reason is above the highest degree of sense, and the lowest degree of renewing grace transcends the highest degree of reason, because this in the highest degree is but human and natural, that in the lowest degree spiritual and divine. Therefore you owe more to God for your regeneration than all creatures of the world do for their natural existence. He hath done more for you, in communicating to you his own nature, than if he had made you viceroys over men and angels, and put the whole created world under your feet, without investing you with this new creation.

[3.] And this God hath done for you, when you were in the common lump, and had no more worth in yourselves to move him to it than the rest of the world. No other motive on your part but misery. All the world had the same; for it lay in the like condition. All that you had, all that you were, was proper to move him to a contempt of you, and a loathing you for ever. It was the invention of his own overflowing love, not any persuasion of your worth. What were you, and what was your father's house, that he should thus translate you from the drudgery of sin to the liberty of grace, from a spiritual death to a divine life? Had God called you out of the womb of nothing, unshaped as the great chaos, and asked you what degree of creatures you were willing to be raised unto, would you have presumed to desire God to make you like himself? Yet God in regeneration raised you to a state you durst not ask, above a rational creature, even to a divine, when he had no motive to anything, but to turn you, with Nebuchadnezzar, to graze among the beasts, and partake with devils in the eternal misery of that image you had contracted.

[4.] It is therefore a wonderful and miraculous change. If the framing the body of man be so 'wonderful' a work, Ps. 139:14, and a curious piece of embroidery, how much more admirable is this new formation of the soul into the likeness of God. If we should see a silly fly or a poisonous spider, a clod of earth, or a glow-worm, transformed into a glittering star, it would not be so great a miracle; it would be a change from one natural image to another. But this is a change from hell to heaven, from being a limb of the devil to become a member of Christ, from a worse than Egyptian darkness into a marvellous light. That is but a change of one innocent nature into another; this a change of a nature hateful to God into a nature delightful to him, a corrupt creature into an holy one, a change of something worse than a bare creature into something like the great Creator and Redeemer. This is your change, therefore the highest obligation in the world lies upon you, to praise and glorify God. It is in the day of your regeneration that God hath rolled away the reproach of your corruption and death, as he said of the Israelites when they were circumcised in Canaan, Joshua 5:9.

To quicken you to praise,

First, Often reflect upon your former state. Cast your eyes back upon what you were, that you may be thankful for what you are. Ah, what was I once? An hater of God, and hated by him; one bearing the image of Satan, and delighting in it; a noisome heap of lusts, estranged from God, sold under sin, dead to goodness, an enemy to the law. What a condition was I in then! Good Lord, how astonishing was thy mercy, how wonderful thy love, how great was thy power, to draw me out of this state!

Secondly, Review what you are. What am I now? Here is a new light in my understanding, new inclinations in my will; I can now look upon God with pleasure and run his ways with delight. Christ is my only joy, and Christ is my only gain. My old nature is wearing away, my new nature is rising higher and clearer; now am I freed by the blood of Christ from my guilt, and by the Spirit of Christ from my filth. What shall I render to the Lord for these inestimable benefits towards me? O blessed God!

O dear Redeemer! O infinite condescending Spirit, to work these things for me, in me; to clear such a nasty soul, imprint such a heavenly image, conform me to so excellent a pattern, and by grace to fit me for a glorious eternity! Let then the love of the author, the excellency of the work, the misery of your former state, the happiness of your new, be joined together in your considerations to enhance your praise; and since you live the life of God, be sure to live the life of thankfulness.

(2.) As it is your duty to admire and glorify God for making you new creatures, so it is your duty and advantage too to preserve in its vigour this new nature in you. When Adam's life was infused, he was to preserve it by feeding upon the fruits of paradise, Gen. 1:29. And you must preserve your spiritual lives by the fruits of divine institutions placed in the church. The inner man is to be strengthened; Paul prays to this purpose for the Ephesians, Eph. 3:16, 'that he would grant you to be strengthened with might by his Spirit in the inner man,' which is not, as some understand it, a strengthening of reason, mind, and understanding, The Scripture by heart understands the mind, will, and judgment, but the apostle joins this inner man so with the heart (ver. 17, 'That Christ may dwell in your hearts by faith'), that he doth manifestly put a difference between this inner man and the heart, making one the seat, the other the root in it. The apostle wishes them not a strength of the soul, but a strength of the new man and image of Christ in the soul. The devil is a mighty enemy to it; he hath lost a servant; he will leave no stone unturned to recover him; his servant will be his judge; he will therefore endeavour to overthrow him. Go to God, therefore, for new supplies in the case of Satan's assaults; desire him to put a vigour into your grace, water the seeds, and blow up the divine spark. Our Saviour desired assisting and strengthening grace for Peter, when he foresaw the devil's preparations to worry him, Luke 22:31, 32. So should we for ourselves, and Christ will not be backward to second us in it; yea, he will prevent us, and send in an auxiliary force over and above the standing habit which makes up the new creature. We need the gales of heaven to blow us forward, the concourse of God to his gracious creature, as well as his common concourse to his natural. Is it not the highest reason to engage all in the defence, and strengthening that which is the delight of God, the happiness of the soul, and the envy of the devil? What is worth our care, if this be thought worthy of our neglect? Sloth in preserving and strengthening argues a lesser value of a thing. Would you lose beauty for deformity, health for sickness? Would you lose the pleasures of heaven for the anguish of hell? Preserve this image then from being defaced, and look that Satan draw no more black lines in your hearts. 'Skin for skin, and all a man hath will he give for his life;' eat his own flesh to preserve his life as long as he can. Oh then, if I may so say, soul for soul, and all that you have, you should give and employ for maintaining this spiritual life, which is as much above a natural life as the sun above a dunghill. Blow it up every day, dress the lamps as the priests in the temple. It is for want of this strengthening it, that we have so little liveliness in duty. It is for want of this excitation that we walk so often in darkness. What have we else to do but this? Preservation and strengthening of life is the chief design of men in the world. Is not a divine life of more worth? Let not then the cares of our bodies surpass those for our souls, and our fondness to natural life exceed our affection to spiritual life. We know but in part, we see but as in a glass darkly. The inclinations of our hearts to righteousness are not in their fell strength.

(3.) Grow up to a taller stature. There must be a daily putting off the old man, and a putting on the new, a renewing the inward man day by day, 2 Cor. 4:16. And though at the first regeneration there is the forming all the essential parts of grace, yet afterwards there is a daily augmentation (the Galatians were both knowing God, and known of him, Gal. 4:9, yet of these did the apostle travail, till Christ was formed again, ver. 19), till the design of Christ be fully complied with, and the soul grown up to the measure of the stature of the fulness of Christ, by the participation of his nature. As providence is a continued creation, so growth is a continued regeneration. As a man grows in reason by new improvements, so ought a Christian in grace, by new additions. Things are not ripened at once. The spirits in raw and immature bodies are depressed by gross and earthy mixtures with them, till they are encouraged by the sun and showers, and thereby able to digest the crude parts, and arrive at perfection.

[1.] This must be: Job 17:9, 'The righteous shall hold on his way, and he that hath clean hands shall be stronger and stronger.' The new nature can no more stand at a stay, than a living tree can, till it come up to the measures of its nature. It is the nature of seed to propagate itself, and spread its virtue into branches and fruit. It will be aspiring to that perfection which nature hath allotted to it. If you do not grow, it is a sign there is no life in you. It is but a common gift, or a common grace, at best; the counterfeit, not the reality of the new creature. Living natures do thrive; pieces of art stand at a stay. He is no member of Christ, but as a wooden leg or arm; not knit by any vital band, but some extrinsic ligaments; not fed with the increases of God, because he doth not grow. To content ourselves with a low degree of grace, makes us unworthy of the benefit of regeneration, and below those that pretend to a likeness to God.

[2.] It must be uniform. As it is one habit which is infused, so it equally thrives in all the parts of it. An unequal growth is the effect of a disease, not of nature. As nature causes a proportion of parts in the make, so likewise a proportion of parts in the growth. It is not a growth in faith, and a decay in love; or a growth in love, and a decay in faith. To pretend to the one without the other, is to have an head without an heart, a life without blood or spirits. A natural man may grow in some moral ornaments, as a dead man in hair and nails; but a spiritual vitality shews itself in an equal increase of all the members in the new creature. And it is best discerned by the thriving of those graces which are most contrary to your natural disposition, which cannot so well be discerned in those which have some foundations in moral natures; as humility hath a mild disposition, which by the addition of grace, advanceth to an eminent humility. But a new creature thrives in those graces which were most contrary to his corrupt nature, now over-mastered. The second draught of a picture defaceth not one line or two of the former, but the whole frame, to make it more near the original. And thus a new creature ought to grow as the vine, and revive as the corn, in all the branches and fruits proper to its nature, Hosea 14:7.

[3.] By this we please God and pleasure ourselves. The more illustrious any work is, the more glory redounds to the artist. If the beginnings of the new creation be so amiable as to make heaven itself in love with it, how infinitely will God be pleased to see it grow to maturity among the whirlwinds and storms of temptations; every increase, adding new colours and lustre to this beauty, will renew the jubilee in heaven. Thus will God pronounce it good at first, and very good the nearer it comes to perfection, as he did in the creation of the world. By this growth you will have a greater capacity for heaven; for if the first new creation capacitates a man for glory, the higher it springs, the more beautiful the divine nature grows, the nearer it is to glory and the fitter to be planted in an eternal paradise, the more a right to heaven will appear to yourselves.

(4.) A fourth exhortation. Behave yourselves in your ordinary walk, as new creatures of another rank from the world. It is the inference the apostle makes from the new state wherein the Ephesians were, 'For you were sometimes darkness, but now light in the Lord: walk as children of the light,' Eph. 5:8. You must bring forth fruits meet for regeneration, meet for him by whom you are renewed, as the ground doth herbs, meet for him by whom it is dressed, Heb. 6:7.

[1.] Adorn the gospel, whereby the divine impression is made upon you. The apostle argues against lying, and by the same reason against all sin, from this head, Col. 3:9, 10. The gospel adorns the soul by its impression; the soul should adorn the gospel by its conversation: Titus

2:10, 'Adorn the doctrine of God our Saviour in all things.' Let the writing of the law in the heart appear on the other side of the life, and the divine light in your hearts shine in your outward man, as a candle through a lantern, that God may be glorified, Mat. 5:16. Let not lust and sin, extraneous to the new creature, bear any rule in any action; let no unworthy action reproach your profession. Do nothing unbecoming one who is like him that rules the world, unbecoming that word and gospel which God hath magnified above all his name. Defile not your garments; we can never walk with God but in white, Rev. 3:4, in the whiteness of purity, not in the blackness of sin. Do not any works of Satan with the nature of God upon you. Indeed, we may be ashamed, that when there is so much of the image of Christ in the gospel, there should be so little of the image of Christ in our lives. Walk as those that are enrolled among the spirits of just men made perfect, as those who have the honour to be of the assembly of the first-born; live to God, not to yourselves. The more wicked the generation is you live in, the more it is your duty to shine, as the lights of heaven in the darkness of the earth, Philip. 2:15, and the more it will be your commendation, as it was the praise of Job, that he was upright in the land of Uz, among the race of profane Esau, not among the offspring of praying Jacob: Job 1:1, 'That man was perfect, and feared God.'

[2.] Live above affections to a drossy world, if you would honour your new nature. An earthly spirit cannot be the effect of a heavenly birth. Let not the rattles of your childhood be your present pleasure, or the bewitching world have any influence upon you. The world is no fit boundary for the soul in its natural capacity, much less in its spiritual; it is too empty for an immortal soul, much more for a divine nature. Let not anything on this side God be your darling, but your footstool, to mount you nearer heaven. Value them only as they enable you to do the higher duties of religion without distracting cares, and are subservient to the honouring God in the world. As the new creature was not redeemed with a vile price, so it is not endued with so sordid a nature, as to be much in love with these things. The conquest of this is one of the first fruits of the new birth. 1 John 5:4, 'Whatsoever is born of God, overcomes the world;' there is a mighty antipathy between the world, and anything that is the offspring of God. There cannot be so much ignorance of the things of another world, as to prize so vile a piece, as a house with walls and furniture, infected with a sinful leprosy. Let the inward contempt of the blandishments of it grow up in you; distract not yourselves with cares for it, but trust in God's promise, and leave things to the conduct of his wise providence. It is inconsistent with a new nature to lie at the bottom of this great sea, sucking up weeds and sand, and never peep its head above water, towards heaven.

[3.] Be much in the thoughts and views of the divine original of your nature. Shall the new nature seldom look up to that place whence it descended, or cast its eye upon that beautiful hand that framed it? Surely the new creature cannot be so unnatural. Employ your souls in exercises of an unbounded love to God, a settled delight in him, a high esteem of the righteousness of his nature, and an habitual walking with him; let the esteem of him, and vilifying yourselves, be your daily employment. The looking upon him will transform you more into his image; by this spiritual converse you will partake of a new brightness, and clearer lineaments. Every view will leave a greater perfection upon his image in you, by a reflection of a glory, 2 Cor. 3:18. By this your hearts will be more suitable to those regions of blessedness to which the divine image is hastening. It will make you sweat out some corruption every day, and advance you some steps toward the state of bliss.

[4.] Fix your aims on a state of perfection. You are to walk, not to stand still. Never rest till all that righteousness which of right belongs to that divine nature in you, be conferred upon you; breathe after a more close conjunction with the original. Keep up in a due sprightliness your detestations of sin, which you had when you were first enlivened;

with what a holy indignation you flung away your lusts, with a Get you hence, and, What have I to do any more with idols? Set an edge upon this hatred every day, sharpen your indignation more and more. Preserve in your souls those affections which did rise up in you, when the irresistible charms of divine love did first allure you, when you first cast your eyes upon this new likeness and image of God; quicken them daily, and 'press forward towards the mark for the prize of the high calling of God in Christ.'

[5.] Let your affection be carried to everything which partakes of the same image. There is in all creatures a kindness to those of their own nature; the most ravenous do not prey upon their own species; all men, descending from Adam, having the same nature, have some kindness to those of their own kind; and all descending from Christ have the same nature, the same affections and instincts. It is in love and holiness wherein God doth decipher himself in the soul; he would not be drawn in any other attributes in the heart of man; and thus in the Scripture he publisheth himself in the abstract as holiness and love, delighting to be imitated by his creature in those two perfections, 'God is love, and he that dwells in God dwells in love,' 1 John 4:16. Love is, therefore, the nature of the new creature, and love to the same objects whereon God's love is pitched, first himself, then his image in his creature. So the love of God and that of a new creature go hand in hand together; first, the affections of the new nature stream out to God as the prime and original beauty, then to all new creatures, as they partake more or less of this divine image. This universal charity to God, grace, and good men, is the inseparable property of the new creature, the highest perfection of it, and the beginning of a state of glory. Love all those that partake of this divine nature.

[6.] Endeavour to propagate your new nature to others. It is the property of goodness to be diffusive of itself; and God, the highest goodness, is the most communicative. The divine nature should imitate him in this. No nature but delights to propagate itself. The new nature ought not to be sluggish in it; since the great change lies in the end, since the glory of God is set up as its main intendment, it will oblige it to propagate holiness and righteousness, whereby God is most glorified; for thereby the number is increased to represent him on earth and praise him in heaven. No sooner was Paul renewed, but he endeavours to bring all the world into the same frame. The apostate angels, being revolted from God, labour to sink all the world into the same disposition. Fire communicates by a touch its own nature to all matter that comes near it, and turns the hardest metals into its own likeness. So ought that holy fire in a new creature to labour to convert everything into its own flames. This is a peculiar mark set upon the evangelical times, and the special fruit of a gospel impression: Isa. 2:3, 'Many people shall say, Come ye, and let us go up to the mountain of the Lord, to the house of the God of Jacob.' It should be your endeavour that all about you may be the better for you. Strive to affect your children and servants with a sense of the corruption of nature derived from Adam, and the necessity of being implanted in the new head of the world, and partaking of another nature from him. Thus to be a fellow-worker with God is the most absolute work of grace, as to beget in its own likeness is the most perfect work of nature.

And to persuade you to walk and act as new creatures, consider,

First, The excellency of your birth. It is a birth of heaven, a resemblance to God; do nothing below it or unworthy of it. Is it fit for you to lie among the pots and smut yourselves? The consideration of the relation you bear to God should inspire you with heroic resolutions for his glory. You are the only persons that keep up God's honour in the world, and his final anger from it Whenever you are tempted, reflect upon yourselves, as Nehemiah: 'Should such a man as I' do this? Neh. 6:11. Or as Joseph to his mistress, 'Behold, my master hath committed all that he hath to my hand;' behold, God hath put his divine nature in my heart, and 'shall I do this wickedness?' Consider in every action what that God you call Father by regenerating grace, that Christ who is the great exemplar and copy of the image in you, would do in such cases and circumstances. How unworthy is it for a living man to do dead works! As your life springs from the highest principle, let it be employed for the highest ends. Was ever any prince ashamed of his honour? And shall any new creature be ashamed of the particular badge of heaven upon it; of that righteousness which is the true nobility of his nature? Holiness is the beauty of an intellectual and rational creature; it must then be your highest honour to live conformably to the dignity of your nature.

Secondly, It was the intendment of God you should walk in a nobler manner than the rest of the world. Did God infuse into Adam a soul of a higher nature than that of beasts, to enable him to live only the life of beasts? God intended by the infusion of this new principle, that you should live above the sphere of humanity and the rate of man. How doth the apostle chide the Christians because they did not advance above the life of mere man; and therefore gives them a title chiefly belonging to the unregenerate world: 1 Cor. 3:3, 'Are you not carnal, and walk as men?' Our Saviour expects a more worthy carriage from his children than what barely nature can teach them. He would have them as God, and imitators of him, Mat. 5:44–47, and do something peculiar to this new state, which cannot be done by any unregenerate man in the world. Your holiness is not to be of the common level with the morality of the world, but such as may set forth the 'praise of God,' 1 Peter 2:9; they are a 'chosen generation,' therefore should have choice conversations; a 'royal priesthood,' therefore princes' deportments; a 'holy nation and peculiar people,' therefore should have holy and peculiar behaviours. They should thus be public evangelists, to set forth ἐξαγγείλητε, the graciousness and righteousness of God. There is also the highest obligation, because he hath 'called them out of darkness into his marvellous light.' God intended that their conversations should be such as should amaze the world into a love of holiness, and admiration of that light which gives them such excellent directions, and that nature which enables them to so exact a walk. God's temples were not intended to be made dunghills.

Thirdly, Not to walk as new creatures is a dishonour to God. You that do not walk answerable to your high calling do more highly dishonour him than all other persons. You are quite contrary to his image, and represent God to the world as they would have him, not what he is in his own nature; for by a careless walk the world will judge God to be like you, or you very unlike to God. Is God holy, and you impure; God merciful, and you revengeful; God a God of peace, and you fomenters of malice and contention? To pretend to his image with such qualities is to disparage his nature, and rather degrade God to a likeness to the flesh than to mount up to a true resemblance of him: Ps. 50:21, 'Thou thoughtest I was altogether such a one as thyself.' It is a disgrace to a noble father to have a swinish, clownish, ill-bred person pretend to be his son. But how much is the contrary a glory to Christ, as delicious fruit and choice flowers credit the beams of the sun! What a mighty pleasure is it to God to behold a suitable walk of his new creatures! He loves them, and 'his countenance doth behold the upright,' Ps. 11:7. How much must he, who is holiness itself, take complacency in the holiness of it. If he loves it while in a low degree, no question but he loves it more in a higher exaltation. How does the Holy Ghost repeat Enoch's walking with God twice in Gen. 5:22, 24, to witness his pleasure in it?

Fourthly, Not to walk suitable to your new creation is a mighty disadvantage to yourselves. Though a new creature doth not totally lose his grace if a temptation deflower his purity, yet his grace suffers an impair, and perhaps he may never recover the same degree of grace and comfort he had before. It is a question whether David ever had his sails filled with such strong gales of the Spirit after his fall as he had before. The marks of a disease will hang about us after the disease is cured, and the same stock of health may never be restored again. If you do let your hearts run out at any time to any sinful pleasure, though it may not raze out the image, yet it will make you more unfit for those views of God which can only maintain it. When you come before him, after such a departure, how will your hearts recoil upon you? With what pleasure can you look upon him whom you have so abused in his image in your souls, and in his image in his law? Besides, every unworthy walk detracts somewhat from the weight of that crown you might otherwise expect to be reserved in heaven for you, and makes it of a greater alloy. But if you keep close to the law in the word, and the law in your hearts, what communications will you have from God? What inward touches and feelings of him? How hastily will he run to meet you half way, and kiss you with the kisses of his mouth? 'Thou meetest him that rejoices and worketh righteousness,' Isa. 64:5. How intimately will he wind himself into the secret corners of your hearts, as John 14:23, 'and make his abode with you;' and like fire in every part of iron, fill every part of the new man with a glowing and divine heat?

Fifthly, Such an exact walk will mightily stop the current of sin. It may justly be feared, the sins of many have taken too much heart from the unsuitable carriages of professors. But a walk according to the rule of the new creation might inflame others to godliness, at least stifle some corrupt motions, suspend some inclinations to sin, and for a time bind up the devil in them. This is the greatest charity to the world; by other benefits we advantage particular persons, by a holy example all that behold us. It strikes an awful reverence into the hearts of men, as being a ray of God; what the gospel enjoins are things comely, and of good report, many of them lovely and illustrious, even in a carnal eye; therefore such expressions of a gospel impression would engender admirations of it, cast a lustre upon the truth of God; men will look upon such works with reverence,* and 'glorify God in the day of their visitation' or conversion, as Calvin understands it. To be a holy people is to be 'sought out,' they are both joined, Isa. 62:12. Many by seeing the holiness of the church in gospel times shall be induced to give up their names to the Lord; it will tend more to the regeneration of others than a thousand sermons; it will raise the reputation of Christianity, and cause them to believe it to be of a divine extract; it would stir men up to a holy emulation to be like them. And beholding the law of God transcribed in the life, it would convincingly answer the cavils of the world, and demonstrate the commands they count grievous to be in themselves practicable. But whither is this gospel ornament we have been speaking of fled? Where is it to be found? How few walk as new creatures, 'as becomes the gospel,' however they profess it, and pretend a zeal for it!

Exhortation 2. To those who lie still buried in the ruins of the old Adam, who carry the image of beasts in their lives, or of devils in their hearts, or both, such I would advise earnestly to seek this new creature state. Let not your hearts be besotted to a neglect of it, and stupefied into endless torments, which will, as surely as you live, be the dreadful issue, if this be not attained. To be so long under the gospel, and retain the obstinacy of an old nature to God, is a high aggravation. Talk not of sparing the old man; it is your enemy, wound it to death, use the utmost severity towards it; put it off, leave not a rag, if possible, behind; send it away, as Abraham did Hagar, and without so much as a bottle of water, to despoil it of any hopes of return. But, alas, how do you cherish and hug this enemy! How do you value it, as if it were a part of yourselves; as if you could not live without poison, or be happy without misery! How do you bid the new man stand far from you, as if it were a real torment to be in the arms of Christ, and the new creation your disease, not your felicity! Though you were the most unblameable in your lives, free from any pretence of an accusation there, what were you without this change, but devils in the garb of angels of light, poison in fair cabinets, and the natures of serpents in the bodies of men? What is become of your souls? Are they so immersed in flesh, that nothing of spirit can make impressions upon them? Have men quite forsworn the attaining any other excellency than what mere nature bestowed upon them? What deformity do you find in God, that you slight his image, which should be imprinted on you? What frightful thoughts have you of the Spirit that solicits you? How come your souls so senseless of their real happiness? Oh what a happy thing were it, if this day Christ were formed in all our hearts; that though we are nasty dunghills, worse than the stable wherein our Saviour was born in the flesh, we might become the sanctuary of our Lord and his Spirit; it is then the angels would renew their song at the birth of Christ in the heart as well as that in the world, 'Glory to God in the highest,' peace and eternal good will to such a soul. If you have any strugglings in your hearts, any convictions upon your consciences, and make not a further progress, these will be so far from being your advantage, that they will add an emphasis to your damnation.

Let me use some motives to press you.

(1.) Shall not the loathsomeness and misery of your present state startle you? It is a nature that makes you 'the children of wrath,' Eph. 2:3. Were your old natures acceptable to God, what need any change? But the requiring this change demonstrates the old nature to be abhorred by God. This nature is the devil's filth, the serpent's poison, a deformed leprosy; it is the pain, anguish, torment, rack of every man that dies in it; it smells rank of hell. Is not another nature then desirable? When you commit some grievous sin, to which you are not accustomed, are you not dejected? Do you not think worse of yourselves for it? And are you not pleased when you can escape it? If the reformation of one sin be a desirable thing, how much more the reformation of the whole nature! For if a drop of that filth bubbling up in the life be so loathsome, what loathsomeness is there in the heart, where the fountain springs! What gall of bitterness must be in the root, when a little of the fruit is so bitter to your taste!* Corruption is the dishonour of your natures, the poison of your souls, the cause of all your unhappiness. It is this that banished you from paradise, ravishing away your pleasures, subjected you to vanity, the wrath of God, the hatred of angels, and tyranny of devils; it is this that hath deformed your souls. Despoil yourselves of this cursed old man, give yourselves no rest till you have conquered it; never say, it is incorporated in your entrails and marrow. Where the question is about your everlasting happiness, let no excuse prevail.

(2.) Shall not the excellency of another state allure you? It is the excellency of any piece of art to come nearest its original; that star is most glorious that doth most partake of the sun's light and power. The very light of nature tells us the state wherein we are is not our perfection; something the soul flutters at beyond this, though it naturally under-stands not what it is. Is it not, then, the happiness of the soul to be reduced to its true centre, to be reinstated in an unspotted nature, to return to a due respect to those ends for which it was made, to have the understanding conversant about the loveliest object, the will inclined to the most amiable goodness, and the affections twining about it, and growing up with it? Can it be anything else but the highest excellency, to live the life of God; to have the image of God wrought upon you, and your souls conformed to his holiness? Can that be an imperfec-tion, which makes you like an infinite righteousness? It was the highest perfection of man to be made according to the image of God, wherein God, as in a glass, might see a resemblance of himself. Is it not then a desirable thing to have it drawn again with more lively and lasting colours, after sin and Satan have so basely defaced it? All other things are not the perfection of man's nature; for whatsoever else there is, is possessed by beasts or devils; the pleasures of sense, by beasts; the endow-ments of knowledge, by devils; but the divine nature by neither. This therefore, which neither devils can be blessed with, nor beasts capable of, is only the perfection of the soul, more excellent than the soul itself, since that which perfects is more excellent than that which is perfected by it. Original corruption destroys your health, sullies your purity, enslaves your liberty. Regeneration restores your health, expels your filthiness, and knocks off your fetters. Let the excellency of this better state prevail with you.

(3.) Will the honour of the thing allure you? Where shall you meet with so honourable a relation? It is more honour to be a new creature in rags than a carnal prince in purple, though the greatest in the world, for you will then be settled heirs of all the promises. Is it not, then, more glorious to partake of the nature of that God, who created and commands the world, than by the force of the old nature to be slaves to sordid lusts, which are both a drudgery and a disease? As a spirit is more excellent than the body, so a spiritual being and frame is more honourable than a fleshly.* There is a greater relation between God and a new creature than between natural fathers and sons. The sons of men have but a little particle of the vile matter and flesh of their fathers, but a renewed man hath the whole divine Spirit in him; and by virtue of this, all things will, one time or other, rise up and call you blessed; you will be more allied to Jesus Christ, by the inward formation of him in your hearts, than the blessed virgin by the conception of Christ in her womb, Luke 11:27. She was more happy by partaking of Christ in her heart, than by conferring a flesh on Christ from her body. What an honourable thing is it to be moulded into the divine likeness! Can you be more glorious, unless you were gods?

(4.) Will pleasure charm you? View it here. Pleasure must necessarily follow this new state, as light the sun; there is no state without a pleasure pertaining to it. Pleasures of sense belong to a life of sense; intellectual pleasures to a life of reason; divine pleasures to a divine nature. 'All the ways of wisdom are ways of pleasantness,' Prov. 3:17. An infinite perfection is attended with an infinite happiness; the more lineaments, then, you have of the divine perfection, the more tastes you will have of the divine happiness. God hath an infinite pleasure in his own perfections; it is his felicity to enjoy himself, to view himself. Pleasure then must naturally result from this image drawn in the soul; and as naturally, I conceive, according to the degrees of it, as the pleasure God hath in his own holiness and love. The pleasure of heaven is the perfection of holiness; therefore there is a pleasure also attending the draught of it here; an imperfect pleasure from the imperfect form of it, as a perfect pleasure from the completing of it in glory. What want can there be of pleasure, if you come into this state? Will you not be conversant about the highest object, and that with your choicest faculties? Can this be without some communications of the pleasure of God, as well as his nature? You will find a pleasure in the very strugglings to get into this state, much more in it.

(5.) Do you profess yourselves enemies to the devil? Why then will you gratify him by continuing in an old nature? He keeps a jubilee when he can draw men into great sins, and bind them under them; his main industry is to make men like himself, and continue them in that likeness. The whole world, that are not of God, lie wrapped up in the devil's image: 1 John 5:19, 'The whole world lies in wickedness, or 'in the wicked one,' Ἐν τῷ πονηρῷ; more consonant to the former verses. Satan and natural men lie nugging together, though the latter dream not of it. His intent in assaulting man in paradise was to destroy the righteousness of his nature; his design now is to hinder the restoration of it, by keeping men off from the means, making them have false thoughts of the unpleasantness of it, as though it were a state injurious to man's tranquillity, by suppressing convictions, which are the first portals to the courts of blessedness. Oh, gratify not the devil; fly from his image, that you may fly from his misery.

(6.) Why will you cross your own sentiments, when sober reason in you may have leave to speak? What do you think was the end for which you came into the world? Was it to serve the devil or God? Whose image is it most rational for you to hear? Are there not innate desires in man to be as God? Adam desired it unlawfully; the same spirit runs through the veins of his posterity. God has shewn you a way in his word whereby you may lawfully desire it, and successfully accomplish it. Do not all creatures, one way or other, instruct you in it? Do they not all run back to their fountain; rivers into the sea, that they may have a new formation in it; beams retracted to the sun; and why not the soul to God? Do they not all declare the glory of God? And shall man stand alone? And what way is there for him to declare God's glory, but by the reformation of his nature? You once had this desirable nature in your first head, and lost it; you may have the re-possession in the second head, and for ever preserve it. You cannot deny your obligation to have it, therefore you cannot deny your duty to seek it. You know your souls received their original from him; you likewise know that there is an obligation to return to him. As the spirit naturally returns to God who gave it, so it cannot be happy in that return, unless it first morally return to God, to be formed like him.

(7.) Nothing else can advantage you if you want this new-creature state. You can no more enjoy happiness by Christ without it, than Adam did in paradise, in the presence of God, with the nakedness of his nature. His being in paradise, the richer part of the whole lower creation, could neither heal him nor content him, after the loss of the purity of his nature. In that happy place his conscience racked him. There he fled from his Creator, which in his innocent nature he never attempted to do; and all the pleasures of that place could not restore him to God's favour or his own peace, without the promise of a seed, and by that seed the restoration in part of his former image.

(8.) Lastly, take this for your encouragement, it is attainable by the meanest person, Col. 3:11. In the new creation 'there is neither Greek nor Jew, circumcision nor uncircumcision, barbarian, Scythian, bond nor free; but Christ is all and in all;' that is, there is no distinction of any. The eloquence of the Greek, or the rudeness of the barbarian; the uncircumcision of the Gentile, or the circumcision of the Jew; the baseness of the slave, or the liberty of the freeman, doth neither advantage nor disadvantage them in this work of the new creation; and he names

Scythians, as being the rudest and most unpolished among all the known Gentiles.* No natural endowments advantage us; no worldly indigencies hinder us. The soul of the meanest is as capable of the new creation as the soul of the highest. There is nothing required to the putting on the new man, which is not attainable by the one as well as the other; yea, sooner by those of the meanest endowments, as wanting that fuel for their pride, which is the chief hindrance to a gospel impression. God values nothing but his own image; neither is he any more taken with the glittering parts and wisdom of men than our Saviour with the glory of the temple, which his ignorant disciples did so much admire.

Quest. But what means must be used to obtain this excellent privilege?

Ans. It is indeed the work of God, yet means may be used.† He that observes precepts of morality shall gain moral habits; and by practising acts of temperance become temperate. So he that follows the rules given in the word for attaining the new creation, shall have it produced in him; and the more assuredly, because it is not produced by him but by God, who is more able to create new hearts in us than the unregenerate man is to work a moral reformation.

For means:

1. Be deeply sensible of original corruption. View yourselves in the glass of Adam; reflect upon the fall, and the dreadful consequences of it; take an exact account of the enmity of thy nature, as the word represents it. We must acquaint ourselves with our sin and misery, and have self-emptying thoughts, before we can seek after a new creature. Man is apt to think his nature good enough; and this makes him the more miserable and wretched, and causes him to think there needs no change, Rev. 3:17.

2. Be deeply humbled before God. Lay yourselves low before him, and abhor yourselves in dust and ashes. Complain of your corrupt nature; melt before God, dissolve into tears. When you are weary and heavy laden, sensible of it by contrition, Christ will give rest by regeneration.

The heart must be melted before it be made new. Pride must be humbled; we must be vile in our own eyes, as well as vile in our own nature. 'The Lord is nigh to them that are of a broken heart,' Psalm 34:18.

3. Often meditate of the excellency of this state, as it is represented in the word. Men hear and forget; they leave behind them what they have heard; they hide it not in their hearts; therefore doth not the word profit them. Think often of the honour of being a new creature, as well as the necessity of being a new creature; if you have any thoughts arising of resting upon your knowledge, or morality, or good meaning, say to your soul, as the apostle in another case, O my soul, 'covet earnestly the best gifts, yet shew I unto thee a more excellent way.' If any imagination arise which flatters you with hopes of being in Christ without an inward change, regard it as an angel from the bottomless pit, sent from the great impostor to seduce you from your happiness.

4. Fixedly resolve not to be at rest till you procure it at the hands of God. Perhaps you may have had some resolutions before, and some diversion hath chilled those purposes; waver not with uncertain velleities between inclination and aversion. Content not yourselves with sluggish wishes, and yawning desires, but put heart and hand to the work. Set vigorously to it, and those sons of Anak, those seeming terrifying difficulties, will fly before you. Where doth the Scripture tell you, that God will neglect his laborious creature, and stand by without assisting him in his serious endeavours? No, no; God will not be wanting in his power, nor the Spirit in his operations, if we firmly purpose and strongly pursue. 'God is near to all that call upon him in truth,' Psalm 145:18; that is, to all that call upon him with a true purpose and desire for his mercy: he is near by his merciful presence, not by his essential presence only. Fool not away your vows in vain mirth, nor drown your resolutions in sensual pleasures. Say as David in another case, 'I have sworn, and will perform it,' that I will in good earnest endeavour that I may become a new creature, Psalm 119:106.

5. Pray. Regeneration is against the inclinations of old nature; intermit not therefore to call earnestly for help from heaven; it is best attained upon the knee. God is the foundation of all vitality; the life of grace is no less the effect of his breath than the soul of Adam. Go to Christ, in whom, as in a steward, is treasured up a fulness of grace, to dispense to him that seeks it. Beg earnestly of the Spirit, who is the officer appointed, the great limner to draw this image in us. Why can you not go to Christ as well as the leper, and lie sobbing before him, 'Lord, if thou wilt, thou canst make me clean,' thou canst change my nature? Do it constantly, do it fervently, and take notice with what inspirations you will be filled. But do you solicit him for this mercy at all? Has God one breath from thee in a whole week to this purpose? Have you, since you heard it, pressed from the necessity of it, made your case known to God? Has there been one groan, one sigh for it? What a stupid creature is man! Time will not always last; God will be solicited for it, and it is fit he should. An old nature is like an old devil, it cannot be cast out without fasting and prayer. The great changes of the soul are chiefly wrought in prayer and the word: our very looking up to God and upon God in humble prayer makes a gradual transformation in our souls: we never are in the mount with him, but our souls (as Moses his face) look quite of another hue and colour. By frequent converse with friends, we grow more into an imitation of the excellent qualities we perceive in them. Converse with God in frequent prayer and meditation, and you will grow more and more into a holy likeness to him.

6. Attend diligently upon the word. To pray to God to renew you, and slight the word which he hath appointed as an instrument to effect it, is to dishonour God; for while you pray to him to be a father to beget you, you contemn him as a governor, by neglecting the means he hath appointed for such ends. As the devil formed himself in the soul by man's listening to and sucking in his temptation, so Christ forms himself in the soul, by our sucking in the milk of the word, as the disposition of the

nurse is by the milk conveyed to the infant. It is wrought by the gospel, 1 Cor. 4:15, 'for in Christ Jesus I have begotten you through the gospel.' Not by the word of God at large, which consists of law as well as gospel. So the regenerations of old were wrought, not by the law, but by that of gospel mixed in that administration. By this means you may get a spiritual knowledge, and discard that ignorance which is the foundation of an alienation from the life of God, Eph. 4:18, 'alienated from the life of God through the ignorance that is in them, because of the blindness of their hearts.' Study the promises, and plead them before the Lord, for 'by these you are made partakers of the divine nature,' 2 Peter 1:4. Resist not any divine impressions, by a sluggishness and a listlessness. Be not in love with your spiritual death, nor cherish the bondage to sin in your will, when God makes motions to enliven and enlarge you. Welcome the breathings of the Spirit. Open your souls, as some flowers do for the sun; drink in the drops of heaven, as the earth doth the rain; and when the Spirit quickens you by its influences, quicken the Spirit by your earnest supplications, Cant. 4:16; make much of him, persuade his stay. Breathe, O blessed Spirit, upon this wilderness. Never leave till it be changed into a fruitful garden, both pleasant to, and fruitful for, my blessed Creator and gracious Redeemer.

A Discourse of the Efficient Cause of Regeneration

Which were born, not of blood, nor of the will of the flesh,
nor of the will of man, but of God.—JOHN 1:13.

THIS evangelist so plainly describes the deity of Christ, and in so
majestic a style, in the beginning of the chapter, that the accidental
view of it in a book lying open by neglect, was instrumental for the
conversion of Junius, that eminent light in the church, from his atheism.

We shall take our rise only from ver. 9, 'That was the true light, which
lighteneth every man that comes into the world.' John Baptist, who, ver.
6, &c., was to bear witness of this light, was a light by our Saviour's
assertion, 'a burning and a shining light,' John 5:35, but not that 'true
light' which was promised, Isa. 49:6, to be 'a light to the Gentiles, and
the salvation of God to the ends of the earth.' The sun is the true light
in the heavens and of the world; not but that other stars are lights too,
but they all receive their light from the sun. Christ is called the true light,
by nature and essence, not by grace and participation: 1 John 5:20, 'We

know him that is true; and we are in him that is true, even in his Son Jesus Christ,' the natural light and Son of God.

1. True, as opposed to types, which were shadows of this light.

2. True, as opposed to false. Philosophical lights, though esteemed so, are but darkness, and ignes fatui, in comparison of this.

3. True original light, ratione officii, illustrating the whole world with his light. Whatsoever is light in heaven or earth, borrows it from the sun; whosoever is enlightened in the world, derives from him 'which lighteth every man that comes into the world.' Some join coming into the world, to light, and read it thus, 'He is the light coming into the world, which lighteth every man.' The Greek is something ambiguous, and it may be referred to light, though not so commodiously. But the translation which we have hath been followed in all ages of the church; and is contended* for only by those who deny the deity of our Saviour, or are somewhat affected to them that do.

How doth Christ light every man that comes into the world?

1. Naturally. So Calvin; the world was made by him, and therefore that which is the beauty of the world, the reason of man, was made and kindled by him. As all the light the world hath had since the creation flows from the sun, so all the knowledge which sparkles in any man is communicated by Christ, even since the creation, as he is the wisdom of God, and as mediator, preserving those broken relics of the fall: Prov. 20:27, 'The spirit of man is the candle of the Lord,' lighted and preserved by him. The light of nature, those common notions of fit and just in men's consciences, those honest and honourable principles in the hearts of any, those beams of wisdom in their understanding, though faint, and like sparkles raked up in ashes, are kept alive by his mediatory influence, as a necessary foundation for that reparation which was intended in his first interposition.

2. Spiritually. So not only the Socinians, but some very sound, understand it; not that all are actually enlightened, but,

(1.) In regard of power and sufficiency, he hath a power to enlighten every man; able to enlighten, not a few, but every man in the world; as the sun doth not light every man, though it hath a power to do so, and doth actually light every man that shuts not his eyes against it.

(2.) Actually, taking it distributivè, not collectivè; that whosoever is enlightened in the world, hath it commmunicated from Christ; as Ps. 145:14, 'The Lord upholds all that fall, and raises up all those that are bowed down;' as many as are upheld and raised, are upheld and raised by God. He doth indeed 'shine in darkness,' his light breaks out upon men, but they are not the better for it, because 'the darkness comprehends it not'; as when there is but one schoolmaster in a town, we usually say, he teaches all the boys in the town; not that every individual boy comes to school, but as many as are taught, are taught by him. I embrace the former, because the evangelist seems to begin with his person, as God; his office, as mediator; and then descends to his incarnation; and it is a sense which puts no force upon the words. And I suppose that every man is added, to beat down the proud conceits of the Jews, who regarded the Gentiles with contempt, as not enjoying the privileges conferred upon themselves; but the evangelist declares, that what the Gentiles had in natural light, and what they were to have in spiritual light, did, and was to come from him, who would disperse his beams in all nations, ver. 10. And therefore 'he was in the world,' before his coming in the flesh, in regard of his virtue and efficacy, by the spreading his beams over the world, enlightening men in all ages and places with that common light of nature; he was near to every man; 'in him they lived, and moved, and had their being;' but the world by their natural wisdom knew him not, and glorified him not. 'The world was made by him, yet the world knew him not.' Ingratitude hath been the constant portion of the mediator, from the world; they knew him not in past ages, knew him not in the present age of his coming in the flesh; they did not acknowledge him with that affection, reverence, and subjection that was due to him.

He aggravates this contempt of Christ,

1. By the general right he had, 'he came to his own,' Ἐις τὰ ἴδια, ver. 11, meaning the world, it being put in the neuter gender. The whole world was his property and his goods, yet they knew not their owner. In this, worse than the ox or ass.

2. By the special privileges conferred on those to whom he first came, and from whom he should have the most welcome reception; implied in these words, 'and his own,' ὁι ἴδιοι, in the masculine gender, his own people, that had been his treasure, to whom he had given his law, entrusted with the covenants and oracles of God, these 'received him not.' His own, some say, as being peculiarly committed to him, the angel of the covenant; whereas other nations were committed to angels to receive laws from them. His own flesh and blood, who expected a Messiah, to whom he was particularly sent, as being the lost sheep of the house of Israel. Christ is most rejected where he proffers most kindness. Those of Tyre and Sidon, those of Sodom and Gomorrah, would not have used him so ill as Capernaum and Jerusalem, his own people. He descends to shew the loss of them that rejected him, the benefit of those that received him: ver. 12, 'But as many as received him, to them gave he power to become the sons of God, even to them that believe on his name.'

Where is,

1. The subject: those that received him.

2. The benefit: the dignity of sonship.

3. The manner of conferring this benefit: 'gave them power.'

4. The instrumental cause: 'believe on his name.' Though his own rejected him, they lost a dignity which was conferred upon those that received him: he lost not his pains, for he gathered sons to God out of all parts of the world. 'To as many as received him.' It was not now peculiar to the Jews, who boasted of being Abraham's seed, and to have the covenant entailed upon them to be the people of God. It was now conferred upon those who were before Lo-ammi and Lo-ruhamah, Hos.

2:23. It was nothing but faith on his name that gave men the privilege of being the sons of God, and this was communicated to Gentiles as well as Jews. Power: not a power, but a dignity, as the word properly signifies. Not a power if they would, but a will, for they were born of the will of God. Faith brings men into a special relation to God; which faith is more than an assent and giving credit to God; for to believe on God, to believe on his name, is a phrase peculiar to Scripture. 'To become the sons of God;' some understand this of sonship by adoption, but the following verse gives us light to understand it of a sonship by regeneration. St Paul uses the word adoption, but St John, both in his gospel and epistles, speaks more of the new birth, and sonship by it, than any of the other apostles; 'who were born not of blood,' or 'of bloods.' He removes all other causes of this, which men might imagine, and ascribes it wholly to God. This place is variously interpreted. 'Not of blood.' Not by natural instinct, saith one; not by an illustrious stock. The Jews imagined themselves holy by their carnal generation from Abraham in a long train of ancestors. Grace runs not in a blood. It is not often a flower growing upon every ability; 'not many wise, not many mighty.' Not hereditary by a mixture of blood. Natural generation makes men no more regenerate than the rich man in hell was regenerate by Abraham, his natural ancestor, whom he calls 'father Abraham.' Religious parents propagate corruption, not regeneration; carnal generation is by nature, not by grace; by descent from Adam, not by implantation in Christ. Abraham had an Ishmael, and Isaac an Esau: man begets only a mortal body, but grace is the fruit of an incorruptible seed. 'Nor of the will of the flesh.' Not by human election,* as Eve judged of Cain that he should be the Messiah, or Isaac of Esau that he should be heir of the promise, as the Jews say. Not by a choice of those things which are necessary, profitable, or delightful to the flesh;† not by a will affected to the flesh, or things of the flesh. Not by any sensual appetite,‡ whereby men used to adopt one to bear up their names when they wanted posterity of their own. I would rather conceive it to be meant of the strength of nature, which is called flesh in Scripture; not by legal observances, the ceremonies of the law being called carnal or fleshly ordinances, Heb. 9:10. It is not a fruit of nature or profession. 'Nor of the will of man.' Calvin takes the will of the flesh and the will of man for one and the same thing, the apostle using two expressions only to fix it more upon the mind. I rather judge it to be meant thus: not by natural principles, or moral endowments, which are the flower and perfection of man as man. It is not arbitrary, of the will of man, or the result naturally of the most religious education. All the power of regenerate men in the world joined together cannot renew another; all the industry of man, without the influence of the heavens in the sun and rain, cannot produce fruit in the earth, no, nor the moral industry of men grace in the soul; 'but of God,' or the will of God; his own will: James 1:18, 'Of his own will begat he us,' exclusive of all other wills mentioned before. It is the sole efficiency of God; he hath the sole hand in it; therefore we are said to be both begotten and born of him, 1 John 5:18. It is so purely God's work, that as to the principle he is the sole agent; and as to the manifestation of it, he is the principal agent. Not of the will of the flesh, that is only corruption; nor of the will of man, that at best is but moral nature. But whatsoever the meaning of those particular expressions is, the evangelist removes all pretences nature may make to the efficiency of this regeneration, and ascribes it wholly to God.

1. There is a removal of false causes.

2. A position of the true cause.

(1.) The efficient, God.

(2.) The manner, by an act of his will.

Shewing thereby,

[1.] No necessity in him to renew us; no motive but from himself.

[2.] No merit on our parts. Man cannot merit, say the papists, before grace; no child can merit his own birth, no man grace.

Doct. 1. Man, in all his capacities, is too weak to produce the work of regeneration in himself.

It is subjectively in the creature, not efficiently by the creature, neither ourselves nor any other creature, angels, men, ordinances.

Doct. 2. God alone is the prime efficient cause of regeneration.

Doct. 1. For the first. Man, in all his capacities, is too weak to produce the work of regeneration in himself. This is not the birth of a darkened wisdom and an enslaved will. We affect a kind of divinity, and would centre ourselves in our own strength; therefore it is good to be sensible of our own impotency, that God may have the glory of his own grace, and we the comfort of it in a higher principle and higher power than our own. It is not the bare proposal of grace, and the leaving the will to an indifferent posture, balanced between good and evil, undetermined to the one or the other, to incline and determine itself which way seems best to it. Not one will, in the whole rank of believers, left to themselves. The evangelist excepts not one man among them; for as many as received Christ, as many as believed, were the sons of God, who were born; which believers, every one that had this faith as the means, and this sonship as the privilege, were born not of the will of the flesh nor the will of man.

For the proof of this in general,

1. God challengeth this work as his own, excluding the creature from any share as a cause: Ezek. 36:25–27, 'I will sprinkle clean water upon you, I will cleanse you, I will give you a new heart, I will put a new spirit into you, I will take away the heart of stone, I will give you a heart of flesh, I will put my Spirit into you.' Here I will no less than seven times. Nothing is allowed to man in the production of this work in the least; all that is done by him is the walking in God's statutes by virtue of this principle. The sanctifying principle, the actual sanctification, the reception of it by the creature, the removal of all the obstructions of it, the principle maintaining it, are not in the least here attributed to the will of man. God appropriates all to himself. He doth not say he would

be man's assistant, as many men do, who tell us only of the assistances of the gospel, as if God in the gospel expected the first motions of the will of man to give him a rise for the acting of his grace. You see here he gives not an inch to the creature. To ascribe the first work, in any part, to the will of man, is to deprive God of half his due, to make him but a partner with his creature. The least of it cannot be transferred to man but the right of God will be diminished, and the creature go shares with his Creator. Are we not sufficient of ourselves to do anything? and are we sufficient to part stakes with God in this divine work? What partner was the creature with God in creation? It is the Father's traction alone, without the hand of free-will. 'None can come, except the Father, which hath sent me, draw them,' John 6:44. The mission of the Mediator, and the traction of the creature, are by the same hand. Our Saviour could not have come unless the Father had sent him, nor can man come to Christ unless the Father draw him. What is that which is drawn? The will. The will, then, is not the agent; it doth not draw itself.

2. The titles given to regeneration evidence it. It is a creation. What creature can give itself a being? It is a putting in a law and a new heart. What matter can infuse a soul into itself? It is a new birth. What man did ever beget himself? It is an opening the heart. What man can do this, who neither hath the key, nor is acquainted with the wards? Not a man knows the heart; it is deceitful above all things, who can know it?

3. The conveyance of original corruption doth in part evidence it. We have no more interest of our wills in regeneration, than we had in corruption. This was first received by the will of Adam, our first head, thence transmitted to us without any actual consent of our wills in the first transmission; that is conveyed to us from the second Adam, without any actual consent of our wills in the first infusion. Yet though the wills of Adam's posterity are mere passive in the first conveyance of the corrupt habit from him by generation, yet afterwards they are active in the approbations of it, and production of the fruits of it. So the will

is merely passive in the first conveyance of the grace of regeneration, though afterwards it is pleased with it, and brings forth fruit meet for it.

4. Scripture represents man exceeding weak, and unable to do any thing spiritually good. 'So then, they that are in the flesh cannot please God,' Rom. 8:8. He concludes it by his so then, as an infallible consequence, from what he had discoursed before. If, as being in the flesh, they cannot please God, therefore not in that which is the highest pleasure to God, a framing themselves to a likeness to him. The very desire and endeavour of the creature after this, is some pleasure to God, to see a creature straggling after holiness; but they that are in the flesh cannot please him. 'Can any good thing come out of Nazareth?' was said of our Saviour. So may we better say, Can any good thing come out of the flesh, the enslaved, possessed will of man? If it be free since it was captivated by sin, who set it free? Nothing can, but 'the law of the Spirit of life,' Rom. 8:2. To be 'sinners,' and to be 'without strength,' is one and the same thing in the apostle's judgment: Rom. 5:6, 8, 'While we were yet without strength;' afterwards, 'while we were yet sinners;' he doth not say, We are without great strength, but without strength, such an impotence as is in a dead man. Not like a man in a swoon, but a man in a grave. God only is almighty, and man all impotency; God only is all-sufficient, and man all-indigent. It is impossible we can have a strength of our own, since our first father was feeble, and conveyed his weakness to us; by the same reason that it is impossible we can have a righteousness of our own, since our first father sinned: Isa. 43:26, 27, 'Declare, that thou mayest be justified. Thy first father hath sinned.'

5. This weakness is universal. Sin hath made its sickly impressions in every faculty. The mind is dark, Eph. 4:18; he cannot know, 1 Cor. 2:14; there is a stoniness in the heart, he cannot bend, Zech. 7:12; there is enmity in the will, he cannot be subject, Rom. 8:7. As to faith, he cannot believe, John 12:39. As to the Spirit, the worker of faith, he

cannot receive; that is, of himself, John 14:17; acknowledge Christ he cannot, 1 Cor. 12:3. As to practice, he cannot bring forth fruit, John 15:4. The unrighteousness introduced by Adam poured a poison into every faculty, and dispossessed it of its strength, as well as of its beauty: what else could be expected from any deadly wound but weakness as well as defilement?* The understanding conceives only such thoughts as are pleasing to the law of sin; the memory is employed in preserving the dictates and decrees of it; the imagination full of fancies imprinted by it; the will wholly submitting to its authority; conscience standing with fingers in its mouth, for the most part not to speak against it; the whole man yielding itself and every member to the commands of it, and undertaking nothing but by its motions, Rom. 6:19.

6. To evince it, there is not one regenerate man but in his first conversion is chiefly sensible of his own insufficiency; and universal consent is a great argument of the truth of a proposition; it is a ground of the belief of a deity, it being the sentiment of all nations. I do not speak of disputes about it from the pride of reason, but of the inward experience of it in any heart. What more frequent in the mouths of those that have some preparations to it by conviction, than I cannot repent, I cannot believe, I find my heart rotten, and base, and unable to any thing that is good! There have been instances of those that would elevate the power of man, and freedom of will in spiritual things, who have been confuted in their reasonings, and acknowledged themselves so, when God hath come to work savingly upon them. Indeed, this poverty of spirit, or sense of our own emptiness, insufficiency, and indigence, is the first gospel grace wrought in the soul, and stands in the head of all those noble qualifications in our Saviour's sermon, as fitting men for the kingdom of God: 'Blessed are the poor in spirit; for theirs is the kingdom of heaven,' Mat. 5:3. And God in the whole progress of this work keeps believers in a sensibleness of their own weakness, thereby to preserve them in a continual dependence on him; and therefore sometimes withdraws his

Spirit from them, and lets them fall, that they may adhere more closely to him, and less confide in themselves.

2. What kind of impotency or insufficiency is there in the soul to be the cause of this work?

Ans. 1. It is not a physical weakness for want of faculties. Understanding we have, but not a spiritual light in it to direct us; will we have, but no freedom to choose that which is spiritually good. Though since the fall we have such a free will left, which pertains to the essential nature of man, yet we have lost that liberty which belongs to the perfection of human nature, which was to exercise acts spiritually good and acceptable to God.† Had the faculties been lost, Adam had not been capable of a promise or command, and consequently of ever sinning after. In Adam, by creation we were possessed of it. In Adam, by his corruption, we were stripped of it; we have not lost the physical but the moral nature of these faculties; not the faculties themselves, but the moral goodness of them. As the elementary heat is left in a carcase, which yet is unfit to exercise any animal action for want of a soul to enliven it; so, though the faculties remain after this spiritual death, we are unfit to exert any spiritual action for want of grace to quicken them. If man wanted faculties, this want would excuse him in his most extravagant actions: no creature is bound to that which is simply impossible; nay, without those faculties, he could not act as a rational creature, and so were utterly incapable of sinning. Sin hath untuned the strings, but did not unstring the soul; the faculties were still left, but in such a disorder, that the wit and will of man can no more tune them, than the strings of an untuned lute can dispose themselves for harmony without a musician's hand.

2. Neither is it a weakness arising from the greatness of the object above the faculty. As when an object is unmeet for a man, because he hath no power in him to comply with it; as to understand the essence of God; this the highest creature in its own nature cannot do, because God dwells in inaccessible light; and it is utterly impossible for any thing but God to

comprehend God. If man were required to become an angel, or to rise up and kiss the sun in the firmament; these were impossible things, because man wanted a faculty in his primitive nature for such acts: so if God had commanded Adam to fly without giving him wings, or to speak without giving him a tongue, he had not been guilty of sin in not doing it, because it was not disobedience, for disobedience is only in what a man hath a faculty to do; but to love God, praise him, depend upon him, was in the power of man's original nature, for they were not above those faculties God endued him with, but very correspondent and suitable to him. The objects proposed are in themselves intelligible, credible, capable to be comprehended.

3. Neither is it a weakness arising from the insufficiency of external revelation. The means of regeneration are clearly revealed in the gospel, the sound is gone into all the earth, Rom. 10:18, and the word of the Lord is an apprehensible object; it is 'near us, even in our mouths,' Rom. 10:8; 'the commandment of the Lord is pure, enlightening the eyes,' Ps. 19:8. If the object were hid, the weakness lay not on the part of man, but on the insufficiency of revelation; as if any thing were revealed to man in an unknown tongue, there were an insufficiency in the means of revelation.

But, 4, it is a moral weakness. The disability lies chiefly in the will, John 5:40; what is there, 'You will not come to me,' is, ver. 44, 'How can you believe?' You cannot, because you will not. Carnal lusts prepossess the heart, and make their party in the will against the things of God; so that inward propensities to embrace sin, are as great as the outward temptations to allure to it, whereby the soul is carried down the stream with a wilful violence. In this respect he is called dead, though the death be not of the same nature with a natural death; for such a one hath not the natural faculty to raise himself; but this is an impotency arising from a voluntary obstinacy; yet the iniquity of a man binds him no less powerfully under this spiritual captivity, than a natural death and insensibility keeps men in the grave; and those fetters of perversity they can no more knock off, than a dead man can raise himself from the grave. By reason of those bands they are called prisoners, Isa. 42:7, and cannot be delivered without the powerful voice of Christ commanding and enabling them to go forth: Isa. 49:9, 'That thou must say to the prisoner, Go forth.' The apostle lays the whole fault of men's not receiving the truth upon their wills: 2 Thes. 2:10, 'They received not the love of the truth;' they heard it, they knew it, but they loved not that which courted them. It is not seated in any defect of the will, as it is a power of the soul; for then God, who created it, would be charged with it, and might as well charge beasts to become men, as men to become gracious.* Man, as a creature, had a power to believe and love God; to resist temptations, avoid sin, and live according to nature; but man, as corrupted by a habit derived to him from his first parents, and increased by a custom in sin, cannot believe, cannot love God, cannot bring himself into a good frame; as a musician cannot play a lesson when he hath the gout in his fingers. When the eyes are full of adultery, when the heart is full of evil habits, it 'cannot cease to sin,' it cannot be gracious, 2 Pet. 2:14.

Now, these habits are either innate, or contracted and increased.

(1.) Innate. By nature we have a habit of corruption, fundamental of all other that grow up in us. Man made a covenant with sin, contracted a marriage with it; by virtue of this covenant sin had a full power over him. What the apostle speaks of the marriage between man and the law, Rom. 7:1–4, is applicable to this case. Sin as a husband, by way of covenant, hath a powerful dominion over the will, and binds it as long as sin lives; and the will hath no power to free itself, unless a higher power make a divorce, or by the death of the husband. This is the cause of man's obstinacy against any return to God, the will is held in the cords of sin, Prov. 5:22. The habit hath obtained an absolute sovereignty over it: Hosea 5:4, 'They will not frame their doings to turn unto their God.' Why? 'For the spirit of whoredoms is in the midst of them,' that is, in their hearts. This adulterous or idolatrous habit holds their wills in chains, and acts them as a man possessed by the devil is acted according to the pleasure of the devil. The devil speaks in them, moves in them, and doth what he pleases by them. And which binds the will faster, this habit is not in a natural man by way of a tyranny, but a voluntary sovereignty on the part of the will; the will is pleased and tickled with it. As a woman (to use the similitude of the Holy Ghost in that place) is so overruled by her affections to other lovers that she cannot think of returning to her former husband, but her unlawful love plays all its pranks, and riseth with that force against all arguments from honesty and credit, that it keeps her still in the chains of an unlawful lust; so this is not a habit which doth oppress nature, or force it against its will, but by its incorporation, and becoming one with our nature, has quite altered it from that original rectitude and simplicity wherein God at first framed it. It is a law of sin, which having razed out the purity of the law of nature, commands in a greater measure in the stead of it. Hence it is as natural to man, in his lapsed state, to have perverse dispositions against God, as it is essential to him to be rational. And the chariot of that weak remaining reason left us, is overturned by our distempered passions; and the nobler part of man is subject to the rule of these, which bear down the authority both of reason and God too. That one sin of the angels, howsoever complicated we know not, taking place as a habit in them, hath bound them for ever from rising to do any good, or disentangling themselves from it, and may perhaps be meant by those 'chains of darkness' wherein they are reserved and held to the judgment of the great day, having no will to shake them off, though they have light enough to see the torment appointed for them.

(2.) New contracted and increased habits upon this foundation. Custom turns sin more into another nature, and completes the first natural disorder. An unrenewed man daily contracts a greater impotency, by adding strength to this habit, and putting power into the hands of sin to exercise its tyranny, and increasing our headstrong natures in their unruliness. It is as impossible of ourselves to shake off the fetters of custom, as to suppress the unruliness of nature: Jer. 13:23, 'Can an Ethiopian change his skin? or a leopard his spots? then may you also do good that are accustomed to do evil.' The prophet speaks not here of what they were by nature, but what they were by custom; contracting thereby such a habit of evil, that, like a chronic disease, could not be cured by any ordinary means. But may he not accustom himself to do good? No; it is as impossible as for an Ethiopian to change his skin. Those habits draw a man to delight, and therefore to a necessity, of sinning. The pleasure of the heart, joined with the sovereignty of sin, are two such strong cords as cannot be untwisted or cut by the soul itself; no, not without an overruling grace. It was a simple wound in Adam, but such as all nature could not cure, much less when we have added a world of putrefaction to it. The stronger the habit, the greater the impotency. If we could not raze out the stamp of mere nature upon our wills, how can we raze out the deeper impressions made by the addition of custom? If Adam, who committed but one sin, and that in a moment, did not seek to regain his lost integrity, how can any other man, who by a multitude of sinful acts hath made his habit of a giant-like stature, completed many parts of wickedness, and scoffed at the rebukes of conscience?

Let us now see wherein this weakness of our wills to renew ourselves doth appear.

1. In a total moral unfitness for this work. Grace being said to make us meet for our Master's use, it implies an utter unfitness for God's use of ourselves before grace. There is a passive capability, a stump left in nature, but no fitness for any activity in nature, no fitness in nature for receiving grace, before grace; there is nothing in us naturally which doth suit or correspond with that which is good in the sight of God. That which is natural is found more or less in all men; but the gospel, which is the instrument of regeneration, finds nothing in the nature

of man to comply with the main design of it. There is indeed some compliance of moral nature with the moral precepts in the gospel, upon which account it hath been commended by some heathens; but nothing to answer the main intendment of it, which is faith, the top grace in regeneration. This hath nothing to commend itself to mere nature, nor finds an internal principle in man that is pleased with it, as other graces do, as love, meekness, patience, &c. For faith strips a man of all his own glory, brings himself from himself to live dependently upon another, and makes him act for another, not for himself; and therefore meets not with any one principle in man to shew it countenance: 'No good thing dwells in the flesh,' Rom. 7:18. There may be some motions lighting there, as a fly upon a man's face; but they have no settled abode, and spring not up from nature. If the apostle, who was renewed, found an unfitness in himself to do that which was good, how great is that unfitness in a mere natural will, which is wholly under the power of the flesh, and hath no principle in it correspondent to spiritual truth, to renew itself! If this regeneration had any foundation in nature, it would be then in most men that hear the gospel, because there is not a general contradiction in men to those things which are natural; but since there is no good thing dwells in any flesh, how can it be fit of itself to be raised into a conformity to God, which is the highest pitch of the creature's excellency? The Scripture represents us not as earth, which is fit to suck in showers from heaven; but as stones, which are only moistened in the superficies by the rain, but answers not the intendment of it. Adamants are unfit to receive impressions; and the best natural heart is no better, like a stone, cold and hard. The soul with its faculties is like a bird with its wings, but clogged with slime and clay, unfit to fly. A barren wilderness is absolutely unfit to make a pleasant and fruitful garden. There is a contractedness of the heart till God enlarge and open it, and that in the best nature. Acts 16:14, Lydia, it is said, worshipped God; there was religion in her, yet the Lord opened her heart for the gospel. Can anything be more indisposed than a fountain that is alway bubbling up poison? So is the heart of man, Gen. 6:5. The least imagination rising up in the heart is evil, and can be no better, since the heart itself is a mass of venom. If the renewed natures find so much indisposition in the progress of sanctification, though their sails be filled with grace, how great must it be where corrupt nature only sits at the stern! As when Satan came to tempt our Saviour he found nothing in him, no touchwood in his nature to take fire by a temptation, so when the Spirit comes, he finds no tinder in man to receive readily any spark of grace. This unfitness is in the best mere nature, that seems to have but a drop of corruption: a drop of water is as unfit to ascend as a greater quantity.

2. There is not only an unfitness, but an unwillingness. A senseless sluggishness and drowsiness of soul, loath to be moved. No man doth readily hold out his arms to embrace the tenders of the gospel. What folding of the arms! yet a little more slumber, a little more sin. Man is a mere darkness before his effectual calling: 'Who hath called us out of darkness,' 1 Peter 2:9. His understanding is darkened; the will cannot embrace a thing offered, unless it have powerful arguments to persuade it of the goodness of that thing which is offered; which arguments are modelled in the understanding, but that being darkened, hath wrong notions of divine things, therefore cannot represent them to the will to be pursued and followed. Adam's running away from God to hide himself, after the loss of his original righteousness, discovers how unwilling man is to implore God's favour. How deplored is the condition of man by sin! since we find not one prayer put up by Adam, nor can we suppose any till the promise of recovery was made, though he was sensible of his nakedness, and haunted by his conscience: 'I was afraid, because I was naked: and I hid myself,' Gen. 3:10. He had no mind, no heart, to turn suppliant unto God; he runs from God, and when God finds him out, instead of begging pardon by humble prayer, he stands upon his justification, accuseth God to be the cause by giving him the woman, by

whose persuasion he was induced to sin. What glass will better discover the good will of nature to God than the first motions after the fall!

3. There is not only an unfitness and unwillingness, but an affection to something contrary to the gospel. The nature of outward objects is such, that they attract the sensitive appetite, corrupted by sin, to prefer them before that which is more excellent; the heart is forestalled by an inordinate love of the world, and a pleasure in unrighteousness: 2 Thes. 2:12, they 'believed not the truth, but had pleasure in unrighteousness' (Ευδοκήσαντες), a singular pleasure. Where the heart and the devil agree so well, what liking can there be to God or his will? Where the amity between sin and the soul is so great, that sin is self, and self is sin, how can so delightful a friend be discarded, to receive one he thinks his enemy! This weakness ariseth from a love to something different or contrary to what is proposed.* When a man is so tied to that object which he loves that he minds not that contrary object which is revealed by a fit light, as a man that hath his eyes or his heart fixed upon a fair picture, cannot observe many things that occur about him; or if he doth consider it, he is taken so much with the things he loves, that he seems to hate the other; that though he doth count it good, yet compared with what he loved before, he apprehends it as evil, and judges it evil, merely by the error of his mind,—a practical, affected, and voluntary ignorance. So though a man may sometimes judge that there is a goodness in the gospel and the things proposed, yet his affection to other pleasures, which he prefers before the gospel, causes him to shake off any thoughts of compliance with it. Now, all natural men in the irons of sin are not weary but in love with their fetters, and prize their slavery as if it were the most glorious liberty.

4. There is not only unfitness, and unwillingness, and a contrary affection to the gospel, but according to the degrees of this affection to other things, there is a strong aversion and enmity to the tenders of the gospel. This enmity is more or less in the heart of every unrenewed man;

though in some it is more restrained and kept down by education, yet it will appear more or less upon the approaches of grace, which is contrary to nature. As a spark as well as a flame will burn, though one hath less heat than the other, there is the same nature, the same seminal principles in all. The carnal mind, let it be never so well flourished by education, is enmity to God; and therefore 'unable,' because unwilling, 'to be subject to the law,' Rom. 8:7. By nature he is of the devil's party, and hath no mind the castle of his heart should ever come into the hands of the right owner. It is in every faculty. Not one part of the soul will make a mutiny within against sin, or take part with God when he comes to lay siege to it; when he 'stretches out his hands,' he meets with a 'rebellious and gainsaying people,' Rom. 10:21. It can converse with anything but God, look with delight upon anything but that which is the only true object of delight. It can have no desire to have that law writ in his heart whose characters he hates. All the expressions in the Scripture denoting the work of grace, import man's distaste of it; it is to deny self, crucify the flesh. What man hath not an aversion to deny what is dearest to him, his self; to crucify what is incorporated with him, his Isaac, his flesh? The bent of a natural heart, and the design of the gospel, which is to lay man as low as the dust, can never agree. A corrupt heart, and the propositions of grace, meet together as fire and water, with hissing.* The language of man, at the proposals of the gospel, is much like that of the devils, 'What have we to do with thee? Art thou come to destroy us?' Luke 4:34.

5. This aversion proceeds on to a resistance. No rebels were ever stouter against their prince than an unrenewed soul against the Spirit of God: not a moment without arms in his hand; he acts in defence of sin, and resistance of grace, and combats with the Spirit as his deadly enemy: 'You always resist the Holy Ghost; as your fathers did, so do ye,' Acts 7:51. The animosity runs in the whole blood of nature; neither the breathings of love, nor the thunderings of threatenings, are listened unto. All natural men are hewed out of one quarry of stone. The highest

rock and the hardest adamant may be dissolved with less pains than the heart of man; they all, like a stone, resist the force of the hammer, and fly back upon it. All the faculties are full of this resistance: the mind, with stout reasoning, gives a repulse to grace; the imagination harbours foolish conceits of it; in the heart, hardness and refusing to hear; in the affections, disgust and displeasure with God's ways, disaffection to his interest; the heart is locked, and will not of itself shoot one bolt to let the King of glory enter. What party is like to be made for God, by bare nature thus possessed? Nature indeed doth what it can, though it cannot do what it would; for though it resist the outward means and inward motions, yet it cannot efficaciously resist the determining grace of God, any more than the matter of the creation could resist the all-powerful voice of God commanding it to receive this or that form, or Lazarus resist the receiving that life Christ conveyed to him by his mighty word. God finds a contradiction in our wills, and we are not regenerate because our will hath consented to the persuasions of grace; for that it doth not do of itself; but the grace of God disarms our will of all that is capable to make resistance, and determines it to accept and rejoice in what is offered. Nature of itself is of an unyielding temper, and removes not one scale from the eye, nor any splinter from the stone in the heart; for how can we be the authors of that which we most resist and labour to destroy?

6. Add to all this, the power of Satan in every natural man, whose interest lies in enfeebling the creature. The devil, since his first impression upon Adam, hath had the universal possession of nature, unless any natural man free himself from the rank of the children of disobedience: Eph. 2:2, 'The spirit that now works in the children of disobedience;' where the same word ἐνεργεῖν is used for the acting of Satan, and likewise for the acting of sin, in Rom. 7:5, as it is for the acting of the Spirit, Philip. 2:13. In whom he works as a spirit as powerfully according to his created strength, as the Holy Ghost works in the children of obedience. As the Spirit fills the soul with gracious habits to move freely in God's

ways, so Satan fills the soul (as much as in him lies) with sinful habits, as so many chains to keep it under his own dominion. He cannot indeed work immediately upon the will, but he uses all the skill and power that he hath to keep men captive for the performance of his own pleasure: 2 Tim. 2:26, 'Who are taken captive by him at his will,' or for his will, Εἰς τὸ ἐκείνου θέλημα. It is in that place a dreadful judgment which God gives some men up to for opposing the gospel, taking away his restraints, both from the devil and their own hearts; but more or less he works in every one that opposeth the gospel, which every unrenewed man under the preaching of the gospel doth; he is the strong man that keeps the palace, Luke 11:21. Can the will of man make a surrender of it, at God's demand, in spite of his governor? What power have we to throw off these shackles he loads us with? 'We are as weak in his hand as birds in a fowler's. What will have we, since we are his willing slaves? The darkness of nature is never like by its own free motion to disagree with the prince of darkness, without an overpowering grace, able to contest with the lord as well as the slave; for by the fall he is become prince of the lower creation, and holds it in chains too strong for weakness to break. How great, then, is man's inability! How unreasonable is it to think that the will of man, possessed with such unfitness, unwillingness, affection to other things, aversion to the gospel, resistance of it, and in the devil's net, can of itself do anything towards its recovery, from that it counts no disease, or to turn to that which it accounts its burden? If unspotted and sound nature did not preserve Adam in innocency, how can filthy and crazy nature recover us from corruption? If it did not keep him alive when he was living, how can it convey life to us when we have not a spark of spiritual life in us? Man was planted a 'noble vine,' but turned himself into 'a degenerate plant;' nothing that hath decayed can by its own strength recover itself, because it hath lost that strength whereby it could only preserve itself.

1. Man cannot prepare himself for grace.

2. He cannot produce it.

3. He cannot co-operate with God in the first work.

4. He cannot preserve it.

5. He cannot actuate it.

1. Man cannot prepare himself for the new birth.

I shall premise a few things for the better understanding of this,

(1.) Man hath a subjective capacity for grace above any other creature in the inferior world; and this is a kind of natural preparation which other creatures have not. A capacity in regard of the powers of the soul, though not in respect of the present disposition of them. A stone or a beast are not capable of habits of grace, no more than of habits of sin, because they want rational natures, which are the proper seats of both. Our Saviour did not raise trees or stones to life, though he had the same power to do that as he had to raise stones to be children to Abraham; but he raised them that had bodies prepared, in part, for a receptacle of a soul. As there is a more immediate subjective capacity in a man newly dead for the reception of life upon a new infusion of the soul, because he hath all the members already formed, which is not in one whose body is mouldered into dust, and hath not one member organised fit for the acting of a rational soul. These faculties have a spring of natural motion in them, therefore are capable of divine grace to make that motion regular; as the wheels of a clock out of order retain their substance and their motion if their weights be wound up, but a false motion unless the disorder of the spring be mended. Man hath an understanding to know, and, when it is enlightened, to know God's law; a will to move and run, and, when enlarged by grace, to run the ways of God's commandments; so that he stands in an immediate capacity to receive the life of grace upon the breath and touch of God, which a stone doth not, not the most sparkling jewel any more than the meanest pebble; for in this it is necessary rational faculties should be put as a foundation of spiritual motion. Though the soul be thus capable as a subject to receive the grace of God, yet it is not therefore capable, as an agent, to prepare itself for it or produce it; as a piece of marble is potentially capable of being the king's statue, but not to prepare itself by hewing off its superfluous parts, or to raise itself into such a figure. If there were not a rational nature, there were nothing immediately to be wrought upon. If there be not a wise agent and an omnipotent hand, there were nothing to work upon it.

(2.) Besides this passive capacity, there are more immediate preparations. The soul, as rational, is capable to receive the truths of God; but as the heart is stony, it is incapable to receive the impressions of those truths. A stone, as it is a corporeal substance, is capable to receive the drops of rain in its cavities; but because of its hardness is incapable to suck it in, and be moistened inwardly thereby, unless it be softened. Wax hath a capacity to receive the impression of the seal, but it must be made pliable by some external agent to that purpose. The soul must be beaten down by conviction before it be raised up by regeneration; there must be some apprehensions of the necessity of it. Yet sometimes the work of regeneration follows so close upon the heels of these precious preparations, that both must be acknowledged to be the work of one and the same hand. Paul on the sudden was struck down, and in a moment there is both an acknowledgment of the authority of Christ, and a submission to his will, when he said, 'Lord, what wilt thou have me to do?' Acts 9:6. The preparation of the subject is necessary, but this preparation may be at the same time with the conveyance of the divine nature: as a warm seal may both prepare the hard wax, and convey the image to it, by one and the same touch.

(3.) Though some things which man may do by common grace may be said in some sort to be preparations, yet they are not formally so, as that there is an absolute causal connection between such preparations and regeneration. They are not causœ dispositivœ of grace, not disposing causes of grace. Grace is all in a way of reception by the soul, not of action from the soul. The highest morality in the world is not necessary to the first infusion of the divine nature. Mary Magdalene was far from the one, yet received the other. If there were anything in the subject that was the cause of it, the tenderest and softest dispositions would be wrought upon, and the most intelligent men would soonest receive the gospel. Though we see them sometimes renewed, yet many times the roughest tempers are seized upon by grace; and the most unlikely soils for fructifying God plants his grace in, wherein there could be no preparations before. It is not with grace as it is with fire, which gives as much heat to a stone as to a piece of wood; but the wood is sooner heated than the stone, because it is naturally disposed, by the softness and porousness of its parts, to receive the heat. Moral nature seems to be a preparation for grace; if it be so, it is not a cause howsoever of grace, for then the most moral person would be soonest gracious, and more eminently gracious after his renewal, and none of the rubbish and dregs of the world would ever be made fit for the heavenly building. There seems to be a fitness in morality for the receiving special grace, because the violence and tumultuousness of sin is in some measure appeased, the flame and sparks of it allayed, and the body of death lies more quiet in them, and the principles cherished by them bear some testimony to the holiness of the precepts. But though it seems to set men at a greater nearness to the kingdom of God, yet with all its own strength it cannot bring the kingdom of God into the heart, unless the Spirit opens the lock. Yea, sometimes it sets a man further from the kingdom of God, as being a great enemy to the righteousness of the gospel, both imputed and inherent, which is the crown of the gospel: to imputed, as standing upon a righteousness of their own, and conceiving no need of any other; to inherent, as acting their seeming holiness neither upon gospel principles, nor for gospel ends, but in self-reflections and self-applauses. What may seem preparations to us in matters of moral life, may in the root be much distant and vastly asunder from grace; as a divine* of our own illustrates it, two mountains whose tops seem near together may in the bottom be many miles asunder. The foundation of that which looks like a preparation may be laid in the very gall of bitterness; as Simon Magus desiring the gift of the Holy Ghost, but from the covetousness of his heart. Other operations upon the soul which seem to be nearer preparations, as convictions, do not infer grace; for the heart, as a field, may be ploughed by terrors, and yet not sown by any good seed. Planting and watering are preparations, but not the cause of fruit; the increase depends upon God.

(4.) There is no meritorious connection between any preparation in the creature and regeneration. The Pelagian opinion was,† that by a generous love of virtue we might deserve the grace of God, and the farther assistance of the Spirit, we first (say they) put our hearts into the hands of God, that God may incline them which way he please; and by thus making our wills depend on God, we merit help from God, and make ourselves worthy of him. Whether this be the opinion of any now, I know not. This is to assert, that man gives first to God, and then God to man in way of requital. What son can merit to be born? What desert before being? Nothing can be pre-existent in the son which merits generation by the father. The fair hand of moral nature can no more induce God to confer on man the state of grace, than the deed of conveyance of a manor, fairly drawn, can dispose the lord to pass it away.* In what part of Scripture hath God indulged mere nature with any promise of adding grace upon the improvements of natural abilities? Whatsoever conditional promise there is, supposeth some grace superior to nature in the subject as the condition of it. We do not find that God hath made himself a debtor to any preparation of the creature.

But there is no obligation on God by anything that may look like a preparation in man. For,

[1.] If man can lay any obligation on God, it must be by some act in all parts his own, for which he is not in the least obliged to God.

Thinking is the lowest step in the ladder of preparation. It is the first act of the creature in any rational production, yet this the apostle doth remove from man, as in every part of it his own act: 2 Cor. 3:5, 'Not that we are sufficient of ourselves to think anything as of ourselves, but our sufficiency is of God.' The word signifies reasoning. No rational act can be done without reasoning; this is not purely our own. We have no sufficiency of ourselves, as of ourselves, originally and radically of ourselves, as if we were the author of that sufficiency, either naturally or meritoriously. And Calvin observes that the word is not αὐτάρκεια but ἱκανότης, not a self-ability, but an aptitude or fitness to any gracious thought. How can we oblige him by any act, since, in every part of it, it is from him, not from ourselves? For as thinking is the first requisite, so it is perpetually requisite to the progress of any rational act, so that every thought in any act, and the whole progress, wherein there must be a whole flood of thoughts, is from the sufficiency of God. We cannot oblige God after grace, much less before, for when grace is given there must be constant effluxes of grace from God to maintain it; and the acts of grace in us are but a second grace of God. How can we then oblige him by that which is not ours, either in the original or improvement? If when a man hath given to another a rich gift he must also give him power to preserve it, and wisdom to improve it, the person cannot be said by his improvement of it to oblige the first donor. What hath any man that he hath not received? 1 Cor. 4:7. The apostle excludes everything in us from the name of a donation to God. If there be no one thing but is received from God, then no preparation to grace but is received from him. The obligation then lies upon the receiver, not upon the donor. But may we not oblige God by the improvement of such a gift? The apostle includes everything, challengeth him to name any one thing which was not received, which will contain improvements as well as preparations. If we have power to improve it, wisdom to improve It, hearts and opportunities to improve it, all these are by way of reception from God.

[2.] If man can lay any obligation upon God, it must be by some pure, spotless act. This cannot be; no pure act can spring from man. God hath taken an exact survey of the whole world in its dark and fallen state, and could not, among those multitudes of acts which spring from the will of man, find one piece of beauty, one particle of the divine image, for he hath pronounced this sentence upon them, with repetition, too, as his infallible judgment: 'There is none righteous, no, not one: they are all gone out of the way, they are together become unprofitable; there is none that doeth good, no, not one,' Rom. 3:10–12. The most refined nature derived from Adam was never found without fault; a pure virtue is a terra incognita. The productions of nature are always evil. If not one action be fully good in the nature of man, what meritoriousness can there be in any preparation of nature for the grace of God? Can the clearest virtue that ever was since Adam oblige God to pardon its own defects, that is, the defects of that very act of virtue? Much less can it challenge a higher degree of grace to be transmitted to it.

[3.] If any preparation were our own, and were pure, yet being natural, how could it oblige God to give a supernatural grace? If there be anything of meritoriousness, it is only something of the same kind with the work in a greater degree, but there is no proportion between natural acts and supernatural grace. There is no one scripture, or one example, declaring grace to be given as a reward to mere nature, or any act of nature. God indeed, out of his infinite righteousness, and equity, and goodness, hath rewarded some moral acts with some worldly advantages, or the with-drawing some judgments threatened, as Ahab's reprieve from judgment upon his humiliation, 1 Kings 21:27, 29; and the temporary pardon to Nineveh, upon their submission to the prophet's threatenings, Jonah 3:8–10. But what obligation lies upon God to reward men doing thus with superadditions of grace? for there is no proportion between such a moral act and so excellent a reward. We may as well say that a coal by glowing and sparkling may merit to become a star; or that the orderly laying the wood and sacrifice upon the altar might merit the descent of fire from heaven to kindle it.

[4.] If there was any obligation on God, by any preparations of nature, then such acts would be always followed with renewing grace. There would be an obligation on God's righteousness to bestow it. And if it should be denied, the creature might accuse God of a failure in justice, because he gave not what was due. God sure would observe that rule of justice which he prescribes to man, not to detain the wages of a hireling, no, not for a night. Were grace a debt upon the works of nature, God were then obliged not only to pay it, but pay it speedily, it being exact righteousness so to do. But we see the contrary. Publicans and harlots are raised and beautified, while pharisees lie buried in the ruins of nature. These preparations are many times without perfection. The pangs of conviction resolve sometimes into a return to the old vomit, and make no progress in a state of life and grace. The apostle's rule will hold true in the whole compass of the work, Rom. 6:11, 'If it be of works, then it is no more grace.' So much as is ascribed to any work or preparation by the creature, so much is taken from the glory of grace, and would make God not the author, but assistant, and that too by obligation, not by grace.

[5.] From this it follows, that man doth not prepare himself by any act of his will, without the grace of God. What preparation can he make, who is so powerfully possessed by corrupted habits, which have got so great an empire over him, struck their roots to the very bottom of his soul, entrenched themselves in the works of custom, that if he goes about to pull up one, his arm shakes and his heart faints? How strongly do these rooted habits resist the power of grace! How much more easily do they resist the weakness of nature in confederacy with them! What is said of the remnant of Jacob as a 'dew from the Lord,' as 'the showers upon the grass,' that it 'tarrieth not for man, nor waits for the sons of men,' Micah

5:7, may be said of the grace of God; it waits not for the preparations and dispositions of the creature, but prevents them. It is a pure gift; though we are active with it, yet we are wholly indisposed for it. We can no more prepare ourselves to shine as stars in the world, than a dunghill can to shine as a sun in heaven. What preparations doth God wait for in the heart of an infant when he sanctifies it? If 'without Christ we can do nothing,' John 15:5, then no preparations without Christ; for they are something, and very considerable too. There is no foundation to think there should be any preparation in the creature, as of the creature.

First, The first promise of redemption and regeneration intimates no such thing in man to either of them: Gen. 3:15, 'I will put enmity,' &c. The putting enmity into man against Satan is promised by God as his own work. There was a friendship struck up, a confederacy made, the devil entertained as a counsellor; God would now break this league, he only puts enmity into the heart against Satan: 'It shall bruise thy head,' &c. The bruising the serpent's head is wholly the act of Christ. It, not the man or the woman, but the promised seed. As there were no preparations in the creature to that which Christ acted in the flesh, so there are no preparations in that creature for what Christ is to do in his Spirit. He bruised Satan in his flesh upon the cross without any preparations in the creature; and so he bruiseth Satan in the heart, by his Spirit, without any preparations on the creature's part. For anything I see, had man in the state of innocency been sensible that his dependency, as to any good, and motion to good, ought to be upon God, and he to have waited upon God for his change and confirmation, he might have stood; but when he would practically assert the liberty of his own will in a way of indifferency to good and evil, he fell. And by the way, those that assert the freedom of their own will naturally, without the grace of God, either common or special, seem to me to justify Adam's first affected independency of God.

Secondly, God is as much in the new creation as he was in the old. Not only the creation of the matter, but the preparation of it to receive the form, was from God; neither the matter, nor any part of it, prepared itself. If nothing prepared itself to be a creature, how can anything prepare itself to be a gracious creature, since to be a new creature is more than to be a creature; and every preparation to be a new creature is more than any preparation to be a creature? The new creation differs, I must confess, from the old creation; but it is such a difference which makes it rather harder than easier.

First, The object of the old creation was nothing, the object of the new is something; but a thing that hath no more active disposition to receive a new form, than nothing had.*

Secondly, The object of the first creation was a simple and pure privation; the object of the second is a contrary form, which resists the work of God: there was only an action of creation in the first, there is an action of destruction in the second; the destruction of the old form and the creation of a new. Is it likely that any nature would voluntarily prepare itself for its own destruction? God in the first creation found no disposition in the subject to entertain a form; here he finds a contrary disposition to resist the form.

Thirdly, What preparation had any of those we read of in Scripture from themselves? What disposition had Paul, when he was struck down with a heart fuller of actual enmity than he had at his birth? Did the apostles expect any call from their nets, or set themselves in a readiness before they heard that call? A voice from Christ was attended with a divine touch or power upon their hearts; both the preparation and the motion itself took birth together. And what preparations are there in Scripture, but are attributed unto God? If a conviction be thorough and full, and consequently a preparation, it must refer to that Spirit which our Saviour asserts to be the principal cause of it, John 16:8, 9, 'When he is come,' that is, the Comforter, 'he will reprove the world of sin.' It is laid wholly upon this, as the end of the almighty Spirit's coming, whereby it is not likely men would be convinced without him. Is there any desire or prayer for it? Even this, if true, is from the Holy Ghost; 'no man can call Christ Lord, but by the Holy Ghost,' 1 Cor. 12:3. Did any of those our Saviour cured of bodily infirmities, prepare themselves for that cure? Neither can any man prepare himself for his spiritual cure.

Fourthly, What thing in all the records of nature ever prepared itself for a change? All preparations in matter for receiving any form arise not from the matter itself, but from some other active principle, or the new form in part introduced, which by degrees expels the old; as in water, when heat comes in the place of cold, the preparation is not from the water, but from the new quality introducing itself. The grace of God is to the soul as form is to matter. The body is formed in the womb, for the reception of the soul, but not by the embryo, but by the formative virtue of the parent, fashioning the parts of the body to make it a fit lodging for the soul; or, as some think, the soul itself, as the bee, fashions its own cell; but howsoever it is not from itself. The preparations of Lazarus to rise were from the voice of Christ, not from the stinking body of Lazarus. The nature of all is alike. That one lute is better prepared for an harmonious touch, is from the musician's skill, not any art of its own. If one man of the same nature with another be endued with rich morals, it is from the common grace of God exciting natural light, and the common notions of fit and just; as the reason one vine of the same kind brings forth more generous fruit than another, is from the stronger influence of the sun. All nature assents to this truth, that nothing doth prepare itself for a change.

Fifthly, If man did prepare himself for grace, it would be a disparagement to God, it would violate the sovereignty of God. It would be derogatory to the majesty of God to have his grace depend upon the conditions and previous preparations in the creature; it would lay the foundations of grace in a man's self, and impose a necessity in God to come in with further grace, and make his actions dependent upon the actings of the creature. The beginning of faith would be from us, and the supplement from God; the work of grace would be of him that 'wills and runs,' and not 'of God that shews mercy,' Rom. 9:16. It would change the whole tenor of the Scripture, and make conversion not God's drawing of us, but our traction of God; for he that doth dispose himself to grace, is in some sort the cause of that grace, as he that doth dispose the subject for such a form is in a sort the cause of that form. If the preparations were from the will of man, man would begin the noblest work that ever was wrought, and God would be made no more than an attendant upon the creature's motion; whereas the very beginning in the will, as well as the perfection, is ascribed to God: Philip. 2:13, 'God works in you both to will and to do of his good pleasure.' God's good pleasure is the original cause of this work upon the will, not the will's good pleasure. The work then depending on God's good pleasure, excludes any dependency on the will of man; it is therefore called a creation, to shew God's independence upon anything as to this work.

Sixthly, Where should this preparation begin? in what part of the soul? Shall it begin in the understanding?* That hath lost the reins whereby it governed the lower parts of the soul. Nothing is more discomposed in its acts than that faculty. It is well compared to a charioteer or coachman fallen from his box, and his feet entangled in the reins of the horses, which hurry him about.† The sensitive appetite, like a wild horse, hath got the bit between his teeth, runs about, and draws the understanding after it. Indeed a charioteer that hath lost the government of his horses endeavours to remedy that violence; he cries out, makes all resistance, hath a will to help himself; but the understanding is so far from resisting, that it takes pleasure in the disorder of the passions; it prompts the will to follow them, and this is properly to be a servant to sin. Shall it begin in the appetite? How can that incline to range itself to the order of reason? It hath no reason itself, it submits not to the laws of reason; it hath got the mastery of it, and hath prescription for its dominion, of a long standing, ever since the fall. The dominion of sin is in the understanding, will, appetite, whence all of them are called flesh, so that all the motions of the soul depending upon them, the slavery must needs be voluntary. Therefore neither the understanding conceives, nor the will wills, nor the appetite desires, anything against themselves; how, then, should the will, which is captivated by a corrupt understanding and disorderly affections, recover itself, when it must necessarily be under the guidance of one of these jailors? Suppose the understanding were illuminated, are those evil habits in the will corrected barely by the illumination of the understanding? If they are corrected, why doth not the will alway follow the dictate of the understanding? But, alas! those evil habits determine the will to evil, as good habits determine it to good; for it is the nature of habits to incline the faculties to those things which are suitable to the nature of those habits; therefore as long as it remains under the command of those evil inclinations, it is impossible it should pass from evil to good. But that the will hath evil inclinations, appears by the Scripture calling the whole man flesh; else corruption would not be universally seated in the soul, but only accidental in the will, from the darkness of the understanding. But certainly, as Adam in innocency had an habitual holy disposition in his will, so man, in his fall, hath a corrupt inclination in his will, an habitual quality, whereby he drinks iniquity like water, Job 15:16. What power of the will can take those cords off which hold it prisoner, whereby it must be prepared for a free motion?

To evidence this further, we shall consider,

1. That man doth not naturally, neither can, understand the new birth.

2. He cannot desire it. Understanding and desire are necessary preparations to any rational change a creature can make in itself.

1. Man cannot understand it. This is necessary to a change. Whatsoever is done by the will, must be done by the impulse of some other faculty. Sensitive appetite cannot instruct the will to this work. Sense is not capable of reason, much less of religion, though it be the portal to

both. The will can never be moved to any good thing, unless the mind propound it as good and amiable. The act of thinking must precede the act of believing, for we cannot believe without thinking of what we believe. It is less to think than understand. If we cannot, then, do that which is less in the preparation, we cannot do that which is greater, especially when it is impossible to will without thinking; and thinking is a necessary means to willing. He that cannot prepare himself for a good thought, how can he prepare himself for a gracious habit? What ability have we to any act of faith, when we have no ability to any thought of faith? We cannot by the strength of nature understand it, if we consider,

(1.) The first blot caused by sin was upon the understanding. Man was first deceived by the sophistical reasonings of the serpent. The first effect of sin was to spread a thick darkness upon Adam's understanding. Though the whole house, and every beam of it, fell together, yet this faculty was first unfastened, and brought all the rest to ruin. As soon as ever he ceased from glorifying God as God, a darkness was brought upon his foolish heart: Rom. 1:21, 'When they knew God, they glorified him not as God, but became vain in their imaginations, and their foolish heart was darkened,' where the apostle describes the state of man in corrupt nature after his fall. Folly first in the heart to desire the forbidden fruit, and then darkness came upon the understanding. Their διαλογισμοὶ, their reasonings, became empty and contradictory; their primitive light departed, and darkness, as a privation, took place. What true motion can there be in the will, when there was so thick an obscurity in the understanding? Where there is but a false knowledge in the mind, there can be no true motion in the will. There must then be a restoration of this light, before there can be any preparation to a good act of the will. Adam recovered not this light by his own strength, no, nor by the outward declaration of the gospel in the promise; for no outward object proposed to the understanding confers any power upon the faculty. How can it then be recovered by our strength, since we have rather added to the scales than diminished them? For,

(2.) There is a darkness transmitted from him to the understanding of every man by nature. The light is darkened in the heaven of the soul, the more spiritual part of the mind, Isa. 5:30, as the prophet speaks in another case. Our understandings are so closed up with the thick slime of sin, that we cannot see the beauty of gospel truths; 'darkness comprehends not the light,' John 1:5. Though the light of the sun did shine a thousand times brighter than it doth, and strike upon the face and eyelids of a man with the greatest glory, yet if there be a spot upon the apple of his eye, if he wants a seeing faculty, he can apprehend nothing of it. Hence the apostle prays for the illumination of the understanding of the Ephesians, chap. 1:17, 18, and that they might have 'a spirit of wisdom and revelation in the knowledge of God.' And our Saviour tells them that they 'must be taught of God,' John 6:45, by an internal teaching of the Spirit, as well as by himself in an oral instruction. What a thick cloud was upon Nicodemus his mind, when he discoursed with him about regeneration, who was the ablest teacher to illustrate it to his fancy and understanding! It is not such a darkness as if he might understand the mysteries of heaven, if he would exert the strength of his own reason. This would be only as a man shutting his eyes who had a visive faculty; but it is such a darkness as cannot be expelled by flesh and blood, or anything arising from it: 'Flesh and blood,' saith our Saviour to Peter, 'hath not revealed it unto thee, but my Father which is in heaven,' Mat. 16:17. Flesh and blood includes everything in opposition to God. Our Saviour had externally owned himself, in the face of the Jews, to be the Messiah, the Son of God; but besides this, there was an inward illumination granted to Peter, for the apprehending and embracing so great a truth. There is not only a darkness upon the minds of those who have no outward revelation of the will of God in Christ, but upon those who are in the midst of the sunbeams: Deut. 29, 'Yet the Lord hath not given you an heart to perceive, and eyes to see, and ears to hear, unto this day.' They wanted not the beams. No people in the world had the ordinances of God besides them; but they wanted an organ fitted to receive and use them, which was not in their power, but is mentioned as the gift of God. God promises to make his people to know his ways. What needs that, if they could know them without him? We have indeed the light of the gospel, we have also a faculty, but without an eye disposed for the light, we enjoy no benefit by it. Now who ever heard that darkness could prepare itself for its own expulsion? It cannot comprehend the light, much less prepare for the reception of it. Who ever heard of one born blind, in a capacity to prepare himself for sight? We are blind in naturals, much more in spirituals. The most polished reasons among the heathens, both for knowledge in naturals and prudence in civil affairs, doated, and with all their wisdom knew not God.

(3.) There is an unsuitableness and a contrariety in the mind of man to the gospel, which is the instrument of regeneration. There is a mighty distance between the spiritual object and the natural faculty. The understanding, though never so well furnished with natural stuff, is but natural, and flesh; the object is supernatural and spiritual; therefore the richest mere nature can no more attain to the knowledge of spiritual things, than the clearest sense can attain to the knowledge of rational. Though every man 'by nature hath the things contained in the law,' Rom. 2:14, 15, yet no man hath by nature the things contained in the gospel. The gospel hath not the same advantage in the hearts of men as the law hath, for it finds nothing of kin to it. Though a natural heart hath some broken pieces of the law of God deposited in it, yet there is not the least syllable of Christ or regeneration writ in the mind by the hand of nature. The understanding therefore naturally cannot prepare itself for the reception of the gospel, because it hath not any principle in it which suits the doctrine of it. It seems a ridiculous thing to the wisest carnalist, who receives not the things of God, because, out of the pride of natural wisdom, he counts them foolishness, 1 Cor. 2:14. Hence not many wise are renewed in their minds. Had the gospel truth been as agreeable to reason as the other common notions imprinted in man, it would have been preserved in the world longer than it was, since, without question, Adam did communicate to his posterity the notion of a redeemer, which did soon die among them, because not consonant to that reason they had derived by nature from Adam. It was a knowledge given to Adam by revelation, not imprinted in his nature by creation. Besides, there is a contrariety in the mind to the truth of the gospel. As we say of liberty, so of enmity. Though it be formally in the will, yet it is radically in the understanding. The mind is the seat of those hostile principles which act the will against God, Rom. 8:7. The mind of man regards the things of God as unpleasant, and an intolerable yoke and hard bridle. Let light, the most excellent thing in the world, glare upon a man that hath sore eyes, he will turn away from it, or shut his eyes against it; for though he understands the worth of it, yet it hath a quality offensive to him. So is the gospel to those notions settled in the distempered mind. Men give not credit to the declarations of the gospel; 'Who hath believed our report?' hath been the voice of God's messengers in all ages, Isa. 53:1. No man, unless known by all never to speak truth, but is more believed than the God of infallible and unerring truth! What principles, then, are there in the understanding to prepare it for the reception of that which is so contrary to its ancient inmates?

(4.) Besides this, the natural levity of the understanding doth incapacitate it to prepare itself. It is with the understanding as with a line, the farther it is stretched out the weaker and more wavering it is. So is the understanding, being at a distance from God. How do vain thoughts intrude into the mind! No man can keep a door locked against them. We feel them rushing upon us while we endeavour to avoid them. We are confounded and overwhelmed by them, and drawn to things against our own resolutions. Man hath not the command of his own heart, so much as to think steadily of a divine object. How can he then prepare his own heart, when he cannot without grace fix in any holy meditation which is necessary for the renewal of it, since nothing is more discomposed in its acts than the mind of man, which is always dancing about, like cork in the water, or feathers in the air? Whence should come any preparation to good order, but by some super-natural ballast, to establish it from fluctuating? This disease every man is sensible of, and whatsoever disease is inherent in nature cannot be cured by any preparations by that nature which is wholly overgrown with it.

(5.) Hence it follows that a natural mind hath no right notion of grace. To the right notion of a thing is required suitableness, pleasure, and a fixedness of the mind upon it. A natural mind wants all these. How can it then prepare itself for that which it hath no knowledge of? And without knowledge it cannot commend it to the will. The apostle asserts a plain cannot in this business: 1 Cor. 2:14, 'He cannot know them, because they are spiritually discerned.' Being destitute of the Spirit, they cannot discern the things of the Spirit. Sense can discern things sensibly, not rationally. Reason can discern things rationally, but not spiritually. The light whereby a natural man judges of the things of the gospel is a star-light or a moonlight, which gives not a distinct view of the object. The evil disposition must be removed from the mind, before the object be entertained according to its worth. As if any natural object have such excellent qualities in it, that if it be embraced it will draw the will and affections after it; yet if the mind be ill-disposed, and doth not judge of the object according to the merit of it, it will refuse it. Offer a man gold who understands not the worth of gold, it will not allure him. Man with his eyes is spiritually blind, and with his ears is spiritually deaf. So God calls the Gentiles, which were to be brought to Christ for a restitution of their eyes: Isa. 43:8, 'Bring forth the blind people that have eyes, and the deaf that have ears.' Such can no more judge of the excellency of spiritual things than a blind man can have regular conceptions of colours, or a deaf man of the excellency of music. If 'no man can call Jesus Lord, but by the Holy Ghost,' 1 Cor. 12:3; if no man can have a magnificent conception and speech of Christ, but by the Spirit giving him both that conception and utterance, he cannot have a notion of the formation of Christ in the heart without the gift and impression of the same hand. What preparations, then, can arise from nature, when the mind can have no conception of Christ but by the Spirit of God?

Well, then, to conclude this. What preparations can there be in nature, since we cannot understand the things of God, when yet we have more clearness in our understanding to see them than we have force in our wills to love them and embrace them? It is in the understanding that the common notions, which are the grounds of knowledge, are deposited. There is less of ignorance in our understanding than of enmity in our will. The eye can see further than the arm can reach. If therefore we cannot think or understand, by all that help of common notions, without the grace of God, how can we then prepare our wills for it, to comply with it, and renew that faculty which is chiefly possessed with a contrariety to it?

2. As we cannot understand it, so we cannot naturally desire it. What is not spiritually discerned cannot spiritually be desired. Not but that according to those unformed conceptions which men have of it by common grace, there may be some weak velleities, but they are wishings without a will, not desires according to the value of the thing. Mercy first breathed on our first parents, before they breathed after that. The first motion came from God. So soon were they turned obstinate enemies against their Creator, without any thoughts of turning suppliants, though they had not lost the conceptions of their late integrity, which if they had, they had been wholly insensible, without any trouble of conscience. What desires can we naturally, then, have for it, who have far weaker conceptions of that happiness than they had immediately after they lost it? We cannot desire what we do not apprehend. A beast cannot desire to be a man, because he hath no conceptions of the excellency of

the human nature above his own. No nature can ever affect that which is contrary to it. No flesh can ever desire its own crucifixion. If we seek, we shall find; if we ask, we shall receive; but who first toucheth the heart to seek or to ask? If we cannot think a good thought of ourselves, how can we think so good a thought as a desire of regeneration? To say, then, we can desire the new creation of ourselves, without some kind of grace, is to assert another doctrine than what the apostle Paul asserted to those already regenerate. The first will, which is the necessary spring of all actions, is wrought by God, Philip. 2:13. The frame of man's will and desire stands to another point: John 8:44, 'The lusts of your father you will do.' The best renewed man 'knows not what to pray for as he ought,' without the instruction of the Spirit, Rom. 8:26. We cannot give our hearts a lift to heaven, or breathe out an unutterable groan, without the help of an infinite Spirit. The root of man's affections grows downward, not upward. What breathings can be expected in a soul choked up with sin? There was no motion of the church till 'the hand of her beloved was put in by the hole of the door,' and made a motion in her bowels, Cant. 5:4. The church owed no obligation to her free will and her own predispositions. There is not a smoke in the heart to heaven without a spark first from heaven; not a step till God enlargeth the heart. Velleities are from common grace, under the preaching of the word; fervent and saving desires are from special grace, by the hand of the Spirit. So that there are no preparations from nature to this, since both our apprehensions of it and desires of it spring not out of that stock.

The second main thing is this, As man cannot prepare himself for it, so he doth not produce and work it in himself. This is evident from the former. If he cannot make any preparation, which is the less, he cannot cause any actual production of it, which is the greater.

But to evidence it more, let us spend some time in this.

As it doth not depend upon the will of man in the preparation, so neither in the production.

I shall evidence it, first, by arguments drawn from the consideration of God.

If this work depended upon the will of man, as the first cause in the production, it would deprive God,

1. Of his sovereign independency. If man's will were the first cause of regeneration, God would not be the supreme independent cause in the noblest of his works. This work is nobler than creation in respect of the price paid for it. The world was made without the death of anything to purchase the creation of it. But the divine image is not restored without the death of the Son of God, every line in this new image being drawn with his blood. Is there anything happens in the world but by the conduct and efficacy of his providence? Do all the motions of the heavens, the productions of creatures, the universal events of nature, depend upon the will, power, and wisdom of God? And shall the soul, the most excellent of the lower creatures, bearing the characters of God's wisdom and goodness upon it (the acts of the soul in the way of religion, being the noblest acts it can produce), be left wholly to itself in the production and management of these? Shall God, the supreme cause in everything else, be an inferior and secondary cause in this affair? It is 'not he that plants, nor he that waters, but God that gives the increase,' 1 Cor. 3:7. God is the first cause, upon whom man depends in all kind of actions, much more in supernatural actions, chiefly in the understanding and will, upon which faculties no creature can have any intrinsic influence to cause them to exercise their vital acts. If the will of man were the first cause, God would be an attendant to the creature in the noblest works. God would not then be the first mover, but man. The will willing would then be the cause of God's working, not God's working the cause of the will's willing and choice. God's working would be consequent upon the will, and so the effect of the will's free motion. Man would then be the dispositiva causa in relation to God. It would make God the second cause, and represent him expecting the beck, and the preparations of

man, before he did exert any act. It would make God to will that which man wills, and make God to will that which man may reject. It would follow that God concurs not to regeneration by way of sovereignty, but by way of concomitancy. It would not be a victorious but a precarious grace, which is against the whole tenor of the Scripture, which represents God as holding in his hands the first links of all second causes: Rom. 11:36, 'For of him, and through him, and to him, are all things.' He is the first governor of all the wills and powers of the creatures, the first cause of all motions. He orders all, without being ordered by any. Now this is below the majesty of God, to be conducted in his motion by the will of the creature; to have the purposes of his goodness brought into act by an uncertain and slippery cause. How can it be conceived that God should put his hand to the more ignoble works of nature, and turn over the noblest work of the new creation to the airy will of the creature.

To conclude; God must either be precedent in his operation to the act of the will, or follow it. If precedent, we have what we would; if subsequent, then God is a mere attendant upon the motions of the creature, and a servant to wait upon man. This is to advance free will to the throne of God, and depress God to the footstool of will; this is to deify the creature, by placing the crown of the sovereign independency of God on the head of free will.

2. It puts a blot upon the wisdom of God. If God expects the determination of the will of man, whether he shall act or no, then God is disposed by the will of man to the intention of his end. But it is very inconsistent with that unfathomable and unerring wisdom, to have the attainment of his end depend upon an agent wherein nothing is wrapped up but folly and madness, Eccles. 9:3. This is to make his power depend upon weakness, and his gracious ends towards his creature hang upon the extravagancies of one distracted, which no wise man would be guilty of. Is God in all things else a God of power and wisdom, working all things in number, weight, and measure, springing up every motion in

the lower world, by an unblameable counsel? And shall he leave the forming of the image of his Son, wherein his wisdom is most seen, to the slight irregular will of man, which hath neither weight nor measure in itself? This would make the immutable counsel of God depend upon the mutability of the creature; which would be inconsistent with the wisdom of man, who chooseth the firmest means he can for the conduct of his designs; for if man wills this day, then God wills; if man reject it the next day, then he rejects that which God wills. So God's will must be at uncertainty, according to the will of man. How shall his counsel stand upon so tottering a bottom? How shall he do all his pleasure if it were a mere dependent upon the pleasure of the creature, contrary to what he is pleased positively to assert: Isa. 46:10, 'My counsel shall stand, I will do all my pleasure.' The apostle doth couch these two arguments together: Eph. 1:11, 'Who works all things according to the counsel of his own will;' he argues (1) from the power of God, 'who works all things,' whereby our own works, and power, are excluded, and God asserted to be the supreme cause of everything, in an efficacious and energetical manner, as the word ἐνεργεῖν signifies. (2.) From his wisdom, 'according to the counsel of his own will,' wisely and justly, and therefore not according to ours, wherein there is nothing but folly and evil. This excludes all our own wills in the first work. Now, to assert that this beautiful image were brought forth upon the stage of the heart by the will of man, as the first cause, would destroy God's prerogative, and represent his operations under the conduct of our own counsel and will, not of his own. Certainly if there be a secret and wise Spirit of providence, running through the whole world to preserve his honour in his works, as certainly there is, the most honourable declaration of them in the heart cannot be thought to be left to the conduct of wild and hare-brained nature.

3. If the will of man were the prime cause of regeneration, it would deprive God of his foreknowledge and prescience; it would make that foreknowledge, which is certain and infallible, merely contingent. For if

the will of man were wholly left to its own determination, the motions of
the will were doubtful and uncertain, till the will doth determine itself;
and so God's knowledge of them would be uncertain, for it is clear, that
from a thing wholly uncertain, there cannot arise a certain knowledge.
Therefore, God could not be said certainly to foreknow the conversion
of man, if the efficacy of grace depended upon so contingent a cause
as the liberty of man's will; for then it might not be, as well as be; the
will might not embrace it, and so the knowledge of God be but merely
conjectural,—a knowledge unworthy of a deity, which must be supposed
to be omniscient; a knowledge depending upon a peradventure, or at
best, it is but a very likely it will be so. This would be a debasing the
deity to an opinionative knowledge, which could not be certain, because
depending upon so indetermined and wavering a cause. God cannot
know this or that man's regeneration from eternity, but he must see it
infallibly in himself willing it, or in the causes of it, irresistibly producing
it.* But if the efficacy of grace depends upon the will, then God doth not
certainly determine the regeneration of man. And for God to foreknow
that which he himself hath not determined, and when nothing in the
creature, nor anything in the circumstances, doth determine it, is to
make God see that (as one saith) which neither in the creature nor in
himself is to be seen.

Obj. Some may object, How doth God come to foreknow sin, for that
depends upon the liberty of the will?

Ans. It would be too long to inquire into this, I shall only at present say
this, it is certain God doth foresee every sin, otherwise the evil acts of men
could not be predicted. Our Saviour could not then have foreknown
what the scribes and priests would do to him, as he doth foretell: Mat.
16:21, 'Christ began to tell them how many things he was to suffer of the
chief priests and scribes.' And since God cannot fail in his predictions,
but they will certainly come to pass, the hearts of the Jews could do
no other thing, supposing the prediction, than what Christ doth here

foretell, for their wicked wills would certainly determine themselves that way. And God, by a concurrence of causes which he had linked together in his hand, orders things so, that meeting with the corruption in their wills, their wills determine themselves to such actions there foretold; yet is not God therefore the author of sin. For sin being no positive thing, cannot have an efficient, but a deficient cause; and God determines the withdrawing of his common grace, and the ordering of such and such circumstances, and so did foresee how a free creature, with that corruption in his heart, would determine himself in such occasions, when involved in such circumstances. But now in the work of regeneration, outward circumstances cannot cause any determination of the will, because those outward circumstances of grace meet with nothing in the heart full of corruption, to take part with them, which outward circumstances of sin do. Therefore since there can be no foresight of God in this case, depending upon the concurrence of outward circumstances, unless there were something in the heart which did suit them, the determination of the will cannot proceed from them, but from God himself, willing and determining the will by a positive influx of his grace. The determination of the will to sin comes from within, from its natural corruption concurring with such occasions, which, joining together, determine the will to it. Therefore God foresees what a free creature will do; but there being no principle in the will by nature to correspond with any gracious external circumstances, it cannot determine itself to grace, because it wants a principle of determination within itself, the corrupt habits determining it quite otherwise. Sin proceeds not so much from the liberty as the captivity of the will; and God knowing the corrupt frame, can foresee what man in such a frame will do upon occasion; as we may easily resolve that an habitual drunkard will be drunk when he hath sensual objects placed before him.

4. Another consideration is this: to make the will of man the efficient of his regeneration, is to make the truth of God a great uncertainty.

(1.) First, In the covenant he made with Christ. If his having a seed depended upon the will of man, the promise of God to give him a seed might be null and void; for at least it must be granted possible, that not one man under heaven would have accepted of his terms; and then his coming to save had been in vain, because there was a possibility that not one man would have embraced the salvation offered. Since the number of rejecters of him is greater than the number of receivers, it is likely the less number, if left to their own wills, would have followed the greater, since the prevalency of evil examples above good ones is every day evident. It had not been, then, 'the pleasure of the Lord shall prosper in his hand,' Isa. 53:10, 11, but the pleasure of man shall prosper in the hand of the will of man. The great resolve of God, the priesthood of Christ, the design of drawing a generation of persons out of the world to praise him, had hung upon a mere hap-hazard and a may-be, if it had depended only on man's will; and God should have waited the leisure of free will, to see whether the most glorious design that ever was laid should prosper, and whether he should have been a God of truth, or a liar to his Son. Though our Saviour bad laid the foundation of our redemption in his own most precious blood, yet he must have depended on our will for the fruits of his purchase; it had been a great uncertainty whether he had seen one grain of fruit for all his expense. He might have been a king without one subject, or the destruction of one potent enemy he came to conquer, not one sin subdued, not one devil cast out of any soul. This might have been; for though by God he was made a king, yet according to the other assertion, it depended on the will of man whether he should have one subject to own his authority; and, if so, God had been very unwise to enter into covenant with him, and Christ very unwise to come upon such grand uncertainties at the best, when it was a question whether any one person should have enjoyed the fruits of his death. How can it enter into any man's heart, that so great a contrivance as the sending of Christ to be the means of salvation, with such great promises to see the fruits of his death in a seed to serve him, should depend in the main fruits and effects of it on any thing undetermined by the will of God; that so great a weight should hang upon so thin a thread as the will of man?

(2.) In the promises he makes to men. How could God promise that so absolutely as he doth, Ezek. 36:26, 'A new heart will I give you,' if this work did depend upon the will of man, which might frustrate the truth of God in his promise? And when God knew there was no principle in their hearts that could rise higher than to shame and confusion, not to so excellent a work as regeneration, as is intimated, ver. 32, 'Not for your sakes do I do this: be ashamed and confounded for your own ways, O house of Israel;' what reason was there for God to depress them to confusion, if they had had power to renew themselves? If this promise of God depended not upon any thing in them in the first making, it could not depend upon any thing in them in the full performance of it. We must either make God a liar, or unwise, or remove any efficiency in the will of man as the first cause. What blasphemy would it be to say, that God was so unwise as to promise that which depended upon the power of another, whether it should be wrought or no; that God could not be certainly true to his word, unless free-will assisted him!

5. It despoils God of his worship, in those two great parts of it, prayer and praise.

(1.) Prayer. With what face can any solicit God for that grace, which he conceives to be in his own power to have when he will? It is a mocking of him to desire that strength of him, which he hath given us already, inherent in our nature. If it were the work of our wills, it would require only the excitation of them, not any application to God. Who begs for what he hath? Who desires an alms that hath thousands in his purse? As prayer would be a vain thing in any man that should deny a providence overruling the affairs of the world, so it would be as vain a thing to call upon God for grace, if the whole affair of regeneration were left to the conduct of man's will. The end of God's making promises of a new heart, and a new spirit, is to be inquired after to do it for us, Ezek. 36:26, 37. The natural consequent, then, of asserting the power of our own wills, is not to call upon God, but direct our desires to another cause, to solicit our own wills, not God. It would not be, then, according to the language of the church, 'Turn thou us, O Lord, and we shall be turned;' 'Draw me, and I will run after thee,' Lam. 5:21, Cant. 1:4, but, I will turn to thee, and then shalt thou be turned to me; I will run after thee, and draw thee to myself. The royal authority, and power of God, and his glory in granting, is the foundation of prayer; therefore the Lord's prayer is concluded with this, as an argument to move God to grant what is asked, 'Thine is the kingdom, the power, and the glory;' that is, thou art rich and powerful, and hast all sorts of blessings to bestow. With what face can any one go to God with these words in his mouth, when he ascribes the kingdom, power, and glory, in so great a work, to his own will? We can never pray in confidence to God for it; for all confidence is wrought by a consideration of the will of him we pray to, to accomplish what we desire, and of his power to effect it. What confidence, then, can we have in his will particularly to work it for us, if we conceive he hath left it to our hands, as the proper work of our own wills? This was the ground of our Saviour's supplications, with strong cryings and tears, that 'God was able to save him,' Heb. 5:7: able naturally, in respect of his power; able morally, in respect of his truth to his promise. If God were careless in this concern, and had cast off all from his own hands, on the hand of free will, God might well say to any man, as he did to Moses, 'Why criest thou unto me? Speak to the children of Israel that they go forward,' Exod. 14:15. Why cry you to me? You may do it yourselves. Go forward with your own wills. The natural language of man to God would not be, Lord, let thy kingdom come, thy will be done, give me a new heart; but, I will have thy kingdom come, I will have thy will be done, I will procure myself a new heart, I will change my heart of stone into a heart of flesh.

(2.) Praise. It doth deprive God of this part of his worship also, praise even for his greatest blessings. If our own wills did produce this work, the greatest cause of glorying would be, not in God, but in ourselves. We have as little ground to praise God, if it be our own work, as we have to pray to him for it. All that can be said is, that we have ground to praise him for the means of regeneration; and this is no more ground than they have that are not regenerate under the enjoyment of the same means. If a man could give himself a natural being without God, he could be his own creator, his own foundation; so if he could give himself a spiritual being without the grace of God, he would be a god to himself; for in this case he would really do more to his conversion than God. If God offer grace equally to all, and the pliableness of one man's will to receive it above another were from himself, he would then owe an obligation to himself, but no more to God than the other that rejected it owes. The apostle, by asking the question, 'Who hath made thee to differ? And what hast thou that thou didst not receive?' 1 Cor. 4:7 (though it be meant of a difference of gifts, yet it is argumentum a minori), clearly implies, that what difference there was between them and others, was not of their own planting, nor grew up from the stock of nature. But if regeneration be wrought by a man's own will, it is not God that makes the difference, therefore the glory doth not belong to him. He is the author of a general call, therefore the glory of that pertains to him, it is true; but yet as much from the damned that have lived under the gospel, as from the glorified saints in heaven, because the special entertainment of this call was not from the efficacy of God's grace, but the liberty of man's will; for, according to this assertion, the love of God would be equal both to the damned and saved, and would not shine with a fairer lustre in heaven than it doth in hell. The apostle wisheth the Philippians to 'work out their salvation with fear and trembling;' and encourageth them by this argument, because God is the author of all that good which they do.* If the determination of the will, then, is from itself, is it not a brave ground to glory in ourselves? How shall any man give God the glory of his salvation? If it be said, God did enlighten their understandings by the preaching of the gospel, this is an illumination common to all; and the reason some believe and others not, is not from the gift of God, but from themselves; how can we give God a peculiar praise for that wherein there is no difference between the best and the worst of men? But the apostle saith, God gives us to will, that is, the operation of our will, and not only the illumination of the understanding; therefore, that our wills do terminate in that which is good, we hold of God; the apostle doth not say, God hath given us power to will, but produced the will in us, and that of his good pleasure. If, therefore, God work no more in one than in another, there is no place for God's good pleasure, because there is no difference. Let us see with what kind of language the praise of God would be clothed, according to the doctrine of free will.† A renewed man may say thus: Lord, I give thee thanks, that thou hast conferred upon me a supernatural grace; but thou didst also give as much grace to my neighbour; but I added something to that which thou didst supernaturally give me; and though I received no more than he did receive from thee, yet I did more than he, since he remains in his sin, and I am regenerate; therefore I have no more obligation to thee and thy grace, than he that believes not; for, Lord, thou didst not make me differ from the other, because he had equal gifts with me; but I made myself to differ, because I superadded my own velle to thy divine assistance. How much of the glory of God would be pared off by such a half-witted praise as this! How low would be the acclamations of glorified saints in heaven! What foundation of pride in the creature, contrary to the intendment of the gospel, which is chiefly to humble man, if man were the cause of the most excellent work in himself! It would write vanity in a great measure upon that excellent exhortation of the apostle, 'Let him that glories, glory in the Lord,' 1 Cor. 1:31, since there would be a bottom for flesh to glory in his presence, contrary to the design of God in his works, ver. 29, which is, 'that no flesh should glory in his presence.'

Arg. 2. The second sort of arguments is drawn from the nature and state of man.

1. In creation. Man did not create himself; to be a new creature is more than to be a creature. As man contributed nothing to nature, so neither can he contribute anything to grace, any more than a passive capacity in respect of faculties, which yet are the gift of God to him, nothing of his own acquisition. The soul, though framed with all its faculties, is as little able to engrave the image of God upon itself, as the body of Adam, formed with all its parts and members, was able to infuse a living soul into itself; there is no reason therefore to attribute our creation to God, and regeneration, the glory and excellency of a creature, to ourselves. I know such similitudes ought not to be strained too high; yet when this doctrine agrees with other parts of Scripture, we may form an argument from this metaphor of creation whereby regeneration is expressed in Scripture. It is confessed by most, if not all, that no creature, not an angel, can be an instrument in the very act of creation of another thing, much less the chief efficient of its own creation; for creation is an act of omnipotency, and an incommunicable property of the Deity, not to be delegated to any creature. The creation of man, in a state of such perfection as to be endued with the image of God, was a greater work than simply the creation of his body or the essential faculties of his soul, yea, greater than the creation of the whole world, because the attributes of God did more lively appear in him, and particularly his holiness. The restoration then of this righteousness to man, after it is lost, is a greater work than the first creation of his body and soul, it being the same thing with the conferring at first his original rectitude upon him. If man therefore could create this in his own soul after it is lost, he would do a greater work than simply the creation of a world. Surely there is as much power and wisdom required to the new-creating righteousness in the heart, after it

is perished, as there was in the placing it there at first; and then it will follow that none can new create it but an infinite wisdom, power, and holiness. If man therefore can create it in itself, he must have a wisdom, power, and holiness equal to that of God his first creator, for what could not be done by any creature at the first conferring it, but it was necessary that it should be a work of infinite power, cannot be done by a less power now, because the work is every whit as great; and no less power is requisite to a second creation of a thing after it is perished, than was necessary to the first creation of it, since this power of creation cannot be derived to any creature. As when life is gone from a fly, and the body of it dried and shrivelled up, all will grant that the restoring life to this fly must be done by an omnipotent power. The case is the same with us by nature; spiritual life, upon the fall, was wholly fled, no good thing dwells in our flesh, Rom. 7:18, not one thing spiritually good; that which is born of the flesh is flesh, wholly flesh in every part of it. If the making a living fly or worm is above the power of nature, much more the creating of so glorious a fabric as grace in the soul. Man might as well have implanted the divine image in his soul at first, as restore it after it was lost. To ascribe such a power to man to raise himself is a greater power than Adam had by creation, because to restore a man's self from death to life is greater than to preserve the vital principle he hath already, and act naturally from it.

2. In the state of innocency. Let us consider man in that, and it will appear he is unable to renew himself. If man did not keep himself up, with so great a stock of natural rectitude in paradise, how can he recover himself and that stock after it is lost? 'Man in his best estate is vanity; all Adam is all vanity.'* In the estate of pure nature, he is vanity in respect of his mutability, much more vanity then in his fallen state, from the experience of which Adam rightly called his second son Abel, vanity, Hebel, the word used here. How soon did the breath of the serpent melt the impression upon him! And if he did not by his innocent will preserve that purity which he had received, how can he by his corrupt will recover

that purity which he hath lost? If Adam had had a will to 'preserve, he might have stood, but in losing his will he lost his power; if he did not maintain his will in his rectitude, nor (as some say) could not without the grace of God, how can he, by the mere force of his own will, restore that lost rectitude to himself? If an universal integrity stood in need of grace to preserve it, an universal depravation stands in need of a more vigorous force than that of our will to eject it. If Adam, who had no disorders in nature to rectify, did not stand by his own will, it is not likely that we, who have strong habits to conquer, can be restored by the strength of our own wills. What nature did not do when it was sound, it is not likely to do a greater thing when it is wounded. We cannot now have more power than Adam had in innocency; but he was not then endued with a power to regenerate himself if he should fall, but death was pronounced, both spiritual and eternal. If temptations corrupted him, and if he, being in a good condition, did not maintain himself in it, but pass from a good condition to a bad, how can we, by the only liberty of our will, pass into a good one? Are temptations less powerful now than before?† Is the devil less vigilant to take all occasions to subvert us? Suppose our wills were not so evil as they are, would it not be more easy for the enemy to draw the will to himself, when it is irresolved between two parts, when the guide of it is so easy clouded, than it was to draw Adam's will to evil from that good to which he might readily have determined himself? Adam had the greatest advantages human nature, in a natural way, was capable of; he was created with a fulness of reason. But how long do we converse with sense, which fastens upon temptations, before we come to a use of reason! After we are come to some smatterings of reason, and a growth in it, as we think, what whisperings and impulses to sin do we feel! What an easiness to embrace incentives, a deafness to contrary admonitions! What languishing velleities, and palsy desires at best, for that which is good; a mighty mist and darkness upon our understandings, irresolution in our wills? How can we with all these fetters be able of ourselves to put ourselves into a better state, and act against nature, which is impossible any creature can do but by a superior power!

3. Consider man also in the state of corruption.

(1.) If the will of man by nature were the cause of regeneration, it would follow that corruption were a cause of regeneration. 'The imagination of the heart of man is only evil, and that continually,' Gen. 6:5. That which is evil, therefore, cannot be the cause of that which is man's greatest happiness. All actions are according to those innate qualities and habits which the agent hath; all corrupted things act no otherwise than corruptedly, because every act hath no more in it than what the principle, which is the spring of the action, conveys to it. If the heart, then, be wicked, it cannot do anything but what is wicked, and a wicked act can never be the foundation of regeneration. If a corrupt man, as corrupt, can be the cause of regeneration, then he can act graciously, not only without a gracious habit, but by and from a corrupt habit. If the acts are corrupt, the product of them must be corrupt, for man, in renewing himself, must act either as corrupt or good. If as good, then he was renewed before he set about the renewing himself. The question will then be the same, How came he by that restoration to goodness? If as corrupt, then corruption is the spring of the noblest happiness of the creature. It would then follow that a man can perform acts of life before he lives; that vital acts may be exerted by dead principles; that sanctification can grow up from an unsanctified root; and that the will, with its old corruption, can be the cause of its elevation to another state; and that the old creature can perform a new creature's act before it be a new creature. Then a carnal mind, while it is carnal, may be subject to the law of God, which the Scriptures say it cannot be, Rom. 8:7. Then those that are in the flesh may please God in an high manner, by the renewing themselves. This would be more strange than if we should see a crab-tree bring forth pomegranates; a corrupt tree would then bring forth good fruit, and that the highest fruit, contrary to our

Saviour's assertion, Mat. 7:18. It would follow that the stony heart would be the cause of the fleshly, and so an effect would rise from a cause quite contrary to it, and the complying principle in man be wrought by the resisting principle. It is as much as if the fire should cool, and the water burn, by their own innate qualities. If the will of man corrupted be the cause of principles of grace, then the old creature brings forth the new.* The image of the devil is the cause of producing the divine nature, and hell the cause of an heavenly principle. It would follow that an act of one kind can be produced by an habit of a contrary nature, and that a man can act graciously before he be gracious. Before grace, no action is essentially good, because there wants a gracious principle, whence it most receive its denomination as good. One act, then, of corrupted man, or a multitude of acts, cannot be the cause of grace, because they all centre in that denomination of evil. How the acts of the will, whereof not one can be called good till the will hath a good principle, can produce so noble a work and habit as grace is, is not easily intelligible. Our being engrafted into the good olive tree is contrary to nature, Rom. 11:24. Nature cannot naturally contribute to that which is opposite to it. We are wild by nature; our new implantation is contrary to nature. A good nature, therefore, cannot be the natural effect of a wild nature.

(2.) Since corruption, the power of man is mighty weak in naturals and morals, much more certainly in spirituals.

[1.] In naturals. No natural body that lies under a grievous disease can repair itself by its own power without some external assistance. A wounded member must be beholding to oils and plants for a cure. No man can cast out a disease when he will. He may be sick when he will, by eating that which is contrary to nature; but the cure doth not depend upon his will, but upon physic. Outward medicines must recover that which he lost by his own wilfulness. The will indeed is conditio sine qua non; there must be a will to use the means, or a man must be forced to use them, as we deal with madmen and children which are unwilling to take physic. But who ever heard of a man that could cure himself by his own will without the application of medicines? How can the soul then be restored to its vital integrity, by its own force? How can it change its own temper without some superior power operating upon nature? 'Man is like a wild ass's colt,' Job 11:12. What wild creature ever tamed itself? If any say that the will of man, by the use of outward ordinances, can cure itself, it is answered, Those ordinances are operative, not in a physical but moral way, and therefore such an efficiency as is in plants and drugs cannot be expected from them. There must be an operation of our own wills to make them efficacious. But what shall cure the will where the disease principally lies, and the love of the disease is seated? Who shall remove the beloved inclination from the will? Can nature cast out nature, or Satan cast out Satan? What can make us willing? When we are made willing, the cure is half wrought, as, when a madman is willing to be cured of his infirmity, you can hardly count him any longer mad. The evil principles in the will will never aim at their own destruction. If this work of regeneration were only the curing of a man that were sick or wounded, it could not be done by the power of man's will, but by the application of some external medicine, though nature did concur with it. But it is not a sickness but a death, therefore cannot come under the influence of the will of man in the first work. Shall a man have more power to cure his soul of mortal sins, than to cure his body of mortal wounds?

[2.] In morals. Whence comes that intemperance, incontinence, luxury, which overflows mankind, who are carried to those things which impair health, even in meats and drinks, against the reluctancy of reason, whose will is led not by reason but appetite, and choose not like men but beasts, under the notion of pleasant and gustful? Is not this from the will conducted by appetite?* The temperance and continence opposite to this is not in Scripture counted part of the extraction of nature, but the gift of God: 1 Cor. 7:7, 'But every man hath his proper gift of God, one after this manner, another after that,' speaking of continence. That which is God's gift is not merely the fruit of human will; for in the apostle's language they seem to be opposed, viz., to be from God, and from ourselves; to be God's gift, and yet our own. In Eph. 2:8 there is a plain antithesis, 'Not of yourselves: it is the gift of God.' It is the same expression of that moral virtue of continence as it is of the divine grace of faith; 'it is the gift of God.' We are nothing in morals without God, no more than a beam is when the sun is clouded or withdraws its light. Shall we, then, allow a greater power to man in spiritual things than the Scripture doth in morals? Shall the one be the gift of God, and the greater the acquisition of nature? Cannot the clay form itself into a vessel of moral honour? Shall it, then, be able to form itself into a vessel of grace? If we are not intrinsecally sufficient of ourselves to exercise a moral act, since our natures are so overgrown with corruption, we are less sufficient of ourselves to exercise a supernatural act without a divine motion. Can anything assume an higher nature than what it originally hath? Man hath assumed a lower nature than that wherein he was created, which no creature besides him in this lower world hath. Since he hath brutified himself, and cannot moralise himself without common grace, how can he advance himself into a participation of the divine nature without special grace? How can man, so habitually evil, ascend up to an higher nature?

[3.] In this corrupt state of man, any one sin beloved will hold a man down from coming to God. It is impossible for a man, wedded in his heart to his riches, and bemired in earthly confidences, to enter into a renewed gospel state. 'How hard is it,' saith our Saviour, 'for them that trust in riches, to enter into the kingdom of God!' Mark 10:24, 25. This one corruption commanding in the heart, will hinder any resurrection by the power of nature, for on man's part Christ pronounces it impossible for such an one to enter into the kingdom of God, ver. 27, that is, into a gospel-state; and that upon the score of this single sin, which only appeared at this time in that young man. The like he pronounceth of another sin, that of ambition: John 5:44, 'How can ye believe, which receive honour one of another?' That one fancy of the Jews, of a temporal conquering Messiah, did so possess their brains, that it barred the door against all the power of our Saviour's miracles; and the bare objective proposal of him, though unanswerable by reason, could not remove this rooted fancy. One sin in the will, hath more power than any imagination in the fancy. When Adam disfigured his nature by one sin, he had no strength to recover himself, though his righteousness was but very lately fled from him. We need not question his recovery of it, had it been in the power of his will to will it, and the power of his nature to regain it. If one sin, then, in the will, is a bar against the power of nature, what are all those lusts which swarm in the heart of man, and swell up this lake of natural venom in the soul? If one fetter stakes down a man to an impotency and impossibility, how great is man's weakness under all those fetters which every day he loads himself with! One string about a bird's leg will keep it from flying away, much more many.

Arg. 3. Another sort of considerations, is from the state of man under the gospel.

1. If regeneration depended on the will of man, what is the reason more do not receive the gospel than are seen by us to receive it? If the faculty of believing were given to all, then all would believe upon the promulgation of the gospel, because the gospel is 'the power of God to salvation,' Rom. 1:16. If it be the power of God in the outward preaching of it, then all would believe. If all do not believe, then some other secret power attends it, which makes it efficacious in one, not in another; it is 'to them that are saved' only, 'the power of God,' 1 Cor. 1:18; to others, though of great reason, foolishness. If the strength of arguments be the cause in one, what is the reason those arguments have not force upon another? What is that which makes the difference? All men have reason; and what is common reason doth conduct all men

more or less. If men could open the eyes of their mind to understand the excellency of gospel proposals, what is the reason that among those great multitudes to whom it is preached, so few in all ages have embraced it, though the things proposed are in themselves desirable, and suit so well, in respect of the blessedness promised, to the natural desire of man for happiness! When it was preached by the apostles, it was edged with miracles, attended with a remarkable holiness, yet they complained that few received their report. Even in that age, and succeeding ages, men have been so far from receiving it, that they have scoffed at it, persecuted with all their fury the professors of it. It hath been thus despised, not only by the meanest and blindest sort of people, but by men of the most elevated understanding among the heathen philosophers, that could pierce into the depths of nature; and by the Jews too, who had the Messiah promised to them, expected him about that time, had so many prophecies deciper- ing him, which all met with their accomplishment in his person; who were also amazed at the miracles he wrought in his life, and those which accompanied his death. Doth not all this shew the natural blindness of man, that there is need of some higher power to open his eyes, be- sides the objective proposal, that he may acknowledge the excellency of those things which are presented to him? Do we not find men ready to acknowledge reason upon other accounts, to be wrought into warm affections by pathetical speeches? Why are they not as ready in this, if it were in the power of their own understandings and wills? Do we not find the wills of men averse from it, though in their consciences they approve of the doctrines of it? What is the reason a man is renewed at one time, and not before, when he hath heard the same arguments inculcated many a time? Many drops would not work it before, and one drop works it now in an instant. Is it from the power of reason in man? What reason is there, then, that he should be mastered by one reason now, who was not mas- tered by the same reason, and many more as strong, formerly? Whence comes that light into the mind? What is the reason such a man was not regenerate before, when he hath in some fits meditated upon former arguments, and afterwards one effects it, by a secret insinuation, without any previous meditation, and a sudden turn of the will is wrought? Can this be supposed to be from the will principally? Rather from some divine spirit spreading itself over the soul, and opening the passages of it which were before shut. That place, Mat. 11:21, where our Saviour speaks of the Tyrians and Sidonians, if the gospel had been preached to them, they would have repented in sackcloth and ashes, doth not prove the power of man to renew himself, but that they would have testified some outward humiliation, as Ahab did at the threatening of Elijah;* or rather, Christ exaggerates the hardness of the Jews' hearts in comparing them with the Tyrians in a hyperbolical manner of expression; as we do when we reproach a man for unmercifulness, we say, Had I entreated a Turk or barbarian as much, I should have bended him; not that we commend the humanity of the Turks, but aggravate the cruelty of those we have to do with. The proposal of an object is not sufficient without the inspiration of a will, whereby that concupiscence which masters that faculty may be overpowered.

2. If regeneration were the fruit of man's will, what is the reason that men convinced by the preaching of the gospel, and under great terrors too, find themselves unable to turn to God? What is the reason they are not presently renewed? Would they be torn with such horrors, and bear about them such racks in their consciences? Would they fill heaven and earth with complaints, were it in their own power to make themselves such as God commands them to be? If this were found in the more ignorant sort of people, the reason then might be charged upon their want of knowledge; but men of great wits and insight are filled with those complaints when God begins to rebuke them. And such as have a great deal of grace, as David, when God charges sin upon him: Ps. 51:10, 'Create in me a clean heart; renew in me a right spirit;' why should they solicit God for renewing grace, were it in the power of their own hand?

Would any that fear God, as David did, mock him at such a rate, as to desire that of him which they are able to do without him? Were there a natural power in man to turn himself, why did not Judas, after his conscience lashed him, go to his Master's knees to desire pardon, rather than to the gibbet? He had long experience of the merciful disposition of his Master; he had not grace given him to incline his will to such an act; yet Peter was turned after his denial of his Master; was there anything more by nature in him than in Judas? Or did Peter do that by the strength of his own will, which Judas did not do? No; the Scripture assures us, it was from the prevalency of Christ's prayer, a secret influence from Christ's look, stirring up that grace that was already in his heart; he might else have gone out cursing his Master as long as he had lived: 'No man can come to me, except the Father draw him,' saith our Saviour; though he be convinced, there must be the Father's traction as well as conviction to complete the work. All drawing implies a resistance, or at least a heaviness and indisposition in the thing so drawn, to come of itself. There is much difference between the proposal of the object, and the cause of our entertaining it. The object is the final cause which puts us upon motion; the object moves the will as an end, but it gives no power to move. If a man hear of an alms to be distributed at such a place, and he knows he stands in need of it, and hath a desire to go to receive it, this knowledge of the necessity of it will not give him legs to go, if he be lame and unable to go; and he that doth go to receive the alms, the desire to receive the alms puts him upon motion; but the intention of receiving the alms was not the efficient cause of that motion. If he had not had strength in him from some other cause than the alms, he could never have gone. Our motion to God must proceed from some higher cause than barely the proposal of the object, and a conviction by it.

4. Argument is drawn from the condition of the regenerate themselves. They are not able to rid themselves of the remainders of sin, much less can natural men of the body of sin. From the impotency after grace,

we may rationally conclude a greater weakness in a natural man that hath not one spark of grace within, to be blown up from any breathing of grace from without. The flesh lusts against the spirit in a regenerate man; how peaceably doth it enjoy its dominion in a natural man, where there is no spirit to control it, and lust against it? Regenerate men 'cannot do the good they would,' and they 'do the evil which they hate,' Rom. 7:15, 19, though they have a law of grace in their mind, set up in contradiction to the law of sin in their members. How can a natural man, then, do so good a thing as the renewal of himself, and the destruction of his sin, who hath no will to the one nor hatred of the other, who hath the law of sin flourishing in him, and delights to read the characters of it and perform the wills of the flesh! If there be such an inability in a renewed man, who hath a relish of God and the goodness of the law, who hath sin in part mortified, and cast out of the mind, to the members and suburbs, how much greater must the inability and resistance be where there is nothing but opposing flesh! What need the apostle issue out such heavy complaints: 'O wretched man that I am, who shall deliver me from the body of this death?' Rom. 7:24, if he had power in his own hands to free himself from this oppressing sin? If Paul, a living tree in God's garden, having both the root and sap of grace, be so wretched, so weak and unable to free himself from those suckers, how wretched then is a dead rotten stake, which hath no spiritual root! How can he free himself from a total spiritual death, when this great apostle could not free himself from a partial spiritual death by all that stock of grace already received? If a good man finds it so laborious a task to engage against the relics of nature, and manage an open hostility against the wounded force of his sensual appetite, much more is it a difficult task for a natural man to row against the stream of unbroken nature, when the natural resistance is in its full strength, and the bent of nature standing point-blank against God. If a well-built and well-rigged ship, with her sails spread, can only lie floating upon the waves, and make no way till a fresh wind fills the sails, surely the rough timber that lies upon the ground can never fit and frame itself into a stately vessel.*

5. It is against the whole order which God has set in the world, for any thing to be the cause of itself, or of a higher rank of being than what it has by nature. No effect is nobler than its cause; grace is more noble than nature. A seal cannot convey any other image than what is stamped upon itself, and no further than its own dimensions; neither can nature stamp anything of grace upon the soul, because it hath no such image engraven on it by God. Nature, though never so perfect in its own kind, can never produce a thing of higher perfection than itself; a plant can never produce a beast, nor a beast a man, nor a man an angel. No natural quality can be changed in any subject by itself, but by the introduction of some other quality superior to it. The fire can never freeze while it is fire; water cannot part with its coldness without some superior acting upon it; and can those that are naturally bad ever become spiritually good but by an almighty power? No nature can exceed its own bounds, because nothing can exceed itself in acting. Whatsoever a natural man doth is but natural, and can never amount to grace, without a change of nature and addition of a divine virtue. If any thing could rise above its own sphere, it would be stronger than itself. Nothing can never make itself something; the best apostle counts himself no better,—2 Cor. 12:11, 'I am nothing,'—and entitles grace the sole benefactor of all his spiritual good, 2 Cor. 12:20. What thing ever gave itself its own shape? Every piece of art is brought into figure by the workman, not by itself. Conformity to Christ is a fruit of the election of God, not first of the choice of our own wills. Rom. 8:29, 'Whom he did foreknow he also did predestinate to be conformed to the image of his Son.' The first link of the chain in the providential and in the gracious administration is in the hands of God. Hence in Scripture the gracious works in the soul run in the passive for the most part: 'Ye are justified, ye are sanctified; 'not you justify or sanctify yourselves; though sanctification and purging and working out

salvation is ascribed to them that have received grace and life, as acting afterwards for such ends, and producing such effects by the strength of grace received from God, and grace accompanying that first grace in its acts.

As we have proved that man by his own strength cannot renew himself, let us see whether he can do it by his additional capacities.

1. Man, by the help of instituted privileges, doth not produce this work of regeneration in himself, without a supernatural grace attending them. Ordinances cannot renew a man, but the arm of God, which doth manage them, edgeth them into efficacy, as the arm that wields the sword gives the blow. Means are the showers of heaven, but they can no more make the heart fruitful till some gracious principles be put in, than the beams of the sun, the dews of heaven, and the water-pots of the clouds, can make a barren ground bring forth flowers, without a change of the nature of the soil, and new roots planted in it. All the spectacles in the world cannot cure a man's eyes, he must have a visive faculty to make use of them. Our faculty must be cured before we can exercise it about objects or use means proper to that faculty. All persuasions will not prevail with a dead man; the fairest discourses, the most undeniable arguments, the most moving rhetoric will not stir or affect him, till God take away the stone from the grave and raise him to life. The report of the prophets will do no good without the revelation of God's arm, Isa. 53:1, because all those things do not work in a physical way, as drugs and plasters, which attain their end without any active concurrence of the patient, but in a moral way; the will therefore and nature must first be changed before those can do any good. You can never by all your teachings teach a sheep to provide for winter, as an ant doth, because it hath no such instinct in its nature. If any thing were like to work upon a man, the most stupendous miracles were most likely to produce such an effect upon the reasons of men; yet those supernatural demonstrations without a man only cannot make him believe a truth.

Miracles are a demonstration to the eye as well as preaching to the ear; though they be confessed to be above the strength of nature, yet all the spectators of them are not believers: John 12:37, 'But though he had done so many miracles before them, yet they believed not.' Many of those that saw our Saviour's works did not believe his doctrine; nay, they irrationally ascribed them to the devil, when they could find no reason in the nature of them to charge them upon such a score. The raising Lazarus from the dead was as high a miracle as ever was wrought; yet, though many of them believed, yet others did not, but accused him to the pharisees, who thereupon more vigorously took counsel to put him to death, John 11:45, 46, 47, 53, though they acknowledged that he did many miracles. They had reason as well as others; the miracles were undeniable, as being acted before many witnesses; the natural force of them upon all reasons was equal, the considerations arising from them unanswerable. There were evil habits in the will, not removed by grace, which resisted the unanswerable reason of the miracles. What made the difference between them and those that believed? Why did not the wills of the enemies follow the undeniable reason, as well as the wills of others? Miracles may astonish men, but cannot convert them without a divine touch upon the heart. 1 Kings 18:39, the people were astonished by that wonderful miracle of fire falling from heaven and consuming the sacrifice, and licking up the water in the trench; and some reverential resolutions were produced in them: they fell upon their faces and said, 'The Lord he is God;' they shewed their zeal in taking Baal's prophets, and helping, or at least suffering, Elijah to slay them; yet those people revolted to idolatry, and continued so till their captivity. The easiness of faith upon the apparition and instruction of one risen from the dead was the opinion of one of the damned: Luke 16:30, 'If one went to them from the dead, they will repent;' but this opinion was contradicted by Abraham, ver. 31, who positively asserts, 'If they did not hear Moses and the prophets, they would not be persuaded though one rose from the dead.' If their wills were obstinate against the means God had appointed for their conversion, the same wills so corrupted would be as obstinate against the highest sort of miracles. If that, then, which is above the hand of nature to act, and bears the character of omnipotency upon the breasts of it, doth not work upon men's hearts and wills of themselves, surely nature itself cannot turn the heart to God.

The two great dispensations of God are law and gospel; neither of these can of themselves work this.

(1.) The law. The law will instruct, not heal.* It acquaints us with our duty, not our remedy; it irritates sin, not allays it; it exasperates our venom, but doth not tame it; though it shews man his miserable condition, yet a man by it doth not gain one drop of repentance. It tells us what we should do, but corrects not the enmity of our nature whereby we may do it. The apostle takes notice of the enmity of man to the law: Rom. 5:6, 7, 'Yet enemies,' 'yet sinners.' That yet may refer to what he had spoken of the law in the chapter before. Though men had had so much time from the fall to recover themselves, and had so many advantages by the law and the ceremonies of it, yet all those years spent from the foundation of the world had produced no other effect than the weakening of them; as creatures that are wounded, by their strugglings waste their own strength. Yet sinners, till this time sinners, whereby the load of sin which lay upon the world was made more heavy by the continual addition made to those heaps. The offence did rather abound by the law than was diminished: Rom. 5:20, 'The law was given that sin might abound.' Though it made a clear discovery of the will of God, yet it rather aggravated sin; it added no power to perform that will. The motions of sin were exasperated by it, ex accidenti, and brought forth fruit unto death; all the means by the law for the repressing of sin did rather inflame it. Sin could not be overcome by it, because the law was 'weak through the flesh;' that is, had not so much power as sin had; it was like a little water put upon fire, which did rather enrage than quell it: Rom. 7:8, 9, 'Sin revived' when the law came, it had a new life, and the apostle found himself utterly unable to overpower it. There were, ver. 5, 'motions of sin,' παθήματα, not only a power in sin, but an enraged power, which adds to the strength of a person; 'sin slew him: taking occasion by the commandment,' ver. 10, and a dead man is wholly at the disposing of his conquerors. The law was 'holy,' it had an impression of God's holiness upon it, Rom. 7:12–14, there was also equity and conveniency in it, it was 'just and good,' and though these were considerations enough to spur men on to rid themselves of this tyrant sin, yet they could not, they had not strength enough to do it; though it was holy, just, and good, yet it was not strong enough to rescue them; and the reason of it, the apostle lays upon the difference in the nature of both: ver. 14, 'We know that the law is spiritual, but I am carnal, sold under sin;' there was an enmity in his nature to it, and therefore he must lie under the power of it till a mighty deliverer stepped in to conquer it. Do we find any better effect of the ceremonial law, which was the gospel in a mask, and which was the instrument of all the regenerations among the Jews? How few do we find renewed among them under that means which they enjoyed solely, and no other nation in the world partners with them in it! How frequent were their revolts, and rebellions, and idolatries, inconsistent with regeneration, we may read in Joshua and Judges. The inefficaciousness of means appears evidently in that nation which had greater advantages than any in the world besides; the covenants, sacrifices, oracles of God, warnings by prophets, yet so frequently overgrown with idolatry from the time of their coming out of Egypt to the Babylonish captivity, and ten tribes wholly cashiered for it.

(2.) The gospel. Though the veil of ceremonies be taken off from it, and it appeareth open faced, yet till the veil be taken off the understandings of men, it will produce little fruit among them, 2 Cor. 3:14. The gospel is plain, but only 'to him that understands,' Prov. 8:9, as the sun is clear, but only to him that hath an eye to see it. The gospel itself cannot remove the blindness from the mind. The proposal of the object works no alteration in the faculty, without some acting on the faculty itself. The beams of the sun shining upon a blind man make no alteration in him. The Jews, to whom the gospel was preached by our Saviour himself, could not believe, because God blinded their eyes, &c., John 12:39, 40. There must be a supernatural power, besides the proposal of the object, to take away this blindness and hardness which is the obstruction to the work of the gospel. Though the Son of God is come, and the gospel be preached, yet the understanding whereby we know is given us by him: 1 John 5:20, 'And we know that the Son of God is come, and hath given us an understanding, that we may know him that is true;' the light of the gospel shines upon all, but all have not an eye given them to see it, and a will given them to embrace it. The mere doctrine of it doth not regenerate any man;* some have tasted of the heavenly gift, that is, have had some understanding of Christ, who is the heavenly gift, the Son given to us, Isa. 9:6, and are partakers of some common illumination of the Holy Ghost, yet are not regenerate. Was not the gospel preached to the Jews, even by the mouth of our Saviour whom they crucified? And was it not preached to the Gentiles by the mouths of those apostles whom they persecuted? Were there not proposals that suited the natural desires of men for happiness, yet did not many that seemed to receive it, receive it not in the love of it? If God himself should appear to us in the likeness of a man, and preach to us as he did to Adam, if he did not overpower our hearts with an inward grace, he would do us no good at all by his declarations. We do not read of any work immediately upon Adam at the promulgation of the gospel by God himself, though it appears that afterwards there was, by his instructing his sons to sacrifice, and his expectations of a Messiah. But we certainly know that our Saviour, God manifested in the flesh, declared the gospel in his own person, and found no success but where he touched the heart inwardly by the grace of his Spirit. All mere outward declarations are but suasions, and mere suasion cannot change and cure a disease or habit in nature. You may exhort an Ethiop to turn himself white, or a lame man to go; but the most pathetical exhortations cannot procure such an effect without a greater power than that of the tongue to cure nature; you may as well think to raise a dead man by blowing in his mouth with a pair of bellows. Judas had enjoyed the best means that ever were, yet went out of the world unrenewed; and the thief upon the cross, who never perhaps was in any good company in his life till he came to the cross, nor ever heard Christ speak before, was renewed by the grace of God in the last hour.

2. Neither can a man renew himself by all his moral works, before faith. Our calling is not according to our works, but 'according to God's own purpose and grace,' 2 Tim. 1:9. Paul, before his conversion, was 'blameless as to the righteousness of the law,' Philip. 3:6, yet this was loss; a bar rather to regeneration, than a means to further it. For all this legal comeliness he ranks himself, before his conversion, in the number of the dead: Eph. 2:5, 'When we were dead in sins;' not you, but we, putting himself into the register of the dead. Whatsoever works a man can morally do before faith, cannot be the cause of spiritual life; they are not vital operations; if they were, they were then the effects of life, not the cause; the Scripture makes them the effects of grace: 'created to good works,' Eph. 2:10. What is an effect cannot be the cause. The best works before grace are but a refined sensuality, they arise from self-love, centre in self-satisfaction, are therefore works of a different strain from those of grace, which are referred to a higher end, and to God's well-pleasing. In all works before grace there is no resignation of the soul to God in obedience; no self-denial of what stands in opposition to God in the heart; no clear view of the evil of sin; no sound humiliation under the corruption of nature; no inward purification of the heart, but only a diligence in an external polishing. All those acts cannot produce an habit of a different kind from them. Let a man be stilted up with the highest

natural excellency; let him be taller by the head and shoulders than all his neighbours in morality, those no more confer life upon him than the setting a statue upon an high pinnacle, near the beams of the sun, inspireth it with a principle of motion. The increasing the perfection of one species can never mount the thing so increased to the perfection of another species. If you could vastly increase the heat of fire, you could never make it ascend to the perfection of a star. If you could increase mere moral works to the highest pitch they are capable of, they can never make you gracious, because grace is another species, and the nature of them must be changed to make them of another kind. All the moral actions in the world will never make our hearts, of themselves, of another kind than moral. Works make not the heart good, but a good heart makes the works good. It is not our walking in God's statutes materially, which procures us a new heart, but a new heart is in order before walking in God's statutes, Ezek. 36:27. Our regeneration is no more wrought by works of our own than our justification. The rule of the apostle will hold good in this, as well as in the other: Rom. 11:6, 'If it be of grace, it is not of works; otherwise grace is no more grace;' and faith is 'the gift of God, not of works, lest any man should boast,' Eph. 2:9. And the apostle, Titus 3:5, opposeth the 'renewing of the Holy Ghost' to 'works of righteousness.' He excludes works from being the cause of salvation; and would they not be the cause of salvation, if they were the cause of the necessary condition of salvation?

Prop. 3. As man cannot prepare himself to this work, nor produce it, so he cannot co-operate with God in the first production of it. We are no more co-workers with God in the first regeneration, than we were joint purchasers with Christ in redemption. The conversion of the will to God is a voluntary act; but the regeneration of the will, or the planting new habits in the will, whereby it is enabled to turn to God, is without any concurrence of the will. Therefore, say some, we are active in primo actu, but not in primo actus; or we are active in actu exercito, but not in actu signato. Some say, the habit of faith is never created separate from an act, as the trees at the creation of the world were created with ripe fruit on them; but the tree, with the power of bearing fruit, and the fruit itself, were created at one and the same time by God. Yet though the habit be not separate at first from the act, yet there is no co-operation of the creature to the infusion of that habit, but there is to the act immediately flowing from that habit; for either that act of grace is voluntary or involuntary. If involuntary, it is not a gracious act; if voluntary, it must needs be; since the tone of the will is changed, then the creature concurs in that act; for the act of believing and repenting is the act of the creature. It is not God that repents and believes in us; but we repent and believe by virtue of that power which God hath given us. In the first act, therefore, there is a concurrence of the creature; otherwise the creature could not be said to repent and believe, but something in the creature, without or against the will of the creature. But in the first power of believing and repenting, God is the sole agent. Jesus Christ is the sun that heals our natures, Mal. 4:2; the rain that moistens our hearts: Ps. 72:6, 'He shall come down like rain upon the mown grass.' What co-operation is there in the earth with the sun to the production of flowers, but by the softness it hath received from the rain? It would else be parched up, and its fruits wither. The Holy Ghost doth by his own power make us good trees; but we afterwards, by virtue of that power, work together with him, in bringing forth good fruit.* Yet this is also a subordinate, not a co-ordinate working; rather a sub-operation than a co-operation.

1. The state wherein man is at his first renewal excludes any co-working with God. The description the apostle gives of a state of nature excludes all co-operation of the creature in the first renewal: Titus 3:3, 'For we ourselves were sometimes foolish, disobedient, deceived, serving divers lusts and pleasures, living in malice and envy, hateful, and hating one another.' And Eph. 2:2, 3, 'Among whom we all had our

conversations in time past, in the lusts of our flesh, fulfilling the desires of the flesh and of the mind.' Every man is naturally taken up in the fulfilling the desires of the flesh; not only the Gentiles, to whom Paul writes, but himself; for he puts himself and the rest of the Jews in the number. In the second verse it was 'ye walked;' in ver. 3, it is 'we all;' and in Titus 3:3, 'we ourselves.' We who had the oracles of God, that had greater privileges than others, were carried out with as strong an impetus naturally, till grace stopped the tide, and after stopping, turned it against nature. When the mind was thus prepossessed, and the will made the lusts of the flesh its work and trade, there was no likelihood of any co-operation with God in fulfilling his desires, till the bent of the heart was changed from the flesh and its principles. The heart is stone before grace. No stone can co-operate with any that would turn it into flesh, since it hath no seed, causes, or principles of any fleshly nature in it. Since we are overwhelmed by the rubbish of our corrupted estate, we can no more co-operate to the removal of it, than a man buried under the ruins of a fallen house can contribute to the removal of that great weight that lies upon him. Neither would a man in that state help such a work, because his lusts are pleasures; he serves his lusts, which are pleasures as well as lusts, and therefore served with delight. There is naturally in man a greater resistance against the work of grace, than there is in the natural coldness of water against the heat of the fire, which yet penetrates into all parts of the water.

2. Regeneration is a new principle. What operation can there be before a principle of action? All co-operation supposeth some principle of working; as actus secundus supposeth actum primum. But a man, before his first regeneration, is blind in his mind, perverse in his will, rebellious in his affections, unable to know the truth, unable to do good, dead in sin. If he does co-operate with God before the habit be settled, then we can act before we have a power to act. We can please God in taking his part, and joining issue with him, before we have a gracious principle;

which is contrary to the Scripture, which tells us we are first begotten of God before we can keep ourselves, or exert one act for the bettering ourselves: 1 John 5:18, 'He that is begotten of God keeps himself.' The preservation of ourselves, and every act tending thereto, follows the infusion of the first principle. And the apostle Paul implies, that God works in us to will before we work: Philip. 2:12, 13, 'Work out your own salvation with fear and trembling; for God works in you both to will and to do,' &c. The apostle supposeth not any operation in them before, because he supposeth not their working without God's giving them a will, the act of volition. The working of the creature supposeth some divine work first upon the will. Did the dust of the ground, whereof Adam's body was formed, co-work with God in figuring it into a body? or doth the body contribute any more than a passive receptivity to the infusion of the rational soul? Lazarus did not concur with Christ till his powerful voice infused life and strength into him. His rising and walking was from a power conveyed, wherein Christ did work; but there was no co-working in him in the conveyance of that power. We do not say that a man co-works with the sun in enlightening a room, because he opens the shuts which barred out the light; the opening whereof is no cause of the sun's shining, but a conditio sine quá non. But do we so much in the first renewal? It is God alone who darts his beams, and opens our hearts too, to admit it: Acts 16:14, it is said, 'the Lord Opened Lydia's heart.' The will cannot concur in the actual infusion of a gracious principle, because it hath no spark in itself by nature, suitable to that principle which is bringing it into the soul itself. The shining of God into the soul is compared to the chasing away that darkness which at the first creation was over the face of the deep: 2 Cor. 4:6, 'For God, who commanded the light to shine out of darkness, hath shined in our hearts, to give the light of the knowledge of the glory of God.' What co-working was there in that darkness to remove itself, but a necessity upon it to obey the command of God, who had the sovereign power over his own works? If the creature did co-work with God at first, it could no more be said to be dead than a man asleep may be said to be dead; and grace were only an awakening, not an enlivening.

3. If there were any co-working of the will with God in the first infusion of grace, God would not be so much the author of grace as he is of nature in any other creature. The creature would share with him in the first principle of its action, which no creature in the world can be said to do. It would rather be a concourse of God than a creation; but all the terms whereby God sets forth himself in the work of regeneration import more than a bare concourse or a co-operation with the creature: 'I will take away the heart of stone; I will write my law in their hearts; I will put my Spirit into them,' are loftier expressions than are used to signify a co-working only. He appropriates the whole work to himself, without interesting the creature in any active concurrence, any more than at his creation.

4. If the will of man did co-work with God in regeneration, it would then share part of the glory of God. The whole glory would not belong to God, which he challengeth to himself in Scripture. He were then but an half Saviour, an half new-creator. We should be in joint commission with him, by the power of our own wills, in the first motion. If creation and resurrection are acts of an almighty power, man co-operating with him in the very act of creation and resurrection would partake with God's almightiness, and in some sort be co-equal with him, and a joint partner with God in a work which required almightiness for the effecting it. Surely since the same power which raised Christ from the dead works first in every believer for his spiritual resurrection, he contributes no more to it than the body of Christ in the grave did to its resurrection, which was a work not of his humanity, but divinity. Plucking out of the power of Satan is an effect of the power of grace, and God's gift, 2 Tim. 2:25, 26. God first 'gives repentance, that they may recover themselves out of the snare of the devil.' A slave, whose hands and feet are laden with

fetters, can contribute nothing to his deliverance but a will and desire to be delivered; nor that, if he be in love with his fetters, which is the case of every one of us by nature, who are as fond to be in the devil's custody as he is to have us. What co-operation can there be in this case? Whatsoever is an act of mercy, and an act of truth in God, he is to have the sole praise of; it doth not in any sort belong to the creature. The psalmist emphatically excludes man from it: Ps. 115:1, 'Not unto us, O Lord, not to us, but unto thy name give glory, for thy mercy, and for thy truth's sake.' Not unto us, twice repeated, but to thy name give glory. Do believers beg of God the giving glory to himself, and not unto them; and will they contradict their prayers, by sharing the praise with God? This is expressed for deliverances. Much less doth any praise and glory belong to the creature for the most excellent deliverance of all, from the power of sin, Satan, and death.

5. How can men co-work with God in the first regeneration, when they must needs acknowledge that in the progress of it they are oftener hinderers than furtherers of it? If God did not work more strongly in us than the best of us do in ourselves, and breathe a willingness into our wills, after regeneration, we should come short of salvation for all the first stock. How often do the best complain of their disability! Is it not frequent in the mouths of Christians in all ages as well as of Paul: Rom. 7:18, 'To will is present with me, but how to perform that which is good I find not'? How easily are our purposes shaken, and our strength staggers! Can we then co-operate with God, when we have no purpose, no strength? Let every man's experience speak for himself, how apt he is to check the motions of the Spirit; to let our Saviour stand and knock, and not open. What strugglings of the body of death! What indispositions in an holy course! Is there not often a kind of rustiness of soul, cold damps in spiritual duties? What faint hands in any holy work! What ebbs and floods, ups and downs in his heart! What feeble knees in his walk! What hung-down heads in laying hold of Christ in repeated acts

of faith! What frequent returns of spiritual lethargies! And all this after habitual grace. If our co-operations with God after grace received, are but a remove from non-acting, next neighbours to no working at all, we must conclude it to be worse with man before grace was settled in the soul, and that there was no active concurrence with it in any manner of acting; otherwise there would be as much co-operation before the implantation of habitual grace as after, which is hard to be imagined, that a man should be no stronger with grace received than under the want of it.

Prop. 4. Man by his own strength cannot actuate grace after it is received. To what purpose did the saints of old pray to quicken them, if they stood not in as much need of exciting grace from God as of renewing grace: Ps. 80:18, 'Quicken us, and we will call upon thy name;' Ps. 119:25, 27, and many places in that psalm. The new creature is little better than an infant in the best, and cannot go unless God bear it in his arms, as he speaks of Ephraim, Hosea 11:1, 3. They cannot move unless led by the Spirit. The child hath a principle of motion in it, but cannot go without the assistance of the nurse; nor the soul, without the assistance of God, actuate that principle of grace. Habitual grace is the instrument, not the principal agent. A sword, though it hath an edge, cuts nothing till it be moved by some strong arm. The first principle of the motion of grace resides in God. Purification in its progress is attributed to faith as an instrument, but to God as a principal agent. It is said, Acts 15:8, 9, 'God gave them the Holy Ghost, as he did to us, and put no difference between us and them, purifying their hearts by faith.' Yet the will of man concurs in this actuating of faith, as a subordinate cause: 1 John 3:3, a man is said to 'purify himself by hope.' A well-rigged soul, with its habit of grace spread, as well as a ship with its sails, must wait the leisure of the wind before it move. Paul acknowledges his acting for the service of God to be not from himself principally: 1 Cor. 15:10, 'Yet not I, but the grace of God which was with me.' It was the grace of God used me as an instrument; the glory must not stick to my fingers; it was the grace of God with me, affording strength and help to that grace which was in me. If this concourse of God be necessary in all natural actions, it is much more in the spiritual frame of the soul to keep it up, and to keep it acting. It is not we that work to will and to do, but God works to will and to do. It is to be considered that the apostle writes to them that are in a state of grace, exhorting them to a progress in salvation, depending upon God, who works the after will and the after doing, as well as the first will and compliance with the grace of God. Do we not find renewed men not able, with all the grace they have, to quicken themselves sometimes in duty? What is the reason they lie spiritless before God, often with breathings, sighs, and groans for quickening, and it is far from them? They stir themselves up, meditate, summon up all the powerful considerations they can, yet find themselves empty of a spiritual vigour. Surely there is some principal power wanting to spirit their grace, and make them leap in duty; some invisible strength hath withdrawn itself, which did before conduct and breathe upon them, and fill their souls with a divine fire. They find it not in the power of the hand of their own will to actuate and quicken the grace they have, much less is it in the power of any man's hand to renew himself, The work of grace is not only a traction at the first, but a continual traction, as conservation is a continual creation: 'Draw me, and we will run after thee,' Cant. 1:4. The church there speaks it as regenerate, desiring a continual traction from God, as the first ground of her race after Christ. Life she had, for she promiseth to run; yet this race she could not begin nor continue, without traction from God.

Prop. 5. Man cannot by the power of his own will preserve grace in himself. Our Saviour's prayer to his Father, John 17:11, 15, to 'keep them,' imports, that they were too weak to keep themselves: 'Unless the Lord keep the city, in vain doth the watchman wake,' Ps. 127:1. Unless God preserve the soul, all the watchfulness of habitual grace will be to little purpose. All creatures, if God hide his face, are troubled, Ps. 104:29, much more the new creature, whose strength doth more necessarily depend upon God, because of its powerful opposites. Were it not for the assisting grace of God, the unruly lusts in our hearts would soon bear down habitual grace in the best. How many temptations are prevented which we cannot foresee! How many corruptions are restrained, which the best grace cannot fully conquer! How is the tide and torrent of these waters beaten back, which otherwise would go over our heads! The poor will of Adam preserved him not against a temptation, when he had no indwelling corruption to betray him; nor did the will of the angels, who had no temptation, keep them from forsaking their habitation. How can any renewed man, alive with all his grace, merely by the strength of his own will, keep himself from sinking down in the lake of his old corruption? He that would ask the fallen angels in the midst of their torments, what was the reason of their fall, would receive no other answer but that their strength was unsuccessful, because it depended upon their own will.* The knowledge of the gospel and evangelical impressions are never like to keep up without the Holy Ghost: 2 Tim. 1:14, 'That good thing which was committed unto thee, keep, by the Holy Ghost,' not by thine own strength. If we cannot keep a form of sound words, which, as it is knowledge, is more agreeable to the natural appetite of man, without the Holy Ghost, much less can we preserve grace in us, which is more stomached by corrupt nature. Neither are good frames like to be preserved in us without God's keeping: 1 Chron. 29:18, 'Keep this in the imagination of the thoughts of the heart of thy people.' Our hearts will not let any good motion sink into them, unless God give a pondus to his own motion. If, then, regenerate men are unable of themselves to actuate and preserve grace received, much more inability is there in a natural man to gain that which he hath not a spark of in his own nature, but an enmity to.

Quest. But, do you divest man of all power, all freedom of will? Is he able to do nothing in order to regeneration?

Ans. We do not divest man of all power; therefore, before we consider what power belongs to man, we may consider,

(1.) Man simply in his fall. So man lost all his natural ability by his first sin, and was the meritorious cause of his losing supernatural grace, which God by a judicial act removed from him; and in this state man had no ability unto anything morally good. Nothing was due to Adam but the state of the devils, who have no affection to anything morally good, but alway do that which is in its own nature evil, and always sin with evil intentions. Adam would have been thus, had the threatening, according to the tenor of it, been executed; there had been no common affections, no more light in his understanding than what might have served for his torment; as wicked men, after death, are deprived in a judicial way of that light in their minds, those velleities and good motions which sometime hovered in them, those affections which were here exercised now and then towards God. The sentence given against Adam is then pronounced against them, and they laid under the final execution of it, which was to die the death: Gen. 2:17, 'Thou shalt surely die;' a death of all morality, all affections to anything that hath the resemblance of goodness. It might be a prediction of what would be in course, as well as what would be inflicted in way of judicial recompence. None of these things can be looked for in Adam, or any of his posterity, as fallen; not a grain of life, or anything tending that way, was due to him, but only death.

(2.) Man is to be considered as respited from the present suffering this sentence by the intervention of Christ; whereby he is put into another way of probation. So those common notions in our understandings, and common motions in our wills and affections, so far as they have anything of moral goodness, are a new gift to our natures by virtue of the mediation of Christ. In which sense he may be said to 'taste death for every man,' Heb. 2:9, and be 'a propitiation for the sins of the whole world.' By virtue of which promised death, some sparks of moral goodness are preserved in man. Thus his 'life was the light of men;' and he is 'the light that lightens every man that comes into the world,' which sets the candle of the Lord in the spirit of man a-burning and sparkling, John 1:9, and upholds all things by his mediatory as well as divine power, Heb. 1:3, which else would have sunk into the abyss. By virtue of this mediation, some power is given back to man, as a new donation, yet not so much as that he is able by it to regenerate himself; and whatsoever power man hath, is originally from this cause, and grows not up from the stock of nature, but from common grace.

Which common grace is either,

[1.] More general, to all men. Whereby those divine sparks in their understandings, and whatsoever is morally praiseworthy in them, is kept up by the grace of God, which was the cause that Christ tasted death for every man: Heb. 2:9, 'That he by the grace of God should taste death for every man;' whereby the apostle seems to intimate, that by this grace, and this death of Christ, any remainders of that honour and glory wherewith God crowned man at first are kept upon his head; as will appear, if you consider the eighth Psalm, whence the apostle cites the words which are the ground of his discourse of the death of Christ.

[2.] More particular common grace, to men under the preaching of the gospel. Which grace men 'turn into wantonness' or lasciviousness, Jude 4. Grace they had, or the gospel of grace, but the wantonness of their nature prevailed against the intimations of grace to them. Besides this common grace, there is a more special grace to the regenerate, the more peculiar fruit of Christ's mediation and death for them. All this, and whatsoever else you can conceive that hath but a face of comeliness in man, is not the birth of fallen nature abstracted from this mediation. Therefore when the Gentiles are said to 'do by nature the things contained in the law,' it is not to be understood of nature merely as fallen, for that could do no such thing; but of nature in this new state of probation, by the interposition of Christ the mediator, whose powerful word upheld all things, and kept up those broken fragments of the two tables of law, though dark and obscure. And considering God's design of setting forth the gospel to the world, there was a necessity of those relics, both in the understanding, and affections, and desire for happiness, to render men capable of receiving the gospel, and those inexcusable that would reject it. So that by this mediation of Christ, the state of mankind is different since the fall from that of the evil angels or devils. For man hath, first, a power of doing that which is in its own nature good; secondly, a power of doing good with a good intention; not indeed supremely for the glory of God, but for the good of his country, the good of his neighbours, the good of the world, which was necessary for the soldering together human societies, so that sometimes even in sins man hath good intentions. Whereas the devil doth always that which in its own nature is evil, and always sins with evil intentions.* Without this mediation, every man had been as very a slave to sin as the devil; though he be naturally a slave to sin, yet not in that full measure the devil is, unless left in a judicial manner by God upon high provocations.

There is then a liberty of will in man; and some power there is left in man. And here I shall shew,

1. What kind of liberty this is.

2. That there is some liberty in man.

3. How far the power of man by common grace doth extend.

Quest. First, what kind of liberty this is.

Ans. 1. The essential liberty of the will remains. Liberty is of the essence of the will, and cannot be taken away without extinction of the nature of man; it is free from compulsion, otherwise it were a not-will, which liberty doth not consist in a choice of good or evil. For even under this depravation it cannot choose evil qua malum, as such. It can choose nothing but what appears to it under the notion of good; though it many times embraceth that which is materially evil, yet the formal consideration upon which it embraceth it is as good, either in reality or in appearance; as the sight in every colour sees light. And when it is carried out to that which is really evil, and only apparently good, it is by force of those habits in the understanding, which make it give a false judgment; or, by the power of the sensitive appetite, which hurries it on to the object proposed, but alway it respects in its motion everything as good, either an honest, pleasant, or profitable good.

Ans. 2. Though the essential liberty of the will remains, yet the rectitude whereby it might have been free only to that which was really good is lost. Man by creation had a freedom of will to choose that which was really good, yet had a mutability, and could choose evil; and by choosing evil rather than good, sank his posterity into this depraved liberty which now remains. Though since the fall man is preserved in his natural freedom, and cannot be forced, yet he hath not a power to will well, because that righteous principle whereby he did will well is departed from him;† yet because the essential freedom due to his nature remains, whatsoever he wills he wills freely, so that though something the will wills may be materially good, yet it wills that good in an ill manner, for being overcome naturally by sin man can do nothing but according to that law which sin, as a master that hath conquered him, imposeth upon him: 2 Peter 2:19, 'They themselves are the servants of corruption: for of whom a man is overcome, of the same is he brought in bondage.' And of all men in a state of nature, though under common grace, the apostle pronounceth, Rom. 3:11, that 'there is none that seeks after God;' that is, in any thing they do, though never so good, they seek not God but themselves. 'There is no fear of God,' no respect to God 'before their eyes,' ver. 18, whence it comes to pass, that by reason of this dominion of sin nothing can be done well. Hence man is said to be dead; not that the life which doth constitute the nature of the soul is taken away, but that which renders it fit for performing actions pleasing to God; for such a life doth consist, not in the nature of the soul or will, but in that habitual integrity which was in man by creation. As the body when it is dead doth not cease to be a body, but ceaseth to be animated, by the separation of the soul from it, so the soul may be truly said to be dead, though the power of the soul be not taken away. If the spiritual rectitude in that power which did constitute it spiritually living be departed, by the removal of this righteousness, the will is not free to spiritual things, though it be to natural. It is 'free among the dead,' as the psalmist speaks of himself, Ps. 88:5; free to dead works, not to living; to this or that dead work, to any work within the verge of sinning, as a bird in a large cage may skip this way and that way by its natural spontaneous motion, but still within the cage.

Ans. 3. Therefore, though man hath lost this liberty to good, he retains a freedom to the commission of sin, under the necessity of sinning. This freedom is a power of choice and election of a thing, which differs from that spontaneity which is in beasts, who act by instinct, without any reasoning in the case, because they want a reasoning power. Though man be under a necessity of sinning, yet it is not a necessity of constraint, but a necessity of immutability, which is consistent with liberty, though the other be not. A creature may be unchangeably carried to good or evil, and yet be free in both: to good, as the angels and glorified saints cannot will to sin, because their wills ere immutably determined to good. They cannot but praise and love God, yet they freely do both; and our Saviour did freely do that good which he could not but do by reason of his hypostatical union, otherwise he could not have merited, for all merit requires the concurrence of the will. To evil; the devils cannot will to do good, because their wills are unchangeably determined to evil, yet they sin as freely as if there were no immutable necessity upon them. So man cannot but naturally sin in all that he doth, yet he is not constrained to sin, but sins as freely and voluntarily as if there were no necessity upon his nature to corruption,—as freely as if God had not foreseen that he would do so. Man sins with as great a pleasure as if he were wholly independent upon the providence of God; and the more a man is delighted with sin, the greater freedom there is in it. Hence the Scripture lays sin upon the choice of man: Isa. 66:3, 4, 'They have chosen their own ways, and their soul delights in their abominations.' They were their own ways, that is, ways proper to corrupt man; but they chose them and delighted in them. Man is voluntary under his depravation, free in his aversion from God; a free necessity, a delightful immutability. The will cannot be compelled to will that which it would not, or not to will that which it would. When sin ariseth from a settled habit, the freer is a man in his sin; and though he cannot act otherwise than according to that habit, yet his actions are most voluntary, because he is the cause of that habit which he acquired by evil acts, and by succeeding acts testifies his approbation of it.

2. That there is some liberty in man, some power in man. Not* indeed such a power as the Jews thought man had naturally, of exercising himself about anything that God should reveal, without the infusion of a new power, to enable him to act that which God required by supernatural revelation. Some power and liberty must be allowed,

(1.) To clear the justice of God. No just man will punish another for not doing that which was simply and physically impossible; and 'shall not the Judge of all the earth do right?' It is a good speech of Austin, If there were not the grace of God, how could the world be saved? If there were not free will, how could the world be judged? If man were divested of all kind of liberty, he might have some excuse for himself; but since the Scripture pronounceth men without excuse, Rom. 1:20, some power must be granted to clear the equity of God's justice. No man sins in that which he is under an inevitable constraint to do, and so would be unjustly punished. It doth not appear that God doth condemn any man simply for not being regenerate, but for not using the means appointed to such an end, for not avoiding those sins which hindered his regeneration, and which might have been avoided by him if he would, though indeed every unregenerate man will be condemned. The pouring out the wrath of God upon man is principally for those sins which they might have refrained, and had sufficient reason against: Eph. 5:6, for 'because of these things,' that is, for those gross sins which they might have avoided, mentioned ver. 5, 'comes the wrath of God upon the children of disobedience,' ἀπειθίας; men that would not be persuaded, which obstinacy was in their will. As these are the causes of God's wrath, so these will be alleged as the principal reasons of the last sentence. And our Saviour in his last judgment doth not charge men with their unregeneracy, but with their omissions of what they might have done, and that easily; and commissions which they might have avoided, Mat. 25:41–43, with their not feeding his members when they were hungry, &c., which were things as much in their power as anything in the world. And the reason Christ renders of the sentence passed upon men, to depart from him, was their working of iniquity: Mat. 7:23, 'Depart from me, you that work iniquity;' that work it voluntarily, and work that you might have forborne. Though unregeneracy doth exclude a man from heaven, as a condition without which a man cannot come there, yet nothing of this is mentioned in the last sentence. If man had a firm will to turn to God, and had not then a power conferred upon him to turn, I know not what to say; but man hath no will to turn, yea, he hath no will to do those things which he might do. Supposing man hath a power to avoid such and such sins, he is justly punished for not making use of that power. Nay, supposing he had no power to avoid them, yet if his will be set to that sin he is justly condemned, not for want of power, but for the delight his will took in it. From which delight in it, it may be gathered that if he had had a power to have shunned it, he would not have shunned it. If a man be assaulted by murderers that will cut his throat, if he will not use his power against them, but take a pleasure in having his throat cut, is not this man a self-murderer, both in the judgment of God and man? Let me use another illustration, since the end of all our preaching should be to humble man and clear God. If a man be cast out of an high tower, and be pleased with his fall, would he not be justly worthy of it, and to be neglected by men, not because he did not help himself in his fall, for that was not in his own power, but because he was mightily pleased and contented with his fall, and with such a pleasure, that if he had been able to have helped himself he would not? So though man be fallen in Adam, yet when he comes to discern between good and evil, he commits the evil with pleasure. So that supposing he had no power to avoid sins, yet he is worthy of punishment because he doth it delightfully. Whence it may be concluded, if he had had power to avoid it, he would not, because his will is so malignant.

(2.) Without some liberty in the will, free from necessity of compulsion, man would not be capable of sin, nor of moral goodness. No human law doth impute that for a vice, or a virtue, to which a man is carried by constraint, without any power to avoid. Where anything is done without a will, it is not an human action. Beasts therefore are not capable of sin, because they want reason and will. If man had not liberty of will, he would be as a beast, which hath only a spontaneous power of motion without reason. Sin could not be charged upon man, as God doth all along: Ps. 95:10, 'It is a people that do err in their hearts and Ps. 119:21, 'Thou hast rebuked the proud that are cursed, which do err from thy commandments.' It had been no error in them, if they had not done it voluntarily. The erring from God's commandments ariseth from pride of heart, they had not else deserved a rebuke. Who would chide a clock for going wrong, which hath no voluntary motion? Man without a liberty of will could not be the author of his own actions, and sin could no more be imputed to him, than the irregular motion of a watch can be imputed to the watch itself, but rather to the workman or governor of it. Without a voluntary power, man would be as an engine, moved only with springs; and human laws, which punish any crime, would be as ridiculous as Xerxes' whipping the sea, because it would not stop its tide. Neither were any praise due to man for any moral virtue, no more than praise is due to a lifeless picture for being so beautiful, or to the limner's pencil for making it so: the praise is due to the artist, not to the instrument.

(3.) Without some liberty and power of motion in the will, all the reason of man, and those notions in the understanding, left by the virtue of Christ's mediatory interposition, would be to no purpose. The reason why men do err is because they do not take right ways of judging according to those means they have: 'Ye err,' saith our Saviour, 'not knowing the Scripture, nor the power of God,' Mat. 22:29. They have a faculty of judgment, and means whereby to judge, which would prevent errors. There is therefore some suitable power in man to follow the judgment of reason, if he will. He would be in vain endowed with that power of reasoning, if there were not a power of motion in some measure suitable to that reason. The authority of judging in the understanding would be wholly insignificant; all debates about any object proposed would be to no end, if the will had not a liberty to follow that judgment. How can God make appeals to men as he doth, if they had not a power of judging that they ought to have done otherwise, and might have done otherwise than they did? Though man hath not a sufficient light left in his nature for salvation, yet he hath such a light of reason in him to which he might be more faithful in his motions than he is, otherwise the apostle could not have argued from that light the heathens had to their conviction, as he doth, Rom. 1:19–21, &c., and manifests their unfaithfulness to that truth which God had manifested to them, and manifested in them in their nature. Most sins do arise from the neglect of being guided by that light which is in men.

(4.) The glory of God's wisdom in the government of the world would not have been so conspicuous, if some liberty had not been allowed to the will. It is no great matter to keep in order an inanimate thing, as a clock that must obey a necessity; God would have been but like a good clock-keeper only, as one* saith. But how much doth it make for the wisdom of God, to make the free motions of his creature, the various humours in the will of man, centre at last in his own glory, contrary to the will and design of the creature; that they have their natural motions, their voluntary motions, and God superintends over them, and moves them according to his own will regularly, according to their nature, without crossing them? 'The determinate counsel of God,' in the death of our Saviour, and the free will of Pilate and the Jews, meet in the same point: God acting wisely, graciously, justly; their wills acting freely and naturally, reduced, without injury to their nature, to the due point of God's will.

Quest. 3. The third question, How far doth the power of man by common grace extend?

Ans. As in a body deprived of the soul there is some power of growth left in the hair and nails, so some power is left in the soul, though it be spiritually dead. As a regenerate man by special grace hath a power of doing that which is spiritually good, so a natural man by common grace hath a power of doing things morally good, if he will. God keeps the key of regenerating grace in his own hands, and unlocks what hearts he pleases, and brings in a vital spirit into whom he pleases; but there is by common grace an ability in men to do more than they do, but that they harbour, cherish, and increase those vicious inclinations in their own souls. But let it be remembered that this power is not to be abstracted from God's common grace, as the power of a renewed man after grace is not to be abstracted from special grace, nor the natural powers of motion to the actual motion, not to be abstracted from God's general providential concourse.

(1.) Man hath a power by common grace to avoid many sins: I say, a power by common grace; for sometime, upon the neglecting the conduct of natural light, God pulls up the sluice of his restraining grace, lets out the torrent of their natural corruption upon them, which forcibly hurries them to all kind of wickedness; as it is said, Rom. 7:24, 25, 'Wherefore God also gave them up to uncleanness, through the lusts of their own hearts; for this cause God gave them up to vile affections.' Wherefore, and for this cause, that is, for going contrary to that natural light they had, God let the lusts of their own hearts, which he had restrained, have their full swing against them. In this case sin can no more be avoided, than a man can stop a torrent.

Again; though a man, as he is in a state of nature, cannot but do evil, yet he is not necessitated to this or that kind of sin, but he may avoid this or that pro hic and nunc in particular, though he cannot in general; as a man who hath the liberty of walking where he pleases in a prison, he may choose whether he will come into this or that walk within the liberty of the prison; but let him move which way he will, he is a prisoner still.

Quest. If it be said, if a man hath power to avoid this or that sin, why may he not avoid all?

Ans. I answer, If he had power to avoid all, he would be restored to the state of Adam. But the reason is this,† the power to avoid this or that particular sin ariseth from a particular cause, the natural subjection of appetite to reason, the lightness of temptation; or if the temptation be more vehement, the stirring up reason and pressing considerations against it; but the power to shun all sin depends upon the subordination of the faculties one to another, in the due order of their creation, and an universal subjection of them to God. Though a man, by a careful watch, may withstand a particular temptation, yet as long as he is alienated from God, and hath corrupt habits in him, which are prone to sinful acts, he will one time or other, by some sudden temptation, be carried out according to his natural inclination, before he is able to premeditate, and set reason on work. And sometimes the motions to sin come in such troops, that he cannot stir up his force against all, so that while he is combating against one, another comes behind and surpriseth him. As another Romanist illustrates it,* a vessel hath three holes to leak at; a man with two hands may stop two of them, which he will, but the third will remain open of necessity. None will say that the devil can avoid all sin in general, and become holy for the future, because his will is determined to sin, but this or that individual act of sin he may; for he may choose whether he will assault this man or that with such a temptation, or whether at this time or another. As if two commands were given to the good angels, and it be left to their wills whether they will do that or the other, though they cannot but do good, because their wills are so determined, yet they have a liberty to choose which command they will at present follow. And the reason of this is this: there is no physical necessity upon a man to this or that sin, as there is that the fire should burn. Lusts only offer themselves; they have no force upon a man, but by his own will; they have no authority from God to compel him; then God should be the author of sin. Satan can give no commission to them to break open our hearts; and though he be a strong adversary, he cannot break them open. If the door be open, it is our own act. Is there any necessity upon a man to run into this or that infectious company, or drink brimful cups, till he hath drowned both his reason and sentiments of morality? Hath he not power to quell many incentives to sin? Shew me that man in the world that, upon serious consideration, would say, it is utterly impossible for him to avoid this or that particular sin when he is tempted to it. What men do in this case, they do willing, though a strong temptation may be the first motive of it. It is said, Hos. 5:11, 'Ephraim willingly walked after the commandment,' though the first motive to it was the command of their prince Jeroboam.

To evidence this, let me do it by some queries, which may both satisfy that we divest not man of all power, and prevent the ill use men may make of this doctrine, to encourage sluggishness.

1. Cannot you avoid this or that foreseen occasion of sin? Cannot he that knows how prone he is to overthrow his reason when the wine sparkles in the glass, avoid coming within the sight of it? What force is there upon his legs to go, or his hands to take the cup? Can we not starve those affections we have to this or that particular sin, by neglecting the

means to feed them? If a man stood by with a drawn sword to stab you if you went into such a place, could you not forbear going in? What is the reason? Fear. And why might not a natural fear of God, heightened by consideration, be of as much force with you as the fear of man, unless atheism hath swallowed up all sentiments of a Deity? Do you not rather wish for opportunities, and court a temptation? put your heads out of the window, with Sisera's mother; why is the chariot of the devil so long a coming? It is said, Prov. 21:10, 'The soul of the wicked desires evil.'

2. Have you not a power to avoid gross sins? Is there any force upon men, to open, sensual sins? Have they not a power to abstain from fleshly lusts? Has not the will a commanding power over the members? What hinders it from exercising that power? The members are not forced, but they are 'yielded up' by consent of the will to sin, Rom. 6:19. Had not Achan as much natural power to forbear taking the wedge of gold and the Babylonish garment, as the rest of that vast number of the Israelites? Not one of their hands touched any of the spoil. Had he not as much power as any of them to have restrained his hands, though he could not quench his covetousness? The law of nature tells us, we ought not to do that to another which we would not have done to ourselves. Have we not as much power to observe this as the Gentiles, who did by nature the things contained in the law? Why may not a man's will command his tongue to speak that which is true, as well as that which is false? Is there not power to control it from speaking blasphemy, and belching out cursed oaths? Cannot you command the hand to forbear striking another wrongfully? Has not a murderer power to keep his sword in his scabbard, as well as to sheath it in his neighbour's bowels? Can any man say, that there was one gross sin in the whole course of his life, but he had a power to avoid it if he would? Forbearance of gross sin consists in a naked omission and a not acting, which is far more easy than a positive acting, and every man hath a power to suspend his own act.

3. Did you never resist a temptation to a particular sin? Why may you not then resist it afterward if you will, since the same common grace attends you? If the will be disengaged one moment from a sin under a great temptation, why not another moment from sin, under a less temptation? No temptation can overpower your strength, unless the will freely shake hands with it: Acts 5:3, 'Why hath Satan filled thy heart, to lie to the Holy Ghost?' His meaning is not, why Satan hath done it, for Ananias could not render a reason of that; but why didst thou suffer Satan to fill thy heart? If you have given a check to Satan before, is it not as easy to say again, 'Get thee behind me, Satan'?

4. Have you not power to shun many inward sins? Man, where he hath least power, yet he hath some, viz. over his thoughts. We cannot, indeed, hinder the first risings and motions of them, which will steam up from the corrupt fumes and lake whether he will or no; but cannot we hinder the progress of them? Is there not a power to check the delight in them if we will, or divert our thoughts another way, not listen to their suggestions, and hold no inward converse with them? Though you cannot hinder their intrusion, may you not hinder their lodging? 'How long shall vain thoughts lodge within you?' Jer. 4:14. Sure we have a power by common grace to forbear any conference with the motions of flesh and blood.

5. When you do sin, had you not many assistances against it, which if you had hearkened to, you might have avoided it? Were there not previous dissuasions from that inward monitor, conscience? When sin hath been enticing you on one hand, and conscience warning you on the other, have you not more willingly listened unto the pleasant reasoning of sin, than the wholesome admonitions of conscience? Can you not as well listen to what conscience as to what sin doth propose? But have you not wilfully scorned its judgment? Have you not raged against it with a confidence in sin (which is the case of the foolish sinner, Prov. 14:16, 'The fool rageth, and is confident'), and would 'not consider any of the

ways of God' it minded you of, Job 34:27, and gave no more regard to its sober dictates, or its louder pressings, than you have to the barking of little curs in the street? Why could you not, with those assistances, have avoided that particular act of sin? The fault was clearly in your wills. Can you not rather choose a cup of wine, than a cup of poison? clear streams, than muddy waters? Besides those assistances, you might have had more, if under the batteries of temptation you had sought to heaven for them. Might you not, then, have avoided this or that sin, when yon had such assistances, and might have had more?

6. Have you not avoided sin upon less accounts and considerations? The heathen philosopher could observe, that men may live better than thcy do.* The wrestlers and champions in the Olympic games lived most temperately and continently during that time, to be more fit for the gaining the prize. May not rational considerations do as much, if excited in your minds, as an ambitious desire of honour and affection to victory did in them? Had not Saul a power to withdraw his hand from the unrighteous persecution of David before, as well as when he was sensible of David's kindness in sparing his life when he might have killed him? A drunkard under the disease and pain caused by his sin, can forbear his cups; doth his disease confer any power upon him more than he had before? No; why could he not then have forborne his drunken revellings? Can men be restrained from some sins by the eye of a man, the presence of a child? What power do their eyes confer upon them? They only excite that which they had before. Cannot men forbear a sinful act for a sum of money if it were proffered them, or in the presence of a king, who is said to 'scatter away evil with his eyes,' Prov. 20:8, or in a visible and imminent danger? If a gibbet or a stake were set before men, that they should be immediately executed if they did not forbear such a sinful action, or if they did not go to hear a sermon; can any be so foolish, to think that the glister of gold, the penalty of the law, the sight of a gibbet, should confer

a power upon you which you were not before possessed with? It is not then the want of power to avoid sin, but the want of will.

7. Why doth conscience check any man after the commission of sin, if it were not in his power to avoid it? All those actions which fall under the cognisance and check of conscience, are actions in our own power, and within the verge of our wills. For the pain of conscience is of another kind than that pain or grief which is raised by those accidents we could not avoid. It ariseth from the liberty of the will, and galls the soul when it considers, that that which it hath done was in its power to be done otherwise. This is the common language of men upon the regrets of conscience: I might have done otherwise, I was warned by my friends; I slighted their warnings, I had resolutions to the contrary, but I stifled them. All men have laid the fault upon themselves, and what is universal consent hath a truth in it; the consciences of all men would not gall them for that which they had no power to decline. Indeed, if men were necessitated to sin, they could not be tormented in hell, for the torment there is conscience acting rationally, and reflecting upon them for their wilfulness in the world. If man had not a power to refuse sin, conscience would have no ground for any such reflections to rack and torment them. And it is observable, that natural men, somewhat awakened upon a deathbed, are not so racked by their consciences simply for not being regenerate, as for not avoiding those sins which were hindrances, and not using those means which were appointments of God for such an end, because those were in their power; but they wilfully embraced the one, and as wilfully refused the other.

Prop. 2. Man hath a power, by common grace, to do many more good actions (actions materially good) than he doth. Evangelical works we cannot do without union to Christ; so himself saith, 'Without me you can do nothing,' John 15:5; nothing according to the order of the gospel, nothing spiritually, nothing acceptably, because no such fruits can arise, where faith, the root of such works, is wanting. Though man be much crippled in regard of morals, yet he is not wholly dead to them, as he is to spirituals. A man may 'break off his sins by (moral) righteousness, and his iniquity by shewing mercy to the poor;' by taking off the yoke of oppression, and restoring of what he hath rifled, which counsel Daniel gives to Nebuchadnezzar, chap. 4:27. Though a sick man cannot do all the acts of a sound man till he be perfectly cured, yet he hath some power of acting some things like a sound man, remaining with his disease. The young man in the Gospel (yet out of Christ) morally kept the law; so may men under the gospel keep the outward and material part of the precept. There are not only some common notions left since the fall, but also some seeds of moral righteousness in the nature of man. The Gentiles did not only, by nature, in part restored, know the things written in the law, but they did by nature do them, Rom. 2:14; upon this stock they bore many excellent fruits. What patience, chastity, contempt of the pleasures of the world! What affections to their country, and bowels of compassion to men in misery! And what devotion in the external worship of their gods, according to their light, were exemplary in them, though only under the conduct of nature! And these works, though they were not according to the exactness of the law, and failed also in the manner of them, and could not please God for want of faith, yet so far as they were agreeable to the law of nature, and in regard of the materiality of them, were not offensive to God. This moral righteousness of theirs was only external, and rather an image of righteousness than a true one. Abimelech had a natural integrity, which God acknowledges to be in him, and did arise from his moral nature, though he also appropriates to himself the restraint of Abimelech, and his concurrence with an approbation of that moral integrity: Gen. 20:6, 'I know that thou didst this in the integrity of thy heart: for I also withheld thee from sinning against me, therefore suffered I thee not to touch her;' □□□□□ □□I gave thee not up to touch her. If men did nourish a moral integrity, which they might do, God would concur with them to preserve them from many crimes. If those which were only under the guidance of natural light had so much power to do many moral acts by a common grace, is man's power less under the gospel, whereby they have an addition of a greater light to this natural? If man was able to do so much by the light of nature, there can be no inability brought upon him under the light of the gospel, unless men, by their sluggishness and obstinacy, provoke God judicially to deprive them of that power, and withdraw his hand from them, and so give them up to all kind of wickedness, as it is the dreadful case of many in these days. Man may keep the law of nature better than he doth, and for not keeping that he is condemned.*

Prop. 3. Men have a power to attend upon the outward means God hath appointed for regeneration. Though man cannot renew himself, yet he hath a natural power to attend upon the means God hath afforded. Though a man hath not power to cure his own disease or heal his wound, yet he hath power to advise with others, and use the best medicines for his recovery. There is not an outward duty a renewed man doth, but a natural man hath power externally to do it; though what is essentially good in all parts, cannot be done without special grace, yet what is externally good may be done by the assistance of common grace. Have you not passions, fear, love, desire, grief? Why cannot you exercise them about other objects than ordinarily they are employed about? Why can you not make hell the object of your fears, and heaven the object of your desire? Why might not Esau have wept for his sins, as well as for the loss of the blessing? Might he not have changed the object if he would? Why may we not exercise our inward affections more in our attendance on God? Is not a little excuse sufficient to put off from duty, a great excuse not sufficient to keep you from committing sin? Great business must be laid aside for sin, not the least laid aside for God. Every little thing is a lion in the way then. Do you not many times rack your minds to invent pleas for neglect of duty? Why can you not set them on work to consider reasons to move you to service? Have we not power to be more serious in the use of means than we are? We can be so when some affliction presses us, or conscience gnaws us. Neither of these furnishes us with a new power. Conscience is like the law, acquaints us with our duty, but gives us no strength. The charge God brings against Ephraim was, that he 'would not frame his doings to turn towards God,' Hosea 5:4; he would entertain no thoughts, not one action that had the least prospect towards repentance; he would use no means for that end, or have a look that way. If a man will not do what is in his power, it is a sign he will not be renewed. Can he pretend to a desire to live, who will not eat, and endeavour to prevent foreseen dangers? Or can he pretend to a desire to build, that will not use materials when he may?

There are two great means: hearing the word, and prayer.

(1.) Hearing the word. Have not men power to go to hear the word, to hear a sermon, as well as to see a play? Have they any shackles upon their feet, that they cannot carry them to a place of worship as well as to a place of vanity and sin? Can you not as well read the Scripture as a romance? Hath not the will a despotic power over the members of the body? How came Herod to have more natural power to hear the word, and to hear it 'with pleasure,' Mark 6:20, than other men have? May you not strive against diversions, resist carnal affection, rouse up your souls from their laziness, and endeavour to close with the word? How smilingly would God look upon such endeavours? If men do not, it is out of a natural sluggishness and enmity of will, not for want of power if they would. Men do not what they might. Certainly he doth no more desire regeneration who neglects and despiseth the great instrument of it, than he can be said to desire his own preservation, who neglects medicines proper for the cure of his disease.

(2.) Prayer. I do not mean a spiritual prayer, which is by the special assistance and indwelling of the Holy Ghost, but of a natural prayer by common instinct; such a one as the apostle puts Simon Magus upon, who he knew was destitute of any air of the Spirit to breathe out, as being 'in the gall of bitterness and bond of iniquity,' Acts 8:22, 23, yet supposeth him to have a power in some manner to express his desires to God; or such a power that was common in heathens, upon any distress to run to their altars, and fill their temples with cries to their gods. You cannot pray in the Holy Ghost, but you may send up natural and rational cries to God. Did not Jonah's mariners cry every man to his god? Have you not as much power to cry to the true God as the heathens to false ones? There is the natural prayer of those mariners, as well as the natural integrity of Abimelech, which was not a new-covenant integrity. Can you not be as devout as the publican, and cry, with more seriousness of affection than generally men do, 'Lord, be merciful to me a sinner'? When men are upon a death-bed, ready to take their leave of the world, they can then cry. It is not their death-bed inspires them with power, more than they had before, but they have more mind, and see a greater necessity of crying to God. They have more power in the time of their health, by how much the habit of sin wanted that strength which hath been acquired by a continuance of acts till the time of their sickness; for the fewer sins have been committed, the less is the power impaired. Though God hath kept other things in his hand, yet he hath given us a power of begging, if we will use it as a means to obtain them. Can you not kneel down before God, and implore his assistance? Can you not acknowledge before him that it is impossible for you to change yourself, but that your eyes are upon his grace; that you cannot attain by your own strength a spiritual heart; that you will seek nowhere else for it but from his hand; and that you will not be at rest till he hath put in his hand and dropped upon your hearts? Can you not thus cry out, Oh that I were a renewed person! as well as cry out, Oh that I were rich and honourable in the world! Had Paul a new tongue when he cried out, 'Who shall deliver me from the body of this death?' Was it not the same member wherein he had breathed out threatenings against the disciples?

Prop. 4. Man hath a power to exercise consideration. He hath seminals of jus and æquum, and a power of judging according to them: Luke 12:57, 'Yea, why even of yourselves judge you not what is right?' Our Saviour checks them for not making use of their natural power; in the searching their own consciences, and judging their own acts, as well as they did in discerning the face of the sky, and what weather would follow. There is a power of consideration in a rebellious heart; for God acknowledges it in a rebellious nation: Ezek. 12:3, 'It may be they will consider, though they be a rebellious house.'

1. Can you not reflect upon yourselves? Every man hath a reflexive faculty; otherwise he is not a man. Reflection is the peculiar privilege of a rational creature, without which he is not rational. The Pharisees could reflect upon themselves, and say, 'Are we blind also?' John 9:40. Can you not then take a survey of your past lives; cast up the accounts of your souls, as well as your books? Can you not view your particular crimes, with the aggravations attending them? Yea, you can, if you would. Can you not look back upon the means you have neglected, the love you have slighted, and the light you have shut your eyes against? As long as a man hath reason, he may use his reason in these things as well as in others. Why may he not reflect upon himself in spiritual concerns, as well as civil affairs in the world? Cannot he, by comparing the face of his soul with the glass of the word, understand his own state, and by self-reflection come to an understanding of his own lost condition and weakness?

2. Can you not consider the word? Cannot your reasons be employed about the objects the word offers, as well as the objects the world offers? Though you cannot act spiritually in the duties of religion, can you not act rationally in them, as men? Are you endued with a rational soul, to consider the proposals of worldly affairs and concerns, and can you not exercise the same power in considering the proposal made to you by the gospel? The gospel is not only spiritual, but rational. As long as you have a thinking faculty, can you not consider what the reasonable

meaning of it is? Though you have not a spiritual taste, you have a rational understanding; why may it not be busied about one object as well as another? The natural repentance of the Ninevites at Jonah's preaching, implied the consideration of his threatening sermon. Why is there not a power in you to think of what is proposed to you out of the word, as well as you can think of what you read of a mathematical or philosophical book, or some history? The power is the same in both, the faculty the same. As the object proposed adds no power to the faculty, so it takes away no power the faculty already hath. Surely man is not such a block or stone, but he may turn these things over and over, press them upon his own soul, which may make way for the sensibleness of his state, and putting the will out of its sinful indifference. What any natural man hath done, that may all under the same means do, if they will. Why may not the veriest wretch among us humble himself at the hearing of the word, as well as wicked Ahab? 1 Kings 21:27, 29, 'When Ahab heard these words, he rent his clothes. Seest thou how Ahab humbleth himself?' He discovered an external humiliation, after the consideration of the threatening denounced by the prophet.

3. Can you not cherish, by consideration, those motions which are put into you? There is not a man but the Spirit strives with, one time or other, Gen 6:3. Hath not man a power to approve any good counsel given him, if he will? Have you not had some supernatural motions lifting you up towards God, and pressing obligations upon you, to walk more circumspectly? Why might you not have cherished them, as well as smothered them? Why could you not have considered the tendency of them, as well as have considered how to divert and drown them, by engaging in some sensual lust? Was the power of consideration lost? No; you could not then have cast about in your minds, by what means you should be rid of them, or how you should resist them. Have you not wilfully rejected them, even when consideration hath been revived at a sermon? And yet you did industriously let that good motion die for want

of blowing up the spark, by following on the consideration which was raised upon its feet. When you have 'begun well, who did hinder you' from a further obedience? 'This persuasion comes not of him that calls you,' Gal. 5:7, 8. There was no necessity upon you, to fortify yourselves in your corrupted habits against the attempts of the Spirit. Could you not as well have fallen down before the throne of grace, to have begged grace to second them, as kicked at them, and spurned them away? Was it want of power to do otherwise? or was it not rather your own obstinate wilfulness? Since I appeal to you, whether your own consciences have not tugged at you, and spurred you on at such seasons, why could you not then beg of God, that such a good motion might not have departed out of your coasts? Because a man cannot renew himself, therefore to lie down in sluggishness is not the design of this doctrine.

4. Can you not consider those notions you have by natural light? Man hath a conscience which minds him of moral good, and pulls him from evil. No man can deprive himself of these. It will check in those things wherein others commend us, and commend us in those things wherein others accuse us. May we not observe the motions of conscience within us? May we not consider the charge it brings against us for any act committed, so as to avoid the like for the future; and the excusations of conscience, in commending us, so as to do the like acts for the future? As we have a law without us, which we may consider, so we have a conscience within us, which witnesseth to the equity of the law, accusing us for what we do contrary to it, and excusing us for what we do in observance of it, Rom. 2:15; and this in man's corrupt state. Cannot man then observe the dictates of conscience? Can he not find out the sense of this law in his mind, though it be much blurred? Cannot he act like a man, in following the dictates of this rational principle, as well as like a beast follow the allurements of sense? No rational principle in man puts him upon evil, but upon moral good; whatsoever draws him from good, or puts him upon evil, are principles common to him with one brute

or other, profit, pleasure, honour, all which are found in some beast or other. Why may not a man then consider the rational reports of his own conscience, as well as the brutish whisperings of sense? But doth not man endeavour to shuffle off his conscience, and is mighty jolly when it keeps silence, or when he can stop its mouth with an excuse? Do not men wilfully choke the sentiments of it, and keep the truth deposited in their souls, in unrighteousness, Rom. 1:18; and like the scorner, 'hear not its rebukes,' Prov. 13:1? Whatsoever man hath by the relics of natural light, he may think of. He knows by nature there is a God; he knows something of his attributes, and of his law; may not those be his morning thoughts? Is he not stirred up sometimes to contemplate on them? May he not do it at other times, since this common grace is always with him, and leaves him not till he leaves valuing and embracing its divine assistances? Let it be remembered, that in all this which man may do, the power is to be ascribed to common grace through a mediator, keeping up by his interposition the pillars of the earth, and preserving some relics of natural light, and the seeds of moral righteousness in man; not in the least to be ascribed to bare nature; and that man's corrupt will, stuffed with sinful habits, is the cause he makes no use of this power.

Quest. 2. If we have not an ability to renew ourselves, why doth God command us to do so? And why doth God make promises to men if they will turn? Is not this a cruelty? as if a man should command another to run a race, and promise to reward him if he did, and yet bind him with fetters that he cannot run? Both the command would be unjust and the promise ridiculous.

Ans. In general. God may command, and his command doth not signify a present ability in man.

(1.) He may command, because we have faculties suited to the command in respect of their substance. For the death of a sinner was not a physical death, but a moral. Man lost not his faculties, but the rectitude of them; he lost the purity of his sight, the integrity of his will, but not the understanding and will itself.

(2.) God's command doth not signify a present moral ability to perform it. God's command, which acquaints us with our present duty, is no argument of a present power; for if a command signified more than the duty man owes, it signified more than a command in its own nature could signify. God's command to us to renew ourselves implies no more an ability inherent in the creature to do so than Christ's voice to putrefying Lazarus, 'Lazarus, arise, come forth,' John 11:43, implied a power in Lazarus to raise himself; or his speech to the palsied cripple, 'Arise, take up thy bed,' implied a power in himself to do it himself before a supernatural conveyance of it. Do not men exhort every day to sobriety those that have contracted a profound habit of drunkenness and lust, that philosophy doth acknowledge it is not possible for them to abstain from; yet no man accuseth those that exhort them of impertinence, nor those that chastise them of unjustice. God's commands are not the measures of our strength, but the rule of our duty, and do not teach us what we are, but what we should be.

But to clear this more particularly:

God may command, though man hath not a present moral ability to renew himself. For

[1.] First, Man once had a power to do whatsoever God would command him; he had a power to cleave to God. He had not else, in justice, been capable of any such injunction; there had been ground of a complaint and charge against God, if man had been created defective in any of those abilities necessary for his obedience to this command. The command is just; God would not else have imposed it, because of his righteousness; and every man's conscience testifies that it is highly just he should honour God, love God, and cleave to God. If it were just, then man was capable to perform this command; for man, as a rational creature, is capable of a law, and cannot be governed otherwise; and no law could be given so proper for him as to stand right to his Creator. Since, therefore, the law was just in itself, and since God did justly impose it, man was certainly created by God in a capacity to observe it. No question but God, who furnished other creatures with an ability to attain their several ends, and perform the orders God had set them in at the creation, was no less indulgent to man. He that was not deficient to the lower creatures would not be deficient to the noblest of his sublunary works. He would have been worse in his rank, without a sufficient stock, than other creatures were in theirs. There would not have been a physical goodness and perfection suitable to his station in the world, and his excellency above other creatures. How could God then have pronounced him good, among the rest of his works, if there had been in his creation a natural inability to answer the end of his creation? If God had created man in such a state that he could not do righteously, and yet commanded him to do righteously, and, because he did not, punish him, he would have been unjust; as if a man should command another to reach a thing too high for him, and that when his hands were tied behind him, and because he did not, boat him. This would have been the case had not man had power at first to do righteously. Had man preserved himself in that created state, no just command of God (and it was impossible any unjust command should have proceeded from infinite righteousness) would have been too hard and too high for him.

[2.] God did not deprive man of this ability. Man was not stripped of his original righteousness by God, for man had lost it before ever God spake to him, or passed any sentence upon him after his fall: Gen. 3:10, 'I was naked.' If God had taken it away without any offence of Adam, he might have expostulated the ease. It had been alike unjust, as if God had never given him power at first to observe the command he enjoined him. It would have been unreasonable to require that of man which God himself had made impossible. But God did not take away man's original righteousness.* If God had taken it away before man's fall, then man was unrighteous before he fell; and God, taking it away from him while he was perfect, had made him, of an holy and righteous man, unholy and profane; as he that deprives a malefactor of his sight, for his demerit, makes him of seeing blind. If God took it away after he spake to Adam in the garden, it would then follow that Adam was righteous after his fall till God deprived him of it, and so was innocent while he was sinful, and strong while he was weak. God did not take it away from him before, but had told him that the loss of it would be the natural consequent of his eating the forbidden fruit, Gen. 2:17; nor after, for after we find only temporal punishments threatened. God indeed did judicially deny him the restoration of it, which, as a governor and a judge, he might justly do, resolving to govern him in another manner than before. So that it would be an unjust imputation on God to say, God cut off man's legs, and then commanded him to run, and come to him. What if God did foresee that man would fall; was God therefore the cause of his fall? God's prescience, though it is infallible, is not the cause of a thing, no more than our foreknowledge that the sun will rise to-morrow morning is a cause o rising of it.

[3.] Therefore, since God did not deprive man of it, it follows that man lost it himself; and not barely lost it, but cast it away. He did voluntarily, by an inordinate intention of will, cast away this original perfection, and fell a-hunting after his own 'inventions,' Eccles. 7:29. He did not stick to that command God had given him, nor implore God's assistance of him, as by his natural ability he might have done. He consulted not with his command upon the temptation, but was very willing to cast off that righteousness wherewith God had endowed him, for an affected godhead. Man readily swallowed the bait; he did not debate the business with Eve, 'She gave to her husband with her, and he did eat,' Gen. 3:6. So that the fault was wholly in himself, and his present state voluntarily contracted; for though the devil tempted him, yet he had no power to force him. He was easily overcome by him, for it was not a repeated temptation, but a surrender at the first parley.

[4.] Therefore God's right of commanding, and man's obligation of returning and cleaving to God, remains firm. God's right still remains. God gave him a portion to manage, though man prodigally spent it. God may challenge his own. Cannot a master justly challenge that commodity he sent his servant with money to buy, though he spent it in drunkenness and gaming? God gave Adam a sufficient stock; he trifled it away. Must God's right suffer for his folly, and man's crime deprive God of his power to command? The obligation to God is natural, therefore indelible; the corruption of the creature cannot render this first obligation void. Righteousness is a debt the creature, as a rational creature, owes to God, and cannot refuse the payment of it without a crime. Who deprived him of the power of paying? Himself. Should this voluntary embezzlement prejudice God's right of exacting that which the creature cannot be excused from? A debtor, who cannot pay, remains under the obligation of paying. The receipt of a sum of money brings him into the relation of a debtor, and not his ability to pay what he hath received. Such a doctrine would free all men who were unable to pay from being debtors, though the sums they owed were never so vast. That judge would be unjust that would excuse a prodigal debtor, because he could not pay when sued by his creditor. No doubt but the devils are bound to serve God, and love him, though by their revolt they have lost the will to obey him. If, because we have no present power, our obligation to turn to God and obey him ceased, there would be no sin in the world, and consequently no judgments. Who will say, that if a prince had such rebellious subjects that there were little hopes to reclaim them, he should be therefore bound not to command them to return to their duty and obedience? If it be reasonable in a prince, whose rights are limited, shall it not be reasonable in God to exact it, who hath an unbounded right over his creature? Either God must keep up his law or abrogate it, or, which is all one, let it lie in the dust. His holiness obligeth him to keep up his law; to abrogate it, therefore, would be against his holiness. To declare a willingness that his creature should not love him, should not obey him, would be to declare that which is unjust, because love is a just debt to an amiable object and the chief good, and obedience to a sovereign Lord. Must God change his holiness because man hath changed his estate? The obligation of man remaining perpetual, the right of God to demand remains perpetual too, notwithstanding the creature's casting himself into an insolvent condition. If man still owes this duty to God, why may not God exact his right of man? Much more may God call for a right use of those means and gifts he hath, as a benefactor, bestowed upon man since his fall. No man will deny this right to God upon serious thoughts. These new gifts and means were given him not only for himself, but for his Lord, to improve for his glory. God may justly require the right use of those moral principles and evangelical means for the ends for which he appointed them.

[5.] It will appear more reasonable, because God demands no more; nay, not so much as he required of Adam in innocency. It is but obedientia redintegrata, a return in part to that perfect holiness which was inherent in man, and to that obedience in part which was in a great measure due to God. As when a prince demands the return of rebels, he demands a restoration of that subjection which they paid him before. God required a perfect obedience in the first covenant, he requires not so much in the second, so that for want of it a creature shall be cast off; but a sincere obedience is required, though not in degree perfect. Adam had a fundamental power in him to perform that obedience which is required, in faith and repentance, the two great parts of regeneration. Faith is nothing but an embracing and accepting of Christ the mediator. Adam had a power of believing and accepting Christ for his head, had he been proposed to him in paradise, as the mediator of consistency and confirmation, and the vinculum of holding him for ever close to

God. Had not Adam a power to accept him under this notion, as well as the good angels have accepted him for their head, and worship him as mediator; that is, pay him an obedience as mediator when he comes into the world, Heb. 1:6. Had he not a fundamental power to grieve, though since sin was extraneous to a state of innocency, he could not have exercised that grief for himself, repentance being extraneous to obedience, and unmeet for him in a sinless state? Suppose God had commanded him to grieve for the sins of the fallen angels, Adam having this passion in his nature, might have done it. He might have known what sin was in them, and might have grieved for the dishonour of God by them; even as our Saviour did grieve for the sins of others, Mark 3:5, who knew no sin himself. And in grieving for his own sin, there was only a change of the object.

[6.] It is yet more reasonable if we consider, that every natural man thinks he hath a power to renew himself, and turn to God when he will; practically, though not all of them notionally. What reason then hath man to quarrel with God, and accuse him of demanding that which he thinks he can give to God, and will not at present, but take his own time to do it, when he sees it fit? This practical opinion runs in the veins of every natural man under the gospel, as well as in the heathens, which appears by the general wilful delays of men about their eternal concerns, by their vows and resolutions upon the blows of conscience of reforming their lives, and becoming new men without having recourse to the grace of God, or taking any notice of him in their resolves. This I think is a clear case. 'Yet a little more sleep,' saith a man, that thinks he can rise time enough when he will, and despatch his business in a moment, Prov. 6:10. With what face can man accuse God of not giving him power, when he thinks he hath power enough himself? or be angry with God for demanding his debt, when he thinks himself in a solvent condition? No man will blame another for requiring that of his servant, which his servant boasts he hath power in himself to do. The Israelites thought so when they said, Exod. 24:3, 'All the words which the Lord hath said we will do,' without any applications to the grace of God to enable them. All men are like Israel in this; only the regenerate are most sensible of their own impotence, and scarce any man else.

[7.] From all this it follows, that God is not bound to give grace to any; and where he doth bestow it, it is an act of his sovereign pleasure. If God hath given man power, and never took it away, but it was cast away by man, therefore God's right is not prejudiced, but he may justly demand of man what once he gave him power to do, especially since it is less than what man at first owed him; and when man thinks he hath power to pay him, it will evidently follow, that God is not bound to give any new power. If God were bound to give a new power to accept of the gospel, he were then unjust not to confer it; if he be not bound, it is of mere grace that he bestows it. God proposeth pardon to all upon such conditions, but he is not bound to give the condition to any; he commands all to renew their obedience to him, but he is not bound to renew any one person. He gives the command to turn, as a lawgiver and governor; he gives the grace to some to turn, as a benefactor. It is grace therefore, not debt. When God confers it, it is an act of his compassionate mercy; when he denies it, it is an act of his just sovereignty. He may, if he please, 'suffer all nations to walk in their own ways,' Acts 14:16. Yet if he please to propose the means of grace to any, the very knowledge of those mysteries of heaven is a peculiar gift, as well as the outward proposal: Mat. 13:11, 'To you it is given to know the mysteries of the kingdom of heaven, but to them it is not given.' If we improve reason to the highest, God is not obliged to give us grace, no more than if a beast improved sense to the highest, he were bound to give him reason. Though if there could be a man found in any age of the world, who did improve reason to the utmost of his power, I would not doubt God's giving him the addition of supernatural grace, out of the largeness of his bounty, though still there is no obligation upon God, because man doth no more than his duty.

And that God doth not give grace to all to whom the means are offered, and yet doth command them to turn, and promise to receive them;—

(1.) It doth not entrench upon his sincerity in his proposals. His proposals are serious, though he knows man will not receive them without an over-powering grace;* and though he be resolved not to give the assistance of his grace to every one under those means, but leave them to the liberty of their own wills. The gospel is to be considered as a command ordering men to believe, or as a promise alluring men to be renewed, by representing to them the happiness of such a state. Consider it as a command, God is serious in it, though he resolve not to give grace to all to whom the precept comes, for under this consideration of a command it is a declaration of man's duty, and a demonstration of God's sovereign authority. Doth God's resolution of not giving grace weaken the obligation of man to his duty, or diminish God's authority, or give ground to man to charge him with insincerity? Consider it as a promise, doth it hinder God's seriousness in it if he resolves not to give the condition of it to all? It is sufficient to shew God's seriousness in it, to declare, that if men will be regenerate, it will be very pleasing to him; that he will make good to them what he bath promised; that if they be renewed, he will make good every tittle of the promise to them; and if they will seek, and ask, and knock, he will not be wanting to them to assist them.

(2.) It doth not disparage his wisdom to command that to man which he knows man will not do without his grace, and so make promises to man upon the doing it. If man indeed had not a faculty naturally fitted for the object, it might entrench upon God's wisdom to make commands and promises to such a creature as it would be to command a beast to speak. But man hath a faculty to understand and will, which makes him a man;† and there is a disposition in the understanding and will which consists in an inclination determined to good or evil, which makes us not to be men, but good or bad men, whereby we are distinguished from one another, as by reason and will we are from plants and beasts. Now the commands and exhortations are suitable to our nature, and respect not our reason as good or bad, but simply as reason. These commands presuppose in us a faculty of understanding and will, and a suitableness between the command and the faculty of a reasonable creature. This is the reason why God hath given to us his law and gospel, his commands, not because we are good or bad men, but because we are men endued with reason, which other creatures want, and therefore are not capable of government by a command. Our blessed Lord and Saviour did not exhort infants, though he blessed them, because they were not arrived to the use of reason; yet he exhorted the Jews, many of whose wills he knew were not determined to good, and whom he told that they would die in their sins. And though God had told them, Jer. 13, that they could no more change themselves than an Ethiopian could his skin, yet he expostulates with them why they 'would not be made clean:' verse 27, 'O Jerusalem, wilt thou not be made clean? when shall it once be?' Because, though they had an ill disposition in their judgment, yet their judgment remained, whereby to discern of exhortations if they would. To present a concert of music to a deaf man that cannot hear the greatest sound were absurd, because sounds are the object of hearing; but commands and exhortations are the object, not of this or that good constitution of reason, but of reason itself.

(3.) Neither doth it disagree with his justice. It is so far from being unjust for God to demand what men are obliged to do, though he knows that they will not do it, that God would be unjust to himself if he did not demand it, if he let men trample upon his rights without demanding restitution of them. If a prince sets forth edicts to rebels to return, and promise them pardon upon their returning, though he knows they are rebelliously bent, that they will not entertain a thought of coming again under his sceptre, but will still be in arms, and draw down his wrath upon them, will not all interpret this to be an act of clemency and goodness in the prince? Neither is God an accepter of persons, because he doth not give grace unto all; for may he not do with his own what he please without injustice? Those to whom we give alms have reason to thank us; those to whom we give not an alms have no reason to complain; we have gratified the one, but we have done no wrong to the other. We are all by nature criminals, deserving death; should God leave us in that deplorable estate wherein he found us, can we accuse him of injustice? Those that by grace are snatched out of the pit, have reason to acknowledge it an admirable favour, as indeed it is; those that are destitute of grace, and by their own wilful rejection left to sink to the bottom, cannot impute their unhappiness to him; for he left them not without witness; he presented them the word, exhorted them to hearken to him; but, instead of paying their duty, they fiercely rejected him, abhorred his exhortations, and gave themselves over to sin and vice. If a man proclaim by a crier that such that can bring such a mark shall receive such an alms, he sends this private mark to some; they come and receive an alms. Had he not power to do what he pleased with his own, to send his distinguishing token to whom he pleased? What injustice is done to the other, to whom he sends not this mark?

We have shewn that God may command. Let us see why God doth command, when he knows man hath no power to renew himself?

1. The first reason is,

To make us sensible of our impotency. The design of God is not to signify our power to perform it, but sensibly to affect us with our inability, that we may be the better prepared for a remedy; as the moral law was given with such terrifying marks, to make men despair in themselves, and the ceremonial law annexed to it, to give some glimpse of a Mediator in whom they might have strength. And therefore when the Israelites were so affected, Deut. 18:16–18, as to desire not to hear the voice of the Lord in that manner, nor to see that great fire any more which attended the law, that they might not die, he commends them for it: verse 17, 'They have well spoken that which they have spoken.' God is highly pleased with this sense of their own inability to answer the terms of the first covenant, since it makes them fly for help and supply to the prophet of the second covenant. The cabalists therefore say, that the law was given to take away the venom of the serpent;* that is, not that we should fulfil the law, but that we might learn how far we were swerved from the duty we owed to God, and how unable to gain the happiness we had lost. A conceit of self-sufficiency secretly lurks in every one of us; we should think ourselves gods to ourselves if we saw not the picture of our own weakness in the spirituality of the command. Therefore, though we cannot ourselves perform this command of regeneration, it is necessary it should be directed to us, to make us abject in our eyes, and strip us of all confidence in the flesh, which is the first step toward a being endued with the Spirit; to make us hang down our proud plumes, and sink into that despair in ourselves, which is necessary to the superstructure of a saving faith. It is necessary the law should be commanded, to make sin appear exceeding sinful, to give us a true prospect of ourselves in the glass of the command: the rectitude of it shews us our crookedness; the holiness of it, our impurity; the justice of it, our unrighteousness; the goodness of it, our wickedness; and the spirituality of it, our carnality and fleshliness. God doth not command us (though we have no power) to upbraid and triumph over us, but to lay us low, and humble us.

2. To make us sensible of the grace of God, and urge us to have recourse to it. It is necessary that man should understand the perfection of divine righteousness, and what the condition of man was before the fall, that thereby he may understand the necessity of the remedy, and be more willing to come under God's wing than Adam was to keep under it; but without a sense of his own weakness man would never come to God.

God commands us, not that he expects we should renew ourselves, for he knows we cannot; but that being acquainted with our feeble frame, we should implore his grace to turn us, and have recourse to him, who delights to be sought unto and depended upon by his creature. That this command of renewing ourselves, and returning to our due obedience, is given to this end, is evident by the promise of the gospel, which did accompany the command, both to encourage and direct men where to find assistance for the performance of what the first covenant exacts, and the second accepts. Therefore, with the commands of the law, there is the promise of a great prophet to teach them, an ordaining typical sacrifices to relieve them; and the gospel, under the mask of the ceremonial law, attended the fiery and impossible commands of the moral. God might have exacted his right without making any promise, it had been summum jus; but God exacts not his right now, but with a promise; where there is jus in one, and remissio juris in the other. And very frequently in the Scripture, where the command is given to shew us our duty, yet a promise is joined to it, to shew that though obedience be our duty, yet sanctification is God's work, as Lev. 20:8, 'Ye shall keep my statutes and do them;' whereupon it immediately follows, 'I am the Lord which sanctify you.' The precept is to acquaint us with our duty; the promise, to acquaint us with the sight of a gracious ability; the precept minds us of our debt, the promise minds us of the means to pay it: what is required in the precept is, encouraged in the promise. Every precept, being a part of the law, is to 'shut us up' to faith, and to 'bring us to Christ,' Gal. 3:23, 24. God makes us amends; that as he requires of us what we lost by another's fault, he hath provided us a remedy by another's righteousness, which we never performed; and by his own Spirit, which we never purchased, if we will but seek it. If God did work it in us without commanding us to work it ourselves, we could not have a foundation to make such sensible acknowledgments of his grace and omnipotent kindness. It is our work as a due debt; it is God's work as a fruit of his grace; Isa. 26:12, 'Thou hast wrought all our works in us.' The promise, therefore, of a new heart and a new spirit, is made indefinitely; none are aimed in it, nor any excluded, that will but seek it. And supposing they are predictions rather than promises, yet they run in the nature of a promise: they are to be pleaded, for God 'will be inquired after concerning them;' and the fulfilling of them to the soul is as pleadable as the fulfilling other prophecies to the church; the grounds of the plea are the same in both, the truth of God: Ezek. 36:37, 'Thus saith the Lord God, I will yet for this be inquired of by the house of Israel, to do it for them;' which may reasonably be concluded to respect the whole antecedent promising discourse of God.

3. These commands and exhortations are of use to clear the justice of God upon obstinate sinners. God is a judge, and judges by law; commands therefore are necessary, because a rational creature is only governable by law. If God were not a lawgiver, he could not be a judge; his judicial proceedings depend upon his legislative power. Men being to be judged by their works, must have some law as the rule of those works; and his law is no more than the first law in innocency, that is, to return to obedience and righteousness. These commands and exhortations are the whips and scourges of perverse consciences, whereby they are galled while they obey not the motions of them, and render them inexcusable and unworthy of mercy in despising the conditions God requires of them, and make the case of Sodom 'more tolerable in the day of judgment' than the condition of such men, Mat. 11:24. We are apt to bring an unreasonable charge against God of cruelty and injustice, as though his punishments did not consist with righteousness. God therefore shews us our duty, and demands it of us, and it is confessed by us to be our duty; man is therefore deservedly punished, because he doth wilfully cherish the old nature in him, the fountain of all sin; he hath the truth, and he holds it in possession, but in unrighteousness, therefore the wrath of God is justly revealed from heaven against that unrighteousness of his, Rom. 1:18. God calls sinners, though he knows they will not renew

themselves, as men send servants to demand the possession of a piece of ground, though they know it will not be delivered to them;* but they do it that they may more conveniently bring their action against such a person that will not surrender. So upon God's command to men to be renewed, his justice is more apparent upon their refusal; as he sent Moses to Pharaoh, though he knew before that Pharaoh would not hearken to him. This punishment is only accidental to the gospel, it becomes the savour of death per accidens, because of the unbelief of those that reject it;† the gospel is designed for the salvation of men, not for their condemnation. If the corruption of man produceth condemnation to himself, must God abstain from doing good to the world? There is not a man but abuseth the light of the sun which shines upon him, and the mercies God gives him, and thereby brings wrath upon himself, and God knows they will do so; would we have God, therefore, to put out the light of the sun, and divest the earth of its fruitfulness? Shall God lay aside his right of commanding, and take away the preaching of the gospel, and so excellent a thing as the happy revelation of his gracious promises and exhortations, because many men by their wilfulness bring the just wrath of God upon them for their refusal? Will any man accuse our blessed Lord and Saviour, when he comes to judgment, that he did them wrong to come and die for mankind, and cause the news and ends of his death to be published, and exhort sinners thereupon to believe in him? Surely men's consciences shall be full of convictions of their own wilfulness, and the equity of God's justice thereupon.

4. The commands and exhortations are of use to bring men to God, according to the nature of rational creatures, and also to keep them with God. Man not having lost his reason, though he hath lost his rectitude, cannot be drawn to God in a rational way but by cords proper to man; for he is a creature governable only by laws, and therefore must have laws suited to his nature; and commands and exhortations are so, for the weakness brought upon men to answer them is by their own defection.

God doth not bring men to him by instinct, as he brought the beasts to Adam, or the creatures into Noah's ark; such a conversion would not be reasonable, nor spiritual, nor agreeable to God, no more than the obedience of the beasts to Noah.* God therefore draws men by commands, and promises, and exhortations thereupon convenient to the nature of man, accommodated to the rational capacity of the creature; for man being created after the image of God, ought to be conducted and governed after another manner than other creatures. The grace of God therefore working suitably to the nature of man, cannot be conceived by us in any other way than in this of commands and exhortations. And when men are renewed, the commands for perfect regeneration are still incumbent upon them (though they cannot attain it in this life), to stir up their hearts to an exercise of that gracious ability they have to walk in the ways of holiness, and to that end to a reliance on the grace of God. The promises are given to them to inflame them to a love of holiness, and to shew them where their chief strength lies; this appears plainly to be the intent of the Spirit of God in that command and promise, Philip. 2:12, 13, 'Work out your own salvation; for it is God that works in you to will and to do.' He writes to those already regenerate, Work out your salvation, use your gracious power, and be encouraged by the assistance God gives you. Use your own power as if there were no grace to help you in the performance; depend upon the grace of God which works in you both to will and to do, as if you had no power at all of any motion in yourselves.

So that to sum up the whole of this later discourse, the impotence of man doth not excuse him.

1. Because the commands of the gospel are not difficult in themselves to be believed and obeyed. If we were commanded things that were impossible in their own nature, as to shoot an arrow as high as the sun, or leap up to the top of the highest mountain at one start, the very command carries its excuse with it in the impossibility of the thing

enjoined. But the precept of regeneration and restoring to righteousness is easy to be comprehended; it is backed with clear and manifest reason, and proposed with a promise of happiness which is very suitable to the natural appetite of our souls. To command a thing simply impossible is not congruous to the wisdom, holiness, and righteousness of God; it would not be justice, but cruelty. No wise man will invite another man by any promises to do that which is simply impossible; no just judge will punish a man for not observing such a precept; no righteous and merciful person would impose such a command. But these commands of the gospel are not impossible in their own nature, but in regard of our perversity and contumacy. The command of righteousness was possible when first given, and impossible since by our own folly; impossible in our voluntary corrupted nature, and by reason of our voluntarily cherished corruption. The change is not in the nature of the law, but in the nature of the creature; and what is impossible to nature is possible to grace, and grace may be sought for the performance of them.

2. Because we have a foundation in our natures for such commands, therefore man's weakness doth not excuse him. It had been unjust for God to have commanded Adam in innocency to fly, and give him no wings; this had been above Adam's natural power, he could not have done it, though he would fain have obeyed God, because his nature was destitute of all force for such a command. It would be strange if God should invite the trees or beasts to repent, because they have no foundation in their nature to entertain commands and invitations to obedience and repentance; for trees have no sense, and beasts have no reason to discern the difference between good and evil. If God did command a man that never had eyes to contemplate the sun, man might wonder, since such a man never had organs for such an action. But God addresseth himself to men that have senses open to objects, and understandings to know, and wills to move, affections to embrace objects. These understandings are open to anything but that which God

doth command, their wills can will anything but that which God doth propose. The command is proportioned to the natural faculty, and the natural faculty proportioned to the excellency of the command. We have affections, as love and desire. In the command of loving God and loving our neighbour, there is only a change of the object of our affections required; the faculties are not weak by nature, but by the viciousness of nature, which is of our own introduction. It is strange, therefore, that we should excuse ourselves, and pretend we are not to be blamed, because God's command is impossible to be observed, when the defect lies not in the want of a natural foundation, but in our own giving up ourselves to the flesh and the love of it, and in a wilful refusal of applying our faculties to their proper objects, when we can employ those faculties with all vehemence about those things which have no commerce with the gospel.

3. Because the means God gives are not simply insufficient in themselves. God doth afford men beams of light; he makes clear discoveries, as it is, Rom. 1:19, 'He hath shewed it to them, ἐφανέρωσε, 'it is manifest in them.' He displays in their hearts some motions of his Spirit, produceth some velleities. The standing of the world under the cries of so many hideous sins, is a daily sermon of God's kindness and patience in bearing up the pillars of it, and is a standing exhortation to repentance; as Rom. 2:4, 'The forbearance, long-suffering, and goodness of God leads to repentance.' The object is intelligible: 'The word is near us, in our mouths, in our hearts;' it is apprehensible in itself, Rom. 10:6, 7. The revelation is as plain as the surface of the heavens, Ps. 19:1–3, applied to the preaching of the gospel, Rom. 10:18. That men are not renewed, and turned to God, is not for want of a sufficient external revelation, but from the hardness of the heart; not from any insufficiency of the means, but the pravity and wickedness of the soul to whom those means are offered. The commands and means of the gospel are no more weak in themselves than the law was; but weak through the flesh, by reason of the

inherent corruption man hath fastened in himself, Rom. 8:3. Would not the hundredth part of any revelation of some worldly object, connatural to man's corrupt heart, be sufficient in itself to put him upon motion to it, and embraces of it? The insufficiency doth not lie in the external means, for the gospel is an act of mercy and grace; the call is an act of kindness. It is clear to man that God offers; it is clear that God will accept, if man will embrace his counsel; and shall this be said to be insufficient, because man will reject it?

4. Because this impotence in man is rather a wilfulness than a simple weakness, therefore man's pretended weakness doth not excuse him from the command. It is not a weakness arising from a necessity of nature, but an enmity of will, whereby some other apparent good is beloved above God, and some creature preferred before him. There is a double impotence, merœ infirmitatis, which is a want of power in the hand, when there is a readiness in the will to perform;* or malignitatis, which is seated in the will and affections, whereby though a man hath a power to perform, yet he cannot because he will not; he will abhor any return to God, and will not be whetted by his promise to any endeavour. A simple impotency deserves pity, for it is a rational excuse; but an obstinate perversity is so far from an excuse that it is an aggravation. The deeper the habit of obstinacy, the more inexcusable the person.* What a ridiculous excuse would this be, to say to God, (1.) that I ought not to be obliged to restore myself to righteousness, and obey the command of the gospel, because I am of so perverse a disposition that I will not obey, and will not be restored; or (2.) that God is bound to restore to him that will to obey and renew himself, otherwise he is guilty of no crime.† The first would be ridiculous, and both impious. What hinders any man from being regenerate under the call of the gospel, but a moral weakness, which consists in an imperious inclination to evil, and a rooted indisposition in corrupt reason and will to believe and repent? And here the Scripture lays it upon the hardness of the heart, Rom. 2:5, and a rebellious walking after our

own thoughts: Isa. 65:2, 'I have spread out my hands all the day unto a rebellious people, which walk in a way that was not good, after their own thoughts.' We are impotent and cannot, because we are rebellious and will not. For since man hath an understanding capable to weigh arguments on both sides, and see the advantage of the good proposed, and the disadvantage of the evil tempting, if he doth the evil, and refuses the good, is not the fault clearly in his will? And when by a custom in sin we ripen the power of our evil habits, we contract an impossibility of doing the good required, and casting out the evil forbidden. This doth in no sort excuse us, because it is an inability contracted by ourselves.† God himself threatens punishment to the Israelites, when he confesseth that they could not attain to innocence:‡Hosea 8:5, 'My anger is kindled against them: how long will it be ere they attain to innocence?' ;□□□□□ □□ How long can they not? Purity or innocence. They had raised such an habit in them, by casting off voluntarily the thing that is good, ver. 3, that they could not divest themselves of it, which was so far from excusing them that it sharpened the anger of God against them.

5. This weakness doth not excuse from obedience to this command, because God denies no man strength to perform what he commands, if he seek it at his hands. No man can plead that he would have been regenerate, and turned to God, and could not; for though we have not power to renew ourselves, yet God is ready to confer power upon us if we seek it. Where did God ever deny any man sufficient strength, that did wait upon him in serious and humble supplications, and conscientiously used the means to procure it. A man cannot indeed merit grace, or dispose himself for it, so that it must by a natural necessity come into his soul, as a form doth into matter upon dispositions to it. But if a man will do what he can do, if he will put no obstacle to grace, by a course of sin, would not God, out of his infinite bounty to his creatures, and out of that general love whereby he would have all men saved, and come to the knowledge of the truth, give him special grace? Hath not our Saviour

made a promise in his first sermon to the multitude, that God 'will give good things to them that ask him,' with a much more than men give good gifts to their children, Mat. 7:11. They were not only his disciples that he preached that sermon to, but the multitude, comparing it with Mat. 5:1, and Mat. 7:28. Hath not God declared, that he 'delights not in the death of a sinner,' Ezek. 33:11, and doth he not out of his infinite goodness condescend to beseech us to be reconciled to him? Will not the same infinite goodness bow itself down to form a new image in them that use the means to be reconciled and conformed to him, as much as they can? Has not our blessed Saviour already given a testimony of his affection to such endeavours, in loving the young man for his outward observation of the law, Mark 10:21, who wanted but one thing only to pass him into a gracious state, the refusal whereof barred him of it? And shall not he have a choicer affection to those that strive to observe the rules he hath left in his gospel? Will he not be pleased with such motions in his creatures towards their own happiness? Will he not further that wherein he delights? Think not therefore to justify yourselves at the bar of God for your sloth, because you are too weak to renew yourselves. It will not help you then. The question will then be asked, Did you ever seriously beg it, as for your lives? Did God ever desert you when you would fight against sin, when you set yourselves seriously and dependently on him for grace? God gives us talents, but by our sloth we embezzle them. It is upon that score Christ lays it, Mat. 25:26, 'Thou wicked and slothful servant.' God hath not promised to furnish you with more talents, when you improve not the talents you have already; non-improvement of them cuts off all pleas men may make against God upon the account of their impotence. As there never was a renewed man, but acknowledged his regeneration as a fruit of God's grace, so there was never any man that can say, he did use his greatest industry in trading with the talents God intrusted him with, and God refused him the supply of his special grace. If you have not a new heart and a heart of flesh, ask your own hearts whether ever you did seriously inquire of God to do it for you. God never fails them that diligently seek him.

For the use of this:

1. For information.

(1.) See the strange misery of man by his fall. We cannot be the authors of strength to our own souls, since we are despoiled of that vital principle which constituted us spiritually living in the first creation. How are we sunk many degrees below other creatures, who alway have, and still do answer the ends of their creation, when we, wretched we, have lost both the will and power to answer the end of ours? We can understand, will, move, but not as man in innocency could. In ourselves we are nothing, we have nothing, can bring forth nothing spiritually good and acceptable to God; a mere composition of enmity to good and propensity to evil, of weakness and wickedness, of hell and death; a fardel of impotence and conceitedness, perversity and inability, every way miserable unless infinite compassion relieve us. We have no more freedom than a chained galley slave till Christ redeem us; no more strength than a putrefied carcase till Christ raise us; an unlamented hardness, an unregarded obstinacy, an insensible palsy spread over every part, a dreadful cannot and will not triumphing in the whole soul. The heart turned into pleasure with its own wounds and chains is an amazing misery both to good men and angels, because it is so great, and yet unbewailed. To see a man endued with a soul so rare, even with its crack, that the heathens thought it to be a particle of God; an understanding that can peer into heaven, fathom the earth by contemplative inquisitions, yet cannot strike up a spark of enlightened reason about everlasting happiness; that that reason, which understands a worldly interest, should be so blind, so weak, about a heavenly bliss! A short-sighted mind, that cannot cast a look so high as to spiritual things, nor rise up in one holy thought without the grace of God; a perverse will, that cannot commission one spiritual desire; a weak arm, that cannot strengthen itself to grasp and hold one spiritual gift; a dry wilderness, that cannot issue out a tear till God open the fountain of the great deep of grace to flow in upon it; a hard heart, that relents not under afflictions on earth, nor could under the flames of hell without grace! What a woful thing is it to be miserable, and have no strength to be happy! to look into a law, and behold it wholly spiritual, and to reflect upon our souls, and behold them wholly carnal! Rom. 7:14, to find a command of regeneration in the judgment of our own consciences, just for God to impose, good for us to receive, and an utter inability to square ourselves according to it!

(2.) See the vast power of sin. It is this that hath cast its infectious roots so deep in our souls, that it is impossible for us to pluck up this degenerate plant.* The first defection from God was of that nature, that it did per se, of itself, produce an inability in us, as sickness doth in a body, or disjointing a member doth weakness in a man; otherwise man, after he had sinned, had been found in strength, and had had a power to do good, till God by punishment had taken away that power, and inflicted a contrary weakness, which would be very absurd to affirm. Adam threw off the royal robe of righteousness; and in all those ages which are run out since, man could not find by all the inquiries of nature how to put it on again without a supernatural strength. This sin that hath taken hold of us, keeps us down, that we cannot lift up our heads to divine knowledge, or reach out our hands to perform any divine precept; it is this has emptied us of our treasure, stripped us of our strength, made us as poor as Job upon the dunghill, and as feeble as the cripple at the pool; and which is worse than this, hath not only deprived us of our health and strength to cure ourselves, but of our will to be healed by another; and possessed us with such a frenzy that we are friends to our madness, and enemies to those that would deliver us from it; we are all possessed with a legion of devils, that makes us cry out against Christ before we be turned to him, Mark 5:7. It is this first poison diffusing itself in the heart of Adam has made us all by nature a generation of vipers, and infected our very tongues, that we cannot, being evil, speak that which is good; that is, perfectly and spiritually good, as it is Mat. 12:34, 'O generation of vipers, how can you, being evil, speak good things?' and poisoned our souls at the very root, that not one grape of grace can grow upon the thorn of nature. All the coin of our actions bears the impression of the evil treasure in our hearts, Luke 6:43–45.

(3.) We may from hence see the groundlessness of any conceits rising in us, of the power and freedom of our own wills to anything spiritually good. This conceit reigns in most men's hearts naturally; it is a legacy left to our natures by the will of Adam. The not submitting our wills to the will of God, in a way of humble waiting upon him, is the source of the misery of mankind; such imaginations will creep up in our hearts, that our understandings can aspire to all knowledge, our wills spring up in grace, as naturally as a clear fountain in pure waters. The cause of such conceits is the ignorance both of the depth and largeness of the wound original sin hath made in all our faculties. Paul, while a pharisee, without question was of this mind, and cried up the liberty of the will as much as he cried down the truth of the Christian religion; he was 'alive without the law once,' Rom. 7:9. But when he takes out the lesson of the sinfulness of natural concupiscence, Rom. 7:7, the experience of his slavery, and being sold under sin, grew up with the notion of the extent of original corruption, and he found himself a mere dead man, as may be observed in several passages in Rom. 7. Every man is born with this conceit, since we find the only peculiar nation God had in the world asserting it in the whole body of them, in the face of God, Exod. 24:3. When Moses told them all the words and judgments of the Lord, all the people answered with one voice, 'All the words which the Lord hath said will we do;' and ver. 7, 'All that the Lord hath said will we do, and be obedient.' Not one man among them duly sensible of natural slavery, nor making any application to God for grace to keep them; but as confident of the strength of their mutable wills as if they had as much power as the first man in innocence. This vain confidence hath its bitter root in the imagination of all Israel; and that it may not appear to be a sudden and rash passion, they assert it again more solemnly upon second thoughts: ver. 7, 'All that the Lord hath said will we do, and be obedient.'

[1.] It is a high piece of pride. To boast of a great estate, when a man hath not a farthing in his purse, is very ridiculous, or for a slave to brag of liberty, with his chains upon his hands and feet. What a vain self-reflection is it when we are bound naturally in our sins, as a slave in his shackles, with Satan's padlock upon us, till the Son make us free indeed! John 8:36. It is the very moth of pride which ate out the beauty of Adam's garment, who, whilst he would stand upon his own bottom, laid the scene of his own ruin; he affected to be his own conductor, and proved his own cut-throat; and aspiring to an independency on God, fell down into the dungeon of slavery to, and dependency upon, Satan. It is a pride like that of Adam's, an invasion of God's property, an affecting to be that by ourselves which we can only be by Christ; it is an arrogance like that of the Babel builders, to think by this slime of nature to raise up a spiritual building as high as heaven. We sin over again more formally the sin of Adam, by affecting an equality with God.

[2.] It is a disparagement to God. It is an unquestionable idolatry, and never yet practised, to set up any creature as the author of the temporal good of the whole world. Is it not more to set up many thousands of free wills as the authors of the spiritual good of the creature, to make every man's will an idol? Is the robbing God of the glory of his grace less criminal than the divesting him of the glory of his outward work? Or are the works of grace in the soul more inconsiderable than those of nature? It disparageth God's grace; it makes his grace subsequent, not preventing; it makes the highest spiritual work to be the seed of man, not the seed of God. If this conceit takes place in your hearts, God is like to be without much praise from his creature. Peter will be no more beholden to God than Judas, Paul no more than Simon Magus; both had the outward revelation, and so both owe a praise to God; but what further debt of praise did Paul owe to God, if his regeneration sprang forth into being by the power of his own will, without any further contribution from God than an objective proposal? It takes off the crown of glory from the head of Christ; for though it will be acknowledged that he bruised the head of the common serpent by the power of his death, yet the destruction of the works of the serpent in our hearts, which is our immediate happiness, was wrought by the seed of free will. It would be strange that the apostle Paul should be so over-seen, to give such praise to the grace of God manifested to him, if he had not been particularly beholden to that for the turning of his heart. By this God is beholden much to the creature's will, in being a great cause of keeping up the interest of God in the world, which had no footing, notwithstanding his revelation, without the compliance of man's will, untouched by any supernatural grace. Such a conceit of man's power seems to envy God the glory of his whole grace. And such a bitter root of this, I doubt, may be one secret cause that we are so heart-tied and tongue-tied in the praises of God for his grace.

[3.] It takes away a great part of the glory of the Spirit's work in the worlds Was his convincing the world of sin and righteousness only external, by the objective proposals of the word, and fitting the apostles for the propagation of that convictive revelation? Was he to stand only as a spectator, to behold which way the motion of free will would cast the balance? Is be to preserve grace in the heart? and is there not more need of his creating it there, than preserving it after? Is there more danger of the devil's quenching the flame kindled in the soul, than there was of its first touch upon the heart? Is he a Spirit of grace only to propose it, not to work it? The Spirit makes no verbal proposal of it, that is by man; if an inward proposal barely by applying it to the understanding, has not man as much power to do that, as to work it in his will? How can it be a well of water springing up to eternal life, if it works nothing efficaciously upon the heart? This secret pride and conceit in the heart may be a cause we make so few applications to the Spirit of God, taking little notice of him in our attempts.

[4.] It puts a bar to all evangelical duties. It makes us cleave to ourselves rather than to God, and presume upon our own strength rather than rely upon his. The heathens (as Seneca) asserted, that it was a silly thing for a man to desire that of heaven which he had power to do without it. Why should we go to him for renewing grace, when it is in our own power to renew ourselves? May it not be said to us, as it was in another case, 'Why trouble you the master?' As long as we think we can spin a righteousness out of our own bowels, we will never go to Christ for a robe of his weaving, though never so rich. And while we think we can rear a stately spiritual building by our own skill, we shall never desire the art of another workman. Our Saviour would have nothing to do with his fulness, if we stood in no need of it; and what need had we of it, if we could despatch this great business of grace ourselves? This secret imagination in the heart is one cause of the neglect of duties, especially prayer, or of a slightness and coldness in it.

[5.] This conceit endangers a man's destruction, by encouraging a delay of using the means necessary to this work in God's ordinary course. What sensualist would not delay using means for repentance, who conceits he can repent when he will, and that to will is in his own power? This makes men think they have a key to unlock heaven at their pleasure, and have the command of the treasuries of grace; and therefore are afraid to attend upon evangelical means, for fear they should be put upon serious reflections too soon. The common sentiments of men are a sad evidence of this; you shall hear many acknowledge their weakness in other things, but not in this; they cannot leave such a coarse of sin, they cannot pray with so much affection, yet their hearts are right; they can repent and believe when they will; that is in their own power; which makes them sluggish and careless at the calls of God. But what a folly this is, let Solomon witness, who sets the fool's cap upon such confidence; 'He that trusts in his own heart is a fool,' Prov. 28:26; it is to trust in a weathercock that is mutable with every wind of temptation. To depend upon our wills, is to depend upon the oldest and the most certain bankrupt in the world, that broke as soon as it was set up, many ages since, and never recovered itself. Who told you, therefore, that you can melt the stone within you at your pleasure? that you can cast the strong man out of your wills without a stronger than he? But suppose the grounds were rational, and that you had a power to cure yourselves; the consequent is very irrational, for that cause to delay it; for what man in his wits would endure a wound or deformity many years, because he can heal or beautify himself at his pleasure in a moment? Take heed therefore of such fancies of your own power to regenerate yourselves, and upon that account to neglect that which you have power to do; but imitate Ephraim with all speed, notwithstanding your cheating imagination, and cry out, 'Turn thou me, and I shall be turned,' Jer. 31:18.

(4.) It informs us, that regeneration is not wrought merely by moral suasion, or only by exhortations; then it would principally be the work of the will of man. Our Saviour had a will to preach to all in Jerusalem, but he had not a will to quicken all: John 5:21, 'the Son quickens whom he will;' so that it depended upon his inward operation, not only upon his outward exhortations. It is true there is a suasion in the ear by the word, but the persuasion is in the heart by grace; the suasion in the word may cause some rational reflections as a moral cause, but no spiritual motion towards God as a physical cause. Men are not disputed or exhorted, but created into grace; the proposal of a good by the understanding is not always embraced by the will, unless it be a good suitable and connatural to those habits in the will. Where, therefore, there is no suitable habit planted in the will, rational reflections in the mind and conscience are not like to prevail much.

[1.] If it were only by suasion and exhortation, the most eloquent preaching were like to do most good. Whereas it never was God's method to found conversion upon the 'words of man's wisdom,' though 'enticing' in themselves, but upon the 'demonstration and power of the Spirit,' 1 Cor. 2:4. The most eloquent preaching would then most fill the gospel nets. And the reports of that rhetorical prophet Isaiah would have been soon believed, which were not so, because 'the arm of the Lord was not (alway) revealed with them,' Isa. 53:1. If any words, as words, were like to have an edge to cut deep into the soul, they must be the words of our Saviour; since 'never man' (even in the judgment of some of his enemies) 'spake as he spake.' But though 'his lips were full of grace,' Ps. 45:2, most of his hearers' hearts were empty of it under his ministry; not the eloquence and pressing reasons of Christ, nor the wrath of God revealed from heaven, can reclaim the heart of man, without the power of grace. The Pharisees were prouder under Christ's melting bowels, and the Jews harder under God's wrathful blows, Isa. 1:5; neither hearing nor feeling will prevail upon hardened souls.

[2.] What bare exhortations can work upon a dead man? Can a well composed oration, setting out all the advantages of life and health, raise a dead man, or cure a diseased body? You may as well exhort a blind man to behold the sun, and prevail as much. No man ever yet imagined, that the strewing a dead body with flowers would raise it to life; no more can the urging a man, spiritually dead, with eloquent motives, ever make him to open his eyes and stand upon his feet. Did our Saviour come out of his grave, or could he ever have done it, by mere suasion, without the power of God to raise him? Eph. 1:19, 20. The working of mighty power is a title too high for the capacity of mere moral exhortations. A mere suasion doth not confer a strength, but suppose it in a man, for he is only persuaded to use the power which he hath already.

[3.] Doth not daily experience testify the contrary? Have you never discoursed with some profane, loose fellow, so pressingly, that he seemed to be planet-struck at every reasoning, shaken out of his excuses for his sinful course, yet not shaken out of his sin; that you might as soon have persuaded the tide at full sea to retreat, or a lion to change his nature, as have overcome him by all your arguments. Have you not seen many at a stand in sin, by the force of some convincing reasons, return again to their vomit? Have not many tears at command in anything that concerns themselves, the loss of some estate, or some dear friend, but in the things of God, in his dishonours, as dry as the parched earth? That you may almost as soon extract water out of a rock, as repentance for sin out of their stony hearts. So that it is not the faint breath of man, or the rational considerations of the mind are able to do this work, without the mighty pleadings and powerful operations of that great Paraclete or Advocate, the Spirit, to alter the temper of the soul.

[4.] There is no likelihood that any man in the world would be renewed, if it were only by moral suasion. Satan's logic would be stronger than God's; his arguments would more suit our imagined interest, and our real enmity against God; his persuasions would find more kindred in the principles of our minds and habits of our wills to take fire by him, than the suasory allurements of God, which will meet with nothing in our hearts but contrariety to them. The deceitfulness of sin within us, and the subtilty of Satan without us, both being active as well as persuading adversaries, would fix us in our rebellion, without a contrary power, as well active as exhortative; and God would do no more towards our restoration than Satan doth towards our destruction, since the devil can only propose to us, not by any physical touch incline our wills. We are wholly inclined to him in our own natures, in love with the knife that cuts our throats, and too fond of our shackles ever to knock them off. The will is so enamoured with its corrupt habit, that were this work left barely to self-will, and no other power employed in it than exhortative, not one person were every likely to come unto God.

[5.] If it were wrought by suasion, the will would have the whole praise of the work. For suasion or exhortation is nothing else but the proposing arguments to the understanding; but the motion, according to those arguments, is wholly from the will, which hath a power to receive them or refuse them.* God, indeed, would be the first speaker, but not the first agent; God would be only the assisting cause, as all moral causes are; he would only assist the motion of the will, not cause it. The motion of the will is a physical act; if, then, the physical act be from the will, and God only the moral cause, the will will be the greater sharer in the work; for moral causes are in vain without a physical effect in those things they work morally upon: as all the reasoning of one man with another will be to little purpose, if there be not a physical motion of the will of that person to comply with the other's reasoning. If, therefore, the reasoning part be only from God, and physical motion from man, the most debauched wretch, under the preaching of the gospel, is as much beholden to God as the highest believer, who had both the same suasions and exhortations; for though the suasion was from God, the persuasion was from their own wills. God only made the revelation, and was afterwards a spectator, not an actor.

(5.) Information. We may draw a conclusion hence whereby to judge of the truth of doctrines. Man cannot renew himself. Whatsoever doctrine doth depress and humble man and advance the glory of God, is true, it answers the main design of the gospel, which all centres in this, that man is to be laid low, and God to be exalted as the chief cause. It pulls man from his own bottom, and transfers all the glory man would challenge into the hands of God; it lays man in the dust at God's footstool. That doctrine which crosses the main design of the gospel, and encourageth pride in man, is not a spark from heaven: 'No flesh must glory in God's presence,' 1 Cor. 1:29. The doctrine of justification by works is thrown down by the apostle with this very argument as a thunderbolt: Rom. 3:27, 'Where is boasting then? it is excluded by faith;' that is, by the doctrine of the gospel; boasting would be introduced by ascribing regeneration to nature, as much as it is excluded by denying justification by works; the doctrine of the gospel would contradict itself, to usher in boasting with one hand whilst it thrust it out with the other. Our Saviour gave this rule long ago, that the glorifying God is the evidence of truth in persons: 'He that seeks his glory that sent him, the same is true,' John 7:18. By the same reason also in things and doctrines; and indeed, Christ speaks it in relation to his doctrine, as appears, vers. 16, 17. All truth gives God the pre-eminence in all gracious works; the first creation, the progress and top-stone, are the works of this great Bezaliel, this mighty artificer, both the first draught and the last line. To confound nature and grace together, is to join the creature in commission with God, and make them co-heirs in the glory which is only due to the only wise and almighty Creator.

Use 2 is for exhortation. 1. To the regenerate. If this doctrine be true,

1. Then ascribe nothing to flesh. (1.) Not to yourselves. No more praise is due to us than to gold for being melted by the fire and wrought by the workman into a vessel of honour; it is due to the skill of the artificer, not to the vessel itself. When the reparation of human nature was to be wrought by the gospel, when the crooked should be made straight, and the rough places plain, then should flesh be as grass, when the Spirit of the Lord should blow upon it; yea, the people, those that are God's peculiar ones, by reason of privileges, are grass, Isa. 40:4, 6, 7, they should be nothing in themselves, that God might be all in all: the Spirit of God blows upon all their self-confidences. If God be the God of all grace, what share have our wills in it then? He calls, he opens the heart, he strengthens, be perfects; all the grace we have is his 'treasure,' 1 Peter 5:10. He first delivers from Egypt; preserves in the desert; conducts to a footing in Canaan. Grace triumphs in the whole work, from Dan to Beersheba, from the beginning of the work to the end. What glory can belong to us? We will, it is true, but God gives that will; we work, but God bestows and stands by that power to work; what have we then to do with the praise? It is 'in his light we see light,' Ps. 36:9. The rays whereby we have a glimpse of him are not darted from us to him, but from him

to us. The light in the air springs not from itself, but from some other body enlightening it; how can any good be ascribed to us, where there is nothing but insufficiency and defect? It is to belie the Lord, to entitle a work of omnipotency to so infirm a cause; it is worse than the pharisee, who, in the midst of his boasts of his own moral righteousness, thought a tribute of praise due to God: 'Lord, I thank thee, that I am not as other men are,' Luke 18:11. Shall we entitle God the author of our beings, and ourselves the creators of our spiritual beings? Is it less to have an elevation of our faculties, and an animation of them by a new virtue, than to have simply the faculties themselves? If the creature be unable of itself to move without a dependence on God in way of common providence, much more unable is it to move without dependence on God in a way of supernatural vitality. The glory of the act is as little due to man as the glory of the first habit.

Now, 1, review yourselves, consider what you were before regeneration, what after it; and then, how can you ascribe anything to yourselves?

(1.) What you were before regeneration. Was not sin as deeply rooted in you as any other, which made you as incapable to raise yourselves as the wickedest man in the world? Were you not prisoners in chains, captives under locks and bolts, when grace first set up its standard for your recovery? How thick was the darkness of your minds? how stout the perversity of your wills? how impetuous the violence of your sinful affections? Did they not all conspire together to make as stout a resistance against the work of the gospel as any others? Can you then say, that because God saw you more inclinable to grace than another, that he drew you? You were created; did you bring clay enough to compose the least particle of flesh about you? You are new created; what part of the new man was formed by your direction? Did you bring grace enough of yourselves to form one holy thought, or send out one holy desire? Did your own will single you out of that multitude of degenerate men of better natures than yours, left still in their own nothingness? Was it nothing but your own will that planted you in the nursery of the invisible church, that made you capable of a divine union? Were not other men's reasons as strong as yours? the means they enjoyed greater? their moral disposition sweeter? What was the reason their wills did not bend themselves as well as yours? What is the reason they did not hold out their hands to catch this all-necessary grace? Did this noble birth cost none any pains but yourselves? Was this goodly fabric reared by your own wills? Look on it; methinks it is a piece too comely and noble for human skill.

(2.) What are you since your regeneration? What, do you find no rebellion of the law in your members against the law of the mind? Are there not powerful allurements of the flesh? Are your thoughts alway flying up to God, and hovering about him? Are you alway nimble in your praise of him? or not rather lifeless many times under the breathings of the Spirit? Why are you thus? Did you first by your own force begin this noble conquest of sin? And can you not by the same power make a better progress? Did you breathe a life into yourselves when you had not a spark, and can you not blow up this spark into a greater liveliness? Surely then this work was not at first the birth of your own wills. Do you not yet find some scale and thick matter upon your understandings that you cannot pick off? some darkness in your minds, as there is some in the air after it is enlightened? Are there not obstructions in your wills? no shackles upon the executive power? Can you not remove that darkness with that great light you have? nor unlock those fetters by the strength of your habitual grace? Can then the first powerful entrance of it, the fall of the first scale from the understanding, be judged to be the work of your own hands? or the first teeming of your wills with grace to be the effect of your own power? View yourselves well in both states, and you will find no ground whereon to build so much injustice towards God, and pride in yourselves, but must needs acknowledge that God and not yourselves have wrought all your works in you, Isa. 26:12, not only your temporal advantages, which the church there means, but your spiritual, and much more spiritual than temporal.

To stave off any ascribing to yourselves, consider,

[2.] He that ascribes it to his own will hath great reason to question whether he be regenerate or no. He may well doubt whether he understands or feels what it is, since those in Scripture who have been most experimented in it, and therefore are the most competent judges, have most highly magnified the grace of God, and most deeply vilified themselves; they have given the glory of it so entirely to God that they have not let a grain of it stick to their own fingers. Thus David often, 'Thou hast quickened me.' The apostle Paul owns his effectual call to be owing to the 'grace of God,' Gal. 1:15, and to an abundant 'grace in Christ,' 1 Tim. 1:14; he was a persecutor, but his faith and love was from the abundance of the grace of God, and that in Christ too, not from any thing in nature. Peter is not behind him in the admiration of it: 1 Peter 1:3, 'Blessed be the God and Father of our Lord Jesus Christ, who, according to his abundant mercy, hath begotten us again.' And it is that the church in the times of the gospel prophesied of: Ps. 100:3, 'It is he that hath made us, not we ourselves;' made us his people, as it follows, 'We are his people, and the sheep of his pasture,' 'not we ourselves.' Whenever the naughtiness of their hearts hath been ready to launch out to self-praise, they have turned the tide quickly to the grace of God. When Paul had owned grace as the cause of his spiritual being, 1 Cor. 15:10, and began to speak of his labouring more abundantly than they, he flies back in haste, as one that had gone beyond his line, 'Yet not I, but the grace of God which was with me;' another, 'Yet not I:' Gal. 2:20, 'I live, yet not I, but Christ lives in me.' There is no mention of any in Scripture that ever in this case did sacrifice to their own net.

[3.] If a man be regenerate, such a boasting of himself is very dangerous. Though it may not rifle you of the new nature, yet by the just judgment of God, it may cloud the comfort of it. If such a man be renewed, this pride is but a prologue of some dark veil to be drawn between him and the light of God's countenance, between him and the sight of his own grace. A swelling up in pride presageth a sinking down in desertion. If God be not owned by you to be the God of all grace in you, he will not own himself to be the God of all comfort to you. Grace follows humility, and some shrewd shock attends spiritual pride; it is such an idolatrous robbing God of his glory (whereof he is most jealous), and giving it to another, that he will not let it pass without a remark. The clouding of your grace will be the fruit of the smothering of his glory. For since the main intendment of the gospel is to humble, God will humble you if any grace be in you. If the Spirit of grace hath breathed upon your souls to renew you, he will blow upon your grass to consume it, Isa. 40:7, he will pull down those proud thoughts and strong holds, and cause your vain confidences to wither and come to nothing. Ascribe it not therefore to yourselves; be not so presumptuous, as, while you allow God to be the author of the being and motion of a little fly, to cry up your own wills as the chief cause of grace, a work more excellent than the material world.

2. Ascribe nothing to instruments, either men or means. It is not of the will of man, not another's will. Without the efficacious working of the Spirit, the gospel itself is but as a dead letter, the Spirit only quickens it. It is not outward teaching and blowing which of itself will kindle these sparks; an instrument cannot act without the strength of an agent to manage it; the chisel forms the stone into a statue, but according to the skill and strength of the artificer moving it. It is not the breath of man, and a few words out of his mouth, can produce so great a work as the new creation; this might be a reason why God chose so weak an instrument as man to preach the gospel, to evidence that the great work was not from the weakness of man but the power of God.

Exhortation 2. Let us be humbled under our own natural impotence and inability, and keep up this humiliation. There is danger of the pharisee's pride climbing up into the heart, even after regeneration. Renewed men have instructions to humility above other men; their sin may strike them low, because it is the growth of their own nature; their grace may keep them low, because it is no plant of their own setting; sin, because it is originally theirs; grace, because it is originally none of theirs; it is no beam of their own understanding, no stream from the fountain of their own will. If we think believingly and fruitfully of Christ at any time, we cannot but think of our own weakness, nothing in him but minds us of it; our weakness to obey the law was the cause of his coming; our weakness to satisfy God was the cause of his dying; our inability to repair and support ourselves was the cause of his fulness. His death minds us of our impotence to redeem ourselves, his grace minds us of our impotence to renew ourselves. The more we grow up in the new birth, the more deeply sensible shall we be of our impotence. Oh, let this text be writ in our hearts, 'Not of the will of the flesh, nor of the will of man.'

3. Resolve nothing in your own strength. The power to believe and be renewed is a power 'given,' not inbred, Philip. 1:29; our strength is deposited, not in the cracked cabinet of our own wills, but in the treasures of Christ. Our purposes are weak without grace to strengthen them, our resolutions vanishing without grace to establish them. If we should be left to the sails of our own faculties, without the breath of the Spirit to fill them, we should lie wind-bound. The will can never in this life be so firm but the allurements of the great tempter will make inroads upon us and overset us, without the special grace of God to establish and strengthen us. As we are not to do anything for our own glory, so we are not to do anything in our own strength. As we must not be our own end, so we must not be our own principle; the power the best have is but derived, the stream must know it is but a stream still. The actual exercise of Paul's ability grew from strength in another hand, 'I can do all things through Christ strengthening me,' Philip. 4:14; all things by him, nothing by himself. When the Israelites went out with God, no sons of

Anak, no walls of Jericho, nor chariots of iron could stand before them. When they trusted in themselves, nothing could be resisted by them. The devil was certainly none of the lowest rank of angels; he had a great clearness of gifts, yet he falls for cleaving to his own will and strength, not to the grace of God. And Adam, in depending upon himself, lost himself and his posterity. For us to undertake the government of ourselves is like a ship without a pilot, to be dashed soon against a rock. To lean on our own wisdom and will, is to lean on broken reeds, deceitful supports; self-confidence is the worm of grace, conceit of a spiritual fulness in ourselves is the way to an emptiness of spiritual comfort. Self-will and self-wisdom are the great idols of the soul, and some little images of them are in the hearts of the best men, which they are ready sometimes to fall down before and worship; they would oppose temptations themselves, do duties themselves by the strength of habitual grace, without regard to the strength of God, the great support of it.

4. Therefore live dependently upon God. Do you not find how apt you are to stagger at every temptation; how weak your wills are to good; how easily your purposes are broken, the thoughts of God few and distracted, your motions heavy in divine ways? Is there not, then, need of a constant looking unto God, as they did upon the brazen serpent, for the healing of our natures, while the wound remains imperfectly cured? All bodies on the earth, though they have a principle of motion in themselves, yet dependently upon the heavenly bodies. If the motions of the heavens should cease, that all motions in the earth would cease too is the opinion of philosophers. Without dependence on the grace of God and fulness of Christ, we sink into weakness and impotency, as a beam expires into duskiness upon the clouding of the sun. It is God only can be a 'dew to Israel,' Hosea 14:5. Think not of bringing forth the after-fruits of grace without his influence, no more than you could plant in yourselves the first root of grace without his power: the same breath of the Spirit must blow the fire up as well as kindle it. As by our

own wills we should never turn to God, so without the continuance of efficacious grace we should quickly start from God. 'As you have received Christ, so walk in him,' Col. 2:6. You received him by faith, walk in him by faith. This is the reason of the different thrivings of one Christian above another, under the same means. One endeavours to act upon his own bottom; the other clings to the vine. Christ knew the things of God by lying in the bosom of the Father; we come to know and do the things of God by lying in the bosom of the Son. All natural effects, if taken off from the influence of their own cause, by which they live and increase, lose their power and die. The soul separate from God, by non-exercise of faith, loses its strength, become stiff and inactive. How often do we return to our wonted coldness, bring forth lazy fruits, creep like snails in the ways of God, without the spur of quickening grace! And we want it because we do not seek it; for though we be armed with the whole armour of God, helmet, shield, breastplate, yet prayer and supplication must be added as a mark of our necessary dependence: Eph. 6:18, 'Praying alway with all prayer and supplication.' Then will the Spirit endue us with a fresh vigour, confirm our languishing wills, restrain the flames of natural corruption, and excite the fear and faith of God in the heart.

2. The second branch of the exhortation, to those yet in a natural condition.

1. Endeavour to be sensible of your natural impotence. Be deeply humbled at the feet of God, strip yourselves (as much as in you lies) of the conceitedness of reason and pride of will. Every man is born with high conceits of himself and his own power; it being a natural evil, should cost us the deeper humiliations. Consider yourselves by nature under the dominion of sin, the demerit of wrath, the curse of the law, the hatred of God, and a feebleness to help yourselves in this wretched condition. View yourselves often in the glass of the law, bring the spiritual word and the carnal heart together, and behold the beauty of the one and deformity of the other; let all the nasty corners of the heart come under the

examination of that purity, and then let the carnal mind hang down at the thoughts of your inability to frame yourselves according to a spiritual law. The view of our natural condition cannot work regeneration in us, but it is some kind of preparation towards it. 'The law is a schoolmaster to drive to Christ,' Gal. 3:24. It works not this grace, but it fires a man out of himself, shews him how much he differs from the holiness of God, and is an occasion for casting about and looking after some remedy, whereby he may be made like to God, and of earnest crying for the showers of grace. Be sensible also of your contrariety to the grace of God; our wilfulness against it is worse than our emptiness of it. God 'will teach the bumble his ways,' Ps. 25:9, those that are sensible of their own insufficiency to guide themselves.

2. Make use of the power you have. Man (as hath been shewn) hath some power by those restored relics of nature. There is no plea therefore to lie snorting upon a bed of sluggishness. We must not expect a divine assistance will fly to us from heaven while we play the sluggards. Though God doth rouse up some on the sudden, before any previous act of their wills, yet we must not expect God will use the same methods to all. Our own power must be stirred up and exerted as much as may be. To be faithful in a little is the way to be made ruler over much. Though the top of nature cannot merit grace, yet if nature struggles to come to the top it may find an invisible hand helping it up step by step. The damnation of most men will not be for the fault of their first parents, but for the abuse of their own power, the perverseness of their wills, and neglect of what they might have done towards the seeking of God. Though Moses had a promise of victory over Amalek, yet Joshua must fight, and the Israelites stand to their arms. God saves not men in ways encouraging their laziness. 'The sluggard desires and hath nothing; but the soul of the diligent shall be made fat,' Prov. 13:4. The sluggard hath nothing but lazy wishes, not active endeavours. If it be not worth the having, why do you desire it? If it be worth the desiring, why not worth the seeking?

(1.) Avoid those sins you have power to avoid. Every sin, though never so little, doth increase our weakness, as every wound doth the distemper of the body. It makes us weigh down towards the centre of sin. Every grain cast into the scale makes it the more unable to rise. As a virtue which is risen to that height that it cannot degenerate into vice is most worthy of praise, so the vice that possesses the soul so deeply as to incapacitate it to the doing good, being contracted by ourselves, is the more worthy of wrath.

(2.) Use the means appointed by God. Though we are torches which cannot light ourselves, yet we may bring ourselves to the word, which may both melt and kindle us. Though the giving rain and the increasing the fruits of the earth be from God, yet no man ever held ploughing, and sowing, and pruning unnecessary. The work of grace is the work of the Spirit, who is a 'wind which blows where it lists,' John 3:8. But may we not wait for those gales? May we not spread our sails and watch for the successful breathings? How do you know but whilst you are waiting upon God in an humble posture, God may unlock your hearts, and pour in the treasures of his grace? Acts 10:44, 'While Peter yet spake these words, the Holy Ghost fell on all them which heard the word.' If you will not harden your hearts to-day, God may soften your hearts to-day: Heb. 3:15, 'To-day, if you will hear his voice.' These are the times wherein God parleys with the soul, and inclines it to the happy surrender. Though the power is God's, as the water is the fountain's, yet he hath appointed the channels of his ordinances through which to convey it: 'Ministers by whom you believed,' 1 Cor. 3:5. The gospel begets instrumentally, God principally, 1 Cor. 4:15. God calls by the gospel, 2 Thes. 2:14. As God is the governor of the world, yet it is by instruments and second causes, which he clasps together to bring about his own designs. He that doth not use these means may fear that God will never work savingly upon him, for it is an utter refusing any acceptance of this grace, or anything tending to it. This is to be peremptory, never to do ourselves any good, or receive any from God. In despising the means, you despise the goodness of God. As God gave up the heathens to themselves, because they were 'unthankful,' Rom. 1:21, for that light of nature and means which they had, so if we use the means of the gospel with thankfulness to God, God may give himself up to us. But by neglect of them we take the larger strides to destruction, and the same dreadful sentence may be pronounced against us as against them in Ezek. 24:13, 'Because I have purged thee,' that is, offered thee means whereby thou mightest have been purged, 'and thou wast not purged, thou shalt not be purged from thy filthiness any more; but in thy filthiness thou shalt die.' The using the means afforded by God hath a common illumination, and a 'taste of the heavenly gift' attending it, Heb. 6:4.

[1.] Use the means fervently, with as much ardour as you set upon anything of worldly concern; do it with all your might, since the eternal blessedness of your soul depends upon it: Eccles. 9:10, 'Whatsoever thy hand findeth to do, do it with thy might.' Stir up your souls to hear and meditate, as David doth to bless: Ps. 103:1, 2, 'Bless the Lord, O my soul; and all that is within me, bless his holy name.' Employ all your faculties in this useful work; bring your hearts as near to the word as you can, screw up your affections to what you meditate upon, check your hearts when they begin to rove. Consider your own particular case in anything you hear; and let the word be as a delightful picture in the view of your minds continually; let every evangelical object excite your inbred affections.

[2.] Use the means dependently. Objective proposals are not useless, because God hath ordained them; though they are not always successful, unless God doth influence them. The means do not work naturally, as a plaster cures a wound, or a hatchet cleaves wood; nor necessarily, as fire burns; for then they should produce the same effects in all, as fire doth in combustible matter; but as God pleases to accompany them with his grace, and edge them with efficacy, they must be used with an eye to God, building with one hand, and wrestling with God with the other. Men speed best in ordinances as they strive in prayer. There are promises to plead before you come to hear: Exod. 20:24, 'In all places where I record my name, I will come unto thee, and bless thee.' The promise was made to the whole nation of Israel, the visible church, therefore pleadable by every one of them; and fix it upon your hearts, that as the death of Christ only takes away the guilt of sin, so the grace of Christ only takes away the life of sin, and the death of nature.

3. Pray earnestly. Entreat God to send his grace; beg of him to issue out a divine force, and a quickening power, to enlighten your minds, incline your wills. Lie at his feet, groan, wait till this work be wrought in your soul. How do you know, but while you are looking up to God, God may come down to you? Can a man be wounded, and not cry for plasters? Can he be shipwrecked and not cry out for some vessel to relieve him? Let such a voice frequently issue from you, 'What shall I do to be saved?' Is there no balm for a wounded soul, no hope for a distressed sinner, no city of refuge for one pursued by wrath and vengeance? Do you pray for daily bread? Why do you not for special grace? Are there no rational pleas you can urge? Is there not a fulness of arguments in the word? Why do you not then use those arguments God hath put into your hands? Why do you not spread his own word before him? Put him in mind how his thoughts were busy about the work of redemption, and that the regeneration you desire of him was the great end of that, and a thing pleasing to him? Why do you not reason with God, to what purpose he sent his Spirit into the world, but to do this work in the hearts of men which you are now soliciting him for; and that you come not to beg any alms of him, but what he freely offers himself? You may daily read such arguments in the word, where a revelation is made of them; you may daily plead them: if you do not, it is not your cannot, but your will not. Cry out of the blind eyes you cannot unscale, the iron sinew you cannot bend, the false heart that will not go right, and the fallen nature which cannot reach so high as a holy thought. Surely

God will not be deaf to the natural prayers of his rational creatures put up to him with a natural integrity, no more than he is to the cries of animals, to the voice of the lion seeking for his prey, into whose mouth he puts, by his providence, what may satisfy it. God gives the Spirit to them that ask him; not to the idle, lazy, and peevish resister of him and his grace. If you have power to regenerate yourselves, why do you not do it? If you have not, why do you not seek it? Is the way of heaven shut to you; or rather, do you not shut your own hearts against it? Have you sought it earnestly, and can you say God denies it you? No man can say so; there is a promise for it: James 4:8, 'Draw near to God, and he will draw near to you;' he speaks it to sinners, as it follows, 'Cleanse your hands, you sinners.' You can pray for other mercies, why not principally for this particular determination of your wills to God, above all other things? Lord, give me to will and to do. Never leave off praying till God hath crowned your petitions with success; and be encouraged to seek to him, whose great business in the world was to destroy the works of the devil, whose principal work was the spiritual death of man. If you have such earnest desires in your souls, that you would rather have it than the whole world, and esteem it above all worldly wealth or honours, be of good comfort, some of the rubbish of nature is removed; the steams of such desires shall be welcome to God, and the Spirit's commission shall be renewed to breathe further upon your souls. Desire as vehement as hunger and thirst shall be satisfied, if our blessed Saviour's promise be true, who never deceived any, or broke his word: Mat. 5:6, 'Blessed are they that hunger and thirst after righteousness: for they shall be filled.' A fulness attends a sense of emptiness, accompanied with hungering desires. But I am afraid few people put up their petitions to God for it; that I may say, as Daniel of his nation, 'all this evil' of unrighteousness and sin is 'come upon us' by our depraved natures; 'yet made we not our prayer before the Lord our God, that we might turn from our iniquities, and understand thy truth,' Dan. 9:13.

4. Nourish every motion and desire you find in your hearts towards it. Have you not sometimes motions to go to the throne of grace, and beg renewing grace of God? Do you not find such tugs and pulls in your consciences? Is there not something within you spurs you on? Kick not against it, nor resist it, no, nor smother any spark of an honest desire in your hearts; be constant observers of lessons, your natural consciences, or whatever any other principle set you. Natural notions are not so blotted, but they remain legible; would men be more inward with themselves, than abroad with the objects of sense, which draw their minds from pondering that decalogue writ in their souls. There is not the wickedest man under the gospel, but hath sometimes more bright irradiations in his conscience than at other times, but they are damped by a noisome sensuality; he hath some velleities and heavings, some strugglings against the solicitations of unrighteousness, some assents upon the presenting of virtue; for as grace is not always so powerful in a good man as to stifle temptation, so neither is corruption so powerful in a wicked man as always to beat back those motions to good which rise up in his soul, whether he will or no. As the law of the mind is not always so sovereign in a gracious man, but that it is affronted by the law of the members, so neither is the law of the members so absolute in a wicked man, but that it is somewhat checked by the law of nature in the mind. Are there not upon hearing the word, or reflecting upon yourselves, some wishings, some inward velleities which partake of reason, and the nature of that faculty which represents the necessity of it to you? As there is some kind of weak knowledge left in us since the fall, there is also something of a weak desire. Cannot these desires be improved and represented to God? Why is not the grace of God fulfilled in you? Because you persevere not in these desires, you quench the sparks of the Spirit, and willingly give admission to Satan to chase them out. Shut not your eyes then against any light, either without or within you, which may provoke God to withdraw this grace from you. How do you know but, upon using

the means, praying earnestly, observing inward motions, God may give you an actual regeneration? The neglect of these is a just reason for God to refuse you any further gift; and may take off all things which you may think to bring against him in your own defence. The use of them hath been beneficial to many, and no example can ever be brought, that God hath condemned any that conscientiously used the means of salvation. Therefore I say again, if any man use the means, pray earnestly for this grace, observe the motions of the Spirit in him, he will not want a superadded grace from an infinitely good, tender, and merciful God.

Two doctrines were raised from these words.

1. That man, in all his capacities, is too weak to produce the work of regeneration in himself.

This I have despatched, and now proceed to the

2d Doct. God alone is the prime efficient cause of regeneration.

It is subjectively in the creature, efficiently from God. Ezekiel's dry bones met not together of their own accord, Ezek. 37:5, 6, or by chance, but were gathered by God, and inspired with life; and not only the last act of life, but the whole formation of them in every part, he doth particularly own as the act of his own power. And doing every part of it by degrees, they should know, by that admirable work upon them, that he was God: 'I will cause breath to enter into you, and you shall live. And I will lay sinews upon you, and will bring flesh upon you, and cover you with skin; and you shall live, and you shall know that I am the Lord.' This work doth as much discover the glory of his deity, and speaks him God in a more illustrious manner than the creation of the world. We know him to be the Lord Jehovah by his creation of the world; but a clearer knowledge of him in his power is added by his regeneration of the soul. The sinews, flesh, skin, all the preparations to grace, are from God, as all the preparations of that mass of clay for the breath of life in Adam were from the power of God, as well as the living soul itself. Most do understand it of the recovery of the Jews from the captivity of Babylon;

but certainly it hath a higher import and respects the time of the gospel, and the renewing of life in the soul of all the Israel of God. (1.) Because the prophecy extends further than the two tribes captivated in Babylon; for, verse 11, the bones are said to be 'the whole house of Israel,' who despaired of ever seeing any good, complaining that their bones were dried: ver. 11, 'Our hope is lost, we are cut off for our parts.' Which could not be rationally the complaint of the Jews, who had a promise that, after seventy years' captivity, they should return, and therefore their case was not so desperate. (2.) Because, verse 14, he speaks of 'putting his Spirit into them;' meaning thereby that work he had spoken of in the former chapter, Ezek. 36:7, which certainly, being a covenant of grace, respected the times of the gospel. If it be said that it is meant of forming the church, it must also be meant of forming every member of it, since the least member of Adam was formed by God, as well as the whole body. Certainly, if renewed men, after some great falls, having still the root of habitual grace in them, cry to God, out of a sense of their own insufficiency, for the creating a clean heart, as David doth, Ps. 51:10, 'Create in me a clean heart, O God, and renew a right spirit within me;' if he then, who had this root remaining, and had some sparks which presently were blown up upon Nathan's speech to him, cries out for a new creation, what need hath he then of an almighty breath who hath not any warm ashes of grace or any one string of a spiritual root in his soul! Whatsoever, therefore, is holy, good, and spiritual in us, we owe to the new-creating grace of God. All graces are his χαρίσματα, his free donatives, over and above his common largesses to nature, a present from his infinite liberality.

I shall shew,

I. That God is the efficient.

II. That it is necessary he should be so.

III. From what principles in God it flows.

IV. How God doth it.

V. The use of it.

I. That God is the efficient.

1. God doth always appropriate this work to himself.

(1.) In the first promise, Gen. 3:15, 'I will put enmity,' &c. In which promise is included the whole work of redemption, and new creating man under another head, with another nature, which should not comply with the designs of Satan, or gratify the great enemy of God and mankind by unravelling the work of God, and subjecting himself to misery. It was necessary to our happiness that the league between Satan and us should be broken, that we should turn to God, hate the works of the devil, and join with the interest which Satan endeavoured to overthrow. And God promises that he would do it; he challengeth it as his own work: 'I will put enmity;' he leaves it not to men or angels to begin this hostility. Every one, therefore, that is at a true variance with Satan is 'God's workmanship, created in Christ,' by a second creation, as well as he was created to a natural life in Adam by the first creation, and 'created to good works, that he may walk in them,' Eph. 2:10. That is, is fashioned by God to walk in ways contrary to those of Satan, which is the greatest enmity we can express to the devil, who envied God a service from the holiness of Adam's nature. And Satan having made that conquest, and gained man to be his friend, it is not easy to conceive how any lower power could unfasten this knot, and set them at variance, since the devil had both wit enough to humour man and strength enough to keep him.

(2.) In the times of the gospel. No less than seven times I will he doth affix to his promise of the covenant, as hath been observed before, Ezek. 36:25–27. What seed was left to keep up the name of God among the Jews was of his begetting: Rom. 9:29, 'Except the Lord of Sabaoth had left us a seed,' cited out of Isa. 1:9. Their standing was not their act, but God's: and 1 Kings 19:18, 'I have left me seven thousand, all the knees that have not bowed to Baal.' Others were left to themselves; these were signally wrought upon by his grace. Others are but instruments;

God is the principal agent in all the seed of the church scattered in the whole earth: Hosea 2:23, 'I will sow her to me in the earth,' alluding to the name Jezreel, which signifies the seed of God. If ever the sons of Japhet, 'dwell in the tents of Shem,' it must be by God's 'persuasion,' Gen. 9:27. The word rendered enlarge signifies to allure. The Spirit of grace is of God's effusion, Zech. 12:10; it is God's pouring out a Spirit of grace on them before their looking up to God. (Where, by the way, observe a signal testimony of the deity of Christ; 'They shall look upon me whom they have pierced;' he that pours upon them the Spirit of grace is he whom they pierced, which was the Lord Jehovah, verse 8; for where in your Bibles LORD is written in great letters, the Hebrew word there is Jehovah; the highest name of God is here attributed to Christ.) And even in the last times he will still be the only agent in it. When God speaks of the Jews' dispersion, under which they are at this day, he owns this work upon their hearts at last to be an act of his own power and of covenant mercy: Deut. 30:6, 'The Lord thy God will circumcise thy heart,' &c., which some of the Jews understand of the time of the Messiah. God will challenge this work as his own right to the end of the world.

2. Christ appropriates it to God, and acknowledges it to depend only upon his will. Had any other cause been in conjunction with God, our Saviour would not have deprived it of its due praise, nor with so much thankfulness and amazement admired the gracious pleasure of his Father as he did,—Mat. 11:25, 'At that time Jesus answered and said, I thank thee, O Father, Lord of heaven and earth, because thou hast hid these things from the wise and prudent, and hast revealed them unto babes: even so, Father, for so it seemed good in thy sight,'—at that time, after he had been discoursing of the judgments upon them for their refusal of the gospel, worse than Sodom and Gomorrah. It was God's pleasure not to reveal it to them, and God's justice to punish them for refusal, because they wilfully refused it. The outward teaching was to all in the ministry of Christ, the inward revelation only to few according to the

good pleasure of God. Christ was the outward teacher, but God the inward inspirer. That others are not renewed by him is not because he cannot, for he is Lord of heaven and earth, but because he will renew some and not others. Our Saviour refers it here only to the good pleasure of God; he had erred much in ascribing it to God, if he had had the assistance of any other cause. Why this part of the clay he had created was formed into the body of Adam and not another, had no other cause but his pleasure; why this part of corrupted Adam is formed into a temple, a divine image, and not another, can be ascribed to no other but the same cause. He that formed Adam in the earthly paradise, forms every believer in the church, the spiritual paradise, and neither hath a co-worker nor motive without himself.

3. The Scripture everywhere appropriates it to God. They are therefore called his saints, Ps. 34:9, as being sanctified by him as well as belonging to him, 'his people,' 'the branch of his planting,' 'the work of his hands,' peculiarly his, as being created for his glory, 'that I may be glorified,' Isa. 60:21. Their fitness by grace for glory is the work of his bands. The vessels of wrath are fitted for destruction, not by God, but by themselves, Rom. 9:22. But the vessels of mercy are prepared by him, ver. 23, 'He had before prepared unto glory.' Adam lost himself, but whosoever of his posterity are recovered are 'wrought by God for glory,' 1 Cor. 5:5. It is observable that the apostle ascribes this in the whole frame of it to God: 1 Cor. 1:30, 'But of him are you in Christ Jesus, who of God is made unto us wisdom, righteousness,' &c., because he would remove all cause of boasting in the creature. He did not only set forth Christ at first as a principle of righteousness, and redemption, and sanctification, but engrafted in him, whosoever is in him, for the enjoyment of those privileges, and made him not only in general to the world, but to us, in the particular application, a principle of sanctification as well as righteousness. Union with Christ, engrafting in him, new creation, putting into another state, are all purely the work of God. He

hath no sharer in it. As Christ trod the wine-press alone in the work of redemption, so God engrafts men alone into this vine. As Christ was the sole worker of redemption, so is God the sole worker of regeneration. In him we are created, but solely by God's skill; Christ the vine, and believers the branches, the one planted and the other engrafted by the same husbandman, John 15:1, 2; he only planted and dressed Christ for us, he only plants and dresseth us in Christ. It is 'by his own will,' not any other, that 'he begat us,' James 1:18. 'Of his own will,' his own good pleasure was the motive, his own strength the efficient. Hence he is called 'the Father of spirits,' Heb. 12:9, not so much (as some interpret it, and that most probably) as he is the Father of souls by creation, as by regeneration, which adds a greater strength to the apostle's argument for submission to him and patience under his strokes. He keeps in his own hand the keys of the heart, no less than the key of the womb, which was alway acknowledged to be in the hands of God. It is with this prerogative of God that Jacob silenceth Rachel, when she so impatiently cried out for children, as if she had a resolution to kill herself if she had them not, with this, 'Am I in God's stead?' Gen. 30:1, 2. He only opens the womb of the soul as well as that of the body, impregnates it with grace, and brings forth the fruit of holy actions, as Philo in his allegory descants upon the place. The Jews perhaps meant no less in that saying in their Cabala,* Abraham had not had Isaac if a letter of the name of God had not been added to his name; the power of God, a letter of his name, must go to regeneration. It is appropriated to none but God in Scripture: to the whole Trinity, without the conjunction of any creature; to the Father as the author, therefore called 'Our Father;' to Christ, as the pattern; to the Spirit, as the inspirer of that grace whereby we are made the sons of God. The very heathen have acknowledged this; some philosophers have affirmed, that the great virtue, wherein they placed the happiness of man, could not be had but by the favour of God, and all thought their heroes to be born of their gods.

And the Scripture affirms that,

(1.) All preparations to this work, as well as the work itself, are of God. The removing indispositions, and the putting in good inclinations, is the work of the same hand; the taking away the heart of stone, as well as the giving a heart of flesh. He removes the rubbish as well as rears the building; razeth out the old stamp and imprints a new; destroys sin, which is called the old man, and restores the new by the quickening of the Spirit. The preparations of the dust of the ground to become a human body, had the same author as the divine soul wherewith he was inspired.

(2.) All the parts of the new creature are of God. Faith, which is the principal part of it, is 'the faith of the operation of God,' Col. 2:12; not but that love and other graces are wrought by God, but in this grace, which is a constitutive part of the new creature, God comes in with a greater irradiation upon the soul, because it hath not one fragment or point in nature to stand upon, carnal reason and mere moral righteousness being enemies to it, whereas all other graces are but the rectifying the passions, and setting them upon right objects. Yet all these, too, own him as the author. Our knowledge of God is a light growing from his knowledge of us; 'we know God' because we 'are known of him,' Gal. 4:9. The elective act of our wills is but a fruit of his choice of us: John 15:16, 'You have not chosen me, but I have chosen you;' our willing of him is a birth of his willing us, our love a spark kindled by his love to us. God first calls us my people, before any of us call him my God, Hosea 2:23. The moon shines not upon the sun till it be first illuminated by it. God first shines upon us before we can reflect upon him; he calls us before we can speak to him in his own dialect; our coming is an effect of his drawing, and our power of coming an effect of his quickening. Every member in Adam was a fruit of his power, as well as the whole body; every line drawn in the new creature is done by his pencil as well as the whole frame.

(3.) The acts of the new creature. God doth not only give us the habit of faith, but the act of faith: Philip. 1:29, 'Unto you it is given in the behalf of Christ, not only to believe, but also to suffer for his sake.' By believing is meant the act of believing, as by suffering is meant not only the power of suffering, but actual suffering; as the fruits upon the trees at the first creation were created as well as the tree which had a power to bear. The very attention of Lydia to the gospel preached by Paul was wrought by God, as well as the opening of her heart, Acts 16:14. Our walking in his statutes is a fruit of his grace, as well as the putting in his Spirit to enable us thereunto. The very act of motion is made by the head and heart; if there be a failing of spirits there, if any obstruction that they cannot reach the indigent part, the motion ceaseth. David acknowledged God his continual strength in his holy pursuits, 'My soul follows hard after thee,' Ps. 63:8. But what was the cause? 'Thy right hand upholds me.' His life and power issued out from the right hand of God. The graces of God's people stand in need of the irradiations of God, like the Urim and Thummim, before any counsel could be given by them.

(4.) The continuance both of the power and acts are from God. Habitual grace is called the 'fear of the Lord' put into the soul; the continuance of it is by his constant sustentation, it is that we may not depart from him, Jer. 32:40, 'from upon him,' from leaning upon him, or believing in him, as the word □□□□imports. If that fear put in did once depart from us, we should no longer cleave to God; we stick to him only because he ties us to himself, and cannot be continually with him unless he 'holds us by his right hand,' Ps. 73:23. The grace that is wrought, as well as the gospel which instrumentally wrought it, is 'kept by the Holy Ghost,' 2 Tim. 1:14; he begins every good work, and he performs it. He was the sole active cause in the creation of the faculties, and the principal cause in preserving them; he is the sole cause of the elevation of the faculties, and the preservation of them in that elevated state. As the virtue of the loadstone is not only the cause of the first attraction of the steel, but of its constant adhesion, therefore it is said: 1 Cor. 1:21, that 'God doth establish us,' not hath done, to note the continual influence of his grace upon us. It was the dropping of the two olive trees that constantly fed the lamps in the candlesticks, Zech. 4:2, 3. Take this new birth in all the denominations of it, it is altogether ascribed to God. As it is a call out of the world, God is the herald, 2 Tim. 1:9; as it is a creation, God is the creator, Eph. 2:10; as it is a resurrection, God is the quickener, Eph. 2:5; as it is a new birth, God is the begetter, 1 Peter 1:3; as it is a new heart, God is the framer, Ezek. 36:26; as it is a law in the heart, God is the penman, Jer. 31:33; as it is a translation out of Satan's kingdom, and making us denizens of the kingdom of Christ, God is the translator, Col. 1:13; as it is a coming to Christ, God is the drawer, John 6:44; as it is a turning to God, God is the attracter.

II. The second thing; it is necessary God should be the efficient of regeneration. He is, or none.

In regard of God.

1. As he is the first cause of all things. He is the creator of the lowest worm, and the highest angel; the glimmering perfections of the least fly, as well as the more glittering eminencies of the angelical nature, are distinct beams from that fountain of light and power. Shall not he then be the cause of the divine motions of the will, as well as of the natural motions of the creatures? Every perfection in a rational creature, or any other, supposeth that perfection to be somewhere essentially; every impression supposeth a stamp that made it, every stream a fountain from whence it sprang, every beam a sun, or some lucid body from whence it darts. Whence should this gracious work then be derived? Not from nature, which is contrary to it; not from Satan, who is destroyed by it. It must be then from God, since it must have some stable and perfect cause. He who was the cause of all the grace in the head is also the cause of all the grace in the members. The same sun that enlightens the heavens enlightens the earth. The grace that Christ had was 'the gift of God,'

John 3:34, much more must it be his gift to us, though we had souls as capacious as his. If the head derived not his grace to himself, the members cannot; for Christ being a creature, in regard of his humanity, must necessarily be dependent; for to make any creature independent upon God is to advance it above the degree of a creature-state, and make it God's fellow, yea, to have a godhead in itself, as being the first principle of its own being. To say any creature can move to God, without being moved by God, or live without his influence, is to make the creature independent on God in its operations; and if it be independent in its operations, it would be so consequently in its essence;* besides, if it be not created by him, it may subsist without him, it stands in no need of his quickening. The believers in Scripture were very unadvised then to pray to God for his quickening and establishing grace, if he were not the enlivener and author of it. His power works in preservation as well as creation, John 5:17, and whatsoever is dependent on him in preservation is dependent on him in creation and the first framing. And if it doth not depend upon him in preservation, it is not his creature, but it is a god. All creatures have a dependence upon something immediately superior to them. The moon receives her light and chief beauty from the sun, which else would be but a dusky body; the earth its influence from the heavens. In artificial things the little wheels in a watch depend upon the greater, that upon the string,† that in its motion upon the hand that winds it up. The higher any creature is, the more immediately it depends upon God in its production; the waters brought forth the fish, but God himself formed man.

2. As he is the promiser of it. The divine promise is only fulfilled by a divine operation, it is necessary then for the honour of his truth to be the performer of it. All his promises concerning this matter run in that strain, I will: Hosea 2:19, 'I will betroth thee to me for ever; I will betroth thee to me in righteousness, in judgment, in loving-kindness, and in mercy: I will even betroth thee unto me in faithfulness; and thou shalt

know the Lord.' The Lord promiseth by this of knowing him all gracious works upon the soul, regeneration, faith, &c., for this knowledge is an effect of the covenant which God promises in that great copy of it: Jer. 31:34, 'They shall all know me, from the least of them to the greatest.' It is not a simple abstracted knowledge, for so the devils know God, and Christ crucified, but such a knowledge that implies faith and love, and a new frame of soul. It is necessary his power should make good what his goodness hath promised. It was not necessary any word of promise should go out of his mouth, there was no engagement upon God to do it, but it is necessary this promise should be performed; though he were free before he promised, yet he is not free after he hath promised, because his truth engageth him to perform it, and perform it as his own act, as much as his mercy moved him to promise it as his own act. As mercy made it, so his mercy is as pressing for the performance; and there comes in a superadded obligation from that of his truth over and above his mercy, to perform it in the same manner he promised it, and in all the circumstances of it. So that, supposing (which cannot be supposed) that his mercy should repent of making it, he would not be true if he did not perform it; besides, it consists not with his truth not to perform that by himself which he hath promised by himself, nor with his wisdom to leave that to an uncertain cause at the best, and, further, a cause utterly unable (as every creature is) to produce that which he had promised to do with his own hand, as the cleansing the soul, pouring clean water upon it, pouring out a spirit of grace, writing the law in the heart, which imply his own act principally in this affair, in concurrence with the means he hath ordained to that end. The performance of God's promise is as infallible as the cause that made the promise. No power can perform that for another which he promises himself to do; for the thing itself may be done by another, yet not being done by the party promising to do it, it is not truly done, and in conformity to the promise made. If it were possible then to be done by any but a divine hand, it would not be done truly, because

God promises it as his own act, and therefore the working it must be his own act in conformity to his truth.

3. As he hath the foreknowledge of all things. It is necessary God should foreknow everything future, and that shall come to pass. This is a perfection necessarily belonging to God; and to imagine the contrary is to frame an unworthy notion of God, and infinitely below the great creator and governor of the world. He therefore wills everything, for if he foreknew anything before he willed it in itself, or in its necessary causes, he foreknew nothing. If he did not will it, how can it come to pass? Therefore he did not foreknow that it would come to pass. If he did foreknow it, then he willed it, otherwise his foreknowledge depended upon an uncertain cause, and he might have judged that to come to pass which never might; unless the cause be determined by God, it is merely contingent. He willing therefore a work of grace in such and such persons, did foreknow that it would be wrought, because he did will that it should be, and his working is done by an act of his will: Rom. 8:29, 'Whom he did foreknow, he did predestinate to be conformed to the image of his Son.' The foreknowledge of God being stable and infallible, and being in this case a foreknowledge of what makes highly for the glory of all his attributes, can have no dependence upon an uncertain and fallible cause, but upon a cause as stable as his foreknowledge, which is his will, himself. His foreknowledge of this is not a foreknowledge of it in any created cause, but in himself as the cause; because, as it will appear further, no created cause could accomplish it.

In regard of the subject of this new birth.

1. In regard of the subject simply considered, the heart and will of man, none can work upon it but God, or have any intrinsic influence to cause it to exercise its vital acts. Angels, though of a very vast power, cannot work immediately upon the heart and will of any other creature, to incline and change it, by an immediate touch. All that they can do towards any moving the will, is by presenting some external objects,

or stirring up the inward sensitive appetite to some passion, as anger, desire; whereby the will is inclined to will something. But the stirring up those natural affections in an unregenerate man, can never incline his will to good; for being the affections of the flesh, they are to be crucified. Angels also may enlighten the understanding, not immediately, but by presenting similitudes of sensible things, and confirming them in the fancy; but to remove one ill habit from the will, or incline it to any good, is not in their power. God gave an angel power to purge the prophet's lips with a coal from the altar, Isa. 6:6, 7; but that was done in a vision, and a symbol or sign only that his uncleanness was removed. A coal could have no virtue in it to purge spiritual pollutions from the spirit of a man. Neither can man change the will; men by allurements or threats may change, or rather suspend the action of another, as a father that threatens to disinherit his son; or a magistrate that threatens to punish a subject for his debauchery, may cause a change in the actions of such persons; but the heart stands still to the same sinful points, and may be vicious under a fair disguise. He only that made the will, can incline and 'turn it as the rivers of waters; the heart of the king is in the hands of the Lord,' Prov. 21:1, and so is every man's heart kept in the hands of him that created it, both cabinet and key.* No man knows the heart; no, the heart itself knows not everything which is in it. God knows all the wards in the heart, and knows how to move it. If a man could turn the heart of another, it could only be in one or two points; it cannot be conceived how he should alter the whole frame of it, make it quite another thing than it was before. The spirit of man being 'the candle of the Lord,' Prov. 20:27, not to give light to him, but lighted by him, can only when it is out be relighted, and, when it burns dim, be snuffed by the same hand. Or, suppose for the present he could do this, it must be with much pains and labour, many exhortations and wise management of him upon several occasions. But to do this by a word, in a trice, to put a law into the heart in a moment, and give the hidden man of the heart possession of the will, that a man knows not himself how he came to be changed, this whole work bears the mark and stamp of God in the forehead of it. Men may propose arguments to another, and he may understand them if he hath a capacity, but no man can ever make another have a capacity who is naturally incapable; it is God only can make the heart capable of understanding, he only can put a new instinct into it, and make it of another bent; it is he that renews the spirit of the mind to enable it to understand what he doth propose, and elevates the faculty to apprehend the reason of it.

2. In regard of the subject, extremely ill qualified. Can any question the divinity of the work, when stones are made children to Abraham; when waters of repentance are drawn out of a hard rock; Aaron's dry rod made to bud and blossom, and bring forth fruit, Num. 7:8; when souls deeply allied to the kingdom of darkness are translated into the kingdom of light? To see habits strengthened by custom, in a consumption, and hearts filled with multitudes of idols in several shapes, casting them out with indignation, and flourishing with new springing graces, it is too great a miracle to be wrought by the hand of any creature. Could anything but the arm of the Lord change the temper of the thief upon the cross, to advance further in the space of an hour in the kingdom of God, than all the apostles had done in the three years' converse with their Master;† to confess him, when one of the most eminent of them had denied him; to be more knowing in an instant, than they had been in a long time; and acknowledge his spiritual kingdom, when they even after his resurrection, and just before his ascension, expected a temporal one? Acts 1:6, 'Wilt thou at this time restore the kingdom to Israel?' If a Socrates, or a Cato, or those braver lights among the heathen, were turned to God, the interest of God in the work might upon some seeming ground be questioned; but when the leviathans in sin, drunkards, extortioners, adulterers, men guilty of the greatest contempt of God and the light of nature, in whom lust had kept a peaceable possession in its

empire for many years, are thoroughly changed, who can doubt but that such must indeed be 'washed and sanctified by the Spirit of our God'? 1 Cor. 6:11. What can this be but the will of God, since their hearts were so delightfully filled with evil, that they had no room nor love for any holy thought? It is not conceivable that where sin hath made such a rout, and cut and slashed all morality in pieces, things should be set in order there, but by a power stronger both than sin and the law, from whence sin derives its strength. It is no less than a divine miracle to renew an habituated sinner.

(3.) In regard of the nature of this new birth. It is a change of nature; a nature where there was as little of spiritual good as there was of being in nothing before the creation. It is a change of stone into flesh; a heart that like a stone hath a hardness and settledness of sinful parts, a strong resistance against any instrument, an incorporation of sin and lust with its nature. Where the heart and sin, self and sin, are cordially one and the same, none can change such a nature but the God of all grace, who hath all grace to contest with all the power of old Adam. No man can change the nature of the meanest creature in the world; he may tame them, bring them to part with some of their wildness, but he cannot transform them. If no man can transform the lowest creature from one nature to another, much less can any but God transform man into another nature.

This nature is changed in every believer; for it is impossible a man should stand bent to Christ, with his old nature predominant in him, any more than a pebble can be attracted by a loadstone, till it put on the nature of steel. An unrighteous nature cannot act righteously, it must therefore be a God, who is above nature, that can clothe the soul with a new nature, and incline it to God and goodness in its operations. Now to see a lump of vice become a model of virtue; for one that drank in iniquity like water, to change that sinful thirst for another for righteousness; to crucify his darling flesh; to be weary of the poison he loved for the purity he hated; to embrace the gospel terms, which not his passion but his nature abhorred; to change his hating of duty to a free-will offering of it; to make him cease from a loathing the obligations of the law, to a longing to come up to the exactness of it; to count it a burden to have the thoughts at a distance from God, when before it was a burden to have one serious thought fixed on him, speaks a supernatural grace transcendently attractive and powerfully operative. Heavy elements do not ascend against their own nature, unless they be drawn by some superior force. To see a soul weighed down to the earth, to be lifted up to heaven, must point us to a greater than created strength that caused the elevation. These acts are supernatural, and cannot be done by a natural cause; that is, against the order of working in all things, for then the effect, as an effect, would be more noble than its cause.

(4.) In regard of the suddenness of it. Peter and Andrew were called when they thought of nothing but their nets; and Paul changed by a word or two, who before was not only unwilling, but rebellious. Some have gone into a church wolves, and returned lambs. This change comes upon some that never dreamt of it, and hath snatched them out of the arms of hell; upon others who have resisted with all their might any motion that way, and were never greater enemies to any, than to those that would check their sinful pleasures with such admonitions; and yet these have been on the sudden surprised. What ground is there to ascribe any of this, but to a divine work? Many have dropped in unto a sermon with no intention to stay, who have felt God's hook in their souls; have leaped like fish out of their element for a while, and God hath catched them in his hand. Have you never heard of some who have gone to make sport with a convincing sermon, or to satisfy lust with unclean glances, who have been made prisoners by grace before their return? This quickness of the soul in coming to Christ was promised to be the fruit of the gospel: Hosea 3:5, 'They shall fear the Lord and his goodness,' when they should 'seek the Lord and David their king.' The word □□□ signifies not only to fear, but to hasten; both significations may be joined together in the sense of the verse. They shall make haste to fear the Lord and his goodness; surely the power that performs it, is the same with the goodness which promised it. Thus some of the disciples have followed Christ at the first call, and moved readily to him, as iron to the loadstone. For a man that was at a great distance from God, and any affection to him, to be filled on the sudden with a warm love and zeal for him, when nothing of interest could engage him (and sometimes it hath been with loss of friends, estate, yea, life too), is as great a discovery of a divine hand, as if a fly were changed into the shape and spirit of a hero; because a spiritual change is more admirable than a natural; and the more by how much the enmity, which was greater, is driven out, for a choice affection to rise up in its stead. The season when such a work is wrought is more significant of a divine force, when men have been in the heat and strength of the pursuit of their sinful pleasures, being then torn out of the embracements of lust with an outstretched arm of God.

(5.) In regard of the excellency of the new birth. Is it reasonable to think that the image of God should be wrought by any other hand than the hand of God, or the divine nature be begotten by anything but the divine Spirit? Since none but man can beget a child in his own likeness, none but God can impart to a soul the divine nature. It is not a change only into the image of God with slight colours, an image drawn as with charcoal; but a glorious image even in the rough draught, which grows up into greater beauty by the addition of brighter colours. 'Changed,' saith the apostle, 2 Cor. 3:18, 'into the same image from glory to glory;' glory in the first lineaments as well as glory in the last lines. Is it not too beautiful then, even in the first draught, to be wrought by any pencil but a divine? It is next to the formation of Christ, for it is an initial conformity to him. God is the fountain of all our good things. If 'every good and perfect gift comes from him,' James 1:17, shall not the best of beings be the author of the best of works? If believers are 'light in the Lord,' Eph. 5:8, they are no less light from him and by him who is the

'Father of lights.' It is a 'heavenly calling,' Heb. 3:1, therefore a heavenly birth. The new heart, the spiritual house wherein God dwells, as well as in the heavens, was not made with a less power and skill than the earth, which is his footstool, or the heaven, which is his throne. If none be able to make God a footstool, much less a throne, as Jerusalem, the church, is called in the times of the gospel, Jer. 3:17. (The embroideries and ornaments of the material tabernacle were not made by common art, but by a Bezaleel inspired by the Spirit of God, Exod. 31:3); can any but himself rear up a temple for the God of heaven to dwell in? 1 Cor. 3:9. Or is the spiritual house of God fit to be made by any but by that God that dwells in it? It was according to the image of God that we were first created; it is according to the image of Christ that we are new created, Rom. 8:29. Who understands the image of the Son but the Father? Who knows the Father but the Son, and he to whom the Son will reveal him? The new creature, according to the copy, can only be wrought by him to whom the copy is only visible. It is for the honour of God to allow him to be the framer of all creatures in the rank of beings. Is it not a dishonour to him not to acknowledge him the framer of the new creature in the rank of spiritual beings, since the later is more excellent than the treasures of the earth or the stars of heaven, than body or soul; since the image of God consists not so much in the substance of the soul as in a likeness to God in a holy nature? Eph. 4:24. To be a righteous regenerate man is more excellent than to be a man; the most glorious effect, then, must have the most glorious cause. One beam of this divine image is too excellent to be the workmanship of any but a divine hand. The very first regenerate thought, to the last dropping off of impurity, is from the same hand. The first drawing us from sin, much more the stripping us of it, is more admirable than the drawing us out of nothing.

(6.) The end of regeneration manifests it to be the work of God. It is to display his goodness. Since this was the end of God in the first creation, it is much more his end in the second. What creature can display God's goodness for him, or give him the glory of it, without first receiving it? Goodness must first be communicated to us, before it can be displayed or reflected by us. The light that is reflected back upon the sun by any earthly body beams first from the sun itself. Both the subject and the end are put together in Isa. 43:20, 21, 'The beasts of the field shall honour me, the dragons and the owls: because I give waters in the wilderness, to give drink to my people, my chosen. This people have I formed for myself; they shall shew forth my praise.' The Gentiles shall have the gospel, who are beasts of the field for wildness, dragons for the poison of their nature, owls for their blindness and darkness. The waters of the gospel shall flow to them to give drink to their souls. This people have I formed for myself. Even beasts, dragons, owls, if formed for himself, they could not be formed but by himself, who only understands what is fit for his own praise. How can such incapable subjects be formed for such high ends, without a supernatural power? So in Isa. 60:21, 'The branch of my planting, the work of my hands, that I may be glorified.' Planted by God, that God might be glorified by them. As God only is the proper judge of what may glorify him, so he is the sole author of what is fitted to glorify him. Nothing lower than the goodness of God can instil into us such a goodness as to be made meet to praise, serve, and love him; such a holiness as may fit us to be partakers of the inheritance of the saints in light, and enjoy him for ever. As infinite wisdom formed us in Adam, and moulded us with his own hand to be a model of his perfection, so are we no less his workmanship in Christ by a second creation to good works, which, as they are ordained by the will of God, so they are wrought in us by the skill and power of God; what is ordained positively by him and for him is wrought by him. The whole world consists but of two men and their offspring: the first man, Adam, the second man, Christ; both they, and all in them, created by God. It is a forming a creature for himself for his own delight. What delight can God take in anything but himself, and what is like himself? Man in his best estate is vanity. As his being is, so are his operations. Vanity, and the operations flowing from thence, are no fit object for the delight of an infinite excellency and wisdom. What pleasure can he have in those things which are not wrought by his own finger? Who knows how to dress anything savoury and pleasant to God but his own grace? Can a finite thing touch an infinite being to enjoy him without the operation of an infinite virtue? Can God delight in anything principally but himself, as he is infinitely good; or in other things but as they come nearest to that goodness? Whatsoever hath a resemblance to a superior being must be brought forth into that likeness by something superior to itself.

Now since the ends of this work are so high as to fit us for his praise, his delight, and a fruition of him; since it is to bring the interest of God into the soul, set him up highest in the heart who before was trampled under our feet, enthrone him as king in the soul, cause us to oppose all that opposeth him, cherish everything that is agreeable to him, this must be his work or the work of none.

(7.) The weakness of the means manifests it to be the work of God. How could it be possible that such weak means, that were used at the first plantation of the gospel, should have that transcendent success in the hearts of men without a divine power? That a doctrine attended with the cross, resisted by devils with all their subtilty, by the flesh with all its lusts, the world with all its flatteries, the wise with all their craft, the mighty with all their power, should be imprinted upon the hearts of men; a doctrine preached by mean men, without any worldly help, without learning, eloquence, craft, or human prudence, without the force, favour, or friendship of men, should get place in men's hearts without a divine inspiration, cannot well be imagined. If it be said there were miracles attending it, which wrought upon the minds of men, it is true; but what little force they had in our Saviour's time the Scripture informs us, when they were ascribed to Beelzebub, the prince of devils. Though miracles did attend it after the ascension of our Saviour, yet the apostle ascribes not so much to them as the means, as he doth to the 'foolishness of preaching;' it was that which was the 'power of God,' 1 Cor. 1:18; it was that 'whereby God saved them that believe,' 1 Cor. 1:21. But the greatest change that ever was wrought at one time was at the first descent of the Spirit, by a plain discourse of Peter's, Acts 2, extolling a crucified God before those that had lately taken away his life, those that had seen him die, a doctrine which would find no footing in their reasons, filled with prejudice against him, and had expectations of a temporal kingdom by him. Must not this change be ascribed to a higher hand, which removed their rooted prejudices and vain hopes, and brought so many as three thousand over at once? If there be 'diversities of operations, it is the same God that works all in all,' 1 Cor. 12:6. He conveys this 'treasure in earthen vessels, that the power might appear to be of God, and not of men,' 2 Cor. 4:7. Such weak means as earthen vessels cannot work such miraculous changes. Therefore perhaps it was that the preaching of Christ in his humiliation had so little success attending it, that nothing should be ascribed to the word itself, but to the power of God in it. To evidence that success depended on the good pleasure of God, who would not make his preaching in person so successful as that in his Spirit, which appears by Christ's thanksgiving to his Father for revealing these things to babes, and not to the wise: 'Even so, Father, for so it seemed good in thy sight,' Luke 10:21. Have you never heard of changes wrought in the spirits of men against their worldly interest, when they have been made the scorn of their friends, and a reproach to their neighbours? Can the weakness of means write a law so deep in the heart, that neither sly allurements nor blustering temptations can raze out; that a law of a day's standing in the heart should be able to mate the powers of hell, the cavils of the flesh, and discouragements from the world, when there are no unanswerable miracles now to seal the gospel, and second the proposals of it with amazement in the minds of men? The weakness of the means, and the greatness of the difficulties, speaks it not only to be the finger but the arm of God, which causes the triumphs of the foolishness of preaching. When the proposal crosses the interest of the flesh, restrains the beloved pleasure, teacheth a man the necessity of the contempt of the world, and that men should exchange their pride for humility, the pleasure of sin for a life of holiness; for a man not only to cease to love his vice, but extremely to hate it; to have divine flights, when before he could not have a divine thought; to put off earthly affections for heavenly, and all this by the foolishness of preaching, it is an argument of a divine power, rather than any inherent strength in the means themselves.

(3.) The differences in the changes of men evidence this to be the work of God, and that it is from some power superior to the means which are used. As God puts a difference between men in regard of their understandings, revealing that to one man which he doth not to another, so he puts a difference between men in regard of their wills, working upon some and not upon others, working upon some that have known less, and not working upon some that have known more, some embracing it, and others rejecting it. We may see,

[1.] The difference of this change in men under the same means. One is struck at a sermon, when multitudes return unshaken. Why is not the case equal in all, if it were from the power of the word? How successful is Peter's discourse, closely accusing the Jews of the murdering of their Lord and Saviour, which is the occasion of pricking three thousand hearts? Yet Stephen using the same method, and close application of the same doctrine, Acts 7:52, had not one convert upon record. While Peter's hearers were pricked in their hearts, these gnashed with their teeth, ver. 54. The corruption of the former was drawn out by the pricking of their souls, the malice of the latter exasperated by the cut of their hearts. What reason can be rendered of so different an event from one and the same means in several hands, but the over-ruling pleasure of God? The reasons were the same, set off with the same human power; the hearers were many of the same nation, brought up in the reading of the prophets, full of the expectations of a Messiah; they had both reasons and natural desires for happiness, as well as the other, yet the one are turned lambs, and the others worse lions than before; the bloody fury of the one is calmed, and the mad rage of the other is increased. The grace of God wrought powerfully in the one, and lighted not upon the other. Two are grinding at the same mill of ordinances, one is taken and another is left. Man breathes into the ears, and God into what heart he pleases.

[2.] The differences in the changes of men under less means. One is changed by weaker means, another remains in his unregeneracy under means in themselves more powerful and likely; some are wrought upon by whispers, when others are stiff under thunders. The Ninevites by one single sermon from a prophet are moved to repentance; the Capernaites, by many admonitions from a greater than all the prophets, seconded with miracles, are not a jot persuaded; some remain refractory under great blasts, while others bend at lighter breathings. One man may be more acute than another, of a more apprehensive reason; yet this man remains obstinate, whilst another becomes pliable. Whence doth this difference arise, but from the will of God drawing the one, and leaving the other to the conduct of his own will, since both will acknowledge what they are advised to, to be their interest, to be true in itself, necessary for their good, yet their affections and entertainment are not the same? Some of those Jews who had heard the doctrine of Christ, seen the purity of his life and the power of his miracles, admired his wisdom, yet crucified his person; they expected a Messiah, yet contemned him when he came; when the poor thief who, perhaps, had never seen one miracle, nor heard one sermon of our Saviour, believes in him, acknowledges him to be the Son of God, whom he saw condemned to the same death with himself, and dies a regenerate man under great disadvantages. A figure (saith one) of all the elect, who shall only be saved by grace, and a clear testimony of an outstretched arm of grace. Those that our blessed

Saviour admonished only as a doctor and teacher were unmoved, none stirred but those he wrought upon as a creator.

[3.] Difference of the success of the same means in different places. How various was the success of the apostles in several parts of their circuits! Paul finds a great door of faith opened at Corinth, and in Macedonia, and his nets empty at Athens; multitudes flocking in at one place, and few at another. He is entertained at Corinth, stoned at Lystra, Acts 14:19, in danger of his life at Jerusalem, while the Galatians were so affected with the gospel, that they could have 'pulled out their eyes' for him. The apostle was the same person in all places; the gospel was the same, and had a like power in itself; men had the same reasons, they were all fragments from the lump of Adam: the difference must be then from the influence of the divine Spirit, who rained down his grace in one place and not in another; on one heart, and not on another; who left darkness in Egypt, while he diffused light in Goshen.

[4.] Difference in the same person. What is the reason that a man believes at one time under the proposal of weak arguments, and not at another under stronger? It is not ex parte objecti, for that was more visible and credible in itself, when attended by strong arguments, than when accompanied with weaker. Perhaps God hath stricken a man's conscience before, and he hath undone that work, shaken off those convictions; he hath contended with his maker, and mustered up the power of nature against the alarms of conscience; struggled like a wild bull in a net, and broke it, and blunted those darts which stuck in his soul; he hath afterwards been screwed up again, and the arrow shot so deep, that with all his pulling he could not draw it out. What but a divine hand holds it in, in spite of all the former triumphs of nature? How come convictions at last to be fixed upon men, which many a time before did but flutter about the soul, and were soon chased away? And God by such a method keeps up the honour of his grace in men after regeneration, and teaches them the constant acknowledgment of his power in the whole management. Do we not daily find that the same reasonings and considerations which quicken us at one time in the ways of God stir us not at another, no more than a child can a millstone; that we are quickened by the same word at one time, under which we were dull and stupid at another; and the same truth is deliciously swallowed by us, which seemed unsavoury at another, because God edgeth it with a secret virtue at one time more than another? Hereby God would mind us to own him as the author of all our grace, the second grace as well as the first. Upon all these considerations this can be no other than the work of God. Can a corrupt creature elevate himself from a state of being hated by God, to a state of being delighted in by him? Satan's work none can judge it to be; the destroyer of mankind would never be the restorer; the most malicious enemy to God would never contribute to the rearing a temple to God in the soul, who hath usurped God's worship in all parts of the world. Good angels could never do it, they wonder at it; the wisdom of God in thus creating all things in Jesus Christ is made known to them by it, Eph. 3:9, 10. They never ascribed it to themselves; if they did, they could never have been good, their goodness consisting in praising of God, and giving him his due. Good men never did it; the first planters of the gospel (whereby it is wrought) always gave God the praise of it, and acknowledged both their own action, and the success, to be the effect of the grace of God, and upon every occasion admired it, Acts 11:21, 23. It was 'the hand of the Lord' and 'the grace of God.'

III. The third general head, from what principles in God it flows, or what perfections of God are eminent in this work of regeneration. What is observable in the forming Christ in the womb of the virgin, is observable in the forming Christ in the heart of a believer: grace to choose her to be the holy vessel; sovereignty to pitch upon her rather than any other of the lineage of David; truth to his promise in forming him in the womb of a virgin, and one of the house of David; wisdom and power in the formation of him in a virgin's womb, above the power of nature; mercy bears the first sway as the motive of the decree, but in a way of sovereignty to call out some, and not others; truth to himself obligeth, after sovereign mercy had made the resolution; wisdom steps in to contrive the best way to accomplish what mercy had moved, and sovereignty had decreed; holiness riseth up as the pattern; and power rides out for the execution. Mercy moves, sovereignty decrees, truth obligeth, wisdom counsels, holiness regulates, power executes.

1. Mercy and goodness is a principal perfection of God, illustrious in this work. 'Born not of the will of man, but of God,' of the will of his mercy. Plato thought that heroes were born ἐξ ἔρωτος θεῶν, the love of God; divine love brings forth an heroic Christian into the world; all outward mercies are streams of God's goodness, but those are but trifles if compared with this. There is as much of God in imparting the holiness of his nature as in imputing the righteousness of his Son. We are justified by Christ, quickened by grace, saved by grace; grace is the womb of every spiritual blessing. To be delivered from places and company wherein we have occasions and temptations to sin, is an act which God owns as the fruit of his mercy: 'I brought thee out of the land of Ur of the Chaldees,' Gen. 15:7, an idolatrous place; it is a greater fruit of his goodness to be delivered from a nature which is the seed-plot of sin. 'He heals our backslidden nature,' because he 'loves us freely.' It is therefore called grace, which is not only goodness and mercy, but goodness with a more beautiful varnish and ornamental dress.

(1.) Therefore in this take notice of the peculiarity of mercy. Such a goodness that not one fallen angel ever had, or ever shall have a mite of; neither did mercy excite one good thought in God of new polishing any of those rebellious creatures; mercy cast no eye upon them, but justice left them to their malicious obstinacy. That the rivers of living water should refuse to run in such a channel, or flow out of such a belly, to run in the heart of a man more muddy! As peculiar grace pitched upon the very flesh of Christ, to be united to the second person, so the like grace pitches upon this or that particular soul, to be united to the body of Christ. That singular love which chose Christ for the head, chose some men in him to be his members: 'Chosen us in him,' Eph. 1:4. And the anointing which is upon the head is poured out by such a peculiarity of love upon the members, not only by an act of his power as God, but by an act of appropriated goodness, thy God, Heb. 1:9. God anoints his fellows with that holy gracious unction, as their God, not only as God; for anointing him as the head, under that particular consideration, he anoints also his fellows, his members, under the same consideration too, because he is as well their God, the God of the members, as well as the God of the head, for they are his fellows in that unction; the difference lies in the greater portion of grace given to the human nature of Christ. And the apostle Peter, 1 Peter 1:3, intimates in his thanksgiving to God, that God begat us as the Father of our Lord Jesus Christ: 'Blessed be the God and Father of our Lord Jesus Christ;' the paternal affection he bears to Christ being the ground of the regeneration of his people; the paternal affection first pitching upon Christ, then upon others in him. Indeed, it is a peculiar affection. In his mercy to the world, he acts as a rector or governor; in that relation he proposeth laws, makes offers of peace, urgeth them in his word, strives with men by his Spirit, enduing men with reason, and deals with them as rational creatures; he uses afflictions and mercies, which might soften their hearts, did they not wilfully indulge themselves in their hardness. This is his rectoral mercy, or his mercy as a governor, and as much as his relation of a governor can oblige him to. If men will not change their lives, is God bound as a governor to force them to it, or not rather to punish them for it? But in regeneration there is a choicer affection, whereby, besides the relation of a governor, he puts on that of a father, and makes an inward and thorough change in some which he hath chosen into the relation of children. As a father, who cannot persuade his son lying under a mortal distemper to take that physic which is necessary for saving his life, will compel him to it, open his mouth, and pour it in; but as he is a governor of his servant, he will provide it for him, and propose it to him. To do thus is kindness to his servant, though he doth not manifest so peculiar an affection as he doth to his son. God governs men as he is the author of nature; he renews men as he is the author of grace; he is the lawgiver and governor; it doth not follow that where he is so he should be the new creator too; this is a peculiar indulgence.

(2.) As there is a peculiarity of mercy, so there is the largeness of his mercy and goodness in this work. It was his goodness to create us, but a full sea of goodness made us new creatures: 1 Peter 1:3, 'Who according to his abundant mercy hath begotten us again to a lively hope,' κατὰ τὸ πολὺ αὐτοῦ ἔλεος. His own mercy, without any other motive; much mercy, without any parsimony; not an act of ordinary goodness, but the deepest bowels of kindness, an everlasting spring of goodness, an exuberancy of goodness. The choice love he bears to them in election cannot be without some real act; it is a vain love that doth not operate; one great part of affection is to imitate the party beloved; but since that is unworthy of God to imitate a corrupt creature, he performs the other act of love, which is to assimilate us to himself, and bring us into a state of imitation of him, endowing us with principles of resemblance to him. It is abundant mercy to love them; it is much more goodness to render them worthy of his love, and inspire them with those qualities, as effects of his love of benevolence, which may be an occasion of his love of complacency. Worldly mercies do many times, yea, for the most part (if you view the whole globe of the earth) consist with his hatred, but this is a beam from a clear sun. At best other benefits are but the mercies of his hand, this of his heart. In those he makes men like others of a higher rank, in this like himself.

[1.] It is a goodness greater than that in creation. It is more an act of kindness to reform that which is deformed, than to form it at the beginning, because it is more to have a happy than a simple being. To

repair what is decayed is a testimony of greater goodness than at first
to raise it. Creation is terminated to the good of a mutable nature,
regeneration is terminated to a supernatural good, and partaking of the
divine nature. The creation was an emanation of his goodness, never
entitled the work of his grace. Man's first uprightness was an impress of
God; his second uprightness is far more pleasing to him, as being the fruit
of his Son's death, wherein all his attributes are more highly glorified. It
is a regeneration 'by the resurrection of Christ,' 1 Peter 1:3; that being
the perfection of it, includes his death, which is the foundation of it, as
the perfection of a thing includes the beginning. God pronounced all
the structures of the first creation good, but not with those magnificent
titles of his delighting in it, forming it for himself, that it might shew
forth his praise, which expressions testify a greater efflux of his goodness
in this second creation. Nor did Christ ever say his delight was in that,
or in that one man Adam, but in the sons of men, of apostate Adam, as
to be redeemed and renewed by him after their apostasy: Prov. 8:31, 'My
delights were with the sons of men.' What sons of men? The exhortation,
ver. 32, intimates it, those that are his children renewed by him, that
hearken to him and keep his ways. God pronounced it good, but not his
treasure, his portion, his inheritance, his segullah, his house, his diadem.
All those things which he made, even the noblest heaven, as well as the
lowest earth, he overlooks and speaks slightly of them: Isa. 66:1, 2, 'All
those things hath my hand made, and all those things have been,' &c.,
to fix his eyes, ‚□□□□upon a contrite spirit, a renewed nature. He speaks
of them as things passed away, and is intent only upon the new creation;
values it above heaven and earth, and all the ceremonial worship. What
is the object of his greatest estimation partakes of a greater efflux of his
goodness to make it so. And the apostle Peter aggrandiseth this abundant
mercy in regeneration, from the term, 'unto a lively hope;' not such
an uncertain hope as Adam had when he was fullest of his mutable
uprightness; a living hope, ἐλπίδα ζῶσαν, that grows up more and more

into life, till it comes to an inheritance that fades not away as Adam's did. Surely there is more of bowels in the Spirit's brooding over a sinful soul, to bring forth this beautiful frame, than in brooding over the confused mass to bring forth a world.

[2.] All the grace and goodness God hath is employed in it. In the creation you cannot say, all the goodness of God was displayed, as not all his power nor all his wisdom: for as to his power he might have made millions of worlds unconceivably more beautiful and more wisely contrived; for though there be no defect of wisdom and power, yet neither of those attributes were exerted to that height that they might have been. So for his goodness, he might have made millions of more angels and men than he did create, with as (and more) illustrious natures; for a man may conceive something more than God hath displayed in the creation, as to the extensiveness of his perfections at least. But in this God hath displayed, as it may seem, the utmost of his grace, for no man or angel can conceive a higher grace than what God shews in this, of beginning in man a likeness to himself, and perfecting it hereafter to as high a pitch as a creature is capable of. Therefore called 'unsearchable riches of Christ,' Eph. 3:7. A further good cannot be imagined or found out than what is there displayed. Therefore the apostle Peter speaks of God as effectually calling us into his eternal glory by Christ, under the title of 'the God of all grace,' 1 Peter 5:10, which calling includes all preparation for glory. All grace doth not less fit us for it, than call us to it; there is more of grace in fitting us for it than barely in calling us to it; and the call itself hath more of grace in it than the giving the possession of that inheritance you are called unto. It is not so high a favour in a prince actually to set his royal bride in the throne with him, as to call her to and prepare her for so high a dignity. To prepare a soul for it by regeneration is an act of pure grace; to give it after a preparation for it, is an act of truth as well as grace; nothing obliged him to the first, his promise binds him to the latter. What if I should say, this renewing of us, and subduing our sins in us, is a greater act of grace than a bare remission! Micah 7:18, 19, seems to favour it. To pardon us is an act of his delightful mercy; but to subdue our iniquities is an act of his tenderest compassion. Mercy is there joined with pardon, and compassion with subduing. And the latter expression, 'Thou wilt cast all their sins into the depths of the sea,' may refer to both those acts of grace, against the guilt and filth of sin.

[3.] The freeness of his mercy is manifest in it. It is as free as election: Eph. 1:3, 4, 'Who hath blessed us with all spiritual blessings' (of which regeneration is none of the meanest), 'according as he hath chosen us in him,' καθὼς ἐξελέξατο. It is as free in the stream as it is in the fountain. Jesus Christ is as freely formed in us, as we were freely chosen in him; as freely, quoad nos, as to us, not in regard of Christ, who merited the former though not the latter. It is his own mercy, 1 Peter 1:3, 'his own will,' James 1:18, not moved by any other, as we do many things by the will of others when our own are not free, in which are mixed acts. It is in regard of this freeness called grace. Supposing God would create man, and for such an end as to enjoy blessedness, he could not create him otherwise than with an universal rectitude, because, had God created him with a temper contrary to his law, he had been the author of his sin. Some therefore call not the righteousness of Adam grace, because it was a perfection due to his nature upon his creation. But there was no necessity upon God to bestow new creating grace, after he had stripped himself of the righteousness of his first creation. And also supposing God will restore man to that end from which he fell, and refit him for that blessedness, he cannot fit him otherwise than by restoring him to that righteousness, as a means of attaining that blessedness. Yet both these are free, because the original foundation of both is free. God might choose whether he would create man when he was nothing, and choose whether he would restore man when he was fallen. Yet there is more freedom in this latter than in the former, in regard of the measures of the new created righteousness, and in regard of the immutability of it, in regard also of demerit. Adam's dust, before creation as it could merit nothing, so it had an advantage above us that it could not lie under demerit. But we, after the fall, are in a state of damnation, children of wrath, so that regeneration is not a creating us from nothing, but recovering us from a state worse than nothing. In regard that man was miserable, he was capable of mercy; but as he was a criminal, he was an object of severity. That is free mercy to renew any man by grace, when he might have damned him by justice, to work him for glory when he had wrought himself for damnation. The apostle therefore excludes all works whatsoever from any meritoriousness in this case: Titus 3:5, 'Not by works of righteousness which we have done, but according to his mercy he saved us, by the washing of regeneration, and renewing of the Holy Ghost.' I say, he excludes all works, because not one work, as good, was in being before the renewal of the soul, for so verse 3 plainly implies, when he concludes all men, himself too, in a state incapable of doing anything that was good; the honour of his truth indeed excites him to perfect it, but his grace only, without any other motive, moves him to bestow it. All the grace you have in regeneration sprung only from this; the righteousness you are arrayed with, the flames of love in your hearts, the flights of your faith, cost you nothing, they were all the births of love. Goodness decreed all when you were nothing, grace formed all when you were worse than nothing, your faith is 'the faith of God's elect,' Titus 1:1. New creatures were chosen to faith by grace, and by the same grace was faith formed in the womb of the soul; electing grace preceded, renewing grace followed, the stream cannot be merited when the spring was free. Regeneration is an accessory to election. No man can merit the principle, therefore not the accessory.

2. As mercy and goodness, so the sovereignty of God, is illustrious in this work. 'Of God,' in the text, is 'of the will of God.' The covenant runs in a royal style: 'I will put my Spirit into them; I will give a heart of flesh,' of my own free motion and good pleasure, like the patents

of princes. God reserves this in his own power, to give to whom he pleases; Cameron saith,* that faith, which is a great constitutive part of regeneration, was not purchased meritoriously by Christ's death; and though Christ doth give us faith as well as repentance, yet he doth that, not as considered as a satisfier of God's justice in his death, but as God's commissioner in his exaltation, being empowered by God to give the conditions upon which they agreed together in the first compact about the work of mediation, unto all those that God had given him to satisfy for. Whether this opinion be well grounded or no, I will not determine; yet the making it depend solely upon election, and to be given as a fruit of election, that hereby we may be partakers of Christ, makes it more fully depend upon the sovereignty of God. God renews when he pleases: 'The wind blows where it listeth,' John 3:8. To some he affords means, to others not; he deals not with every nation as he dealt with Israel. In some, he works by means; to others, he gives only the means, without any inward work; it is his pleasure that he works upon any one to will, his good pleasure that he gives to any one to do: Philip. 2:13, 'of his good pleasure.' Some hear the word, others the Spirit in the word; some feel the striking of the air upon their ear, others the stamp of the Spirit upon their hearts. Who chose this rough stone to hew and polish, and let others lie in the quarry? Who frames this for a statue, a representation of himself, and leaves another upon the pavement? What doth all this result from, but his sovereign pleasure?

(1.) No ultimate reason can be rendered for this distinction, but God's sovereignty. We can render an immediate reason of some actions of God: why the heavens are round, because that is the most capacious figure, and fittest for motion; why the sun is the centre of the world, as some think, because it may, at a convenient distance, enlighten the stars above, and quicken the things below; why our hearts are in the midst of our bodies, because they may more commodiously afford heat to all the members; so also, why God loved Adam, because he saw his own image in him;

why he sends judgments upon the world, because of sin; why he saves believers and condemns unbelievers, because they receive the grace of Christ, those reject it.† We have not recourse immediately to God's will for a reason; the nature of the things themselves affords us one, obvious to us. But no reason can be rendered of other actions of God but his good pleasure. Why he chose Abraham above other men, and delivered him from Ur of the Chaldees; why Israel above other nations, since all other men and nations descended from Adam and Noah, and they were in their natures equally corrupt with others; they were not in themselves better than others, nor other nations worse than they; so in Esau and Jacob, why the elder should serve the younger, since they both issued from the same parents, lay in the same womb, were equally depraved in their nature, had original sin equally conveyed to them by their parents: no reason can be rendered but the will of God. So, if it be asked, why men are condemned, because they do not believe.* Why do they not believe? Because they will not. God hath given them means and faculties. If you ask, why God did not give them grace to believe and turn their wills, no other answer can be given but because he will not. It is his free will to choose some and not others. Election is put upon his pleasure: Eph. 1:5, 'Predestinated according to the good pleasure of his will;' and the making known the mystery of his will is put upon his pleasure: Eph. 1:9, 'Having made known unto us the mystery of his will according to his good pleasure.' As God regards us absolutely, it is rather mercy than his good pleasure. Why hath he changed our wills? Because he loved us, and bare good will to us in his everlasting purpose, to which he was incited by his own mercy. But if we compare ourselves with others, and ask, why he renews this man and not that, then it is rather an act of the sovereign liberty of his will, for there cannot be the result of any reason from any thing else; he pitches his compassion where and upon whom he pleases. The apostle joins mercy and this sovereignty of his will together: Rom. 9:15, 'I will have mercy on whom I will have mercy; and I will have compassion on whom I will have compassion.' He is so absolute a sovereign, that he will give no account of these matters but his own good pleasure. Why he renews any man is merely voluntary; why he saves renewed men is just; why he justifies those that believe is justice to Christ and mercy to them; but why he bestows faith on any is merely the good pleasure of his will. The pharisees believed not, because they were not of Christ's sheep, John 10:26; that is, they were not given to Christ by the Father, as is intimated, verse 29. And the prosperity of those which are given to Christ is resolved wholly into the pleasure of God: 'The pleasure of the Lord shall prosper in his hand,' Isa. 53:10. In all our searches into the cause of this, we must rest in his sovereign pleasure; our Saviour himself renders this only as a reason of his distinguishing mercy, wherein himself doth, and therefore we must, acquiesce: Mat. 11:27, 'Even so, Father, for so it pleased thee.'

(2.) He may well do so, because he is no debtor to any man in the way of grace. There is nothing due to man but death; that is his wages; the other is a gift: Rom. 6:23, 'To you it is given to know the mysteries of the kingdom of heaven, to them it is not given,' Mat. 13:11. Who shall control him in the disposal of his own goods? 'Who shall say unto him, What dost thou?' Grace is his own treasure; if he gives the riches of it to any, it is his pleasure; if he will not bestow a mite on any man, it is no wrong; 'if any man hath given to him, it shall be recompensed to him again,' Rom. 11:35. It is not unjust with God to deny every man grace; it is not then unjust to deny a great part of men this grace: 'Who hath enjoined him his way?' saith Job; or, 'Who can say, Thou hast wrought iniquity?' Job 36:23. He is not to be taught by man how to govern the world, neither can any man justly blame him, if they judge aright of his actions. Though every man is bound to endeavour the conversion of others, and every good man hath so much charity that he would turn all to righteousness if he could, and though the love of God is infinitely greater than man's, it cannot be argued from thence that therefore God should renew every man.† This charity in man is a debt he owes to his neighbour by communion of blood, upon which the law of charity is founded, which obligeth him to endeavour the happiness and welfare of his neighbour; but God is free from the engagements of any law, but the liberty of his own will; he is under no government but his own; he hath none superior, none equal with him, to enjoin him his way, and to prescribe him rules and methods. If he gives any favour to man, it is his pleasure; if man improves it well, God is not indebted to him, and obliged to give him more, no more than a father is bound to give his son a new stock, because he hath improved well the first he hath entrusted him with; it depends only upon his pleasure.

(3.) God's proceedings in this case do wholly declare it. In the first gift of his people to Christ, he acted like a God greater than all in a way of super eminent sovereignty: 'My Father which gave them me is greater than all,' John 10:29. He acts as a potter with his clay; he softens one heart, and leaves another to its natural hardness. He converts Paul a persecutor, but none of the other pharisees who spurred him on in that fury and commissioned him to it; he snatcheth some from the embracements of lust, while he suffers others to run their race to hell. David, by grace, is made a man after God's own heart, and Saul left to be a man after his own will; some he changeth in the heat of their pursuit of sinful pleasures, others he wounds to death by his judgments. The reason of the latter is deserved justice; the reason of the other is undeserved pleasure. He chooseth the mean things of the world to be highest in his favour, and passes over those that the world esteems most excellent. 'Not many wise, not many mighty,' is his sovereign method. The amiable endowments esteemed by the men of the world have no influence upon him. He acts in this way with his own people; he gives sometimes to will, when he doth not give presently to do; he distributes greater measures of grace to one than to another; he sometimes excites them by his grace, sometimes lets them lie as logs before him, that he may be owned by them to be a free agent. And further, it must needs be thus, because God doth not work in regeneration as a natural agent, and put forth his strength to the utmost; as the sun shines, and the fire burns, ad extremum virium, unless a cloud interpose to hinder the one, or water quench the other, but as an arbitrary agent, who exerts his power according to his own will, and withholds it according to his pleasure. For there are two acts of his sovereign will: one whereby he doth command men to do their duty, promises rewards, and threatens punishment, but the subject is to be disposed to do God's will of precept. Here comes in another act of his sovereignty, whereby he wills the disposing such and such hearts to the accepting of his grace, and doth will not to give others that grace, but leave them to themselves. This we see practised by God almost in every day's experience.

3. The truth of God is apparent in this work. Truth to his own purpose: 1 Tim. 1:9, 'Who hath called us with a holy calling, according to his own purpose and grace, which was given us in Jesus Christ before the world began.' Sovereignty first singles this or that man out; and truth to that firm and immutable counsel, and that resolve in his own mind, steps in to excite his holiness, wisdom, and power, to make every such person conformed to the image of his Son. It was not from any truth respecting any condition annexed to any promise he had made which he might find in the creature, for the apostle plainly excludes it, 'not according to our work'; for what motion can our work in a state of nature cause in God but that of anger and aversion, arising from truth to his threatening, the condition whereof is fulfilled by us, but not one mite of good fruit that could as a condition challenge this great work at the hands of the truth of God by virtue of his promise. His truth to his threatening would have raised up thoughts of destroying men; his truth to his purpose carried on his design of effectually calling them. It is not an engagement of truth to his creature, but of truth to himself. So that if you ask why he hath called Peter, Paul, and others, since many better conditioned than they have

rejected the gospel, the answer is, because he had so purposed in himself; and he is faithful, and cannot deny his own counsel, for that were to deny himself, and that eternal idea in his own mind: 2 Tim. 2:13, 'He is faithful, and cannot deny himself,' in regard of his purpose, in regard of his absolute promise. Truth to his promise; his promise to his Son, for so Titus 1:2 is principally to be understood: 'In hope of eternal life, which God, that cannot lie, promised before the world began.' There was a donation of some made to Christ, and a donation of grace to Christ for them, deposited in his hands as a treasure to be dispensed to every one of them in their proper time. His truth comes in upon this double donative: a donative of grace to them in Christ, before the world began, which would be but as a useless rusty treasure, if not bestowed upon those for whom it was entrusted in his hands; a donative of some, according to this purpose, to Christ, whose death, and resurrection, and purchase, would be ineffectual, if those thus given were not in time engrafted in him, and renewed by him, to be made partakers of all that which he purchased and preserved for them. Jesus Christ was to have a seed by covenant, a people to be conformed to his image. The issue then of forming a people for his seed, is the effect of God's truth to Christ. And consequent to this antecedent purpose in himself, and promise to Christ, he gives him an order to bring in those that were thus designed to be his sheep, which he calls his sheep by right of donation, before they were renewed: my sheep, by right of gift from my Father, mine by right of purchase at my death, mine by right of possession at their effectual call, these I must bring in; not I may, but I must; and they shall hear my voice: John 10:16, 'Other sheep I have; them also I must bring, and they shall hear my voice,' not they may, but they shall be inclined to comply with my word and call. Satan and their own lusts shall not hinder them from coming unto me, but they shall be overruled by a powerful Spirit. So that there is truth to his purpose, truth to his promise to Christ, truth to the depositum in Christ's hands, truth to his word published, that he would give a new heart. So that whatsoever heart his work is wrought in, it is a manifest effect of the truth of God to himself and his Christ. The gift of grace, in possession, is a necessary consequent of that gift of it, in purpose, before the world began.

4. The wisdom of God appears in this work. The secrets of wisdom shine forth in the great concerns of the soul in Christ, who is made wisdom principally to us in our sanctification, as well as righteousness and redemption. Wisdom in the imputation of righteousness, in the draught of sanctification, and in the perfection of it in a complete redemption; wisdom, like thread, runs through every part of the web. The new birth is the great wisdom of the creature; by this he becomes wise, since the Scripture entitles all fools without it. The inspiration of this wisdom can own no other but divine wisdom for the author. It is his own wisdom; for 'Who hath been his counsellor?' Rom. 11:34. He works all things according to the counsel of his own will, freely, wisely; a work of his will, a work of his understanding: Eph. 1:11, 12, 'Who works all things according to the counsel of his own will, that we should be to the praise of his glory,' that the glory of the Father may shine out in us. If all things are thus wrought with the choicest counsel, much more the rarest work of God in the world. If all things are wrought with counsel, because he will have a praise from them, much more that from whence he expects to gather the greatest crop of glory. The bringing us to trust in Christ is for the praise of his glory; a glory redounds to him, because there is nothing of our own in it, but all his; a farther glory redounds to him, because it is in the wisest manner. It is to the praise and the glory of his goodness in the act of his will; to the praise of the glory of his wisdom in the act of his counsel. There was a mystery of wisdom in the first secretion and singling out this or that person; a revelation of wisdom in the preparations to it, and formation of it. If there be much of his counsel in the minute passages of his providence in the lowest creatures, which are the subjects of that providence, much more must there be in the framing the soul to

be a living monument of his glory. It is not a new moulding the outward case of the body, but the inward jewel wrapped up from the view of men; the spirit of the mind, which, being more excellent, requires more of skill for the new forming of it.

(1.) The nature of the new birth declares it to be an effect of his wisdom. It is a building a divine temple, a spiritual tabernacle, for his own residence: 'ye are God's building,' 1 Cor. 3:9. Strength will not build a house without art to contrive and proportion the materials; skill is the chief requisite of an architect. The highest pieces of art come from the most excellent idea in the creature. The beautiful fabric of grace is modelled by the wisest idea in God; that which is glorious in the erection, supposeth excellent skill in the contrivance. Every renewed man is a 'lively stone:' 1 Pet. 2:5, 'Ye also as lively stones,' every one of you polished and carved by the wise Creator for an everlasting statue. It is he that hath 'wrought us to the self-same thing,' 2 Cor. 5:5, κατεργασάμενος; polished us and curiously wrought us, who were rough stones, covered with the rubbish of sin. As a wise builder, he lays the foundation in sound habits, whereon to raise a superstructure of gracious actions. The counterpart in the heart is no less a fruit of his wisdom than the law in the tables of stone; wisdom in the first framing the law, wisdom also in the deep imprinting of it. That which enlightens the eyes, and makes wise to salvation, can be entitled to no other original cause than divine wisdom. The soul is a rational work of God.* Surely, then, that which is the soul of the soul, the glory of the creature, the preparation for happiness, more pleasing to God than the brightest nature, than the natural frame of the highest soul, that which is the pleasure and delight, must be the fruit, too, of infinite wisdom. Bare effects of power are not the immediate objects of God's special delight.

(2.) The means of it declare it to be a fruit of his wisdom. Christ the exemplar hath the treasures of wisdom; grace copied from it is part of those treasures. The gospel, the instrument, is 'the wisdom of God,' as well as 'the power of God,' 1 Cor. 2:7. Divine skill framed the model, reared the building, no less sows the seed in the heart. What did partake of wisdom in the contrivance, progress, all the parts and methods of it, partakes of the same in the inward operations of it upon the soul.

(3.) The manner of it speaks it to be so. In regard of the enemies he hath to deal with, there must be prudence to countermine the deep and unsearchable plots of the powers of darkness. As there is the strength of sin within, the might of Satan without, as fit subjects for his power, so there are the stratagems of Satan, the subtleties and deceits of the flesh, as a fit occasion for his almighty skill against hellish policy. In regard also of his working upon the soul, he works upon those that are so contrary to his design without imposing upon their faculties; he moves them according to their physical nature, though contrary to their moral nature; he makes us do willingly what we would not; he so tunes the strings that they speak out willingly what naturally they are most unfit for. The Spirit acts wisely in the revealing to us the knowledge of Christ, as Eph. 1:17, 'The spirit of wisdom and revelation in the knowledge of him,' which may note the manner of his acting in the revelation, which is the first work of the soul, as well as the effect it doth produce, though I suppose the effect is principally meant. Some question the wisdom of God in acting so upon the will as not to leave it to its own indifference in this change. What reason is there to question his wisdom? Do not the angels in heaven admire God's wisdom as well as his grace, who hath immutably fixed them to that which is good? Do they question the wisdom of God for so happy a confirmation of them against that indifference which destroyed some of their fellows by creation? But is there not an evident art in this work, to make the will willing that had no affection to this change; to fit the key so to all the wards that not one is disordered; to move us contrary to our corrupt reason, yet bring us to that pass to acknowledge we had reason to be so moved; to move our faculties one by another as wheels in a watch; to present spiritual, things with such an evident light as engageth our understandings to believe that which they would not believe before, and our wills to embrace that which our affections gainsay? It must therefore be a fruit of divine skill since it is a fruit of divine teaching, John 6:45.

(4.) There is a greater wisdom in it than in the creation of the world. The higher the work riseth, the more of skill appears. It is a divine art to make man to live the life of plants in his growth, the life of beasts in his sense, the life of angels in his mind; more it is then to make him live the life of God in his grace. Man in his body partakes of earth, in his soul of heaven, in his grace of the heaven of heavens, of the God of heaven. The grace in the hew birth is nearer the likeness of God than the figure of men in the first birth. God therefore doth more observe the numbers and measures in the second creation than he did in the first. Man was the most excellent piece in the lower creation, therefore more of art in the framing of him than in the whole celestial and elementary world. The glorious bodies of sun, moon, and stars had not such marks upon them. The nearer resemblance anything hath to God, the more of wisdom as well as power is signified in the make of it.

5. The holiness of God is seen in this work. The day of God's power breaks not upon us in the change of our wills, without his appearance in 'the beauties of holiness,' Ps. 110:3. The Spirit is called a spirit of holiness, not only as he is the efficient, but as he is the pattern, and like fire transforms into his own nature; for that which is born of the Spirit is spirit. The law in the tables of stone was an image; the law in the heart is an extract of God's holiness. Our first creation in a mutable state was according to his own image, Gen. 1:26. Our second creation is more exactly like him, in a gracious immutability. The holiness in Christ's human nature was an effect of the holiness of God; the holiness we have then in resemblance to Christ, must be a fruit of the same perfection. If we are renewed according to his image, it must be according to his holiness. To be merciful and just, is to have a moral image; to be holy, is

to have a divine. The apostle intimates this in his exhortation, we must be holy in serving him, because he was holy in calling us: 1 Peter 1:15, 'As he which hath called you is holy, so be ye holy,' &c. In this respect, God calls himself, not only a holy one, but the holy one of Israel: Isa. 43:15, 'I am the Lord your holy one, the creator of Israel, your king.' He is not only holy in himself, but displays his holiness in them, by an act of a new creation. By creator is not meant, his being the creator of them, as he is of all, even of wicked men and devils; but implies a peculiar relation to them, as distinguished from others. He is the creator of devils, holy in his actions towards devils, but not their holy one by any inward renovation, or consecrating them to himself, as he is the holy one of Israel. As he is a God in covenant, he is our God, therefore our God as he is a holy God, as well as he is a powerful God, communicating the one as well as the other in a covenant way; therefore the prophet Habakkuk joins them both together, 'O Lord my God, my holy one,' Hab. 1:12. His holiness is no less necessary for the felicity of his people, than his mercy and power. What happiness could his mercy move, his wisdom contrive, or his power effect, without the communication of his holiness? Mercy could not of itself fit a man for it, nor power give a man possession of it, without holiness attiring him with all those graces which prepare him for it. God, as sovereign, chose us; as merciful, pardons us; as wise, guides us; as powerful, protects us; as true, makes good his promises to us; but as holy, cleanseth us from our old habits, makes us vessels of honour, filled with the savoury and delicious fruits of his Spirit, his pleasant things. The implantation of grace in the heart, is no less an effect of his holiness, than the preservation of it is, which our Saviour intimates, when in his petition for it he gives his Father rather the title of holy, than of any other attribute: John 17:11, 'Holy Father, keep through thy own name.'

6. The power of God appears in this work. 'Since the world began was it not heard that any man opened the eyes of one that was born blind,' John 9:32; neither was it ever heard that any man could open the

understanding of one that was born dark. Everything that pertains to life and godliness, of which regeneration is not the meanest, is the work of divine power: 2 Peter 1:3, 'According as his divine power hath given to us all things that pertain to life and godliness, through the knowledge of him who hath called us to glory and virtue;' glory and virtue, by a hendiadis, for a glorious virtue; and the apostle adds, that this calling was an effect of a glorious power; it is not εἰς, but διὰ, through glory and virtue; the same preposition διὰ, which, as joined with knowledge, is translated through; as much as to say, through a glorious virtue or power, both ἀρετὴ and virtus signifying valour and strength in their several languages. When God hardens a man, he only withdraws his grace. But a divine virtue is necessary for the cure of our hereditary disease. There is no great force required to cut a dead man, but to raise him requires an extraordinary power. We may as well deny this work to be a new creation, a resurrection, as deny it to be an act of divine power. There is a word that calls; there is also a power to work: 1 Thes. 1:5, 'Our gospel came not unto you in word only, but also in power, and in the Holy Ghost;' that is, the power of the Holy Ghost. There was not only grace in the word, to woo, but the power of the Holy Ghost in it, to overcome the heart. There is not only an act of an almighty Spirit, but an act of his almightiness. The hand of the Lord created the world, 'the heavens are the work of his fingers,' Ps. 8:3; but grace is the work of 'his arms,' Isa. 53:1. It may be said of the first grace in the new birth, as it was of Reuben, Gen. 49:3, it is his 'might, the beginning of his strength, and the excellency of his power.' Though ministerial gifts were as excellent as Paul's, whose preaching was with demonstration and power, and who knew the readiest ways to men's hearts, if a man ever did, yet 'the excellency of the power was of God;' and when he brandished his spiritual weapons, they were only 'mighty through God,' 2 Cor. 10:4. Though the declaration was his, yet the working was Christ's, Rom. 15:18; none of his people are willing, till the day of his power, Ps. 110:3.

(1.) It is as great, yea, greater power, than that put forth in creation. It is as great; it is the introduction of another form, not in a way of any action or fashion, but in such a manner as was in the creation, that is, by the mighty operation of God; otherwise it could not be called a new creature, though it might be called a new thing. You call not that which is made by the art or power of man, as a watch, a clock, a house, a new creature; for there is nothing of creation in them, but art and industry, setting the pieces of matter, created to their hands, together in such a form or figure. But this is called a new creature, not so much in regard of the newness of the thing, but in regard of the power that wrought it, and the manner of working it, being the same with that of creation. And being termed so, it implies the exerting an efficacious power; for creation is not wrought by a cessation of action (which would be in God, if the will were only the cause of it) but the employment of an active virtue.* God doth not hold his hand in his bosom, but spreads it open, and applies it to an efficacious action. Since it is a new creation, it implies a creator, and a creative power; creation cannot be without both. It is a greater power expended in regeneration than in creation; more power morally in this, than physically in that. One word created the world; many words are combined for the new preparation of the heart. It is easier to make a thousand glasses, than to set together one that is dashed in pieces. It is easier with God to make a world (quoad nos, as to our conception, for all things are alike easy with God), and create thousands of men with his image, as bright as Adam's, than to bring that into form which is so miserably defaced.

[1.] First, In regard of the subject, sin hath turned man into a beast, and omnipotency only can turn a bestial man into angelical and divine. There is a less distance between the least dust and the glorious God, than there is between the holy God and an impure sinner; sin and grace are more contrary to one another, than aliquid and nihil, something and nothing. A straw may with less power be made a star, than a corrupted sinner be made a saint. In creation, God was only to put in nature, here he is to put off one that is strong, and to bring in another altogether strange and new; it is hard to bring a man off from his old stock, and as hard to make him nakedly to trust Christ. It is more difficult to make a man leave his sin, than to change his opinion, since men are more in love with habitual wickedness, than with any opinion whatsoever. In regard of the indisposedness of the soul. There is some foundation for a natural religion, there being general notions of God and his attributes, which would administer some conclusions that he was to be feared and reverenced; and according to these notions many checks of conscience, which would induce men to some moral behaviour towards God. But in the setting our hearts right to God, and creating them in a mediator, there was not the least dust in nature to build upon. In the creating of Adam's body, there was some pre-existent matter, the dust of the ground, whereof his body was by a divine power made and organised; but we meet with no pre-existent matter for the formation of the soul, which made him a rational creature; that indeed was the breath of God, not engendered by any concurring cause in nature. There is no pre-existent matter in the creature, of which this image is formed, though there be a pre-existent subject to receive the impression of it; it is not the rearing anything upon the foundation of nature, but introducing a nature wholly new, which speaks almightiness. In regard of the contradiction in the subject. The stream of man's natural reason, the principles of self, whereby he is guided, run counter to it; there is a pride of reason which will not stoop to the gospel, which in man's wisdom is counted foolishness. Man is an untamed heifer, a wild ass that snuffs up the wind, full of hatred to the ways of God, guided by gigantic lusts, which make as great a resistance as a mountain of brass; stoutness of heart, strong prejudices against the law of God; fierceness of affection, drinking iniquity like water; universal madness, resisting the spirit, hare-brained imaginations; forwardness in the will, forwardness to evil, perversity against good; can anything, less than an almighty power, make a universal cure? It is more easy to make men stoop to some victorious prince, and become his vassals, than to bring men to a submission to God and his laws, which they entertain with contempt and scorn. Nothing obeyed God's word in the creation; though it contributed not to his design, yet it could not oppose him; it could not swell against him, because it was nothing. But every sinner is rebellious, disputes God's commands, fortifies himself against his entrance, gives not up himself without a contest. This pride is hereditary, it bore sway in the heart ever since Adam's fall, and hath prescription of as long a standing as the world to plead for possession. What but infinite power can fling down this pride at the foot of the cross, make the heart strike its swelling sail to Christ, and become nothing in itself, that Christ may be all life in him, and all righteousness to him? It is only possible to God to make a camel, with this bunch on its back, pass through a needle's eye; no less than divine power can bring down these armies of opposite imaginations, which have both multitude and strength (and no man knows either their number or strength), and the whole frame of contradiction against the grace of Christ. Our Saviour intimates this creative power in that thanksgiving to his Father: Matt. 11:25, 'I thank thee, O Father, Lord of heaven and earth,' &c. Christ, in all his addresses to his Father, used attributes and titles suitable to the business he insisted on. The revelation of divine knowledge to babes, the moulding their hearts to receive it, was an act of God as he is Lord of heaven and earth, putting forth an infinite power in the forming of it. If God were the author of grace in the hearts of those babes, persons better disposed, and nearer the kingdom of heaven, as he was Lord of heaven and earth, then there must be some greater power than that of the creation of the world put forth to conquer the wise and prudent, whose wisdom and prudence stands armed in the breaches of nature to beat off the assaults of the gospel.

[2.] In regard of the opposition of the present possessors. The chasing out an armed devil, that hath kept the palace in peace so long, must be by a power superior to his own, Luke 11:21, 22. This great Goliath hath his armour about him, hath had long possession and dearest affections; the impulses of natural concupiscence take his part; he hath his alluring baits, his pleasing proposals; the world and the flesh are linked with him in a league to hinder the restoration of the soul to Christ, and the restoration of God's image to the soul. A threefold cord is not easily broken. It must be a power superior to those three great powers in conjunction, that must bind the strong man; and casting him out, and spoiling his goods, are acts of power, Mat. 12:29. Satan is too strong to be easily cast out, and the flesh loves him too dearly to be easily divorced from him; he is never like to lay down his arms by persuasions; though all the angels in heaven should entreat him, he would not give up one foot of his empire. Nay, though what God doth propose hath a greater weight of goodness, pleasure, and profit in itself, than what those three great impostors can offer, yet, since reason is weak, and mightily corrupted under the conduct of sense, which hath an alliance with Satan's proposals, and first sucks them in, it is not like to meet with any entertainment, as being against the interest of the flesh; and the will being backed with two such powerful seconds, as Satan and the world, to assist it in its refusals. Indeed, if he that is in the regenerate, were not greater and more powerful than he that is in the world, they would not be able to resist his allurements and subtilties, 1 John 4:4. The triumphs of Christ at his ascension declare his power in his acquisition; with a strong hand he broke the chain of sinners, and 'led captivity captive' before he gave gifts to men, Ps. 68:18. He doth the like in giving grace to the heart; he rides upon his white horse in the power of almighty grace, when he conquers the enmity in the soul, as well as when he overcomes the enemies of his church, Rev. 6:2.

(2.) It is a power as great as that which wrought in the resurrection of Christ. It is considerable how loftily the apostle sets it out: Eph. 1:19, 20,

'And what is the exceeding greatness of his power to us-ward who believe, according to the working of his mighty power, which he wrought in Christ when he raised him from the dead, and set him at his own right hand in heavenly places.' Exceeding greatness of his power, ὑπερθάλλον, with an hyperbole, according to the working or efficaciousness of his mighty power, noting the infusion of faith in the soul by a powerful impression, 'according to the working of the might or strength.' One word was not enough to signify the great power working: it is strength with a greater edge upon it; as when a man would fetch a mighty blow, he stirs up all his strength, sets his teeth an edge to summon all his spirits to assist his arm. The power of God in creation of nature is never in the whole Scripture set forth so magnificently as his power in the creation of grace is in this place. The apostle picks not out any examples of God's power in his ordinary works, or that power in lesser miracles which exceeded the power of nature, to illustrate this power by. He doth not say, It is that power whereby we work miracles, or speak with tongues: no; neither is it that power whereby our Saviour wrought such miracles when he was in the world. It is a more illustrious power than the giving sight to the blind, speech to the dumb, hearing to the deaf, yea, or life to a putrefied carcase; this is an extraordinary power. But yet this gracious power is higher than all this, for it is as great as that which wrought the two greatest miracles that ever were acted in the creation, as great as the raising Jesus Christ perfectly dead in the grave, and having the weight of the sin of the world upon him; and as great as that power, which, after the raising of him, set him in his human nature at his right hand, above principalities and powers, above the whole angelical state; as much as to say, As great as all that power which wrought the whole scene of the redemption, from the foundation-stone to the top-stone. It is such an unconquerable power, whereby God brings about all his decrees which terminated in Christ. Some say this power is not exercised in the begetting faith, but in the faithful after faith is begun. It is very strange that a less power is necessary to beget, than to preserve a thing after it is brought into being. And the same power is requisite to raise the heart of the morallest man under heaven out of the grave of corrupted nature, as well as those that are furthest in their dispositions from God. As, had not our Saviour had the weight of the sins of men upon him, had he been dead but an hour or two, lain in the grave with a litle loose or light sand cast upon him, it would have required infinite power to have restored him to life. The apostle mentions this in other places, though not so highly as in this: Rom. 6:4, 'That like as Christ was raised up by the glory of the Father, even so we should walk in newness of life.' It must be understood thus. Even so we, being raised up by the glory of the Father, should walk in newness of life. And it may be partly the meaning of the apostle Peter, 1 Peter 1:3, 'Who hath begotten us to a lively hope by, or through, the resurrection of Jesus Christ from the dead,' not only as the foundation of our hopes, but by a power conformable to that which raised Christ from the dead. I would only by the way note, that this infers a higher operation than merely an exhortation and suasion; for would any man say of a philosopher that had taught him morality, that he had displayed in him the exceeding greatness of his power, only upon the account of advising and counselling him to reform his manners, and live more soberly and honestly in the world? Our Saviour esteemed this one thing greater than all the other miracles he wrought, and declared himself to be the Christ more by this than by any other. When John sent to know who he was, he returns no other account than the list of his miracles: 'The blind see, the lame walk, the lepers are cleansed, the deaf hear, the dead are raised, to the poor the gospel is preached,' Luke 7:20. That which brings up the rear as the greatest is, 'the poor εὐαγγελίζοιται are evangelised; 'it is not to be taken actively of the preaching of the gospel, but passively, that they were wrought upon by the gospel, and became gospelled people, transformed into the mould of it, else it would bear no analogy to the other miracles; the deaf hear, and the dead were raised; they had not exhortations to hear and live, but the effects were wrought in them; so those words import not only the preaching of the gospel to them, but the powerful operation of the gospel in them. This greatest miracle in the catalogue is the only miracle our Saviour hath left in the world since the cessation of all the rest.

I have insisted the longer upon these perfections in God apparent in this work.

1. To stir up every renewed person to a thankful frame towards God, that he should engage his choicest attributes for the good of a poor creature. To what purpose did the apostle so long and so highly speak of the power of God in raising them from a spiritual death, but that they should acknowledge it, and admire God for it? It cannot but raise high admirations and adorations of God, to consider how mercy moved for them, sovereignty called them out, wisdom modelled them, holiness cleansed them, and power framed them.

2. To stir up deep humility. It is a plain declaration of our miserable estate by nature, and the difficulty of emerging out of it, impossible for any creature to effect. Had not God been infinitely merciful, wise, holy, true, and omnipotent, and put forth his power to free men from a slavery to sin, not a man had been able to escape out of it; and these two, admiration of God, and humiliation of self, are the two great acts of a Christian, which set all other graces on work. Mercy speaks us very miserable, wisdom declares us fools, holiness unclean, and power extremely weak.

3. How mightily will it give a ground to the exercise of faith! He that is deeply sensible of this work of holiness and power in him, cannot but trust God upon his deed, as well as before he did upon his word. As you go to the promises without you, consider also the counterpart of the promise within you, and the efficacy of that power which wrought it. You have a ground of faith within you; the power extends to every one wherein this work is wrought: 'What is the exceeding greatness of his

power to us-ward who believe;' this the apostle speaks to all the believing Ephesians.

4. Therefore look much into yourselves by way of examination, to observe the actings of God's wisdom, holiness, and power within you. The want of this makes many gracious persons live disconsolately. Paul was certainly diligent in his observation, since he speaks so feelingly and experimentally of it. It is the way to answer Satan's objections, silence unbelieving thoughts, when you can trace the steps and operations of them in you; it would make you strive for an increase of this work of regeneration, that you may feel in yourselves more evidences of the holiness and power of God.

5. Those that want it may well despair of attaining it by themselves and their own strength. Divine wisdom and power are exerted in this work, and men may as well think themselves able to raise a dead man, yea, Christ from the grave, and set him at the right hand of God, as do this by their own strength. If we want an eye or a hand, all the creation cannot furnish us with either. How can any power but that which is infinite give us an eye to look to Christ within the veil, and a hand to clasp him in heaven?

6. It directs men where to seek it, and to seek it earnestly. At the hands of God, since infinite wisdom, holiness, and power, are necessary for the production of it. With earnestness, because it is so transcendent a work, hath so many perfections of God shining in it, that creature-strength and wisdom is utterly unable to frame and raise it; and with hopes too, if they earnestly seek it, since God hath hereby declared himself infinitely loving, in the combination of so many attributes for the effecting of it. Plead, therefore, the glory of God in these his attributes, and if God give you a heart to seek it, it is a probable argument he will give you that grace which he hath given you a heart to desire.

IV. Quest. How God doth this?

1. This work is secret, and therefore difficult to be described. The effects are as obvious to a spiritual sense, as the methods of it obscure to our understandings; secret as the original of winds, sensible as the sound and bluster of them, John 3:8. If a dead man were raised, he would not know the manner how his soul returned into the body, how it took its former place, and made up a new union, yet he would know that he lives and moves. A gracious soul knows that he was carnal, and now spiritual; blind, and that he now sees. He finds strength instead of weakness, inclinations to good instead of opposition, sweetness in the ways of God instead of bitterness. The methods of grace are obscure as those of nature: Eccles. 11:5, 'Who knows the way of the spirit, or how the bones grow in the womb of her that is with child? even so thou knowest not the works of God who makes all.' The manner of the formation of Christ in the soul is as undiscernible as the formation of a child, or the manner of Christ's conception in the womb of the virgin, both which are fearful and wonderful; as it is said of the first, Ps. 139:14; 'Who can declare his generation?' Isa. 53:8; that is, the generation of Christ, either in his person or in his people. We cannot give a satisfactory account of the natural motions of our souls, how one faculty commands another, how the soul governs the several parts of the body, what the nature of the action of our mind is in contemplation and reflection, how our wills move the spirits in the body, whereby the members are acted in their motion, and the functions of life performed. Much more undiscernible are the supernatural methods of the Spirit of God. We know ourselves heirs to the corruption of the first Adam by the inbeing of it, the light of the grace of the second Adam discovers itself in the soul, but the manner of the descent of either is not easily to be determined. The loadstone's attracting of iron is the best representation of this work; the soul, like that, moves sensibly, cleaves strongly to God; but wherein this virtue consists, how communicated, both in that of nature and this of spirit, dazzles the eye of reason.

2. Yet this is evident, that it is rational; that is, congruous to the essential nature of man. God doth not deal with us as beasts, or as creatures destitute of sense, but as creatures of an intelligent order.* Who is there that believes in Christ in such a manner as heavy things fall to the earth, or light things fly up to the air, or as beasts run at the beck of their sensual appetite, without rule or reason? If the Spirit of God wrought so upon man, this were to lay our faculties asleep, not to act them, but to act only upon them; this were to invert the natural order by creation, to raze out the foundations of virtue, and deny the creature the pleasure of his condition, who, according to such a manner of operation, could not understand his own state, no more than a brute can the harmony of music, or the pleasing variety of colours. But grace perfects our souls, possesseth them with new principles, moves one faculty by another, like the motions of the wheels in a clock or watch; like the common course of providence, wherein he orders all affairs according to the dependence of them one upon another by creation, without making any inroad upon the natural rights of any creature, but preserving them entire, unless in some miraculous action. He diffuseth a supernatural virtue into the soul, not to thwart it in that course of working he appointed it in the creation, but to move it agreeably to its nature as a rational being. As the sun conveys a celestial virtue upon the plants, drawing them forth by its influence according to their several natures, so the Holy Ghost introduceth a supernatural principle into men, whereby they act as reasonable creatures in a higher strain. What methods our Saviour used in the first declaration of the gospel, he uses in the propagation of it in the hearts of men. The same reason that is used in writing the indenture is used in writing the counterpart. He might, by his omniscient wisdom, have found the way to the secretest corner of every man's heart, and by his power have set up what standard he pleased in every part of the castle, without proposing the gospel in the way of miracles and arguments; but he transacts all that affair in such a manner, that men might be moved in

a rational way to their own happiness. He required a rational belief, as he gave rational evidences: John 10:37, 'If I do not the works of my Father, believe me not;' that is, the works that none but one empowered by God could do. God, that requires of us a reasonable service, would work upon us by a reasonable operation. God therefore works by way of a spiritual illumination of the understanding, in propounding the creature's happiness by arguments and reasons, and in a way of a spiritual impression upon the will, moving it sweetly to the embracing that happiness, and the means to it which he doth propose; and indeed without this work preceding, the motion of the will could never be regular.

God doth this by a double work.

1. Upon the understanding.

2. Upon the will.

1. Upon the understanding. The opening the eyes precedes the conversion from darkness to light, in God's operation as well as in the apostles' commission, Acts 26:18. The first appearance of life, when God raiseth the soul, is in the clearness and distinctness of its knowledge of God, Hos. 6:2, 3. And the apostle, in his exhortation to the Romans, tells them the way for the transformation of their souls was by the renewing of their minds: 'Be ye transformed by the renewing of your minds,' Rom. 12:2. The light of the sun is seen breaking out at the dawning at the day, before the heat of the sun be felt. As the action of our sense is to sensible objects, so is that of our soul to spiritual. Our eye first sees an object before our hearts desire it, or our members move to it; so there is an apprehension of the goodness of the thing proposed, before there be any motion of our wills to it; so God begins his work in our minds, and terminates it in our wills. In regard of this, as a state of nature is set forth under the term of darkness, so a state of grace is often termed light, that being the first work in the new creation, as it was the first word of command in the old, 'Let there be light,' 2 Cor. 4:6, Col. 3:10, and is therefore called a renewing 'in knowledge,'

or unto knowledge or acknowledgment, ἀνακαινούμενον εἰς ἐπιγνωσιν. If you consider the Scripture, you will find most of the terms whereby this is set forth to us have relation to the understanding. The gospel itself is called knowledge, Luke 1:77, wisdom, 1 Cor. 1:30. What faculty in man is appointed for the apprehending of a science to gain wisdom, but the understanding? That whereby we receive the gospel is called 'the spirit of the mind,' 'the eyes of the understanding' and 'sight,' which is put before believing: John 6:40, 'Every one which sees the Son, and believes on him.' The work of grace is called 'revelation,' Gal. 1:16, 'illumination,' Eph. 1:18, 'translation from darkness to light,' 'opening the heart.' The action of our minds being enlightened, is called 'comprehending, Eph. 3:18, and 'knowledge,' 2 Peter 1:2. All respect the understanding as the original wheel which God primarily sets in order,* from whence he doth influence secondarily all the other faculties which depend upon its guidance, God preserving hereby the order which he instituted in nature. Therefore, when the understanding savingly apprehends the deformity of sin, the will must needs hate it; when it apprehends the mercy of God, and the beauty of holiness, the will must needs love him; and the higher the degrees of this saving illumination are in the mind, the stronger and firmer are the habits and acts of grace in the will. This illuminative act of the Spirit is before, prior natura, the other of inclining the will, for the understanding is first exercised about the word, as verum, true, before the will is concerned in it as good. The understanding takes in the light of the gospel, which, by the working of the Spirit, is reflected upon the will, whereby it is changed into the image of Christ, whose gospel it is: 2 Cor. 3:18, 'Beholding as in a glass the glory of the Lord, we are changed into the same image.' The first act is of the mind, which is the eye of the soul; where the apostle intimates, that the whole progress, as well as the first change, is wrought in this manner.

This is wrought,

1. By removing the indisposition and prejudices which naturally are in the mind. As a wise physician which orders his medicines for the removing of the principal humour. Chains of darkness must be broken, films upon the eye must be removed, which hinder the act of vision; for what the eye is to the body, that the understanding is to the soul. The darkness of ignorance is promised in the covenant to be scattered: 'They shall all know me, from the least to the greatest of them,' Jer. 31:34. This being a law in the inward parte, the eye must be cleared to read it, as well as the heart cleansed to obey it. The object being spiritual, requires a spiritual disposition in the faculty for the reception of it. This is called in Scripture a giving eyes to see, and ears to hear, Deut. 29:4, and the revealing things not only by the word, but by the Spirit, 1 Cor. 2:10, which, in regard of rectifying the reasons and judgments of men, is called a 'spirit of judgment,' Isa. 4:4, 'and shall have purged the blood of Jerusalem from the midst thereof, by the spirit of judgment, and the spirit of burning:' a spirit of judgment, as it is light in the understanding, removing the darkness; a spirit of burning, as it is heat in the heart, thawing the hardness. It reduceth the mind into a right order, and teacheth it to judge between truth and falsehood, between good and evil, the want of which is the cause of sin; whence sins are called ἀγνοήματα, Heb. 9:7, errors, as arising from error in judgment. Since the mind is filled with fogs, and incapable to perceive the splendour of divine truths, God acts upon the mind by an inward virtue, causing the word proposed to be mixed with an act of faith, which he begets in the soul, whereby it apprehends the excellency of that state presented to it in the gospel. As there is a manifestation of his name in the word, so there is an operation of his grace, an internal teaching by God, as well as an external by the gospel; the proposal of the word by man, the opening and fitting the heart by God: John 6:45, 'Every man that hath heard, and hath learned of the Father, comes unto me.' Christ taught all by his ministry, the Father only some by his Spirit. Learning of God goes before coming to Christ,

and those two acts are plainly distinguished: Isa. 6:9, 10, 'Hear and not understand.' The lock of their minds was to be opened, as well as that of their ears; the prophet's voice could unlock the one, the Spirit only had the key of the other. Men may enlighten as moral causes, God only as the efficient cause, to root out the inward indisposition. The Spirit also removes the prejudices against Christ as undesirable, against holiness as troublesome; takes down the strength of corrupt reasonings, pulls down those idols in the mind and false notions of happiness, out-reasons men out of their inward thoughts of a happiness in sensual pleasures, pride of life, mammon of honour or wealth, which are the root of our spiritual disease, and first to be cured. In this there is a manifest difference between the working of Satan and the operation of God; he sets his battery against the affections, because the entry is there easiest; God breaks in upon the understanding, which, being the chief fort, will quickly be a means to reduce the lesser citadels. And when the work begins in removing the blindness, it is the way to a true conversion; when it begins only in the affections, it is a prognostic of a quick starting aside. In an outward exhortation, God acts suitably to our nature, since we are endued with understanding and will; but in acting upon us within, he doth remedy the vice of our nature, since our reason and will are corrupted.

(2.) It is wrought by bringing the mind and the object close together. Sight is produced in a blind man by drawing off the scales from his eyes, and the recourse of spirits to the eye necessary for sight; besides this, there must be outward light, and objects coloured by that light; and from the eye so disposed within, and the thing discovered without, ariseth the action of sight.* So from the preparation of the understanding, and the application of the object, ariseth this action of spiritual vision. There is a double opening, one of the gospel, the other of the understanding; our Saviour did both, he 'opened the Scriptures,' Luke 24:32, and 'opened their understandings,' ver. 45, that there might be a mutual entrance, that the word might dwell in their hearts, and their hearts have admission into the word. The Spirit shews the great things of the gospel to the soul: John 16:14, ἀναγγελεῖ, 'He shall receive of mine, and shew it unto you,' not in general, but bring them near to them, to make them view 'and know the things that are freely given to them of God,' 1 Cor. 2:12, the benefits of the death and resurrection of Christ. He repeats them again and again, that there may be an evidence in the mind that they are the royal gifts of God. There is a knowledge, before this work of the Spirit, but as of things at a distance. Many know the things proposed in the gospel, but they know it not as a glorious gospel, nor see the wonders in this law, till the Spirit brings that and the faculty close together. As a man may discern a statue or picture at a distance, but till the eye and the objects meet close together, it cannot discern the beautiful work-manship upon them with any affection to them. Not that a man knew nothing, or knows new reasons of those things which he knew before; but there is a nearer, and therefore clearer, representation of them, which is demonstratio ostensiva, whereby he knows them in another manner than he did before. As a man may know the promises before, but they were not brought so near to him as to taste them; taste being an addition to knowledge, whereby a man knows that sensibly which before he only knew notionally. It is one thing to know a mechanical instrument, and another to know it in the operation of it, when it is applied to its proper use. It is like a man that hath his understanding more cleared by seeing mathematical demonstrations, and lines drawn, than by all the rules of art in his head.

(3.) By fixing the mind upon the subject so closely presented. The Spirit settles that light and the object so in the mind, that it can no more blow it out than puff out the sparklings of a diamond, or than an artist endued with the habit of some art can divest himself of his skill. Many men have some convictions of truth, but flashy and uncertain, and which slip from their minds. But when the Spirit opens the heart, it holds the object to the mind, and the mind to the object; starts one holy thought after another about the truth it hath darted in, makes the mind peer about it, and take notice of every lineament of that truth that we eye, and those thoughts lie down, rise up, and walk with us. When Lydia's heart was opened, she 'attended to the things spoken by Paul,' Acts 16:14, her whole heart cleaved to them. In this respect the Spirit is a remembrancer, making the soul ponder and beat over again with all intenseness of mind the goodness and truth of those things in the gospel which are brought unto it, that the heart is, as Paul was, 'bound in spirit to Jerusalem,' Acts 20:22. The thoughts of that journey did so haunt him and follow him, as the shadow doth the body, that no arguments of friends, nor fear of danger, could divert him; the soul is bound by them, one consideration overtaking another, and all at work beating upon the mind. Hence consideration is put before conversion: Ezek. 18:28, 'Because he considers and turns away from all his transgressions.' And it is called the 'ingrafted word,' fastened to the soul as a graft to the stock; when the heart is opened by the Spirit, the word is inserted in and bound to it, and at last the heart becomes one with the word, and grows up with it.

(4.) By bringing the soul to an actual reasoning and discourse upon the sight of the evidence. God convinceth the judgment with reasons proper to evidence the truth and goodness of what he doth propose, and that with pregnant and prevailing demonstrations, which give a competent satisfaction; therefore called the 'demonstration of the Spirit and power,' 1 Cor. 2:4, that is, a spiritual and powerful demonstration. When the eye is opened, and the revelation made, and held close and fast to the soul with a divine demonstration, that this is the only means to elevate him to a high condition, and at last bring him to a blessed immortality, the understanding is moved to compare the force of those arguments, and consequently judgeth that true which before it counted false and foolishness, and comes by the help of this spiritual light to reason spiritually, and spiritually to discern the proposition made to it.

It compares its natural state with the happy state offered to it, its own ignorance with that light, its own misery with that mercy. God will not have man, that is so far above a beast, do anything without reason; for this would be to do it brutishly, though the thing done were never so good, When men act as men, they follow the judgment of the best reason they can. And shall man, that was created a rational creature, be renewed without reason, when the very work is to advance him to the true state of a reasonable creature, and his reason is enlightened by the Spirit, that it may rightly judge of the demonstrative arguments it offers to him? Is there not as much reason for the guidance of the will in the highest concern, as for the conduct of it in affairs of a lower sphere? Man was first enducd with reason, that he might rationally serve God; and his depraved reason is reformed, that he may rationally return to God. If, therefore, he act like a man in other things, he doth not surely act like a brute in this; but the Spirit excites that reason he hath enlightened to judge of those excellent things he doth propose, and the strength of the arguments he backs them with, which are so clear and undeniable that they cannot be refused by a mind divested of those indispositions which drew out before a contempt of them. The change in the will being an election and choice, cannot be made without convincing and satisfying reasons which induce it to that choice, and justify the election it hath made. That can hardly be called faith, when a man believes that which he doth not think upon the highest reason was his duty to believe.* And indeed what man is there that cannot allege some reason why he is induced to this or that act? God moves men by presenting things to the understanding under the notion of good, honest, profitable; and when the understanding is enlightened to judge of things in some measure under the same notion that God proposeth them, a man's own reason cannot but upon a view of them assent unto them, and that assent is followed with a change, according to the degrees of that illumination, if it be a saving one. Upon this account that our own reason is excited to judge of the proposal, our faith can no more be said to be a human faith, or the work to proceed from our own power, than it can be said to be sensitive because it comes by hearing; for though faith depends upon hearing and reasoning, as upon natural powers, yet the light whereby the faculties are acted is wholly supernatural, and from the Spirit of God.

(5.) Hence follows a full conviction of the soul. Both the knowledge of its own misery, and the amiableness of the gospel offer, whence issues a weariness under the one and desires for the other. By this enlightening, the soul sees sin in its empire, God in his wrath, Satan in his tyranny, and the hardness of the stone within him; he sees the law accusing, sin triumphing, heaven shut and hell open, God ready to judge him, and his soul every way deplorable. He sees also in the gospel how Christ hath expiated sin, answered the demands of the law, stills the clamours of conscience, satisfied the justice of God by bearing his wrath; hereupon the soul closes with Christ, and is born again. Here are heaps of sin that cannot be numbered, on the other side are riches of mercy that cannot be reckoned; there is sin to damn, here is a Christ to save; heaven and hell, sin and Christ, damnation and salvation, are presented in their proper colours, and pressed upon the understanding, which beholds all by a clear light. And thus, by the illuminative virtue of the Spirit, the soul is laid at God's foot in a sense of its misery, and then drawn into Christ's arms by a sense of his grace. This is wrought by a convictive persuasion, for so the word ἐλέγχειν signifies, John 16:8, which causes both a sight of sin and a sense of righteousness, and produceth a full assent in the understanding.

2. The next faculty wrought upon is the will. The will is inclined, as well as the understanding enlightened, whereby spiritual things are approved with a spiritual affection; the same hand that darts light into the mind, puts heat into the will. After the act of understanding hath preceded in a serious consideration, and thorough conviction, the act of the will, by virtue of the same Spirit, follows in a delightful motion to the

object proposed to it; it is conducted by light, and spirited by love; the understanding hands the object to the will, as necessary to be embraced, and the arms of the will are opened to receive it, as the eyes of the mind are to behold it.

For the understanding of this, take these propositions.

Prop. 1. There seems to me to be an immediate supernatural work upon the will, as well as upon the understanding: not that the understanding is only enlightened, and the will follows the dictate of that without any further touch of the Spirit upon it; but the will, as it is the will, and therefore cannot be forced, there is need of a moral cause which may determine it according to its nature, and draw it by the cords of a man. When a master instructs a youth in his trade, he doth it by arguments morally; when he holds his hand with the instrument in it, and directs the motion, he acts physically; so doth the Spirit exhort us to spiritual motion, telling us inwardly which is the way, that we may walk in it, and take our wills by the hand, as it were, and lead them in the way they are to go. A nurse's tongue and exhortation is not enough to make a child to go, because of the weakness of its limbs; nor the light in the understanding sufficient to move the will, wherein there is an habitual weakness and contradiction. How did God work up the wills of the Egyptians to lend their jewels to the Israelites, but by some immediate touch.* Their reason might have furnished them with many more arguments against it than it could for it. They knew the Israelites had been highly injured, and that very lately, too; that they could not but have a deep sense of their oppression, and intentions of revenge, as far as their power extended. They knew that the Israelites prepared for flight, and might more than conjecture that they intended never to return or send their jewels to them; for what need had they of so many goods barely to sacrifice in the wilderness? How were their wills thus bended against so many arguments against this action, and without any strong reasons to move them to consent to such a desire of the Israelites? How must this be but by the efficacious power of God, not forcing their wills, but taming their fierceness, softening them by a secret instinct, and exciting them to a grant of the Israelites' request? The apostle saith, God 'gives to will.' If there were not a particular act upon the will, it had better been said, God gives to understand and know, and man to will and do. After the evidence set up in the understanding, there is a secret touch upon the will, opening and enlarging it to run the way that is proposed in an excellent and charming manner. As the power of God raiseth every part of Christ, so the same power raiseth every faculty of the soul; it was also a physical power, since mere exhortation would never have effected it.

(1.) The Scripture intimates this in the terms whereby it signifies this work to us, as creation, resurrection, regeneration, new birth, all which denote some physical operation distinct in each faculty in the new creation, as there was in the first; not only the law in the mind to direct, but the heart of flesh to comply, is God's act. The fleshy heart is wrought by him, as well as the knowledge of the mind lighted by him. In generation something is removed, another thing introduced; in regeneration then of the will, there is consonant to that an eradication of corrupt habits, and an implantation of gracious ones. It is called a 'giving a heart,' a 'circumcision of the heart to love God,' Deut. 30:6. Love is an act of the will, though it supposeth a knowledge of the amiable object in the understanding. If faith be principally in the will, as I think it is, as to consent; and the words leaning, resting, coming rather note an act of the will than an act of the understanding; there is then an operation of God upon the subject, viz. the will, in the implanting of it.

(2.) The will is corrupted as well as the understanding. The works of the flesh issue from both; if the corruption were only in the understanding, then that being removed, the will would be regenerated. As in a watch, if the fault be only in one wheel, that being mended, the whole frame is rectified; but if there be a flaw in all, the mending of one, though the principal one, which moves the rest, will not set every wheel right, without a particular application of art to restore them to their due frame. Was not original righteousness subjectively in the will as well as in the mind? Did not a stoutness in the will succeed in the place of that righteousness, as well as darkness in the place of light? Must not there then be a habit of mollifying grace bestowed upon the one as well as a habit of enlightening truth set up in the other; an inclination to good in the will, and an aversion from evil, as well as the knowledge of both? The corrupt proneness in the will is the cause that it is easily excited to evil by the persuasion of the devil and the world; and is there not need of an inward rectitude in the will to bias it to a free embracing and close adherency to the good proposed to it by God, that his grace may be efficacious in every part? This work is a quickening a man under a universal spiritual death; the will was dead, as well as the mind dark, which must have life instead of its deadness, as the other hath light instead of its darkness; and if they be two distinct faculties, then there are two distinct acts of the Spirit, though they depend one upon another. There is no less power requisite to make us spiritually willing than to make us spiritually knowing, since the corrupt habits in our wills are rather stronger than the prejudices in our understandings; therefore there seems to be a distinct act in removing the resistance from the one as well as expelling the darkness from the other. As the Spirit takes away the wisdom that was sensual, earthly, and devilish, so it divests the will of that disposition whereby it was enamoured on that devilish wisdom of the flesh, and makes it willing to cut off the right hand and right eye, to deny sin, which is the very self, and engage in an irreconcilable quarrel against all that which engrossed its choicest affections.

(3.) If the understanding hath such a power, by virtue of its illumination, without an act also of the Spirit upon the will, and a particular application of the understanding to the will, and the will to the understanding, why did not Adam's will follow his understanding? His understanding was clear, without darkness; his affections first made the rebellion; sense was the leader, and the will the follower. Eve's under-standing was not silent under the temptation of Satan; her knowledge was actuated in that speech, 'God hath said, You shall not eat of it, neither shall you touch it, lest you die,' Gen. 3:3. She cites the word, her understanding must needs concur with it, unless it were corrupted and darkened before the fall. Where lay the resistance? In the affections, and the will which sided with them. Why may not the will, possessed with those evil habits, resist the understanding imperfectly restored to its primitive light, as well as Adam's will did where there was no scale or film upon the eye of his soul? And likely his affections had kept their due order, if the will had preserved its due dependence upon reason, and its sovereignty over the sensitive part. Do we not find that our wills are oftener in contradiction to the true sentiments of our understanding, and in conjunction with the affections, than in a due subordination to the one and commanding over the other? Is it not frequently seen that men of much light, knowledge, and gifts of reason, answer not the end of that illumination, and are without a will to turn to God? Besides, since corruption came in by the way of the affections, when the understanding was clear, how can regeneration of the will come in by the illumination of the understanding, without a particular operation upon the will and affections? If it be said, the will follows the dictate of the understanding, why did it not so in Adam? If we were perfectly restored, as Adam was in innocency, without the grace of God in our wills, as well as light in our understandings, we were not like to keep up in due order.

(4.) God in his other creatures gives not only a light and fancy in nature, but endues them with such principles that incline them to their motion, as connatural to them. Why, then, shall we not think, since the will is an habitual power, that when the will is moved to supernatural ends, it is endued with such a supernatural habit, whereby it may be sweetly and readily moved to the chief good as its proper object?* Are there not corrupt habits in the will, which the Scripture calls 'lusts,' and 'the works of the flesh,' Gal. 5:19–21, which the Spirit mortifies as well as those of the mind? Why not, then, gracious habits set up in the room of the other in this faculty as well as in the other?

(5.) If there were not a physical operation and habits in the will, what would become of infants, who cannot in that state be renewed without such a kind of working? They are not capable of moral-exhortation, we cannot conceive any other way the Spirit hath to work upon them, but by such a physical operation, putting habits into their wills, whereby they are renewed and sanctified; they are capable of the habit, though not of the act. We never find our Saviour spending any exhortations upon infants, but he took them in his arms and blessed them, and told us that of such is the kingdom of heaven; and if the kingdom of heaven be of such, there is some operation upon them different from this method of working only upon their understanding.

(6.) If there were not some operation of the Spirit upon our wills, regeneration and conversion would be more our work than God's. If the Spirit terminates his working only upon the understanding, and the will be moved by the understanding alone, without any conjunction of the Spirit in the work upon the will, then the Spirit doth not immediately concur to the chiefest part of regeneration, but as it illuminates the mind; for the chief part of renewing grace is in the will; so it would be more our work than God's, if the moral only were his, and the physical operation only ours. It was in a less affair than this, wherein David blessed God for the people's willingness, offering so freely, acknowledging it indeed the people's act, but by God's overruling their wills, 1 Chron. 29:13, 14.

(7.) God is all in all in glory: 1 Cor. 15:28, 'When Christ shall have delivered the kingdom to his Father, God then shall be all in all;' all in their understandings, all in their wills; he shall be the immediate cause of all things, and govern and dispose all things by himself, and for himself; binding the souls of all the glorified by everlasting ligatures to himself; all in all to the glorified, all light in their understanding, all love and delight in their will, objectively, efficiently. What efficacy he hath in glory, shall we deny him in grace in every particular faculty?

Prop. 2. Yet this work, though immediate, is not compulsive and by force. It is a contradiction for the will to be moved unwillingly; any force upon it destroys the nature of it; if it be forced, it ceaseth to be will. It is not forced, because it is according to reason, and the natural motion of the creature; the understanding proposing, and the will moved to an embracing; the understanding going before with light, the will following after with love. The liberty of the will consists in following the guidance of reason; to have a liberty to go against it, is the greatest misery of the creature. That is properly constraint, when we are compelled to work contrary to the natural way of working; there is no constraint by force, but there is a kind of a constraint by love, because the Spirit accompanies this operation with so much efficacy, that instead of that sadness we should have in a thing we were forced unto, there is an unspeakable joy and contentment in the soul; it not being possible to taste so much of the love of God, to be delivered from so fearful a condemnation, to be brought to so glorious a hope, without being seized upon with much pleasure and delight. God changeth the inclination of the will, but doth not force it against its inclination; the will, being a rational faculty, cannot be wrought upon but rationally. Since the main work consists in faith and love, it is impossible there can be any force; no man can be forced to believe against his reason, or love against his will, or desire against his inclination. Belief is wrought by persuasion; no man can be persuaded by force. It cannot be conceived, that the will should will against the will. No man can be happy against his will, all happiness consisting in a suitableness of the object to the faculty; those things that in themselves are the greatest pleasures of the world, if they please not a man, cannot confer any happiness upon him. The Spirit never works thus, because 'where the Spirit of the Lord is, there is liberty,' 2 Cor. 3:17; he destroys not the liberty, but reduceth it to will more nobly than before. Besides, the liberty of the will doth not stand in indifference to this or that thing, for then the will would lose its liberty every time it hath determined itself to any one thing, because after the determination it would be no longer indifferent to the other. But the liberty of the will consists in being carried out according to the dictate of the practical judgment, and not by a blind instinct. God doth not deal with us as stones and logs, or slaves, whom the whip makes to do that which they hate in their hearts; but conducts us in ways agreeable to our nature; he calls, saying, 'Seek you my face;' and inclines the will to answer, 'Thy face, Lord, I will seek,' Ps. 27:8. That God who knows how to make a will with a principle of freedom, knows how to work upon the will, without entrenching upon, or altering the essential privilege he bestowed upon it; he that formed us, as a potter doth his vessel, knows very well the handles whereby he may take hold of us, without making any breach in our nature.

Prop. 3. It is free and gentle. A constraint, not by force, but love, which is not an extrinsic force, but intrinsic and pleasant to the will; he bends the creature so, that at the very instant wherein the will is savingly wrought upon, it delightfully consents to its own happiness; he draws by the cords of a man, and by a secret touch upon the will makes it willing to be drawn, and moves it upon its own hinges. It is sweet and alluring; the Spirit of grace is called 'the oil of gladness;' it is a delightful and ready motion which it causes in the will; it is a sweet efficacy, and an efficacious sweetness. At what time God doth savingly work upon the will, to draw the soul from sin and the world to himself, it doth with the greatest willingness, freedom, and delight follow after God, turn to him, close with him, and cleave to him, with all the heart, and with purpose never to depart from him: Cant. 1:4, 'Draw me, and we will run after thee.' Drawing signifies the efficacious power of grace; running signifies the delightful motion of grace; the will is drawn, as if it would not come; it comes, as if it were not drawn. His grace is so sweet and so strong, that he neither wrongs the liberty of his creature, nor doth prejudice his absolute power. As God moves necessary causes, necessarily; contingent causes, contingently; so he moves free agents freely, without offering violence to their natures. The Spirit glides into the heart by the sweet illapses of grace, and victoriously allures the soul: Hosea 2:14, 'I will allure her, and speak to her heart;' not by crossing, but changing the inclination, by the all-conquering and alluring charms of love, as a man doth that person whom he intends for his spouse; for to that he alludes, because in the latter part of the chapter, he speaks of the consummation of his marriage with the church: ver. 16, 'In that day thou shalt call me Ishi.' In what day? In the day that he should allure her, and speak to her heart. God puts on the deportment of a lover in changing the frame of the will. The Spirit is as one that leads the way into truth (the Spirit 'shall guide you, ὁδηγήσει, into all truth,' John 16:13); not drags; he opens the heart, not by a forcible entry, but as a key that fits every ward in the lock. The attraction of the will is much like that of iron by the loadstone, which had no motion of itself till the powerful emissions of the loadstone's virtue reached it, and then it seems to move with a kind of voluntariness; there is no force used, but a delicious virtue emitted, which doth, as it were, both persuade and enable it to join itself to its beloved attracter. There is a secret virtue communicated by God, which, as soon as it toucheth the soul, puts life and delightful motion into it, which before lay like a log. It embraceth Christ as its portion, and passes a decree, that it will keep his words: Ps. 119:57, 'Thou art my portion, O Lord: I have said that I will keep thy words.'

Prop. 4. It is insuperably victorious. What the mouth of God speaks, what his will purposeth, his hand doth fulfil, 1 Kings 8:24. It is not a faint and languishing impression, but a reviving, sprightly, and victorious touch. As the demonstration of the Spirit is clear and undeniable, so the power of the Spirit is sweet and irresistible; both are joined, 1 Cor. 2:4. An inexpressible sweetness allures the soul, and an unconquerable power draws the soul; there are clear demonstrations, charming persuasions, and invincible efficacy combined together in the work. He leaves not the will in indifference.* If God were the author of faith only by putting the will into an indifference, though it be determined by its own proper liberty, why may not he also be said to be the author of unbelief, if by the same liberty of this indifference it be determined to reject the gospel? For in the same manner God is author of one motion of the will as well as of the other, if he doth no more than leave the will in an œquilibrium. This irresistibleness takes not away the liberty of the will. Our Saviour's obedience was free and voluntary, yet necessary and irresistible. He could not sin in regard of the hypostatical union, yet he had a greater aversion to sin than all the angels in heaven. Is not God freely and voluntarily good, yet necessarily so? He cannot be otherwise than good, he will not be otherwise than good. So the will is irresistibly drawn, and yet doth freely come to its own happiness. The soul is brought over to God, and adheres to him, not by a necessity of compulsion, but of immutability. As the angels necessarily obey God, not by compulsion, but from an immutable love. A sinner is necessarily a servant to sin, a regenerate man necessarily a servant to God; both by a kind of necessity of nature. Our main business, then, is to see what new enlightenings there are in our minds by the Spirit in the gospel, what tastes and relishes we have of divine truths, how our wills are allured to a sincere and close compliance with the proposals of God in the gospel, what vigour is in them. This is God's method, to work first upon the understanding, then upon the will. That work which begins first in the affections, without light dawning and breaking in upon the mind, and growing up by consideration and inquiries into the gospel is to be suspected, and is not like to be durable.

This is the Scripture method, and every regenerate person may find it more or less in himself.

V. The use is,

1. For instruction.

(1.) If God alone be the author and efficient of the new birth, then it doth instruct us how insufficient a good education of itself is to produce this work in the soul, and how unfit to be rested on, without a further work. I doubt many may rest upon a religious education, without searching and inquiring into themselves what further work of God hath been wrought upon them. God hath entrusted parents with a power of instructing their children, but reserves the power of renewing grace to himself. If parents may set the object before them, God only can give them a spiritual eye to discern it; if they may inform the understanding, a divine touch only can bend the will; if they may lay the wood of spiritual lessons together, yet the fire to kindle them in the heart, and consume the lusts, must descend from heaven. Education may correct, but not extirpate the malignity of nature; good instruction, meeting with an orderly constitution, may sow the seeds of moral virtue, and restrain natural corruption, but not weed that out of our nature, or plant the root of grace, any more than the skilful management of a beast can change its natural inclination, though it may curb it. The folly bound up in the heart of a child is too strong for the wisdom of man, and is wholly to be expelled by the wisdom which comes down from heaven, set up in the heart by Christ, who is the wisdom of the Father. The little stars of precepts glittering in the mind, cannot make the young plants sprout up with their heads towards heaven, without the influence of the sun. Christ, the Sun of righteousness, fixed in the soul by the Spirit, can do more than all the stars of moral instructions in the world. Timothy had as religious instruction from his religious mother and grandmother as any in the world, both being believers, 2 Tim. 1:5; yet Paul calls him his 'own son in the faith,' 1 Tim. 1:2, as having 'begotten him in the gospel.' Those instructions did not beget him, though they might facilitate the evangelical work which was wrought by the gospel in Paul's ministry. Therefore the apostle manifestly distinguisheth between instructors and fathers: 1 Cor. 4:15, 'Though you have ten thousand instructors in Christ, yet have you not many fathers: for in Christ Jesus I have begotten you through the gospel.' He distinguisheth their instructions from Christ, the efficient cause, and himself through the gospel, the instrumental cause. Yet such instruction is not to be neglected when children are capable; God may set home that by the gospel, which hath been sucked in in younger years. Men may as well turn their backs upon the hearing the word, because it is insufficient without the operation of the almighty grace. Instruction and prayer should go hand in hand together; but take heed of resting upon a good education.

(2.) It instructs us that regeneration doth not depend merely upon the word, if God alone be the efficient cause of it. It depends upon the inward efficacy of the Spirit. Had it depended upon the power of the apostles, or the outward demonstration of the word, they would have converted all that they had preached to, they would not have suffered any to have remained obstinate against the gospel; charity would have obliged them to the exercise of their power; and their power would have made their charity effectual. As God doth seldom work without means, so means can never work without God. David had the law of God in his hand, but could not learn it without God's teaching; therefore he prays, Ps. 86:11, 'Teach me thy way, O Lord: I will walk in thy truth.' And in many places of the 119th Psalm he takes notice, that all spiritual knowledge comes from God, though in the way of his precepts: ver. 98, 'Thou through thy commandments hast made me wiser than mine enemies'; and ver. 104, 'Through thy precepts I get understanding.' While we use the means, our eye should be upon God. Thomas had his fingers upon our Saviour's wounds, but his thoughts upon Christ's divinity: 'My Lord, and my God.' Food maintains the body, but by virtue of the soul animating it, and enabling it to concoct that food. The Spirit of God is the soul of the gospel, and of all means, to make them efficacious; and with this power of the Spirit the weakest means can effect more than the greatest means without it, which, indeed, can produce little or nothing.

Peter's sermon, Acts 2, was but short, but improved by the Spirit to the conversion of three thousand souls. Means can do nothing of themselves to change the heart. When the disciples had two ordinances representing the death of Christ, i.e. the passover and the Lord's supper, pride, the great enemy to regeneration, put up its head above water; they quarrelled 'who should be greatest,' Luke 22:24.

(3.) There is no reason to confide in our own purposes and resolutions, or any strength of our own, if God alone be the efficient cause of regeneration; for it depends not upon our resolves without the grace of God. Satan fears not our vows; he knows, without grace they are but as light feathers, easily to be puffed away by him; but sparks, which, without his breath, the flood of corruption in our souls would extinguish as soon as they begin to appear. How can our resolves without grace renew us, when Peter's resolve, with his inherent grace, could not defend him? who, after his boasting, when certainly he sincerely meant what he said, fell so shamefully, that he stood in need of a new conversion. How soon do we, after a transient awakening, fall to nodding in our spiritual sleep? If grace be not present with us to cure our lethargy, our purposes are as empty sails hoisted by us; the breath of the Spirit only fills with a full gale for motion. We can never 'stedfastly look into heaven, and see the glory of God,' unless we be 'full of the Holy Ghost,' Acts 7:55. Stephen's eye would have been twinkling, had not the divine Spirit fixed it. How soon will a slight blast of a temptation shake a building; which hath no other foundation but the moveable sand of our own purposes, when as slight a temptation shook the image of God out of Adam with all its brightness, who was built with God's own hand, with a power also to keep himself! Adam could not be without purposes of obedience when he heard the precept, yet with a slender temptation came tumbling to the dust, and fell as low as hell. A vain confidence in our own resolutions is so far from being a cause of this spiritual birth, that it is rather a hindrance, and part of the pride of nature, that must be demolished, and to be reckoned as one of the eldest things among these old things that are to pass away. Trust not, therefore, to yourselves; look up daily for the divine influence; lean not to your own understanding, though in part enlightened; confide not in your own wills, though in part inclined to the best things; pursue nothing in your own strength.

(4.) It is an injury to God to associate any thing with him in this work, which he challengeth as his own production. Would it not be a disparagement to deny him the sole efficiency in one of the noblest works of his wisdom and holiness? That he who wrought the comely fabric of the first creation by his power and wisdom, without a co-partner, or deputing any of the highest angels to bring the world into form, should not have the honour of a work which bears the stamp of a higher wisdom and power than the whole creation! That he who contrived the models of the little creatures in the world, should leave this to the foolish contrivance of any creature! Why should we imagine that the divine image, upon whom the highest blessedness of the creature depends, should be of so little value in the judgment of God's infinite wisdom, as to be turned over from the care of so wise a workman, to the capriciousness of a light and uncertain will, more blind and mutable than Fortune the heathen goddess? It is more (we have heard) to frame so excellent a piece as the new creature is, out of the rubbish of sin, than to frame the whole celestial and elementary world out of a rude mass of matter; since there is a greater gulf to be shot between corruption and grace than between nothing and the beautiful structure of heaven and earth; and, therefore, we may less disparage him, in denying him the title of creator of the world, than that of the creator of a new heart, since he hath promised by his own mouth to do it with his own hand. The apostle cannot be charged with ignorance, but knew what he said in that comprehensive thanksgiving for 'all spiritual blessings in Christ;' if all, then one of the highest, the new creation, is not intended to be left out of the roll of spiritual blessings, associating none with God, as the principal, but Christ as the Mediator, conveying this grace by his Spirit, according to the orders of the Father: 'Blessed be the God and Father of our Lord Jesus Christ, who hath blessed us with all spiritual blessings in heavenly places in Christ,' Eph. 1:3.

(5.) See from hence how excellent a thing it is to be born again, if God be the sole efficient of it! Whatsoever God is the author of in his ordinary works, is excellent in its kind; they are all the effects of his will; this is an effect of his gracious will. Other generations are by the will of man, wherein the will of God concurs with them; this is solely by the will of God, without any concurrence of the will of man in the first work, called therefore by way of excellency, 'the faith of the operation of God,' Col. 2:12, not a gift conveyed by angels, but his Spirit. A grain of grace of God's planting is more worth than millions of gold of man's getting; a more worthy gift than all the gold of Ophir, which God gives to men by their industry, who shall never see his face; but this by his own Spirit in order to glory. It is a royal gift he reserves in his own hands, to bestow upon those that were his favourites in his eternal purposes; it grows not in every man's ground, neither is it sown in every man's field. The soul is more excellent than the body, not only in respect of its nature, but in respect of its immediate author. God is called particularly, 'The Father of spirits,' not of bodies, though he is so; but in the production of bodies he acts by the hand of nature, in the production of the soul by his own hand. In that work he acts by the intervention of second causes; in this, without serving himself of any other efficient cause but his own will. If the soul, as being the only work of God, is therefore more excellent, then certainly a new-born soul is more excellent than anything in the world, in regard God is the author of it in a more peculiar manner, by the operation of his choicest affections.

(6.) If God be the efficient of regeneration, then there is a necessity of the influence of God in all the progress of grace. It is yet imperfect, the same hand that planted it must also water and dress it. There is a tough sinew left in man's will, which makes him halt after he hath the new name of Israel put upon him; a weakness of faith, a coldness of love, a faintness of zeal. What he is the creator of, is nursed by his providence; what he is the new creator of, is fostered by a succession of grace. The scripture therefore appropriates all to him: he is the God that calls us, the God that anoints us, the God that carries us, the God that establisheth us, the God that keeps us, and the God that perfects us. He is the author of grace in its first issue, its fruitful sproutings, its delicious ripenings; it depends upon him in creation, preservation, augmentation, as well as natural things depend upon him in all their progressive motions, from one degree to another, as the author of nature. When nature was most unspotted, grace was necessary to preserve and fix it in that state. Adam needed the assistance of grace with the embellishments of nature. The same power that inspires us with life, inspires us with a perpetual continuation of it. If the tide that turns the stream of the river desert it, and return to its own channel, the river will return to its natural current. Our hearts will decline, our life languish, unless fed by that supernatural efficacy which did first produce it. The plants cannot grow merely from their own internal form, nor trees bring forth their pleasant fruits without the influence of rain and sun, feeding and hatching their innate spirits, and drawing them out to make a show of themselves in flowers and fruits; and when they are brought forth, they stand in need of the same rain to fill them, the same sun to ripen them.

(7.) If God be the efficient, &c., we see whither we are to have recourse in all the exigencies of the new creature; to whom, but to the author of those beginnings of eternal life! God is all, in all parts of this glorious work: 'The God of all grace, who hath called us into his eternal glory, make you perfect, strengthen, stablish, settle you,' &c., 1 Peter 5:10. There is need of preserving, strengthening, increasing, quickening, and perfecting grace.

These you need, and these must be sought, and will be had from the same goodness and power by which you were new born.

[1.] Preserving grace.

First, God only can give it. There is a necessity of it; as God rears it, so he only can keep it from pining away. Plants will wither if the rain do not descend; the flame will be extinguished if fuel be not added. There is as much a necessity of a constant influence to keep up this new nature, as there is of the sun to preserve the horizon from that darkness which would invade it upon the turning its face to other parts of the world. The perpetual duration of renewing grace is not essential to grace, for then Adam and the angels had stood by virtue of their grace, for nothing ever loseth its essential property; but it is by an additional grace, distinct from the first grace wherein our regeneration doth consist, as the preservation of the creatures in their natural beings is by an act of God distinct from his creative act. The first grace God gives now is a bounty to his creatures, but it is further an obligation upon himself, not as it is grace, or as it is his own work, for Adam's grace which failed was wrought by his fingers, inspired by his breath, but as it is a new covenant grace which alters the condition of it. God's finger writ the law in the heart, and his breath can only blow the dust off, that would fill the engraved letters.

Secondly, God will preserve it. Job would argue with God, and ask him, 'Is it good unto thee that thou shouldest despise the work of thine hands?' Job 10:3. Is it agreeable to his goodness and wisdom to slight and neglect the work of his own heart; not a fruit of his common liberality to the creation, but a choice fruit of his redeeming love? His common love, as he is the author of nature, preserves the old creation; much more his special love, as he is the author of the new nature, will preserve the new creation. His general goodness made the world, but his gracious goodness formed the soul; the one is more splendid than the other, therefore the effect more durable. Mercy compasseth the godly about, Ps. 32:10, like bulwarks that surround a city for its defence, against the assaults of spiritual enemies. A higher providence attends man than other creatures, because he is of a more noble constitution; upon the same account a higher providence must attend the new creature, as being far more noble than mere man. God embraceth all creatures in his arms with a common love as creatures; he lays the new begotten ones in his bosom by a special love. His power too is to be considered. He will not want a power to preserve that which he did not want power to new create. The power being the same that raised Christ from the dead, which raised any from their natural condition, will have the same issue, since it never suffered Christ to return to the grave again, neither will it suffer any new born soul to return to a spiritual death. Every new creature is the Father's by purpose, and by actual traction; they were his before they were Christ's. The Father draws them to Christ; and the power of Christ will be as eminent to preserve them, as the power of the Father was to draw them. Why were the creatures brought, by that instinct God put into them, into Noah's ark, but to be preserved from the destroying deluge? Why did he take pains to write the law anew in the heart, if he would suffer it to be dashed out again? If he would not preserve his own work, why did he not let the soul lie wallowing in its old filthiness, and forbear the expense of those fresh colours he hath new drawn his image with? It seems to be a greater power to take off all that load of sin which lay upon you, than to preserve you from having so great a burden again upon you. It is not reasonable to think that God should be at so much cost, only to restore man to Adam's mutable condition, whereby to incur a greater condemnation.

[2.] Strengthening grace. This we need, as well as preserving grace. It is God that strengthens us in the inward man; by that strengthening grace the new creature can do all things, without it nothing. Through him we are more than conquerors over principalities and powers, Rom. 8:37, 38. Strength to mount up to heaven as an eagle, to run our race without weariness, to walk without fainting, to combat difficulties without sinking fears, is only to be had by waiting upon the Lord, who is the fountain whence all these flow, Isa. 40:31, and by his grace confers a supernatural fortitude: Isa. 40:31, 'But they that wait upon the Lord shall renew their strength; they shall mount up with wings as eagles: they shall run, and not be weary; they shall walk, and not faint.' Look not therefore for strength in your new nature; look for it in God, in that Spirit which first renewed you, since that glorious power is imparted to strengthen you, which was at first employed to new-create you. This was the matter of the apostle's prayer for the Colossians, and this should be ours: Col. 1:9, 11, 'Strengthened with all might, according to his glorious power.' There is much weakness in us, a medley of lusts, an army of enemies, but the way is open for us to that glorious power, to endue us with a new vigour, which first seized upon us with an insuperable efficacy; our shattered and weakened sins shall not be able to resist that glorious power now, which they could not stand the shock of when they were in their full strength. 'God will be a sun and a shield,' Ps. 84:11, a sun to dispel our darkness, a shield to secure us from darts; a sun against the allurements of the world, defeating them by a charming light; a shield against the affrightments of the world, overpowering them by an irresistible force; the sun that gave us life, the shield that secures our strength. The glorious power which we need in our progress lies in the same arm which wrought our deliverance, and from thence must be fetched. It is only by him that we have strength to tread down the wicked one's temptations, and those fiery darts are made as ashes under the soles of our feet, Mal. 4:3.

[3.] We need increasing grace; and that is from God. The increase depends upon him, as well as the first planting. When we want it, he is the fountain from whence we must draw it; so did the disciples, Luke 17:5, 'Increase our faith,' or add to us faith, προσθὲς ἡμῖν. Every new spring, fresh bud, spreading blossom, is an addition by his influence. When we have it, we must acknowledge his sole hand in it; so the apostle did when he saw the growth of the Thessalonians' faith, and the abounding of their charity: 2 Thes. 1:3, 'We are bound to thank (ἐυχαριστεῖν ὀφείλομεν) God always for you, because that your faith grows exceedingly.' He did it by obligation: no such tie had lain upon him had God left them to increase it themselves. The new fruits you bear is from his new purging, as the first power to bear was from his planting, John 15:2. If you would thrive, it must not be by your own, but by the increases of God; 'God gives the increase,' both in the outward administration and inward operation of the gospel, 1 Cor. 3:7. Faith, in every assent, is conducted by that power which first settled it in the heart, and without it cannot commence any higher degree. As every spark of spiritual life is by his kindling, so every sparkling of that spark is by his blowing. Look for it at God's hands, beg of him to write that law deeper, which his fingers first engraved in your hearts. It is God's being 'a dew to Israel' makes him grow up in beauty as 'the lily and the olive tree,' in strength 'cast out his roots as the cedars of Lebanon.' Hosea 14:5–7. If you would grow up as calves of the stall, you must lie under the healing wings of the Sun of righteousness: Mal. 4:2, 'Unto you that fear my name shall the Sun of righteousness arise with healing in his wings,' &c. That Sun which by his beams conveyed into you a spiritual life, can only by the same heat influence you to a taller growth. Every drop of the knowledge of his will till you come to be filled, every mite of wisdom and spiritual understanding, is to be drawn from him only, Col. 1:9 both the additions of knowledge and the deeper impressions and lively sproutings of what we know.

[4.] Quickening grace. This also we need. As our life, so the liveliness and activity of grace depends upon the divine influence; a divine motion is necessary to elevate our souls to those actions which are supernatural; our grace depends upon God in actu secundo, as well as actu primo. As God first puts a nature into creatures (in the exercise as well as the being) and then quickens them by his providential concurrence in those acts suitable to their nature, which acts are therefore natural to those creatures, so by a gracious concurrence he doth quicken the new nature in the soul to the exerting of gracious operations, according to that nature he hath endued it with. As he tunes the strings by his skill to fit them for a divine harmony, so he enlivens them by his touch to make what music he pleases; every heavenly prayer, every gracious groan, every start of spiritual affection, is from the Spirit tuning, quickening, assisting against infirmities and deadness. There must be a continued drawing to make a continued running. 'Draw us, and we will run after thee,' Cant. 1:4. It was the church, the gracious church, the spouse and dove of Christ, yet sensible of her own inability to quicken her pace to new communion with Christ, without fresh communications first from him. There is a bias in the soul to direct it in a right motion; there must be a hand without to put it upon that motion; Christ must 'put his hand in at the hole of the door' before a lazy soul, though gracious, will stir at his call, Cant. 5:3; or as a child; which hath a principle of motion, must be assisted and quickened by the nurse before it can move a step. Grace is more prevalent to keep us from sin than excite us to holiness, yet neither can be done by it without new quickenings; our motion is in him and by him, as well as our life, spiritually as well as naturally: Acts 17:28, 'In him we live, move, and have our being;' the old stock must have continual supply. 'Without Christ we can do nothing,' John 15:5; without him we cannot have grace in the plant, nor grace in the fruit. As the soul excites the spirits in the eye to an act of vision,—if they be not quickened by their governor, though things be before our eyes they see nothing,—so the Spirit of God excites, as it were, the spirits of grace to their particular acts, faith to apprehend and love to work. The goodness that made the promise guides the hand of the soul to fasten upon it: Ps. 119:49, 'Remember the word unto thy servant, upon which thou hast caused me to hope.' As God makes the promises, so he makes the meeting between the soul and the promise; every motion proceeds from God's touch upon the heart enlarging it, therefore our dependence must be upon God's grace: Ps. 119:32, 'I will run the way of thy commandments when thou shalt enlarge my heart.' I will run, not by my own strength, but by the hand of God enlarging and enlivening my heart. Indeed, if God did not give to act as well as implant the habit, he would give no more to us in the new covenant than he gave to Adam in the old, who had a power to do, but not the act of doing; his power was from God, but the act of obedience depended upon himself, and for want of actual abedience he fell. We see whence we must derive our quickenings; we want them because we expect them from the new nature in us, not from the author of that nature, and the concurrence of his grace with it, and depending upon habitual more than actual grace is the cause of our having many a slip. We are as dead lumps, notwithstanding all the grace we have, if God did not cause a free life to spring up in us by successive breathings.

[5.] Perfecting grace is only from God. He is the finisher of what he is the author of, Heb. 12:2, and in our spiritual warfare supplies us with new recruits, till the combat end in victory, and the victory in triumph. He will come 'as the former and the latter rain,' Hosea 6:3: as the former rain to open the womb of the earth, and the latter rain to ripen the fruits of the earth. As he hath laid the foundation of mount Zion, so he will perform the whole work in it; he fulfils the work of faith with the same power wherewith he begins it, 2 Thes. 1:11. The power which caused the resurrection of Christ caused his ascension; he had his forty days upon the earth, after his resurrection, before he was taken up to glory. There is a continuance of a believer in the world after his resurrection from a spiritual death, but the same power which caused his spiritual resurrection will as surely cause his heavenly ascension. That arm that brought him out of Egypt will conduct him to the limits of Canaan, the flourishing pastures of the promised land. Grace is the first gift, glory is the latter; glory follows upon the heels of grace: 'He will give grace and glory,' Ps. 84:11. Grace to fit for glory, and glory to reward his own grace; all grace till it ends in glory. God must be sought and depended on for this; we cannot will our perfection without grace, as we cannot will our regeneration without grace; God gives the will, the progressive as well as the initial Will. Then seek only to God, depend upon him only, for the warmth of his goodness, to bring those chickens to perfection which he hath gathered under his wing; his affections are not tired, it is a pure disinterested love mingled with no defects; his wisdom and power is no less able to perfect than his love is to incite him to it.

Use 2. The second use is of comfort.

Is God the author of regeneration? He that is the God of all grace is the God of all comfort too. Where he is the one, he will be the other. As he creates the soul to good works, so he creates it to heavenly consolations. When God acts as a God of justice toward sinners, he appears as a terrible God in his punishments; when he acts towards saints as a God of grace, he appears as a comforting God; he fills the one with all terrors, prepares the other for all comforts; he calls you by a new creation into his eternal glory, and sends therefore some sparkles of glory into the soul here. Are you born of God? You approach in excellency as near to Christ as a creature's capacity will admit. Christ was his natural begotten son, believers his spiritually regenerated children. Christ is 'the first born,' but 'among many brethren,' Rom. 8:29; that Christ 'that sanctifieth, and we that are sanctified, are all of one,' Heb. 2:11; of one nature, say some; of one Father, say others; therefore 'he is not ashamed to call them brethren;' one nature doth not so much make us brethren as one father. Christ was not regenerated, but generated; he stood not in need of the other, because the first generation failed not; neither could he, being God; he is the exact image of his Father's person, and so particularly of all his attributes, because he partakes of his essence. Believers are the living images of God's holiness, not partaking of all his attributes, but of that.

Particularly,

(1.) God will rejoice in his own work. If he rejoiced in the first planting of his image at the creation, he will no less rejoice in it at the restoration;

and with more gladness embrace the son that is returned from death to life, by returning from his debauched course, than that son that remained with him all the while. Why doth he renew the face of the earth by the mission of his Spirit, but that he may rejoice in his works? 'Thou sendest forth thy Spirit, they are created: and thou renewest the face of the earth. The glory of the Lord shall endure for ever: the Lord shall rejoice in his works,' Ps. 104:30, 31. If God shall in time rejoice in the earth, wherein he had little joy after the creation of it, and soon repented of his work, he will rejoice in the noblest work, in the frame of his image, which, next to Christ, makes all other works of the lower creation pleasant to him. He 'creates Jerusalem a rejoicing, and her people a joy,' and he will rejoice in the new creation of his people, in the people he hath new created, Isa. 65:18, 19.

(2.) He will destroy all enemies to his own work. How will his love pierce into every part, and employ his power in destroying the enemies of his work; whip buyers and sellers out of his spiritual temple, cast out all their remaining rubbish; let not his house be always a den of thieves, that shall rob God of his glory, and his temple of its beauty! That God that can raise men five thousand years ago dead as easily as one dead the last minute, can remove all the bands of corruption, though never so strong. If he hath raised you from death, he will lift you up from all the remainders of death; the grave-clothes which yet remain about you, shall be in time untied, as well as the soul unloosed from the principal bands of death. Though there be in you a 'spirit that lusteth to envy,' as well as a spirit that lusts to love, yet 'God gives more grace,' James 4:5, 6. Lusts will down, corruptions fall in time before his grace, darkness must hide its hated head, when that word breaks louder from his lips, 'Let there be light.' The promises of a thorough sanctification belong to you, as well as the promises of a perfect remission. If God be the teacher, no matter what the scholar is; if God be the workman, no matter what the matter is; if God be the guardian, no matter what the enemies are; nothing is too rugged for his skill, or too hard for his power.

(3.) He will order all things for the good of his own work. 'They shall not labour in vain; for they are the seed of the blessed of the Lord,' Isa. 65:23. He did not want grace to restore them, he will not want comforts to support them. Their very afflictions shall be ordered to preserve the work of his own heart in them; and while he prunes and cuts, he will purge away the luxuriant corruptions, that his vine may be more beautiful and delicious. And if he doth chasten you sharply, it is that you may be nearer 'partakers of his holiness,' Heb. 12:10.

Use 3. The third use is of exhortation.

1. To the renewed.

(1.) Walk humbly. Swell not big, as if your own power had procured it, let not pride spread its sails in your souls. Consider, you are creatures still, though new creatures. As God put into you whatsoever you have of natural existence, so he hath put into you whatsoever you have of spiritual; you are dust still by your natural creation, though new formed by the Spirit. There is nothing of grace, no act of grace, but you receive mediately or immediately from God. You opened not your own eyes, nor thrust back the lock of your own hearts, nor can call one spark of that spiritual life you have, your own creature; it moved not at your beck, obeyed not your orders; it is when God saith Go, that it goes, and Do this and that, Settle upon this or that soul, and it doth it. How humble should you be, since grace doth nothing in any but by God's order, not your own. God works in us, we add nothing to God. The melted wax receives the stamp from the seal, but the wax adds nothing to the seal. 'What hast thou that thou hast not received?' 'If thou didst receive it, why dost thou boast as if thou hadst not received it?' 1 Cor. 4:7. Grace is God's communication to you, not yours to yourselves. What is received, is not your own work, but another's gift; were it desert, we had reason to boast; but being a gift, we have no reason to grow big. Lie therefore before him in your own nothingness. Renewing grace first lighted upon you when you were humble; and grace in its increase flourishes when the soul is in the same posture.

(2.) Ascribe all that you are, as renewed creatures, to God. Ascribe it wholly to him; let self rub off every filing of this gold from its own fingers. 'Not unto us, not unto us, O Lord, but unto thy name be the praise,' Ps. 115:1. The repetition removes the glory far from themselves. If praise be comely for an upright person, it is most comely in the greatest cause that can happen to him, Ps. 33:1. Account yourselves therefore nothing, and God and grace all; and let no shoutings be heard in your souls while God is rearing up the divine temple, but those of Grace! Grace! Zech. 4:7, both in the foundation and superstructure, till he comes to the top stone. Your breathing after God is but the effect of his breathing after you; the moon hath no light of herself, but what she receives from the sun; nor any creature a spark of grace, but what is derived from the Father of lights. God's purity is as the sun, your grace as a beam from that sun, not primitive in your nature, but derivative from God. Were it not from grace, Saul had never been Paul, nor Peter a penitent, nor Mary a convert, nor Zaccheus a Christian, nor hadst thou ever been brought to the sweetness of a spiritual life, or advanced to the state and comforts of another world. Did you will to run till mercy moved your wills and spirited the feet of your souls? Your will, your race, was nothing; God's grace was all, Rom. 9:16. Was it not his word of command, Let there be life? Was it not his invincible power battered down the strongholds of sin? Oh seriously think, O Christian, that dry and desert heart of thine could never have been mollified and watered by rocky nature, nor virtue ever bud and blossom in that barren soil, unless the soil were mended, as well as the plant fixed, by some powerful hand. Bless God, therefore, since had it not been for him, you had never been humbled, never been renewed, never reached so high as a holy desire, or a penitential tear, but lain till this day, and for ever, bemired in fallen nature.

That you may know what reason you have to bless God with the highest praises, consider,

[1.] What your obligation is, how great! What good would your creation have done you since your fall without a new creation by the same hand? It must have rendered you miserable without this, and could never have rendered you happy but by the intervention of this. Without this you might have been his sons and daughters by creation, and devils by corruption. The heathens were God's offspring, as they were rational creatures, Acts 17:28, and the devil's children, as they were corrupt creatures. You might have had the image of God in a glimmering reason, without his image in a divine holiness. Was it not a greater obligation to restore that with kinder circumstances which you had wilfully thrown away, when it was in no wise due to you, than it was at first to bestow it? There was something like debt at first; supposing God would create a rational creature, integrity and innocency was naturally due to it, in regard of the holiness and wisdom of God, unless he would have been the author of the creature's sinfulness; but since that voluntary defection, the restoration was in no sort due, therefore the obligation greater. If God had created a thousand worlds, and given you the lordship of them for some millions of years, had this been such a kindness as to afford you a new nature, whereby you will be eternally happy in a likeness to God and enjoyment of him? As the work of redemption, so this of regeneration, darkens the glory of the work of creation; since more of grace, wisdom, power, holiness, are the springs of it, the obligation must be far greater; the difference is as great as between heaven and earth. Will you not bless God for making you creatures, for recovery from a fit of sickness? Is the obligation less in delivering you from a spiritual death? Is not the reason of blessing God greater for the second creation than the first, since it is the same skill adorns you with his image in the new creation, which beautified man with that image at the first?

[2.] Was there not as much unfitness in you as in the worst of men by nature? Not one good disposition grew upon nature, but all was the work of preventing grace. Could; then, the iron gates of your hearts fly open of themselves? Or could any else but a God break them open? Was not your nature carried as violently to sin as any, perhaps not into such brutish sins as others, yet more refined and devilish? If you did not launch out into the grossest sins, you owe your preservation to restraining grace. That Socrates was better and wiser than another, was from God, in the acknowledgment of a heathen, who saith he was chosen to virtue, Κατὰ τοῦ Θεοῦ χειροτονίαν, by the divine suffrage. Were your strings better? Sure they were of God's tuning. Man was not more unfit for a natural being before God created him, than the best man in the world was for a spiritual being, till God wrought him with his own finger. Was not the worst in the world naturally as fit for it as yourselves? Did any better thing dwell in your flesh than in theirs, to give grace entertainment? Did not grace at first make its way, conquering, and to conquer, and not one blow struck by you to facilitate the victory? Nay, were you not so far from having a grain of grace by nature, that there was nothing but opposition and rebellion against the Author of it? Did you not want everything to make you lovely in God's eye? Nay, did you not hate him while he had a love of benevolence towards you? And have you not reason to bless him then, that he would not disdain to look upon you, such an impure and rebellious creature? Perhaps your case was the same with hers, Hos. 2:5, who said, 'I will go after my lovers.' She decreed to follow her idols, and was resolved not to be reclaimed; but God resolved otherwise, ver. 6, 7, who would not leave her till he had made her change her base and unworthy resolution for better: 'She shall say, I will return, &c.' And was it not a happy resolution in the divine breast, not to suffer you to run mad and furiously to hell? What an irrecoverable condition had you been in if God had not spake a powerful word, 'Hitherto thou art gone, but no further shalt thou go!' Were you not once in your blood, and pitied by no eye, when God said, Live? And can you not wonder at the mercy of his lips, and raise your notes above an ordinary strain? Read over the records of the first work upon thy heart, and see if anything were written there with thy own finger. The very sense of thy own wretchedness was God's writing on thy heart; thou wast weighed in the balances and found wanting; lighter than vanity, nothing of thy own to concur with God, but folly and misery.

[3.] If grace found thee unfit and rebellious, there could then be nothing of the least desert; and this should make you cast a wondering eye at the greatness of God's kindness. Man's voluntary defection, without any violence offered to him, had rendered him unworthy of any recovery; you did no more deserve it than the worst devil, who shall never have one line of it drawn upon him. Not one previous disposition, not one sigh or groan for it, could be discerned, much less the draught itself. Your true earnings were nothing but that death you lay under. The unloosing any band of it, or knocking off any fetter, was merely free grace. Is there not, then, reason to bless the Lord, when an undeserved power hath been put forth to new create you, when a deserved power might have buried you for ever under your own ruins? Suppose you had been the most exact moralists in the world, the supernatural grace of the new birth could not be deserved by you, because nothing can be merited but by an act as excellent as the reward. No man can merit by any act a thing of a greater value than the act itself; but this grace is of another order, and far superior to any moral natural work. Indeed, upon covenant, if a man doth such a thing, he shall have such a reward; the thing promised may be challenged upon the performing the condition, but cannot be said to be merited, because the act was inferior to the reward in the true value of it; but this grace could neither be merited nor challenged at God's hand upon a condition, since he had made no promise in this kind to give you a right to such a demand. It is one thing to be capable of it, another thing to have a just right. A sinner in the state of sin is capable of being changed, but not capable of having a right to that change. Well, then, you could never deserve such a mercy; and will you prize it and bless God for it?

[4.] Since you did not deserve it, no, nor the proposals of it, consider what a condition you had been in had God left you to yourselves, or put your wills only into an indifference. Had it been by a mere suasion, or a naked proposition of the truth, I suppose you are so sensible of the mutability of your wills, that you might well believe you should scarce have complied with God. Your security at best had been but as good as Adam's, who had his posse but not his velle. What furious passions and devils in your souls were set against him! and had you been left to your own choice, you would not have stirred one foot to follow his chariot. If you did 'purify your souls in obeying the truth,' it was 'through the Spirit,' 1 Peter 1:22; and all the faith you have was from the same fountain, Acts 18:27, 'which believed through grace.' Put it to yourselves: Do you think your hearts were not so stout, that nothing but divine grace could mollify them? Do you think there would have been any heat or warmth in you unless God had kindled the flame? Can yon imagine your frozen hearts would have melted but by a divine breath? It was happy for you that God would put your wills beyond an indifference, and deal with you by the same power as he dealt with Christ, not leaving him or you in a doubtful state between life and death. How happy was it for you that God would be conqueror, and surmount your resistance, tame your force, scatter your counsels, level your mountain, and bring your fierceness under the yoke; that he would not wait your choice and leisure, but make the event certain; that he had mercy on you, because he would have mercy; that he would turn the stream of your hearts by the overmastering tide of his grace, and overpower the flesh in the chief parts of your souls, and secure the rational powers of mind and will for himself! How glad may you be of the loss of that indifference that secures your happy estate for ever! Who that is in favour with a prince would not willingly have his will fixed to please him, and dread nothing more than such an indifference, whereby he might hate his prince and lose his favour?

[5.] Is there not reason you should bless God, when he hath dealt thus graciously with you, and not with many others in the world; why any of you should be raised up to a spiritual life, when you see many others near you stretched out in a spiritual death; why one upon the same bench and not another; why one should be gathered with his arm, and another left to the jaws of the devouring lion; why you should have any choice fruit grow in any of your hearts, when thorns and briers grow in every hedge? That God should have afforded you means of regeneration, and not to most others in the world, is a ground of blessing and praise; much more that he should afford you the grace of regeneration, and not to many others under the same means. He hath not dealt so with every nation in giving them the means, Ps. 147:19; he hath not dealt so with every person in giving them the grace. That wind that blows where it listeth hath left other dry bones to remain dry still, passed by others more civil and of sweeter conversations; drawn his image in one, and left others to tumble down to hell in the likeness of Adam, wherein they were born; overlooked one that was not far from the kingdom of heaven, and laid hold on another that was many leagues further from Christ. The Spirit of God only makes this distinction: he will pour out his grace in Galatia and Macedonia, and not suffer it to be known in Bithynia: Acts 16:6–8, 'And they essayed to go into Bithynia, but the Spirit suffered them not;' cause it to rain in one city, on one person, and not on another; call one out of the grave, and leave others under the bands of death and in the dregs of human nature. You see your calling, and you may see how distinguishing it is, 'not many wise after the flesh, not many mighty,' 1 Cor. 1:26. Can you see this and not bless the caller, the renewer? A less favour wrought so much upon David's heart that he would bless God in spite of mocks and scoffs, 2 Sam. 6:21. Oh rich discriminating grace! Where any are peculiar monuments of grace, they should have peculiar notes of praise. What reason can others have to bless God, if such should have no hearts to bless him for so great a mercy? All are under God's will of precept, all are under his will of promise, if they perform that precept; but all are not under his will of purpose, to give them strength to perform that precept.

[6.] It is to be considered, too, with what pains and patience God wrought this work in your hearts. You may best know what ado God had with your hearts before they were thus formed according to his will. Were they not as clay to the potter, which needed much tempering before they were fit for use? Did God find that pliableness in you that the devil found? Had he a cordial welcome at the first proffer? Do you not remember resistance enough to make you for ever ashamed that ever you should put the blessed God to that toil? And yet you know not the thousandth part of that resistance God knew was lodged in your nature. Do you not remember how he met you at every turn, hedged up your perverse way with thorns, before he could be admitted to speak a word to your heart; how he answered one objection after another, whereby you would have stifled his work? Can you remember this, and not admire the mercy that took such pains with so unprofitable a heart? It is called a resurrection, but it is more. Before the resurrection of the body, one part of man lives and waits for reunion though the body be crumbled into very dust; but there is no life in you naturally: so little in you to take part with God, that even that which is the glory of man, his mind, and reason, and wisdom, were in arms against this work, as well as the sensitive and brutish part; for 'the carnal mind was enmity against God,' Rom. 8:7. What was your language to God at first, but like that of the hellish spirit in the man in Luke 4:34: 'What have we to do with thee?' Yet he dealt with you as the sun with the earth, which scatters the mists it sends out to choke its light, and spreads its warm wings over the face of the world. So doth God; though men offend him with the steams of their sins, and uncivilly command him to depart from them, yet he leaves them not till he hath made them willing that he should do them good.

[7.] The work itself requires admiration and blessing in regard of the excellency of it. It is more admirable than all the miracles of nature; the whole world can no more compare with it than a dunghill can equal the worth of a rock of diamonds; all blessings which make you happy spiritually and eternally are wrapped up in it. What can God give greater than his own nature? What are you capable of more than what he hath done and will do upon that foundation? If God had only given thee knowledge, thou mightest have been a devil for all that; but the new nature makes you equal with angels. What man or angel could you be born of with so great advantage as to be born of God? There is no higher being to be born of. What can he do more than thus to beget you? You are new-born according to that image after which his only Son was eternally begotten; conceived by that Spirit whereby Christ was conceived in the womb of the blessed Virgin; raised by the same almighty hand whereby the great pattern of the new birth was raised from the dead. It is the highest elevation of human nature to be united to the Son of God, and to be made like to that glorious image. Greater gifts cannot be than these two, Christ to descend to partake of human nature, and the creature elevated to partake of the divine. If you will not loudly bless him for this, what can God do that shall deserve your praise, since a greater he cannot confer, more full of the spirits of his favour towards you?

[8.] May there not be some circumstances in your particular new birth that may raise your hearts to blessing and praise? Perhaps thou wert 'born in a day,' as his promise is of a nation, Isa. 66:7, 8, and without those racking pains which attend the new birth of many. He did not take thee by the throat, nor arrest thee with legal terrors, but breathed upon thee with a gentle wind; conceived and formed thee in a little space of time, that thou wert within the prospect of heaven before thou thoughtest thyself out of the suburbs of hell, and brought thee forth a man-child before thou didst imagine thyself to be delivered. Was it not mercy to renew thee without worrying thee; to melt thee by a gentle fire of love, not break thee piecemeal by the hammer of wrath, that thou should scarce discern the lance from the balsam, and the wound from the plaster? Perhaps he arrested thee in a full course of sin, in some desperate career, when some plot was laid for a high piece of wickedness. It had been an act of his power hadst thou been brought up in some religious family, tutored in the ways of religion by a choicer education; but perhaps God took thee from the very steams of hell, when thou hadst not one thought of him, and he might have let thee alone as well as he did others of thy companions. It had been admirable power to turn clear water into wine, but more to turn stinking and putrefied water into a generous wine. Do not the visible characters of mercy and power in such a case call for more praise at thy hands? Can any other cause have a pretence to put in for a share in thy acknowledgments?

[9.] You are not without many examples to move you to this acknowledgment. Our Saviour himself could not regard the centurion's faith without astonishment. He wondered at that in his humanity which he wrought himself by his divinity, Mat. 8:10. And when Peter professeth his faith in him by acknowledging him to be the Son of God, Christ presently owns his Father as the author of it: Mat. 16:17, 'Flesh and blood hath not revealed it unto thee, but my Father which is in heaven.' Angels sang both at the first and second creation, and shouted for joy when the corner-stone thereof was laid, Job 38:6, 7. When they saw its beautiful order, they then shewed themselves to be the sons of God indeed, in glorifying their Father for his incomparable works. The second creation being more glorious than the first, is not celebrated by them with fainter shoutings; if God hath then hallelujahs for you, it is fit he should have hallelujahs from you. If angels speak loud, it is not fit you should speak low; it is their concern, as they are God's friends and servants; your concern, as you are his workmanship, of his own carving. The saints in all ages of the church have led the way in this acknowledgment. The elders, made kings and priests on earth, in a conquest of Satan and their own hearts, crowned with a blessed grace, cast down their crowns at the feet of God: Rev. 9:11, 'For thou hast created all things, and for thy pleasure they are and were created,' both the present new creation and the old. 'Thou hast loosed my bonds,' Ps. 116:16. What follows? 'I will offer to thee the sacrifice of thanksgiving.' And God's renewing David's youth like the eagle's, his changing him into a new man, saith Jerome, is one argument of David's praise, Ps. 103:5. Add to this, heathens* have acknowledged it to be the work of God; one examining the reason why Homer calls virtuous men δίους, answers, Because goodness was not a work of art, but ἔργον Διὸς. If divining and mystical knowledge be θείᾳ τινὶ ἐπιπνοίᾳ, by divine inspiration, shall we say of virtue it is ἔργον τέχνης θνητῆς, the work of man's art? Where do you find any like Nebuchadnezzar, gazing upon the divine formation in his own heart, and proudly crying out, 'Is not this great Babylon which I have built?' Doth such language drop from a David's mouth? No; but 'thou hast quickened me.' Or from Paul? No, 'by grace I am what I am.' Every inch, every spark, every joint of the new man is from grace.

[10.] If you do not acknowledge it to God, and bless him for it, you may justly suspect you are not born of him. It is the nature of true grace to reflect back upon God, as it is of a sunbeam shining upon a wall to reflect back upon the sun. Blessing God for it, is a character of a renewed man. It is an evidence of the ruin of the contradiction of nature against God, when man can strip himself of all, and own God the prime fountain of what he is and hath. If a man boast of his being the cause of a new birth in himself by any work of his own, it is a shrewd sign he is not renewed, because by such boasting he crosses the main end of the gospel, which is to stain the pride of man, and debase him to the dust from all grounds of glorying in himself, How jealous was the apostle in this case, and therefore backs his assertion again and again, that he might beat man's hands off from fingering anything of God's glory: Eph. 2:5, 'By grace you are saved;' again, vers. 8, 9, 'and that not of yourselves: it is the gift of God.' Once again, 'Not of works.' And the reason why he is thus earnest, was perpetually to discountenance self-confidence, 'lest any man man should boast.' The design of God in all gospel dispensations, is to pull away the stool whereon the flesh sits to glory: 1 Cor 1:29–31, 'That no flesh should glory in his presence.' It would seem strange that the new birth, a main gospel work, should be wrought without promoting a gospel end. To have a new birth, and such a flourishing pride, opposite to the end of it, is a contradiction. If the doctrine of faith doth exclude boasting, as Rom. 3:27, boasting is 'excluded by the law of faith,' the grace of faith also will exclude it; where the new birth is wrought, pride, the great enemy to it, will surely be captivated. We are then something in and by God, when we are most nothing in ourselves.

Well, then, be much in the work of praising God, who shined into thy heart when it was dark, and sealed instruction to thee; who took away the stony heart, and introduced one of flesh in the room; who manifested a day of power in the night of your weakness. Can you, dare you, to ascribe it to yourselves? Let God then have the praise. It is our fault we are more in complaints of what we want, than acknowledgments of what we have. Oh, rob not God of his deity, pretend not yourselves partners with him in the least of the stock. The more you return the glory of his grace, the more will he return the comfort of it to you; the more you give him that glory he is so jealous of, the more he will give you that grace he is so liberal of.

(3.) A third duty for those that are renewed. Acknowledge God in all the changes you see in others. Miracles must be regarded. It is greater for the apostles to act with new hearts than to speak with new tongues; greater than to stop the sun in its course, which would set all the world upon an astonished gaze. Shall any such miraculous work be done in our view, and we stand only as stupid spectators, and not render to God that glory which is due to him for his choicest work? As the sight and consideration of the material creation kept up the notion of the being of

God as creator, so the consideration of his works upon the souls of men will quicken thy sentiments of God as a new creator. One is an argument to prove the power of his essence, the other an argument of the power of his grace. Noah doth not bless Shem first for that act of filial duty shewed to his father, but blesses God as the author of that modesty Shem had shewn in covering his father's nakedness: Gen. 9:26, 'Blessed be the God of Shem.' When a great number were turned to Christ, Barnabas presently cast up his eye to the grace of God, 'he saw the grace of God,' Acts 11:21–23. Let every Lazarus you see raised from the grave raise up your faith to a higher elevation, and dress it in a jubilee attire. When you see a new temple reared to God, own it as the Lord's doing, and let it be marvellous in your eyes.

(4.) Be content with every condition your new creator shall cast you into. Discontent at any of God's dispensations doth ill become one whom God hath new begotten to a glorious inheritance. What can he do more than he hath done, and what he will do upon that foundation? All that he acts is to further that which he hath so powerfully and mercifully begun. What son would repine at the losing a rattle, as long as he is born to a never-fading inheritance? If grace hath put forth a power to new create you, it will not use that power otherwise than for your good. It may contradict your carnal desires, not your spiritual interest. Well may any man be content with the jewel that is left, though the casket be lost. All things are too light if put into the balance with the new birth: the dearest husband or wife, the sweetest children or friends, the most flourishing inheritance; study, therefore, contentment in the worst condition upon this ground; you know not how soon you may be put to practise all your skill. Do you not see the heavens gathering blackness over your heads? A new birth, that allies us to God as his children, will be of more force to settle us, than calamities can be to discompose us; for never was child so dear to an earthly, as a new created soul is to its heavenly Father.

(5.) Walk worthy of the author of it. A verbal acknowledgment will signify little without a real imitation of the virtues of him 'that hath called you out of darkness into his marvellous light,' 1 Peter 2:9. A holiness is to be expressed by you, like the holiness of that God who hath renewed you. Let no devilish or brutish carriage be yoked with a divine birth, indeed it cannot; the bespotting corruption of the world will not agree with the regeneration of the soul; the stains of the flesh are inconsistent with the purity of the new nature. Belial and Christ, God and Satan, are not joint begetters; Satan's impure breathings upon you should not be admitted to mix with the breath of God. A new nature by grace must not imitate a brutish nature by sin; a soul born of God must not be fashioned according to the world. If you differ from the world in your nature by grace, differ from the world also in your carriage by holiness. It is uncomely for one born of God to be taken with the foolish, flaunting pride of the world, more than the pattern God hath set him; that is, to imitate beasts, not a heavenly Father. The world is little, nothing, vanity in the eye of God; so should it be in the eye of a divinely begotten soul. Use the world as travellers an inn, to lodge, not to dwell in, to accommodate you in your journey to that Father of whom you were born. Let a heaven-born nature be attended with heavenly flights, longing for that happy state wherein nothing but the divine nature shall be seen in you, as nothing but fire is seen in melted gold.

(6.) Mourn for your imperfections. Give God his due, and grieve for your defect in paying him his own. The soul in creation comes pure out of God's hand, but it is poisoned by the flesh, and the impurity in the sensitive part of man. Though your grace be from God, yet your imperfections are from yourselves. The waters that run through sulphur and alum mines flow from the sea, but the ill taste and scent are communicated by the matter it mixes with in its passage. God is the author of your faith, but not of the weakness of your faith; the author of your love, but not of the coldness of your love; the author of your zeal, but not of the faintness of your zeal. Chide your hearts, therefore, for your weakness, as Christ did his disciples for their slowness in faith. 'Rejoice with trembling,' Ps. 2:11, rejoice in what you have, and mourn for what you want and come short in. Reason you have, since there is too much of the power of nature remaining with our best grace, so that it may be said of it, as Lot of Zoar, What grace hath enclosed is but a little one.

Exhort. 2. To those that are not born of God. You see at whose hands you are to seek it. God was the first contriver of the gospel, the first preacher of the gospel, the sole artist in any gospel operation. No man can come except the Father draw him; not some men, but no man; every man must therefore seek to this great attracter. It is a vanity of human nature, that every man loves to be αὐτοδίδακτος, his own teacher; and no less a vanity it is, that every man loves to be αὐτογέννητος, his own begetter. Men glory in the knowledge they get without a teacher, and no less glory in any change they can hammer out without a spiritual Father. As he that scorns to be taught by another shall surely have a fool to his tutor, so he that thinks to gain spiritual life by himself, shall be sure to have death for his quickener. No man would seek life from death, or light from darkness, and the best natural man is no better. The glory of the Lord must rise upon us, before we can rise out of our death in sin: 'Arise, and shine, for thy light is come, and the glory of the Lord is risen upon thee,' Isa. 60:1.

(1.) Seek it only at the hands of God. It is not to be had by outward rules, but divine influence; the streams of life must come from him, since with him only is the fountain of life: Ps. 36:9, 'I will give a heart of flesh;' I alone, without any other co-ordinate cause, either man or angel. He only hath the key of the heart, as well as that of the womb; confide not in yourselves. Adam was a root to convey sin and death, but no root to convey spiritual life. Corruption comes by propagation from him, grace only by spiritual regeneration from God. Would any wise man seek for water in a desert, or for grace from himself, who is naturally a dry wilderness? What toad, naturally full of poison, ever made himself sweet and wholesome? As Christ was by the grace of God made partaker of our nature in his incarnation, so by the same grace only can we be made partakers of his nature by regeneration. We are naturally weeds; if ever we be flowers in God's garden, the transformation must be God's act alone.

Seek it of God. But,

[1.] In the use of means, not abating anything of thine own industry. Seek, while God offers it; hold your mouth under the fountain while it runs. Moses hewed the tables, but God wrote the law. God promised David and Gideon victory, but not with their hands in their pockets, but their arms and armies about them. Moses must fight with the arms of Israel, but pray to the God of battles and victory. We must with one hand use the directions God hath given, and lift up the other in spiritual supplication for success upon them. Therefore let not the doctrine of God's being the cause of the new birth encourage your laziness and sloth. This sloth among men Chemnitius thought to be the occasion of Pelagius his error, who, seeing the laziness of Christians, thought to correct it by making them think highly of their own strength; but that was a dangerous extreme.

[2.] Yet let your eye be solely upon God in the use of them, since all the means in the world cannot do it without him. Unless God pull up the flood-gates, no water of life can stream into the soul; means can no more of themselves cast out death than the disciples could cast out some devils; but Christ was able to do what they could not. All the angels in heaven and men upon earth have not been able, these almost six thousand years, to make one fly; yet all the angels and the whole frame of the world were made by God in six days. Men speak to the sense, God to the heart; they to the understanding, and God into it; men argue with the will, and God persuades it. All the clamours of the whole nation of the Jews, yea, of all the men in the world, would not have made Lazarus stir out of the grave, had not our Saviour spake the word, 'Lazarus, come forth.' How often do the clouds of heaven drop upon men, yet they still remain as a dry chip, their stony hearts perhaps moistened with some transient flashy affections, but not mollified into flesh. Pray therefore to God, before the use of any means, Lord, breathe life so powerfully upon me, that I may walk before thee, and never find myself again in a natural winding-sheet. Let thy voice, Lord, be heard and felt by me as the voice of thy Son was by Lazarus. To use means without a seeking to God for his blessing, is to be exercised in divine institutions with an atheistical spirit. He is an atheist that expects nourishment from his meat without God's benediction, and he no less that runs to means without lifting up his heart to God, thinking to get grace conveyed by the means without God's operation.

(2.) Direction. Plead much with God from the glorious attributes he honours in this work. Lord, here is a subject for thy power to work upon. God made the heavens when there was nothing but a rude mass; he brought forth the sun, moon, and stars, with all their glory, out of the barren womb of nothing. Is thy heart worse than nothing, more contradictory to God than nothing? It is so. Assume an argument from hence: Lord, here is a subject for thy power above what was manifested in creation; there is not a more tough heart in the world than mine; lose not the opportunity of displaying the greatness of thy power, since there is scarce a heart more stout and unwieldy than mine is. Lord, bestow a vital principle upon me; thou didst it to the lifeless body of Adam; thy power will be more magnified in the breathing upon a lifeless soul of a son and daughter of Adam. In the same manner plead his wisdom and holiness. Plead also the enmity thy sin hath against him, the wrong it hath done him, in spoiling the creation, changing the end of it, hindering thee from thy natural duty, and that it is not for the interest of his glory to let sin bear such a sway and dominion, and usurp his room in one who would fain be another man.

(3.) Be deeply sensible of the corruption of thy nature; the want of this is the cause there is so little sense in men and women of the absolute necessity of the grace of regeneration, and a change of nature. Therefore labour to see yourselves in a forlorn condition by spiritual death. Look upon your great fall as a son of Adam, a slave of Satan, and possessor of a hellish nature, and at a vast distance from God and happiness.

(4.) Grieve not the Spirit in any of his operations. Quench not the sparks of the Spirit in any previous preparations and dispositions to this new birth. Be pliable to his breathings; hoist up your sails to receive his gales; when he knocks, open thy heart as wide as may be, push it to the furthest point, that there may be no remora; let all the house be free for his triumphant entrance. Since thy strength is too weak for it, beg of him at such a season to break it open; set upon prayer at such a season, and leave not till you have prayed your spirits up and your resistance out. How ungrateful and foolish is it to grieve that Spirit, who offers to form you into a new birth, and bring the life and joy of heaven into your heart! This is the only means to recover the loss you had by the fall of Adam, and surmount all the misery of it. Seek to him; he that can gather the dust of your bodies, if blown to the further part of the world, and knit it together, can overcome the filthy and deadly noisomeness of your souls; he can make a barren wilderness to become pools of water, a lump of vanity a garden of pleasure, a heap of rubbish to sprout up a new-born sun. If you would therefore be animated with a spirit of life, you must approach the beams of the sun,* and lie under the rich and enlivening influences of it.

A Discourse of the Word, the Instrument of Regeneration

Of his own will begat he us, with the word of truth, that we should be a kind of first-fruits of his creatures.—JAMES 1:18.

I HAVE chosen this text to treat of the instrument of the new birth.

The apostle having advised them (verse 13, 'But let no man say when he is tempted, I am tempted of God: for God cannot be tempted to evil, neither tempts he any man') not to charge God as the author of any temptation to evil, shewing it to be contrary to the nature of God, who is infinite goodness and righteousness; for as he cannot be tempted with evil, so neither can he tempt any man; and declaring the true cause and spring of all evil to be inherent in ourselves, even that lust which is riveted in our nature, which he calls our own lust,—verse

14, 'But every man is tempted, when he is drawn away of his own lust, and enticed,'—he takes occasion from thence to shew the order of sin's working. Sin is first conceived by that original corruption in our nature, and formed and brought forth into action; and when it is finished, and grows into a habit, it 'brings forth death,' verse 15. To remove this error, which some in those days had sucked in out of a natural self-love that man hath to excuse himself, and remove the cause of sin far from him, the apostle shews that God is the author and fountain of all the good we have: ver. 17, 'Every good gift and every perfect gift is from above, and comes down from the Father of lights, with whom is no variableness, nor shadow of change.' God being the infinite Father of lights, who hath no eclipses or decreases, no shadows or mixtures of darkness, but alway shines with a constant and settled brightness, of this goodness hath given a great evidence, in conferring the choicest mercy upon us, even a new begetting through the gospel, and thereby the relation of children to him, that we might be consecrated to him as the first fruits and a peculiar portion. Of his own will, βουληθεὶς; by his mere motion, induced by no cause but the goodness in his own breast. (1.) To distinguish it from the generation of the Son, which is natural, this voluntary; of his own will, not naturally, as he begat his Son from eternity. (2.) Not necessarily, by a necessity of nature, as the sun, to which he had compared God before, doth enlighten, and enliven, when matter is prepared to receive his quickening beams; but by an arbitrariness of grace. (3.) Not by any obligation from the creature; the will of God is opposed to the merit of man. The new creation answers to election; the first purpose was free, the bringing that purpose to execution is free; whatsoever obligation there is, results not from the creature, but from himself, his own immutable nature, which hath no variableness, nor shadow of change. 'Begat us,' ἀπεκύησεν, or brought us forth; for the same word ἀποκύει, ver. 15, is translated, 'brings forth.' 'By the word of truth,' a title given to the gospel both in the Old and New Testament: in the Old, Ps. 45:4, 'And in thy majesty ride prosperously, because of truth,' or 'upon thy word of truth;'* in the New Testament, Eph. 1:13, 'In whom you also trusted, after you heard the word of truth, the gospel of your salvation.' So 2 Cor. 6:7, and 2 Tim. 2:15. And it is called truth by way of excellency, as paramount to all other truth. (1.) Either, by an Hebraism, the word of truth; that is, the true word. (2.) Or rather, by way of eminency, as containing a higher truth, more excellent in itself, more advantageous for the creature, than any other divine truth; wherein the highest glory of God, the sure and everlasting happiness of the creature, is set forth; a word which he hath 'magnified above all his name,' Ps. 138:2.

And called the word of truth.

1. In regard of the author, truth itself; and the publisher, he who was 'the way, the truth, and the life.'

2. In opposition to all false doctrines, which can never be the instruments of conversion; for error to convert to truth, is the same thing as for darkness to diffuse light, or water to kindle fire.

3. In opposition to the windy and flashy conceits of men, which can no more be instrumental in the begetting a Christian, than mere wind can beget a man.

4. In opposition to the legal shadows; the gospel declares the truth of those types. Both the law and prophecy were but as a dim candle 'in a dark place,' 2 Peter 1:19, but this as a sun shining out at noonday. All other discourses did stream to this as their great ocean, wherein they were to be swallowed up. The law was the word of truth, but referred to the gospel as the great end of it. This contains the whole and ultimate purpose of God, for saving men by Jesus Christ, and in him enriching them with all spiritual blessings, and not by the works of the law; and thus the Spirit, which enlightens and seals instruction upon our souls, is called 'the Spirit of truth,' John 14:17, as it is called a Spirit of holiness, as it makes us holy; a Spirit of grace, as it makes us gracious, or as it declares the grace of God. Some by the word of truth understand Christ,

the essential and uncreated λόγος, Word, as it is understood by some in 1 Peter 1:23, 25, 'By the Word of God, which lives and abides for ever; and this is the Word which by the gospel is preached to you.' Possibly it may be meant of Christ, who by the gospel is declared and preached to be the mediator between God and man, appointed to raise up those that are given to him. Others by the word there, mean the will of God of giving grace in Christ, which is manifest in, and expressed by, the gospel. But here it is evidently' meant of the gospel, because of the inference the apostle makes: ver. 19, 'Be swift to hear;' that is, prize the word, wait upon the means with all readiness; 'slow to speak,' to utter your judgment of it, or be wise in your own conceit, whereof a readiness to speak peremptorily in divine truth is sometimes an evidence; 'slow to wrath' and passion, which hinder any profit by the word. 'That we should be a kind of first fruits of his creatures;' the chief among his creatures. The first fruits were the best of every kind to be offered to God, whereby they acknowledged God's gift of them, and desired his blessing upon them, and were given as God's peculiar right and portion. It was commanded in the law, Deut. 18:4. It was a custom among many of the heathens. To offer them was a token of thankfulness; not to offer them, was accounted a sign of atheism and profaneness.* The new creature is God's peculiar portion taken out of mankind; and it bespeaks duty too: being consecrated to God by a new begetting, they should serve God with a new spirit, new thankfulness, new frames.

We see here,

1. The efficient of regeneration, God; 'he,' the Father of lights.

2. The impulsive or moving cause, 'his own will.'

3. The instrumental cause, 'with the word of truth.'

4. The final cause, 'that we may be a kind of first fruits.'

The doctrine I am to handle is,

Doct. That the gospel is the instrument whereby God brings the soul forth in a new birth.

The Scripture doth distinguish the efficient and instrumental cause by the prepositions ἐκ, or ἐξ, and διὰ. When we are said to be 'born of the Spirit,' it is, John 3:5, ἐκ πνεύματος; 1 John 3:9, 5:1, ἐκ Θεοῦ; never διὰ πνεύματος, or διὰ Θεοῦ; but we are nowhere said to be born of the word, or begotten of the word, but διὰ λογου, by or with the word, 1 Peter 1:23; and διὰ ἐυαγγελίου, 1 Cor. 4:15, I have begotten you 'through the gospel.' The preposition ἐκ or ἐξ, usually notes the efficient or material cause; διὰ, the instrumental or means by which a thing is wrought. Sin entered into the heart of Eve by the word of the devil, grace enters into the heart by the word of God; that entered by a word of error, this by a word of truth: 'Ye are clean through the word I have spoken to you,' John 15:3, whereby our Saviour means the word outwardly preached by him, for it is the word spoken by him. Not that it had this efficacy of itself, but as an instrument of their sanctification, rendering them ready to every good work. The holiness, therefore, which it begets, is called the holiness of truth, Eph. 4:24, opposed to the ἐπιθυμίαι τῆς ἀπάτης,' lusts of deceit,' ver. 22. Lusts grow up from error and deceit, and holiness of the new man grows up from truth. The gospel administration, in regard of the effects of it, is called 'the kingdom of God,' Mark 1:14; it erects the kingdom of God in the world and in the hearts of men, and called the regeneration: Mat. 19:28, 'Ye which have followed me in the regeneration;' the gospel administration being a creating of 'new heavens and a new earth,' Isa. 65:17. This is the triumphal chariot, wherein Christ rides majestically to the conquest of hearts: Ps. 45:4, 'And in thy majesty ride prosperously, because of truth,' ,□□□ □□□ □□a psalm the Jews themselves understand of the Messiah. The word of his truth is the support of his kingdom, whereby he awes sinners into submission. Peace from heaven, and the health of our nature, is 'the fruit of the lips,' though of God's creation, Isa. 57:19. It is like the dew or mist which watered the ground, and prepared the earth for the formation of Adam's body, into which God breathed afterwards a living soul, Gen. 2:6, 7.

I. For explication, take some propositions:

1. It is not the law that is this instrument. The law, taken in general for the legal administration prescribed to the Jews, was instrumental for renewing, because there was a typical gospel in that Judaical administration: Heb. 4:2, 'For to us was the gospel preached as well as unto them.' They were evangelised, Ἐυαγγελισμενοι, as the word signifies. The Judaical administration was compounded of law and gospel: the moral law, as a covenant of works; the ceremonial law, representing the covenant of grace. The law of God, or gospel among them, is said to convert the soul, Ps. 19:7. But the law, taken as a covenant of works, was not appointed for renewing the soul, otherwise what need had there been of enacting another law for that work?* And those that say the law is instrumental in conversion, or inflaming our affections to obedience, say that all the benefits by it are to be ascribed to the covenant of grace in Christ. It is true, the law considered in itself is preparatory to cast men down, and shew them their distance from God and contrariety to his command; but the law without the gospel never brought any man to Christ. Whatsoever it doth in this case is not of itself, but by the mingling the gospel with it, which spirits it to such an end. Though the law did not encourage sin, yet it gave no help against it, but left the soul under the dominion of it, which is evident by the apostle's inference: Rom. 6:14, 'Sin shall not have dominion over you; for you are not under the law, but under grace.' Hence the property of the law, which is meant by 'the letter,' 2 Cor. 3:6, is to kill, but 'the Spirit' gives life; that leaves under the severity of justice, after sin had entered; but the spiritual administration, wherein the Spirit works, is to quicken and renew the soul, and make it able to get above the guilt and power of sin. The apostle, therefore, wholly excludes the law: Gal. 3:2, 'Received you the Spirit by the works of the law, or by the hearing of faith?' that is, the word of faith, as the gospel is called, Rom. 10:8. By Spirit is meant, saith Calvin, the grace of regeneration, as by faith is meant the doctrine of faith. I might have preached (as if

the apostle had said) the works of the law till my lungs had been worn out, and the renewing Spirit would never have entered into you by that fire, but it descended upon you in the sweet gospel dew. The gospel is therefore called the 'ministration of the Spirit,' and the 'ministration of righteousness,' 2 Cor. 3:8, 9. It is the chariot or vehiculum wherein the Spirit rides, the proclamation by which it is declared, the channel through which it is conveyed. The law discovers the righteousness of God as well as the gospel; but that demands a righteousness from the creature, the gospel confers a righteousness upon the creature; the law shews us God's righteousness in his nature, the gospel shews us God's righteousness in his nature and grace. The law is a hammer to break us, the gospel God's oil to cure us; the law makes sin live and our souls die,—Rom. 7:9, 'When the commandment came, sin revived, and I died,'—the gospel makes sin die and our souls live; the law awakens the lion, the gospel lets out his blood. At the best, the terrors of the law do chain up our furious affections, but the sweetness of gospel mercy changeth them. The law prepares the matter, the gospel brings the new form. That was appointed for the rule of our walk, not for the restoration of our life. And they are the promises of mercy which are the motives to return; rebels will not submit to their prince as long as they know they shall have no quarter.† Hue and cry makes the thief fly away the faster. By the 'great and precious promises,' we 'are made partakers of the divine nature,' 2 Peter 1:4. The promises of the law being conditional, belong not to us without fulfilling the condition, of which we are incapable of ourselves. The law, therefore, since the fall, is destructive, the gospel restorative, and the promises of it the cords whereby God draws us.

2. The gospel is this instrument. It is an instrument to unlock the prison doors, and take them off the hinges; strike off the fetters, and draw out the soul to a glorious liberty. It is by the voice of the archangel men shall rise in their bodies; it is by the voice of the Son of God in the word that men rise in their souls. Nothing else ever wrought such

miraculous changes. To make lions become lambs, Isa. 6:6, Hosea 4:13; beloved idols to be cast away with indignation; to make its entrance like fire, and consume old lusts in a short time: these have been undeniable realities, which have created affection and astonishment in some enemies as well as friends. It hath a more excellent instrumentality in it than other providences of God, because it is a higher manifestation. Every creature conducts us to the knowledge of God, by giving us notice of his power, wisdom, and goodness, Rom. 1:20. The declaration of his works in the world is instrumental to make men seek him, Acts 17:27. Every day's providence declares his patience, every shower of rain his merciful provision for mankind, Acts 14:17, every day's preservation of the world under a load of sin manifests his mercy. The heavens have a tongue, and the rod hath a voice; the design of all is to lead men to repentance, Rom. 2:4. If these, therefore, be some kind of instruments upon the hearts of considering men, the gospel being a discovery superior to all these, in manifesting not only a God of nature, but a God of grace, must be designed to a choicer and nobler work. The heavens and providence are instruments to instruct us, this to renew us.

It is an instrument; but,

(1.) It is not a natural instrument, to work by any natural efficacy, as food doth nourish, the sun shines, or the air and water cools, or as a sharp knife eats if it be applied to fit matter. If it were thus natural, it would not be of grace. Though the shining of the sun, or the healing by a plaster, are acts of the goodness and mercy of God, yet the Scripture calls them not by that higher title of acts of grace. If the operation were natural, the gospel would never be without its effect wheresoever it were preached; as the sun, wheresoever it shines in any land, doth both enlighten and warm. Our Saviour then would have had more success, since the gospel could not have greater natural efficacy than from his lips; yet the number of his converts were probably not much above five hundred, for so many he appeared to after his resurrection, 1 Cor. 15:6, when many thousands in that land heard his voice, and saw his miracles. Christ, who was alway able to give himself success, would not, perhaps for this among many other reasons, to advance his spiritual above his corporal presence, and to prevent any thoughts of any natural virtue in the word, without the power of the Spirit working by it. Every day teaches us, that though many see the glass of the gospel, yet few see the glory of God in that gospel. Were it natural, then, that all that hear it were not renewed, would be more miraculous than that any are; as it was more a miracle that the sun should stand still in Joshua's time, against its natural course of motion, than that it moves every day in the heavens. If it were a natural instrument, it must then have life in itself; but how can the voice of a man, or the words and syllables in a book, be capable of receiving spiritual life, which they must have before they can naturally convey it to others?* Were it a natural instrument, it would have the same effect upon the soul at one time as at another. But doth not daily experience witness, that the word shines at some particular times upon the soul with a clearer ray than at other times, that such a soul hath thought itself in another world (as it were), and that too when it hath been much clouded by the weakness of the instrument declaring it? Lastly, were it natural, the wisest men, men of the sharpest understandings, could not resist it; no man can hinder the sun's shining upon him, when he is under the beams of it; it would warm him whether he would or no; yet have not such been the most desperate opposers of it in all ages of the world, as well as in the times of the apostles? It is not then a natural, but a moral instrument, which will follow afterwards, when we come to consider how it works.

(2.) It is the only instrument appointed by God to this end in an ordinary way. God hath made a combination between hearing and believing, Rom. 10:14, 17, so that believing comes not without hearing. The waters of the sanctuary run only through the channels of the gospel; the mines of grace are found only in the climates of the word. Why doth not air nourish? Because God did not set that, but meat, apart for such an end. Though God could by his almighty power bless air to this end, yet in an ordinary way he hath fixed his blessing on these natural causes of his own ordaining. God hath appointed second causes for natural operations; if we would be warm, God hath appointed fire and sun to warm us; he could do it immediately, by spreading a lively heat in every member, as well as he gave at first a power to fire to burn; but he uses natural instruments in natural effects, and likewise spiritual instruments in spiritual productions. God may flow in an extraordinary way upon the soul by a divine breath without any instrument, as he did immediately upon the prophets, or as he gave light to the world the three first days of the creation without a sun, but since only by the sun and stars. But God seems here to have fixed his power: Rom. 1:16, the gospel is 'the power of God to salvation;' not that his power shall alway attend it, but that he will exert his power, at least ordinarily, only by it; no other organ through which the wind of the Spirit shall blow, no other sword which the Spirit shall manage but this, Eph. 6:13. Though our Saviour prayed upon the cross for some of his greatest enemies, who had their hands embrued in his precious blood, though he was heard, yet his prayer was not answered but through Peter's ministry, to grace the first spiritual discovery of the gospel. Nothing else can have that efficacy. Had every man in Israel made a brazen serpent, and looked upon it when they had been stung, they might have looked till they had groaned their last, before they had met with any cure, because only one was of God's appointing. To a cast of an eye upon that, he had only promised his healing virtue, in that only then he had lodged his power.

(3.) It is therefore a necessary instrument.

[1.] In regard of the reasonable creature there must be some declaration.* God doth not ordinarily work but by means, and doth not produce anything without them which may be done with them. God doth not maintain the creatures by a daily creation, but by generation; he maintains that faculty of generation in them by the means of health and nourishment, and that by the means of the fruits of the earth, and doth all this according to the ordinance he fixed at the creation, when he appointed every kind of creatures their proper food, and bestowed his blessing upon them, 'Increase and multiply.' So according to the method God hath set of men's actions, it is necessary that this regeneration should be by some word as an instrument, for God hath given understanding and will to man. We cannot understand anything, or will anything, but what is proposed to us by some external object; as our eye can see nothing but what is without us, our hand take nothing but what is without us, so it is necessary that God by the word should set before us those things which our understandings may apprehend, and our wills embrace. Now we believe things as we conceive them true, or not believe them as we conceive them false. We love, desire, delight in things, as we conceive them honest or profitable; we hate, we refuse, or grieve, as we conceive them dishonest, or troublesome, or hurtful to us; whatever we are changed by in our understandings, wills, and affections, is represented to us under some of these considerations. To make an alteration in us according to our nature of understanding, will, and affection, it is necessary there should be some declaration of things under those considerations of true, good, delightful, &c., in the highest manner, to make a choice change in every faculty of the soul, and without this a man cannot be changed as a rational creature; he will otherwise have a change he knows not why, nor to what end, nor upon what consideration, which is an unconceivable change in a rational creature.

[2.] It is necessary the revelation of this gospel we have should be made. There is a necessity of some revelation, for no man can see that which is not visible, or hear that which hath no sound, or know that which is not declared. There is also a necessity of the revelation of this gospel, since faith is a great part of this work. How can any man believe that God is good in Christ, without knowing that he hath so declared himself?

Since the Spirit takes of Christ's, and shews it to us, there must be a revelation of Christ, and the goodness of God in Christ, before we can believe. Though the manner of this revelation may be different, and the Spirit may renew in an extraordinary manner, yet this is the instrument whereby all spiritual begettings are wrought; the manner may be by visions, dreams, by reading or hearing, yet still it is the gospel which is revealed; the matter revealed is the same, though the formal revelation or manner may be different. Paul's regeneration was by a vision, for at that vision of the light, and that voice of Christ, I suppose him to be renewed, because of that full resignation of his will to Christ, Acts 9:6, yet the matter of the revelation was the same, that Christ was the Messiah, for so Paul understands it, in giving him the title of Lord. Though God may communicate himself without the written word to some that have it not, yet according to his appointment, not without a revelation of what is in that word.

[3.] This necessity will further appear, if we consider that it always was so. Adam and Eve were the first after the fall wherein God did constitute his church, whose regeneration and conversion were wrought by that promise of the seed of the woman made to them in paradise; God surely putting an enmity in the heart of those to whom this first promise of an enmity was made, upon which promise a sacrifice followed, which some ground on Gen. 3:21, 'God made them coats of skins' of beasts, which the word □□□signifies, and is never taken in Scripture otherwise than for the outward skin of a beast. And, indeed, it is not likely that 129 years should be between the promise and the first sacrifice, for some think Abel was killed by Cain in the 129th year after the creation; for it is certain 130 years after the creation Seth was born, Gen. 5:3.* And this is confirmed, Heb. 9:22, 'Neither the first testament was dedicated without blood.' The first testament was of ancienter date than the Jewish service ordained by Moses; and some ceremonies, as sacrifices, and distinction of clean and unclean beasts, were in use before, Gen. 8:20, so that there seems to be a sacrifice representing the Messiah, for the dedication of the first testament, which Adam had received from God and transmitted to Abel, whom he taught the way of sacrificing. What regeneration Adam had was by this word of the gospel. Had not Adam believed it, he would not have delivered it to Abel; and Abel had not sacrificed, unless he had been taught so by his father, or immediately by God; but most likely by his father, because God doth not use extraordinary means, when ordinary will serve. And Abel was regenerate, for it is said 'by faith he offered' this sacrifice, Heb. 11:4; and it was faith in Christ, faith in the promised seed, for all of them in that catalogue, Heb. 11, did eye Christ by faith, as well as Moses, of whom it is particularly expressed, ver. 26, that 'he esteemed the reproach of Christ greater riches than the treasures of Egypt.' Considering all this, it is evident, that the ancient restoration was by the revelation of Christ and the gospel as the only necessary means. Abraham, it is likely, had some external word in his father Terah's family, by tradition from the patriarchs, and had the revelation of the promise made to him by God, Gen. 18:19. And it was wrought then in an ordinary way by instruction; for, for that Abraham is commended; and no doubt but Isaac and Jacob did the same, so that all along this change of the heart was wrought by a declaration of the word of the gospel.

(4.) It seems to be the standing instrument of it to the end of the world. Some indeed think the conversion of the Jews shall not be by the declarations of the word in a way of preaching and instruction, as the Gentiles were brought in, but by a visible appearance of Christ, which they ground upon Zech. 12:10, 'They shall look upon him whom they have pierced,' they shall see Christ in the clouds as pierced by them; and understand Paul's conversion by an extraordinary light shining round about him, and a voice from heaven, to be a type and pattern of God's manner of the future conversion of the Jews, which is intimated, 1 Tim. 1:16, that the mercy he obtained was 'a pattern for them which should hereafter believe on him to life everlasting.' Whether this be so or no, yet however the conversion is by a revelation of that which is the matter and substance of the gospel, it is the revelation of Christ himself; and if, like Paul's conversion, by a voice, as well as by sight, by instruction as well as apparition; but it seems to me to be the perpetual standing means of regeneration. The fruits of our Saviour's ascension shall endure to the end of the world, and the enduing men with gifts for the building him a spiritual house is a great end of his ascension, Ps. 68:18, compared with Eph. 4:8, 9, 'Thou hast ascended on high, thou hast led captivity captive, thou hast received gifts for men; yea, for the rebellious also, that the Lord might dwell among them.' He receives gifts upon his ascension, for the subduing and changing the hearts of the rebellious, that they may be a fit habitation for God, who dwells in them by his Spirit; these gifts being the fruit of so glorious an ascension, and a rich donative to him for the accomplishment of his undertaking in the world, and being given for the smoothing, polishing, and fitting rude stones to combine together for a temple for the Lord to dwell in (which is the reason why he keeps up the world). As long therefore as God hath a temple, and any stone to polish, these gifts will remain in the ministry of the word, and be exercised in order to so great a building; and we may infer also by the way, that it is not likely that God doth dwell in any, but such who are so subdued and formed by the ministry of the word, which is the fruit of Christ's ascension. It seems also to have an ancienter date, and founded upon the covenant of redemption between the Father and the Son. All that prayer in the 17th of John seems to me to run upon those articles agreed on between them. Those that were given to Christ were given to keep his word: John 17:6, 'Thou gavest them me, and they have kept thy word.' Which word was given to Christ by God in order to be given to them: ver. 8, 'I have given them the word which thou gavest me.' And in his prayer for their sanctification, ver. 17, he seems to intimate that this was the ordinary method then subscribed to by both, and the settled means of sanctification; he doth not only propose his desire for their sanctification, but the means, 'through thy truth,' and specifies what he means by truth, 'thy word is truth.' And what he did here pray for, for them that were then with him, he did for all that should hereafter believe, ver. 20; and though this be meant of a further sanctification of those that were already regenerate, yet it will, I think, evidently follow that if the word by agreement between the Father and the Son be the instrument of every degree of sanctification, it must be also of the first; since there can be no faith, but refers to the object believed, and the ground why it is believed, whence 'belief of the truth' is joined with the 'sanctification of the Spirit,' 2 Thes. 2:13; besides, ver. 20, all belief for the future was to be through the word, 'through their word.' Let me add another inference from this; what an excellent argument is this to plead in prayer, before you go to hear or read the word; Lord, was not this an article of agreement between thee and thy Son? Was not this the desire of our Saviour, who knew the best means of sanctifying?

[5.] It is necessary, by God's appointment, for all the degrees of the new birth, and all the appendixes to it. When God shews his own glory for a further change, he represents the species of it in the glass of the gospel: 2 Cor. 3:18, 'Beholding as in a glass the glory of the Lord, are changed into the same image, from glory to glory.' It is the ministration of the Spirit in all the acts of the spirit. If the Spirit quicken, it is by some gospel precept; if it comforts, it is by some gospel promise; if it startles, it is by some threatening in the word. Whatsoever working there is in a Christian's heart, it is by some word or other dropping upon it. If any temptation which assaults us be baffled, it is by the word, which is the sword of the Spirit. The life of a Christian is made up of increasing light, refreshing comforts, choicer inclinations of the heart towards God. By the same law whereby the soul is converted the heart is rejoiced, and the eyes further enlightened: Ps. 19:7, 8, 'The law of the Lord is perfect, converting the soul, making wise the simple, rejoicing the heart, enlightening the eyes.' The Spirit makes the word not only the fire to kindle the soul, but the bellows to blow; it is first life, then liveliness to the soul. It is through the word he begets us, and through the word he quickens us: 'Thy word hath quickened me,' Ps. 119:50, 93. It is by the word God gathers a church in the world; by the same word he sanctifies it to greater degrees, Eph. 5:26. It is the seed whereby we are born, the dew whereby we are refreshed. As it is the seed of our birth, so it is the milk of our growth, 1 Peter 2:2. Faith comes by hearing, and salvation after faith by the 'foolishness of preaching,' 1 Cor. 1:21. It helps us after we have believed through grace, Acts 18:27. Our fruitfulness depends upon our plantation by this river's side. The influence of other ordinances depends upon it. Sacraments that nourish and increase, are not efficacious, but by virtue of the word;* they have their dependence on the word, as seals upon the covenant. The word is operative without sacraments; sacraments are not operative without the influence of the word, they are only assistants to it. This quickens and increaseth habitual grace, as well as it was the instrument first to usher it into the heart: Eph. 5:26, 'That he might sanctify and cleanse it with the washing of water by the word.' As God will have the mediation of his Son honoured in the whole progress and perfection of grace as the meritorious cause, the efficacy of the Spirit as the efficient cause, so he will have the word in every step to heaven honoured as the instrumental cause; that as Jesus Christ is all in all, as the chief, so the word may be all in all as the means. As God created the world by the word of his power, and by the word of his providence bid the creatures increase and multiply, so by the word of the gospel he lays the foundation, and rears the building, of his spiritual house.

4. As it is not a natural instrument, but the only instrument appointed by God, and therefore, upon these and upon other accounts, a necessary instrument, so it is an instrument which makes mightily for God's glory. The meaner the appearance of the instrument, the more evident the power and skill of the workman. It would be miraculous for a man to

raise up another from death, by a composition of medicines syringed down the throat, but a greater miracle to raise him by speaking a word. In the new birth there is nothing sensible to man but the word, the other causes are secret; like the wind, you know not whence it comes, nor whither it goes. The instrument being weak in itself, none can claim any share with God in the glory of the work. But were there a natural strength in the means, much of the honour would be pared from God, and assumed by the creature. It is like the trumpet in the right hand of Gideon's soldiers, and a pitcher with a lamp in the left. Upon the blowing of the trumpet and the breaking of the pitcher, the enemies fled; and God would have the means but small, but three hundred of thirty-two thousand, that Israel might not vaunt, and say, Mine own arm hath saved me, Judges 7:2. It had not been so admirable for Samson to have killed so many with a sword or spear, or if the walls of Jericho had fallen flat by the force of some battering engine; but it was wonderful to see them tumble at the blast of ram's horns. Is it not the same to see strongholds, high thoughts, Goliath-like corruptions, and spiritual death itself, fly before the voice of the word? To see a man like the Babel-builders, swelling and rearing up his own confidences against God, to have all the former language of his soul confounded by a word; to think of other objects, speak in another strain, descend from self to dust, deny pleasure, embrace a crucified Christ; that carnal reason should be silenced, legions of devils driven out, a massy Dagon fall before an ark of wood, that hath nothing in it but the rod of Aaron and the pot of manna: in such weak means is the power of God exalted, and no other cry can reasonably be heard but 'This is the Lord's doing, and it is marvellous in our eyes.' So it was more glorious for our Saviour to turn many of the Jews to him after his death than in his life, to bring them to believe by a word, upon a person they had crucified as a malefactor, than if he had brought them to believe while he was attended with a train of miracles. The power of his miracles might seem in their eyes to be extinct with his death, since he that delivered others did not deliver himself from the hands of his murderers. He now honours both his own words and their faith, in bringing them to believe by the preaching of men, who did not believe by the word from his lips, attended with the seals of so many glorious miracles.

5. Consider, as it is an instrument, so but an instrument. God begets by the word; the chief operation depends upon the Spirit of God. No sword can cut without a hand to manage it, no engine batter without a force to drive it. The word is objective in itself, operative by the power of the Spirit; instrumental in itself, efficacious by the Holy Ghost. The word of Christ is first spirit and then life: 'The words that I speak unto you, they are spirit, and they are life,' John 6:63. The word is the chariot of the Spirit, the Spirit the guider of the word; there is a gospel comes in word, and there is a gospel comes in power, 1 Thes. 1:5. There is a publishing of the gospel, and there is the 'fulness of the blessing of the gospel,' Rom. 15:29. There was the truth of God spoken by Peter and Paul, and God in that truth working in the heart: Gal. 2:8, 'He that wrought effectually in Peter to the apostleship of the circumcision, the same was mighty in me towards the Gentiles.' The gospel in itself is like Christ's voice; the gospel with the Spirit is like Christ's power raising Lazarus; other men might have spoke the same words, but the power of rising must come from above. It then successful when an inward unction drops with the outward dew, when the veil is taken from the heart, and the curtain from the word, and both meet together, both word and heart; when Christ kisseth with the kisses of his mouth, and the man embraceth it with the affections of his heart. The light in the air is the instrument by which we read, but the principle of that light is in the sun in the heavens. The word is a rod, a breath, but efficacious in smiting and slaying the old man, as it is the rod of Christ's mouth, the breath of his lips, Isa. 11:3; a rod like that of Moses to charm us, but as it is the rod of his strength, Ps. 110:2; a weapon, but only 'mighty through God,' 2 Cor.

10:4; a seed, but brings not forth a plant but by the influence of the sun. The word hath this efficacy from the bleeding wounds and dying groans of Christ. It is by making his soul an offering for sin that he sees the travail of his soul in his new born creatures. By his blood are all the promises of grace confirmed; by his blood they are operative. The word whereby we are begotten was appointed by God, confirmed by Christ, and the Spirit which begets us was purchased by the same blood. To conclude: the word declares Christ, and the Spirit excites the heart to accept him; the word shews his excellency, and the Spirit stirs up strong cries after him; the word declares the promises, and the Spirit helps us to plead them; the word administers reasons against our reasonings, and the Spirit edgeth them; the word shews the way, and the Spirit enables to walk in it; the word is the seed of the Spirit, and the Spirit the quickener of the word; the word is the graft, and the Spirit the engrafter; the word is the pool of water, and the Spirit stirs it to make it healing.

II. Quest. How doth the word work?

1. Objectively, as it is a declaration of God's will, as it doth propose to the understanding what is to be known, in order to salvation hereafter and practice here, as it doth declare the purpose of God to save only by Jesus Christ the Mediator, and by him to deliver us from sin, Satan, and whatsoever is contrary to everlasting happiness; and thus is significative of something to our minds and understandings. The Spirit gave us an eye to see, and the word is the light which discovers the object to the eye. The Spirit gives us an organ, but something must be proposed for that organ to exercise itself about, otherwise there is no use of the understanding in any rational operation; which certainly there is, for though the object is supernatural, and the inward work upon the mind supernatural, yet the proposal of the object to the mind is made in a rational manner. The word doth objectively propose life and death in a way suitable to the nature of man, that he may rationally choose life: 'I have set before you life and death, blessing and cursing, therefore choose life,' Deut. 30:19.

Both the blessings of the gospel and the curses of the law are presented in the word, that the one may be chosen, the other avoided. The word is proposed under various notions: as true, and so it is the object of the speculative understanding; as good, so it is the object of the practical understanding and will; as profitable, so it is the object of the appetite and affections. When it is received into the speculative understanding, it is a preparation to the new birth; when it is received into the practical understanding and will, it is the new birth. It discovers the wonders in God's own heart, his Son, and his promise; the Spirit demonstrates it, and gives power to embrace it. It first presents the promise, and then answers the pleas the stubborn heart makes against it, yet by the same gospel; it fetches demonstrative arguments from that quiver to satisfy a cavilling understanding, and motives from thence to overcome a resisting will; it silenceth the fears, points to the way, excites the soul to an acceptance of Christ, all by this gospel, and so draws us, as a man draws a child, by presenting some alluring object to him. The Spirit immediately himself touches the soul, but by the word, as an instrument proposing the object, and drawing out the soul into an actual believing. The two chief parts of the word are,

(1.) The discovery of our misery by nature. The heart is ripped open, our putrefied condition in our blood evidenced, our deplorable state unfolded, and thereby the conscience awakened to sensible reflections. It dissects the heart, discovers the secret reserves, unravels the thoughts, pursues sin to its fastnesses, and pulls and brings it out, as Joshua the kings to execution: 1 Cor. 14:25, 'And thus are the secrets of his heart made manifest, and so falling down on his face he will worship God, and report that God is in you of a truth.' It opens sin to the very bowels, discovers the inward filth, takes off its beautiful disguise, its silken covering, and shews the running ulcer under it. It discovers the forlorn estate by nature, and the insufficiency of flesh and blood to inherit the kingdom of God. Let the word be whispered by the Spirit in the ears of a ruffling sinner, and the curtains which obscured his sin from his eye drawn open, that he may see what a nest of devils he hath, what astonishment will it raise in him! How will he stand amazed at his own folly! How will he loathe that self which before he so vehemently loved!

(2.) A second discovery is of the necessity and existence of another bottom. It discovers our misery by nature, and our remedy by Christ, the plague brought upon the world by the first Adam, the cure brought to the world by the second. It proclaims a peace concluded between God and the humbled sinner, by his Son, the great ambassador, confirmed by his blood, assured by his resurrection. It shews him the fountain of death in his sin, the fountain of life in Christ, the free streams and gracious communications of it. The promise discovers the gracious nature of God, his kindness to man, the openness of his arms to receive him, and thus bring the soul off from itself to the foot of God and the bottom of the cross. When the word like fire and the heart like tinder come close together, the heart catcheth the spark and burns. From the word reconciliation and peace step out and meet the soul, it finds the kisses of Christ's mouth inspiring it with life, the box of the gospel promises broke open, the window of the gospel ark opened, and the dove flying out of it into the desert heart. The word proposeth things as they are in reality, and the soul knows things as it ought to know, 1 Cor. 8:2. It understands the unavoidable necessity and the infallible excellency of the things proposed; it sees the rocks and shelves wherein the danger lies, and a compass whereby to steer, a road wherein to lie safe at anchor; whereupon he relents for his sin, is astonished at divine kindness, rejoiceth at the promise as before he trembled at the threatening, and hath far other thoughts of God than he had before, in which act divine life is breathed into the soul.

2. The word seems to have an active force upon the will, though the manner of it be very hard to conceive. It is operative in the hand of God for sanctification. The petition of our Saviour, John 17:17, 'Sanctify

them through thy truth, thy word is truth,' seems to intimate more than a bare objective relation to this work; it both shews us our spots and cleanseth them. It is a seed. Seed, though small, is active; no part of the plant retains a greater efficacy; all the glory and strength of the plant, in its buds, blossoms, and fruit, are hidden in it. The word is this seed, which being settled in the heart by the power of the Spirit, brings forth this new creature. It is a glass that not only represents the image of God, but by the Spirit changeth us into it, 2 Cor. 3:18. A sword that pierceth the heart, Heb. 4:12, yea, 'sharper than a two-edged sword, dividing asunder the soul and spirit.' It is a fire to burn. The Spirit doth so edge the word that it cuts to the quick, discerns the very thoughts, insinuates into the depths of the heart, and rakes up the small sands from the bottom, as a fierce wind doth from the bowels of the sea. It is God's ordnance to batter down strongholds. Though it be not a natural instrument to work necessarily, yet it is likened to natural instruments, which are active under the efficiency of the agent which manages them; and this also, in the hands of the Spirit, works mighty effects. The 'sanctification of the Spirit and belief of the truth' are joined together, one subordinate to another, 2 Thes. 2:13. The Spirit efficiently infusing holy habits; the word objectively and actively—objectively, as outwardly proposed; actively, as inwardly ingrafted;—it at least excites the new infused gracious principle, and produceth our actual conversion and believing. As the pronouncing excommunication in the primitive times filled the person with terror; and no question but upon the same account the authoritative pronouncing the pardon of sin by the apostles, though only declarative, might have a mighty operation upon the soul in filling it with joy; yet both, as managed by the Spirit, concurring with his own ordnance. So that the word is mighty in operation as well as clear in representation; for an activity seems to be ascribed to it by the Scripture metaphors. The chief activity of it is seen in that likeness which it produceth in the soul to itself. Seeds have an efficacious virtue to produce plants of the same kind with that whose seeds they are; so the word produceth qualities in the heart like itself. The law in the heart is the law in the word transcribed in the soul; a graft which changeth a crabbed stock into a sweet tree, James 1:21; like a seal it leaves a likeness and impression of itself; it works a likeness to God as he is revealed in the gospel, for we are changed into the same image. What image? The same image which we behold in that glass, 2 Cor. 3:18; not his essential image, but the image of his glory represented in the gospel for our imitation. The word is the glory of God in a glass, and imprints the image of the glory of God in the heart. It is a softening word, and produceth a mollified heart; an enlightening word, and causes an enlightened soul; a divine word, and engenders a divine nature; it is a spiritual word, and produceth a spiritual frame; as it is God's will, it subdues our will; it is a sanctifying truth, and so makes a sink of sin to become the habitation of Christ. To conclude: this is certain: the promise in the word breeds principles in the heart suitable to itself; it shews God a father, and raises up principles of love and reverence; it shews Christ a mediator, and raises up principles of faith and desire. Christ in the word conceives Christ in the heart; Christ in the word, the beginning of grace, conceives Christ in the soul, the hope of glory.

III. The Use. 1. Information.

1. How admirable, then, is the power of the gospel! It is a quickening word, not a dead; a powerful word, not a weak; a sharp-edged word, not dull; a piercing word, not cutting only skin deep, Heb. 4:12. What welcome work doth it make, when a door of utterance and a door of entrance are both opened together! It hath a mighty power to out-wrestle the principalities of hell, and demolish the strongholds of sin in the heart. It is a word of which it may be said, as the psalmist of the sun, Ps. 19:6, 'His circuit is to the ends of the earth, and there is nothing hid from the heat thereof.' No part of the soul is hidden from a new birth by the warm beams of it, when directed by God to the soul. What a powerful

breath is that which can make a dead man stand upon his feet and walk! If you should find your faces, by looking in a glass, transformed into an angelical beauty, would yon not imagine some strange and secret virtue in that glass? How powerful is this gospel word, which changeth a beast into a man, a devil into an angel, a clod of earth into a star of heaven!

(1.) It is above the power of all moral philosophy. The wisdom of the heathens never equalled the gospel in such miracles; the political government of the best states never made such alterations in the hearts of men. How excellent is that gospel which hath done that for the renewing of millions of souls, which all the wit and wisdom of the choicest philosophers could never effect upon one heart! All other lectures can do no more than allay the passions, not change them; bring them into an order fit for human society, not beget them for a divine fellowship; not draw them forth out of a principle of love to God, and fix them upon so high an end as the glory of God that is invisible. This is the glorious begetting by the gospel, which enables not only to moral actions, but inspires with divine principles and ends, and makes men highly delight in the ways they formerly abhorred. What are a few sprinklings of changes moral philosophy hath wrought in the lives of men, to the innumerable ones the gospel hath wrought, which were such undeniable realities, that they were never openly contradicted by any of the most violent persecutors of the Christian religion, and were alway the most urged argument for the truth of the gospel in the ancient apologies for it? How long may we read and hear mere moral discourses, and arrive no higher than some reformation of life, with unchanged hearts; have sin beaten from the outworks, yet retain the great fort, the heart!

(2.) Above the power of the law. The natural law sees not Christ, the Mosaical law dimly shews him afar off; the gospel brings him near, to be embraced by us, and us to be divinely changed by him. The natural law makes the model and frame of a man, the Mosaical adds some colours and preparations, and the gospel conveys spirit into them. The natural law begets us for the world, the Mosaical kills us for God, and the gospel raises up to life. The natural law makes us serve God by reason, the Mosaical by fear, and the gospel by love. It is by this, and not by the law, those three graces which are the main evidences of life are settled in the soul. It begets faith, whereby we are taken off from the stock of Adam, and inserted in Christ; hope, whereby we flourish; and love, whereby we fructify. By faith, we have life; by hope, strength; by love, liveliness and activity. All these are the fruits of the gospel administration.

(3.) Its power appears in the subjects it hath been instrumental to change. Souls bemired in the filthiest lusts, have been made miraculously clean; it hath changed the hands of rapine into instruments of charity, hearts full of filth into vessels of purity; it hath brought down proud reason to the obedience of faith, and made active lusts to die at the foot of the cross; it hath struck off Satan's chains, and snatched away his captives into the liberty of God's service; it hath changed the most stubborn hearts. The conversion of a great company of those Jewish priests that were most violent against it and the author of it, is ascribed to the power of the word: Acts 6:7, 'And the word of God increased, and a great company of the priests were obedient to the faith.' How many were raised to life by Peter's sermon! More souls turned than words spoken upon record. It subdues the will, which cannot be conquered but by its own consent. Light can dart in upon the understanding whether a man will or no, and flash in his face though he keep it in unrighteousness. Conscience will awaken and rouse them, though men use all the arts they can to still it. The will cannot be forced to any submission against its own consent; the power of the gospel is seen in the conquest of the will, and putting new inclinations into that.

(4.) The power of it is seen in the suddenness of its operation. In a moment, in the twinkling of an eye, like the change at the last resurrection: 1 Cor. 15:51, 52, 'We shall all be changed, in a moment, at the last trumpet.' How have troops of unmastered lusts fled at the voice of the gospel trumpet, like a flock of frighted birds, and left their long-possessed mansion! How have the affections, which have sheltered so many enemies against God, been on the sudden weary of their residence, and abhorred what they loved, and loved what the moment before they abhorred! How have welcome temptations been upon this sudden change rejected, a despised Saviour dearly embraced, a furious soul tamed, a darling self crucified, and a soul open to every temptation strongly fortified against it! How frequent are the examples, in the first times of Christianity, of men that have been almost as bad as devils one day, one hour, and joyful martyrs the next; and as soon as ever they have been begotten by it, asserted the power of it in another new birth by flames!

(5.) And this hath been done many times by one part, one particle of the word. One word of the gospel, a single sentence, hath erected a heavenly trophy in a soul, which all the volumes of the choicest mere reason could never erect; one plain scripture hath turned a face to heaven that never looked that way before, and made a man fix his eye there against his carnal interest. One plain scripture hath killed a man's sins, and quickened his heart with eternal life; one word of Christ, remembered by Peter, made him weep bitterly, and two or three scriptures, pressed by the same Peter upon his hearers, pricked their hearts to the quick. How hath hell flashed in the face of a sinner, out of a small cloud of a threatening, and heaven shot into the soul from one little diamond spark of a promise! A little seed of the word, like a grain of mustard seed, changed the soul from a dwarfish to a tall stature! This the experience of every age can testify.

(6.) And this power appears in the simplicity of it. Savonarola* observes, that when he neglected the preaching of the Scripture, and applied himself to discourses of philosophy, he gained little upon the hearts of people; but when he came to illustrate and explain the Scripture, the minds of people were wonderfully inflamed and excited to a serious frame; and that when he discoursed in a philosophical manner, there was a non-attention, not only of the more ignorant, but the more learned sort too; but when he preached Scripture truths, he found the minds of men mightily delighted, stung with divine truth, brought to compunction, and a reformation of their lives, which shews, saith he, the power of the word, acting more vigorously than all human reason in the world. And indeed Scripture, and Scripture reason, is the wisdom of God; all other reason is the wisdom of man. God will depress man's wisdom and advance his own. It works as it is 'the word of God which lives and abides for ever,' 1 Peter 1:23. To wrap a fine piece of silk about a sword, or gild a diamond, is to hinder the edge of the one, and the lustre of the other.

2. Information. The gospel is then certainly of divine authority, since in this 'God hath set a tabernacle for the Sun' of righteousness to move in, as the heavens are the tabernacle for the material sun, Ps. 19:4. That word that raises the dead, must needs be the word of no less than God. Our Saviour's discovery of men's thoughts argued his deity. The word's discovery of the inward workings of the heart, and the alteration it makes there, evidenceth a divine stamp upon it. God would never have made a lie so successful in the world, or blessed it in making those alterations in men, so comely in the eye of moral nature, so advantageous to human society, as the principles it instils into the minds of men are. A lie would never have been blessed to be an instrument of so much virtue and truth; it would not consist with the righteousness of God's government, or his goodness and truth as governor, to bring the hearts of men into so beautiful an order by a deceitful gospel. What word ever had such trophies! What engine ever battered so many strongholds! If the lame walk by the strength of it, if the dead are raised by the power of it, if lepers are cleansed by the virtue of it, if impure souls are sanctified, dead souls enlivened, are we to question its divine authority? Should a word work such wonderful effects for so many ages, that had no stamp of divine authority upon it? Would all those witnesses be given by God to a mere imposture? Let the victories it hath gained evidence the arm that

wields it. What sword was used at the first conquest of the world through grace, but this of the Spirit? How soon was the devil, with all his heap of idols, fain to fly before it! How soon was the devil, with all his pack of lusts, forced to leave his habitation in the hearts of men! Is not that of divine authority that so routs the enemies of God, puts sin to flight, expels spiritual death, breaking the bands of that worst king of terrors; that had skill to find out sin in its lurking holes, and power to dispossess that, and introduce spiritual life into the soul? Can that be a thing less than divine, that restores man to his due place as a creature respecting his Creator, referring all things to his glory; that implants the love, fear, hope of God in the mind; that makes man, of a miserable corrupt creature, to become divine; that roots out the vices of hell, and stores the soul with the virtues of heaven? Can such a gospel be termed less than a divine word of truth? If there be any word that can so change the nature, and transform wolves into lambs, let it have the honour and due praise when it is found out; but whatsoever the atheism of the world is, that never felt the powerful efficacy of it, you surely that have felt it a mighty weapon to conquer the devils that once possessed you, and an instrument to new beget you when you lay in your blood, should entertain no whisper against the divine authority of it, but count it the power and wisdom of God, as, indeed, it is in itself, and in its effects upon souls, Rom. 1:16. It is said there to be 'the power of God to salvation.' Upon that account the apostle was not ashamed of it; neither should we, but conclude as the same apostle saith, 'If I be not an apostle, yet to you I am an apostle.' So if the gospel be not in itself the gospel of God, surely it is so to you who have been renewed.

3. Information. It shews us the reason why the gospel is so much opposed by Satan in the world. It begets those for heaven whom he had begotten for hell. It pulls down his image and sets up God's; it pulls the crown off his head, the sceptre from his hand, snatches subjects from his empire, straitens his territories, and demolisheth his forts, breaks

his engines, outwits his subtilty, makes his captives his conquerors, and himself, the conqueror, a captive; it pulls men 'out of the kingdom of darkness, and translates them into a kingdom of light,' Col. 1:13. And all this, as it is a word of truth, opposed to his word of deceit, whereby he hath cheated mankind and deceived the nations; that we may well say of him, as the apostle of death, 'O death, where is thy sting?' 1 Cor. 15:55. O hell, where is thy sting? O Satan, where is thy victory? This slays Satan and revives the soul.

4. We see then how injurious they are to God, who would obstruct the progress of the gospel in the world; that, as the papists, would hinder the reading and the preaching of the word. Whose seed are they, but the seed of that dragon, that would as well hinder the new birth as devour a divine-begotten babe 'as soon as ever it were born,' Rev. 12:4. Such would hinder the greatest and most excellent work of God upon the souls of men, would have no spiritual generations for God in the world. Such envy Christ a seed, and God a family; they would despoil him of a family on earth, though they cannot of a family in heaven. In banishing the word, they would banish the grace of God out of the world, and leave no place in a world drowned with ignorance, where this dove should set her foot. Those that would take away the seed, would not have a spiritual harvest, but reduce souls to a deplorable famine, lock them up in the grave, and keep them under the bands of a spiritual death.

5. It informs us, that the gospel shall then endure in the world, as long as God hath any to beget. Men may puff at it, but they cannot extinguish it; it is a word of truth, and truth is mighty, and will prevail. It was a mighty wind wherein the Spirit came upon the apostles, to shew not only the quick and speedy progress of the gospel, as upon the wings of the wind, but the mighty force of it, that men can no more silence the sound of the gospel than they can the blustering of the wind. It shall prevail in all places, where God hath a seed to bring in, a people to beget. Those given to Christ shall come from far: 'from the east,' Isa. 49:12, 'and from

the west, and from the land of Sinim' (now, I think, called Damiata, in Egypt). The word, being the instrument, shall sound everywhere, where he hath sons and daughters to beget for Christ. As long as Christ doth retain his royalty, 'his mouth shall be a sharp sword,' Isa. 49:2. That is the first thing concluded on between God and Christ, before they come to any further treaty, which is expressed in that chapter. As Christ shall be his salvation to the ends of the earth, so shall the word be the instrument of it to the end of the world: the 'polished shaft' is 'hid in his quiver.' As he is a light to the Gentiles, so the golden candlestick of this gospel wherein this light is set, shall endure in spite of men and devils. Since his promise of a seed to Christ stands sure, the word, whereby he begets a generation for him, is as sure as the promise, and shall not return void: Isa. 55:11, 'but it shall accomplish that which he pleases, and it shall prosper in the things whereto he sent it.' Never fear then the removal of the gospel out of the world, though it be removed out of a particular place, since it is a word of truth, and an instrument ordained to so glorious an end.

6. It is a sign, then, God hath some to beget, when he brings his gospel to any place. He hath a pleasure to accomplish, and it shall not return unto him void. Prosperity is entailed upon it for the doing the work whereto he sent it. Since then it is appointed an instrument, in the hand of the Spirit, for a new begetting, it will be efficacious upon some souls where it comes; for the wise God would not send it, but to attain its main end upon some hearts. God never sends his word to any place, but it is received and relished by some as the savour of life. It looseth the bands of spiritual death in some, and binds them harder upon obstinate sinners; to them that perish it is the savour of death. In every place the gospel was savoury to some: 2 Cor. 2:14, 15, 'God made manifest the savour of his knowledge,' by the apostles, 'in every place.' Wherever this seed is sown, the harvest hath been reaped, either more or less. It is fruitful at Corinth, for there God had much people, Acts 18:10. It is not fruitless at Athens, though the harvest was less; most mocked, but some believed,

and but one man of learning and worldly wisdom, Acts 17:32, 34. When God sends John in a way of righteousness, if the pharisees believe not, God will, make a conquest of publicans and harlots: Mat. 21:32, 'John came to you in the way of righteousness, and you believed not: but the publicans and harlots believed him.' The net of the gospel is not cast wholly in vain, but from the time of its coming, to the time of its removal, some souls have been catched, though not of the most delicious fish, yet of the worst sort.

7. It informs us, what an excellent thing is a new birth! The end is more desirable than the means; this is the chief end of all the ordinances of God in the world. The gospel had never been revealed but for this intent; this is the design of the Spirit's operation in any gospel administration. All the lines of the word are to draw the lineaments of grace in the heart. This must be a noble and excellent thing, for which chiefly the oracles of God sound in the world, for which so great a light is set up in the gospel. All the love of Christ breathes in the gospel; the whole Testament is sealed by his blood; the perpetual workings of the Holy Ghost, the preaching of the word, the celebration of the sacraments, are in subserviency to this end; the one to make us live, the other to make us grow. How unconceivably excellent is that, how valuable in the eye of God, how advantageous to the happiness of men, that is, the design wherein so many divine operations meet!

8. What a lamentable thing is it, that so few should be new begotten by the word of truth! How many are there among us that understand not what a new begetting and birth is, no more than Nicodemus when he discoursed with our Saviour! What a deplorable thing is it that the word should be preached, and so little regarded! that not only an hour's, but many years' discourses should pass away (as the psalmist speaks of our lives) 'like a tale that is told!' Ps. 90:9. How miserable is that man that hath the objective cause of the new birth, without the effective! It is the word of truth. What will become of you, if you prefer a word of

error before it; if you prefer the devil's killing suggestions before God's reviving oracles? What doth the word of truth move you to, but to a new birth? Why will any man struggle against it? Every resistance of the word is a resistance of God himself. It is God hews by the prophets, Hos. 6:5; it is God offers to beget by the word; every reluctance then against the word, is a reluctance against God. The word will either bring in a new form of grace, or a new form of torment. If the inworking of the one be rejected, the inworking of the other cannot be avoided; it will either cut the bands of a spiritual death, or cut the sinews of our souls. That piece of timber that hath not its knots cut off for the building, shall be cut in pieces for the fire. A new life waits for them that obey the gospel; an endless death for them that reject it; they that obey not the gospel, know not God, 2 Thes. 1:8. And what is reserved for such, but revenging flames in another world? It would be happy for such, that they had never heard of a renewing gospel. Every gospel discourse that might have been the cause of a spiritual life, and a divine cordial, if sucked in, rejected, will be a bitter drug in that potion which shall be drunk in an eternal fever.

9. Hereby you may examine whether you are new begotten. It is the word of truth whereby God begets. In this word he opens the glory of his grace, and through this he conveys the power of his grace. The conquests of Christ were to be made by the word, and it was so settled at the first constitution of him as Mediator and Redeemer: Isa. 49:2, 'He hath made my mouth like a sharp sword.' It was by this the hearts of men were to be conquered. And what heart is not subdued by the sword of his mouth, is not subdued by the power of his arms. Some word or other was the instrument to beget you (I speak of people grown up). The apostle's interrogation is a strong negative. There is no believing without hearing, Rom. 10:14. Hearing goes before believing; he lays it down as a certain conclusion from his former arguing: 'So then faith comes by hearing, and hearing by the word of God.' If you conclude yourselves new begotten, how came you by it? Is it by the word, or no? That is God's ordinary

means. If you be not renewed by this, it is not likely you are renewed at all; no other instrument hath God ordinarily appointed to this end. Afflictions may plough men for it, but the word is the only seed that renews the face of the earth. All false notions or presumptions of the new birth must be brought to this touchstone; it is a misshapen and monstrous birth, that is not by a seed of the same kind; the law in the heart hath no seed of the same nature with it to engender it, but the law in the word, that word which we properly call gospel; the word of truth, not the word of philosophy, which is a word of uncertainty; God's word, not Plato's word. If a thousand beasts had been consumed by common fire, not one of them had been an holocaust, a grateful sacrifice, unless consumed by the fire of the altar which came down from heaven. Moral wisdom is not that fire, hath not that eminent descent from heaven; it is not that speech from heaven whereby our Saviour is said yet to speak, Heb. 12:25. A little spark kindled by the voice of Christ from heaven, from whence he yet speaks in the gospel, is more worth than all the bonfires in the world, kindled by the sparks of moral wisdom. Those qualifications which grow of their own accord, without the word, are like the herbs which sprout in wild places without any tillage, which are of a different kind than what are planted and watered in a garden, and overlooked by the care of man. If your dispositions you boast of were not planted by the word, how fair soever they may look, they are but a wild kind of fruit; therefore, it concerns you to look back upon yourselves, think what word it was whereby you were begotten. If no particular word can be remembered, if your regeneration were wrought insensibly in your younger years, examine what suitableness there is between the word and your souls, whether your hearts are turned into the nature of it. The measures of grace are according to the measures of the word. If you cannot remember the first glorious entrance of it, you must see for the rich dwelling of it. An inhabitant may enter into our houses unseen, but he cannot dwell there without our knowledge; the lines of the word will be seen in the heart, though the particular pencil whereby they were wrought may not be remembered.

10. It instructs ministers how to preach. It is the word of truth, the gospel, that must be the main matter of our preaching; and those things in the gospel that have the greatest tendency to the new begetting men, and working this great change in them, and driving it on to greater maturity. The instrument of conversion is not barely the letter of the word, but the sense and meaning of it, rationally impressed upon the understanding, and closely applied to the conscience. The opening the word is the life of it, and the true means of regeneration. If any man would turn his servant or child from a course of sin, would he discourse to them of the nature of the sun and stars, their magnitude, motions, number, and qualities? This would be nothing to the purpose; his way would be to shew them the deformity and danger of their sin. The word of truth is God's instrument, and it should be ours; what is the end of the word, should be the end of our preaching. It was through the gospel the apostle begat the Corinthians; not that the preaching of the law is excluded, but it must be preached in order to the gospel as a preparation to it. Whatsoever in the word of truth doth prepare for the new birth, produce it, cherish it, preserve it, centre in one and the same end. How careful and industrious should we be to beget children to God, that we may present them, and say, 'Here am I, and the children, which thou hast given me.' The new birth will be your joy, and crown, and you will be ours, 1 Thes. 2:19, 20. Aaron's sons are called the generations of Moses, as well as Aaron, Num. 3:1, though none of his natural sons are reckoned; Aaron's by natural generation, Moses's perhaps by a spiritual regeneration and instruction.

Use 2. Of exhortation.

1. Highly glorify God for the word of truth, which is so great an instrument. How thankful should we be for an invention, to secure our estates from consuming, houses from burning, bodies from dying! The

gospel, the word of truth, doth much more than this: it is an instrument to beget a soul for God; an instrument whereby God makes himself our Father, and us his children. It is but an instrument; let not the glory be given to the instrument, but to the agent. As it is an instrument, let it have part of your affections, but nothing of the glory that belongs to God; love the truth, but glorify and bless the God of truth, that hath ordained it to be so excellent an instrument,

(1.) Bless God in your hearts. [1.] That ever you had the word of truth made known to you. How many millions sit in a spiritual darkness, without so much as the means of a new begetting! Millions never heard the sound of it, nor ever will. [2.] Much more that it hath been successful to any of you. Have you any thing in your spirits that bears witness to the truth of it? When you read or hear it, do you find something of kin to it in your souls, and feel something within you rise up and call it blessed? How should you read and hear it, with eruptions of thankfulness to God for it, hearty embraces for it, and fervent ejaculations to God to work more in you by the power of it! Why hath the word grappled with any of our souls, and not with others; arrested any of you in a course of sin, and left others to walk in their own ways, to run down silently like the streams of a river, till swallowed up in an ocean of death? The apostle Paul heard the voice, others with him only a sound of words, Acts 9:9, 7, 22:9; some have heard a sound of words, without the voice of God in it, while others have heard a divine voice in a human sound. The wind hath blown upon many, God in that wind only upon few; some have received air, whilst others have received spirit and life; some have only the body of the word, while others feel the spirit and power of it in their hearts. Shall not God be glorified for this? Had it not been for him, and his Spirit, words had been only words and wind to all as well as to some.

(2.) Glorify God in your lives. As you feel the power of it in your hearts, let others see the brightness and efficacy of it in your actions. The new born creature should principally aim at the glory of God, since the instrument whereby he is begotten was first published for the 'glory of God in the highest,' Luke 2:14. What is produced by the efficacy of such an instrument must have the same end, viz. the glory of God in the practice of holiness. A holy gospel imprinted can never leave the heart and life unholy. A gospel coined for the glory of God, when wrought in the heart, can never suffer the soul to aim chiefly at self, but at the great end for which the gospel was first discovered. The gospel of holiness and truth in the heart will engender sincerity and holiness in the life.

2. Prize the word of truth, which works such great effects in the soul. Value that as long as you live, which is the cord whereby God hath drawn any of you out of the dungeon of death. Never count that foolishness by which God hath inspired you with the choicest wisdom; and never count that weakness which hath made any of you of dead, living; and of darkness, light; and of miserable, happy by grace. If a soul be worth a world, and therefore to be prized, how precious ought that to be which is an instrument to beget a soul for the felicity of another world! How should the law of God's mouth be better to us than thousands of gold and silver! Ps. 119:72. How should we prize that word whereby any of us have seen the glory of God in his sanctuary, the glory of God in our souls! When corruptions are strong, it is an engine to batter them; when our hearts are hard, it is a hammer to break them; when our spirits are imposthumated, it is a sword to cut them; when our hearts are cold, it is a fire to inflame them; when our souls are faint, it is a cordial to refresh them, it begins a new birth and maintains it. It is the seed from whence we spring, 1 Peter 1:23, the glass wherein we see the glory of God, 2 Cor. 3:18. By the waters of the sanctuary, we have both meat for nourishment, and medicines for cure, from the tree that grows by its streams: Ezek. 47:12, 'The fruit thereof shall be for meat, and the leaf for medicine.' Have a great regard to it, keep it in the midst of your hearts, for it is life, Prov. 4:21, 22.

3. Pray and endeavour for the preservation and success of the word of truth. Were there a medicine that could preserve life, how chary should we be in preserving that? The gospel is the tree, whose leaves cure the nations, Rev. 22:2. It was a blessing God endued the creatures with, when he bid them increase and multiply, Gen. 1:22. It was an evidence that he intended to preserve the world. If the gospel get ground in the hearts of men, it is an evidence it shall continue in spite of the oppositions of men or devils.

4. Wait upon God in the word. Where there is a revelation on God's part, there must be a hearing on ours. Sit down therefore at the feet of God, and receive of his words, Deut. 33:3. (1.) Despise it not; he that contemns it never intends to be new begotten, since he slights the means of God's appointment; he that intends an end, will use all means proportionably to his desires for that end; he that contemns it never was renewed. Habitual grace being wrought by it, cannot, but in its own nature, have a great affection to it. He that loves Christ cannot but love all the methods of his operations. (2.) Despise it not because it is but an instrument: say not, because God is the chief agent, therefore you need not come to the word. Our Saviour knew that 'man did not live by bread alone, but by every word that proceeds out of the mouth of God,' Mat. 4:4. Did he therefore neglect means for preserving his life? Because God gives the increase, should not the husbandman plough and sow? If God doth not work upon you by the means, you can have no rational hopes he will do it any other way. What though ministers can only speak to the ear? John Baptist could do no more, whose ministry was notwithstanding glorious, in being the forerunner of Christ. To neglect it, therefore, is to double-bar your hearts against the entrance of grace, and slight the truth which Christ brought down from the bosom of God.

(1.) Never did God appoint any other way but this. Miracles were never appointed but as attendants upon this. Miracles come after teachings in the great gifts to the church, 1 Cor. 12:7–10. First, the 'manifestation of the Spirit,' 'the word of wisdom and the word of knowledge,' then 'gifts of healing and miracles.' Miracles are ceased, as being not absolutely necessary; but the ministry of the word will last to the end of the world. By the prophets God brings souls out of a state of bondage, and by the prophets he preserves them in a state of grace: Hosea 12:13, 'By a prophet the Lord brought Israel out of Egypt, and by a prophet was he preserved.' Miracles and the resurrection of one from the dead, was never appointed under the legal administration, but Moses and the prophets, Luke 16:13. These were the ordinary means, and if these did not work, miracles were inefficacious.

(2.) God never made any promise but in this way. God promised to circumcise their hearts to love him with all their soul, but in the way of hearing his voice, and observing his statutes, Deut. 30:6, 10, 11. He meets souls only that remember him in his way, Isa. 64:5. And to the preaching of the gospel only, our Saviour promised his presence to the end of the world, Mat. 28:20; the promise is perpetually and immoveably throughout all ages of the world fixed to this command. The promising his presence to the preaching of the gospel, implies that his presence shall be enjoyed only by attendance on the gospel. The gracious workings of the Spirit are by this, they are the words of Christ brought to remembrance by him, whereby he doth so mightily operate.

(3.) No other way did God apparently work by formerly. In the time when God did especially manifest himself to his people by visions, dreams, and apparitions of angels, and in those ways made revelations to them, he converted not any either from a state of nature, or from a particular fall, but by the word. Manasseh's conversion was by the word of the seers, 2 Chron. 33:18; nor was David reclaimed after his fall by an immediate vision, but by the ministry of Nathan; Peter by a look, which revived the word spoken to him, Luke 22:61. The angel that attended the eunuch, Acts 8:26, made no impressions upon him, but was ordered to direct Philip thither to explain to him the mystery of the gospel; and the

Spirit particularly orders him to go near the chariot, ver. 29, but makes no impression upon him but by the ministry of the word. An angel is sent to direct Philip, but Philip is sent to discover Christ. An angel is sent to Cornelius, not to preach the gospel, but to direct him where to send for a teacher, Acts 10:3, 5, 6, the Spirit prepares Peter to go, vers. 19, 20, and likewise prepares Cornelius for his reception; God prepares the jailor by an earthquake, but renews him not but by the ministry of Paul, Acts 16:26, 32. In the times of the gospel there was first to be a teaching of God's way, before a walking in his paths, Isa. 3:3. The arm that made heaven and earth makes the new heart and new spirit, but by a word as well as them. The net of the gospel is only appointed to catch the fish; though the fish that had the tribute-money in its mouth was immediately for the service of Christ, yet he would not use his power to bring it to the shore, without Peter's casting out the net. Christ first brings souls to the net, and by the net to himself.

(4.) God hath always blessed this more or less. Moses' rod in Moses his hand hath wrought miracles, Christ's rod in the Spirit's hand hath wrought greater; the new creations have been always by it, and the after-breathings of the Spirit through it. By this he makes men righteous, holy, sincere, in a way of eminency, as the morning light which increaseth to a perfect day, and no longer as a morning cloud which quickly vanisheth, Hosea 6:5, which some understand of a gospel promise mixed with that discourse. How hath the light of the beauty and excellency of God, flashing upon the understanding from the glass of the gospel, filled the will and affections of many with desire and love to that glory it represents, and that state it offers! The very leaves of it, the profession, hath healed nations, and brought human societies into order, and the fruit of it hath been the cure of many a soul. Wait therefore for the falling of this fruit. Grace is a beam from the Sun of righteousness, but darted through the medium of gospel air; a pearl engendered by the blood of Christ, but only in the gospel sea. It hath not been without its blessing to others, it hath raised men from death to life. Is the virtue of the seed expired? or the strength of the Lord grown feeble? If ever therefore you would have the image of God in inward impressions of grace, and outward expressions of holiness, you must look for your transformation in and by the gospel. All the other knowledge in the world cannot give a man a right notion of the new birth, much less produce it. Look not after enthusiasms, nor expect it in new ways; 'to the law and to the testimony,' ways of God's appointment. The Jews could not expect an angel to bring them soundness of limbs, but by the pool; nor we the Spirit to infuse grace into us, but by the word. It is from the mercy-seat only God speaks to Israel; wisdom's gates are the places where to expect her alms, Prov. 8:34. Wait therefore upon the word, wherein the Spirit of God travails with souls.

Quest. How shall we wait upon the word, so as that we may be new begotten by it?

1. Wait upon the word frequently. Be often in reading and hearing, and meditating on it. Men set upon these works as if they were afraid they should be new born too soon, or prejudiced in their concerns and contentments in the world, as if they feared the mighty wind of the Spirit should blow away their beloved dross too fast, as if it were a matter of indifferency to be like their Maker. If you had gold not thoroughly refined, would you not cast it again and again into the fire? If filth not wholly purged, would you not use the fountain again and again? Those that are in the sun are coloured and heated by it, and have things more visible; those that are much in the word, see more of the wonders, feel more of the warmth, receive deeper impressions, are endued with the grace and holiness of truth, have a purer flame in their affections for heaven. How do you know but an opportunity missed, might have been the best market? How do you know but the Spirit might have joined himself to the word, as Philip to the eunuch's chariot, while he was reading? 'While Peter yet spake those words (it is said), the Holy Ghost

fell upon all them which heard the word,' Acts 10:44. What words? Even the marrow of the gospel, ver. 43, 'that through his name, whosoever believes in him shall receive remission of sins.' God may have a portion ready for us, and we go without it, because we are not ready to receive it. We must not expect a raven to bring us food upon a bed of sluggishness. Do it the rather, because you may live to see such times, wherein Bibles may be as much shut as they are now open, wherein (as in former times) you may be willing to give a large parcel of your goods for one chapter of it. We read of some that have given a load of hay for one chapter of St. James. Be frequent in waiting upon the word.

2. Let your hearts be fixed upon that which is the great end of the word. New begettings are the end of the gospel. Come, then, with minds fixed upon this end, and desires for it. Regard it not as a mere sound of words, but as an instrument of the noblest operations in the soul. If this be the great work of the gospel, we ought to read and hear it, with desires to be enlivened where we are dead, quickened where we are dull, be made new creatures where we are yet but old, taller creatures where we are yet but of a low stature; not only to have our understandings instructed, but our hearts changed; to inquire after God to behold the beauty of the Lord, Ps. 27:4, that we may be transformed into it; to look for God, who is in the word of a truth, for the kingdom of God comes nigh to you in the gospel. That was the word that Christ, when he sent his disciples out first to preach, bid them speak unto men, Luke 12:9. Men usually get no more than they come to seek. He that goes to market, intending only to lay out his money upon some trifle, returns for the most part with no better commodity. Zaccheus got upon the tree to meet with Christ, and so noble an end wanted not an excellent success; that day came salvation into his house, Luke 19:9. When the Jews did not mind the end of sacrifices, and regarded not the things God principally looked for in them, God slighted them, and they went without any divine operations upon their souls by them, Isa. 1:11, 13, 14. When our ends

suit the gospel, then are we like to feel gospel influences. We come with wrong ends, and, therefore, return with unchanged hearts; we come for a sound, and go away with no more. One end therefore in coming should be to gain this new begetting, or increase the growth of the new creature; our ends are not else conformable to the ends of God in it; therefore, as the earth sucks in the rain, and the roots in the earth attract it unto themselves that they may bring forth fruit, so should we open our hearts to receive the showers of the word with an aim at a new birth, or a further growth. As this is finis operis, so it should be finis operantis.

3. Mind the word in the simplicity of it, and that in it which tends to that end. Some men are more taken with colours than truth, more enamoured with words than matter, fill themselves only with air, and neglect the substance. Such are like those that are pleased with the colours of the rainbow, more than with the light reflected, or the covenant of God represented by it. No man is renewed by phrases and fancies; those are only as the oil to make the nails of the sanctuary drive in the easier: in Eccles. 12:11, 'Acceptable words,' joined with 'words of truth,' are as the 'fastening of the nails,' both 'given by one shepherd.' Words there must be to make things intelligible; illustrations to make things delightfully intelligible, but the seminal virtue lies not in the husk and skin, but in the kernel; the rest dies, but the substance of the seed lives, and brings forth fruit; separate, therefore, between the husk and the seed. The word doth not work as it is elegant, but as it is divine, as it is a word of truth. Illustrations are but the ornaments of the temple, the glory of it is in the ark and mercy-seat. It is not the engraving upon the sword cuts, but the edge; nor the key, as it is gilded, opens, but as fitted to the wards. Your faith must not stand in the wisdom of men, but in the power of God, 1 Cor. 2:5. It is the juice of the meat, and not the garnishings of the dish, that nourishes. Was it the word as a pleasant song, or as a divine seed, that changed the souls of old, made martyrs smile in the midst of flames? It was the knowledge of the excellency of the promise, and

not worldly eloquence, made them with so much courage slight gibbets, stakes, executioners; they had learned the truth as it is in Jesus.

4. Mind the word as the word of truth. Take it not upon the account of persons, value it for its own sake, as it is a word of truth. It is neither Paul nor Apollos, but God that gives the increase. Value it not by men; it is no matter what the pipe is, whether gold or lead, so the water be the water of life; the word hath an edge, because it is the word of God, not because it is whetted upon this or that grindstone. Some will scarce receive a truth, but from one they fancy; as if a man should be so foolish as to refuse a medicine which will preserve his life, because it is not presented to him in a glass which he hath a particular esteem of. To receive or refuse any truth upon the account of the person, is a sign of carnality, and the way to remain carnal; upon this account the apostle pronounceth the Corinthians again and again carnal, 1 Cor. 3:4. Despise not the meanest instrument. Our Saviour in his agony was comforted by an angel, much more inferior to him who was the Lord of angels, than any minister can be to a hearer. Mr. Peacock, being fellow of a college, in great despair, when some minister had been discoursing with him, and prevailing nothing, offering to pray with him, No, says he; dishonour not God so much, as to pray for such a reprobate. A young scholar of his standing by, answered, Surely a reprobate could not be so tender of God's honour; which words prevailed more to the bringing him to believe than all that the other had spoken. When men turn their backs upon the word, because the mouth doth not please them, they turn their backs upon God, John 13:20, and perhaps upon their own mercy. When any have respect to the man more than the word, God will leave them to the operation of the man, and withdraw his own.

5. Attend upon the word with an eye to God. Look not for the new birth only from the word. It was the folly of the Jews to think to find life in the Scriptures without Christ; life in the letter, without the original of life, John 5:39, 40. 'Except the Lord build the house' (that is the

temple), 'they labour in vain that build it,' Ps. 127:1. Without God all our endeavours to build a spiritual temple are like the strivings to wash a blackamore white. No believing the word, though preached a thousand times, without God's revealing his arm, Isa. 53:1. It is not the file that makes the watch, but the artist by it. No instrument can act without the virtue of some superior agent. It is the altar that sanctifies the gold, and Christ that sanctifies the ordinances. Paul may plant by his doctrine and miracles; Apollos may water by his affectionate eloquence; but God alone can give the increase by his almighty breath. Man sows the seed, but God only can make it fructify. The richest showers cannot make the ground fruitful, but as instruments under God's blessing. It is not said the prophets did hew them, but God by his prophets, Hosea 6:5. Then have your eyes fixed upon God. It is the word of his lips, not of man's, whereby any are snatched out of the paths of the destroyer, as well as kept from them. Man's teachings direct us to Christ; God's teachings bring us to Christ; man brings the gospel, at most, to the heart, the Spirit only brings the gospel into the heart; man puts the key in the lock, God only turns it, and opens the heart by it; man brings the word of truth, and God the truth of the word into the soul; man brings the objective word of grace, God alone the attractive grace of the word. If where there is already the new birth, the soul must be fixed on God for further openings, much more where it is not yet wrought. David had an excellent knowledge, yet cries out for the opening of his eyes to see the wonders in God's law. It is God only can knock off the fetters of a spiritual death, and open the iron gates, that the King of glory may enter with spiritual life. If any, therefore, will regard the word more than as an instrument, as a partner with God in his operation, he may justly leave you to the weakness of that, and deny the influx of his own strength.

Therefore let the word be attended with prayer.

(1.) Before you wait upon God in any ordinance, plead with him as Moses did in another case, 'To what purpose should I go, unless thy presence go with me?' What can the letter do without the Spirit, or words without that powerful wind to blow them into my heart? None can have life by the bread of the word, without the blessing of God. As man brings the graft, desire God to insert it. As God hath promised gifts to his church, so he promised his own teachings: Heb. 8:11, 'All shall know me, from the least to the greatest.' Urge God with his own promise, desire him to open his mouth, and to open your hearts; his mouth to breathe, and your hearts to receive. When men overlook God, he makes a separation between the word and his own quickening presence. The end doth not necessarily arise from the means; and, therefore, in the use of them, there must be a fiduciary recourse to the grace of God. In the time, too, of waiting upon God, let there be ejaculations; let your hearts be continually lift up to God; let your expectations be from him. We should be like Jacob's ladder; though the feet stand in Bethel, the house of God, our heads should reach to heaven in all our attendances.

(2.) After you have been at the word. God is the great seer, Christ the great prophet; we should go to him for the repetition of things upon our hearts; we may have that wind afterwards by prayer, which we felt not so stiff at hearing. The operations of truth, as well as the knowledge of it, are best fetched out upon our knees by earnest prayer. How do you know but, while you are praying, the fire may descend from heaven, and transform you into a divine likeness? Thus you will make God the Alpha and Omega of his own ordinances, in your acknowledgment of him, as well as he is so in himself.

(3.) Rest not in bare hearing. Look for God in the ordinances as he is the living God, who lives in himself, and gives life to men and means: Ps. 84:2, 'My soul longs for the living God;' there is a strength and glory of God to be longed for in the sanctuary; no means are to be rested in or used, but as to lead to such an end for which they are fitted. To rest in the word heard, or read, is to make that our end, which God hath appointed only as the means. The word is sweet, but as it is the pipe through which

God and his image, God and his grace, which is sweeter and higher than all ordinances, stream to the soul. Rejoice in the word, but only as the wise men did in the star, as it led them to Christ. The word of Christ is precious; but nothing more precious than himself, and his formation in the soul. Rest not in the word, but look through it to Christ.'

6. Attend upon the word submissively. It is not the hearer, but the humble hearer, shall find the power of the word working in him; as it is not the speaking a prayer, but the wrestling and struggling of the heart with God in prayer, receives a gracious answer. The humble are the fittest subjects for grace, those that lie upon the ground with their mouth close to the pipe. 'He gives grace to the humble.' Resign yourselves up to the word, struggle not against the battery it makes, nor the wind that blows; receive every stroke till you see the frame of the new creature. Let a silence be imposed upon the flesh, and self bowed down to the dust, while Christ the great prophet speaks. Be not peevish, nor expostulate with God's sovereignty, as they did: Isa. 58:3, 'Wherefore have we fasted, and thou seest not? Wherefore have we afflicted our soul, and thou takest no knowledge?' Acknowledge God a free agent, submit to his sovereign pleasure. A truly humble bow to God will prevail more than all the saucy expostulations of proud flesh. In hearing the word, pick not here a part, and there a part, as suits your humour, but consider what really is God's will, and submit to it. Cornelius was of this resigning temper when the Spirit descended upon him: Acts 10:33, 'We are here present before God, to hear all things that are commanded thee of God.' An humble soul, saith Kempis, by the grace of God, understands more the reasons of eternal truth in a trice, than a man that hath studied many years in the schools, because he hath the operations of them in his heart.

7. Receive the word with faith. I mean, not the faith which is a part of the new creature, but an assent. There is a rational belief that it is the word of truth, which is in many men that have no justifying faith. Actuate this. The believing the word to be so, to be the word of God, is

the first step to the receiving advantage by it. No man will ever comply with that which he believes not to be true, or believes not himself to be concerned in. It is said by the apostle, Heb. 4:1, 2, 'The word profited not, because it was not mixed with faith.' There was truth in the word, but no firm assent to it in their hearts. There can never be a full compliance with Christ, in order to a new birth, if there be not first an assent to the word. Where there is a defect in the first concoction, there will also be a defect in the second and third. If you do not believe with Naaman, that the waters of Jordan are appointed by God for this end, and not those of Abana and Pharpar, you will never be rid of the spiritual death, no more than he would have been of his leprosy. You never see God in his sanctuary, nor feel God in his power for want of this. Surely as this made our Saviour suspend the power of his miracles, by the same reason it makes him suspend the power of his word: Mat. 13:58, 'He did not many mighty works there, because of their unbelief.' If men did believe there were a place where they might enjoy all earthly delights in a higher measure, at an easier rate, how ambitious would they be of putting themselves into a state to enjoy them? If men did believe the report of the gospel, would they not be full of great undertakings for the enjoyment of the proffers of it? But the gospel, more is the pity, hath not naturally that credit with men that a fiction hath.

8. Observe much the motions upon your hearts while you are attending upon God. If the sails be not skilfully ordered to catch and hold, and make the best improvement of the wind that blows, much of the wind will pass beside it, and the ship lag many leagues behind, or lie wind-bound a long time before it receive a like gale. God hath particular seasons: Heb. 4:7, 'To-day if you will hear his voice.' Sometimes the Spirit is more urging than at another time, and sends his motions thicker upon the heart; let those times be observed, and when there are motions on the Spirit's part, let there be compliance on yours. Catch a promise when the Spirit opens; bind yourselves to an observance of the precept when the

Spirit shews it; let God's drawing be answered with the soul's running; observe what precious oil is dropped through the golden pipes upon the heart, and spill it not; take notice of what sparks light upon you, and lose not the warmth they may convey to your hearts; what beam of light breaks in, let it not be puffed out by a temptation or diversion; observe what is afforded to make your hearts burn, and your corruptions and sinful inclinations cool. Regard not so much your affections, as what touches are upon your wills. Affections may arise from a natural constitution of the body, some tempers being more easily excited to exert affections than others, yet they are not always, nor altogether, to be disregarded, nor are they always to be looked upon as ciphers; but, especially, see what influence the word hath upon the understanding and will chiefly, as well as upon the affections. Judge of yourselves by the inward power and might, by the breakings in of the light, and the sprightly strain of your wills. The might of the Spirit works in the inner man, Eph. 3:16; not in a part of the inner man, but in every faculty. See what compunction there is in your souls, what strong desires in the will. Bare affections are but like a sponge, which will by a light compression let out that water which it so easily sucked up. Men may' receive the word with gladness' without having any root of spiritual grace, Mark 4:16, 17. When men regard only particular affections, they usually sit down in those sparks of their own kindling, and look not after a thorough change. Or if you find such affections, see whether those affections are raised rather by the truth than the dress; whether they be kindled by the consideration of those attributes of God, his mercy, goodness, wisdom, holiness, which have a great hand in the new birth; whether by the deep consideration of our Saviour's death and resurrection, the great designs of the gospel; whether the motion be orderly, first, understanding, then will, and afterwards affections. This is a genuine flame, kindled by a fire which comes down from heaven, working upon all the parts of the soul. A bare work upon the affections is rather a strange and carnal fire.

Observe, therefore, what tender blades bud and shoot forth in the higher faculties of your souls.

9. Press the word much upon your hearts after hearing. How great is the neglect of this application of the word of truth! Men will spend hours in hearing, and not one minute in serious reflections; as if the word in their ears, or a receipt in their pockets, could cure the disease in the heart. This is the worm at the root of all our spiritual advantages. What is only dashed upon the fancy, or lightly coloured, may soon be washed off. The soil must be made tenacious of the seed by the harrow of meditation, which hides it in the heart, and covers it with earth; for want of being laid deep, and banded by serious meditation, the seed takes no root, because there is not much earth about it, Mark 4:5, 6, 16. How can food nourish your body, unless t be concocted by natural heat? or spiritual food enliven you, unless concocted by meditation? The shepherds, after they had heard the news of Christ's incarnation from the mouth of the angel, reflected upon their duty, Luke 2:14, 15. Words must be kept some time upon the mind, and rolled over and over again, before they can work any sensible change, because the heart naturally hath an averseness to God and his word; as the strongest physic must be in the body some time, and be wrought upon by the stomach, before it can work upon the humours. How do you know, but while you are musing, a divine fire may sparkle in your souls, and Christ rise in your hearts? Grapes must be pressed to get out the wine that will cheer the heart. Put the question to your soul, in every part you can remember, as our Saviour did to Martha, John 11:25, 26, 'I am the resurrection and the life. Believest thou this?' There is such a thing as the new birth: believest thou this? It is necessary to be had: believest thou this? God only can work it: believest thou this? And so for every divine truth. Leave not thy soul to its vagaries, hold it on to the work, press it to give a positive answer whether it believe this or that truth. Put not yourselves off with a slight answer to the question, but examine the reasons of your belief of it. Look

upon yourselves as really concerned in the word you hear, otherwise it will no more affect you than if you should tell an ambitious man, gaping after preferment in England, of a wealthy place fallen in Spain, which will not engage his thoughts, as being out of his sphere and at too great a distance. To have a listlessness to such duties, or any spiritual duty, after hearing the word, which is the food of the soul, shews a great corruption within, as the heaviness in the body, and corrupt vapours in the mouth, shew the badness of concoction.

10. Labour to have the savour of truth upon your spirits, as well as the notions of it in your heads. The kingdom of God consists not in word, but in power; the new birth consists not in a bare notion, but in spiritual savour. The highest notional knowledge comes far short of experimental; the knowledge a blind man hath of light and colours, by hearing a lecture upon it, is but mere ignorance to the knowledge he would have if his eyes were opened. Endeavour to have the savour of Christ's ointments, Cant. 1:3, and inward sense exercised, Heb. 5:14. The apostle distinguisheth knowledge and judgment, Philip. 1:9. Knowledge is a notion in the head, judgment, or αἴσθησις, is the sense or savour of it in the heart. What a miserable thing is it to spend our lives without a taste! Knowledge is but as a cloud that intercepts the beams of the sun and doth not advantage the earth, unless melted into drops, and falling down into the bosom of it; let the knowledge of the word of truth drop down in a kindly shower upon your hearts, let it be a knowledge of the word heated with love.

I might have added more; bring plain hearts to the word, put off all disguises. Moses took off his veil when he went into the presence of God. Bring not flesh and blood as your counsellors; these are no friends to a new birth. And come with love; love makes the strongest impressions upon the soul.

It might here be also worth the inquiry, why so few are renewed by the word of truth in this age; why the gospel has no more powerful effect among us, as in former ages? It is a wonder to see a man begotten by the word, as it was a wonder for the woman to bring forth a man-child, Rev. 12. When our Saviour was brought into the temple, not a man but Simeon knew knew him; no question but many pharisees, doctors, and gentlemen were walking there, but none but Simeon knew him, to whom he was revealed, Luke 2:22, 25; the rest looked upon him as an ordinary child. Formerly men flocked to Christ as the doves to the windows. The sword of the Spirit was never unsheathed, but it cut some hearts; the word seems now to have lost its edge and efficacy, which ought to be considered and laid to heart.

Many causes may be rendered; I will only hint a few.

(1.) Taking religion upon trust. Old customs are hardly to be parted with: 'Every man will walk in the name of his God,' Micah 4:5. To root out false conceptions in religion, which either education, fancy, or humour have rooted, is very difficult.

(2.) A conceit of the meanness of the word, whereby there is a secret contempt of it, and so a formal and customary use of it.

(3.) A conceit of men, that they are new born already. Many think their condition good, because of their civil honesty. Though that be a very comely and commendable thing, yet security in it kills its thousands. Many, because they are free from the common pollutions of the world, and possessed with many amiable virtues, never consider how much their hearts are stored with an enmity against God. Such count their righteousness their gain, and think it a sufficient bribe for God's mercy.

(4.) A conceit that to be new born is but to change an opinion. A change of opinion may look like faith, as presumption doth, but it is not faith. The devil holds some men in the chain of sublimated speculations, which hinder the working of the most spiritual and influential truths.

(5.) Pride of reason, frequency of disputes. It is a rational age, an age overgrown with reason, and the Scripture tells us, 'Not many wise,' &c. The truths of God are very much turned into scepticism.

(6.) The common atheism that so much prevails among us. How should men regard a discourse of the new birth, a begetting to God, when they scarce believe there is a God at all, but their own lusts, to be like unto? How should they be wrought upon by the word of God, that scarce believe there is any God to reveal a word, and that there is no word of God?

(7.) Hardness of heart, occasioned (through the just judgment of God) by the frequency and unprofitable hearing of the word. The word is most operative when it comes first into a nation or town. When the heart is not broken by hearing the word of truth, it becomes more hardened and compact in sin. Many other reasons might be rendered, but I have held you too long upon this subject.

www.ingramcontent.com/pod-product-compliance
Lightning Source LLC
Chambersburg PA
CBHW051255120626
46547CB00015B/1958